Dilemmas of Democracy & Dictatorship

Place, Time,
and Ideology in
Global Perspective

Dilemmas of
Democracy &
Dictatorship

Michael S. Radu

Transaction Publishers
New Brunswick (U.S.A.) and London (U.K.)

Library of Congress Catalog Number: 2006040441
ISBN: 0-7658-0313-5
Printed in the United States of America

Library of Congress Cataloging-in-Publication Data

Radu, Michael.
    Dilemmas of democracy and dictatorship : place, time, and ideology in global perspective / Michael S. Radu.
        p. cm.
    Includes index.
    ISBN 0-7658-0313-5 (alk. paper)
        1. International relations. 2. World politics—1989- 3. Political violence—Case studies. 4. Terrorism. 5. Globalization. I. Title.

JZ1305.R39   2006
327.1—dc22   2006040441

CONTENTS

ACKNOWLEDGMENTS

This volume was made possible by the help I have received from the Foreign Policy Research Institute in Philadelphia, whose institutional patience I have often pushed to the limits. Most importantly, I am grateful to FPRI's Trudy Kuehner for her extensive editorial help and to my intern, Ludwika Chrzastowska for her dedication and hard work in putting it together.

INTRODUCTION

INTRODUCTION

In May 1981, the day I was to defend my Ph. D. thesis at Columbia (on the foreign policies of the then-Marxist African states—Angola, Mozambique, Benin, and Congo/Brazzaville), I got a call from another, somewhat older, Columbia alumnus, at the time director of the Foreign Policy Research Institute (FPRI), inviting me to come to Philadelphia to interview for a possible job. At the time, my only known chance—and it was just a chance—for a job was a vague possibility at a small western university. Naturally, I went to Philadelphia. I was hired, part time, among America's oldest (founded 1955) think thanks. By the end of that year, after receiving a grant from the Reagan administration, part-time became full-time and I became a fixture—for better or for worse—at FPRI. FPRI was less known outside Philadelphia than its journal, *Orbis* (which I have seen in libraries from Valparaiso, Chile, to Johannesburg and Bucharest) until the Internet age, when FPRI's e-notes began to bring it the attention it deserves. At any rate, some of the FPRI people, especially Alan Luxenberg, now vice president, were there when I started, and still make it a great place to think and write.

Because my mother was born in Rockford, Illinois, to Romanian emigrant peasants from Transylvania, then part of Habsburg Empire (my father was Romanian), I managed to emigrate from Ceausescu's Romania, leaving behind a thick Securitate (secret police) file. Once in America, I started as a typical immigrant, speaking no English but with an almost finished Ph. D. in Romania (with a thesis ambitiously titled "The relationship between scholastic philosophy and Gothic art in Western Europe") and two university degrees (in history and philosophy—the latter meaning, mostly, Marxism-Leninism) under my tightening belt. Once at FPRI, I started doing what, in Romania, I only dreamed of doing—traveling. Indeed, under Ceausescu I was not even allowed to travel to the Soviet Union, so great was the regime's fear of my defection. They had good reasons to mistrust me—after all, as a student I published the first Romanian translation of Heidegger, which almost got me expelled from the university; wrote about Caravaggio on the anniversary of the Communist Youth Organization—a no-no, since the revolutionary post-Renaissance painter was also a murderer and thus a bad example for the "new communist" man; and made numerous other missteps.

Sometimes that desire to travel gave (and, I suspect, still does) FPRI heartburn—especially since my travels were mostly to Central and South America

1

and Subsaharan Africa, poor countries that were amazingly expensive for Western travelers. Indeed, when, as in Brazzaville in 1983, there is only one Western-owned and run hotel/restaurant in town, the price is high, but there is no choice unless you want to frighten your health care provider back home. But expense is no longer an issue: Paris and even Madrid have by now caught up with Brazzaville and Lagos as the most expensive cities in the world.

In all events, over the past twenty years I did travel to some forty countries. Besides Latin America and Africa, I made repeated incursions into both "old" and "new" Europe (if Romania, Bosnia, Moldova and Croatia are indeed "new")—and an interesting trip to Southeast Asia as a UN elections monitor in Cambodia in 1993. The latter was an interesting experience in more than one sense—indeed, while I have served as elections monitor elsewhere (Guatemala, Romania, Peru), that was my first and hopefully last experience as a temporary UN employee.

As a monitor of Cambodia's first free elections, I was only supposed to be an observer—until the last possible moment, when the UN realized that the locals simply could not run anything that could be observed. Thus my fellow monitors and I were told, basically, that we would have to run the election—in my group's case, in the Kompong Cham area. Incompetence was only matched by corruption and inefficiency—and that was UN's largest operation ever. The leader of that operation was later appointed to Bosnia, only to be finally fired for running the same sort of operation there.

As an East European would-be academic, Columbia Ph.D. or not, I realized early on that making East European communism my specialty was not something I could do in the prevailing academic atmosphere—be "balanced," meaning remove any trace of anticommunist "bias" from my research Since I was not prepared to make concessions on that issue, I directed my attention to Third World areas, some of which, like Southern Africa and Central America, have attracted me for a long time. And so I began my study of political violence—the very essence of Marxism Leninism.

In my experience, American conservatives have always had a serious problem with the realities of the third world—a mixture of ignorance, of consistently being taken advantage of by a Left that knows much more and understands little, and of Pollyanna-ish confusion of desires with realities. One does not need to know anything to claim that Salvadorans or Peruvians, black South Africans or Turkish Kurds or, now, Iraqis and Afghans, are hungry for democracy—after all, isn't that hunger common to all mankind? Well, not really or, at the very least, it is not that simple.

Long, real-world experience made me far less optimistic on that count. Indeed, a recent Latinobarómetro poll (August 2004) suggests a clear disenchantment of most Latin Americans with democracy—with the usual exceptions of Costa Rica and Uruguay, and one does not need a poll to realize that in most African states, the very concept is both misunderstood and distrusted, for whatever reason—and there are many reasons.

I came to the issue of who engages in political violence, rather than why they do. As a former historian in the field, I always took Lenin seriously—not because of his amateurish attempts to pose as a theoretician but because of his obvious success as a practitioner of violence. And Lenin was right on one issue—the revolution is, and can only be, the result of actions taken by professionals, who must be well educated, amoral (the revolution defines its own morality) and "represent" rather than—indeed, opposed to—being part of the "proletariat." That explains why Lenin (and Stalin and Mao, both even more simplistic "theoreticians" and even more successful practitioners) was the Bible of third-world self-proclaimed revolutionaries, from Ethiopia's Mengistu Haile Mariam to Congo's Marien Ngouabi to Angola's Agostinho Neto. Certainly it is not the sophisticated nineteenth-century Germans, even if their names are Karl Marx and Friederich Engels and their treatises are boring.

For quite a while I remained the only person—reactionary, for sure—publishing analyses of revolutionary terrorist or guerrilla leaders in Latin America and elsewhere, suggesting that theirs were frustrated middle-class rather than "popular" movements; that it was a Leninist vanguard of failed or over-ambitious privileged members of the elite rather than some "people's" uprising that defined such groups as the Tupamaros of Uruguay, Montoneros of Argentina, Sandinistas of Nicaragua and the FMLN in El Salvador—not to mention Peru's murderous Shining Path, led by Abimael Guzmán with his a double M.A. and Ph.D. from the San Agustin University in Arequipa. Remove the Leninist cover, and the al-Qaeda nebula, especially its core around Osama bin Laden, and one finds the very same reality—a Saudi millionaire, an Egyptian doctor of aristocratic background, as operational leaders, a well-traveled Egyptian, Sayyid Al-Qutb, as the main ideologue.

For a long time, that analysis was disregarded as avoiding things like "structural violence" and the "root causes" of political violence—what I call the "vegetable explanation"—the tendency to think that parsley, parsnip, and celery roots produce terrorists. By now my then-isolated opinion is on the front pages and in academic sources represented by Yvon Grenier on Salvador, Rohan Gunaratna on Islamist terror groups, etc.—a small contribution to a serious debate.

In Europe I saw abounding contradictions, but from year to year one could feel the rise of anti-Americanism—and I do feel it when talking to French (in France or Belgium) or Spanish (in Madrid) speakers. But while the political disputes between Paris and Washington become more public and obvious, the cooperation between intelligence organizations in the two countries is better than ever; and the French would rather work with the CIA than the disorganized and decentralized Germans. Muslims, if not always Islam as such, are a growing problem for many European countries, with their numbers and growing radicalism making them less and less assimilable.

And when it comes to the Balkans—which are European if any cultural definition is used, with their combination of religious conflict, ancient hatreds, and Subsaharan Africa, poor countries that were amazingly expensive for Western travelers. Indeed, when, as in Brazzaville in 1983, there is only one Western-owned and run hotel/restaurant in town, the price is high, but there is no choice unless you want to frighten your health care provider back home. But expense is no longer an issue: Paris and even Madrid have by now caught up with Brazzaville and Lagos as the most expensive cities in the world.

In all events, over the past twenty years I did travel to some forty countries. Besides Latin America and Africa, I made repeated incursions into both "old" and "new" Europe (if Romania, Bosnia, Moldova and Croatia are indeed "new")— and an interesting trip to Southeast Asia as a UN elections monitor in Cambodia in 1993. The latter was an interesting experience in more than one sense—indeed, while I have served as elections monitor elsewhere (Guatemala, Romania, Peru), that was my first and hopefully last experience as a temporary UN employee.

As a monitor of Cambodia's first free elections, I was only supposed to be an observer—until the last possible moment, when the UN realized that the locals simply could not run anything that could be observed. Thus my fellow monitors and I were told, basically, that we would have to run the election—in my group's case, in the Kompong Cham area. Incompetence was only matched by corruption and inefficiency—and that was UN's largest operation ever. The leader of that operation was later appointed to Bosnia, only to be finally fired for running the same sort of operation there.

As an East European would-be academic, Columbia Ph.D. or not, I realized early on that making East European communism my specialty was not something I could do in the prevailing academic atmosphere—be "balanced," meaning remove any trace of anticommunist "bias" from my research Since I was not prepared to make concessions on that issue, I directed my attention to Third World areas, some of which, like Southern Africa and Central America, have attracted me for a long time. And so I began my study of political violence—the very essence of Marxism Leninism.

In my experience, American conservatives have always had a serious problem with the realities of the third world—a mixture of ignorance, of consistently being taken advantage of by a Left that knows much more and understands little, and of Pollyanna-ish confusion of desires with realities. One does not need to know anything to claim that Salvadorans or Peruvians, black South Africans or Turkish Kurds or, now, Iraqis and Afghans, are hungry for democracy—after all, isn't that hunger common to all mankind? Well, not really or, at the very least, it is not that simple.

Long, real-world experience made me far less optimistic on that count. Indeed, a recent Latinobarómetro poll (August 2004) suggests a clear disenchantment of most Latin Americans with democracy—with the usual exceptions of Costa Rica and Uruguay, and one does not need a poll to realize that in most African states, the very concept is both misunderstood and distrusted, for whatever reason—and there are many reasons.

I came to the issue of who engages in political violence, rather than why they do. As a former historian in the field, I always took Lenin seriously—not because of his amateurish attempts to pose as a theoretician but because of his obvious success as a practitioner of violence. And Lenin was right on one issue—the revolution is, and can only be, the result of actions taken by professionals, who must be well educated, amoral (the revolution defines its own morality) and "represent" rather than—indeed, opposed to—being part of the "proletariat." That explains why Lenin (and Stalin and Mao, both even more simplistic "theoreticians" and even more successful practitioners) was the Bible of third-world self-proclaimed revolutionaries, from Ethiopia's Mengistu Haile Mariam to Congo's Marien Ngouabi to Angola's Agostinho Neto. Certainly it is not the sophisticated nineteenth-century Germans, even if their names are Karl Marx and Friederich Engels and their treatises are boring.

For quite a while I remained the only person—reactionary, for sure—publishing analyses of revolutionary terrorist or guerrilla leaders in Latin America and elsewhere, suggesting that theirs were frustrated middle-class rather than "popular" movements; that it was a Leninist vanguard of failed or over-ambitious privileged members of the elite rather than some "people's" uprising that defined such groups as the Tupamaros of Uruguay, Montoneros of Argentina, Sandinistas of Nicaragua and the FMLN in El Salvador—not to mention Peru's murderous Shining Path, led by Abimael Guzmán with his a double M.A. and Ph.D. from the San Agustin University in Arequipa. Remove the Leninist cover, and the al-Qaeda nebula, especially its core around Osama bin Laden, and one finds the very same reality—a Saudi millionaire, an Egyptian doctor of aristocratic background, as operational leaders, a well-traveled Egyptian, Sayyid Al-Qutb, as the main ideologue.

For a long time, that analysis was disregarded as avoiding things like "structural violence" and the "root causes" of political violence—what I call the "vegetable explanation"—the tendency to think that parsley, parsnip, and celery roots produce terrorists. By now my then-isolated opinion is on the front pages and in academic sources represented by Yvon Grenier on Salvador, Rohan Gunaratna on Islamist terror groups, etc.—a small contribution to a serious debate.

In Europe I saw abounding contradictions, but from year to year one could feel the rise of anti-Americanism—and I do feel it when talking to French (in France or Belgium) or Spanish (in Madrid) speakers. But while the political disputes between Paris and Washington become more public and obvious, the cooperation between intelligence organizations in the two countries is better than ever; and the French would rather work with the CIA than the disorganized and decentralized Germans. Muslims, if not always Islam as such, are a growing problem for many European countries, with their numbers and growing radicalism making them less and less assimilable.

And when it comes to the Balkans—which are European if any cultural definition is used, with their combination of religious conflict, ancient hatreds, and unassimilated historical emotions— the old issue of living with Islam remains unresolved. After a bus trip across Bosnia and a stay in Sarajevo, I would say that the complications are too great for any single solution. The Banja Luka Serbs hated anything American (or foreign), while in Sarajevo the Iranian "Cultural Mission"—a collection of severe looking mullahs—stood on Boulevard Marshall Tito just across the street from Benneton's United Colors. Nobody worked, and everybody expected the EU, U.S. or Japan to "provide aid."

What does all of this mean? What does the Coca-Cola bottle among the crocodiles on a Congo River beach mean? The Iranian mullahs of Sarajevo? The confused Khmers of Kompong Cham asked to do the incomprehensible (i.e., boil their water)? The Soweto teenagers claiming a "right" to good jobs after *apartheid* because they "sacrificed" education over the years they were burning their opponents alive? It means that, globalization or not—and I have a problem seeing it when TV systems, electrical outlets, voltage are incompatible between Paris and Philadelphia, let alone Washington and Darfur—the world is not a village, but a conglomerate of differences. This volume is a collection of views on the world, as diverse and confused as it may often be, is made more complex as the traveler is both a conservative and an immigrant.

PART 1
HUMAN RIGHTS AND OTHER FASHIONS

A world ruled by lawyers and emotional masses? It may seem exaggerated, but the reality is that we are getting there—especially in Europe. Consider the fact that there are more and more important lawyers in the Department of Defense than ever before; that ecologists, Amnesty International, enormous foundations with endowments the size of many national GNPs and most national budgets, influence government policies even on matters of national security; and that "evolving standards" of human rights, undefined but concretely sought by powerful global groups, intend to do the following: force Alabama to apply mushy anti-death penalty "feelings" from The Hague; penalize international corporations for the behavior of the governments under whose laws they operate; punish whole nations for real or alleged sins committed centuries ago; and criminalize warfare as such, as if Philadelphia Quakers took over the entire world.

Worshipping the UN and its subsidiary institutions such as the International Court on Rwanda in Arusha, with a record of some twenty trials in a decade at a cost of almost a billion dollars—is part of this. Never mind that the UN General Assembly decided to form a Human Rights Commission that regularly includes, even as chairs, the likes of Libya, Saudi Arabia, Cuba, and Syria. And never mind that totalitarian, anti-Semitic apologists of the 9/11 attacks such as the Madres de Plaza de Mayo of Buenos Aires are still lionized as a human rights group in Europe and elsewhere. From a noble goal and wish, human rights and those claiming to pursue them have formulated a global ideology and become what can only be described as the Human Rights Establishment.

THE PINOCHET CASE: ANTI-COMMUNISM ON TRIAL

On October 16, Augusto Pinochet Ugarte, Chile's president from 1973 to 1990 and now senator for life, was arrested while he underwent surgery in a London hospital. British authorities decided to honor an Interpol warrant signed by Baltasar Garzón, a Spanish judge. Subsequently, the British High Court ruled the warrant illegal, a decision still subject to a final appeal to a House of Lords committee. Whatever transpires, the episode is worthy of scrutiny in light of its wider implications for the expansion of international jurisdiction over human rights cases. That said, the Pinochet case has little to do with law, and everything to do with the rewriting of history—this time by the losers.

The legal case for the British decision is as weak as it is political. Judge Garzón, a former Socialist member of the Spanish parliament, is a well-known publicity-seeker whose expansive notion of appropriate jurisdiction would make the most liberal American judge proud. Acting independently, he decided to formally accuse Pinochet (as well as former Argentine military leaders) of "the delict of genocide," no less—and provided a list of ninety-one (!) alleged victims of illegal arrest, assassination or disappearance, none of them Spanish. There is no ground in international or Spanish law for the accusation; indeed, Garzón's claims are so bizarre that the office of the Spanish State Prosecutor itself is appealing his arbitrary expansion of his court's jurisdiction. That appeal is based on the fact that whatever crimes may have taken place in Chile more than two decades ago were neither committed in Spain nor by Spanish citizens. Moreover, the appeal questions Garzón's use of the term "genocide"— legally defined as actions intended to eliminate an entire group because of its ethnicity, race or religion.

Garzón himself identified the presumed victims mostly as members of the totalitarian Communist Party or the Movement of the Revolutionary Left (MIR). To call actions against such people "genocide" is worse than bizarre—it is an insult to the victims of real genocide—Jews, Gypsies, Armenians, Tutsis. Garzón's accusation lowers not just legal standards, but moral ones. Unfortunately, it is also part of an emerging pattern and an eventual success for Garzon's "case" against Pinochet would only accelerate it. It has indeed become a habit in the media and the Left everywhere to qualify as "genocide" any real or alleged large-scale abuse of human rights, whether by Serbs in Kosovo or Bosnia, or by military forces fighting insurgencies in Mexico, Peru or Colombia. But just as most murderers are not Stalin or Hitler, most killings in wartime are not genocide. To make the accusation against Pinochet is, however, politically correct and thus an appropriate focal point for media attention and public applause. And herein lies the true meaning of the entire episode.

Garzón's other accusation against Pinochet—that of "terrorism"—is positively Orwellian. A state defending itself against well-known Marxist terrorist organizations—MIR and the Communist Party's armed branch, the Manuel Rodriguez Patriotic Front, both responsible for hundreds of crimes in Chile—becomes "terrorist" while totalitarian terrorists are transformed into "innocent victims."

Pinochet's real problem is not legal: he has visited London before, without difficulty and with the same diplomatic passport. What has changed is the nature and ideology of the British government. Indeed, one could only be amused at the righteousness of the official position of Tony Blair's government, which pretends that the issue is simply legal, not political. Meanwhile, Blair's Trade Secretary and close confidant Peter Mandelson described the idea of respecting Pinochet's diplomatic immunity as "gut wrenching "—a mild statement compared to those coming from the Labour backbenchers. And all this from the very same government that does not seem to find it "gut wrenching" to negotiate with IRA killers of children and women. Nor is it surprising that Margaret Thatcher has publicly attacked London's decision. Thus has the episode cast doubts upon Tony Blair's commitment to the rule of law and reinforced the suspicion that, where human rights are concerned, "international law" is merely a a code word for political correctness.

Through these contradictions it becomes obvious that the real battle, in Britain and Spain as well as for the Left worldwide, is not over legality or morality, but history itself. Pinochet, though long ago replaced as leader of a small and remote nation, remains the most hated man in "progressive" circles throughout the world. The reason is simple: his 1973 coup against the government of Salvador Allende was the first successful overthrow of a Marxist regime by internal forces. It shattered the long-prevailing myth of the historical inevitability and permanence of communist regimes, institutionalized at the time by the Brezhnev Doctrine. Furthermore, during its seventeen years in power, the Pinochet regime not only removed Marxism as a serious political and cultural force in Chile, it also inaugurated a capitalist, and ultimately democratic, revolution that made that country a model for Latin America and beyond. Much to the chagrin of the soundly defeated Left, Pinochet enjoys lasting popularity in former communist countries, and more than two thirds of Chileans today either support or do not condemn him.

And now the Left, from Judge Garzón to the left wing of the Labour Party to Spanish Socialists to the Chilean Communist Party (whose leader is Pinochet's most vocal accuser), sees a chance to recover moral ground and "correct" the historical record. If the general could be convicted of "genocide" and "terrorism," in some court by some judge somewhere—in fact anywhere, and no matter how Orwellian the proceedings—the Left could alleviate its long-simmering frustrations, rewrite history, and turn its moral and political defeat into victory at last. What those on the left seek, in other words, is not the trial of a dictator—would they arrest Castro?—but of anti-communism.

Reprinted with permission from http://www.fpri.org, October 30, 1998

KNOW THY ENEMY

For almost two decades, the Western media has described Argentina's Madres de Plaza de Mayo as a model of "civil society" in the Third World. The group has been lionized in books written in the United States, supported by groups established all over Western Europe, and become rich enough from donations from Western sympathizers to establish "The Popular University of the Mothers" (UBA), an unrecognized pseudo-educational entity in Buenos Aires. The group, and its founder and leader, Hebe de Bonafini, have long been seen as a "natural" for the Nobel Peace Prize. Little attempt, however, has been made to look beneath the surface at the actual nature, ideology, goals, and statements of Bonafini. Like Rigoberta Menchu before her (Nobel Peace Prize winner, 1992), Bonafini's totalitarian past and present have been papered over in the name of political correctness and misguided sympathy.

But like much else, this too may change as a result of September 11. In her characteristically direct fashion, Bonafini created mass confusion and panic among the global human-rights establishment by stating that "in the Twin Towers died the powerful. And the powerful are my enemy; because it is the same that killed my children" (a reference to members of the Montoneros terrorist group killed during Argentina's civil war in the mid-1970s). Asked about the fact that office workers of African, Muslim, and even Argentine origin also were killed, she answered, "What does that have to do with anything?. . .It is true: I am happy and celebrate the fact that this savage capitalism which destroys us has for once been hit. I do not feel sorry over them."

While admitting that there are a few good Americans— like Noam Chomsky and unreconstructed Leninist James Petras—Bonafini made it clear that she hates the American people. Men like Chomsky and Petras are few, while the great majority of Americans are guilty and deserve what they got in September. She concluded: "Now things are clear. Revolution is the only way people can succeed. . .You are either imperialist or Marxist."

Bonafini's sincerity and consistency in her comments cannot be doubted. At least twice she has condemned the United States for "genocide" while on the soil of its adversaries: on visits to Baghdad after the Gulf War and Belgrade during the Kosovo war of 1999. Add to this her sycophantic support for Fidel Castro, and it is clear that she can find no enemy of the United States, no matter how murderous, that she cannot love, as long as it is totalitarian. It is not easy to place oneself to Castro's left, but Bonafini has done just that, since even Fidel condemned the September attacks.

Bonafini's stance provoked a strong reaction among her colleagues, who were perhaps fearful of being tarnished by association. Horacio Verbitsky, a former Montonero supporter himself, a committed Leftist, and one who lost family members to the military crackdown against that terror group, publicly condemned Bonafini's statements—at which point she accused him of being an American agent because his group receives money from the Ford Foundation. Moreover, she added, Verbitsky is a Jew, the implication being that all Jews are American agents. To their credit, twelve faculty members of her own "university" resigned in protest. It is not the first time that manifestations of totalitarianism, anti-Semitism, and anti-Americanism are all wound together; it is what makes Bonafini a kin of Osama bin Laden.

Bonafini's ravings shed light on the oft-overlooked fact that particularly in Latin America, but elsewhere as well, non-governmental organizations (NGOs) that ostensibly advocate human rights have largely become the refuge of the Left—the unemployed and unemployable Marxist radicals "victimized" by the shrinking subsidies to the dysfunctional public sector, and especially public universities, and now subsidized by rich Western foundations, socialist governments, and Protestant or Catholic elements. September 11 and the likes of Hebe de Bonafini helped, if anything, to bring these people out of the woodwork.

In a far less repugnant but still very troubling way, more mainstream groups such as Human Rights Watch and Amnesty International are effectively asking that the United States prosecute its war in Afghanistan with one hand tied behind its back, by issuing rules for comportment for both sides that it can never conceivably expect the Taliban to follow. Issuing demands that the Taliban allow distribution of humanitarian aid and that the United States cease using cluster bombs is just not very fruitful. Framing the conflict in such a way suggest a false moral equivalence that will only damage the NGOs' own reputations. Does Amnesty International or Human Rights Watch really believe that the likes of al-Qaeda would accept their "rules?" After all, Osama bin Laden has just described the United Nations as a "criminal organization" and condemned the Muslim governments participating in it as lackeys of the "infidel."

Nor do such AI and HRW demands as the trial of the victorious Northern Alliance leaders—now seen as liberators by many Afghans—for real or alleged past abuses, or the placing of "human-rights observers" in a country still at war and without a functioning government do any good to their image as hopelessly utopian and arrogant.

Ultimately, the human rights establishment is faced with two equally important and vital problems: how to deal with the Bonafinis in their ranks and how to make themselves relevant post-September 11.

Reprinted with permission from http://www.nationalreview.com, December 3, 2001

HUMAN RIGHTS FIFTH COLUMN

It is an almost daily occurrence that someone—usually but not always from the self-proclaimed "progressive" Left—accuses the Bush administration or its predecessors or the United States in general, of moral inconsistency, incoherence (that, on good days) or, more seriously and frequently, hypocrisy. The main argument is that America is or claims to be built upon principles of extensive individual human and democratic rights, but behaves abroad as if democracy and respect for human rights were matters of political convenience. The evidence they present is supposed to show both the irrationality and incoherence of U.S. policies, and the pernicious impact they have upon some elements of the American body politic and overseas opinions about the United States. Let us take a closer look at one of those.

Over the past decade or so the "human rights establishment" in the U.S. and abroad, made up of non-governmental organizations (NGOs) such as Amnesty International (AI) and Human Rights Watch (HRW), have continually accused various military regimes in South America's Southern Cone (Argentina, Chile, Uruguay, and Paraguay) as well as Brazil and Bolivia, of engaging in a genocidal conspiracy, "Operation Condor," in the mid-1970s. The human rights establishment labels Operation Condor a "crime against humanity" under what its members hopefully describe as "evolving international law," but that is all an ideological claim and no more.

Operation Condor was an informal arrangement among South American military governments and their countries' intelligence services to exchange intelligence and co-operate against the then deadly and internationally coordinated threat from Marxist-Leninist terrorist groups in those countries.

Furthermore, the "progressives" and human rights activists claim, naturally enough, that all this "criminal activity" was at the very least condoned, and probably actively encouraged, by Washington. For public relations purposes, the groups have a poster boy for America's complicity in Operation Condor: it was all the fault of Henry Kissinger, national security adviser and then secretary of state between 1969 and 1977, who according to Christopher Hitchens' *The Trial of Henry Kissinger* (Verso Books: May 2001; excerpted in the *Guardian*, *Harper's* magazine and at the Third World Traveler website), was an immoral, reactionary war criminal.

Operation Condor was simply an agreement between the intelligence organizations of anti-communist regimes to exchange data, extradite or arrest terrorist suspects trying to take advantage of regional freedom of movement, and, yes, in some cases, and often outside the law, to deal with them—to murder them for a partner country. Hence, Chilean terrorists of the MIR (Movement of the Revolutionary Left) were often found dead in Argentina, Montoneros Marxist Leninist terrorists were "disappeared" in Chile or Paraguay, Uruguayan Tupamaros in Argentina, and so on. Some of the countries or regimes involved—

Chile and Argentina being the best example—were traditional enemies. But under the precept of "the enemy of my enemy is my friend," the countries were unified by the Castroist menace to their countries. That menace, coordinated and organized from Havana, was even more international. A Revolutionary Coordinating Junta between Uruguayan, Bolivian, Argentine, and Chilean Marxist terrorist groups was established in Paris in 1976, largely paid for by Havana (and so indirectly probably with Soviet money). Moreover, ever since the mid-1960s Havana was openly organizing, training, and arming sympathetic "revolutionary" groups throughout Latin America.

The clear, violent, and totalitarian threat to both the undemocratic and democratic (e.g., Uruguay) regimes in South America was inherently international. Why was Operation Condor a "crime against humanity" under international law, but not the Tricontinental, OSPAAL (Organization in Solidarity with Peoples of Africa and Latin America), JCR (Revolutionary Coordinating Junta) and other organizations Castro paid for, sponsored, and controlled? Perhaps because the New York Times et al. in the mainstream American and European media have bought the notion that illegally murdering totalitarian terrorists and their logistical supporters is more illegal than Marxist terrorists killing policemen, military personnel, and their families. Or that Fidel Castro is a "progressive" and thus untouchable for the human rights establishment, or that violent totalitarian terrorists are to be seen as "leftist dissidents." "Dissidents" indeed-who killed police, army, and government officials and their families, as well as innocent passersbys, and sought a Stalinist "solution" in the Southern Cone.

Aside from the goals of the "victims" of the 1970s, there are their methods. The Montoneros planted booby traps in infants' cradles. Nor does it seem to matter to AI & Co. that it was the Sandinista regime in Nicaragua that was responsible for the assassinations of Commander Bravo in Honduras and Somoza in Paraguay. The human rights establishment never seems to have considered accusing the Sandinistas of Somoza's or Bravo's murder, nor appreciating

Operation Condor as simply an answer to an equally international, and even more dangerous, threat to national survival than that expressed by such leftist caricatures as Pinochet, etc. The civil wars of South America during the 1970s were wars, and rights get trampled by all combatants in wars—in this case by military gorillas as well as the Castro-backed terrorists.

Ultimately, the fight over who was culpable for Operation Condor is not a matter of "human rights" by any rational definition, but a fight over history. He who controls the interpretation of the past controls the present-and, one may add, has an advantage in defining the terms for the future. Hence, "truth commissions"—whether in South Africa or Guatemala, Peru, or Spain—are simply attempts to manipulate "human rights" fundamentalism in order to reclassify terrorists as "innocent victims," make anti-communism a crime per se, and thus legitimize a long lost and historically defeated "progressive" cause. The issue is not criminality as such-Argentina's military rulers of the 1970s snatched children and completed the ruin of their country started by the "progressive" Juan Peron, and they should have paid for that. But that is not the goal of their "human rights" enemies. Their goal is cleaning up the image of the Marxist terrorists, and such pseudo-human rights groups as the Madres de Plaza de Mayo make no secret of it.

That previously legitimate groups like AI, of which this author used to be a member, give credibility to these schemes only demonstrates how much the rot inside the human rights establishment has advanced, and why its claims to moral authority have to be questioned.

Reprinted with permission from http://frontpagemag.com, August 26, 2002

THE GUANTANAMO HYATT

Camp Delta in Guantanamo Bay, where Taliban and al-Qaeda members continue to be held as "unlawful combatants," continues to attract charges of human rights abuses from the Left. Yet the mothers of eight Russian prisoners the U.S. is holding there have now "begged Washington not to extradite their sons to answer terror charges in Russia, fearing that conditions in their jails and judicial system are even worse than those at Camp Delta." "In Guantanamo they treat him humanely and the conditions are fine," the mother of one of them has said. Her son has written her "there is no health resort in Russia that can compare." And more: Nina Odizheva, the mother of Ruslan, twenty-nine, from Kabardino-Balkaria, wrote several times to the U.S. ambassador, Alexander Vershbow, begging Washington to resist Moscow's calls for extradition. Ruslan wrote to his mother that at Camp Delta "what we see around us is a complete miracle." ("Russian mothers plead for sons to stay in Guantanamo," Nick Paton Walsh, *Guardian*, August 9).

Indeed, the Red Cross has expressed no concern over the detainees' treatment. But this does not stop Amnesty International, Human Rights Watch, and other human rights organizations—that, unlike the Red Cross, do not have access to the detainees—from charging human rights abuses.

Except for the few facts that have been provided by the Pentagon, all we really know about Camp Delta comes from second-hand media reports, reports by detainees who have already been released (some fifteen so far, all Afghans and Pakistanis), and letters from detainees to their relatives. There are some 640 detainees at Guantanamo, citizens of some forty countries.

There are some 640 detainees at Guantanamo, citizens of some forty countries on all continents. While all figures are approximate, it seems that the largest group are Saudis, some 127 of them; thirty-seven Yemenis, forty-two Pakistanis, seventeen Moroccans, seven Kuwaitis, six Algerians, eleven Turks, four Bahrainis, eight Russians, some fourteen from Western Europe (Britons, Swedes,

Belgians, French, Spanish, Danes), some Uzbeks, and two Australians. Some have been interrogated by the intelligence services of their native countries, and all have been by the United States. Virtually all are Muslims, with educational levels ranging from illiterates to advanced degree holders.

U.S. law actually does not apply in Guantanamo, which is sovereign Cuban territory (though Fidel Castro has stated that he has no objection to the United States' using the base for terrorist detention). This does not help the confusion that already exists surrounding the remedies to terrorism available under "international law," but there is no reason, or excuse, for the West to let this inevitable confusion deteriorate into complete chaos.

While most were captured during the 2001 war in Afghanistan, many were arrested subsequently in Pakistan, Africa, or Southeast Asia. Whether because their nations' governments fear reprisals and/or because their legal or prison systems are inadequate, it appears those governments were happy not to have to deal with their Islamic terrorists and to be able instead to dump their terrorist hot potatoes into Uncle Sam's lap.

President Bush recently made it known that six unnamed Guantanamo detainees, who it was later established were British and Australian citizens, would be brought before U.S. military tribunals. Under pressure from London, Washington then assured that the British detainees would not be subject to the death penalty, nor would the Australian, David Hicks—one of the most violent of the lot. That, of course, opens the door for other governments to demand similar treatment for "their" terrorists (as the Saudis already have) and transforms the soon-to-be-established military tribunals into a political circus.

But of course, Camp Delta has already become something of a circus. Sweden's security police chief has described twenty-three-year-old detainee Mehdi-Muhammad Ghezali, a Swedish citizen, as "a confused youth." Confused indeed. In Afghanistan he stood with bin Laden at Tora Bora to the end, before fleeing to Pakistan—presumably, as the same Swedish official would have it, "looking for spiritual fulfillment."

The British do not want their Guantanamo detainees returned to the U.K. for trial because—and this issue is sure to cause a major transatlantic conflict soon enough—there are simply no legal grounds to put them on trial at home. Islamic terrorists with European passports already have good reason to feel safe at home (except possibly for in France and Spain, which have both been burned long and badly enough by Islamic and other terrorism to have implemented relatively harsh counterterrorism measures). After all, most of them are only guilty of credit card fraud or similar crimes at home.

And then there is the issue of the death penalty, opposition to which is a core European value. When forced to choose between extraditing a terrorist tried and sentenced to death abroad (in Jordan, Egypt, Iran, Yemen) and granting him asylum, welfare, and a platform to continue inciting to murder, European governments have consistently chosen the latter. The cases of terrorist ideologues ensconcing themselves in the United Kingdom—or "Londonistan," as it is now aptly called by many—are now legion, the likes of Abu Hamza, Omar Bakri, and Abu Qatada being only the best known. That issue alone is a guarantee that adequate punishment will not be given to international terrorists based in Europe, even if they are extradited to the United States. And that is the main reason Washington's promise to London and Canberra regarding the Guantanamo detainees is a bad precedent.

Ultimately, the issue of Guantanamo's detainees is going to become the issue of Western and civilized approach to Islamist and generally international terrorism—legally and otherwise. Neither the United States, nor, to say the least, the Europeans are yet prepared to deal comprehensively and consistently with the issue, and the counterproductive, indeed irresponsible but powerful influence of "human rights" NGOs only makes a solution more difficult. Perhaps the statements of the Russian detainees and their relatives may raise some questions and quiet some hysterical voices—but so far that should be seen as a remote hope rather than promise.

Reprinted with the promission from http://www.frontpagemag.com, August 13, 2003

JUSTICE FOR A DESPOT

Within hours of news of Saddam Hussein's capture, the global human rights establishment (HRE) had started its campaign on his behalf, in the name of "international justice." Its representatives tell us that the Iraqis are too primitive to assure a fair trial for their tormentor, unless, that is, "international experts" (the HRE of course) run it.

"No Political Show Trial for Saddam Hussein; International Expert Participation Key to Trial," pontificates Human Rights Watch (www.hrw.org). "Give Saddam Prisoner of War status," demands Amnesty International. "The Iraqi Governing Council should partner with the UN to create an accountability process that works," said HRW's Kenneth Roth. "There won't be a second chance to do this right." He is right. That's why we may be glad that President Bush is calling for a public trial in Iraq. Because the Iraqis—and the United States—have a great opportunity to demonstrate the vacuity of the much-trumpeted "evolving international law" on human rights.

By all standards, Saddam Hussein is one of the worst mass murderers of recent times—not an "alleged" or "suspected" murderer. If he does not belong in the company of Stalin, Mao, or Hitler, it is only because there were not enough Iraqis to kill to put him in this first rank. HRW's likening of a trial that has not even begun yet—the Iraqis' trial of this tyrant—to Stalin's show trials of the 1930s is absurd. It casts Saddam's victims in the Stalin role. It is Saddam, not they, who is in that role here. As even HRW admits, his crimes include genocide against Iraqi Kurds, the use of chemical weapons against Iranian troops and Kurdish civilians, large-scale killings after the failed 1991 uprisings, destruction and repression of the Marsh Arabs; and the forced expulsion of ethnic minorities in northern Iraq.

Amnesty supports a "fair trial" for Saddam, but obsessively defines "fair trials" as those that do not involve capital punishment. (Democratic presidential candidate and former general Wesley Clark might wish to note this. He continues to call for Osama bin Laden, if captured, to be tried for 9/11 by the recently formed International Criminal Court, "under international law with an international group of justices. . . Remember, 80 other nations lost citizens in that strike on the WTC. It was a crime against humanity, and he needs to be tried in international court." Obviously Gen. Clark has no idea what the ICC is—that like Amnesty, it is anti-capital punishment—or what it could do. It cannot try terrorist crimes, since terrorism as a crime does not exist under "international law," and it cannot try cases involving events that occurred before it was founded in June 2002).

In all events, let us suppose that the HRE "standards" are applied by the Iraqi court trying Saddam. The court would include "international experts"—that is, European jurists who are opposed to capital punishment. Notwithstanding that Iraq is an Arab country with specific cultural and legal traditions quite different from those of Belgium or Sweden. How would a verdict (life sentence?) from such a tribunal serve such basic principles of jurisprudence as deterrence and punishment to fit the crime in a way that would satisfy Iraqis? It would not. It would only serve as another example of Western imperialism, especially for those Iraqis who were victimized by Saddam. Of course, the readily available targets for retaliation will not be Swedish or German human rights lawyers, but U.S. and coalition troops.

Based on our experience to date with international courts, after a trial of months or years (Yugoslavia's Slobodan Milosevic has been on trial before a UN international tribunal for more than a year and is now running for office in Serbia, and the UN tribunal in Rwanda's seventeen convictions over nine years have cost $80 million a year), Saddam would be found guilty and sentenced to life or many years in prison. Then what? Is the Iraqi government supposed to keep him in isolation, which would earn it the condemnation of the HRE? Or allow him his "rights" according to the HRE, and thus the ability to plot a return to power?

If Saddam Hussein is tried and found guilty of genocide, mass murder, and crimes against humanity, he deserves no less than Adolph Eichmann received: the Israeli law against execution in general notwithstanding, Eichmann was executed. Nor are more recent and relevant precedents lacking—in August 3, 1979, Francisco Macias Nguema, self–proclaimed President for Life and "Only Miracle" of Equatorial Guinea, was executed by a Moroccan firing squad, after being overthrown a few months before in a military coup. At the time of the capture, Macias, who murdered a third of his country's population and forced another third into exile, was in possession of most of the country's treasury. The trial took place in the capital, with observers from Amnesty International, etc. Arrested in December 24, 1989, Romania's communist dictator Nicolae Ceausescu, "the genius of the Carpathians," and his wife Elena, were tried the following day by a military tribunal, found guilty of "genocide," sentenced to death and shot.

Why the Iraqi Governing Council suspended capital punishment is unclear, and was probably misguided, but the Iraqis have the natural right to lift that suspension. The sooner they do, and the sooner Saddam is tried and executed, the better. An ideal Baghdad court would be composed of five judges—a Shia, a Kurd, a Marsh Sunni, a (secular) Iranian, and a Kuwaiti. The longer Saddam lives, the more Iraqis and Americans are going to die—and that, more than utopian "evolving international standards" or AI anti-capital punishment paranoia, should be decisive.

Reprinted with permission from http://www.frontpage.com, December 18, 2003

ABUSING THE CAUSE OF HUMAN RIGHTS

Communism may have collapsed over a decade ago, but its adherents have not gone quietly into the good night. Rather, the intellectual remnants of the Marxist Utopia have reinvented themselves as staunch defenders of "human rights." In Argentina, Chile, Peru, Guatemala, South Africa, and even Spain, radical Marxists are attempting, with great success, to rewrite the history of the violent Left's defeat at the hands of anti-communist forces. The major root cause of these reassessment campaigns is their promoters: embittered die-hards still clinging to the destructive credos of the defeated totalitarian Left.

In Latin America, leftist-dominated public universities such as San Carlos in Guatemala, San Marcos in Lima, and UNAM (The Autonomous National University of Mexico, the world's largest) have shrunk over the past two decades as government expenditures have shriveled and higher education has been privatized. As a result, public schools now compete with private universities such as the Guatemalan Francisco Marroquin University, where educating rather than radicalizing students is the goal. Consequently, many Progressive intellectuals have been forced to leave their traditional university refuges and seek employment elsewhere.

"Elsewhere," increasingly, is the growing constellation of Non-Governmental Organizations (NGOs), largely funded—directly or indirectly—by the European Union (EU), through its rich and usually leftist member governments. Marxists formerly employed by Latin American taxpayers are now active as human rights militants, their salaries underwritten by the EU, the Ford Foundation or radical factions of the Catholic Church and assorted Protestant congregations in the U.S.

In some cases, this recasting of the hard Left as "human rights advocates" and pacifists has even led to unrepentant Marxists receiving the Nobel Peace Prize. Guatemala's Indian and leftist activist Rigoberta Menchú Tum (1992), and Argentine writer Adolfo Perez Esquivel (1980) have both received Nobel prizes. Here is a sample of Esquivel's award-winning "thinking," from a letter to President Bush, dated April 10, 2003:

> The greatest of your defeats is that you will lose the respect of the people of the world, and win rejection in humanity's conscience for all the crimes committed. In this flight to rush onward, you are accompanied by your allies of death: Tony Blair, José María Aznar and John Howard. You hide the true motives of the Iraq invasion and seek to justify massacres in order to seize the oil resources of Iraq, and to dominate the Mideast, and to impose your plans of world hegemony and global dictatorship....You have transformed the United States into a terrorist State.

Equally disturbing is the mainstream acceptance of groups like the Mothers of the Plaza de Mayo of Argentina (openly and unashamedly Stalinist) as noble human rights defenders, even after the Mothers' leader, Hebe de Bonafini, publicly applauded the 9/11 attacks. Incidentally, Bonafini's anti-U.S. vitriol did not prevent her from receiving numerous European "human rights" prizes.

But the most confusing, dangerous and ultimately pernicious campaign of this transmogrified Left is its attempt to rewrite the histories of countries where Marxist totalitarianism failed. Members of Salvador Allende's regime in Chile engaged in acts of murder and terrorism even before Allende's election in 1970. But the dinosaurs of the Communist Party insist upon judging the crimes of the Pinochet era (1973-1990), as if that military regime had overthrown mere liberal democrats rather than professional Marxist terrorists when it ousted Allende from power.

It is the same story in Argentina: those who took part in the various military juntas (1976-80) that destroyed the Montoneros and ERP (People's Revolutionary Army)—both of which were supported, armed, and trained by Castro—were and are being pursued by law enforcement officials, while the defeated Marxist terrorists are not. Yes, some members of the military engaged in real crimes, such as kidnapping infants, for which they should be punished. But not only are the middle-class Montonero and ERP terrorists—the real authors of the Argentinian civil war—seen as victims, their supporters are now the judges of the past.

In Spain, the establishment Left in the media has managed to frame the Spanish Civil War as a victimization of the Left at the hands of Franco. Franco's victims among the Spanish totalitarian Left (most of which was controlled by Stalin from Moscow) are now lionized, while the thousands of priests, nationalists and conservatives and dozens of bishops and nuns, as well as anarchists and Catalan or Basque separatists, murdered by the Communist-controlled Republican regime are largely forgotten.

In Guatemala and El Salvador, where Marxist guerrillas lost civil wars and then entered politics (so far with little success), their fellow travelers in justice and human rights want to put on trial the military and the large majority who supported them during the 1980s. Thus, Menchú's campaign against Efraim Rios Montt, a Guatemalan junta leader in 1983 who had been popularly elected (and defrauded by the military) in 1976, and was also a military victor against the Left in 1970 and again in 1983. The accusation? "Genocide," despite the fact that the victorious military of Rios Montt, his predecessors and successors were mostly Indian, fighting mostly terrorist groups led by Marxist white intellectuals.

In Peru, where the Communist Party (better known as Shining Path) was responsible for some 30,000 dead between 1980-1992, a democratic Commission for Truth and Reconciliation led by leftist intellectuals has managed to place equal blame for the long-running violence on the Communist terrorists and their legitimate adversaries. They even persuaded Peru's President Toledo to apologize for his elected predecessors' crackdown on Shining Path militants. Worse still, the relatives of thousands of murdered Peruvian civilians are being encouraged by left-wing voices to "reconcile" with their Maoist killers. Reconciliation is the last thing that should happen.

In South Africa, the apartheid intelligence and military apparatus was put in the same defendants' box as civil servants, mob murderers and practitioners of "necklacing." Perhaps there is no moral difference between these factions, except that the latter were promoted into the South African security forces after the fall of apartheid.

The common thread running through all these developments is that the very same Left that failed, and was defeated, in its violent campaigns is now trying, with considerable success, to win in the eyes of "justice" and "law" what it lost in the military and public opinion fields. When an entire generation is being taught a false version of the recent past, under the noble rubric of "human rights," an entire future generation of leaders will be unprepared to deal with threats to freedom; when the initiators of the civil wars of the 1970 and 1980s— the spoiled sons and daughters of dysfunctional middle classes in most cases—are seen as innocent victims of uniformed guerillas, rather than terrorist totalitarians, morality and truth are the true victims.

Would Chile be better off now if Allende and his minority clique, rather than Pinochet's free marketers, succeeded in their goals? Would a Marxist El Salvador be better off than the present model? Would a Moscow-controlled Spain, likely a member of the Warsaw Pact, be the thriving European Union member and democracy it is today? The answer to all these questions should be obvious, but instead, the very notions of justice and human rights are being distorted to further an alternative totalitarian history.

Reprinted with permission from http://www.frontpagemag.com,
December 26, 2003

THE HUMAN RIGHTS ESTABLISHMENT DESTROYS HAITI

Liberalism's two flagship newspapers, the *Washington Post* and the *New York Times,* have recently voiced concerns with Haiti's left-wing ruler, Jean Bertrand Aristide—on the editorial page, no less. How have we come to this turn of events? After all, Aristide was put back in power by the U.S. military under President Clinton's comically misnamed "Operation Restore Freedom" in 1994. Aristide is a "progressive" former Catholic priest expelled by his own conservative church, is black and would satisfy the PC Left's portrait of what a Third World leader should be. And still, the very same Aristide, whose 1990 election and 2000 re-election were applauded by leftists everywhere, is now seen with increasing criticism even by the Left's standard bearers. This change has come about because Haiti under the collapsing Aristide regime threatens to raise doubts over the very core of liberal orthodoxy on the Third World.

The basic problem is *not* Bill Clinton's intervention in Haiti (or Somalia, or Bosnia), or Bush's present interventions in Afghanistan and Iraq; it is, in fact, not a partisan problem at all but a cultural American/Western issue: the failed policies of the leftist Human Rights Establishment (HRE) toward the Third World.

Haiti is the perfect case study, but it is far from a unique case: Somalia, the Solomon Islands, Afghanistan, Zaire (oops! The Democratic Republic of Congo), Liberia, Sierra Leone, and a number of others are quite similar. All are pseudo-states enclosing profoundly dysfunctional societies, societies that are beyond repair from within, and too costly to repair from afar. Simply put, this is about the "black holes" of the international system, entire "states" where there is no civil society, no legitimate institution, no rule of law, indeed no law at all—all there is, in most cases, is a vote in the United Nations' General Assembly and a limitless ability to absorb and demand Western aid. All of this is made possible by the equally limitless and nonsensical demands and claims by Western non-governmental organizations (NGOs), who take advantage of the taxpayers' ignorance, gullibility, and innate sympathy for those Third World kids with distended bellies on their TV screens.

A recent piece in the far-left British newspaper the *Guardian* illustrated the NGO dilemma well: "Aid agencies warn of Haiti crisis, but…(as usual) have no solution…fifteen U.K. and international NGOs, including ActionAid and Oxfam, have warned that the economy is collapsing, with a threat to food supplies as transport breaks down exacerbated by a doubling in the price of petrol."

The *Guardian* continued to paint Haiti's developing "situation of ungovernability, of institutionalized violence and of insecurity." This is worsening "the already precarious socio-economic conditions of the population," in a country where about half the population—some 4 million people—have "insecure access" to food and 65 percent live below the absolute poverty line, the NGOs warned. But the agencies said the emergency situation cannot be solved by a massive influx of food aid "without reaching a resolution of the political situation which is the cause….Moreover food aid has traditionally had adverse impacts on the systems and structures of production of the country and can only put at risk the process of sustainable development."

The NGOs have also warned against armed intervention. They said the gravity of the situation in Haiti "must in no way serve as a pretext for the international community to intervene once again, militarily, in the country, particularly at the time when the Haitian people celebrate the bicentenary of its independence dearly acquired through struggle and self-denial." They added: "Any military intervention in the current crisis would not be sustainable if the structural causes of the decaying Haitian social situation were not addressed—notably a social structure which is extremely unequal and polarized, [and] the increasing poverty and social exclusion of the great majority of the population from the spheres of power. We reaffirm that international solidarity with the Haitian people must be characterized by the respect for national sovereignty and the right to the people of self-determination."

Let us translate this into normal, human language: The NGOs say Haiti is a humanitarian mess, the fault lies with Haitians and only they could solve it. On the other hand, they also say that outsiders could not and should not interfere militarily; the West must simply continue an endless supply of aid to Haitians, but never interfere, especially militarily, because Haitians have a sovereign right…to murder each other.

The NGOs affirm this right to slaughter is legitimate, "particularly at the time when the Haitian people celebrate the bicentenary of its independence dearly acquired through struggle and self-denial." Translation: Because black slaves succeeded in establishing a dysfunctional Republic in the Americas in 1804, the outside should "respect" it and do *nothing* about the present collapse of a hopeless descendent of slaves and tyrannical leader of Haiti—Jean Bertrand Aristide—nor the chaos his incompetence has wrought.

In other words, the only role for the West is to pay, subsidize and feed Haitians as they slaughter one another. This is the perfect example of the NGOs' "human rights" and "humanitarian" terminal hypocrisy.

The ultimate responsibility lies with Western academia, which upholds multiculturalism, the notion that all cultures are equal—except the immoral Western one, of course. These noxious notions have become the de facto ideology of the "human rights" and charitable NGOs throughout the world—a combination that could only be called the global Human Rights Establishment (HRE). Somalia is not a "state" and never should have been treated like one. Haiti could not be repaired because the locals choose a tyrant in (relatively) free elections supervised by Jimmy Carter and thus is deemed by the world a "democracy." The Haitians voted for Aristide because, then and now, he represented their "values"—just as they elected Francois "Papa Doc" Duvalier in the 1950s. Indeed, it should be remembered that the only two Haitian presidents ever elected in competitive elections in 200 years were…Papa Doc and Aristide.

Elections, even technically free ones, do not make a democracy any more than a rooster creates the daylight. Values make a democracy, and when they are absent, at least beyond the village or tribal level, elections become just a pretext for Aristides, Talibans, and similar monstrosities. But multiculturalists have told us—and generations of elite university alumni have agreed—that "tribe" is itself a Western racist notion (tell that to the Somalis!) and that political culture is an evil "Orientalist" fiction when it comes to the Arab world—where large majorities still believe that September 11 was the work of the Mossad and CIA.

(Is this attitude toward the Muslim world going to change? Probably so, since multiculturalists now have to deal with a new threat: the presence of those admired Islamist cultures in the midst of the West. It is one thing to explain away Islamic arranged marriages, the general treatment of women, or genital mutilation when it occurs in Saudi Arabia or Central Africa; it is another when the ordinary Joe Six Pack or Pierre hears of it in his neighborhood. Americans have forgotten Somalia—and even the *Black Hawk Down* movie—but the Somali black hole is still there, awaiting another scream for "humanitarian aid" from the HRE—hopefully one not accepted.)

In terms of Haiti, it is one thing for a Randall Robinson or Jesse Jackson to scream "racism" when Bill Clinton had doubts about restoring Aristide (as if his enemies were not *also* black), another for Americans to see that just a murderous gangs—the "Pink Army" in St, Marc, the "Canibal Army" in Gonaïves (now rebaptised as the Front for the Liberation of Haiti), the "Red Army" elsewhere—represented Aristide's "popular support" and are now turning against him.

Unless Haitian1s once again try to invade Florida—and bring their culture, voodoo included, with them—Americans should let Haiti be…Haiti. We should let them sort out their own affairs, rather than attempt to impose a failed national "solution," as Bill Clinton did. We should not continue to entertain the fiction that they are a stable "democracy," as our guilt-ridden leftist academics and HRE functionaries do, and our aid should remain as absent from Haiti as our "imperialist" armies. But at least the academics get it half-right. For once, the NGOs have come up with a recommendation that should be taken seriously. For once.

Reprinted with permission from http://www.frontpagemag.com,
February 25, 2004

DEFENDING THE DEVIL

French celebrity lawyer Jacques Vergès has announced that, "at the request of the (Hussein) family," he has decided to serve as the defense lawyer of Saddam

Hussein at his upcoming trial for genocide and similar charges. The trial, to begin sometime this year, had already promised to be interesting and revealing; but Vergès' presence ensures that it has a chance of becoming an international, ideological and political nine-ring circus.

Concepts such as genocide, terrorism and the right to a fair trial will all come under scrutiny during the trial, enveloped in a fog of Stalinist "anti–imperialism," Vergès trademark. It is thus important to understand who Jacques Vergès is, why is he taking Saddam's case, how he will handle the case and what the implications of the coming judicial spectacle will be.

For those who believe that communism, and even more so, Stalinism, are long dead, Vergès is a living fossil, his ideology a Jurassic Park of twentieth-century criminal thought. Vergès' biography[1] is revealing of a certain trend in European, especially French, intellectual environment, where "justice" is a matter of ideology, fashion and politics rather than morality and law. It is only in such an environment that a lawyer who lost most of his cases (before France abolished capital punishment in 1984, Vergès was nicknamed "Monsieur guillotine," in recognition of the fate of many of his clients) became famous, had his books published by the most prestigious editors,[2] and is taken seriously in his relentless assaults against the very concepts of Western law and democracy.

Jacques Vergès was born in 1925 in Thailand, where his father, Raymond, was serving as a French diplomat. Raymond was a native of the French island department of La Réunion in the Indian Ocean, whose inhabitants are mostly of mixed race (Asian, European, African); his wife, Jacques' mother, was Vietnamese. That racial background gave Jacques a perennial claim to victimhood (or "racism").

In 1937, Raymond Vergès founded the Réunion Communist Party (PCR), the local branch of the metropolitan organization. Jacques' twin brother, Paul, jailed as a young man for the murder of a political opponent of his father, was a deputy for the Party. Since 1996, he has served as a Senator in the French Parliament and remains President of the Regional Council of Réunion and head of the PCR, which has become Thailand's second largest party.

Jacques himself joined the Communist Party as a teenager, and by 1949, was president of the AEC (Association of Colonial Students), a Communist front, where he befriended a fellow colonial student from then-French Indochina, Saloth Sar—better known as Pol Pot. The connection with the Khmer Rouge continues to this day, with Vergès offering to defend Pol Pot's associate and fellow Sorbonne contemporary alumnus Kieu Samphan.

Between 1950 and 1954 Verges was in Prague, then the center of Soviet global propaganda and ideological training, as leader of one of Moscow's youth front organizations. During that period he had the high honor of meeting Joseph Stalin himself.

Upon return to France, Vergès left the Communist Party and began his road to fame as a defense lawyer for Algerian terrorists. The most famous of those, and a case that won him the plaudits of the Left, was that of Djamila Bouhired, who had been implicated in the bombing of an Algiers café that resulted in numerous fatalities. Bouhired was sentenced to death, but the combination of a leftist media campaign and a weak Socialist government led to her release and subsequent marriage to Vergès.

At a time when France was at war, Vergès openly supported, as well as defended, terrorists and their French accomplices. For that reason he was jailed for two months in 1960 and temporarily lost his practicing license.

Since then, Verges' clients have included Nazi criminal Klaus Barbie (sentenced to life in prison); fellow radical lawyer and accomplice of the Baader–Meinhof Gang, Klaus Croissant; terrorist Ilich Ramirez Sanchez a.k.a. Carlos the Jackal (sentenced to life in prison, 1994); ex-Marxist philosopher and convicted Holocaust-denier Roger Garaudy (convicted and fined, 1996); Slobodan Milosevic (2002) and now, logically enough, Saddam.

What do these clients have in common with their lawyer? The same characteristics as another Verges associate, the ex-Nazi, now Islamist sympathizer Francois Genoud—who, as owner of the Arab Commercial Bank in Switzerland, was the apparent paymaster in the Barbie and some Palestinian terrorist cases. They are ideologues and defenders (Garaudy), practitioners (Milosevic, Barbie, Saddam) or would-be practitioners (Bouhired, Kelkal) of mass murder or genocide. Their ideology is totalitarian at its core, and they share yet another common trait of twentieth-century European totalitarianism and present Islamism—hatred of Jews and Israel.

It is this background that gives away Vergès' likely tactics at Saddam's trial and indeed explains his taking up the case. The radical lawyer has waged a life-long campaign against Western values and freedoms, and the fate of his clients is not a major concern to him–they are just replaceable tools for a greater goal. He needs a political platform, not a legal success. Hence, the desire to have Saddam's case tried by the International Criminal Court in The Hague, while fully aware that the court has no jurisdiction over Iraq.

As (mostly self-) appointed lawyer for Milosevic, Vergès has claimed that the International Court trying the Serb leader is inherently illegitimate and biased, because it receives outside donations from George Soros, the United States and Saudi Arabia. Otherwise, he claims, the Court would ask for testimonies from Messrs Clinton, Blair, Schroeder and Chirac, "Because in Dayton they recognized Mr. Milosevic as a respectable and valid interlocutor." Expect the same in a Baghdad court—after all, Defense Secretary Rumsfeld did talk to Saddam in the 1980s, and the West helped him against Iran at the time. As a defender of Palestinian terrorist hijackers of El Al planes in 1969, Vergès claimed that the terrorists' acts were political, not criminal, and the fault of Israeli aggression.

All this combines with Vergès' personal and peculiar views of the justice system in general and of morality itself. Thus, in his book, Beauty of Crime, he writes: "Between the dogs (prosecution) and the wolf (defendants) I'll always be on the side of the wolf—especially when he is wounded."

In many ways Vergès has been a pathfinder for radical lawyers everywhere, with his approach to the defense of terrorists—a path followed by American and German lawyers for decades. He blurred the lines between defense, representation and ideological comradeship with the accused, and tried to transform a legal case against individuals into a global tribune against "the system," to put the court, the judges and democracy on the dock. True to his habit, he has already made it clear that he will try to bring world leaders on the dock in Baghdad—and has already found enablers in the media speculating that such tactics "could be a huge embarrassment for the United States, France and other countries."[4]

That would, of course, depend on the Iraqi judges and rules to be decided in Baghdad. If the clamor by Western human rights groups and defense lawyers succeeds in making the Saddam trial an international affair, they will do what they did for decades—offer Vergès another platform for his anti-Western psychopathic obsessions and Saddam a chance for revenge against his persecutors in Washington and London and, perhaps, a chance to save his skin. If, however, common sense and morality set the rules, Jacques Vergès will not only lose the case—he is used to that—but, given his age, also the last chance to promote the counter values of a century of totalitarian ideologies.

Notes

1. For useful biographical information, go to http://www.essentialresults.com/article/Jacques_Verges
2. Such as *On Judicial Strategy* (1981) ; *The Beauty of Crime* (1988) ; *I Defend Barbie* (1988) and *I Have More Memories than If I Would be One Thousand Years Old* (1999).
3. ST.B., *Le Parisien*, 27 mars 2004, p. 6
4. "World leaders should take stand in Saddam trial: lawyer," in the *Sidney Morning Herald*, December 20, 2003 http://www.smh.com.au/articles/2003/12/19/1071337168638.html?from=storyrhs

Reprinted with permission from http://www.frontpagemag.com,
April 14, 2004

PART 2
EUROPE—OLD, NEW AND THE NEWEST VERSION

THE BALKAN DILEMMAS

The quip that the Balkans have too much history to digest has a lot of merit. What makes the region unique, even in our times of rampant victimology, is that there, everybody sees themselves as victims, and they are all correct: it all depends on the century or decade one is considering. There are no permanent "good" or "bad" guys—the angelic victims of the present were definitely less angelic in the past, and with the region's exceedingly long memories, the difference between centuries is of minimal relevance. Thus Albanians and Greeks have long been seen as oppressors and Ottoman puppets by the Serbs, Bulgarians, or Romanians; the Greeks see themselves as victims of Turkish secular oppression, while Albanians see themselves as victims of Serbian or Macedonian "genocide" and gypsies as everybody's victims, period.

Born and partly miseducated in Ceausescu's Romania, on the fringes of the region, I had enough direct experience with its diverse peoples, idiosyncrasies and deeply rooted myths to be cautious of whatever rhetoric comes from there. Unfortunately, that is not the case with a largely uninformed, emotional and politically correct Western media, intellectuals, and politicians. Even when they do travel or do some (superficial) research on the region, they remain captives of old prejudices, fashionable old books, Western standards and biases, nonsense and false analogies. And the locals miss no opportunity to take advantage of all this. Albanians are the most recent of the region's nationalities to successfully manipulate a Western psychology they know well but do not share and gypsies, or their romantic admirers and defenders, are moving fast to the same level of effective manipulation of the cult of victimology.

Many communist slogans were better received in the Balkans than elsewhere in the old and unlamented Soviet bloc. Collectivism, based on traditional village-based egalitarianism, class envy (if not struggle in the *Das Kapital* sense), artificial and violence-based upward mobility for marginal groups (Jews, gypsies, ethnic minorities of all kinds after 1945), anti-intellectualism—all made it safer for the likes of Ceausescu, Jhivkov, Hoxha, even Tito, than for their colleagues further north, in Poland, the Czech Republic, or Hungary. Religion, whether Orthodoxy, with its inherent anti-Westernism, or Islam's anti-individualism and confusion of state and "church," further facilitated this.

And then there is Turkey—the best of Islam, the best and worst of the Balkans, a universe more than simply a country, large as it is. There, a secular and effec-

31

tive military keeps the standards of civilization against the corrupt political class or a growing, if still bland, Islamism. In Eastern Anatolia, neglected by Ankara's politicians and despised by Istanbul's elites, it is the military who ensure that Kurdish girls go to school against the democratic wishes of their parents, that schools in general are built, that tribal loyalties are diminished—and they do all this quite undemocratically. When Turkish generals started a dinner in Sirnak, close to Iraq's border, with a toast (yes, the alcoholic raki, a local version of anisette), they made a pro-Western political statement—just as their mentioning the fact that many old Ottoman sultans died of cirrhosis, which still agitates the likes of Osama bin Laden. And when military wives on the Iranian border at Van smoke and drink (excellent) Turkish beer, they demonstrate how important the much-maligned (in the West) military is for Turkish secularism, Westernism, and ultimately democracy. Within Turkey, the military are by far the most respected institution, more than Islam, political parties, or any other institution. For almost two decades, the Turkish military and militarized police—the jandarma—fought a profoundly reactionary foe – the Stalinist PKK, whom the Western media, politicians, and academia misunderstood to be "Kurdish nationalists."

THE BURDEN OF EASTERN ORTHODOXY

Eastern Orthodoxy is the major religious denomination in ten European countries, all but one of which (Greece) are former communist states.[3] More so than in the rest of Catholic or Protestant Western Europe, the Orthodox churches of Eastern Europe have long been openly and actively involved in national politics and are intimately and historically connected with the region's dominant postcommunist ideology—nationalism.

Historical Background

Orthodoxy originated in the culturally Greek Byzantine Empire. Spread by Byzantine missionaries, Orthodoxy still recognizes the Greek ecumenical patriarch of Constantinople (Istanbul) as its spiritual guide. However, centuries of anti-Greek sentiments in places like the Balkan states—the result of long centuries of Ottoman Turkish-imposed Greek religious and cultural dominance of those countries—has produced a unanimous rejection of the term Greek Orthodox by the larger bastions of Orthodoxy farther north.

On the other hand, the theology and politics of Orthodoxy were inherited from Byzantium (which also passed along the Cyrillic alphabet, the Old Slavonic language and calendar, etc.). In Byzantium, at least since the beginning of the seventh century, the physical survival of the state and of Greek culture (first against the Zoroastrian Persians, then against the Muslim Arabs, and finally against the Catholic Franks [a generic term for West Europeans]) was inextricably linked to the survival of Orthodoxy and has continued to be linked over the centuries.[4]

A basic distinction should be made between Byzantium—for most of its history a multiethnic empire—and its Orthodox successors, the modern Balkan states, Russia, and Ukraine—all self-proclaimed national states. It is precisely this relationship between the state, the people, and the faith (i.e., the Orthodox Church) that has made the term "Greek Orthodox" so politically incorrect and led to its replacement by "Orthodox," a geographically vague concept.

The state-people-church triangle has never been stable in the history of the Orthodox world. The Byzantine state, as well as its most powerful medieval rivals, was an imperial state, where the distinction between the ruler (who was God-anointed) and the state did not exist. The people enjoyed "rights" only to the extent that they derived from the Orthodox faith. The church, though representative of the people, was expected to support the state and thus be subject to it, a phenomenon long characterized (pejoratively) by Western Europeans as "caesaropapism." Hence Byzantine emperors always appointed patriarchs, whom they also routinely removed, arrested, and occasionally murdered.

The Byzantine *basileus,* starting with the initially pagan Constantine I (324-337), was often the arbiter in theological debates within the Church.[5] His successors, particularly the Serbian, Bulgarian, and Russian tsars (the Slavic spelling of "Caesar"), followed suit. In Russia the tsars, and their latter day counterparts, the Politburo chairmen, simply eliminated the office of patriarch—or reinvented it when politically expedient.

In political and structural ways the link between Byzantium as empire and the Orthodox Church laid open realities beyond imperial control. The loss of the Middle East and Egypt in the seventh century forced Byzantium to accept the steady decline of the established patriarchies of Alexandria, Antioch, and Jerusalem (all three since then under Muslim control). By contrast, the new patriarchal sees, starting with Moscow in 1559 and continuing, during the twentieth century, with those of Serbia, Romania, and Bulgaria, became the centers of national and nationalistic churches. In fact, the very establishment of national states in the Balkans and Eastern Europe, beginning with Serbia in 1812 through Ukraine in 1991, inevitably led to pressures for the creation of national patriarchies as well. Belgrade, Sofia, and Bucharest succeeded—and Kiev is well on the way to doing so. Nor is this overlapping between independent statehood and an independent Orthodox Church a modern invention. In 925 Simeon of Bulgaria (893-927) proclaimed himself tsar, and the next year the bishopric of Ohrid was transformed into a patriarchate. When Serbia succeeded Bulgaria as Byzantium's main political and military rival in the Balkans, Stephen Dusan (1331-1355) proclaimed himself tsar and established a patriarchate at Pec (in today's Kosovo province). As one scholar noted, "For both, Simeon and Dusan, full independence from Byzantium was unthinkable without a church controlled by themselves alone."[6]

Today the Orthodox Church is divided between autocephalous patriarchies in Belgrade, Sofia, Bucharest, Moscow, and Tbilisi, in addition to the historic ones in Constantinople, Alexandria, Antioch, and Jerusalem, and an autonomous Church of America. The nine patriarchies are virtually independent of one another. Orthodox political culture has not changed much since the days of Leo VI (886-912). The divinely anointed emperor (*basileus*, tsar) has been replaced by the more abstract "state," but he (or it) still controls the appointment—and often the replacement—of patriarchs. The church sees itself, and is once again seen by many, as the embodiment of the people—that is, of nationhood and national continuity.

Church and Nationhood

The Orthodox Church in Eastern Europe sees itself and is widely perceived as the historic repository of nationhood, national values, and, quite often, as the savior of a nation's very existence. Without the stubborn presence of the Orthodox Church, the Ottoman Empire's Balkan Christians would most likely have been converted to Islam, a fate which may well have befallen the Russians and Georgians under centuries of Mongol occupation, not to mention, similarly, the Ukrainians under Polish Catholic rule and the Romanians in Catholic or Calvinist Hungarian—ruled Transylvania.

These historic religious conflicts are crucial to understanding the appeal of nationalism to Orthodoxy. For one, unlike the Catholic Poles and Hungarians, neither the Ottomans nor the Mongols really tried to impose their religion on subject peoples. That fact may well explain why the present revival of Orthodox influence and political impact is (Serbia notwithstanding) anti-Catholic or anti-Protestant and not anti-Islamic. Typical is the 1997 Russian law pledging "respect" for Islam, Buddhism, Judaism, and "traditional religions," while imposing rigid limits on Catholic, Protestant, and Evangelical groups.[7] Even among Serbs, where the Bosnian conflict has caused the Orthodox Church to bring back anti-Islamic memories and raise the specter of Islamic fundamentalism, it is the Vatican, through its Croat tools, that is seen as the main cause of Serbian suffering.

Secondly, the sixteenth- and seventeenth-century compromises between Orthodox subjects of the Habsburgs and the Vatican led to the creation of the Greek-Catholic or Uniate churches, combining Catholic dogma and acceptance of Vatican leadership with Eastern Orthodox rules for the clergy (including marriage of priests) and the performance of the Mass in the national language—something the Roman Catholic Church did not acknowledge until the 1960s. The Uniates played an essential role in maintaining the national spirit against foreign cultural inroads, particularly in Western Ukraine and Transylvania. Seen in this context, the relentless hostility of the Orthodox against the Uniates can be explained only by politics and institutional greed, considering the fact that the Orthodox churches were the beneficiaries of Stalin's decision to eliminate the Uniate churches in his realm and transfer their properties and, as far as was possible, their flocks, to the Orthodox.

Orthodox hostility toward the Uniates has deeper cultural roots, including distrust by the former of anything related with the West, with which the Uniates are associated. Indeed, the late Byzantine Empire's church hierarchy made an intentional choice in preferring Islamic Ottoman rule to submission to Rome. The Russian Orthodox Church has for centuries considered Latin a "pagan" and "heretical" language and has often banned its study.[8] Even today the grounds of resentment against the West remain. In the words of Ecumenical Patriarch Bartholomaios, "Above all, Orthodox Christianity is confronted with the zeal of many Western Christians, especially from America, who are spiritually pilfering the house of their brethren."[9] The threat of competition from neo-Protestants, "especially from America," is furthered by the fact that Orthodox clerics such as the late archbishop Iakovos of the Greek Orthodox Church of North and South America, believe such groups as the Assemblies of God, Pentecostals, Mormons, Christian Scientists, Jehovah's Witnesses, and Seventh-Day Adventists "are not of the Christian tradition."[10]

In addition to its historic disputes with Rome and fear of—as well as doctrinal opposition to—Protestantism, Orthodoxy has profound theological and spiritual characteristics that set it apart from most Western political and social traditions. This phenomenon also helps to explain in part its ability to survive and its willingness to collaborate with communist regimes that, in turn, is the key to understanding Orthodoxy's present political standing vis-à-vis neocommunist governments in Eastern Europe.

The Churches under Communism

If there is anything approaching an Orthodox version of the Catholic social doctrine, it is its combination of nationalism, cooperation with the state, and preference for collectivism. For example, the Russian Orthodox tradition as manifested by the nineteenth-century Panslavist intellectuals (Fyodor Dostoevsky among them) and, more recently, Alexander Solzhenitsyn, is inherently hostile to the individualism that has been the center of Western political culture since the Renaissance. Indeed, no Orthodox culture, with the exception of a few isolated figures abroad, has actually experienced the Renaissance and its exaltation of the individual spirit and bourgeois values.

In Romania, in part under Russian influence, during the first decades of the century one of the dominant intellectual currents was dedicated to the uniqueness of Orthodox spirituality and, within it, a particular Romanian system of values, described by its greatest twentieth-century poet and philosopher as fatalistic and bordering on pantheistic, unselfish, and self-sacrificing.[11] Whether the result of Orthodox influence or a cause of its specific dislike of individualism, collectivism, defined as the primacy of the nation over the individual and of the state over group interests, remains a strong element in the social and political behavior of predominantly Orthodox countries, particularly among those social sectors most closely associated with the church.

Thus in Russia, a 1991 Radio Free Europe opinion poll estimated the number of Orthodox believers in the Russian Federation at thirty-seven million, a majority of which were women and those over sixty years of age; furthermore, most lived in rural areas. Orthodox believers were more supportive of existing order and traditions and of forces on the extremes of the political spectrum, and indicated "considerably greater support for two symbols of stability—Stalin and the tsar."[12] Post-1989 polling data in Romania and Bulgaria, as well as Ukraine, suggested similar patterns of social and political conservatism.

While no religion with such strong dogmatic, institutional, and historic traditions could be compatible with official atheism, Orthodoxy has had more in common with Eastern European and Russian communism than any other institutionalized religion and was, as a result, more vulnerable to communist manipulation. Thus, in addition to anti-individualism and anti-Westernism, the Orthodox Church also helped to legitimize the nationalist claims of some communist regimes (during World War II Russia, Ceausescu's Romania, and the late Zhivkov era in Bulgaria), as well as post-1989 neocommunist regimes.

Beyond the ideological, social, and cultural compatibility between the Orthodox churches and ruling Marxist-Leninists, there are more specific and practical reasons explaining the relationships between Orthodox churches as institutions and the communist "Caesars" unto whom they felt historically bound to render what was theirs. Thus, the Orthodox churches generally, although to varying degrees, benefited from communist rule through expanded jurisdiction, relative privileges, freedom to function, and state-enforced restrictions on, or elimination of, historic opponents and new religious rivals.

Naturally enough, the Russian Orthodox Church was the primary beneficiary of greater expansion. The Soviet state under Stalin, and since, has learned from its tsarist predecessors the value of the Orthodox Church as a vehicle for mobilization behind Russian nationalism and imperialism. Thus the Russian Orthodox Church saw its ecclesiastic authority grow in step with Stalin's post-World War II territorial conquests. The Soviet-annexed Western Ukraine and Belarus, Moldova, Northern Bukovina, and Eastern Slovakia, all areas with a heavy and independent Orthodox presence before 1940, were transferred—by order of the state rather than through canonical synods accepted by Constantinople and the other patriarchs—to the jurisdiction of the Moscow patriarchate.[13]

Stalin's territorial acquisitions and post-1945 additions to his newly created Moscow patriarchate not only expanded the latter's jurisdiction enormously but, for all practical purposes, gave it new life. The Orthodox structures in western Ukraine and Moldova inherited by Moscow in 1940 and again in 1945 were far more vital than the moribund Russian Church itself.[14] By 1958 a huge majority of the 13,415 registered Orthodox communities in the USSR came from post-1940 Ukrainian and Romanian territorial annexations: while Moscow had 212 and Leningrad 57 registered communities, Lviv had 2071, and Chisinau (the capital of then Soviet Moldova) had 546.[15] As late as the 1988 celebrations of the millennium of Russian Christianity, out of 6,893 Orthodox parishes in the Soviet Union 4,000 were in Ukraine.[16] Simply put, Stalin not only gave the Russian Orthodox Church a new lease on life by reestablishing the patriarchate, he also provided it with churches, a clergy, and a flock it had lost since Lenin's devastating antireligion campaign. Only most of that flock, clergy, and churches were neither Russian nor willing subjects to the patriarch—then and now.

That reality had significant financial and social implications for the Russian Orthodox Church, none of which are missed by the Moscow patriarchate today. Considering the fact that the Orthodox Church (independent of Moscow) had been massively reestablished in Ukraine and Moldova during their respective German and Romanian World War II occupation, the post-1945 institutional survival of the Russian and Ukrainian Orthodox Churches is, to a large extent, the direct product of Hitler and his erstwhile ally Stalin's opportunistic and strictly political decisions.

While the Russian Church was the only one to significantly expand its jurisdiction and resources at the expense of other Orthodox churches,[17] she and the Romanian patriarchate also expanded their control over millions of believers and thousands of churches previously belonging to the Uniates, with whom they had a vengeful, historic score to settle. Immediately following the expansion of Soviet rule in Eastern Europe after World War II, the regionally important Uniates were banned in Ukraine, Czechoslovakia, and Romania. With the help of the state, Uniate churches, properties, and constituents were transferred to the Orthodox.

Nonetheless, while Stalin's manipulation of territorial jurisdiction in favor of the Moscow patriarchate was relatively easy to enforce (and is still a matter of bitter dispute today), his attempt to destroy the Uniate faith and church failed miserably—as demonstrated by recent events in Ukraine and Romania. Even under communism Soviet and Romanian authorities were aware that most Uniates refused to "become" Orthodox and instead enlarged the ranks of Roman Catholics in Romania and of underground, illegal neo-Protestant groups in both countries.

The Orthodox willingly accepted Stalin's "gifts" and today, following the fall of communism, try to keep those properties. No doubt, the Communist elimination of the Greek Catholics in Ukraine and Romania was perceived as the vindication of a centuries-old rivalry with the Uniate "traitors" and "sellouts" to the "heretic" pope in Rome. Furthermore, the fact that the present pope (the Uniates' leader) is Polish only makes anti-Polish Ukrainians (and Belarussians) less eager to return Uniate property.

In Romania, Bulgaria, and Yugoslavia (prior to the Tito-Stalin break) the Communists did not make the same mistake of Lenin's post-1917 policy of virtual destruction of the Russian Orthodox Church. Hence the Serbian, Bulgarian, and Romanian patriarchates continued their existence. It is not surprising then that despite losing their territorial jurisdiction uncanonically and illegally, the three patriarchs never dissented. In contrast to the destruction of the Uniates in Ukraine and Romania and the draconian restrictions on Roman Catholic activities, the Orthodox, institutionally, were treated far more favorably, retaining some properties, including several monasteries, and obtaining permission for a small number of mostly elderly monks and nuns to maintain monastic life. It should be pointed out that the Orthodox clergy in Eastern Europe also provided a number of martyrs to communist persecution—albeit proportionally fewer than other religions and usually limited to the lower ranks. Lenin's Russia aside, nothing like the physical elimination of the Uniate hierarchies in Romania and Ukraine, or the arrest of Cardinals Wyszynski in Poland, Mindszenty in Hungary, and Stepinac in Yugoslavia occurred against Orthodox hierarchies in post-1945 Eastern Europe.

In addition to the above noted case of the Uniates, the Orthodox in Eastern Europe also benefited from the decades-long persecution of neo-Protestants, their most dangerous competitors. If there was a common denominator on religious politics among the Eastern European communist regimes, it was their universal fear and hatred of Evangelical missionaries. While the Vatican was widely disliked and the Lutherans dismissed as negligible, Evangelicals were positively despised for their uncompromising and decentralized nature, their disdain for certain state demands (military service, for example), and, most of all, for their alleged Western cultural bias. In Ceausescu's Romania in the early seventies this author overheard secret police and Communist party members encouraging Orthodox clergy to be more active in attempting to destroy the Baptists. Even Orthodox-based popular movements, such as the "Lord's Army" in Romania, were persecuted for similar reasons.

The Taint of Collaboration

Despite the apparent threat to their existence and institutional interests, the Orthodox churches and their leaders during the entire communist period established a long record of collaboration with the atheistic Marxist-Leninist governments.

The Russian journal *Ogonek* played a leading role in exposing the close ties between the Soviet regime and leading Russian Orthodox hierarchs, Patriarch Aleksii II among them. The nature and existence of those ties was admitted by the KGB prior to 1991 and roundly criticized by spokesmen of the Russian Orthodox Church Abroad and secular observers alike. The most important leaders of the church were said to be former KGB agents (complete with code names), informers, and even officers.[18] Former KGB major general Oleg Kalugin admitted that upper hierarchs of the Orthodox Church were on the KGB's payroll, and a devastating report from the 1970s (the Furov Report) was made public, describing in detail the methods and success of police control, recruitment, and handling of the church.[19] Considering this past, it is not surprising that during the August 1991 KGB-led, hard-line Communist coup in Moscow Patriarch Aleksii II limited himself to timidly supporting Gorbachev (but not Yeltsin) and did so alone among the top leaders of the church—in sharp contrast with some ordinary priests who actively supported the democratic forces.[20]

Collaboration occurred to such lengths in Bulgaria that in 1991 all of the Orthodox Church's bishops (except for Patriarch Maxim) publicly apologized for their past actions. In July 1996 a formal schism resulted when the repentant clergy elected another patriarch, who decried the "official" church as "Maxim and his gang of cops" who ought to be "replaced by real Christians, not slaves of the socialists."[21]

In Romania, Patriarch Teoctist was Ceausescu's appointee and ardent supporter to the bitter end, even as the dictator was demolishing churches in Bucharest under Teoctist's eyes. Ten days prior to Ceausescu's execution, Teoctist had the dubious distinction of being the last leader of a major institution publicly to express his strong support for the dictator; ten days later, he declared Ceausescu "a follower of Herod" with the blood of innocents on his hands.[22] Briefly removed from office immediately following the fall of Ceausescu, Teoctist was promptly reinstated by the neocommunist Iliescu regime, with which he enjoyed warm relations until the November 1996 elections brought the anticommunist opposition to power. Metropolitan Antonie Plamadeala of Transylvania, Crisana, and Maramures, continues to be the main apologist of collaboration with communism: collaboration, if it ever existed, he preaches, was the price of the Orthodoxy's survival; accusations of collaborationism are "insults against some martyrs."[23]

The response of Orthodox hierarchs to accusations of past collaboration is generally a combination of silence, indignation, partial and implicit admission of guilt, and self-justification. In Russia Aleksii II dismissed accusations as a plot by "atheist and other enemies trying to discredit the Russian Orthodox Church in the minds of people."[24] One of the most peculiar but significant examples of an Orthodox Church's refusing responsibility for collaborationism was the December 1997 demonstration by some three hundred Romanian Orthodox priests and monks, led by the bishop of Lower Danube (an area widely known in Romania as the "red belt" for its electoral support for unreconstructed communists), protesting parliamentary attempts to open the pre-1989 secret police files of the clergy.

Filaret Denisenko, the metropolitan of Kiev and an ethnic Ukrainian, spent most of his long career as an aggressive supporter of the Russian Orthodox Church's systematic attempts to transform the Moscow patriarchate into an instrument of Russian control over all Orthodox believers in the former USSR.

Ukrainians widely resented his rejection of their language and history, and in 1990 he was second runner-up for the Muscovite patriarchal seat. He made a name for himself as a ferocious anti-Greek and anti-Roman Catholic spokesman, as an active international representative of pro-Soviet interests in religious matters (mostly within the World Council of Churches), and as a known KGB agent. At the same time he publicly embarrassed the church with revelations of his many mistresses and illegitimate children. Despite such a past, after 1991 he became a virulent Ukrainian patriot and outspoken opponent of Russian ecclesiastic control over Ukraine.[25]

It should be noted that some members of the Orthodox hierarchy did demonstrate some courage in decrying collaboration and nationalist abuses perpetrated by their churches under communism. Thus, in addition to dissident priests like Polosin and Yakunin, the Russian Orthodox archbishop Chrysostom of Vilnius and Lithuania freely admitted his own, and the Russian Church's collective guilt of silence and collaboration.[26] In Romania Metropolitan Nicolae Corneanu of Banat was the first (and so far the only) hierarch to return Uniate properties under his jurisdiction, saying, "I must confess that as a hierarch, I have witnessed for years many events repugnant to my Christian convictions, without however acting according to the prompting of my conscience. Regrets are obviously superfluous."[27] Jovan Pavlovic, the Serbian metropolitan of Croatia and Slovenia, expressed contrition and wept at the sight of Catholic churches destroyed by Serbs in Croatia.

The last fact raises the legitimate issue of a Yugoslav (i.e., Serbian) exception to the general rule of Orthodox collaboration with communism. In the former Yugoslavia Tito treated the Orthodox Church and the Belgrade Orthodox patriarch as dangerous precisely because they were associated with the regime's main enemy—nationalism, in general, and Serbian nationalism, in particular. Tito considered Croat Catholic and Serbian/Montenegrin Orthodox nationalism as the main threats to his idea of a "Yugoslavia." In many ways the half-Slovene, half-Croat atheistic Tito was the most informed and realistic Communist leader in Eastern Europe in understanding the danger to his (and Communist) rule posed by the overlapping of ethnicity and religion, and he refused to pay the cost of political manipulation of religion. His antiecclesiastic policies, while ecumenical, do serve as a credible argument for the Serbian Church's claim of never having made a basic compromise with the godless Belgrade Marxists. Many Serbs support the current patriarch, Pavle, in his opposition to Milosevic's neocommunism; but like the patriarch, they do so from a more sincere, and thus more dangerous, Serbian nationalist and antidemocratic, anti-Western position.[28]

Postcommunist Church-State Relations

The issue of Orthodox collaboration with communism cannot be separated from its behavior after the latter's collapse in 1989-1991. Politically the church's turn, or return, to nationalism forced her into facing the new state rulers, many of whom, in Romania's, Bulgaria's, and Ukraine's presidential palaces and parliaments and in Russia's Duma, were neocommunist (or self-proclaimed reformed communists or social democrats) or unreconstructed communists seeking an alternate and legitimate ideology (and excuse) for retaining power.

At the same time, the Orthodox Church, seeking her own excuses for past collaboration, found one in "institutional survival and national preservation." Neocommunist regimes and strong opposition parties like Russia's Communists and Liberal Democrats, Romania's Greater Romania (PRM) and National Unity (PUNR) parties, or Serbia's Radicals, were in a similar search. All but the last were made up of former communist high officials, opportunistically converted to nationalism in the absence of anything else. What's more, all supported, encouraged, and strengthened ties with the compromised Orthodox hierarchy. As under communism, the church expected the same advantages and protection against religious enemies, while offering the same, now far more propitious, cover of nationalist legitimacy. This understanding helps explain both the Orthodox Church's excellent relations with neocommunist regimes in Romania, Bulgaria, and Ukraine, and her far more complicated relations with sincere anticommunists in and out of power.

Nationalist legitimacy took the form of spectacular blessings for secular politicians. Former Soviet foreign minister, Politburo member, and Georgia KGB boss Edvard Shevardnadze took the baptism from Georgia's patriarch upon becoming president, and in Romania then president Ion Iliescu (his past as Communist party ideologue notwithstanding) and his half-Jewish, half-Spanish prime minister, Petre Roman, were frequent participants at the Sunday Mass. In Russia, Boris Yeltsin discovered God, and the Communist leaders of the Duma were strong supporters of the patriarchy in its dealings with rebellious Ukrainian, Estonian, and Moldovan churches.

The Orthodox Church's use of national symbols during the *glasnost* and postcommunist eras contributed to the rise of nationalism and was a prescient reaction to its future popularity. In 1988-1989 the Serbian Orthodox Church organized a religious reinternment of the relics of Prince Lazar, the Serbian leader defeated and killed by the Ottomans at the battle of Kosovo Polje in 1389, and provocatively conducted the procession through the Serbian areas of Croatia and Bosnia.[29] Politically helpful to Milosevic and his nationalist claims was the key Serbian Orthodox argument for a Greater Serbia, i.e., the alleged historic mission of the Serbs to protect Orthodoxy from the double threat of Mecca and the Vatican. Even more important for the cause of Serbian nationalism is the church's total opposition to any concession to Albanian irredentism in Kosovo, since it (correctly) regards the area as the historic cradle of the Serbian Church and the home of its most important monuments at Pec, Gracanica, and Decani.

In Romania, whose church has very rarely conducted sanctification proceedings, the most prominent new saint elevated during the past century was the medieval ruler Stephen the Great (1457-1504), admittedly a towering figure but also, and not coincidentally, the national hero of the Republic of Moldova. In Georgia during the *glasnost* period in 1987 the catholicos (patriarch) Ilia II canonized the nationalist poet and politician Ilia Chavchavadze, murdered by the Bolsheviks in 1907. A few years later he threatened excommunication to any Georgian who killed another Georgian, but did not say anything about Georgians murdering non-Georgians, such as Russians, Abkhazians, or Ossetians.[30] The political pressures on the Russian Orthodox Church (coming largely from Zhirinovsky's right-wing group) to sanctify the incompetent tsar Nicholas II, are yet another attempt to use the church for blatantly nationalistic goals.

As a general rule then the Orthodox Church has enjoyed privileged relations with neocommunist and nationalist regimes in Russia and Eastern Europe. By contrast, while the Orthodox Church was also courted by anticommunist and genuinely democratic governments and parties in the region, its relations with them have been far less cozy. All post-1989-1991 states in the region have enshrined the separation between state and church in their constitutions, but not without ambiguities and de facto breaches and allowances for the national church of preference (Catholic in Poland and Lithuania; Orthodox elsewhere).[31] In almost all countries the Orthodox Church has encouraged such breaches. But separation has meant different things at different times; neocommunist authorities interpreted it as meaning protection for the Orthodox Church against all competitors. When Bulgarian Socialists came back to power in 1994, many of the same Bulgarian bishops who expressed public regrets for past collaboration went back on their contrition. Then, following the return to power of the anticommunist Union of Democratic Forces (UDF) in 1997, the Supreme Court denied official registration to Patriarch Maxim's group, while also refusing approval to his rival Pimen's.[32]

The youthful metropolitan of Romanian Moldova and canonical successor to the patriarchal see, Daniel Ciobotea, although seemingly resigned to the concept of church-state separation, also assumes for the church the role of "loyal opponent" to the state's economic and foreign policies (he is equally opposed to communism and capitalism), and is a vocal supporter of Orthodox education in Romanian schools. His church has also assumed the mantle of moral arbiter (while mitigating the issue of past clerical collaboration and moral transgressions as a matter of "corruption and inertia") and succeeded in obtaining preferential treatment from the Iliescu government.[33] Today Hungarians in Romania complain that the Orthodox is the only church receiving a separate budgetary allowance.[34] Not all of the church's demands are acceded to, of course, including Teoctist's most recent scheme to have a grand "National Cathedral of the Reunification of the Motherland" built in Bucharest at taxpayers' expense, which Daniel also supports.[35] On the other hand, ever since 1990 the patriarchy has successfully refused, delayed, and procrastinated on the issue of return of

Uniate properties, flaunting the stated position of successive governments. Though it appears the division of ecclesiastical property in Transylvania may yet be completed without major national political clashes, the issue is so deeply rooted in historic Orthodox arrogance and fears that even the few genuinely anticommunist Orthodox clergymen have opposed Uniate demands for restitution.[36]

In Serbia, the Orthodox Church also tried, and failed, to introduce religious education in public schools, influence television programming, criticize "art that negates truth," and ban abortions.[37] Nor has postcommunist democratization stopped the Orthodox Church from pushing legislation directed against the Uniates, the Vatican, and Protestant missionaries. Indeed, there is a certain unanimity among Orthodox leaders throughout the region regarding what they perceive as a dual threat of internal and external competition, even if the specific nature of those threats differs. In addition to the aforementioned anti-Catholic measures passed in Russia, the Romanian Orthodox Church unsuccessfully pushed anti-Protestant legislation during the Iliescu regime, while the Bulgarian Socialists passed a law in February 1994 requiring legal registration—under strict scrutiny—for nontraditional religious groups, i.e., neo-Protestants. In fact, so strong is the Bulgarian Orthodoxy (whether pro- or anti-Maxim) that even UDF deputies supported the anti-Protestant legislation.[38]

While in Romania and western Ukraine the Uniates are still seen as the main threat to the Orthodox Church, in most of the former USSR it is the presence of competing native-based and foreign-based Orthodox groups that is most bitterly fought. Whether the threat comes from the Russian Orthodox Church Abroad in Moscow or the Moscow patriarchate in Kiev, Orthodox politics and nationalism are still hard to disentangle. What is more, the churches themselves encourage the confusion, and nowhere is that more obvious than in Ukraine.

Independent Ukraine's Orthodox religious politics are deeply enmeshed in the ambiguities of Ukrainian nationalism, border disputes, statehood, and secular politics, which are dominated by Ukraine's idiosyncratic and ecumenical distrust of all of its neighbors: Russians, Poles, Slovaks, Romanians, and, to lesser extent, Hungarians. Ukraine is a case study of a large state with an ambiguous ethnic, historic, and cultural identity, futilely relying on the Orthodox Church to provide unity. The issues of collaboration with the KGB, Russia, and the Soviet Union are as confused and muddled as Ukrainian politics and national identity. Much clearer is the secular power's use of the church as an instrument of state- and nation-building and manipulation of public attitudes.

Ukraine had a real historic claim to being the fountain of Orthodoxy among Eastern Slavs (since the Kiev princes converted in 988) at a time when Russians were a small, irrelevant factor in northern Europe. Never having had her own canonical patriarchate, Ukraine, since the collapse of the weak Kievan state under Mongol assault in the thirteenth century, has been what her name implies—a border state.

Indeed Ukraine is a border between the Catholicism and tolerance of the West and the Orthodoxy and intolerance of the Russian East. In the West large numbers of Orthodox converted to Greek Catholicism as a result of the Union of Brest (1556), and many others retained a fragile but nevertheless lasting autonomy. The eastern Ukrainians, however, lost their ecclesiastical autonomy as early as 1686 when the metropolitanate of Kiev was transferred to the Moscow patriarchate (where, as far as Moscow is concerned, it remains to this date).

An observant analyst of the Ukraine notes that "since 1988 the religious situation changed more in Ukraine than in any other area of the former Soviet Union" with various churches besides the Russian Orthodox maintaining "competing organizations with legally registered parishes."[39] That description oversimplifies the situation, exacerbated by personal, regional, and historic conflicts in the Ukrainian Autocephalous Orthodox Church, the only possible version of a Ukrainian national church.

Little has occurred to support the establishment of an independent Ukrainian Orthodox Church, not even Denisenko's playing the nationalist card with the support of successive neocommunist regimes. The situation surrounding Ukraine's religious predicament remains as unsettled as that of Ukrainian nationalism. In western Ukraine, where the Orthodox Church is bitterly divided among autocephalists abroad and nationalist vs. pro-Russian factions at home, local anticommunist (and anti-Russian) authorities helped Uniate demonstrators retake the important Church of Transfiguration in Lviv in 1989. By the end of that year most former Uniate churches throughout western Ukraine were reoccupied, with both sides resorting to violence.[40]

At the national level, the Ukrainian official position was simply stated by then president Leonid Kravchuk in November 1991: "For an independent state— an independent church,"[41] by which, of course, he meant an independent Orthodox church. Ever since, and notwithstanding government changes in Kiev, the goal of establishing a separate patriarchy in Kiev has remained unchanged, if still unfulfilled. The task has been complicated by the divisions within Ukrainian Orthodox ranks, which replicate ethnic and cultural divisions in the country as a whole. Eastern, and largely Russified areas remain stubbornly loyal to Moscow, while Kiev and the western regions are divided between the followers of the previously exiled leaders of the Ukrainian Autocephalous Orthodox Church and the officially supported (but very few) followers of Filaret.[42] Quite clearly, the status and future of the Orthodox Church in Ukraine is part and parcel of the larger issues of Ukrainian national identity and unity and, equally important, of Kiev's relations with Moscow.

The Orthodox Church and the World Today and Tomorrow

To those who follow Pope John Paul II's innumerable journeys around the world, it may appear strange that the most peripatetic pope in history has never visited any predominantly Orthodox countries, not even those having significant Catholic (Roman or Greek) minorities. The reason, however, is simple: Orthodox hierarchies in those struggling democracies have made such visits politically costly. Hence, Gorbachev's invitation to the pope was undone by the opposition of Aleksii II, and a similar Romanian government intention was derailed by Teoctist's objection to any Vatican role in Romania, including the right to appoint Greek Catholic bishops. The Serbian Orthodox succeeded in preventing papal visits to Belgrade and Sarajevo.

Orthodox churches have a long tradition, preceding communism, of serving as instruments of foreign policy for their governments. That tradition was most obvious and embarrassing during the communist period, when Orthodox churches served directly and unabashedly as tools of Soviet foreign policy. By virtue of their size and (government-provided) financial resources, the Orthodox churches heavily influenced the leftist World Council of Churches, which throughout its history was consistently critical of free markets, liberal democracies, and the United States, in particular. At the same time, they provided support to Soviet protégés among Third World totalitarian regimes and various "national liberation movements." The end of the Soviet Empire has resulted in the Orthodox churches turning their attention from the World Council and its campaigns for peace, disarmament, or Third World revolution, to interests closer to home—and to each other.

The current status of Eastern Europe has helped bring an end to the artificial, Kremlin-enforced "unity" of views among the Orthodox churches. Just as nationalism (especially its anti-Russian versions in Romania and Ukraine) was suppressed during the communist period, so were the national Orthodox churches' abilities to pursue divergent and often opposite interests in international affairs. With the newly acquired independence of the Eastern European nations, both governments and churches have become free to pursue those interests, which, more often than not, coincide on essential aspects: the governments are concerned with strengthening national identity, independence, and influence among their ethnic co-nationals living outside state borders. The churches share all those concerns for institutional and historic reasons, and their role in the traditional alliance with the secular power has been strengthened by their ability to provide an additional, less controversial, voice than normal state-to-state diplomatic relations would allow.

In Russia, for instance, since the collapse of the Soviet Union in 1991, it has become increasingly clear that the Moscow patriarchate, together with the Russian military, is attempting, with some success, to maintain Russian influence within the geopolitical sphere of the former USSR. Thus, while Russia's military, often operating alone, used techniques of destabilization, covert intervention, and intimidation to ensure a presence in nearly every former Soviet republic, the patriarchate is still defending, with great success, the Stalinist legacy which gave it jurisdiction over the entire Orthodox population of the Soviet Union (save for Georgia).[43]

In Estonia, where the situation is quite different, the small Orthodox (and largely ethnic Russian) community, with government encouragement, decided in the 1920s to shift its allegiance from the then dying Russian patriarchate to the ecumenical patriarchate of Constantinople. Following Estonia's occupation by Stalin in 1940, the local Orthodox were forcibly "transferred" back to the Moscow patriarchate. By 1991 the newly independent Estonia did not object to its small Orthodox (and still overwhelmingly Russian) community's shifting their allegiance back to Constantinople. Aleksii II, however, strongly objected. He went so far as to provoke a (temporary?) schism within the Orthodoxy in February 1996.[44] The matter was not resolved until September 1997, with the recognition of Aleksii's jurisdiction over the turbulent Ukrainian and Moldovan Churches by the ecumenical patriarch Bartholomaios, with whom Aleksii had suspended relations.

The Moldovan issue could well serve as a case study in manipulation by conflicting political and secular interests in the Orthodox Church. Moldova, a truncated part of eastern Romania, annexed by Russia in 1812, was transferred to Russian religious authority soon thereafter; recovered by Romania in 1918, it was transferred to the Romanian patriarchate, until its reannexation by Stalin in 1940, at which time it was transferred once again to Moscow's jurisdiction. With the collapse of the Ceausescu regime and the declaration of Moldovan independence two years later, the issue of reunification became active once again. While successive Romanian governments officially recognized Moldovan independence and avoided making any public territorial claims, they have consistently supported Romanian nationalists in Moldova and paid for the education—particularly theological education in Bucharest and Sibiu seminaries—of young Moldovans. Most of those graduates have now returned to Moldova where they comprise some 120 out of about 800 Orthodox clergy. All of them are ethnic Romanians who support the reestablishment of a metropolitanate of Basarabia (the region's historic name), under the authority of the Bucharest patriarchate—the situation that prevailed between 1918 and 1940.

Not surprisingly, the Moldovan government views the situation as a Romanian assimilationist plot. Having nowhere else to go, the government prefers continued allegiance to the Moscow patriarchate (since Aleksii is relatively far away and promises a high degree of autonomy whereas Teoctist is nearby and does not). At the end of 1997 the Moldovan Supreme Justice Court reaffirmed the allegiance of Moldova's Orthodox Church to Moscow, although the decision is still contested and means little to the growing number of younger members of the Romanian ethnic clergy. Considering also that 30 percent of Moldova's population is made up of Ukrainians and Russians, both of whom fear the idea of unification, the religious picture in Moldova today is a perfect reflection of Orthodox ethnic division, with Romanians, the clear majority, divided but leaning toward Bucharest; the Ukrainians, the largest minority, split among the three competing Orthodox churches in the Ukraine; and the Russians steady supporters of Moscow.[45]

In former Yugoslavia the older conflict between the claims of the Serbian patriarchate and the autonomist ambitions of the Macedonian Church—now supported by the government of independent Macedonia—remains unsolved, although in practice Skopje has been independent from Belgrade since Tito's time.[46]

If there was a recent issue in which the Orthodox churches came together it was their clear and consistent support for the Serbs in the Yugoslav conflicts. The Moscow and ecumenical patriarchs supported Patriarch Pavle's repeated claims that the Serbs were victims, that Western military action against them is unfair, and that sanctions against rump Yugoslavia should be lifted.[47] These positions, supported by the Romanian Church as well, albeit more discreetly, faithfully, and not coincidentally, represent the official policies of Russia, Serbia, and Greece. It is highly significant that Ecumenical Patriarch Bartholomaios, while reiterating support for Pavle and denying any joint political strategy between Athens, Belgrade, and Moscow, also purported to detect a religious motivation behind the West's anti-Serb position.[48]

Nowhere in Eastern Europe has the Orthodox Church succeeded in shedding its collaborationist past, adapting to the necessary political and economic change of democracy and free markets, or learning to function in a truly secular constitutional environment. Dangerous radical nationalists in Russia, Serbia, and Romania have embraced the church and have not been rejected. Neocommunists everywhere have used the church in order to polish their newly acquired nationalist credentials—again, with the belated exception of Serbia, without being rebuffed.

History and tradition aside, the reason behind this behavior has much to do with the nature of the present hierarchy in most of Eastern Europe and Russia. Like the recently converted nationalists from the ranks of the former Marxist internationalists, the leaders of the Orthodox churches perceive nationalism as a convenient refuge. By cloaking themselves in that mantle in the name of the Orthodox tradition, Aleksii, Teoctist, Maksim, and Filaret also try to erase the memories of the church's recent behavior and defend their own credibility.

At a time when the majority of Romanians, Ukrainians, and Bulgarians (if not Russians and Serbs) seek integration in a democratic and capitalist Europe, the Orthodox churches are increasingly vocal in their opposition to Western influence—and not just the Vatican's. Individual and minority religious freedom is interpreted as a threat, as are the practical effects of separation between church and state. The Orthodox historic fear of religious competition easily translates into fear of free markets and political debate. Whether a younger generation of leaders could change these trends remains to be seen, but the indications so far are not encouraging.

While Western-style religious freedom is not realistic and should not be expected in the Orthodox East, neither should the ethno-religious absolutist nationalism still advocated by the Orthodox be accepted by the East European states as they try to become part of a Europe they themselves understand to be tolerant, secular, democratic, and capitalist. Whether there is a happy medium remains to be seen. What is unfortunately clear is that the Orthodox churches are not expected to contribute to its discovery any time soon.

Reprinted with permission from http://www.fpri.org, Spring 1998

Notes

1.   These are, in decreasing order of their population Russia, Ukraine, Romania, Yugoslavia (Serbia and Montenegro), Bulgaria, Belarus, Greece, Moldova, Georgia, and Macedonia. Total population exceeds 250 million, with an Orthodox majority ranging from over 90 percent (in Greece and Yugoslavia) to 70 percent in Romania and Ukraine.

2.   Hélène Ahrweiler, *L'Ideologie politique de l'empire byzantin* (Paris: Presses Universitaires de France, 1975), p. 33.

5.   There were two exceptions to this general rule: when the very existence of the Church was in question, during the Iconoclast crisis of the eighth and ninth centuries, and during the fifteenth-century issue of ecclesiastic union with (and under) Rome. In both instances the church won at the expense of the emperor.

6.   Peter F. Sugar, "Roots of Eastern European Nationalism," in *Nationalism in Eastern Europe*, ed. Peter F. Sugar and Ivo John Lederer (Seattle: University of Washington Press, 1971), p. 25.

7.   Associated Press, Internet, June 23, 1997.

8.   Boris Uspensky, "Schism and Cultural Conflict in the Seventeenth Century," in *Seeking God: The Recovery of Religious Identity in Orthodox Russia, Ukraine, and Georgia*, ed. Stephen K. Batalden (DeKalb: Northern Illinois University Press, 1993), pp. 113-17.

9.   Bartholomaios I, interview in *Christian History*, Mar. 2, 1997, p. 2.

10.   *Christianity Today*, Apr. 29, 1996, p. 55.

11.   See Lucian Blaga, *Gândirea Mioritica*, various editions (Bucharest [Bucuresti]), passim. *Gândirea* ("Thought") was a prominent intellectual journal; "Miorita" is Romania's national ballad. See also Keith Hitchins, "Gândirea: Nationalism in a Spiritual Guise," in *Social Change in Romania*, ed. Keith Jowitt (Berkeley and Los Angeles: University of California Press, 1978), pp. 140-78; and James P. Niessen, "Romanian Nationalism: An Ideology of Integration and Mobilization," in *Eastern European Nationalism in the 20th Century*, ed. Peter F. Sugar (Seattle: University of Washington Press, 1995), pp. 273-304.

12.   Mark Rhodes, "Religious believers in Russia," *RFE/RL Research Report*, Apr. 3, 1992, p. 61. Rhodes quotes similar results from a simultaneous survey by the Russian Institute of Sociology.

13.   Nathaniel Davis, *A Long Walk to Church: A Contemporary History of Russian Orthodoxy* (Boulder, Colo.: Westview Press, 1995), pp. 12Ü13.

14.   See Frank E. Sysyn, "Third Rebirth of the Ukrainian Autocephalous Orthodox Church and the Religious Situation in Ukraine, 1989-91," in *Seeking God*, pp. 191-93; and Alexander Webster, *The Price of Prophecy*, 2nd ed. (Washington, D.C.: Ethics and Public Policy Center, 1995), pp. 194-203.

15.   Davis, *Long Walk to Church*, p. 33.

16. To those Ukrainian parishes one should also add some one thousand others in Moldova and other non-Russian republics. See John B. Dunlop, *The Rise of Russia and the Fall of the Soviet Empire* (Princeton, N.J.: Princeton University Press), p. 159.

17. The Romanian Orthodox Church also took jurisdiction over Serbian parishes in the Banat region.

18. Oxana Antic, "Orthodox Church Reacts to Criticism of KGB Links," *RFE/RL Research Report*, June 5, 1992, pp. 61-63.

19. For details and a lucid analysis, see Webster, *Price of Prophecy*, pp. 39-46.

20. Dunlop, *Rise of Russia*, pp. 225-27. According to Davis, *Long Walk to Church*, p. 90, the other hierarchs actually supported the coup.

21. Galina Sabeva, Reuters, Internet (Sofia), Nov. 6, 1997.

22. Cf. Webster, *Price of Prophecy*, p. 112; see pp. 89Ü136 for a detailed account of the Romanian Orthodox Church's subservient relations with the Communist regime.

23. Antonie Plamadeala, interview by Sorin Comorosan, in *Romania. Societate cu raspundere limitata* (Bucharest [Bucuresti]: Editura Cartea Romaneasca, 1995), p. 79.

24. Antic, "Orthodox Church Reacts," p. 6.

25. For Filaret's interesting career, see Webster, *Price of Prophecy*, pp. 44-46; and Davis, *Long Walk to Church*, pp. 80-95.

26. Antic, "Orthodox Church Reacts," p. 62; Davis, *Long Walk to Church*, pp. 95-96.

27. Quoted in Webster, *Price of Prophecy*, p. 103.

28. See Sabrina Petra Ramet, *Balkan Babel: The Disintegration of Yugoslavia from the Death of Tito to Ethnic War*, 2nd ed. (Boulder, Colo.: Westview Press, 1996). Ramet points out that during the initial and apparently successful years of Milosevic's nationalist policies and war in Croatia and Bosnia, the Serbian Church supported him just as much as he used it for his own purposes. It was not until the 1995 Serbian loss of the war in Croatia that the Orthodox Church once again came in conflict with the neocommunist regime in Belgrade, which it blamed for the defeat.

29. Nebojsa Popov, "Serbian Populism and the Fall of Yugoslavia," *Uncaptive Minds*, Fall/Winter 1995-96, pp. 86-87.

30. Fairy von Lilienfeld, "Reflections on the Current State of the Georgian Church and Nation," in *Seeking God*, pp. 225-26.

31. For an early overview of the postindependence position of the Lithuanian Catholic Church see Saulius Girnius, "The Catholic Church in Post-Soviet Lithuania," *RFE/RL Research Report*, Oct. 15, 1993, pp. 43-46.

32. Ibid.

33. Ibid., p. 109.

34. "Liderii UDMR vor solicita in CoCo restructurarea Secretariatului de Stat pentru Culte," in *Ziua* (Bucharest), Dec. 15, 1997.

35. Karin Popescu, Reuters, Internet, Sept. 26, 1997.

36. A good example is former Romanian political prisoner and dissident Orthodox priest Gheorghe Calciu, for whom the Uniates' demand for the return of their properties is "unbrotherly." For Calciu's duplicitous position and a Uniate response, see *Ziua*, Dec. 20 and 24, 1997.

37. Popov, "Serbian Populism," p. 104.

38. *Christianity Today*, p. 5.

39. Sysyn, "Third Rebirth," p. 191.

40. Davis, *Long Walk to Church*, p. 72.

41. Ibid., p. 97.

42. For the truly Byzantine politics of Ukrainian Orthodoxy, see Davis, *Long Walk to Church*, pp. 97Ü102; and Webster, *Price of Prophecy*, pp. 61-69.

43. For still unclear reasons, in the forties Stalin allowed the reestablishment of the office of Georgian patriarch (catholicos). As for the Russian Church, it was accurately described as an "Empire-saving Institution" in Dunlop, *Rise of Russia*, pp. 158-63.
44. *Christianity Today*, p. 55.
45. Unusual for an Orthodox patriarch, Teoctist of Romania has publicly asserted that Moldova is under his, not Moscow's, jurisdiction, a position he further affirmed by appointing as metropolitan of Basarabia a member of the Romanian Orthodox Synod. It became clear that the Bucharest government was prepared to support Teoctist when the chairman of Romania's Senate Security and Defense Commission declared that the Moldovan court's decision was part of an anti-Romanian plot. See *Ziua*, Dec. 19, 1997.
46. Ramet, *Balkan Babel*, pp. 175-77.
47. For details see the sympathetic analysis of Webster, *Price of Prophecy*, pp. 259-73.
48. Quoted in ibid., p. 263.

WHY EASTERN AND CENTRAL EUROPE LOOK WEST

Speaking on C-SPAN on November 26, 1995, former French foreign minister Roland Dumas observed that the erstwhile communist countries of Central and Eastern Europe desire both prosperity (hence their wish to join the European Union (EU) and stability (hence their wish to join NATO). But while the EU's link to prosperity is self-evident, many Western observers find it less obvious why, after the cold war, stability in the eastern half of Europe is dependent upon a Western military and political alliance.

The answer is the potential threat to the region posed by Russia. Given Russia's size and proximity, such a threat is inevitable. Unfortunately, identifying the threat of Russian military aggression as a key motive for joining NATO has become taboo, not only in Moscow, but in Washington. As a result, Central and Eastern Europeans tend to cite membership in NATO as a way of renewing their historical and cultural ties to Western Europe. Apparently, American policymakers find such considerations sufficiently innocent and Moscow-friendly. If so, that can only be because they do not grasp how people in Central and Eastern Europe employ cultural-civilizational terms.[1]

Since the events of 1989-91, which led to Central and Eastern Europe's liberation from Soviet control, the one issue dominating the entire region's geopolitical and foreign policy discourse has been that of redefining the region's identity. This search for identity is occasionally national (particularly in the successor states of the former Soviet, Yugoslav, and Czechoslovak federations) but always cultural And in cultural terms there exists a continuum: from an "East"—defined as things Russian/communist/Soviet, or Turkish/Islamic, or Greek/Orthodox-to a "West," defined as things appertaining to Western Europe and its civilizational outposts, from Austria and Germany, to the United States and Canada, to Australia and New Zealand.

However, this politico-geographical continuum is not merely denotational; for the residents of Central and Eastern Europe, it is also redolent with connotation. "The East" is widely associated with backwardness, poverty, lack of freedom, and foreign domination. "The West" or "Europe" is associated with wealth, freedom, independence, and security. That Russia-and even more so her willing satellite, Belarus—is by all measurable standards far behind almost every Central and Eastern European country in terms of democratic and free-market reforms only serves to increase the perceived gap between Moscow and her western neighbors.

Following their liberation from Soviet rule, all states formerly sharing that dubious "Eastern" history were trying to deny, reinvent, or reinterpret it. Being part of "the East" was simply not acceptable anywhere in the region. Czechs, Poles, Balts, and Hungarians observed that they had universities at a time when Muscovy was still under the Mongol yoke. Even the Bulgarians mentioned that "we gave Russia its alphabet and Christian values!" Some- Bulgarians, Serbs, Russians—pointed to the survival of Orthodoxy to deny any lasting Ottoman influence. Romanians also offered their Romance language as proof of their natural place within Western civilization.

Thus, when Central and Eastern Europeans discuss their desire to join Western institutions in terms of national identity, they may avoid mentioning strategic considerations such as a fear of Moscow—but fear and loathing of Russia are no less in the forefront of their minds. They merely appear under the code word of "the East." And those fears are strengthened by the revival of Russia's long-running identity debate between "Europeanists" and "Eurasianists," between those seeking acceptance by the West and those who wish to preserve an "Asian" identity as well. Present trends in Moscow's foreign policy, symbolized by Foreign Minister Yevgeny Primakov's undertakings, suggest the Eurasianists are winning.

The Forbidden Motive

Throughout most of Central and Eastern Europe, fear of Russia and the memory of Russian domination first prompted the idea of joining NATO. The West, while promising the Central and Eastern Europeans membership in an expanded alliance, has consistently tried to strengthen Russia's president Boris Yeltsin and to avoid even the impression that NATO's enlargement might threaten Russia. This disparity between the motivations of Eastern and Central Europeans on the one hand and Western ambiguity on the other has led to confusion, dissimulation, and diminished credibility on all sides.

What Westerners fail to grasp is that all Central and Eastern Europeans, from top to bottom socially and Tallinn to Tirana geographically, have a vivid awareness of Russia's past and present role as an empire. Slovak president Michal Kovac could have spoken for his counterparts in the region when he stated that joining NATO is his top priority because "I am concerned about the situation in Russia and Ukraine: If the democrats fail to survive there, then our democracies will also be endangered."[2]

Indeed, most Central and Eastern Europeans would not bother to qualify that statement, for the notion that Yeltsin's Russia is a democracy, or on the way to becoming one, is not much accepted among them. In the eyes of virtually all Central and Eastern Europeans, the distinction between Russia and the USSR is a distinction without a difference. Bolshevism was, and is, widely perceived as just another avatar of imperialism in Russia's long history of oppression.

For centuries, virtually all the peoples in the region between Bulgaria and Estonia have been directly, decisively, and negatively influenced by Russian power, culture, and interests. In most cases, Central and Eastern Europeans have resented and tried to reject this Russian influence, which they saw as alien, inferior, and oppressive. Today, despite important differences between them, all of these peoples must cope with the messy and destabilizing territorial, cultural, ideological, and political debris of Russia's—not just the Soviet Union's—historic impact.

As always, there are exceptions. Slovenes and Croats were sheltered first by Austria-Hungary and later by Josip Broz Tito's nonalignment. Albanians were geographically isolated. Serbs and Bulgarians owe their independent statehood in the last century to Russian victories over the Ottomans—something that does more to explain current political alignments than those countries' present neocommunist leadership.

With those exceptions, however, the generalization holds, and the results are what one might expect. Petre Roman, post-Ceausescu Romania's first prime minister and leader of the opposition Social Democratic Party since 1992, expressed an opinion that finds acceptance well beyond his country's borders when he remarked that "we are left with the feeling of a possible revival of Russian imperialism, for reasons that are well-known in our history." For Roman, an enlarged NATO means a new balance in Eastern Europe, as well as a new level of deterrence, "particularly deterrence of the Russian imperialist tendencies."[3]

Thus, the Western perception of Yeltsin's Chechnya adventure as an incomprehensible mistake is not shared in Central and Eastern Europe. It is particularly not shared in Estonia, Latvia, and Poland, where there exists significant popular sympathy for the Chechens. On the contrary, in these countries Chechnya is understood—in accordance with those "reasons well-known in our history"—as yet another proof that Russia has not shed its brutal, centuries-old imperialistic tendencies and appetites.

Nor are developments closer to Central and Eastern Europe, such as the recently announced reintegration of Russia and Belarus, likely to diminish anxiety about Moscow's long-term intentions. The widely influential Polish newspaper *Rzeczpospolita* noted:

> One of the outcomes [of the Minsk-Moscow agreement] will be that the Russian border will once again lie on the Bug River. Russia will thus neighbor directly with the region of counties aspiring to NATO membership. . . .It is self-evident how much room the Kremlin diplomats gain for maneuver.[4]

In the same vein, Vladimir Zhirinovsky's egregiously imperialistic statements are taken far more seriously in Central and Eastern Europe than they are in the West, and not just because of the popular support he enjoys in Russia and among the Russian communities abroad (mostly in the Baltics and Moldova). The primary reason is that Zhirinovsky is what the Central and Eastern Europeans expect from Russian politicians. When in March 1996 the Russian Duma voted to declare void the end of the Soviet Union, the news was received in Central and Eastern Europe less with surprise than with a collective sigh of "we told you so."

Significantly, far from taking offense at Central and Eastern European characterizations, many Russians endorse them. Alexei Podberyozkin, leader of the Spiritual Heritage Movement, a group closely aligned with Gennadi Zyuganov's Communist Party of the Russian Federation (CPRF), stated "Russia is an empire. It is Russia's historic fate that it cannot exist on any other scale."[5]

Contributing to perceptions of Russia on the part of Central and Eastern Europeans are the new school curricula throughout the region, which now relate history without the pro-Russian bias of the communist era. Most galling to Russians, their cherished national myth—that Russia single-handedly defeated Nazi Germany and liberated half of Europe—is being rejected almost everywhere and replaced with the more accurate view that Nazi crimes, exploitation, and domination were simply supplanted by Stalinist terror and alien communist rule. In at least some countries, Nazi Germany is today perceived (as it was at the time) as being no worse than Russia in its destructiveness. Indeed, a principal reason that World War II leaders in the region who aligned with Germany are today rehabilitated—in popular eyes and occasionally in official eyes as well—is because they were, first and foremost, anti-Russian and anti-communist. Such are the cases of Monsignor Alois Tiso in Slovakia, Marshal Ion Antonescu in Romania, Admiral Miklos Horthy in Hungary, Colonel Draja Mihailovic in Serbia, King Boris in Bulgaria, and even the fascist Ante Pavelic of Croatia.

Mirroring this reassessment of the World War II era is the almost universal association of Russia (rather than the Soviet Union) with communism, Stalin's imposition of communist rule throughout the region after 1946, and communism's catastrophic effect on the region. Thus, even in Poland, victimized by the Nazis more than any other European country, anti-German feelings today are far less deep than anti-Russian resentments.

The Russian-Soviet-communist link is still accepted by many Central and Eastern Europeans. As evidence they note that whenever diaspora Russians have had a chance to vote in free elections—in the Baltic states, in Ukraine, in Moldova's Transnistria—they have invariably and overwhelmingly chosen candidates who are extreme Russian nationalists, communists, or both. Such facts tend to weaken the claim of those Russian liberals who argue that it is unfair to treat communism, and particularly Stalinism, as a Russian phenomenon, because Russians were its victims just like everybody else.

Lastly, and despite official silence on the subject, many Central and Eastern European countries still resent deeply Russia's territorial grabs. Present geopolitical and military realities combine with Western discouragement to prevent such feelings from being openly vented, but that does not make them less traumatic or psychologically important.

Poland and Romania were the main victims of territorial mutilation by Russia, but Estonia, Latvia, and Moldova share their resentments, for all had direct and painful experience with Russian/Soviet imperialism. Since 1939, Latvia and Estonia lost both their statehood and some territory to the Soviet Union, while Romania and Poland lost atonal sovereignty and territories to Moscow—Bessarabia and northern Bukovina in the former case; the entire eastern half of the country, including Lvov, in the latter. By contrast, Bulgaria, Slovakia, the Czech Republic, Hungary, Albania, and the successor states of Yugoslavia lost either no important territory to the USSR (Slovakia, Hungary) or none at all.

Western Timidity

In response to Central and Eastern Europe's desire to leave Russia's sphere of influence, the West has consistently displayed timidity. From Washington to Brussels, politicians and analysts have engaged in a dangerous game of self-delusion by tiptoeing around the obvious—that without the menacing presence of Russia there would be no need to expand NATO, no pressure to do so, and indeed no need for NATO at all.

Thus, U.S. Deputy Secretary of State Strobe Talbott wrote that the Russian threat is no more important than "other, equally valid, less provocative reasons for enlargement, which Russia should accept, and even support: the promotion of democracy, free markets, and regional stability."[6] Zbigniew Brzezinski, no fan of Russia or the Clinton administration, has consistently stated that NATO's enlargement is not anti-Russian and that it is actually compatible with a deepened cooperation between the alliance and Moscow.[7]

For Central and Eastern Europeans, the argument that NATO's expansion has nothing to do with the potential threat of Russian aggression is counterintuitive. The notion that the expansion is good for Russia, disregarding a consensus to the contrary within Russia itself, strikes them as insincere,

Not surprisingly, though, upon being subjected to an avalanche of such arguments from NATO officials and respected Western analysts, most Central and Eastern European leaders have felt compelled to repeat them, often against their own beliefs and personal experience, and generally at the risk of sounding unrealistic at home. Hence, the claim that NATO's expansion is not directed against Russia but, in fact, enhances Russian security has been dutifully put forward by all the governments of Central and Eastern Europe. For example, in 1993 then Bulgarian defense minister Valentin Aleksandrov stated, "In our view, Russia has an interest in the stability of our geographic area, hence we can essentially contribute to this stability as a NATO member.[8] Gheorghe Tinca, his Romanian counterpart today, has similarly claimed "Russia's genuine strategic interests require stability in our area, and this can only be ensured by NATO."[9] At least one prominent Hungarian security analyst went even further, claiming that:

> Hungarian fears of a Russian threat in terms of an invasion of Hungary as in 1956 are therefore untenable. If there is a potential Russian threat, it is not likely to be around the corner and Hungary would be only pan of a wider equation-and probably not even the main part.[10]

Slovak prime minister, Vladimir Meciar chimed in by stating that Slovakia neither feels threatened nor does it threaten anybody....It is our goal, program, and intention to become a part of NATO, which currently is the only efficiently operating defense alliance in Europe.[11]

There are two main problems with this approach to the issue of Russia's role in NATO's expansion: credibility and coherence. To deny the existence of a Russian security threat weakens the very case Western proponents of expansion want to make, If enlargement is not intended to provide security to Eastern and Central European states and thus expand the West's own area of security against a resurgent Russian imperialism, there is no valid counterargument to Moscow's position that NATO's expansion eastward is an aggressive move toward Russia. That, in turn, validates Moscow's claim that the enlargement signifies a change for the worse in the very nature of NATO, an alliance that has always proclaimed itself to be defensive.

Proponents of expansion are then reduced to justifying it with the mushy arguments used by Talbott, asserting that the purpose of expansion is "encouraging and solidifying democracy and free-market economies" in Central and Eastern Europe. But if NATO is primarily a vehicle for promoting the growth of democracy and capitalism, why not start by admitting Russia and Belarus, clearly the European states most in need of such encouragement? And how does the Talbott argument fit with NATO's and Washington's publicly held position that only free-market democracies are to be admitted in the first place? Such arguments clearly raise far more questions than they answer, and hardly anyone in Central and Eastern Europe takes them seriously.

Partnership for Peace

As for the Partnership for Peace (PFP), the program that offers former Eastern bloc countries a chance to develop cooperative military relationships with NATO, President Lennart Meri of Estonia compared it with an empty bottle of Chanel No. 5—nice looking but still empty. He may well have spoken for most of his colleagues in the region, but not for all of them. Depending on the country or the government of the day, the PFP is seen as either a satisfactory alternative to NATO membership, a placebo, or a useful tool for domestic political purposes.

When Romania joined the PFP (the first East European country to do so formally), National Peasant Party leader Ion Ratiu, then chairman of the Romanian Chamber of Deputies' Foreign Policy Commission, stated what remains the general consensus in Bucharest:

> This is the best solution we could have hoped for, since the alternative would have been to have the Visegrad countries immediately accepted under the NATO umbrella. In such a situation, we would have been left outside the Western defense system and would have inevitably had to gravitate toward the CIS [Commonwealth of Independent States]. At the same time [the PFP] means that no discrimination is being made between the former communist countries in Eastern Europe.[12]

Ratiu's position is widely shared in Romania: the vague but universal PFP is better than NATO enlargement without Romania, and the only alternative to NATO (or at least the PFP) is Russian domination. President Ion Iliescu warned that admission of only the Visegrad countries to NATO "would not be favorable to either the region's or Europe's stability. Discrimination should not be encouraged."[13] Slovak president Michal Kovac echoed Iliescu, no doubt because his country, albeit a Visegrad state, has a similarly dubious democratic standing. Kovac stated: 'We are not of the opinion that the stability of Central Europe would be served well if full membership would be granted to one of the countries and later to a second, third and fourth."[14]

Iliescu was joined by the Romanian opposition's presidential runner-up, Emil Constantinescu, who claimed "it would be extremely serious to adopt a discriminatory attitude toward Romania."[15] What Iliescu's and Constantinescu's warnings meant was made clear by the Romanian Defense Ministry's spokesman, Mircea Pascu. When asked whether Romania's protracted refusal to sign a treaty with Hungary had anything to do with complicating Budapest's admission into NATO, he admitted "there is a tiny little bit of truth in it."[16]

Not surprisingly, given Bucharest's and Bratislava's strongly shared distaste for Hungary, Pascu's admission was even more bluntly stressed by the Slovak nationalist and neutralist newspaper *Slovenska Republika*, a good indicator of sentiments in at least some government circles:

> If by our nonparticipation in NATO we "bring about" the nonadmission of Hungary, we will weaken considerably the influence of this country in Central Europe. Hungary will be far less attractive for the West, which, vice versa, will strengthen our position.[17]

That Romania and Slovakia now feel entitled to a de facto veto over Hungary's accession to NATO is a result of the alliance's own lack of clarity and its attempts to please everyone. When even timid efforts are made to clarify membership criteria, the reaction from Central and Eastern European capitals threatened with exclusion is rapid. In a December 1994 interview, Mircea Pascu accused unnamed "Western leaders" (clearly Chancellor Helmut Kohl) of "strategic subjectivity" because of their preference for the Visegrad group, "which seem to be the candidates that can be sure they will be admitted" into NATO. That preference was "subjective," in Pascu's opinion, because "there is no difference" between those countries and the others in the region "from the point of view of their development level."[18]

While more sensible Romanian politicians, particularly Roman, seem to be resigned to the idea that Poland and the Czech Republic are the most likely future NATO members,[19] even they are not prepared to see Budapest admitted ahead of Bucharest; nor are Slovak politicians, whatever their ideological hue, prepared to see Budapest admitted ahead of Bratislava. What NATO is dealing with, in short, is a cultural, ethnic, and nationalist minefield, which will become more dangerous the longer present ambiguity on admission criteria continues.

Nevertheless, the PFP is clearly losing its luster. The initial enthusiasm for it on the part of the Romanians, Bulgarians, Slovaks, and other likely losers in the race for NATO membership lay in its promise of at least postponing, if not altogether eliminating, the prospect of selective admittance into NATO. However, except in a few countries, like Moldova and the Ukraine, that never saw the PFP as a door to NATO, Russia's admission to the PFP eliminated most of those illusions.

Indeed, Russia's participation in the PFP has probably destroyed the appeal and credibility of that structure in the eyes of the Central and Eastern Europeans, for it proved that the PFP was not a step toward NATO membership but an alternative to it—and perhaps only a placebo. The result has been a general dismissal of the PFP and a free-for-all rush towards individual membership in NATO—without regard for collective regional, cultural, or civilizational arguments. The Czechs were the first to foresee this trend, followed by the Lithuanians, Poles, Hungarians, and Slovenes.

Thus, Russia's PFP membership, which was likely intended to strengthen the organization, boomeranged by discrediting the structure and speeding up the race to join NATO. Since that race is fundamentally rooted in a fear of Russian imperialism, any attempts by Moscow to prevent NATO's enlargement by strengthening the PFP will be seen as yet another demonstration of such imperialism. So too will Moscow's attempts to blackmail, threaten, or convince Bulgaria, Slovakia, or Romania to stay away from NATO.

Indeed, if there is one thing uniting all governments in Central and Eastern Europe, it is their rejection of the notion that Russia has a right to veto their

NATO membership. That applies even to states—such as Slovakia and Bulgaria—whose governments are friendly to Moscow and whose commitment to NATO membership is doubtful.

In 1993, then defense minister Aleksandrov declared: "Bulgaria does not intend to wait for anybody's [read Moscow's] permission in deciding whether it should join NATO or not. . . .It is up to Bulgaria and to the other NATO member states to decide about the form of our future integration into NATO."[20] Iliescu was blunter still, stating that "it is not up to Russia to define the conduct of other states"[21] The reason for this unanimity, however insincere in some instances, is that all governments in Central and Eastern Europe are now (more or less) freely elected—and thus to some extent responsive to public opinion.

The Historical-Cultural Politics of Integration

Although all countries and peoples in Central and Eastern Europe desire to leave behind a Russia-dominated East, the depth and feasibility of that desire vary among the countries formerly under Russian/Soviet/communist rule and influence. One principal reason has to do with differences in the histories and cultures of the countries. Some countries are simply more "Eastern"; some are more "Western."

The Balkans

Since the outbreak of the Yugoslav wars, the countries deemed Balkan have again come to seem symbolic of everything dysfunctional in Eastern political culture. But the term "'Balkan" in this sense has little relation to the geographers' term. Geographically, the Balkan peninsula is bordered on the north by the lower Danube and Sava Rivers. Yet Romania, the largest country deemed Balkan, lies north of the Danube, while Slovenia and Croatia, both of which deeply resent any association with the term "Balkan," are bisected by the Sava.

Culturally, the term "Balkan" includes those areas that were under some form of rule from Istanbul during medieval and early modem times. Thus, the word signifies long periods of Turkish political domination, but often through the mediation of imposed Greek ecclesiastic and administrative control. In this sense, it subsumes Serbia, Albania, Bosnia, Greece, Bulgaria, Macedonia, and the Romanian provinces of Moldova and Walachia.

This period of Balkan history was characterized by bureaucratic corruption, clientelism, economic backwardness, and rampant ethnic nationalism and regionalism. Five hundred years of such rule could not but leave a lasting legacy, particularly when added to a previous millennium of Byzantine rule or influence possessing many of the same characteristics. To cap the process, this joint legacy of Ottoman and Byzantine political culture was in many cases reinforced by the more recent rule or influence of Byzantium's self-proclaimed heir,

Russia. And this recent period also possessed many of the same characteristics: autocratic rule, an overlap of secular and religious authority, a corrupt bureaucracy, and a lack of political participation by citizens.

In the West, the word "Balkan" has long been associated with unpleasantness in Europe, especially with tribalism and irrational nationalism, ethnic and territorial fragmentation, and a seeming incapacity for responsible self-rule. "Balkan" has also meant a notable inability to forget or forgive real or perceived past injustices and territorial losses, as well as cultural and ideological impositions. For most Western political observers and leaders since Bismarck, the Balkans form an irremediably confused area whose baffling peoples and leaders are prisoners of history rather than students of it.

In an era of political correctness, however, some Western observers have managed to convince themselves that the term "Balkan" amounts to stereotyping and thus should be abandoned.[22] While a few Balkan analysts are willing to accept the condescension of political correctness, others prefer to deny that their countries belong to the benighted Balkans. Romanian analyst Elena Zamfirescu attempts to have it three ways. First, she says, to separate the Balkans from Central Europe is unfair, insulting, and dangerous-politically incorrect, in short. Secondly, Romania does not belong to the Balkans, geographically speaking. And if those two reasons are not sufficient to redeem Romania, the term "Balkans" is meaningless.[23] But it is not only academics who get worked up over labels, far from it. When Bulgaria tried to convene a meeting of Balkan foreign ministers in Sofia in May 1996, Slovenia and Croatia declined the invitation on the grounds that they are not Balkan states.

The converse of denying one is Balkan is to accuse others of being so. Thus, while all nations deny the Balkan label, they frequently use it to describe neighbors or their own national minorities. Gypsies are considered Balkanic everywhere on the peninsula, as are Serbs from Croatia's perspective, Romanians from Hungary's perspective, and Greeks from Romania's perspective. Taking a more positive attitude, Todor Churov, the Bulgarian deputy foreign minister, tried to do some public relations work for the term "Balkans." In 1994, he complained that "attempts are being made [in the West to delineate spheres of civilized compatibly. Ideas were suggested of making culturological divisions between the countries of Europe, based on religious traditions, alphabets, and ethnic features, and according to this, we lie in the eastern orbit." But he went on to point out that Balkanic Greece, the birthplace of the West and the quintessential heir of Byzantium, is now fully integrated into Western institutions.[24]

The Visegrad States

In light of the Balkans' history, the distinction between Visegrad Europeans and Balkan Europeans is real in many ways, not the least important of which are religion and past relations with Russia. Visegrad Europeans are largely Catholic or Protestant, in contrast to the mostly Orthodox Balkan Europeans. Most Visegrad countries—Poland being a partial exception-were part of the Habsburg Empire until 1919 and were thus shielded from Russia's imperial ambitions. In law and politics, the dominant cultural influences were for many centuries Germanic (Prussian, Austrian, Swedish), rather than Turkish or Russian. All these elements, and many more that cannot be quantified, from cuisine to fashion to educational systems to living standards, go far towards explaining current regional differences.

As a result, Europeans less affected by "Eastern" culture—Hungarians, Czechs, Balts, most Poles, Slovenes, Croats, Transylvanian Romanians, and Vojvodina Serbs—do not have the inferiority complex most Balkan people have. If anything, these peoples might be said to suffer from a *superiority* complex vis-à-vis their southern neighbors and Russia. They see their history and political culture as fundamentally Western and mostly Catholic or Protestant. They claim a political culture that includes the rule of law, religious tolerance, a functioning bureaucracy, a rational and efficient economic structure, and a civil society only briefly curtailed by communism.

When Slovenia held its first free election in 1990, the major slogan of the victors was "Europe Now!" and Slovenes are still congratulating themselves on having "left the Balkans" behind. Czechs never tire of pointing out that Prague is west of Vienna. And the main, perhaps only, reason that Croatia refrained horn engaging in a wholesale massacre of Serbs and Muslims is President Franjo Tudjman's obsessive desire to be accepted as part of the West.

Thus, the southeastern Europeans and Ukrainians find themselves patronized by their more Westernized neighbors. Plaintive Balkan protestations that "'we share the same values of democracy, pluralism, and human rights that the countries of that alliance [NATO] do" find only a limited audience.[25]

Still, the real differences between Balkan and Visegrad countries should not obscure the similarities between the groups or the dissimilarities within the groups. Slovakia's politics have a clear "Eastern" flavor, including resistance to market reforms and personalistic politics, as well as restrictions on the media, minorities, and the political opposition, making Bratislava more like Bucharest and Belgrade than it is like neighboring Warsaw and Prague.

The Domestic Politics of Integration

Domestic politics provides a second reason why the desire to leave behind a Russia-dominated East varies in depth and feasibility among the countries of Central and Eastern Europe. The chain of neocommunist electoral victories throughout the region after 1992 cannot be taken as a monolithic rejection of NATO, the EU, Western values and interests, and ultimately of democracy and free markets, Because each country differs in its political culture, ethnic makeup, the ties it has had with Moscow and the West, and its intraregional relations, it would be simplistic and mistaken to link the ruling parties of Poland and Bulgaria just because they are neocommunist. Poland has a history of ferocious anti-Russian sentiment, while Bulgaria is the most Russophile country in Eastern Europe.

Before turning to the domestic politics of Central and Eastern Europe, however, a clear distinction should be made between the universal support for EU membership and the less-than-universal support for NATO membership. Membership in the European Union is widely associated with economic aid and has few if any security or national identity implications. It is expected to provide economic benefits without representing a definitive ideological choice, and it consequently allows those who are pro-Russian and anti-NATO on security and ideological matters to have it both ways. On the one hand, they can burnish their pro-European image domestically and internationally, while not upsetting Moscow. On the other hand, they can identity themselves with those anti-American voices of the European Left that are not openly opposed to EU expansion—such as the Socialist and Green factions in the Strasbourg parliament. For many leftists in Central and Eastern Europe, the combination is unbeatable. Given these complexities, it is possible and useful to distinguish a number of rough categories among the Eastern and Central European states regarding their position vis-à-vis NATO membership.

Countries with a Dominant and Enduring Pro-NATO Consensus

Both Poland and the Czech Republic enjoy certain advantages from being ethnically homogeneous. Elsewhere in the region, national attitudes towards NATO are shaped either by significant internal minorities of another nationality or significant external minorities in another country. The effects tend to be of two sorts. First, ethnic minority parties (with the previously mentioned exception of Russian minority parties) tend to support NATO enlargement far more strongly than majority parties, for the simple reason that membership implies democracy and protection of their rights. Secondly, the existence of ethnic minorities-whether internal or external-helps foster nationalist parties, and these (as well as peasant-based parties, many of which comprise nationalist nostalgics) tend to be either hostile or cool toward the idea of joining NATO.

Poland is the one country in the region where the absolute priority of NATO membership is simply not a matter of polite political debate. All Poles are pro-Western, pro-NATO, and quietly but strongly anti-Russian. The ruling neocommunist party, the Democratic Left Alliance (including President Aleksander Kwasniewski and Foreign Minister Dariusz Rosati), is as committed to NATO—and as prepared to face the Russians on the issue-as were its anticommunist predecessors, Lech Walesa included. When Russian foreign minister Primakov visited Poland in March 1996, Kwasniewski lectured him on the

"Polish state philosophy," one of whose fundamental tenets is NATO member-ship.

Kwasniewski ostentatiously chose Brussels, Bonn, and Paris for his first trips abroad. He also brought oppositionist Bronislaw Geremek, a former dissi-dent historian who is still chairman of the Sejm's Foreign Affairs Committee, with him during his April 1996 trip to Moscow. That trip started at Katyn, scene of the most recent (1940) Russian atrocity against Poles. In addition, the Polish agenda included demands for Russian reparations-for the deportation of Poles after World War II and for the ruination, ecological and otherwise, left behind by Soviet occupation forces,[26] The mere rumor of a Russian proposal to build and control a rail and road corridor from Belarus to the exclave of Kaliningrad provoked a furious nationwide reaction in Poland, perhaps less an vocation of Moscow's intentions—Primakov denied that there ever was such a proposal—as of Polish sentiments.

Because the exclave of Kaliningrad is a part of Russia, Poland may be said to have a border with Russia, a position not shared by any other former Soviet satellite in Europe. That fact, combined with Belarus's de facto return to the Russian fold, makes the Poles even more eager to join NATO.

Like the Poles, the Czechs are unanimous in wanting NATO membership. But whereas Poles seek NATO membership for security and historic reasons, the Czechs' reasons are mostly pragmatic. The consensus in Prague is that NATO accession is a necessary and symbolically important precondition of the Czech Republic's permanently "leaving" the East for the West. Furthermore, the Czechs, starting with Prime Minister Vaclav Klaus, see an American-dominated NATO primarily as a counter to German political and economic supremacy in the region.

The Czech government was the first in the region to challenge openly the notion (briefly entertained in Washington and Brussels) that NATO's enlarge-ment should treat the entire region as a bloc—regardless of the enormous differ-ences between the applicants. Instead, Prague has consistently advocated a case-by-case approach to both NATO and EU expansion, supremely confident of its advantages. As a logical corollary, the Czechs have also successfully blocked efforts by others (Slovakia, Romania, Hungary) to establish effective regional economic and political organizations, seeing them as an impediment to integration with the West and a possible excuse for those opposed to NATO/EU expansion to at least postpone it indefinitely.

Countries with a Dominant but Fragile Pro-NATO Consensus

The countries in this category (Hungary, Romania, and Lithuania) present significant differences yet share a number of common traits that distinguish them from Poland and the Czech Republic, Two of these traits are: (1) the presence of minority-but significant-anti-NATO forces; and, most important,

(2) the perception of NATO membership as a protection against neighbors no less than a protection against Russia.

Hungary-though culturally and historically close to Poland and the Czech Republic, and ethnically homogeneous, has two major problems. Internally, there exists a significant group of basically anti-Western, chauvinistic, and irredentist groups and parties; and externally, a large Magyar diaspora in Romania, Slovakia, and Serbia is seen by those parties as in dire need of protection- from Budapest certainly, from Hungary's future allies if necessary. Thus, the 1990-1994 conservative government of the late prime minister Jozsef Antall was a strong NATO supporter, but he also declared himself the leader of all Hungarians, including the millions living in neighboring countries-a position that made Brussels undeniably nervous and brought Bucharest, Belgrade, and Bratislava to the brink of hysteria.

Antall's neocommunist successor, Prime Minister Gyula Horn, is an equally staunch supporter of Hungary's NATO membership. Despite his personal participation in the suppression of the 1956 Hungarian uprising, Horn has convinced voters that he is as pro-West, pro-NATO, and pro-EU as anyone, while renouncing Antall's threatening claims, Indeed, Horn has concretely demonstrated that he is pro-NATO. Hungary joined the PFP and is working closely with NATO by providing military installations for the alliance's operations in the former Yugoslavia. Budapest is also trying to implement all the measures necessary for admission to NATO, such as civilian control over the military and participation in joint military maneuvers. What is most important perhaps, and most painful for Hungarian nationalists, is that in August 1996 the Horn government finally signed the friendship treaty with Romania, formally giving up the notion of autonomy rights for the almost two million Transylvanian Magyars.

Most Hungarian intellectuals and most of the media are strongly pro-NATO and even more strongly pro-EU. Yet Hungarian nationalist populism is alive and well. The rapidly growing Independent Smallholders' Party of Jozsef Torgyan is now the strongest opposition group, and it is highly skeptical of NATO. The group around Istvan Czurka, a chauvinistic, anti-Semitic former Antall ally, is also active, as are similar xenophobic nationalists like those in Albert Szabo's Hungarian Life and Justice Party. For all of these forces, NATO means outside interference with Hungarian nationalism, particularly as it applies to the huge Magyar diaspora. NATO membership also requires liberal democracy and tolerance, a condemnation of irredentism, and an emphasis on individual rather than collective rights.

As of November 1996, Iliescu's ruling neocommunist party, the Social Democratic Party of Romania, has been in power since the fall of Nicolae Ceausescu in 1989, the longest tenure in all of Eastern and Central Europe. Although party members are publicly pro-NATO, their rhetoric is less than convincing. Both Defense Minister Tinca and Chief of the General Staff General Dumitru Cioflina have made statements (later officially described as "out of context") suggesting that NATO membership is not essential. Cioflina suggested a regional alliance as an alternative. Nor is there anything new in this lack of enthusiasm for NATO membership among some elements of the Romanian military and police. Here is a good example, provided by an outspoken gendarme major:

> Getting into NATO? Why should we join NATO, just to be at the Americans' call? What I'm telling you is that Romanian military men, absolutely all of them in my opinion, regardless of the service they belong to, do not want us to join NATO! Now that the Warsaw Pact is dismantled, what is the need for NATO, after all? What would we have had to do in Iraq, and now in Somalia? What about the independence and sovereignty of those countries? Whose interests would we have served there? Not those of the Americans?[27]

After Iliescu's party lost its majority in the 192 elections, it formed a coalition with extreme nationalists and unreconstructed communists. As the 1996 elections approached and Western pressures mounted, that coalition was formally dismantled-but for how long? Most important, those xenophobic and hard-line communist parties received some 20 percent of the popular vote in 1992. There are also minor elements of opposition, now joined by the government's former coalition partners, whose goal is not liberal democracy at all, but the replacement of Iliescu's regime with a "truly national" system: one that is anti-Russian, anti-Hungarian, anti-Ukrainian, anti-Bulgarian, and ultimately anti-Western.

The liberal Romanian opposition, such as it is, is sincerely pro-Western, in the sense that it expects the "West"—a mythical entity with unlimited amounts of ideas, dollars, and legitimacy—to bring Romania into "Europe" and the liberals to power.

Opportunistic Vacillators

While Iliescu might be seen as largely inclined towards the West, Slovak and, even more so, Bulgarian neocommunist leaders are less-than-sincere vacillators on the NATO enlargement issue, albeit for somewhat different reasons.

In both Slovakia and Bulgaria, the democratic opposition is weak and divided and, although committed to membership in NATO and the EU, has to rely on frail reeds, namely, the presidents of these parliamentary republics: Kovac in Slovakia and the departing Zhelyu Zhelev. Both are under vicious attack from their neocommunist prime ministers, Meciar and Zhan Videnov. As a result, Kovac's future is uncertain and Zhelev, after losing his party's primary to an unknown lawyer, is on the way out. Thus, it appears that Slovakia and Bulgaria may be early quitters in the race for NATO membership. The roots of Slovakia's pro-Russia tilt go beyond Meciar's opportunistic and authoritarian instincts and straight to the heart of modem Slovak nationalism. Prior to 1948, the Slovaks, like the Czechs (but unlike every other people in Eastern Europe), had little contact with and thus no reason to fear or resent Russia or the USSR. The

Soviet-organized Prague coup of 1948 ended Czechoslovakia's exemption on that score, as well as a tradition of mushy Pan-Slavic sympathy, but the effects were not as great in Bratislava as in Prague.

Twenty years later, the 1968 Soviet-led invasion of Czechoslovakia destroyed whatever sympathy for Russia Czechs might have retained, but it too had a much lesser impact on Slovakia, Indeed, the post-1968 regime was not only led by a Slovak, Gustav Husak, but it engaged in a massive redistribution of resources from Czech lands to Slovakia, a process that continued until the collapse of communism in 1989, The relative absence of an intelligentsia in Slovakia, with the anticommunism that came naturally to that group throughout Central and Eastern Europe, also helped lessen anti-Soviet and anti-Russian feelings in Bratislava. Thus, the humiliation, hatred, and anticommunist sentiments of the "Czechoslovaks" after 1968 should be seen in their true context: they were shared by virtually all Czechs but not by most Slovaks. Many gradual Slovaks benefited from the communist era, particularly from the post-1968 industrialization of their previously relatively rural and backward area. Politically, Meciar's Movement for a Democratic Slovakia, while professing pro-NATO and pro-EU commitments, depends upon its coalition partners to stay in power. Those partners, a small communist party and a small nationalist party (Jan Luptak's Association of Workers of Slovakia and Jan Slota's Slovak National Party, respectively), are opposed to NATO membership and are friendly to Russia. Indeed, Luptak, vice speaker of Slovakia's parliament, declared in Moscow that Slovakia should be neutral.[28]

In light of such facts, the repeated statements by Meciar and Foreign Minister Juraj Schenk to the effect that integration into NATO is "an indisputable priority" of Bratislava's foreign policy should be taken with a large grain of salt.[29] That is particularly true when such statements are followed by caveats suggesting NATO should change its nature to assuage Russian fears-demands echoed in Bulgaria—and, even more important, when one considers Slovakia's policy of increased economic and military dependence on Russia. Such ties are part of Meciar's policy of opposing major economic reforms, particularly the dismantling or privatization of Slovakia's mammoth communist-era state enterprises in general and its defense-related factories in particular. That opposition has been present in his electoral platforms from the beginning and is shared by his extreme left- and right-wing allies in the present coalition. Since that position brought him to power twice, it would be unrealistic to expect any change.

As it happens, the survival of those obsolete industries, and therefore the support of their workers, depends upon traditional Russian/CIS markets, for Slovakia (along with Bulgaria) has not significantly diverted its foreign trade westward. On the contrary, it is the only state in Central or Eastern Europe to obtain a major ($150 million) Russian loan. To that one may add Slovakia's decision to continue, indeed expand, its military dependence on Russia by acquiring additional MiG aircraft and continuing to produce parts for export to the CIS.

In Bulgaria, the question of NATO membership is a losing battle for the soul of the nation. Pro-Western elements, centered around President Zhelev, have clearly lost out to Prime Minister Videnov's unabashed Russophiles. The uniquely close ties between the Bulgarian Socialist Party (BSP) regime in Sofia and some of the most unreconstructed Russian hardliners are symbolic of this trend. That Marshal Viktor Kuilikov, former Warsaw Pact commander and now advisor to the Russian Defense Ministry, could state in Sofia, in June 1995, that the Warsaw Pact was strictly defensive, that "it was a collective body, and the USSR applied no pressure to the other members,[30] is significant. Such statements are unlikely to have been made anywhere else west of Minsk. In fact, it is unlikely that Kulikov would have been tolerated anywhere else.

The government's commitment to Bulgaria's long tradition of pro-Russian and pro-Soviet communism cannot be doubted. It is certainly undoubted in Moscow, to a degree that embarrasses even Sofia. Thus, on March 2, 1996, President Yeltsin mentioned Belarus, Kazakstan, Kyrgyzstan, and Bulgaria (alone among Central and Eastern European states) as possible members of a new Russian commonwealth. The statement provoked a storm in Bulgaria, with even pro-regime media complaining about the government's reluctance to reject Yeltsin's vision. On the other hand, when the Russian Duma's chairman Gennadi Seleznev stated in Sofia, on March 26, 1996, that Russia and Bulgaria share common strategic aims and openly supported the idea of Bulgaria's neutrality, there was no official comment from the Bulgarian government.[31] Clearly, Bulgaria is neither interested in nor Rkely to seek NATO membership. On the occasion of Viktor Chemomyrdin's May 1995 visit to Sofia, a pro-BSP newspaper, Duma, gushed enthusiastically "a period in which politicians, merchants, deputies, and ministers tried to undermine not only our geopolitical but also our trade relations with Russia, is behind us. Led by the Bulgarian sense of realism, we broke off with this period.1

By electing the BSP, Bulgarians have reverted to their historic alignment with Russia, for the BSP has never hidden its pro-Russia sentiments, thus suggesting that at least most ethnic Bulgarian voters share those sentiments. Vocal pro-Western and pro-NATO sentiments are to be found principally in the Turkish-dominated Movement for Rights and Freedoms.

Implications for the West

As historic patterns reassert themselves, the pro-Western euphoria of post-1989 is rapidly declining in certain countries—ranging from Belarus to Bulgaria and Slovakia to Romania. One could point also to Moldova and Ukraine, which have chosen neutrality via membership in the PFP because they fear Moscow's reaction if they join NATO. In short, there is a growing feeling in Central and Eastern Europe that NATO will limit its expansion to the Visegrad countries, or perhaps only some of them. Among those left out, emotions ranging from resignation to resentment contribute little to regional stability, at least in the short term. But while it is clear that a selective and limited enlargement would exacerbate cleavages in the region, these cleavages are likely to grow anyway.

Indeed, following the collapse of the Soviet empire, the East-West cleavage in Central and Eastern Europe is deeper than it has been for centuries, and it is growing. Baits, Czechs, Slovenes, and Croats have been rushing Westward, while their Balkan ex-partners have been moving Eastward, at different speeds. No amount of NATO or EU diplomatic obfuscation will change this trend, nor will domestic politic. The drift is so strong that it continues regardless of the parties in power—and will continue, so long as those parties have to submit to elections; hence, the surprising degree of continuity between the strategic thinking of Polish, Hungarian, Slovene, and Baltic anticommunists and neocommunists.

Difficult as it may be for NATO decision makers, these realities should be faced, and the temptation to paper over the East-West cultural gap rejected. The NATO alliance is, after all, a Western alliance. And that places the key factor in NATO's enlargement, opposition by Russia, in a different light. During Mikhail Gorbachev's tenure, and during Yeltsin's first years in power, Moscow played down the East-West cultural gap by talking about a "common European house." But that is not the case anymore. Like the peoples to its west, Russia has returned to historic patterns: facing both Europe and Asia, and bent upon expanding its influence in both directions. Unlike most Western policymakers, Central and Eastern Europeans recognize the extent, depth, and durability of this shift-the naturalness of this return to historic patterns—and act accordingly.

Some, like the Bulgarians and Slovaks, appear resigned, if not happy, with the return of Russian influence and are adapting to it. The Poles, Balts, Czechs, and Hungarians also see a resurgence of Russian influence-and view rapid admission to NATO as their last chance to escape. In light of these strategic assessments, the continuation of NATO's present policy of denying the existence of a Russian threat is untenable and dangerously lacking in credibility. What makes the situation even more urgent is that, as in the late 1930s, no one in Central and Eastern Europe sees a viable alternative security arrangement. At that time, the alternatives were Berlin or Moscow. Today, the alternatives are Brussels or Moscow.

Reprinted with permission from http://www.fpri.org, Winter 1997

Notes

1.   "Article Assesses Russian Arms, NATO Membership," Foreign Broadcast Information Service, Daily Report: East Europe (hereafter, FBIS, EEur), May 23, 1995, p. 4, from Demokratsiya (Sofia), May 19, 1995.

2.   Interview in La Libre Belgique (Brussels), Nov. 3, 1993. This and all subsequent translations are by the author.

3.   "Politicians Welcome NATO 'Partnership,'" FBIS, EEur, Jan. 19, 1994, p. 21, from Romania Libera (Bucharest), Jan. 12, 1994.

4.   "Poland: Daily Comments on Yeltsin-Lukashenka Agreement," FBIS, EEur, Mar. 26, 1996, p. 56, from Rzeczpospolita (Warsaw), Mar. 25, 1996.

5.   Bruce W. Nelan, "The Undead Red," Time, Apr. 8, 1996.

6.   Strobe Talbott, 'Why NATO Should Grow," New York Review of Books, Aug. 10, 1995

7.   For a recent restatement of these ideas, see "A la recherche d'un nouvel ordre de securite. Entretien avec Zbigniew Brzezinski" (In search of a new security order. Interview with Zbigniew Brzezinski Politique Internatiomle, Summer 1995, pp. 130-31

8.   "Defense Minister Views Relations With NATO," FBIS, EEur, Oct. 21, 1993, p. 3, from Chasa (Sofia), Oct. 15, 1993.

9.   Adevarul (Bucharest), Apr. 12, 1995.

10. Istvan Szonyi, "Hungary: A Security Challenge?" International Spectator, Jan.-Mar. 1994, p. 97.

11. "Meciar Discusses Chances of Joining NATO," FBIS, EEur, Sept. 17,1993, p. 16, from Pravda (Bratislava), Sept. 11, 1993.

12. "Politicians Welcome NATO 'Partnership,'" FBIS, EEur, Jan. 19, 1994, p. 21

13. "Eastern Europe Must Join NATO 'Together,'" FBIS, EEur, Dec. 29, 1993, p. 24, from AFP (Paris), Dec. 28, 1993.

14. Quoted in David Ottaway, "Slovakia Joins Neighbors in Call for NATO Entry," Washington Post, Jan. 5, 1994.

15. "Constantinescu Discusses Membership," FBIS, EEur, Nov. 9, 1993, p. 31, from La Libre Belgique, Nov. 8, 1993.

16. "Defense Official Discusses NATO Integration," FBIS, EEur, July 10, 1995, p. 47, from Curierul National (Bucharest), June 28, 1995.

17. "Slovakia: Article Argues Against Joining NATO," FBIS, EEur, May 23, 1996, p. 11, from .Slovenska Republika (Bratislava), May 20, 1996.

18. Curiel National, Dec. 20, 1994.

19. See Petre Roman's intenriew In Jumalel National (Bucharest), May 20, 1996.

20. "Defense Minister Views Relations With NATO," FBIS, EEur; Oct. 21, 1993, p. 3

21. "Iliestu Desires Rapprochement With NATO, EU," FBIS, EEur, Nov. 8, 1994, p. 31, from La Libra Belgique, Nov. 7, 1994

22. R. Craig Nation, "Images of the Balkan in the West," Balkan Forum (Skopje), Sept. 1995

23. Elena Zamfirescu, "Post-Cold War Central Europe and Its Many Maps," Romanian Journal of International Affairs vol. 1, no. 1, 1995.

24. Editorial, Romania Mare (Bucharest), Jan. 26, 1944.

25. "Spokesman Views NATO Membership, Other Issues," FBIS, EEur, Dec. 22, 1994, p. 35, from Dimineata (Bucharest), Dec. 13, 1994.

26. "Poland: Polish, Russian Priorities for Negotiations Differ," FBIS, EEur, Mar. 18 1996, P. 53, from Gazeta Wyborcza (Warsaw), Mar. 15, 1996.

27. Lumea Libera (New York), Jan. 1, 1994.

28. "Slovakia: Kovac Speaks Out Agains Neutrality Option," FBIS, EEur May 30 1996, from SME (Prague), May 28, 1996

29. "Slovakia: Poll Suggests Majority Support Joining NATO," FBIS, EEuc Mar. 18, 1996, firom Slovenska Republika, Mar. 15, 1996

30. "Kulikov Discusses NATO, Security Issues," FBIS, EEur, June 8, 1995, p. 5, from Duma (Sofia) June 5, 1995

31.   See "Bulgaria: BSP To Issue Statement on Yeltsin," IBIS, EEur, Apr. 2, 1996, p. 8, from Duma, Apr. 2. 1996.
32.   "Commentary Examines Relations With Russia," FBIS, EEur, May 23, 1995, p. 3, from Duma, May 18, 1995.

GYPSIES—PARIAHS ON THE DANUBE OR THE LATEST P.C. MINORITY?

On January 17, 2003, the UN Development Program/Regional Bureau for Europe and the CIS (UNDP/RBEC) published a report on the situation of the gypsies of Romania, Bulgaria, Hungary, Slovakia, and the Czech Republic. The "Roma Regional Development Report" ("Roma" is the name the gypsies now prefer for themselves, however historically inaccurate it may be), was immediately picked up by the left-wing European media (see e.g., the *Guardian's* "UN Report says one in six Roma is starving," 1/17).

As the UNDP report itself acknowledges, the problems with assessing the gypsies' real, imagined or indeed self-inflicted problems start with the basic one of defining who is a Gypsy and how many of them are. Gypsies themselves do not agree on this. They are divided along dialectal, tribal, and historic occupational lines. For instance, in Romania, the country with the largest Gypsy population, the gypsies have historically been divided between *caldarari* (caldron makers), *lingurari* (wooden spoon makers), *aurari* (river gold miners), *ursari* (bear trainers) and, most prominent and influential, *lautari* (musicians). Similar divisions apply elsewhere in Eastern and Central Europe. While such distinctions have lost their old meaning, they remain under different forms.

They are also highly opportunistic. Depending on circumstances, Gypsies may declare themselves gypsies in official censuses or declare themselves part of the dominant community in which they live—Hungarian in Hungary or Romanian Transylvania; Czechs in Slovakia; Slovaks in the Czech Republic—whatever is more advantageous. The same goes with religion. In Turkish-dominated areas of Bulgaria they identify themselves as Muslim, while elsewhere (e.g., Romanian Moldova and Wallachia) they are Orthodox. In Transylvania, depending on location, they could be Calvinists, Orthodox, or even Unitarian.

That means that general reports such as UNDP's about the conditions of the Gypsy minority are based on quicksand. Meaningful analysis of a "community" one cannot even define is difficult. As to its size, the Romanian 1992 census counted 409,723 gypsies, while most realistic estimates put that number at 1.5 million and Gypsy militants claim some 2.5 million. Hungary counted 142,836 in its 1990 census and 190,046 in 2001; again, more realistic independent figures are closer to 500,000.

There can be no argument about the historic discrimination against gypsies in Eastern Europe. In the Romanian principalities of Wallachia and Moldova, until the mid-nineteenth century they were serfs to be sold as village communities, families or indeed individuals. Hitler attempted to eliminate them entirely, beginning with the 1938 *Zigeuneraufräumungswoche* ("Gypsy clean-up week") and culminating in the genocide at Auschwitz (what Gypsy collective memories call *Porajmos*). In fact, the percentage of the Gypsy population murdered by the Nazis was probably as high or even higher than the percentage of the Jewish population killed.

As a people (or, more accurately, a collection of disparate groups) originating in India's Gujarat, gypsies were the camp followers of Mongol invaders of Eastern Europe in the thirteenth century. Once within the Byzantine Empire, they adapted the Byzantine self-defining term of *Romaioi* ("Romans" in Greek), given Byzantium's claim to be the direct successor of the (Eastern) Roman Empire. Hence today's historically absurd self-definition as "Roma." Whatever name they choose for themselves (and "Roma" appears to be the most potentially lucrative and thus increasingly the most fashionable one), all gypsies, regardless of their centuries-old differences of dialect and history, define themselves less as an inclusive ethnic group and more as distinct from the *gagea*—the non-gypsies around them. To accept the values and rules of the *gagea* is to cease to be a Gypsy—a policy that has had profound impact on the size of the Gypsy community and its ability to carry its culture forward, since intermarriage with the *gagea* has always been common.

In addition of being the most linguistically adept people in the region, the gypsies have made extraordinary contributions to European music, influencing Hungarian, Romanian, Spanish, Russian, and Balkan music and dance. Spanish flamenco dances and the works of Spain's preeminent poet of the twentieth century, Federico Garcia Lora, are basically Gypsy inspired. And despite nationalist East European claims to the contrary, Romanian, Hungarian, and Eastern Slav (Slovak and Ukrainian) folk music and dances are ultimately heavily influenced by the gypsies.

But then there is the other side: the historic dysfunctional nature of the Gypsy society, which continues to today. While any suggestion that gypsies are a dysfunctional, indeed criminally minded subgroup elicits strenuous denials and counter allegations of racism, it remains the case that in all countries where they are present in a significant number, they are disproportionately represented among the criminal elements. Prior to 1989 their activities didn't go much beyond petty theft; now they have "graduated" into far more serious types of crimes: from robbery to murder and from theft to international drug and illegal migrant trafficking.

Nor can it be simple poverty accounting for this. Sibiu, a fairly large city in Romanian Transylvania, boasts the huge kitsch palaces of "Emperor Julian" and "King" Cioaba of the Romanian gypsies complete with gold-covered roofs. In Bucharest one sees Gypsy gang leaders with huge 18-karat gold chains and enormous rings. But the EU has made them official "victims."

In 2004 the EU will vote on the admission of some of these countries with large Gypsy populations and have to face the obvious: a dysfunctional, criminally oriented "community" that has well learned how to manipulate human rights claims. This community, which has been on the record for centuries as refusing to accept *gagea* rules such as the rule of law, obligatory schooling, and the civic responsibilities of voting, will be free to migrate around and benefit from that same *gagea*, all the way from Helsinki to Lisbon. It will be interesting to see whether authors of articles like "Shame of a Continent" (the *Guardian*, 1/08) on the gypsies' plight hold to their views after their own countries begin to receive large numbers of Gypsy immigrants.

Reprinted with the permission from http://www.frontpagemag.com,
January 21, 2003

WHO IS ABDULLAH ÖCALAN?

On November 13, the Italian police arrested Abdullah Öcalan, founder and leader of the Kurdish Workers' Party (PKK), at Rome's airport. He had just arrived from Moscow with a false passport and, upon arrest, asked for political asylum. Coming at a time when British authorities are detaining former Chilean president Augusto Pinochet, who stands accused by a Spanish judge of terrorism and genocide, the arrest of Öcalan on an outstanding warrant issued in Turkey promises to raise significant questions about European politics, international legal standards, and the very possibility of cooperation in combating terrorism.

Born in 1948 in a village in Eastern Turkey, Öcalan studied political science at Ankara University, where he became a Maoist. By 1973 he had organized a Maoist group—which initially included Kurdish as well as Turkish militants—whose goal was socialist revolution in Turkey. After years of recruiting and indoctrinating followers, the PKK was formally established on November 7, 1978. In the previous year, he committed his first known murder, that of an ideological rival accused of working for the government.

Since then, the group has evolved into a deadly insurgency against Turkey, reaching a strength of some 5,000 by 1992. From his bases in Syria and Lebanon's Bekaa Valley, Öcalan conducted a ruthless campaign, ostensibly for Kurdish independence but, as widely available PKK internal documents suggest, the ultimate goal is the creation of a Maoist state in areas of Turkey, Iran and Iraq. (Skeptics are urged to visit their website at http://burn.ucsd.edu/~ats/PKK/.) Öcalan's ambitions were clearly defined in 1995 at the Fifth Congress of the PKK, where the "Resolution on Internationalism" stated that "By effectively arguing in favor of socialism and by spreading socialist ideas to the people of the region, [the PKK] is the vanguard of the global socialist movement. . ." In 1984 the PKK was a founding member of the Revolutionary Internationalist Movement (RIM), a sort of loosely structured Maoist version of Lenin's Comintern that also includes Peru's Shining Path (Sendero Luminoso).

Indeed, the similarities between the PKK and the Shining Path are striking: like the latter's founder, Abimael Guzman, Öcalan is a Maoist with global leadership ambitions; their tactics are particularly bloody, even by terrorist standards, and the main victims are civilians who refuse to submit to their groups. Frequent targets include teachers, members of village self-defense groups, and elected local officials. So far, since the beginning of its operations in 1980, the PKK is primarily responsible for a war that has left some 30,000 people dead (compared with 25,000 for the Shining Path). In addition, the PKK was responsible for a number of murders of Turks in Germany, which is the reason the German government has also issued a warrant for Öcalan's arrest.

For almost two decades, Öcalan has operated from Syria and Syrian-occupied Lebanon. However, last October, after Turkey very nearly went to war against Syria, Damascus backed down, closed PKK camps and expelled Öcalan. First, he fled to Moscow, where he has enjoyed close relations for decades. While the Russian government denied any knowledge of his whereabouts, on November 4 the Duma unanimously voted to demand that he be given asylum. Two days later, 109 Socialist and communist members of the Greek Parliament—one third of the entire body—issued an invitation to Öcalan to come to Greece as "leader of the world's most oppressed people." The collective invitation, supported by Greece's deputy speaker, Panayiotis Sgouridis, was renewed by a Greek Socialist parliamentarian in Rome, after Öcalan's arrest.

To its credit, the Russian government, under pressure from Turkey and the United States, expelled Öcalan, forcing him to flee to Italy. The terrorist leader's choice was not accidental: Italy's government is dominated by ex-communists of the Party of the Democratic Left and supported by the unreconstructed ones. Sure enough, a prominent Democratic Left leader has already expressed support for Öcalan's request for asylum, while leaders (and parliamentarians) of the Greens and the orthodox communists became his lawyers. In fact, the orthodox communist Giuliano Pisapia, one of Öcalan's lawyers, used to be the chairman of the Italian parliament's justice committee. As the influential Milan newspaper *La Stampa* put it, the communist Justice Minister, Oliviero Diliberto, has a dilemma on his hands: "What would the Italian government do with Abdullah Öcalan, leader of the PKK and the Kurdish resistance, a terrorist for the Turkish and German authorities, who want him in their jails, and a patriot for the Italian Greens and Communists?"

Öcalan's arrest raises serious issues that include, but go beyond that of dealing with terrorism. Judging by the number of his victims, Öcalan is in rarefied company in today's terrorist Pantheon—only Guzm n himself and the other Maoist cum nationalist Vellupilai Pirapaharan of the Tamil Tigers of Sri Lanka are in the same league. That the dominant parties in the Russian Duma and NATO members Italy and Greece openly support and lionize him is disturbing indeed. In Russia's case this suggests that an eventual Communist replacement of Yeltsin could well bring back some of Moscow's worst Cold War habits: support for large-scale international terrorism. As for Greece, it appears that the traditional reflexive support for any enemy of Turkey is reaching dangerously provocative and irrational heights—not a good omen for the stability of the Alliance's southern flank.

Italy already has a bad record in dealing with foreign terrorists: they routinely walk away from its jails, are given asylum or allowed to transit freely. It is also important to see if the ex-communists dominating the government in Rome have indeed become democratic or still share Öcalan's beliefs in "proletarian internationalism," and put them above justice and good sense.

Furthermore, an Italian refusal to extradite Öcalan will irreparably damage Europe's already tense relations with Turkey and make a further mockery of the

European Union's pontifications about "human rights" and international law. Indeed, if Öcalan goes free after a campaign that has left 30,000 dead in the name of Maoism, while Pinochet is put on trial for the deaths of 3,000 in winning Chile's war against communism, then we will know that the European capacity for political hypocrisy has not been exhausted by the fall of the Soviet Union.

Reprinted with the permission from http://www.fpri.org,
November 16, 1998

THE CAPTURE OF ABDULLAH ÖCALAN AND THE FUTURE OF COUNTER-TERRORISM

On February 16, in Nairobi, Kenya, Abdullah Öcalan, the founder and supremo of the Kurdish Workers' Party (PKK), was captured and promptly sent to Turkey to face trial. As the main engineer of a Maoist guerrilla organization, he stands accused of crimes involving the death or wounding of some 30,000 people, and untold economic damage, mostly in Turkey, but also in Iraq and Germany. His arrest raises delicate questions: the political and legal aspects of international counterterrorism; the likely impact on Turkey's internal counterinsurgency campaign; the most appropriate treatment of Öcalan; and the larger geopolitical implications.

The odyssey that culminated in Öcalan's capture is still somewhat obscure but this much seems clear: after Turkey threatened to go to war with Syria last October, PKK bases in that country were finally closed and Öcalan expelled. With the public support of the Russian communists, he had reason to hope for refuge in Moscow. But that failed, and so Öcalan invoked his close ties with the ex-communists ruling Italy, and arrived there demanding political asylum. That request touched off an embarrassing imbroglio during which the new, Social Democratic government in Germany publicly admitted that it was too afraid of PKK terrorism to pursue its own arrest warrant against Öcalan, and the neo-communists in Rome vacillated between longstanding sympathy for the PKK and respect for international law. Ultimately, Italy rejected both Turkey's extradition request and Öcalan's asylum demand, and expelled him. Relentlessly pursued by a succession of Turkish governments from across the political spectrum, the Maoist leader unsuccessfully sought asylum in various European countries—all of which recognized that he was now a liability not worth the risk to their political and economic relations with Turkey or the United States. Finally, after apparently spending a few days at the Greek embassy in Nairobi, Öcalan was either forced out (the PKK version) or left the compound on his own accord (one of the Greek versions), whereupon he was seized and sent to Turkey.

Öcalan's misadventures and the end of his career—and perhaps his life, given the possibility of his receiving the death penalty—are a significant victory for international efforts to control terrorism. Their occasional reticence and outright lies notwithstanding, Kenyan and European governments of all political colors—strongly prodded by Washington, one may add—ultimately concluded that harboring a major terrorist figure was not in their interest. The Turks made it impossible for Öcalan to find asylum in Europe. The Kenyans, already shocked by their victimization at the hands of international terrorism last year (against the U.S. embassy), were naturally ready to avoid a repeat. And the Greek government apparently found (or blundered into) a way of getting rid of a serious problem that could give Turkey a casus belli.

One of the mysteries of the entire episode is the unexpected Turkish knowledge of and preparation for a crisis in East Africa. While this involves a degree of speculation, Ankara probably received intelligence support from at least one of its two key allies—the United States and Israel. Washington has been consistently and publicly supportive of Turkey's extradition demands against Öcalan—whom the State Department has consistently labeled a terrorist—and probably played a major role in convincing Russia, Italy, and the Netherlands to deny him asylum. Furthermore, at least since last year's terrorist bombing of the embassy in Nairobi, there is a strong U.S. intelligence presence in Kenya. As for Israel, a newly close ally of Turkey, it has had good relations with Kenya (including intelligence) for many years, as demonstrated more than two decades ago by the Entebbe incident. (As of this writing, both governments have denied any involvement in the Öcalan capture.)

The role of the Greek government, now attacked by PKK fanatics across Europe for being "responsible" for Öcalan's extradition, is also remarkable. Greek public opinion, particularly on the Left, has for years been supportive of the PKK and Öcalan, for the simple reasons that they are effective at killing Turks and, as Maoists, they are ideologically kindred spirits. Greek public opinion—encouraged by both ruling and opposition parties—remains irresponsibly pro-PKK and hostile to Prime Minister Costas Simitis, who now stands accused of cooperating with Ankara. Whether Greeks in Kenya were misled, tricked, forced, or just wanted to relieve themselves of a major national problem, remains to be seen. What is clear is that Greek involvement remains, well, byzantine.

On the other hand, this victory for law and common sense is clouded by the fact that, the Kenyans aside, no government had the courage to extradite Öcalan to Turkey. Opposition to the death penalty—not applied in Turkey since 1982—was not only a cover for Italy to avoid dealing with Öcalan, it was arrogant and self-righteous. More to the point is the Europeans' fear of PKK terrorism at home—a reasonable fear, as the events immediately following the capture demonstrated. In a clear display of the PKK's extensive penetration of the Kurdish diaspora, militant Kurds engaged in well-coordinated attacks against Greek and Kenyan diplomatic missions throughout Europe—from London to Moscow and from the Netherlands to Switzerland.

According to German intelligence sources, 10,000 of the half million Kurds in Germany are PKK cadres and perhaps another 40,000 can be mobilized. Among the somewhat more than half million Kurds in Europe as a whole, PKK militants are in reality a small minority, albeit a well-organized and violent one. They are also wealthy—which should come as no surprise, given the PKK domination of heroin (and illegal alien) traffic throughout Western Europe. Those lucrative activities have allowed the PKK to fund their London-based television station (MED-TV), an extensive Internet presence, funding of "Kurdish" organizations in Europe and North America, and backing for the now-sputtering PKK military operations in southeastern Turkey and northern Iraq. Thus the PKK is a continental threat, but one that should be treated as a criminal enterprise as much as a political and terrorist organization—very much like Colombia's Marxist insurgents or Peru's murderous Shining Path, the latter an old ally of the PKK.

The PKK's fortunes may now be changing, because the loss of Öcalan, whether through a long prison term or execution, is a terminal defeat—at least within Turkey. Even before his arrest the PKK had been losing its war against Turkey since the end of Syrian support last October. Öcalan's second in command was recently captured; Turkish tactical intelligence has improved dramatically, suggesting popular dissatisfaction with the insurgent movement; Iraqi Kurds have eliminated the PKK's local presence in that country; and without a Syrian base, income from heroin trafficking may have been limited.

Whatever its military and strategic losses, the PKK's public relations campaign has still registered political success in Europe, where Öcalan's lifelong commitment to Maoism has been obscured by a mushy wave of revisionism. PKK terrorists are now hailed as "nationalists," and self-immolating fanatics are treated as "patriots" rather than as a terrible sign of the true potential of a PKK-run state. PKK militants in Western Europe (Germany, Italy, the Benelux countries, France) are still accepted as representatives of "the Kurds," and the existence of a "Kurdish issue" is generally considered a relevant topic for political debate, at least among elites. PKK attempts to internationalize their "cause" enjoy dangerously high levels of support, certainly much greater than any attempt to make the Corsican, Basque, or Irish "issues" a matter for European consideration.

The reasons for such support are many, but the usual extremism of emigres, when compared to those back home, is among the most obvious. Just as Cubans in Miami are more vocally anti-Castro than those on the island, relatively well off Kurds in Berlin find it more attractive to "fight" Ankara than do their compatriots left in eastern Turkey's poor rural areas, particularly when the latter are the ones dying as a result.

Another reason for the organization's success is the tendency among some in the media and in public office to take at face value the PKK's false claims to be nationalist and to represent the Kurds in Turkey. CNN relentlessly and unwittingly repeats the propagandistic portrayal of the PKK as a "Kurdish rebel/guerrilla" organization and Öcalan as a "separatist leader," when all widely available evidence suggests otherwise. In truth, from the beginning of his career in 1978 until the recent crushing military defeats and the loss of his Syrian bases, Öcalan was an avowed Maoist like Pol Pot, and his goal was the creation of a Maoist state throughout the Middle East—not a Kurdish national polity. The overwhelming majority of the PKK's victims in Turkey, including over 5,000 women and children, village leaders, peasant militiamen, and teachers, were in fact Kurds who disagreed with his goals. And among his targets were the authentically nationalist Kurdish organizations in northern Iraq completely lacking in Maoist fanaticism and goals. So much for the romantic—if not intentionally false—notion that Öcalan and the PKK somehow represent the Kurds in Turkey or elsewhere.

European governments—particularly Italy—should clearly take another look at their irrational acceptance of the PKK stance and its place in their countries. Many Kurdish immigrants treated as bona fide "refugees" are hard-headed potential terrorists. PKK activists should not be tolerated, but rather recognized as security threats, and their leaders sent back to Turkey to stand trial.

In terms of the resolution of the "Kurdish issue" in Turkey itself, Öcalan's capture may well be an opportunity not to be missed. With its founder, strategist, and ideologue gone, the PKK could follow the pattern of its ideological kin, the Shining Path. In Peru, the capture of Abimael Guzman in 1992 led to the organization's fragmentation, loss of ideological and political purpose, and ultimate strategic defeat. While chaotic PKK violence in Turkey may continue—and in fact may briefly increase as local leaders try to establish a loyal following through accelerated terror—the PKK's back is probably broken for good. If the Turkish government adopts an intelligent combination of measures such as a generous amnesty for middle-level cadres and rank-and-file PKK members, increases military pressure on the remaining units, and avoids premature triumphalism, the insurgent threat could be eliminated. Current economic development programs in the southeast should be accelerated, and cooperation with anti-PKK Kurdish elements in northern Iraq continued.

On the other hand, Turkey should resist the predictable "human rights" onslaught from the European Left against the proceedings during the forthcoming trial of Öcalan—whatever those proceedings may look like. He should be tried for common crimes, and under no circumstances given the opportunity to transform the proceedings into a political circus. If terrorism is morally and legally wrong—and Öcalan is clearly a terrorist, no matter what his goals may have been—he should be tried as a criminal and not as some kind of "misguided" political activist. The trial of Abdullah Öcalan presents an ideal opportunity for a nation built on democracy (even as imperfect as Turkey's may be) to draw the line, once and for all, between legitimate political activism and murder.

And, in the face of a "victory" it has neither achieved nor planned for, NATO has its hands full of impossibilities.

Reprinted with the permission from http://www.fpri.org,
February 18, 1999

The PKK Strategy in Europe to Place Turkey on Trial

After the arrest of the Kurdish Workers' Party (PKK) "Chairman" Abdullah Öcalan on February 16 in Kenya, and his subsequent transfer to a Turkish jail to stand trial, widespread "Kurdish" demonstrations erupted throughout Europe, Canada, Australia, and the Middle East the very following day.

In the Middle East the protests were centered in Lebanon, Iran, and Turkey, none of which is surprising. Under the protection of Beirut's overlords in Syria, Lebanon has since 1984 been a haven of PKK training and recruitment. And Iran, not exactly a friend of either Kurdish independence or democratic expression, is ruled by a regime for which any weakening of Turkey is welcome. As for Turkey, its southeastern region remains infiltrated by the PKK.

More interesting was the geographic scope of demonstrations in Europe: from Berlin, London, Stockholm, Milan, Rome, Marseille, Amsterdam, and Brussels in the west, to Bucharest and Moscow in the east; and also in smaller cities such as Heilbronn, Dresden, and Leipzig. The targets—all highly prized public relations objectives—were diplomatic missions, mostly Greek, as well as Israeli and Kenyan, and offices of international organizations in Switzerland.

The convenient conclusion, shared by willfully ignorant members of the media and leftist parties in Europe and America, was that these protests abundantly demonstrated universal Kurdish support for the man known as "Apo" and his Maoist PKK. The actual size of the demonstrations, however, suggest a carefully coordinated attempt by a small group bent on publicity. The following figures are taken from pro-PKK internet sources: in Berlin, there were 150 protesters, including children; in Frankfurt fifty, and in Bonn between twenty and thirty—all in a country with half a million immigrants of Kurdish origin, out of an estimated West European total of 850,000. In Milan the protesters totalled twenty, and in Rome a similar number—although there an Italian communist cabinet minister was involved. In London there were fifty, the same number as in Bern, and in Moscow, which historically has been supportive of the PKK, fifteen were arrested in the takeover of the Greek embassy. "Kurdish" protests also took place in Melbourne, Montreal, and Toronto—and a small, quiet, almost invisible group demonstrated in Washington.

In addition to the small turnout there are three other reasons to conclude that these events were neither "spontaneous" nor broadly "Kurdish" but rather the actions of a well-organized underground terrorist organization amply funded through heroin trafficking, racketeering, and illegal alien smuggling operations in Western Europe.

First, it strains belief that "Kurdish" hostage-taking throughout Europe, Canada, and Australia was spontaneous. Even the spectacular acts of fanatical self-immolation had already been rehearsed during Öcalan's initial arrest in Italy last year. The telling evidence of planning is that—contrary to the PKK's long-standing ideological belief that the main enemy is ultimately "imperialism" (i.e., the United States)— there were no attacks against U.S. installations. The reason is clear: the PKK Central Committee controlling the "Kurdish" demonstrations realizes that, after the PKK's military defeat in Turkey, provoking a hostile reaction from the American public and Congress would work against its real strategic goal—a public relations campaign to discredit Turkey.

Second, the PKK strategy of blurring the distinction between the Kurds in the diaspora and its own murderous Maoism should be seen for what it is— another aspect of the public relations campaign. The overwhelming majority of Kurds in Europe and even in Turkey do not support, belong to, or want anything to do with the PKK or "Apo." Those who do should be treated as a security threat everywhere.

Third, as an "internationalist" organization— and one need only check the PKK's 1995 Fifth Congress documents, all freely available on the Internet— the group's ideology and practice is profoundly incompatible with democracy. Sharing the same Maoist legacy with the Khmer Rouge and Shining Path, the PKK is an immediate threat to free societies in Turkey and throughout Europe.

Europe and the United States have to prepare to deal harshly and promptly with the Maoist remnants of Öcalan's organization. Unfortunately, too many European politicians, media outlets, and legal authorities have replaced common sense with romantic "feelings" about the Kurds, an error with potentially catastrophic consequences. It is incomprehensible that MED-TV, a pro-PKK satellite outfit, can continue advocating Öcalan's cause from Belgium under a British licence. It is shameful that self-proclaimed human rights groups should suddenly be preoccupied with Öcalan's "rights" rather than those of his Kurdish victims or Turkish sovereignty. And it is unreasonable for governments not known for their effective justice systems—Russians, Iranians, Italians, and Greeks among others—to be providing advice to Turkey.

Indeed, government responses to the wave of "spontaneous Kurdish reactions" to Öcalan's capture varied, largely in direct relation to the size of their Kurdish community and, more significantly, the nature of the government. In

Romania the anti-communist government had no qualms about beating up the few Kurds trying to demonstrate illegally; the police there were already encouraged by their unexpected success in defeating a pro-communist quasi insurrection by violent miners. In Germany the leftist government, under attack from the opposition and the public for renouncing its own arrest warrant against Öcalan for crimes committed on its territory, threatened to "deport" Kurdish troublemakers. How credible that threat is remains to be seen, but in light of a German intelligence report (done under the previous government) that estimated the local PKK cadres at 10,000 with an additional 40,000 supporters, the PKK threat to domestic law and order is indeed serious.

The PKK's game is obvious: to galvanize a broad spectrum of the European Left on its behalf. On February 25, taking advantage of the funeral of three PKK militants killed on February 17 while trying to take over the Israeli consulate, they managed to assemble a crowd of 8,500 people in Berlin. That demonstration brought together pacifists, the city's ubiquitous street cafe activists, as well as Kurds who appear to have come to express ethnic solidarity with their dead kin rather than ideological support for the PKK. Forty-four were arrested for displaying the banned PKK symbols.

The results, however, may not have been what they expected. The February 25 demonstration in Berlin seems to have been enough for the German government to declare the PKK a "terrorist organization," upgrading its earlier designation of the PKK as a "criminal organization." As for the nervous Swiss, after some fifty (!) Kurdish militants threatened foreign embassies in Bern, and a few others did the same in Geneva and Zurich—again in solidarity with those killed in Berlin—they openly considered using the army for riot control.

The big losers, naturally enough (given their long-standing and not so well hidden support for Öcalan and the PKK), were the Greek and Greek-Cypriot governments—both of which have been involved in the Öcalan imbroglio, to the discomfiture of the European Union. The wave of PKK assaults on their embassies in Europe, even though they turned out to be non-violent, must have been more than disappointing.

Despite the PKK's totalitarian ideology and criminal record, Greek, Italian, British, and German parliamentarians have already gone on record supporting it, and former lawyers for German and Italian terrorists are also openly trying to manipulate European Union concerns about Öcalan's trial. Such actions work quite effectively to the advantage of PKK terrorism and its strategic goals.

The issue, ultimately, is one of historic memory. Too many leftist politicians in Europe (some of whom now share government power) never believed that the Cold War made sense—that Marxism was a threat to freedom, or that "bourgeois" democratic values were worth defending. But the Cold War is not dead as far as the PKK's Maoists are concerned, and they may succeed where the European New Left never did—for they have learned to pick up a new vocabulary without setting aside an old program. They have discovered that their methods, goals, and ideology can all be forgotten, indeed sanctified in the name of "self- determination" and "human rights."

Reprinted with the permission from http://www.fpri.org,
February 26, 1999

IS THE PKK IN TURKEY ON THE ROPES?

The Kurdistan Workers' Party (PKK) has apparently been set adrift. Ever since last February, when Turkey captured the terrorist organization's leader, Abdullah Öcalan, the group has struggled—and largely failed—to maintain any sense of its former military or political cohesion. In this respect the movement's fate mirrors that of Peru's Shining Path, whose rapid and steady decline was linked closely to the capture of its founder and supreme leader, Abimael Guzman. The reason is simple: real and aspiring dictators seldom surround themselves with others of similar talents and charisma.

If the Kurdish group's latest declarations are to be believed, it has transformed itself so much as to be unrecognizable. Öcalan, now sentenced to death, has discovered a vocation as (of all things) a peacemaker. He renounced violence and stated that the PKK's new goal is a culturally autonomous Turkish Kurdistan rather than a communist state of Kurdistan taken from parts of Iran, Iraq, southeastern Turkey, and Syria. And Öcalan, from his prison cell, even ordered PKK terrorists out of Turkish territory beginning September 1.

All of this, naturally, seems quite encouraging, suggesting at last an end to bloodshed that has killed at least 30,000 people—and coming just when weary Turkey is dealing with the trauma of the August earthquake.

There are two problems with that view. One is that Öcalan, forcing his softened voice through the cracks in the prison walls, cannot wield the same control over the organization he once did and so is not necessarily a reliable spokesperson. The other problem is that the PKK's shift is in all likelihood merely a rhetorical mask for other goals. Specifically, the PKK is trying to do the following:

1. Save Öcalan's Skin—His fate is now in the hands of the nationalist-dominated Turkish Parliament, which must confirm his death sentence. Öcalan knows that his anti-violence message, delivered from prison, will ensure massive West European political pressure for a commutation of his sentence. Considering Turkey's need for substantial foreign aid after the devastating earthquake, this may well work.

2. Snatch Political Victory from the Jaws of Military Defeat—The PKK has suffered severe setbacks of late. By the end of this summer, it was reduced to merely 1,500 guerrillas inside Turkey—one tenth of its

strength seven years ago—and lacks high-ranking commanders, all of whom stayed safely outside the country. A trip to the region by this author also suggested that the concentration of Kurds in fewer, but larger, population centers has denied the PKK access to supplies and recruits. Simply put, the PKK inside Turkey is withering on the vine. Claiming a "voluntary" withdrawal under orders from Öcalan simply hides imminent military defeat.

3. Move Its Area of Operations—Borrowing a page from strategists elsewhere, the PKK has realized that it must go "out of area or out of business." Long sustained by support from Turkey's enemies in the region—Syria, Iran, and Iraq—the PKK is now finding itself snubbed. Under military threat from Ankara, last October Syria expelled most of the PKK cadres (including Öcalan) who had established bases there. Iran, under similar pressure and already wary of the PKK's pan-Kurdish claims, is now reluctant to provide the kind of support that it did as recently as a year ago. And Saddam Hussein is unable to do much about northern Iraq, since he does not control the area. The PKK's other supporters—Greece, Armenia, and Russia—are too busy dealing with their own internal problems to be of much help, and in any event could not make up for the loss of important rear bases in Syria, Iran, and Iraq. And Athens' long- standing aid for a terrorist group in a fellow NATO country has rightfully turned into a public relations disaster.

Whither the PKK? The most logical retreat would be into northern Iraq—except that most of the border in that area is under the control of an alliance of pro-Turkish Kurds and the Turkish military, while the rest, in the Hakkari and Van provinces, depends on Iran and its Kurdish protegees in Iraq. Retreat into Armenia, on the other hand, would entail the risk of crossing hundreds of miles of Turkish-controlled territory without even the certainty of admittance once the Kurds reached the border. Armenia is a small country that cannot afford the significant threat from Turkey which it would certainly face if it allowed the PKK to enter. The remaining option is for the PKK to remain hidden and inactive in Turkey—forced to choose between starvation and surrender.

Any Turkish triumphalism at this point, however, would be premature, because the PKK's political fortunes have not exactly mirrored its military troubles. For one thing, the Maoist Kurds can still count on a measure of sympathy in wealthy Western Europe, particularly in Germany, the Netherlands, and Belgium. Some leftists have remained enamored with the PKK's unabashed Marxism, while certain misguided human rights groups are more preoccupied with abuses (real or imagined) by the Turkish police and military than the PKK's own brutal violence. Moreover, Western sentimentalism for the "underdog" (no matter how unsavory) ensures a degree of success on the battlefield of public opinion.

Nor does the PKK face bankruptcy. It remains a very wealthy organization, largely due to heroin trafficking in Western Europe and racketeering among the huge Kurdish diaspora in Germany.

That the PKK's cadres in Europe should be enjoying a degree of success while the militants inside Turkey face such dire straits is just one sign of the fundamental struggle currently going on within the organization. Consider that the PKK is now preparing for its 7th Congress—the second this year alone and the third since 1995; there were only four such meetings between 1978 and 1995. The ongoing struggle for the succession to Öcalan has obviously left the group in a state of severe disarray. The West European branch, which controls the funds and propaganda apparatus, is competing with the militaristic faction in the Middle East, led by the most important remaining founding member of the PKK, Cemil Bayik. Bayik has expressed his doubts about Öcalan's strategy of paying lip service to nonviolence, while another commander, Osman Öcalan (Abdullah's brother), has unsurprisingly toed the line. How far this division will go remains to be seen, but the PKK's future is cloudy at best.

Again, the experience of the Shining Path may be instructive here. After Guzman's capture, that movement split between ideologues on the one side and cocaine-trafficking revolutionaries on the other. Ultimately, the schism proved fatal to both of them.

That precedent unfortunately does not mean that an endgame against the PKK can be played out easily or cheaply in the event of a "militarist/Europeanist" split. The former, on the brink of terminal defeat, may well engage in urban terrorism (bombings, assassinations, and the like) throughout the major urban centers in Turkey, perhaps in alliance with another Maoist terrorist group, the People's Revolutionary Liberation Front (DHKC). At the same time, the savvy European branch of the PKK would no doubt decry the loss of life, while excusing it under the pretext that it was provoked by Turkish "repression," and trying to profit from it by presenting itself as the self-appointed "representative" of the Turkish Kurds, ready for a "political solution." This author's recent experience in Turkey suggests that such political attacks are the most difficult for Ankara to parry effectively.

But Washington—and indeed the European Union—could play a constructive role in several ways. First, they should declare its unambiguous support for Turkey, a vital and loyal ally in a strategically dicey neighborhood. Second, pronouncements by the likes of U.S. Assistant Secretary of State Harold Koh—demanding that Turkey tolerate PKK fronts under the guise of human rights—should be halted, for they can only help to revive the PKK's fortunes and make possible a return to terrorism. Third, "Kurdish" groups in America and Europe that provide logistical and financial support for terrorists should be monitored more closely.

There is no doubt that the PKK is on the ropes. But a decisive split in the organization's already fractious leadership will mean only that a military victory by Turkey does not suffice to slay the multi-headed serpent.

Reprinted with the permission from http://www.fpri.org, September 28, 1999

WHY TURKEY SHOULD NOT HANG ÖCALAN... NOW

The capture of Abdullah Öcalan by Turkish commandos last February ignited a national celebration in Turkey. After all, Öcalan, the supremo of the terrorist Kurdistan Workers' Party (PKK), was held responsible for the deaths of some 30,000 people, half of whom were either innocent civilians (mostly Kurds) or military and police personnel. That capture, however, proved to be only the beginning of the end of Turkey's PKK headache, not the end itself.

On the face of it, the fate of Öcalan should have been a straightforward matter. He was tried under Turkish law, found guilty of treason and separatism—both capital offenses—and sentenced to hang. His appeals to the highest courts and the prosecution were both rejected according to law. All that is left under Turkish law is for the Parliament to approve the sentence and the President of the Republic to confirm it; after that, there is only the hangman.

But Öcalan is no ordinary murderer—and not just because of the enormity of his crimes—nor is his case simply a matter of criminal law. To the contrary, this is a case with enormous political ramifications. How things are handled may jeopardize—or save—thousands of lives in the future.

Since his capture, Öcalan has enthusiastically cooperated with the authorities: he named names, "assumed responsibility" for atrocities, and renounced both "armed struggle" (i.e., terrorism) and secessionism. Furthermore, he ordered some of his followers to surrender (which they did), and all of them to withdraw from Turkey, which most seem to have done. According to Prime Minister Bulent Ecevit, "separatist terrorist acts have greatly diminished [since Öcalan's capture]. They have almost reached zero."

While it is true that the PKK was in decline even before Öcalan's capture—owing both to the loss of its Syrian/Lebanese bases in 1998 and to a dramatic improvement in Turkish counterinsurgency tactics—that decline has accelerated dramatically since Öcalan's capture. A brief outburst of suicide bombings following the capture ceased abruptly, on Öcalan's orders, and a number of violent hardliners have been forced out, the latest being Murat Karayilan, a member of the "Leadership Council" (Politburo).

Obviously, Öcalan's newfound desire for a "political solution" has a lot to do with the prospect of hanging. But equally obvious, and of greater significance, is the fact that Öcalan continues to control the bulk of his organization, if not all of it, and does so while under the supervision of the government. As long as he lives, the remaining PKK leaders cannot solve the succession problem, particularly since Öcalan was founder, strategist, ideologue and tactician all rolled into one. For the PKK leaders and rank-and-file alike, Öcalan's captivity, and the orders he gives from jail, introduce a deadly element into the life of any insurgency: uncertainty as to whether his orders are indeed his, whether they have been accurately transmitted, and whether he has the organization's interests rather than his own in mind.

If the experience of the equally violent Shining Path in Peru following Abimael Guzmán's capture in 1992 is any guide, once such a leader is lost, so are the organization's coherence, motivation, strategic purpose, and operational capabilities. These considerations alone should persuade the Turkish elites that, at the very least, it is not in the country's interest to execute Öcalan— certainly not soon. It is also likely that similar considerations explain the somewhat unexpected silence of the influential Turkish armed forces on this matter. Simply put, military and intelligence professionals appear to believe that Öcalan is far more useful to Turkey alive than dead. Consider, too, that his hanging would likely be followed by indiscriminate and uncoordinated violence by desperate followers seeking martyrdom.

If there are good strategic reasons for keeping Öcalan alive, there are also bad political reasons for doing so. These follow from the fact that the PKK issue has become internationalized, for Öcalan and the PKK enjoy widespread support in Western Europe, particularly in Scandinavia, Belgium, and the Netherlands, where government, leftist parties, and "human rights" groups often overlap. Thus, Italy had Öcalan in its hands in 1998 and let him go; Germany was so intimidated by his threats that it refused to honor its own arrest warrant against him; and Greece for years gave him and his organization refuge, support, and operating bases.

None of this is new or surprising to most Turks or outside observers; what is new is the coincidence of the Öcalan imbroglio with the European Union's decision, at its Helsinki meeting in December, to grant Ankara the status of candidate for EU membership. That means that Turkey has the obligation to obey EU rules and idiosyncrasies in the present in exchange for membership consideration in the future. One of those idiosyncrasies is the West European opposition to capital punishment in general, and in the Öcalan case in particular. That sparing Öcalan is a pre-condition for any further consideration of Turkey's EU membership was made clear by the open threats from one EU spokesman after another—German, Finnish, and Swedish. It may also be added that the Ocalan *cause célèbre* serves as a useful cover for those EU members (Sweden, the Netherlands, and Germany come to mind) who never really wanted a Muslim Turkey in their European/Western club in the first place.

A few years ago, Ankara would have demonstrated that Turkey does not take kindly to outsiders' threats, and Öcalan would have hanged. Today, however, the Turkish political elite is unsure of its own identity and values. Prime Minister Ecevit, a social democrat, is "personally opposed" to the death penalty, and his third most important government partner, former Prime Minister Mesut Yilmaz of the Motherland Party (ANAP), thinks that concessions to Kurdish demands (not necessarily those of the PKK) are the way to EU membership. However, the second largest government party, the Nationalist Movement (MHP) led by Devlet Bahceli, is a strong supporter of Öcalan's execution. So are the opposition Islamist Party (FP), led by Recai Kutan, and the True Path Party (DYP). Meanwhile, President Suleyman Demirel seems to be on his way out, with no clear successor in sight.

With all his options exhausted within the national legal system, Öcalan will appeal to the European Court for Human Rights, which will certainly reject the death sentence and ask for commutation—or worse, a new trial with "European" lawyers representing Öcalan. Incidentally those are the same German and Dutch radical lawyers who "represented" such past "freedom fighters" as the German Baader Meinhof Gang. This could take as long as eighteen months, giving time for a cooling off of the public's emotions in Turkey as well as allowing for a further disintegration of the PKK. While this would benefit Turkey's counterterrorist campaign, it would also set a dangerous precedent for future dealings with leftist and Islamist terrorism in the country.

Turkey's unusual position with respect to Öcalan's fate is that the strategic calculation of national interest happens to coincide with the mushy, moralistic, alien values of the EU. The problem is to do the right thing—spare Öcalan's life at least for now—while not appearing to be caving to external pressures that threaten Turkey's national values, identity, and interests.

This author is no opponent of capital punishment and harbors no doubt that Öcalan richly deserves the noose. But the hanging of Abdullah Öcalan—now, anyway—is not in Turkey's national interest.

Author's note: Since this essay has been published, Turkey has abolished capital punishment and Öcalan's sentence has been commuted to life in prison.

Reprinted with the permission from http://www.fpri.org, January 11, 2000

THE RISE AND FALL OF THE PKK

In 1992 Turkey was in the midst of a war with the Kurdistan Workers' Party (Partiya Karkeren Kurdistan—PKK), whose forces were credibly estimated to be 10,000 strong.[1] In 1996 the journalist Franz Schurmann called the PKK "the biggest guerrilla insurgency in the world," and wrote of its leader, Abdullah Öcalan, that "he alone among Kurdish leaders understands that a social revolution is going on in Kurdish society everywhere. . . . Öcalan will go down in the history books as the Saladin of the late twentieth century."[2] By the summer of 1999, however, senior officers of the Turkish military and *Jandarma* (militarized police) estimated the PKK's total strength inside the country at 1,500 and declining rapidly.[3] In May 2000 the *Turkish Daily News* reported that "PKK armed militants have largely left Turkish territory after the PKK executive council called on them to cease armed struggle and leave Turkey."[4]

What brought about such a dramatic decline in just three years? Three developments provide a short, albeit incomplete, answer: the February 1999 cap-

ture of Öcalan, the PKK's founder and uncontested leader; the increasing disenchantment of Turkey's Kurdish citizens with the PKK's armed struggle; and
dramatic changes in the regional balance of power in the Middle East, which
weakened the PKK's traditional supporters. Of these, the capture of Öcalan in
Nairobi, Kenya, by Turkish commandos was the most obviously devastating
blow, but was in fact symptomatic of military and political troubles that were
years in the making. This is amply demonstrated by the fact that, after fifteen
years of safe haven in Syria, Öcalan was on the run and desperately seeking
asylum in Africa.

The PKK's evident vulnerability in the late 1990s raises the question of the
depth and strength of its support among the Kurdish population, which had
long been considered the source of the party's military and political successes
over a decade and a half. The far from simple answer is that the degree of PKK
support is a matter of definition. While some Kurdish clans actively backed
Öcalan's party, others rejected it and joined the government's efforts to combat
it. Clearly, then, the hitherto widespread impression of the PKK as a grassroots
movement with broad popular support needs revisiting. To arrive at a greater
understanding of the origins, ideology, leadership, and goals of the PKK, this
article will rely heavily on the PKK's own statements and documents—all freely
available on the Internet.[5] Obviously, such material constitutes propaganda
rather than objective analysis, but that does not limit its value. To the contrary,
what the PKK wants the world to know about it says a great deal about the way
it sees itself.

Ideology, Leadership, and Strategy

On occasion, the PKK has presented itself as the defender and chief advocate
of Kurdish nationalism. Its weak claim to such a position, however, reveals not
any true conviction, but rather astute political instincts and sheer opportunism.
Since the beginning, the PKK has been Marxist-Leninist in its ideology, Stalinist
in its leadership style, and Maoist in its strategy for the conquest of power.

Marxism, not Kurdish nationalism, has always defined the PKK. Given that
the founders of the PKK included ethnic Turks as well as Kurds, their common
interest was never based on ethnicity. The history of the PKK, as portrayed in
the records of its congresses prior to Öcalan's capture in February 1999, makes
abundantly clear the party's unwavering loyalty to Marxism-Leninism. Most
important is the "Fifth Victory Congress" of January 1995, which called attention to the importance of ideology in the life of Kurds—and to the PKK in the
progress of socialism across the globe.[6] In the two major documents that emerged
from that congress, the "Brief History of the Kurdistan Workers Party (PKK)"
and the "Party Program of the PKK," the organization portrays itself as the
"vanguard of the global socialism movement, even though the Party hasn't yet
come to power.[7] "Perhaps to shore up its claim to the leadership of socialism

internationally, the program states that the PKK from the very beginning tried to enlist support in other countries; that "a new phase of socialism" has begun; and that the PKK "is the embodiment of one of the most significant socialist movements during this new phase."[8] It is important to consider the timing of that statement—a decade after Mikhail Gorbachev initiated *perestroika* and *glasnost*, and six years after the collapse of the Berlin Wall. What had the PKK to say about those events? It claimed that "Soviet socialism was a kind of deviation," and went so far as to call it "rough," "wild," and even "primitive." By contrast, "the PKK's approach to socialism is scientific and creative."[9]

The arrogance manifest in such declarations can be attributed directly to Öcalan's leadership style, which in its megalomania and iron-fisted grip on power borrows heavily from Stalin. Öcalan, simply put, created a personality cult with himself as its focal point, and has made his own name virtually synonymous with that of the organization he heads. He has always been identified as the sole author of any text of significant ideological impact (including all major documents of the Fifth Congress), the initiator of every political and military campaign, and the uncontested decision maker at the party's helm.[10] And yet Öcalan's personal background would seem to make him an unlikely leader of Kurdish workers, a fact that makes the PKK's purported nationalist aspirations all the more specious.

Öcalan was born in 1948 into a peasant family in the mostly Kurdish village of Omerli. Significantly, his mother was not Kurdish at all, but Turkoman, and it was she (described by Öcalan as an "independent, headstrong, woman") who controlled the household and dominated his "helpless" Kurdish father. Equally notable is Öcalan's statement that his family "was poor and had lost its tribal traditions, but it continued with strong feudal values"[11]—rather a surprising admission from a self-declared socialist leader who claims to be fighting against the "colonial" oppression of Kurds. After studying at a vocational school in the provincial capital of Urfa, Öcalan moved on to Ankara University's School of Political Science in the early 1970s, a period during which Turkish universities were involved in revolutionary activism far more than education. Öcalan spent his time learning political organizing and Marxist doctrine, and he evidently learned well. As he later put it, "I dedicated myself completely to ideological work"—which included political violence, for which he was arrested and imprisoned for a few months in 1973.

The PKK itself was founded in 1978, and Öcalan's continuous control over it was only obtained by ruthlessly eliminating potential challengers to his absolute authority. Those who threatened his leadership or simply disagreed with him faced demotion, expulsion, or death. As he euphemistically described the fate of those unfortunates at his own trial, despite "comprehensive educational and organisational efforts against them, . . . the most deviated ones of them could only be neutralised by internal struggles."[12] According to Chris Kutschera, one of Europe's most active, sympathetic, and knowledgeable analysts of the PKK, "Five or six of [the PKK's] original central committee have been physically eliminated, three others committed suicide, [and] eight are still alive, acting semi-clandestinely. . . . Others have been driven underground."[13] Moreover, the purges continued for years. Kutschera goes on to quote Selahattin Celik, the founder and first commander of the PKK's armed wing, the People's Liberation Army of Kurdistan (Artesa Rizgariya Gele Kurdistan—ARGK): "There were between fifty and sixty executions just after the 1986 Congress. In the end there was no more room to bury them!"[14] Among those "arrested" at that time was Duran Kalkan, who was later released and is now still a member of the PKK Presidential Council. Not surprisingly, perhaps, Kalkan is now rumored to have offered Ankara his surrender in exchange for amnesty.[15] Another reminder of the Stalinist purges of the 1930s is found in the career of Ali Omer Can, a Central Committee member who was arrested and tortured in the PKK's Beka'a jails in 1986 and then released and rehabilitated. After he again broke with the party and tried to establish a rival organization, the "PKK Refoundation," he was assassinated in November 1991.[16]

If Öcalan's leadership style was Stalin's, his strategy for conquest resembled Mao's. The PKK's first goal was to establish a credible military force within Turkey that would be sufficient to challenge the political power of the government. Once that was accomplished, the party would expand its control to Kurdish areas beyond Turkish borders. A unified, socialist Kurdistan could then serve as a base from which to promote socialism within the region and around the world.[17] In other words, the foundation of a Kurdish state was never an ultimate goal in itself, but rather a means to spread socialism.

Specious Nationalism

If a Kurdish state was only, at best, a secondary goal for the PKK, it is important to examine the nature of its purported nationalism. Upon closer look, it becomes clear that the PKK's claim to be "the leading force in the liberation of Kurdistan" is sheer obfuscation. In reality, the organization is not representative of the Kurdish people, nor is it nationalist in any commonly understood sense.

From the PKK's beginnings, there have been several reasons to question its claim to be the legitimate representative of the Kurdish people. First, as noted above, ethnic Turks were a part of the party since its inception, and in the early years the PKK counted as many Turks as Kurds among its members. Secondly, the party's official history acknowledges that already by 1980 it had difficulty recruiting Kurds in Turkey, which suggests that many Kurds' interests—*as they perceived them*—did not coincide with the PKK's own. Thirdly, Öcalan's own background makes him ill suited to be a standard-bearer of Kurdish interests. Not only was his mother of Turkoman origin, but his recent trial made clear that he never learned either of the two major Kurdish languages (Kurmandji and Zaza) and used Turkish in all communications with followers.

Surely the most damaging fact undermining the PKK's position as the representative of Kurdish interests is the party's adversarial and often hostile relationship with Kurds throughout the region. In its efforts to gain recruits and legitimize itself in the eyes of certain segments of the Kurdish population, particularly in Tunceli province, Öcalan's party has not only exploited but exacerbated historic regional divisions and clan rivalries. Kurds under PKK attack have then sought assistance from the Turkish government and joined in its successful counterinsurgency campaign. Partially as a result of this internecine conflict, more Kurdish civilians than Turks have died during the PKK's war against Ankara, which suggests that absolute power matters far more to Öcalan than do the aspirations and welfare of the people he claims to lead. His party has killed Kurds as reprisals for suspected collaboration with Ankara; it has killed Iraqi Kurds during hostilities with the two leading Kurdish groups there; and it has killed Kurds in Europe and Lebanon who disagreed with Öcalan or simply did not support him fervently enough.

Among other tactics, suicide bombings in Kurdish areas have figured prominently in the PKK's terror campaign and contributed to the group's reputation for indiscriminate violence. According to the Turkish government, quoting both internal PKK documents and statements by captured militants, the PKK decided at its Fifth Congress to engage in bombing, and reaffirmed the decision a year later.[18] By 1997 the group had formed "Suicide Guerrilla Teams" that relied on large numbers of potential volunteers. Perhaps not surprisingly, the "volunteers" came from the most vulnerable segments of society: the majority of the early bombings attributed to the PKK were carried out by young, impoverished, and poorly educated women.

The PKK's disregard for human life has also carried over into its collaborative arrangements with governments waging violent campaigns against their own Kurdish populations, most notably in Syria and Iraq, but also to a lesser extent in Iran. The incentive for such collusion is not immediately apparent. One PKK analysis of the general Kurdish situation acknowledges that large numbers of Kurds in Syria "play an active role" in the Kurdish struggle, and Öcalan himself admitted that during the late 1980s Syrian Kurds were an essential part of the PKK's recruitment base.[19] And yet Öcalan has not only refused to provide assistance to Kurds in Syria, he cooperated with the government in Damascus that brutally oppressed them. Similarly, for more than a decade he supported Saddam Hussein's offensives against Kurdish nationalists in northern Iraq (or "South Kurdistan," in PKK parlance). The PKK's machinations have left Kurds throughout the region, who were never united to begin with, more divided than ever.

The real motivation for PKK collaboration can be summed up as strategic necessity. The insurgents have almost always needed outside help and have been willing to accept it from any quarter. The official history of the PKK acknowledges that the group engaged in a "tactical retreat" into Syria in 1980, when Öcalan fled Turkey just ahead of a military coup that culminated in a violent crackdown on Marxists.[20] He and his followers were given relatively free rein in the Syrian-controlled Beka'a Valley in Lebanon, where they thrived. As recently as the early 1990s, the PKK took foreign journalists on Potemkin village tours of bases and training camps there. For Öcalan to have objected to his hosts' treatment of their own Kurdish population would have meant the loss of the PKK's center of operations, without which it would have never been able to threaten extensive areas of southeastern Turkey during the 1990s.

Öcalan's acceptance of safe haven from Syria marked only the beginning of the PKK's heavy reliance upon support from governments that, for reasons of their own, found common cause with it. The Persian Gulf War created a power vacuum in northern Iraq, allowing the PKK to expand its influence there in competition with the existing Kurdish groups, principally the Patriotic Union of Kurdistan (PUK) and the Kurdistan Democratic Party (KDP). Iran, because of its ambiguous position vis-à-vis Kurdish separatism in Turkey and Iraq (but never at home), likewise allowed the PKK to use Iranian territory to open new fronts along Turkey's eastern frontier. With the collapse of the Soviet Union, newly independent Armenia also provided enough help, or tolerance, for the PKK to threaten northeastern Turkey. In addition to these friendly outsiders, Greece supported, tolerated, and encouraged the PKK for more than a decade, as the circumstances surrounding Öcalan's arrest ultimately revealed.[21] It is noteworthy, however, that although outside assistance greatly enhanced the PKK's effectiveness, ultimately it was also a key factor in the party's rapid descent.

In light of the PKK's acceptance of foreign support and open opposition to other Kurds, two questions suggest themselves: On what basis can the PKK claim to be nationalist, and what advantage does it gain from doing so? Despite ample evidence to the contrary, the PKK has gone to some lengths to shore up its claim to represent Kurds—a claim that has required no small amount of logical and linguistic contortions. According to the Fifth Congress documents, the lineage of the Kurds can be traced back to the ancient Medes, who as early as the seventh century B.C. were engaged in a "long struggle which gave rise to a national consciousness," and who "played a leading role in the formation of our national values."[22] But the national consciousness touted by the PKK is not any "bourgeois" consciousness of the Kurds as an ethnically, culturally, or historically distinct group. Rather, the PKK distinguishes "reactionary nationalism" from a "socialist national consciousness" that takes into account "the fact of exploitation . . . a class characteristic."[23] Presumably, then, a Turk of an "exploited" class would be included within this "nation," whereas a Kurdish landowner would not.

This patently Leninist definition of nationalism is incompatible with the usual understanding of the concept, but has nevertheless allowed the PKK to portray itself as a Kurdish nationalist organization since the class-based distinction seems largely lost on outsiders sympathetic to its calls for national self-determination. Thus, although not a single volume has been published in English on the PKK per se, the vast literature on the Kurds tends to assume, without further explanation, that the PKK is the legitimate representative of Kurdish interests. John Bulloch and Harvey Morris, for example, while aware of Öcalan's Stalinist beliefs, still described the PKK as "the latest in a long line of insurgent groups which has tried over the years to obtain basic human rights for the Kurds of Turkey."[24] Michael M. Gunter describes the PKK as "first a Kurdish nationalist movement."[25]

A European Life-Support System

Here the PKK's motivation to be called "nationalist" becomes clearer: the label has proved to be a highly successful part of its public-relations campaign and its principal means of gaining a degree of legitimacy around the world. Specifically, the survival of the PKK has depended not only on the cooperation of the various governments mentioned above, but also on the active support of some Westerners and the Kurdish diaspora in Western Europe. By virtue of its being considered a nationalist organization, the PKK seems to have inoculated itself against at least some of the damage that might be expected to result from reports of its murders, insurgent attacks, and collaboration with dictators. No such news, for example, dissuaded Danielle Mitterand, the radical widow of the former French president, from addressing Öcalan as "Dear President Öcalan" in a 1998 letter, which ended "[R]est assured, Abdullah, that I am committed to be beside you in the bid for peace. Sincerely yours, Danielle Mitterand."[26] As Öcalan's attempts to find political asylum in 1998 and early 1999 proved, he also enjoyed the support of leftist parties in Italy, France, and Greece. The most insidious, if not necessarily surprising, support came from Germany's and Italy's Marxist terrorists, which supported and occasionally even joined in PKK combat operations. At least two German women became PKK members. One was killed in combat, the other was captured in 1998.[27]

Nothing better demonstrates the PKK's public-relations capabilities than MED-TV, a satellite television channel that operated first under a British license from London and later from Brussels. Although it ostensibly existed to promote Kurdish culture, the channel was such a blatant propaganda outlet for the PKK (at a cost of some $200 million per year) that it was eventually expelled from Britain and later lost its operating license in Belgium as well.[28]

Its public-relations campaigns and prominent supporters gave the PKK a measure of legitimacy, but the party also needed something else: funding. It proved so adept at generating money that European assessments generally placed its annual income at between $200 and $500 million in the mid-1990s. Income came from two major sources in Europe. One was the sizable pool of West European Kurdish militants among the émigré population, especially in

Germany. In 1997 Germany's Federal Ministry of the Interior estimated the number of PKK sympathizers in the country at 11,000, and claimed that the PKK possessed an ability to mobilize "tens of thousands" among the 500,000 resident Kurds.[29] The German government further stated that the PKK collected millions of marks at its annual fundraising events, including 20 million marks in 1996Ü97.[30]

The more important source of funds has been criminal activity, especially in Germany, Switzerland, France, Scandinavia, and the Benelux countries.[31] Operating among Europe's 800,000 Kurdish immigrants, the PKK has been involved in theft, extortion, arms smuggling, human smuggling, and heroin trafficking. Infamous for its violence, the PKK is widely known to rely on murder and beatings as enforcement measures. Apparently, its methods have had their desired effect. Some sources estimate the PKK's annual income from criminal activities at $86 million.[32] Recently, the PKK's bankrolls have likely suffered some setbacks due to the military decline of the PKK and factional disputes among the European front's leaders. One PKK representative, for example, disappeared with 2.5 million German marks in party funds and may have made them available to PKK dissidents.[33] Despite those losses, however, the magnitude of the PKK's income suggests that the group remains wealthy. It is also worth noting that in addition to providing considerable financial resources, the PKK's international criminal activities also attest to the organization's sophisticated logistical capabilities.

Foreign political support, well-padded bank accounts, and the backing of thousands of Kurds in Western Europe enabled the PKK to apply immense military and political pressure on Turkey throughout most of the 1990s. Ultimately, however, these same pillars of support pointed up the inherent weakness underlying the PKK's apparent strength. Émigrés and criminals underwrote the PKK, and prominent leftists legitimized it, but their backing never translated into the broad support of Kurds in Turkey, who were better apprised of the party's totalitarian nature.

This constellation of facts provided the kernel of the PKK's undoing, as became apparent in the late 1990s, when much of the external support started to unravel. Most prominently, Turkey's de facto alliance with Israel automatically raised the stakes for Syria's continuing support for the organization.[34] As a result, when in the summer of 1998 Ankara threatened military action because of Syrian aid to Öcalan, President Hafez al-Assad had to back down. In October of that year he expelled Öcalan and closed most PKK camps in Lebanon and Syria, including those along the Turkish border. Suddenly on the run, Öcalan had to find a new refuge farther away from his fighters (whom, one may add, he never personally joined in combat), first in Russia, then Italy and Greece. Pursued by the Turks and denied asylum in Western Europe, he accepted Greek offers to go to Nairobi, only to be captured there by Turkish commandos with Kenyan connivance and probably American and Israeli intelligence help. The

Iraqi government is in no position to offer any significant assistance to the PKK, since it still does not control its own northern territories. Armenia, constrained by its vulnerability to Turkish reprisals, likewise cannot do much even if it were so inclined. Greece, apparently, was stung by the Kenya episode and U.S. criticism, and has made a concerted effort both to mute its traditional hostility toward Turkey and to limit aid to the PKK.

Ankara's Response

Deprived of external support and chronically short of it within Turkey, the PKK was left vulnerable to Ankara's crushing blows. As major insurgencies go, Turkey's campaign against the PKK is one of the few recent examples of clear victory by the state—only Peruvian president Alberto Fujimori's success against the Shining Path and the Tupac Amaru Revolutionary Movement was similarly decisive.[35] It took Ankara sixteen years and cost some 30,000 lives, but success ultimately resulted from a combination of military astuteness, political realism, and diplomacy.

For the first six years of PKK operations, Turkish forces failed to realize the magnitude of the PKK military threat and respond adequately. Among the most effective measures taken was the militarization of virtually the entire southeast. The army and militarized police seized de facto control of daily life and managed to ingratiate themselves with the population at least in part through initiatives such as education programs for girls. But the military also won support because a large portion of the Kurdish population found the protection of the Turkish government far more attractive than the terror of the PKK and its hostility to Kurds of rival clans or differing political views. The most dramatic result of the cooperation between government and people was the "village guards," which were local Kurdish self-defense forces specifically organized to counter PKK operations. At the height of their strength, the village guards numbered some 60,000 armed civilians.

Aside from the changed relationship between the Turkish government and the population, the military also took other tactical and strategic steps to harm the Kurdish rebels. Notable in this regard was the effective use of special forces to pressure PKK groups in their mountain strongholds. In addition, heavy use of air power, mostly helicopters, hindered PKK movements in border areas where limited natural cover left the insurgents vulnerable. The army also launched massive operations in northern Iraq—often in conjunction with local KDP elements—that succeeded in denying the PKK access to its rear bases there. Finally, improvements in intelligence led to the capture of at least three major PKK leaders abroad in 1998 and 1999, the most notable, of course, being Öcalan himself.

To be sure, the Turkish military also benefited from developments that lay at least partially beyond its control. Among the most important of these was the depopulation of the countryside and concentration of Kurdish civilians in de-fensible centers. This dramatic shift occurred for several reasons, including PKK atrocities against civilians (mostly Kurds from clans Öcalan could not control or intimidate), the government's own military operations (damage from air attacks, in particular, forced people to relocate), and the general poverty of the southeast, which the war exacerbated. Local residents fled many of the more isolated areas and migrated to Western Europe, other parts of Turkey, or re-gional centers such as Diyarbakir, Van, and Sirnak. In doing so, they deprived the PKK of the recruitment, logistical, and communications assistance on which it had depended. As Öcalan himself admitted, "The PKK has not succeeded to become a regular armed force," the implication being that the PKK's inability to attract willing recruits forced it to resort to violence and intimidation, which in turn led to indiscipline and indiscriminate attacks against civilians.[36]

Ankara also pursued other policies that greatly enhanced its position vis-à-vis Öcalan's rebels. As noted above, its increasingly assertive regional diplo-macy, backed by credible threats of force, led Syria to expel Öcalan and close down PKK camps on its territory and in Lebanon. Domestically, Turkish lead-ers, from the late president Turgut Özal to the present prime minister, Bülent Ecevit, have gradually come to acknowledge the Kurdish issue as such and—without ever accepting any PKK connection to it—have made concessions on matters related to language and cultural grievances. In addition, the govern-ment has also initiated huge investments in the southeast, exemplified by the $32 billion Southeastern Anatolia Project, to improve the long-languishing region's economic prospects.[37] Indeed, between 1983 and 1992 the southeast received twice as much investment per capita as any other region in Turkey, with total spending during that time on the Southeastern Anatolia Project reach-ing $20 billion.[38]

Lastly, it should be noted that strong diplomatic support from the United States helped to convince a number of West European governments, particu-larly the Netherlands, Greece, and Italy (and to a lesser degree Russia and Armenia), to deny Öcalan political asylum. His failure to find refuge ultimately led him to Kenya and captivity.

The Prisoner Recants?

If the dramatic progress of the campaign against the PKK within Turkey exposed the weaknesses in its support there and the inadequacy of its outside assistance, then Öcalan's incarceration revealed the flaw in the party's Stalinist leadership structure. Once the supreme commander was arrested, rifts emerged throughout the entire organization that threatened its contin-ued existence. Even more important than his imprisonment itself, however, was the effect on the PKK of Öcalan's apparent renunciation of his entire insur-gent campaign.

Ever since his arrest in Nairobi in February 1999, Abdullah Öcalan has made repeated statements contradicting the ideological, military, and political positions he has advocated since the founding of the PKK. To begin with, in his wide-ranging final statement at his trial in June 1999, he acknowledged that Kurdish society in Turkey did not fit his long-standing analysis and strategy. Indeed, he admitted that the PKK "should have taken into account the development the country had undergone both when it was founded and in the 1990s." More astonishing still was his giving up pursuit of "a separate part of a state, something which . . . would have been very difficult to realize—and, if realized, could not be maintained and was not necessary either."[39] In one grand stroke Öcalan delegitimized all PKK positions on matters of ideology, strategy, and tactics. In other words, a socialist Kurdistan—for which the PKK had ostensibly fought for years—was, as Chris Kutschera phrased it, a "mad dream."[40] Not only did Öcalan ask the PKK to stop fighting and withdraw from Turkish territory, but in September 1999 he also ordered the symbolic surrender of a few units to Turkish authorities.

The obvious question is whether Öcalan's statements are representative of true changes of personal opinion or merely an expression of survival instincts, particularly given the prospect of capital punishment. His behavior at his trial hints at the latter, in light of his attempts to lay the responsibility for the PKK's record of violence at the feet of his field commanders by claiming that he was unable to "implement my own ideas and the official tactical line of the organization. . . . Individual or local initiatives were dominant." He even seemed to suggest that his followers' upbringing was at the root of their violence: "[I]t was hard to control the PKK . . . especially when one considers how the individuals [fighting in the PKK] had grown up."[41] He also claimed that he had never ordered or approved of suicide bombings—a dubious denial from the man who once said: "We shall come down to the cities. . . . No matter the price, it is not difficult to get on a bus, to get on an airplane. We have thousands of people who shall go with a bomb around them."[42]

It is probably impossible to determine the degree to which Öcalan's about-face was due to the threat to his own life, or to a realization that the insurgency was a lost cause, or to the collapse of vital Syrian support. What is clear, however, is that, in a manner befitting a Stalinist leader, he made these extraordinary changes without consulting anyone and simply expected the party to accept them. Amazingly enough, the PKK did largely follow Öcalan's lead. Nothing better symbolized the abandonment of the goal of a separate Kurdish state than the decision by the PKK's Presidential Council in February 2000 to drop the word "Kurdistan" from the name of both its dwindling armed wing, the ARGK, and the still-strong international political wing, the National Liberation Front of Kurdistan (Eniya Rizgariya Natewa Kurdistan—ERNK). Thus, the ARGK became the People's Defense Force, and the ERNK became the Democratic People's Union.[43] The personality cult constructed around Öcalan, which had for so long given the PKK its unity, coherence, and purpose, ultimately allowed it to be undermined rapidly.

High-ranking Turkish military officials professed surprise at Öcalan's apparent change of heart.[44] In actuality, however, it matches rather closely the behavior of the Shining Path's founder and supreme leader, Abimael Guzmán, who renounced armed struggle after his own arrest. In both cases the result was similar: the party faithful, having lost their ideological anchor, became confused and descended into factionalism and intraparty violence. The Shining Path suffered defeat; the ultimate fate of the PKK is not yet known.

Many PKK hardliners found Öcalan's newly conciliatory stance intolerable. Subsequent to his orders issued from captivity, and particularly his lengthy concluding statement at trial, dissent within the ranks of the party appeared almost immediately from among Kurds in Europe as well as fighters in and around Turkey. An anonymous group that called itself the "PKK revolutionary line fighters" issued a starkly worded rejection of Öcalan's call for some PKK combatants to surrender to Turkish forces: "At this junction, we will either be simple executor of this plan, and therefore we would kill ourselves, or we will say 'No' with all our force against this liquidation plan."[45] Some of the most prominent PKK hardliners, including former Central Committee members and other leaders, accused Öcalan of no less than "treason." In proof of their opposition to his decisions since capture, they established the "Kurdish Initiative in Europe," which was intended as a possible alternative to the ERNK. They also threw their support to Hamili Yildirim, a Central Committee member and field commander from Tunceli province who refused to obey Öcalan's call for a general retreat.[46] Yildirim joined forces with Turkish Communist Party elements and continued fighting Turkish security forces.[47] Significantly, the dissident group chose January 12, 2000, for one such attack—the very date the Turkish government coalition was to decide whether to execute or give a reprieve to Abdullah Öcalan. In view of Turkish public sentiment in favor of execution, those attacks could be seen as nothing but an attempt to have Öcalan killed. However, Yildirim's rebellion did not last. By May 2000 security forces had killed one of his fellow commanders and wounded Yildirim himself, whereupon he returned to the PKK fold and reintegrated his troops into the PKK's "Public Self-defense Force," although they did not disarm. That outcome, in fact, demonstrates the disingenuous nature of Öcalan's current position: he has ostensibly renounced armed struggle, but continues to encourage "self-defense" and overlooks the PKK forces still active in northern Iraq.

For a group notoriously intolerant of internal dissent, it is not surprising that the PKK leadership has taken exceptional measures to ensure that its orders are followed. The party dispatched Presidential Council member Murat Karayilan to the Netherlands in 1999, ostensibly to seek political asylum, but in reality to enforce Öcalan's will among Kurds in Western Europe.[48] In early 2000 the PKK Presidential Council simply decided to abolish the Free Women's Movement

of Kurdistan (Yekityia Azadiya Jinen Kurdistan—YAJK), which had long sup-
plied the movement with suicide bombers and assassins, because of the YAJK's
leaders' objections to Öcalan's "capitulationist" stance. Intimidation and credible threats of violence are also commonly used to enforce the party line. In
1998 Semdin Sakik, a Central Committee member and ARGK field commander,
was expelled from the party and forced to flee to pro-Turkish areas in northern
Iraq after facing death threats for disagreeing with Öcalan.[49] When it cannot
silence dissidents, the PKK has also tried to discredit them. Sakik, for example,
is now accused by the PKK of having sabotaged Öcalan's 1993 cease-fire declaration by attacking and killing some thirty unarmed Turkish recruits. This
particular claim, however, is belied by the fact that he was reelected to the
Central Committee in 1995—two years after his alleged transgression. In another case, Öcalan tried to destroy his estranged wife, Yesire Yildirim, and her
brother Huseyn (who are not related to Hamili Yildirim), who had been expelled from the party in 1986, by accusing the pair of murdering Swedish prime
minister Olof Palme—an unproven and probably unprovable charge.

Yet for all its efforts, the PKK has still not entirely succeeded in silencing its
disgruntled members. Some of the most telling statements have come from a co-
founder of the ARGK, Selahattin Celik, who was beaten up by PKK supporters
in Cologne after criticizing Öcalan's behavior in captivity. In an interview
given in Germany following that attack, he said,

> Most Kurds simply cannot understand this [Öcalan's statements since his capture].
> And yet no one is allowed to raise their voice in opposition to this new line. While the
> PKK makes one concession after another to the Turkish state, they damn people who
> demand democracy in their own ranks and in Kurdish society.[50]

In a view paradoxically shared by Ankara, Celik went on to state that the
"Kurdish issue could increasingly become separated from the PKK . . . [and]
contradictions could surface within the PKK, which would make internal clashes
unavoidable."[51] In other words, the PKK could lose its relevance and descend
into yet another round of purges.

What Future for the PKK?

Currently, however, as Öcalan faces the (admittedly unlikely) prospect of
execution and his beleaguered party confronts political and military pressure
on almost all fronts, the PKK leadership seems to understand that it cannot
afford costly strife within its own ranks. In an August 2000 interview, Cemil
Bayik, the only remaining PKK founder at large and the most prominent member of the Presidential Council, announced a new strategy that emphasized
"deepening party unity and national unity, adding new circles of friends to
those that already exist, strengthening solidarity with the regional people, and
securing internal peace among the Kurds."[52] It would appear, then, that the PKK

may seek common ground with erstwhile rivals and dissidents. But his statement was by no means completely conciliatory. Bayik, Öcalan's closest collaborator, lashed out at rivals among Kurds in Iraq and had harsh criticism for those within and outside the party who sought to "tear us from our beloved President" and "liquidate the party and the revolution and sell out the people." He went on to declare that the conflict with Turkey was far from over and that the PKK was "carrying on a sacred war with the genuine lords of the manservants"—the "lords" being an apparent reference to Turkey, the "manservants" being collaborators.[53] As those strident words suggest, the "strategic" changes that ostensibly announced the end of the PKK's bid for a separate Kurdish state may have actually been a tactical ploy to buy time for the PKK to regroup. In fact, according to plausible estimates from Jalal Talabani, leader of the rival PU.K. in northern Iraq, the PKK now has approximately 7,000 fighters in Iraq and Iran, and is currently recruiting and rearming. He added, however, that the fighters' morale was low: "I think that if there is an amnesty . . . all of them will come back to Turkey."[54]

The PKK's tenacious survival despite its declining fortunes has, of course, not escaped the notice of the Turkish government. To its credit, Ankara does not trust Öcalan's peaceful intentions or those of his lieutenants still at large and, despite Öcalan's September 1999 announcement that the party laid down its weapons, has given the PKK no quarter. In fact, recent air attacks on targets inside Iraq demonstrate the military's greater willingness to pursue the PKK wherever necessary in order to ensure its final destruction.[55] At the same time, however, Selahattin Celik's prediction has come to pass, and the Turkish government has indeed separated the Kurdish issue from the PKK. The significant political and economic changes mentioned above—most initiated since Öcalan's capture—prove that the PKK has been not an advocate for Kurds, but rather the major obstacle to political and economic development in southeastern Turkey and to Kurdish interests in general. The critical question now is whether the PKK's sympathizers and supporters in Western Europe will make a similar distinction. For only when Öcalan and his followers are deprived of funds and legitimacy will their bloody campaign truly be "neutralized," and only then will peace and genuine reconciliation have a chance for success.

Reprinted with the permission from http://www.fpri.org, Winter 2001

Notes

1.   Franz Schurmann, "Kurdish Leader Is Key Player," *San Francisco Examiner*, Sept. 5, 1996, posted by Kurdistan Web Resources (http://www-personal.usyd.edu.au/~rdemirb1/PUBLIC/Leader.html). Except where otherwise noted, all web sites cited in this article were accessible as of October 2000.
2.   Ibid.
3.   Author's interviews in Sirnak and Van provinces, June 1999.

4.   "PKK Looks for Route Out of Turkey," *Turkish Daily News*, May 18, 2000, posted by the *Kurdistan Observer* (http://homepages.go.com/~heyvaheft1999/18-5-00-TDN-pkk-route-out.html). Many stories from the *Kurdistan Observer* (http://www.kurdistanobserver.com) are archived elsewhere. See especially (http://homepages.go.com/~heyvaheft1999/Archive-News.html) and (http://www.mnsi.net/~mergan95/).

5.   Most of the information here is taken from the PKK's own "Brief History of the Kurdistan Workers' Party (PKK)" (http://www.guerilla.hypermart.net/archives/pkkhist.htm). Site no longer accessible in October 2000, but see note 7 below.

6.   See "PKK Fifth Victory Congress" (http://www.kurdstruggle.org/pkk/information/congress.html).

7.   "A Brief History of the Kurdistan Workers Party (PKK)" and "Party Program of the Kurdistan Workers Party," posted at a PKK web site available through the BURN! Project from the University of California at San Diego (http://burn.ucsd.edu/~ats/PKK/pkk-hist.html and /PKK/pkk5-1.html). The BURN! Project's site, a major publicity outlet for violent Marxist groups around the world, was closed down in 2000 by the administration of UCSD, but was accessible in October 2000. The "Party Program" is also posted by Kurdish Struggle (http://www.kurdstruggle.org/pkk/information/index.html).

8.   "Party Program."

9.   Ibid.

10.   Among other works, Öcalan is identified as the author of the PKK's manifesto, *The Road to the Kurdistan Revolution* (1982), *Problems of the Personality and Characteristics of the Fighter* (1982), 32 volumes of political reports (1981, 1990), *The People's War in Kurdistan* (1991), and *Selected Writings* (5 volumes, 1986-92). See "Biographical Notes on Abdullah Öcalan" (http://burn.ucsd.edu/~ats/APO/apo-bio.html) and "Abdullah Öcalan Biographical Notes" (http://www-personal.usyd.edu.au/~rdemirb1/PUBLIC/serok.html).

11.   Ibid.; see also Öcalan's own account of his life as given during his 1999 trial, "My Personal Status" (http://www.xs4all.nl/~kicadam/declaration/status.html).

12.   "The Final Statements of Defendant Abdullah Öcalan," June 17, 1999, posted by Kurdish Struggle (http://www.kurdstruggle.org/defence/final.html).

13.   Chris Kutschera, "Disarray inside the PKK," *Middle East*, May 2000 (http://www.africasia.com/me/may00/mebf0502.htm).

14.   Ibid.

15.   "Kurdistan: La situación del PKK," *Rebelión*, Aug. 5, 2000 (http://www.rebelion/internacional/Kurdistan_pkk020800.htm).

16.   Kutschera, "Disarray inside the PKK."

17.   "PKK Fifth Party Congress Resolution on the Function of Internationalism" (http://www.kurdstruggle.org/pkk/information/internationalism.html).

18.   Office of the Chief Public Prosecutor, State Security Court (DGM), *Indictment Regarding Accused Abdullah Öcalan* (Ankara: Republic of Turkey, Apr. 24, 1999), prep. #1997/514, principle #1999/98, indictment #1999/78, pp. 56-60.

19.   "Party Program of the PKK. Chapter One: The World Situation" (http://kurdstruggle.org/information/chap1.html). Öcalan neglected to mention, however, that many of those recruits were in fact infiltrators working for the Syrian government. See Michael M. Gunter, *The Kurds and the Future of Turkey* (New York: St. Martin's Press, 1997), pp. 26-27.

20.   "Brief History of the PKK."

21.   Ministry of Foreign Affairs, Republic of Turkey, *Greece and PKK Terrorism* (Washington, D.C.: Turkish Embassy, Feb. 1999) provides an admittedly biased

but largely correct analysis of Greece's support for the PKK and other terrorist groups in Turkey.

22. "Party Program of the PKK. Chapter Two: Kurdish Society" (http://kurdstruggle.org/information/chap2.html).

23. "Nationalism and the Kurdish National Liberation Movement" (http://burn.ucsd.edu/~ats/PKK/nationalism.html).

24. *No Friends But the Mountains: The Tragic History of the Kurds* (New York: Oxford University Press, 1992), p. 168.

25. *The Kurdish Predicament in Iraq: A Political Analysis* (New York: St. Martin's Press, 1999), p. 32.

26. Danielle Mitterand, "An open letter to President Öcalan," Sept. 1, 1998, posted by the American Kurdish Information Network (http://www.kurdistan.org/Articles/dmforpeace.html).

27. See "Juhnke to be Transferred to Amasya," *Kurdish Observer*, Dec. 28, 1999 (http://www.kurdishobserver.com/1999/12/28/hab06.html); and "ERNK Statement on the Death of Andrea Wolf," KURD-L archives, Nov. 29, 1998 (http://burn.ucsd.edu/archives/kurd-l/1998.11/msg00033.html). For more details on German anarchist and "anti-fascist" groups' ties with the PKK, see (German) Federal Ministry of the Interior, *Annual Report 1997* (http://www.bmi.bund.de/publikationen/vsb1997/englisch/v97). The latter web page was no longer accessible in October 2000.

28. MED-TV ceased operations in 1999, but its web site was still accessible as of October 2000 (http://www.med-tv.be/med/med-tv/medhome.htm).

29. Federal Ministry of the Interior, *Annual Report 1997*.

30. Ibid.

31. Ministry of Foreign Affairs, *Drug Trafficking and Terrorist Organizations* (Ankara: Republic of Turkey, Aug. 1998).

32. "Kurdistan Worker's Party (PKK)," International Policy Institute for Counter-Terrorism, Jan. 27, 2000 (http://www.ict.org.il/inter_ter/orgdet.cfm?orgid=20). This source quotes the British National Service of Criminal Intelligence to the effect that in 1993 the PKK obtained 2.6 million pounds sterling from extortion and 56 million German marks from drug smuggling.

33. "Cracks Appear in the PKK," *Turkish Daily News*, Jan. 21, 2000; and Susanne Gusten, "Kurdish Rebel Leader Öcalan at the Mercy of the PKK," Agence France-Presse, Jan. 13, 2000, both posted by the *Kurdistan Observer* at the following addresses (http://homepages.go.com/~heyvaheft1999/21-1-00-TDN-pkk-cracks.html and /~heyvaheft1999/13-1-00-AFP-apo-mercy-pkk.html).

34. See Raphael Israeli's article, "The Turkish-Israeli Odd Couple," in this issue of *Orbis*.

35. The definitive analysis of the Shining Path is to be found in Coronel PNP Benedicto Jimenéz Bacca, *Inicio, Desarollo y Ocaso del Terrorismo en el Peru* (The beginning, development and decline of terrorism in Peru), restricted ed. (Lima: Servicios Graficos SANKI, 2000), vol. 2, pp. 759Ü-65. See also Carlos Ivan Degregori, ed., *Las rondas campesinas y la derrota de Sendero Luminoso* (Peasant self-defense goups and the defeat of the Shining Path) (Lima: IEP Ediciones, 1996). For a recent analysis in English, see Michael Radu, "The Perilous Appeasement of Guerrillas," *Orbis*, Summer 2000, pp. 363-82.

36. "Final Statements of Defendant Abdullah Ocalan."

37. Douglas Frantz, "As Price of Progress, Turkish Villages Are Flooded," *New York Times*, Aug. 21, 2000.

38. Kemal Kirisci and Gareth Winrow, *The Kurdish Question and Turkey: An Example of Trans-state Ethnic Conflict* (London: Frank Cass, 1997), p. 124. For details on

the $20 billion project, see Bülent Topkaya, "Water Resources in the Middle East: Forthcoming Problems and Solutions for Sustainable Development of the Region" (http://www.geocities.com/RainForest/Jungle/1805/gap.html).

39.   "Final Statements of Defendant Abdullah Ocalan."
40.   Chris Kutschera, "Mad Dreams of Independence: The Kurds of Turkey and the PKK," *Middle East Report*, July-Aug. 1994, posted by the Kurdish Information Network (http://www.xs4all.nl/~tank/kurdish/htdocs/lib/dream.html).
41.   "Final Statements of Defendant Abdullah Ocalan."
42.   *Indictment Regarding Accused Abdullah Öcalan*, p. 58. The PKK occasionally mentioned having as many as 3,000 would-be suicide bombers.
43.   "PKK dropping the word 'Kurdistan' from the names of new wings," Associated Press, Feb. 9, 2000, posted by the *Kurdistan Observer* (http://homepages.go.com/~heyvaheft1999/10-2-00-AP-pkk-dropping-kurdistan.html).
44.   Author's interviews with army and *Jandarma* officials in Diyarbakir, Sirnak, Van, and Eruh, June 1999.
45.   "Statement from 'PKK revolutionary line fighters,'" KURD-L archives, Nov. 12, 1999 (http://burn.ucsd.edu/archives/kurd-l/1999.11/msg00000.html).
46.   Kutschera, "Disarray inside the PKK."
47.   "Cracks Appear in the PKK."
48.   Kutschera, "Disarray inside the PKK."
49.   In April 1998 Turkish special forces captured Semdin Sakik in a KDP-controlled part of northern Iraq and brought him to Turkey, where he was tried and sentenced to death. He now, like his former leader, awaits a decision of the European Court of Justice regarding his fate.
50.   Jorg Hilbert, "Interview with Selahattin Celik on the PKK," *Junge Welt*, Sept. 25, 1999, KURD-L archives, Oct. 11, 1999 (http://burn.ucsd.edu/archives/kurd-l/1999.10/msg00002.html).
51.   Ibid.
52.   Cemal Ucar, "Cemil Bayik: We Will Be Victorious," *Özgür Politika*, Aug. 16, 2000, posted by the *Kurdistan Observer* (http://www.mnsi.net/~mergan95/15-8-00-OP-interview.html).
53.   Ibid.
54.   "Talabani: There Is No Assault against the PKK," *Özgür Politika*, Aug. 5, 2000, posted by the *Kurdistan Observer* (http://www.mnsi.net/~mergan95/7-8-00-OP-talabani-ankara-pkk.html).
55.   "Turkey Acknowledges Iraqi Air Raid, Probes Casualty Claims," Agence France-Presse, Aug. 18, 2000, posted by the *Kurdistan Observer* (http://www.mnsi.net/~mergan95/18-8-00-AFP-tky-acknowledges-raid.html).

THE TURKISH PROBLEM—AND HOPE

On November 3, Turks elected a new parliament. Turkey's citizens had eighteen to choose from in the elections, three of which had been in the previous government. Not one of those three parties met the 10 percent of the vote threshold for obtaining seats in the November elections, which were resoundingly won by the Justice and Development Party (AKP), the latest incarnation of an earlier Islamist party. AKP received 34 percent of the vote, giving it 363 seats in the 550-member parliament—just four less than are needed to amend the constitution. The only other party in the new coalition government will be the Republican People's Party (CHP) of Mustafa Kemal Atatürk, the fanatically secularist founder of the Turkish Republic. CHP won 19.3 percent of the vote and will have 178 seats in parliament.

But this is not the victory for Islamists it might appear to be, after the Islamist victories in Morocco, Indonesia, Kuwait, and Bahrain. Understanding the reasons for these results is important if one is to understand the general stakes of the war on fundamentalist Islam terror as represented by al-Qaeda.

Turkey, with 70 million Muslims, has been the only case study of Islam's potential to become compatible with modernity, democracy, and tolerance. Muslim leaders elsewhere who have taken Atatürk as a model, from Afghanistan's King Amanullah in the 1920s to Pakistan's President Musharaf and various post-Soviet leaders in central Asia today, have largely failed. Meanwhile, Turkey had in Tansu Ciller, prime minister from 1993-96, the only female chief of government ever in the Islamic world elected on her own merits, rather than family background. Its military is thoroughly secular and has the constitutional role of protecting Atatürk's secularism, which is supported by some 70 percent of Turks.

Ever since Atatürk imported persecuted German-Jewish professors to establish Turkey's first public universities, banned Islamic garb, and proclaimed that the West was the model to be followed, Turkey has pursued a clear course of moving closer to the West. Some 3 million Turkish citizens now live in Western Europe, concentrated in Germany, the Netherlands, Belgium, and France. A NATO member since 1953, Turkey provided excellent fighters in Korea, and today has the second largest army in the alliance (after the United States), one that has proven itself in successful combat experience since 1984 against the Kurdish Workers' Party (PKK). Sharing borders with Iran, Iraq, Syria, Georgia, and Azerbaijan, it may be situated in the least desirable neighborhood in the world. It has therefore been in its interests to train armies and establish military academies in the Turkic-speaking former Soviet republics in Central Asia, fromUzbekistan, Kazakstan, Kirghizstan, and Tajikistan, all the way to the Chinese borders. The Turkish/NATO air base in Incirlik is a key to any operation in Iraq, and is still used by U.S. and U.K. forces in enforcing air control over northern Iraq.

Considering all this, what is to make of the results of the latest Turkish elections? To begin with, the number of votes cast for AKP, 10.8 million, was slightly below that of invalid and uncast votes, and less than the roughly 20 percent of votes that went to secular parties that did not break the 10 percent threshold individually. This 20 percent is about the same percent of the vote the Islamists obtained the last time they reached power, in 1996.

Second, exit polls and informal talks with Turkish voters suggest that many voted for the AKP because of its clean record in administration in large cities such as Istanbul and Ankara, rather than for its muted religious history. Rejection of the incompetent and corrupt secular regimes had far more to do with

AKP's victory—and CHP's—than the AKP's proposing to lift the army-imposed ban on women's wearing Islamic headscarves at universities and official places.

In fact, the AKP's rhetoric since its victory has been anything but radical. Its de facto leader, former Istanbul mayor Tayyip Erdogan, who was banned from politics for making religious speeches, has all but openly accepted the military's role in preserving secularism. In fact, he compares his party to the German Christian Democrats. Erdogan and the newly installed prime minister, Abdullah Gul, an economist, are moderate in dealing with the Cyprus issue, committed to NATO membership, pro-American, and obsessed with winning Turkey's membership in the European Union.

All of this should allay most concerns about an Islamist takeover in Ankara. Strategic decisions are taken by the National Security Council, where the military and the president have a clear majority; and the new government is openly aware of the limits imposed on it by the society, the elites, the media and, ultimately, the army. Whether those limits will confine the new government from legalizing the wearing of headscarves in public places (which it claims it promotes on the basis of multiculturalism and tolerance) and demoting Turkey's strategic ties with Israel remains to be seen, but the latter in particular is highly unlikely.

Turkey's unspoken strategic alliance with Israel runs deep. Israeli pilots train in the wide-open Anatolian air space, the powerful American Jewish lobby in Washington largely counters the hysterically anti-Turkish Greek and Armenian lobbies, and Turkey sells water to Israel. The mere existence of this alliance serves to contain Syria's rogue regime. In October 1998 Ankara gave Damascus a clear ultimatum—cease and desist from supporting the PKK or else. Without Tel Aviv's saying a word, the implicit threat from south and north compelled Damascus's compliance. PKK camps in Lebanon, Syria's protectorate, were closed down, and PKK leader and founder Abdullah Öcalan was expelled, to be ultimately captured in Kenya, effectively putting an end to the PKK.

And yet Valéry Giscard d'Estaing, chairman of the EU's federal constitution project, stated last month that Turkey is not a European country, and that its accession to the EU would be the end of that organization. Given the increasing internal security and cultural problems posed by the Muslim minorities in Western Europe, Giscard's concerns may seem reasonable. However, the Turkish minority is the least problematic and—at least compared to the Moroccan, Algerian, or Pakistani elements, less likely to be attracted to Islamist radicalism.

The problem is that Turkish elites, including the neo-Islamists of AKP and ordinary Turks, most of whom have some family connections to Western Europe—have made EU membership a litmus test of Turkey's acceptance as a European country. It is highly unlikely that Turkey will ever become an EU member, but its rejection will only force Ankara against its will closer to the Middle East.

For U.S. foreign policy, the impact of the AKP victory in Turkey is marginal: Turkey's support for a U.S. war on Iraq if the UN approves such an action remains unchanged. Domestically, it can only bring better economic management, of which Turkey has a clear need and in European terms, it means better prospects for resolution of old problems such as Cyprus, ties to Greece, and immigration. Ultimately, the AKP leaders represent exactly what Islam everywhere needs: realism, flexibility, and modernization. They can potentially be another example of why the Turkish model is relevant and needed, and why the United States should support it.

Reprinted with the permission from http://www.frontpagemag.com,
December 4, 2002

THE TURKISH TRAGICOMEDY OF ERRORS

After tortuous months of surprises and confusing signals from Ankara, which have brought U.S. relations with one of its most loyal allies to their lowest point in decades, Secretary of State Colin Powell will finally visit Turkey on April 2. State Department spokesman Richard Boucher said Powell would discuss with Turkish officials Turkey's possible sending of troops into northern Iraq, the war on terror, Cyprus, and other U.S.-Turkish relations issues. On the eve of his trip, the signals from Turkey are more confusing than ever. How did relations devolve so rapidly?

The short answer is timing. The war on Iraq and the dramatic but still incomplete change in Turkish politics are unfortunately occurring simultaneously, and both sides, with the Turks in the lead on this, have misjudged and misunderstood each other.

The election of the Justice and Development Party (AKP) led by Prime Minister Recep Tayyip Erdogan by an overwhelming vote in November 2002-the first time in decades that a Turkish party obtained a crushing majority in Parliament-was seen as a radical rejection of a corrupt establishment, rather than an endorsement of the Islamist origins of the AKP. Erdogan himself symbolizes the AKP's own transformation. A former mayor of Istanbul who was jailed for Islamist speeches a few years back, he was constitutionally prevented from running for Parliament until his party's winning the majority in November led to a constitutional change. He has since received 84 percent of the vote in a by-election earlier in March.

Between November 2002 and the by-election, Abdullah Gul (now foreign minister) was officially in charge, while Erdogan was the de facto decision maker. Adding to the confusion was the fact that almost none of the AKP member had any previous parliamentary, let alone ministerial, experience. In the confusion, the parliamentary vote on permitting the deployment of some 60,000 U.S. troops into northern Iraq through Turkey missed the required majority by three votes.

Erdogan was somehow certain that the vote would be easy. His AKP was officially in favor of the American deployment, and Erdogan allowed AKP deputies to vote free from party discipline. A large number of the deputies simply voted against it - a few because of their Kurdish separatist feelings, some because ...they could....The opposition CHP (Republican People's Party—Ataturk's old organization), for whom opposition seems to simply mean all out obstruction, also voted no on the ballot. Considering the security issue at hand, that was quite unusual, but significant for the general change Turkey is going through.

President Ahmet Necdet Sezer acted as a potent free agent against the ruling party, fervently lobbying against the deployment. The military, which traditionally and constitutionally has a decisive say on security matters, kept quiet- at least until after the vote, which discredited a government they never liked anyway given its Islamist roots. Chief of General Staff Gen. Hilmi Ozkok then came forward and publicly stated that Turkey had only two unpleasant choices, supporting the U.S. or not, but not supporting it was the worse of the available choices. For the military (to the extent one can talk of "the military" given how divided, and quite unusually. they are now), the idea seems to be to give the AKP enough rope to hang itself with, so as to be able to accuse it of incompetence and endangering Turkey's security. The strategy is not unlike that of the discredited, old Istanbul political, economic, and elite establishment, which wants to redress its humiliating defeat in November.

But what of the polls CNN cites, which find that 90 percent of Turks oppose the war? Reading carefully, one sees that the very same people who overwhelmingly oppose the war (mostly for economic reasons) also gave Erdogan, a supporter of U.S. deployment, 84 percent of the vote in the largely Kurdish (hence particularly antiwar) Siirt district; and the equally pro-U.S. military still has a 70 percent approval rating, still making it the most respected institution in the country. More seasoned leadership could still have won the day, were Turkey's leaders willing and able to put the nation's larger interests ahead of mob emotions (as Tony Blair or José Maria Aznar were), but obviously this is beyond the reach of the AKP and Erdogan.

In fact, the AKP is largely the party of small merchants from the provinces and metropolitan slums, something the Istanbul elites never miss an opportunity to mention. It has only a limited understanding of security and wider regional or international politics, and the secularists within the Foreign Ministry bureaucracy and military—the natural advisers on such matters—mistrust it. Concerned to what degree the AKP has a hidden Islamist agenda, they are not inclined to help it.

What did Turkey lose by sending such confused signals? Tactically, and most dangerously in the long run from the military/intelligence perspective, it lost the ability to finish off its main enemy, the Marxist/separatist Kurdish Workers Party (PKK), which has retreated over recent years into northern Iraq.

(There are some 7,000 PKK cadres there, as compared to less than 700 inside Turkey proper.) The PKK insurgency that began in 1984 and ended with the capture of the PKK's leader, Abdullah Ocalan, in 1999 led to some 30,000 fatalities. Indeed, the plan initially offered by Washington included having U.S. heavy forces move south from Turkey into Iraq, with Turkish forces cleaning up the PKK stronghold behind.

Economically, Turkey lost some $6 billion in U.S. grants and much more in loan guarantees from IMF loans-money Turkey desperately needs after a decade's mismanagement of the economy. When I visited Turkey in 2001 the lira was at 400,000 to the dollar. When I left Ankara two weeks ago after a follow-up visit, all Turks were millionaires: the lira was at 1,700,000 to the dollar.

Politically, Turkey's support for Saddam (which is what the rejection of the U.S. force deployment amounts to) is a lose-lose proposition. Arabs hate Turks, and always will; Turks despise Arabs; the idea of the overwhelmingly secular Turks expressing "solidarity" with Iraqi Arabs is simply preposterous.

Strategically, Turkey only has one serious friend in the West, the United States, as demonstrated by the November 2002 NATO imbroglio, when France, Germany, and Belgium refused to give Ankara the defensive support it requested. It was only Washington that pressed for a different and better result.

By rejecting a U.S. deployment that would have established a strong northern front against Saddam's regime, Ankara managed only to increase the Iraqi Kurds' influence—the light American forces in northern Iraq are more, rather than less, dependent on Kurdish military support. This is precisely what the Turks did not want to do. Worse still, both Washington and the EU, as well as NATO, now oppose any Turkish incursion into Iraq, even one directed to the PKK—an organization considered terrorist by the U.S. for years and, since 9/11, by the EU as well.

In terms of U.S.-Turkish relations, the damage is enormous. Americans who supported Turkey against powerful Greek and Armenian lobbies feel disappointed; and most of the Pentagon, always the American institution friendliest to Ankara, rightly feels that the Turkish decision, or lack of one, will inevitably lead to American military fatalities, now that a northern Iraqi front has to be established through airborne operations.

But what about the United States? While Turkish indecision bears the largest part of the blame for the current situation, one wonders why the U.S. embassy in Ankara failed to understand the always-complicated Turkish domestic politics. It would appear that Ambassador Robert Pearson was asleep at the wheel, since during the run-up to the war in Iraq, the only high-ranking U.S. officials to visit Ankara were from the Defense Department. This suggests that Washington assumed, erroneously as it turns out, that the traditionally close military-to-military ties with Turkey were enough to "deliver" Ankara.

Secretary Powell's belated April visit to Turkey may or may not contain the damage to bilateral relations, but its immediate goal—preventing a massive

Turkish military incursion into Iraq—is evidence of how far the miscommunication between the two countries was allowed to go.

Ultimately, Turkey has a legitimate right to eliminate PKK strongholds in northern Iraq, hopefully with the support of a post-Saddam regime in Baghdad. On the other hand, Ankara's own indecision has postponed that eventuality, and the price will be paid in Turkish lives. Whatever calculations the Turkish military made regarding the PKK and the possible impact of Iraqi Kurds on U.S. operations were wrong. Ankara is blinded by its fear of an unlikely independent Kurdish state in Iraq, especially if it gets its hand on the oil fields of Kirkuk. But by rejecting the U.S., Turkey only strengthened the hand of the Kurds, making them a far more valued U.S. ally than they needed to be.

But in one amazing development in Turkey, I found on my visit that cabbies as well as establishment figures do something very unusual for Turks talking to a foreigner: they say "We made a mistake." Let's hope that such feelings spread to the antiwar types in Istanbul.

Reprinted with permission from http://www.frontpagemag.com, April 2, 2003

(EVERYBODY'S) TRICKY KURDISH ISSUE

Now that the Baathist regime in Baghdad is gone, the perennial issue of the status of the region's Kurds reemerges. For some countries in the Middle East and Europe—Turkey has some 12 million Kurds, Iraq and Iran over 4 million each, Syria perhaps 2 million, Armenia some small number, and Western Europe perhaps 1 million or so—the Kurds pose a serious problem: To permit the growth of any sentiment for a Kurdish state, in northern Iraq or elsewhere, would ruin any chance of stability in the Middle East, and further weaken NATO as well.

There is little love lost among Turks, Arabs, and Iranians, but there is one issue that unites them: opposition to any form of Kurdish independence whatsoever and anywhere (well, perhaps they could live with a Kurdish state in Berlin). Their shared antipathy to a Kurdish state has recently led to high-level military and political meetings among Damascus, Ankara, and Teheran—not normally the best of buddies.

On the other hand, many in Western Europe and elsewhere have a strong affinity for the Kurdish cause, being emotionally susceptible to the Kurds' claims that they are the largest stateless ethnic group in the world, who were shortchanged when then-Colonial Secretary Winston Churchill failed to establish a Kurdish state in the aftermath of World War I notwithstanding purported promises of same from U.S. president Woodrow Wilson. It is a romantic view of the Kurds shared by many Europeans (most Americans have no idea who the Kurds are or what to do about them), including Churchill's own Tory grandson today. Such indulgence of Kurdish grievances, encouraged by a well-educated and non-representative Kurdish intellectual class in the diaspora, made the Western European Left easily manipulable and willing to support one of the most violent terrorist organizations in recent times, the Kurdish Workers' Party (PKK), a Stalinist group seeking to establish a "true" communist state in south-eastern Turkey as a first step toward a regional bastion of "socialism." The PKK campaign against Turkey (1984–99) left some 30,000 Turkish citizens dead, mostly Kurdish civilians (unfriendly clan and tribal leaders, teachers, police-men, bureaucrats were PKK's favorite targets).

Is it "undemocratic" and "unfair" (whatever that may mean in international politics) to deny 20 million Kurds statehood? After all, one might reason, both Massoud Barzani's Kurdistan Democratic Party (KDP) and Jalal Talabani's Pa-triotic Union of Kurdistan (PUK) are now allies of the coalition forces in north-ern Iraq, with their *pesh mergha* ("those who fight to death") irregulars accept-ing U.S. command in operations there. Might they not reasonably expect a Kurdish state for their trouble?

Not necessarily. Kurdish "national sentiments" are largely a creation of the tiny intellectual elites now active in Western Europe and, to a lesser extent, the United States. The Kurds are divided along so many lines as to make any serious talk about a past, present, or future "Kurdistan" meaningless. While Kurdish languages are indeed separate and fundamentally distinct from Turk-ish or Arabic (they are basically related to Iranian Farsi), these are different languages—and not mutually understandable at that. Furthermore, the funda-mental loyalty of a Kurd, whether in Iran, Turkey, Iraq or elsewhere, is not to a "Kurdish nation" proclaimed by French- or English-speaking, pseudo-Jeffersonian Kurdish émigrés in Paris or London. A Kurd's loyalty is to his family, clan, and tribe, in that order.

That explains why our present "staunch" allies against Saddam (one should remember that over the past decade Barzani has been in bed with Saddam and Talabani with the Teheran ayatollahs) fought each other with a determination worthy of a better cause. That also explains why, despite more than a decade of de facto autonomy and economic progress in northern Iraq, protected by U.S. and U.K. airplanes enforcing a no-fly zone over Iraqi Kurdistan, there are still two Kurdish governments in the region, under PDK and PUK control, respectively.

More disturbing to neighboring Turkey, both the PUK. and the PDK toler-ate, at least occasionally, the presence of some 7,000 PKK, which reestablished in northern Iraq after their founder, Abdullah Öcalan, was captured and they were finally defeated in 1999. The PKK remnants are rich (mostly from their Western European criminal and racketeering operations) and increasingly well armed—a fact that can only be explained by Iraqi Kurds' tolerance of arms smuggling into PKK strongholds. If Ankara is often paranoid about the Kurds in general and the PKK in particular, it is not without reason.

Worst still for the U.S., the autonomous Kurdish authorities in northern Iraq, despite their media-glorified *pesh mergas*, said to be as many as 60,000 strong, were for almost two years patently unable to deal with less than 1,000 Ansar al Islam ("followers of Islam")—al-Qaeda's Arab and Kurdish followers, who are ensconced in a small enclave along the Iranian border. It took U.S. special forces, bombings, and Kurdish ground forces to finish this operation off in three days.

The official U.S. position is that Iraq's "territorial integrity" should be maintained—a way of saying to Ankara, Teheran & Co. that there will be no independent or autonomous state of Kurdistan in Iraq. And, listening to (English-speaking) Kurdish politicians in Suleymanyia and Irbil, one hears the same liturgy that "We just want a federal Iraq." So far, so good, but "federal" means something different in Washington than it does in Ankara (or for that matter in Damascus or Teheran, or likely in whatever regime is established in Baghdad). "Federal" in the Middle East does not connote as it does to us Hawaiians, Tennesseans, and Mexican-Americans in California being different but equally loyal Americans, swearing allegiance to the same flag; it would be a way-station toward a Kurdish state threatening all the nations' territorial integrity.

It should be clear that any U.S. support for an independent Kurdistan, implicit or otherwise, whether an autonomous one or some "federal" Iraq giving Kurds control over northern Iraq (including the oil fields of Kirkuk) would sooner or later unite traditional enemies—Turks, Persians, and Arabs—militarily.

As to the issue of PKK strongholds in northern Iraq, that organization, leaderless as it is since Öcalan's capture, has been listed as terrorist by the U.S. State Department since the 1980s, and belatedly so by the EU after 9/11, and simply has to be permanently eliminated. The U.S. forces in northern Iraq simply cannot do it alone, as Turkey's misguided policies on the war on Iraq have left them. But either Turkey or the Iraqi Kurds must do so soon.

Indeed, Kurdish elements are already reversing Saddam's ethnic cleansing of their people from Mosul and Kirkuk, by removing the Arab settlers, while the significant Turcoman minority feels unprotected—a situation Turkey is unlikely to accept for long. But if Ankara, in a fit of nationalism and anti–Kurdish paranoia, does invade northern Iraq, the chances of a new conflict would increase exponentially, pitting all Kurds against all of Iraq's northern neighbors. Furthermore, such unilateral Turkish action would seriously endanger that country's position within NATO, and thus the alliance itself. Indeed, Germany has already threatened to pull its AWACS crews from Turkey in such an event, and the U.S. has also made it clear that it will not tolerate a massive invasion either.

All this considered, and taking into account European opposition to the war (a contradiction, since Iraqi Kurds have made abundantly clear their virulent anti-Saddam feelings) and romantic tolerance for diaspora Kurds' claims and PKK terrorism, the coalition now victorious in Iraq must make clear that emotions and vague sentiments will have no part to play in Iraq's reconstruction. Simply put, the coalition should consider expressions of outsiders' sentiments about Kurds just as it considered the antiwar demonstrations: politically wrong, irrational, irresponsible, and counterproductive (even if protected as free speech). Westerners should let the Iraqi Kurds live free(r) in a country called Iraq, rather than "feel their pain" and risk havoc throughout the region.

Reprinted with the permission from http://www.frontpagemag.com,
April 16, 2003

TURKEY'S KURDS—BACK TO SQUARE ONE?

Between 1984 and the arrest of its leader, Abdullah Ocalan, in Kenya in 1999, the Marxist-Leninist Kurdish Workers' Party (PKK) was engaged in a major insurgency in southeastern Turkey, leaving some 30,000 dead. Following Öcalan's capture, the party declared a cease-fire and pulled most of its some 5,000 militants into northern Iraq, leaving only some 200 behind in Turkey, where they remained relatively quiet, until a few days ago. The PKK leadership in Iraq has now declared an end to the cease-fire and the resumption of attacks against Turkish targets, beginning September 1.

Despite its change of name—in 2002 it renamed itself the Kurdistan Freedom and Democracy Congress (KADEK)—the PKK remains what it has always been: a totalitarian terror organization seeking a Marxist state in all areas with a Kurdish population (Turkey, Iran, Iraq, and Syria). In the late 1980s it became one of the first terrorist groups to use suicide bombers, engaged in massacres of Kurdish villages opposed to it, and murdered civilians, all with the support of Syria, in whose Lebanon protectorate it had its training and indoctrination camps. This all started to unravel in 1998, when Turkish threats of war forced Syria to close down PKK's camps and expel Öcalan.

Even more important than the Syrian support was PKK's acceptance in Western Europe. Through blackmail, threats, and violence, it continues to collect funds from the hundreds of thousands of Kurds in Germany, the Netherlands, and elsewhere, and it receives massive amounts of money from its drug and illegal migrant trafficking there. The PKK operations in Western Europe were led by relatively well-educated people with extensive international support from governments (Greece having been the most prominent) and groups in Western countries (Germany, Benelux, and Scandinavian states). Some local government, such as the Basques' in Spain, openly supported the PKK, its terrorist methods notwithstanding. Prominent leftist government parties and individuals in Italy, Russia, and Greece publicly helped Öcalan during his failed attempts to find political asylum, and most of the remnants of Germany's Marxist terrorists supported and occasionally participated in PKK combat operations. At least two German women terrorists and PKK members were involved in these Andrea Wolf, a former Baader-Meinhof terrorist who was killed in combat, and Eva Juhnke, who was captured in 1998.

It was European pressure that forced Turkey to commute Öcalan's death sentence to life in prison, and it took 9/11 and strong U.S. demands for the EU to finally declare the PKK a terrorist organization. It is this European romantic sympathy for the Turkish Kurds and its willingness to associate their interests with the PKK's that has allowed the group's remnants to survive in the mountains of northern Iraq.

This makes a complication in the present situation, for both Washington and Ankara. As the major occupying power in Iraq, the United States is technically responsible for developments on that country's territory and thus in theory should be responsible for solving the PKK problem there.

However, for both practical and political reasons, the United States cannot and indeed should not be directly involved. American forces in northern Iraq are already overextended and highly dependent on Iraqi Kurdish cooperation—especially since of all the Iraqi groups, the Kurds are the most cooperative, effective, and sympathetic to the U.S. presence.

Iraqi Kurds have had a long and complicated relationship with the PKK, one that has to be considered by both Washington and Ankara. On the one hand, they have cooperated on and off with Turkey in keeping the PKK out; on the other hand, they are torn by Kurdish ethnic solidarity, deeply rooted antipathy for the Turks, and, more importantly, their economic interests. PKK is a wealthy organization, able to pay well for supplies of weapons to the local Kurds. Furthermore, PKK numbers and effectiveness, at least until recently, were such that Iraqi Kurds have preferred to avoid any head on confrontations, and should not be expected to do so in the future.

That said, it is clearly not in the United States' interest, or the interest of Iraqi stability, to continue allowing the presence of a large, armed, and fanatical alien element in the country, especially one threatening a key NATO ally—Turkey. But the Turks have not helped their own cause. For Ankara, the Kurdish issue is vital, occasionally reaching the level of national obsession. Kurdish separatism is perceived as a threat to the nation's unity, and PKK's Marxism, no matter how well hidden lately, only adds to that perception. Although the Turkish forces badly damaged its morale by capturing Öcalan and have basically broken the back of PKK's infrastructure inside Turkey, only the wholesale destruction of the PKK's Iraqi remnants could truly transform a Kurdish Marxist/ separatist terrorist threat into a strictly domestic political matter. In fact, Ankara has made significant efforts toward that goal, by allowing Kurdish language media, offering amnesty to PKK members, and (mistakenly as it turned out) allowing Öcalan to communicate with his followers.

However, Ankara has also badly mishandled and misunderstood the new situation in Iraq. First, the new ruling party's poor management of a vote to allow U.S. forces to pass through Turkey to northern Iraq led to the parliament's inability to approve the deployment, making life harder for U.S. troops, increasing the importance of Iraqi Kurdish cooperation and influence, and concomitantly reducing Turkey's influence on events in Iraq or Washington's policy there.

Second, Turkey made no serious effort to establish the political and military grounds for dealing with the PKK. Although there are some 5,000 Turkish troops in northern Iraq, and have been for a long time, they are not enough to control a long and difficult border or to permanently disable the PKK. Unpopular as Turkish military action might be, the United States could probably convince the Iraqi Kurdish parties to at least stay neutral in the event of a major and decisive Turkish operation against PKK camps in Iraq. But for that to happen Turkey must provide guarantees to both the Iraqi Kurds and the U.S. that the incursion would only target the PKK and would be temporary.

Finally, Ankara should realize that it cannot have it both ways, refusing to contribute troops to Iraq unless it has the United Nations' blessings (a position suspiciously similar to that of U.S. adversaries within the United States) but claim a right to deal with the PKK in Iraq without mention of the UN.

It is clearly in the interest of the United States, a free Iraq and, most obviously, of Turkey for the PKK to be dispatched to the trashcan of history, where it belongs. Its most recent threat is a sign of desperation and blackmail but is a real threat nonetheless. Because Turkey's recent policies have made an already complicated situation even more complex, it is Ankara's turn to help simplify it. Militarily, only Turkey can finish off the PKK. Let us hope Ankara soon comes to some clarity about this.

Reprinted with permission from http://www.frontpagemag.com,
September 10, 2003

WHO WANTS A GREATER ALBANIA?

CNN's heart-wrenching images and the *New York Times*' strident editorials on the suffering of allegedly innocent Albanian civilians in Kosovo at the hands of the ruthless Serbs have the Clinton Administration on the same kind of meaningless rhetorical and diplomatic offensive as it was in Bosnia and Rwanda, Somalia and Haiti. And the results, as in those cases, are predictable: misguided sentimentalism, outrage, and protest; increased but covert costs for Americans; and complete disregard of the implications of bellicose statements and a diminishing foreign policy stick. The most disturbing of those implications, the Administration's protestations to the contrary, is the inadvertent encouragement by Washington of the creation of a Greater Albania, including Kosovo and areas of Macedonia.

Kosovo, annexed by Serbia in 1912, became a highly autonomous province of the Republic of Serbia under the 1974 Constitution of Yugoslavia—a status it lost in 1989 as a result of Serbian leader Slobodan Milosevic's machinations. Although the more developed Slovenia and Croatia had subsidized Kosovo for decades, the region remained the most backward in the former Yugoslavia. Barely larger than Delaware, Kosovo, even more than Albania itself, largely lacks natural resources. Its young, fast growing, poorly educated, and unskilled population of 2.8 million—80 percent of which is ethnic Albanian, 10 percent Serbian/Montenegrin and the rest of various origins, mostly Gypsy—has no economy to speak of, beyond smuggling, remittances from (mostly illegal) emigrants to Western Europe and the United States, and most recently foreign aid. Simply put, Kosovo is, like Albania, the archetypal social, political and economic basket case—a Haiti in Europe.

Although Kosovo is now largely Albanian, it did not have such a large majority prior to 1912. The high Albanian Muslim fertility rate, in addition to Serbian emigration, helped create the present situation. Nonetheless, Serbian and Montenegrin history, sentiments, and geopolitical considerations are all strong reasons as to why Kosovo should remain part of Yugoslavia. Indeed, the religious and cultural roots of medieval Serbian nationhood are to be found in today's Kosovo: the first Serbian Orthodox Patriarchate at Pec, the great monasteries of Decani and Gracanica, and most importantly, the location of the 1389 lost battle of Kosovo, the source of Serbia's national mythology.

It is easy to dismiss such emotional attachments as irrelevant or obsolete, just because they come from the Balkans, that motherlode of historic delusions; but it is also dangerous to dismiss Serbian motivations, which are truly nationalistic and involve Serbia's most revered institution—the Orthodox Church. Not surprisingly, the Belgrade Patriarchate is at the forefront of Serbian and Montenegrin sentiments on Kosovo. Nor are Serbian and Montenegrin fears of the implications of Kosovo irredentism all emotion—an independent Muslim Albanian Kosovo, or a Greater Albania, would probably provoke secessionist pressures in the Sandjak of Novi Pazaar, the largely Muslim area linking Bosnia and Kosovo—enough to bring relatively liberal Montenegro back into the arms of conservative and nationalist Serbia. Then there is the little matter of international law, which recognizes Kosovo as an integral part of Yugoslavia, as do all world governments, including the United States.

On the other side of the ledger are the Albanians, whether the "moderate" followers of Ibrahim Rugova's Democratic League of Kosovo or those of the increasingly active and violent Kosovo Liberation Army (KLA)—and they all share the same objective—independence as a first step toward joining Albania. The Rugova forces use an increasingly sophisticated public relations campaign, including ubiquitous English language banners during their made-for-TV marches in the capital of Prishtina. The KLA is more direct: it threatens the moderates and, more ominously, it uses civilians as propaganda tools. Its money, arms, and ideas come from (mostly illegal) Albanian emigres in Western Europe and the United States, its leaders seem to be former Stalinist followers of the Enver Hoxha regime, and its ideology is a hodgepodge of totalitarianism, ultranationalism, and contempt for the West and its values.

Indeed, from the murky images coming from Kosovo through the double screens of Serbian censorship and Western media emotionalism, it appears that the KLA has selected a risky, but so far successful, strategy. On the one hand, it engages in a hopeless static "defense" of villages against superior Serbian forces, resulting in heavy civilian casualties, and on the other, it counts on the usual Serbian brutality to make sure that those casualties are widely known (and exaggerated) abroad—in other words creating victims today for the glory of tomorrow—and for provoking a NATO military intervention. And the glory of tomorrow, for the KLA and Rugova alike, is a Greater Albania, which would include large parts of Macedonia (another fragile and largely fictitious Balkan state with its 600,000 irredentist Albanians) as well. Indeed, the U.S. position only encourages the Kosovo Albanians, as well as the violent operators of the KLA, to pursue their maximalist goal.

Albania proper can best be described as a Balkan Somalia. Its Western-installed regime, led by the barely reformed ex-Stalinist Fatos Nano, hangs on to the capital by a thread. Smugglers, criminals, and local clans, in effect, control most of the country. In fact, foreign aid and smuggling—of drugs, emigrants, weapons, and anything else—are Albania's economy. An Albania almost double the size of today's would not only intensify the clan conflicts and corruption that have already destroyed the state, but also magnify mass emigration to Italy, provoke further "humanitarian crises," and require more and more foreign aid. Who needs it? Who needs a Greater Albania? And who will pick up the inevitable bill to keep it afloat?

Officially, the Clinton Administration recognizes that Kosovo is, and should remain part of, Serbia/Yugoslavia, and has even declared the KLA a terrorist organization. On the other hand, it makes no secret of its sympathy for Rugova, and for the Albanian government, whose weakness and duplicity allow the KLA to exist. More seriously, it threatens the Serbs with dire consequences if they defend their territorial integrity, as they have every right to do. Washington demands the withdrawal of Serbian police from Kosovo, protests the mining of the border with Albania, and forces Belgrade into negotiations with Rugova. Symbolically, during his recent trip to the area, Richard C. Holbrooke, the Administration's factotum in the Balkans, did not even see fit to meet with Serbian religious leaders in Kosovo—as if they are not a party to the conflict.

How do these attitudes combine with the provisions of the 1975 Helsinki Accords, forbidding territorial changes by force? Seeking a "peaceful solution" in Kosovo may sound good, but the Administration cannot have it both ways—professing respect for recognized borders while at the same time supporting committed irredentists and condemning the state that tries to protect its borders. If Washington has decided that Kosovo should be independent, then it should explain that decision; if not, it should act accordingly.

By manifesting sympathy for the Albanians and threatening Serbia/Yugoslavia with military intervention for using force in Kosovo, the Clinton Administration (like the Bush administration before it) is making impossible negotiations that might lead to the only solution, if there is one, to the Kosovo problem: the region's autonomy within Serbia/Yugoslavia—that is, a return to the 1974 old Yugoslav status quo. That would mean forcing Rugova, before the KLA completely destroys his political support, to accept a return to the pre-1989 situation. The same should be required from Belgrade. The alternative is more bloody, useless insurgency by Afghan Muslim ideological veterans, Islamic mercenaries, and fanatical volunteers seeking the creation of a Greater Albania, opposed by a brutal, well-armed, and zealous Serbian and Montenegrin state supported by the masses.

The Congress of the United States has the responsibility to ask questions and to compel the Clinton Administration to answer for its decision to push the Serbians into an unacceptable concession of territory to an ethnic group totally incapable of ruling itself, either alone or with its even less prepared brethren, across the mountains in Albania and Macedonia. Meanwhile, Americans should be prepared for a protracted diet of selective CNN images of Serbian atrocities against Albanian "innocents" with no corresponding images of Albanian terrorism, no analysis of the implications of a possible KLA victory, and no analysis of the Serbian motivation for resistance.

Reprinted with the permission from http://www.fpri.org, July 10, 1998

DANGEROUS INCOHERENCE IN KOSOVO

Americans and many Europeans are rightly confused over the Clinton Administration's actions in Kosovo, for those actions neither amount to any sort of "policy" nor suggest a willingness on our part to learn from past blunders (Somalia and Haiti come to mind) and thus avoid repeating them.

Between 1992 and 1995 when Serbia and her then president, Slobodan Milosevic, tried to create a Greater Serbia by adding ethnically Serb territories from Croatia and Bosnia, Washington condemned the action and ultimately bombed the Bosnian Serbs into (temporarily) desisting from such attempts. American policy dictates that borders of recognized European states (Croatia's and Bosnia's) cannot and should not be changed by force, regardless of the ethnic composition of certain areas—a wise principle, considering the alternative: a chain reaction of mass border revisions (from Russia's Caucasus to Azerbaijan's Nagorno Karabakh to Romania's Transylvania). Whether Bosnia Herzegovina's enforced and artificial unity is a realistic proposition in the long run is another question. Secretary of State Madeleine Albright went so far as to openly (and unsuccessfully) interfere in elections there—by what might properly be described as bribery—when she implied this past summer that aid to the Serbs would be conditioned upon the victory of the U.S.-supported candidate during the Serbia entity's presidential election.

The notion of inviolability of borders, unsatisfactory as it may be, not only remains one of the few substantive and generally accepted principles of what goes by the name of international law, but also limits the number of non-viable pseudo-states condemned to become international welfare recipients (Bosnia, Macedonia) or lawless black holes (Chechnya). Furthermore, that very same principle helped justify the Gulf War, U.S. support for the Nigerian government during the Biafra episode, and opposition to the Soviet annexation of the Baltic States.

Today, as if walking in its sleep, the Clinton Administration disregards common sense and American tradition by its misguided actions in Kosovo. Indeed, largely because of media images of Albanian refugees and an admittedly well-founded dislike and distrust of Milosevic, American forces are on the brink of bombing Serbia because it resists a change of its borders by force. Furthermore, to claim, as the Administration does, that military action against Serbia is not intended as support for Albanian secessionism begs the point: it will help the secessionists even if it not intended to do so.

To give Serbia an ultimatum requiring the withdrawal of police and military forces from Kosovo is tantamount to giving the aggressively secessionist Kosovo Liberation Army (KLA) a free hand. Such a withdrawal means the de facto loss of the province. Other key U.S. demands—negotiations with the Albanians and heavily intrusive on-the-ground international monitoring—only further strengthen the secessionists' position. No international forces could control the

Albanian border with Kosovo, and, thus, prevent the KLA from rearming itself. What passes for the government of Albania has neither the interest nor the means to do either.

It is no secret that the KLA aims to create a "Greater Albania" from territories now within the internationally—and U.S.-recognized—borders of Yugoslavia (Serbia's as well as Montenegro's), Macedonia, and probably Greece. As for the Albanian moderates, Ibrahim Rugova's Kosovo Democratic League will "negotiate" with Belgrade but only concerning the timing and conditions of independence. In addition, a campaign of selective assassinations by the KLA against the few pro-Yugoslav Albanians, Rugova's people, and the 10 percent of the population that is neither Albanian nor Serb (mostly Gypsies)—helped to make the separatist threat about the only issue of concern for the Serbian people.

None of the above facts is unknown to the Administration—or to the Serbs. Nevertheless, if NATO bombs are intended to bring about negotiations that lead directly to autonomy for Kosovo, as President Clinton desires, what is there to negotiate if the Albanians don't seek autonomy in the first place? Perhaps what the White House really means by "negotiations" is the postponement of any solution until President Clinton leaves office.

The position of the United States in the Kosovo insurgency represents an ironic reversal of roles vis-à-vis Vietnam. There, we could not win in large part due to the safe haven insurgents had in North Vietnam, itself protected by a superpower. In Kosovo the Serbs cannot permanently defeat the KLA because it has a safe haven—Albania—protected by...us! Such a position would make perfect sense if Washington's goal were a KLA victory, but it makes absolutely no sense if we are serious about describing the KLA as "terrorist" (as the State department did) or about opposing its goal—secession from Serbia. Thus we are prepared to use military force in order to defeat our own stated political and diplomatic goals.

Equally serious and puzzling is the misconception in Washington—shared by the White House and the Republican Congress alike—that the "problem" in Kosovo is Milosevic. If only we could get rid of him, goes the inside-the-Beltway wisdom, all would be fine. Really? The most popular politician in Serbia is Voijslav Seselj—now a deputy Prime Minister. Unlike Milosevic, whose only creed is his own political survival, Seselj is a true (if unsavory) Serbian nationalist. No opposition politician in Belgrade supports a NATO attack or an independent Kosovo, and for one very simple reason—virtually no Serbian citizen does so. Who, then, are we going to turn to once Milosevic is out of power? Unlike the Gulf War, in which only a minority of Iraqis supported Saddam Hussein, an attack on Serbia would mean war with the Serbian people, with or without Milosevic. Is this something we want? Considering the implications (the risk to American lives, the creation of a Greater Albania), that the administration has not, is this something we are prepared for?

Reprinted with the permission from http://www.fpri.org, October 21, 1998

BOMBS FOR PEACE? MISREADING KOSOVO

President Clinton's address to the nation explaining the decision to launch air attacks against Yugoslavia on March 24 revealed several flawed premises. These, in turn, must raise doubts about the wisdom of the bombing campaign.

First, the situation on the ground in Kosovo is far more complex than the Serbian forces' obvious brutality against an innocent and helpless civilian population. In fact, there is a war going on in Kosovo, between the separatists of the Kosovo Liberation Army (KLA) and Serbian forces. Both sides are taking casualties—including innocents. The KLA, far from "innocent," is widely suspected of paying for its weapons with heroin money, and is known to have received training from fanatically anti-Western Islamic fundamentalist veterans of the war in Afghanistan. They have murdered not only Serbs (military personnel as well as civilians) but also ethnic Albanians "guilty" of moderation or opposed to violence. Hence, the "moral imperative" the president mentioned to justify the bombings is, at best, a far more complicated matter than simply protecting "innocent Albanians" by bombing the Serbs.

Second, the proclaimed military goal of the operation—to "degrade" Serbian capability of inflicting casualties on Kosovo civilians—is not very plausible. The only plausible targets of air attacks are heavy weapons: air defense systems, aircraft, and tanks—none of which is particularly useful to Serbia in the type of counterinsurgency campaign it is waging in Kosovo. Counterinsurgencies everywhere rely on small weapons, small units, and good intelligence—all immune to "stealth" aircraft and Tomahawk cruise missiles. As for the Serbian ability to inflict harm on Kosovo Albanians, keep in mind that the most recent true genocide, in Rwanda in 1994, was committed with . . . machetes.

Third, Washington is misreading the political situation in Belgrade. Yugoslav president Slobodan Milosevic—an unreconstructed communist and demagogue—is primarily responsible for the wars throughout former Yugoslavia since 1989. But, on the issue of Kosovo, the far more important fact is that Milosevic is not the main problem, and his removal from power is not the solution.

Simply put, Kosovo has united the Serbs. It is significant that one of Serbia's deputy prime ministers is Vojislav Seselj, a rabid nationalist and anti-communist; and that the leader of the Serbian delegation at the Rambouillet negotiations was Vuk Draskovic, a liberal intellectual and anti-communist. Both of them have in the past been beaten up and jailed by Milosevic's police, and yet they both joined Milosevic on the Kosovo issue, along with virtually all representatives of the opposition, including Vuk Obradovic, a retired general and democratic opponent of Milosevic. Dragoljub Zarkovic, the long-suffering editor of the opposition weekly Vreme, made it clear that, "In this whole business (of Kosovo), as a matter of principle, we shouldn't give a toss for the latest political pirouettes of Yugoslav President Slobodan Milosevic. It is because of him that we are where we are. There is something more important at stake here: the preservation of international order and the preservation of Serbs as a political nation." The true danger is that the bombings, and our entire policy on Kosovo, will result in America and NATO going to war against the Serbian nation—not Milosevic.

Fourth, the bombing will encourage the dreams of the KLA and others of a Greater Albania. What is clear, to the Serbs, Albanians, and objective observers alike, is that the de facto result of U.S. policy on Kosovo, from the Rambouillet Accord to the air campaign, is independence for Kosovo—all of Foggy Bottom's protestations to the contrary notwithstanding. Indeed, if our goal is to disarm the Serbs by destroying their military, or to force them out of Kosovo via Rambouillet, what will be left of our recognition of Serbian "sovereignty" over Kosovo? Sovereignty might be a meaningful concept, of course, if NATO ground forces actually manage to disarm the KLA and control the mountainous Albanian and Macedonian borders through which the Albanian separatists bring weapons and reinforcements—but that is unlikely unless NATO is prepared to take casualties in policing the people we have described as the innocent victims.

The consequence of this policy could be totally destabilizing to the entire region—the very opposite of U.S. intent. An independent Kosovo, soon to join Albania, would instantly create irresistible secessionist pressures in eastern Macedonia, where the 25 percent Albanian minority is already resistive and strongly supports the KLA. If Serbia, with a relatively strong military, could not prevent the creation of a Greater Albania, what chances does Macedonia, with virtually no army of its own, have to do any better? Then, in the face of a Greater Albania carved out of its own lands, what would happen to the Slavic remnant of Macedonia? Remember that neighboring Bulgaria fought (and lost) five wars over that country since 1885. As for the creation of a Greater Albania itself, who needs it, and who will pay the price for it? Albania today has totally deconstructed itself. It has no functioning government, and an economy based strictly on smuggling: of illegal emigrants and heroin to Italy, and of weapons from Europe.

The president correctly stated "we need a Europe that is coming together, not falling apart." What is not clear is how the de facto dismemberment of Yugoslavia and the creation of a larger chaos named Greater Albania would promote that goal.

Finally, there will be a dangerous impact on Bosnia. How could NATO justify the presence of ground troops in Bosnia-Herzegovina, where their clear aim is to prevent a majority of that country's population (the Croats and Serbs) from seceding to Croatia and Serbia, while simultaneously promoting Albanian secessionism in Serbia?

The understandable desire to punish a villainous Milosevic should not take precedence over serious consideration of national interests—even the very limited ones we have in Kosovo. Nor should we be blinded by loose charges of "genocide" that cheapen the moral value of the language of politics. Decrying "genocide," when less than 2,000 people (not all Albanians) have died in Kosovo since 1989, demeans the memory of victims of true genocide: Jews, Gypsies, Tutsis. References to "ethnic cleansing" when proportionally far more non-Albanians than Albanians have left or have been pushed out of Kosovo during the past two decades, also have no place.

Among our united interests is one to which we have paid little attention—respect for Serbia's territorial integrity, based on hard choices. One of those choices is a clear NATO guarantee of Yugoslavia's borders, including Kosovo, in exchange for extensive regional autonomy from Belgrade. Serbian police could be allowed to deploy in strength along the chaotic Albanian border in exchange for Serbian military withdrawal from Kosovo. Macedonia would also require help to control its borders. NATO and/or European Union military police or civilian observers, furthermore, could be deployed in Kosovo to monitor Serbian and Albanian police behavior. European cooperation to at least limit KLA recruitment, arms smuggling, and fund-raising abroad would be another essential element of the deal. Unlike the abortive Rambouillet agreement, which included lip service for Serbia's integrity but would put NATO forces "in country," this strategy would use the Alliance to secure regional borders rather than build new nations. Such measures, rather than "bombs for peace" and winks toward Albanian irredentism, are more likely—though not certain—to bring at least a modicum of stability to the region.

Reprinted with the permission from http://www.fpri.org, March 26, 1999

DON'T ARM THE KLA

A Republican-sponsored bill currently moving through the U.S. House of Representatives asks for U.S. military aid to the Kosovo Liberation Army (KLA, or Ushtria Clirimtare e Kosove—UCK, in Albanian). Despite the bill's prominent supporters—including Senator Joseph Lieberman (D-Conn.) and former national security adviser Zbigniew Brzezinski, both usually lucid observers of the international scene—it is misguided and dangerous.

"Arming" the KLA (as if they are not already armed) would be far more than a mere mistake. It would display both American ignorance of the true nature of the KLA and despair at the failure of NATO air strikes against Yugoslavia. It would also mean that foreign policy would be guided not by the defense of national interest, but by the emotionalism now masquerading as news on CNN.

Some politicians have apparently confused the KLA with the Nicaraguan contras or the Afghan mujaheddin of the 1980s. This author was an enthusiastic supporter of both of those groups, but the KLA is far from the same. Any confusion reflects a bad reading of history—both of the "Reagan Doctrine" and

Nixon's "Vietnamization"—for the KLA is a group with distinctly dubious origins, goals, and methods.

To its credit, the Clinton administration has, thus far, distanced itself from the idea of arming that organization, but its position may be wavering, and it seems prepared to use the growing support for that notion as an additional form of pressure on Belgrade.

Slobodan Milosevic's rather crude, Bolshevik-style propaganda has succeeded in marshalling Serb opinion against all Albanians rather than just the KLA. The Clinton administration, however, should be able to deflect American calls to aid the KLA by presenting the facts about the group it declared a "terrorist organization" last year.

The KLA: Terrorist, Authoritarian Guerrillas

The KLA is, briefly put, a secessionist and irredentist guerrilla organization seeking a Greater Albania carved from territories now belonging to Yugoslavia, Macedonia and Greece. Equally disturbing, some of its founders and leading cadres were associated with the Yugoslavian communist secret police or even the late Enver Hoxha's Sigurimi, a group that made the KGB, at its Stalinist worst, look good by comparison. Moreover, reports have traced KLA support to Iranian, Afghan, and other unsavory sources, including Ossama Bin Laden.

The KLA leadership is largely made up of Albanians from the diaspora (including Switzerland, Germany, and the United States, among others), Albania proper—particularly northern Albania, the area controlled by former president and present warlord Sali Berisha and his Tropoje clans, as well as Kosovo groups. According to the Times of London (see its March 24 edition) and other European publications, the KLA is heavily involved in trafficking heroin, cigarettes, and illegal aliens throughout Europe. Supplementing that income are "contributions" often extorted from Albanian emigres. In conjunction with Albanian criminal organizations, the KLA also controls arms smuggling from Europe into Albania, Macedonia, and Yugoslavia.

Beyond those facts, the KLA's tactics and treatment of Kosovo Albanians should make American aid to the organization unthinkable. Currently, the KLA is recruiting—often forcibly, and even at gunpoint—men of fighting age from among those in flight to the Albanian border, according to reports in the *Los Angeles Times, New York Times*, and *Washington Post*. Other reports, too numerous to dismiss simply as Serbian propaganda, indicate that the KLA fighters were trained by veterans of the Afghan war, all of them anti-democratic and anti-American Islamic fundamentalists.

The KLA has, in fact, never shown regard for democracy. When the Kosovo Democratic League of Ibrahim Rugova— the only democratically elected Kosovo Albanian leader ever— tried to establish its own armed branch (the Armed Force of the Kosovo Republic [FARK]) with bases in Albania, the KLA promptly killed its leader. Nor did the KLA have any qualms about murdering Rugova's collaborators, whom it accused of the "crime" of moderation. Most recently, although Rugova's recent meeting with Milosevic may well have been under duress, the KLA declared Rugova a "traitor"—yet another step toward eliminating any competitors for political power within Kosovo.

Victimhood as Strength

Worse still is the KLA's systematic, insidious use of civilians for its own narrow and cynical purposes. For all its bluster, the KLA does not pose a serious military threat to Belgrade. It is disorganized, fragmented, and clan-based, and has lost every attempt to control specific areas of Kosovo. More shrewd than strong, however, the KLA's leaders realized that atrocities against civilians would provoke not only Western indignation but also action. To that end, in contrast to most guerrilla organizations, the KLA concentrated its operations in populated areas, confident that the typically brutal Serbian forces, especially the irregular paramilitary groups, would eventually retaliate against civilians. A good example is the February 28 KLA murder of Bogoljub Staletovic, the Serbian police chief in Kachanik. His "sin" was that he was one of the few Serbian police chiefs who did his job well and impartially—and was popular with both Serbs and Albanians. His murder radicalized the Serbs and provoked indiscriminate retaliation—a fresh supply of victims for KLA propaganda. Now, military intervention to protect noncombatants has effectively turned NATO into the KLA's air force. Thus, where the KLA could not gain an advantage with its own might, it finessed one with propaganda.

Propaganda will thrive precisely where knowledge is scarce and emotion fills the void—and here the KLA has found a powerful ally in CNN. It was that network's excitable Christiane Amanpour who reported that "adult men are missing from among the refugees," the implication being that they had been murdered by the Serbs. The appearance of many such men among those at the borders—in footage from CNN itself as well as other news organizations—disproved any such notion, and indicated, if anything, that threatening recruiters from the KLA were, themselves, to blame for the dearth of young men in the crowds.

It was also CNN that claimed that Kosovo Albanian leaders in Pristina, such as Rambouillet negotiator Fehmi Agani and journalist Baton Haxhiu, had been killed, and that Ibrahim Rugova had fled from his burnt out house and was in hiding. Other Western media outlets later found that those "dead" may, in fact, be alive, and Rugova, his house apparently intact, turned up with Milosevic on Belgrade TV. Whether any of those individuals are well, or free, is another issue, but the more significant point is that this sort of "coverage" paints an inaccurate picture, and heightens the anti-Serbian sentiment that the KLA depends on.

The Dangers of Despair

In the face of mounting evidence of the inadequacy and costs of the NATO aerial campaign, which has not spared Kosovo but has united Serbs behind Milosevic, NATO's leaders are casting about for alternatives. Whatever the merits of a ground campaign, providing military aid to the KLA, however, is patently wrong-headed. The only reliable outcome of such a policy would be to turn Kosovo into a permanent battleground—because Serbian nationalism will always support attacks against the KLA's objective of a "Greater Albania."

Furthermore, none of the Balkan states around Kosovo would support a KLA-led Greater Albania. Macedonia and Greece justifiably fear the prospect of an independent Kosovo as a precursor to a Greater Albania. Bulgaria, Slovakia, and Romania likewise see that concept as a direct threat to their own national integrity—given their large and geographically concentrated Turkish and Hungarian minorities respectively.

Reprinted with the permission from http://www.fpri.org, April 6, 1999

NATO AND KOSOVO: AFTER "VICTORY," WHAT?

What is NATO doing in Yugoslavia? First, it said it was bombing the Serbs to make them give up their own territory, as called for in the Rambouillet "accords." Instead, it made all Serbs mad, and Slobodan Milosevic stronger than ever.

Then, it was bombing the Serbs to "protect the Albanians in Kosovo"—half a million of whom have now fled the province.

NATO also bombed the Serbs to "degrade" their military apparatus, but the loss of heavy weapons made little difference to the counterinsurgency being conducted in Kosovo by lightly armed forces and paramilitary organizations. What the destruction of the relatively disciplined and professional army did degrade was the one major threat to Milosevic's power.

Finally, we are told, NATO dropped bombs to "prevent" a spillover of the Kosovo conflict into the entire Balkan region. Instead, the influx of refugees and Serbian cross-border attacks on the KLA have increased internal pressures in Albania, Macedonia, and Montenegro. And because bombed-out bridges now obstruct the Danube, serious economic damage awaits Austria, Hungary, Romania, Bulgaria, the Ukraine, and lands beyond.

NATO Should Be Careful What It Wishes For

But suspend both logic and disbelief for a moment, and suppose that NATO somehow succeeds in breaking the Serbian will to retain Kosovo, that Milosevic is dragged in front of a war crimes tribunal (as he should be), and that Kosovo is brought under NATO occupation. Then what? NATO will have "won" for itself nothing but the obligation to oversee an intractable quagmire.

First, there is the problem of refugees. Macedonia, Bulgaria, Greece, and Montenegro cannot afford the political risks of accepting radicalized Kosovar Albanians within their borders. Western Europeans, already beset by Albanian organized crime, will hardly want to grant permanent asylum to more Albanians. At some point, therefore, many Kosovo Albanian refugees will come "back," not to a province but to a NATO protectorate—and they will confront razed villages, decimated infrastructure, and empty pantries. NATO troops (who else?) will have to serve as police, border patrols, and even social workers, all funded, of course, by NATO taxpayers.

If the alliance seeks to hand the various tasks over to Kosovar political leaders, it will have to find them among the KLA because, simply put, there is no one else. The extraordinary system of peaceful paraellel Albanian statehood in Kosovo, established and led by Ibrahim Rugova's Democratic League of Kosova (DLK) since 1991, would have been far more palatable, but was destroyed by the totalitarian KLA's drive to eliminate competitors for power.

But NATO should be more than reluctant to associate itself with the KLA. Notwithstanding the western alliance's promised protection of "minority" (i.e., non-Muslim, non-Albanian) rights, KLA leadership would likely be a nightmare for the 20 percent non-Albanian population—Serbs, Montenegrins, Gypsies, and others. When communist Albanians had the run of Kosovo as an autonomous province of Serbia within Yugoslavia (1974-1989), they were not known for tolerance. The KLA also has ties to supporters of the late Enver Hoxha—Europe's closest friend to Pol Pot.

For its part, the KLA has little interest in Kosovar autonomy, but rather in a "Greater Albania" to be carved from Serbia, Montenegro, Macedonia, and Greece. Internationally recognized borders matter little to the KLA, which has no qualms about launching attacks from Albanian territory. Albania's feeble government already protests Serbian pursuit of insurgents across the international border. If the KLA has a NATO-protected base in Kosovo from which to work, its neighbors should be justifiably worried about their own frontiers, and about the imminence of "Greater Albania." The irony is that not even many Albanians share that goal, and NATO could find itself responsible for intensifying the Albanian civil war.

To be sure, the Rambouillet texts call for NATO to disarm the KLA, but that is sheer fantasy, and Western leaders must realize the impossibility of the task. Moreover, after the alliance's demonization of the Serbs and denigration of their religious and historical claims to sovereignty over Kosovo, KLA fighters will probably think themselves well within their rights to retain their weapons.

An Untenable Occupation

NATO's military challenges by no means stop there, however. Serbian irregulars, incited by that same NATO dismissiveness, will surely take up the
fight where the army leaves off—and they are long familiar with guerrilla tactics. In fact, since the Tito-Stalin break in the late 1940s, Serb-dominated Yugoslavian military doctrine was centered on irregular warfare—what Tito and his
successors called a "protracted people's war." Casual suggestions that NATO
should occupy Kosovo, let alone Serbia itself, display far more than ignorance
of looming bloodshed.

Are Americans, Frenchmen, Italians, Greeks, and Icelanders ready to accept
the price of "victory" in Kosovo? Did anyone think through the aftermath of
Serbian capitulation? It is time to go beyond cheap slogans ("Arm the KLA")
and ask the real question: what if we "win?" The answers, so far, have been
devoid of any sense of consequences and realistic prospects. Americans, our
European allies, Albanians, and Serbs deserve better.

Setting aside the vague and emotional responses that have dominated so
much of the media to date, we are able to discern one unmistakable conclusion:
long-term NATO occupation of an autonomous Kosovo is untenable. First, as
already discussed, the alliance would find itself in the middle of an armed struggle
between the KLA and Serbian irregulars, a position made more awkward by the
inevitable perception that NATO would be protecting the Albanian side.

Second, the growing reticence among Italians, Hungarians, Czechs, and
Greeks makes the resolute continuation of NATO operations highly questionable. Leftist opposition in Western Europe threatens popular support in France
and Germany as well.

Third, NATO will never be able to overcome the reality of ethnic intolerance
in the region. The Albanian Muslim leader in Pristina admits that ethnic coex-
istence between his people and the Serbs is impossible— and, reluctantly, so
does Serbian Orthodox bishop Artemije of Metojia, the custodian of Serbia's
historic and religious grounds in the province.

Fourth, Serbs will never accept Albanian rule over the Metohija ("Church
lands") region, which includes the most important Serbian sites. No one in
Kosovo finds credible the U.S. and NATO assurances of "protection" for the
sites, because everyone understands that NATO occupation will not last indefinitely. NATO's assumption—that protection of minorities and free access to
historic and religious sites could somehow be guaranteed—confuses Kosovo
with Switzerland.

Partition: Unappealing, Workable . . . and Inevitable

The only way to avoid all these pitfalls, and to make sure that a NATO (or
European Union or United Nations) protectorate does not become as perma-

nent as the peace-keeping forces in Cyprus or South Korea (and far less viable), is to stop tiptoeing around the crux of the matter: the future permanent status of Kosovo. Winks to Albanian separatism, ala Rambouillet, won't do; neither will dreams of Kosovo as a Swiss canton—not for the Serbs, not for the KLA.

To what conclusion, then, does all of this lead? The only hope for resolution is the permanent partition of Kosovo along newly established ethnic lines. It is a solution that will make Belgrade and the KLA equally unhappy, but it takes into account the mutually acknowledged reality of ethnic intolerance.

Partition, moreover, can be done according to lines that should be acceptable to both sides. To do so, NATO needs to consult the Serbian Orthodox Church, which it inexplicably excluded from Rambouillet. The Church has been no supporter of Milosevic, but will never sanction the detachment from Serbia of certain areas in Kosovo. In addition, it possesses—and has used—the moral authority to galvanize broad Serbian resistance to any outside threats to those areas, whether from Albanians or NATO. The key to successful partition lies in the fact that the historic lands vital to the Serbs—Pec, the medieval monasteries of Decani, Studenica, Gracanica, and Mitrovica, and the field of Kosovo Polje—have no particular meaning or importance in the KLA's grand strategy. For the KLA, the goal is not to establish an independent Kosovo—which it realizes will not be viable in any case—but a Greater Albania.

Thus, by taking into account the cultural and strategic needs of both sides, the specifics of a viable solution emerge: a partition line starting from the Albanian border south of Decani, moving in a crescent just south of the road to Pec, Prekale to Mitrovica, and then southeast to and including Gracanica. The line is not only plausible, but also defensible by both sides. Some in Serbia will, of course, object to any seizure of their territory, but at least the Church will have no grounds to use its broad influence to mobilize sentiment against the action. The KLA gets a seed that it must learn to cultivate.

Great Powers in Context

Of course, others, including many in the West, will object that partition smacks of "ethnic cleansing," a feeling stirred by Washington's careless language and persistent ignorance of history—especially that of the Balkans.

It is important to remember that "ethnic cleansing" has not always been shorthand for evil. Just a few decades ago the same actions were described far more benignly as "population exchanges" and seen as a natural, indeed useful, long-term solution to perennial ethnic conflicts. How much worse would Indian-Pakistani relations be without the relocation of tens of millions of people following the end of the British Raj? Closer to Kosovo, some six million Germans were thrown out of their homes in Poland and Czechoslovakia in 1945, despite a history of Germans in the region dating back two thousand years. In 1922 one million Greeks were pushed out of Anatolia—where, some 2,500 years ago, their ancestors in Ephesus and Miletus developed philosophy and the cultural foundations of the modern West. At the same time, half a million Turks were thrown out of Greece, despite 500 years of settlement there. The latter two instances were not just accepted, but encouraged and ultimately codified as the Treaty of Lausanne by the Great Powers—the now more reticent France, Italy, and Britain.

The question of NATO's moral, legal, and political consistency, by comparison, is far less easily resolved. The alliance is bombing the Serbs into accepting Albanian separatism, while keeping troops in Bosnia-Herzegovina to prevent Croat and Serbian irredentism. It wants to detach Kosovo from Serbia, but has made no mention of the highly predictable, possibly violent, impact in the Republika Srbska of Bosnia. Furthermore, if ethnicity is the new criterion for territorial statehood, NATO's simultaneous support of the Macedonian government and the KLA—whose expansionism will inevitably encroach on Macedonia— makes no sense.

Consistency of principles will make it impossible to isolate Kosovo from the larger problem: redrawing borders throughout the Balkans along ethnic lines. The territorial status of Bosnia-Herzegovina as well as of Yugoslavia has to be on the table, because a Greater Serbia, including the Serb-populated areas of Bosnia, is just as "legitimate"—or "illegitimate"—as a Greater Albania. This is not something NATO wants to talk about, but it will be forced to. After the bombings and the establishment of a Kosovo protectorate, Serbian nationalism could easily become a violent and permanent factor for regional destabilization—just as in 1914.

This brings us to the final aspect of the Balkan problem. Although it may seem like political heresy, a return to the nineteenth-century method of dealing with the unruly Balkans is the only solution for the foreseeable future. Specifically, there should be an international conference (perhaps in Berlin, as an ironic twist) to redraw borders according to the newly defined ethnic criteria. The peoples of the Balkans would have little input, their behavior having largely disqualified them already. Rather, decisions should be made by the international powers: not the United Nations, European Union, the Conference on Security and Cooperation in Europe (CSCE), or even NATO as such, but individual members with divergent interests in the Balkans and at least some military, political, and economic means to pursue them. Thus, the participants should include the United States, France, Britain, Italy, Germany—and Russia. The latter suggestion has nothing to do with Moscow's pontifications about "inviolability of borders" and "sovereignty"—after all, it is Russia whose troops and machinations keep the secessionist cauldrons boiling in Moldova, Georgia, and Azerbaijan—but with common sense. Stalin could not solve the Balkan problems, and Russia cannot do so now, but it certainly can make any solution impossible.

Reprinted with the permission from http://www.fpri.org, April 19, 1999

NATO'S KLA PROBLEM

The war in Kosovo ended a few months ago, but the practice of "ethnic cleansing" is flourishing, this time perpetrated by ethnic Albanians who are proving even more adept at it than the Serbs. Whereas Serbian brutality and the war itself pushed only about half of the Albanian population into temporary exile, fully 90 percent of the non-Albanian minority (which numbered about 200,000 at the beginning of the year) have now left the region—this, during three months of "peace" and under the oversight of the United Nations and NATO.

Simply and undiplomatically put, the Kosovo Force (KFOR) and the United Nation's viceroy in Kosovo, France's Bernard Kouchner, are losing their half-hearted struggle to maintain the myth of a "multinational" Kosovo.

The reason: the behavior of the Albanians led by the Kosovo Liberation Army (KLA). First, the KLA and its supporters claimed, probably with some justification, that the Gypsy minority of 30,000 participated in the looting of Albanian property during the war. As a result, the entire Gypsy population was successfully hounded out of Kosovo. The larger Serbian minority has been subject to murder, harrassment, and destruction of Serbian historic monuments, churches, and other property. Almost 300 Serbs were killed by Albanians since the end of the war.

And yet somehow, in the face of incontrovertible evidence of these crimes, the KLA-led Albanians have succeeded in maintaining the widespread perception that they are merely the "victims" of Serbian brutality, and as such, must be beyond reproach.

The problem is that the KLA wants to have it both ways—it seeks international recognition as the effective government of Kosovo while simultaneously denying any responsibility for ethnic cleansing. On the one hand, the organization claims to be in control, and its unelected government claims to be the legitimate authority in Kosovo. It has appointed "mayors," has established what it calls a "police force," and generally acts as if it is the government of a sovereign state of Kosovo—which has been its stated goal ever since Albania's collapse in 1997 made unification with that country an unattractive option in the short term.

On the other hand, the KLA military commander, Agim Ceku, claims that whatever abuses against non-Albanians have taken place are the work of rogue elements over which his organization has no control. His political boss, the self-proclaimed Prime Minister of the "Kosovo government," Hashim Thaqi, even sheds crocodile tears over the fate of minorities. No matter that KLA commanders were directing "spontaneous" Albanian demonstrations and attacks on French KFOR troops in Mitrovica. KLA commanders are in tight control of most, if not all, armed Albanian groups in Kosovo and, thus, directly responsible for the killings of Serbs and Gypsies.

Nor has the Albanian leadership earned any credibility for its adherence to the agreements it signed. On June 21, 1999, Hashim Thaqi signed an Undertaking of Demilitarization and Transformation by the UCK (the Albanian acronym of the KLA). Since then, it has violated each and every provision of that document. According to point 10 (a), it was to cease firing all weapons, and yet Albanians even in Pristina fire at will. Point 10 (d) states that the KLA is not to attack, detain or intimidate civilians; nor is it to attack, confiscate or violate the property of civilians. But the KLA "police" are doing nothing but encouraging and participating in the veritable pogroms that now terrorize the Serbs. Article 23 provides for the KLA to surrender its heavy weapons. It has not, and mortar attacks on Serbian peasants have killed dozens.

What should be obvious is that these violations are not emotional outbursts by isolated individuals. Rather, they are part and parcel of a longstanding KLA policy of emptying Kosovo of non-Albanians, a policy unchanged since ethnic Albanians enjoyed political autonomy in Kosovo from 1974 to 1989. Consider that when the KLA had temporary control over the Drenica area in 1998, its first decisions were to ban political parties and expel non-Albanians.

None of this is surprising, and, in fact, the KLA's deeds are fully consistent with its ideology of authoritarianism and ethnic exclusionism. What is completely inexcusable, however, is the response of the international community. Mr. Kouchner said that he was shocked at what he chose to call "Albanian revenge attacks," as if history began with the Serbian expulsion of Albanians. And how could General Wesley Clark's willfully ignorant claim that there is no evidence of KLA involvement in ethnic cleansing be interpreted as anything but permission to finish the job?

True, the KFOR and Kouchner have few choices at this point, and certainly no pleasant ones. Once NATO went to war portraying Serbs as evil and Albanians as angels, it became impossible to admit that there are no angels in Kosovo, but only a shifting balance of evil against evil. To hope, as President Clinton did, for a "multicultural and multiethnic" Kosovo, or to lament the zero-sum game played by both Serbs and Albanians, as Kouchner did, is nonsensical.

The Western powers' misplaced good-vs.-evil dichotomy was already evident last October, when the United States and NATO imposed a de facto capitulation upon Serbia by requiring it to cease counterinsurgency operations against the KLA. It continued with the June 1999 agreement ending the war, which eliminated all Serbian administrative, police, and military presence in Kosovo—everything, in short, but the pretense that the region was still part of Serbia.

NATO's misjudgment was compounded by the fact that, after it eliminated the Serb presence, it was unprepared to replace it. The porous border with chaotic Albania is left to Italian troops—tantamount to making it even more open. And there is virtually no international police presence to challenge the KLA, the promised Fijians (!) notwithstanding. But most egregious is the lack of any long-term strategy to deal with the KLA.

The cold reality is that, except for a few tenuous Serbian enclaves (parts of Mitrovica being the largest), Kosovo is on the way to becoming a purely Albanian area under the de facto control of a profoundly anti-democratic, duplicitous, and violent organization. And Thaqi and co. are no doubt aware that as the minority exodus from Kosovo nears completion, there will be even less incentive for the KFOR to crack down on the KLA. Worse still, the growth of this totalitarian cancer is being encouraged by the KFOR's inability, or unwillingness, to stop it, and paid for by West European and American taxpayers.

But the costs of the "humanitarian" intervention advocated by Clinton, Blair, and Albright will be measured in more than just dollars. The credibility of NATO, the United States, and the United Nations have all suffered severe damage. And within Serbia itself, the Serbian refugees from Kosovo will join those who left Croatia and Bosnia to create a volatile and vengeful mass of some 800,000—10 percent of the electorate—that will be unlikely to support any Serbian government prepared to accept a more democratic and less nationalistic government. Whether Milosevic or the nationalists of Vojislav Seselj will be able to take advantage of these people's frustrations remains to be seen. What is clear, however, is that they have left their homes behind, but not their grievances.

NATO's bombs are only as smart as its leaders, and victory in Kosovo has so far gone to the tyrants.

THE PROBLEM OF "LONDONISTAN":
EUROPE, HUMAN RIGHTS, AND TERRORISTS

All the perpetrators of the September 11 attacks had some direct link with Western Europe: the leader, Mohammed Atta, and the other three pilots were all linked to an al-Qaeda cell in Hamburg; and the alleged twentieth hijacker, Zakarias Moussaoui, is a French citizen recruited in London. Since September, authorities in Spain, the United Kingdom, France, Germany, Belgium, the Netherlands, Italy, and Bosnia have arrested over 100 al-Qaeda operatives or recruits—compared with less than a handful caught in the United States.

An in-depth analysis of European reactions, statements, and media comments since September 11 suggests that there is only limited understanding of the causes of this terrorism or why the terrorists have found Europe to be a hospitable environment. More important, there is little if any realization in Europe politically and culturally (as distinct from among the intelligence communities) of why these terrorists are a threat to Europe. Ultimately, the whole issue is perceived of as an American problem. (Except, of course, that the EU and America's NATO allies claim a political right to be consulted on the nature and scope of the war on terrorism and a moral right—indeed an obligation—to criticize the United States' conduct of that war and its treatment of captured terrorists.)

On February 6, French foreign minister Hubert Vedrine commented on Washington's "simplicity" for centering its foreign policy on the issue of international terrorism. This is of course from a country where anti-Americanism is a national pastime. But there are also divisions between the U.S. and Europe on the Israel-Palestinian conflict. Witness the widespread pro-Palestinian and often anti-U.S. demonstrations from Stockholm to Milan. With some laudable dissenters (Spain, Denmark, and Italy), the EU also refuses to acknowledge such terrorist groups as the Turkish PKK for what they are: responsible for mass murder in Turkey, a European country, NATO ally, and candidate for EU membership.

All of this raises the basic issue of the balance between the allies' rights and responsibilities within the alliance, and here the asymmetry is enormous. While Britain did provide useful military help in the Afghan campaign and Prime Minister Blair has been Washington's staunchest supporter, more often than not he had to do so against resistance from members of his own Labour Party, including cabinet colleagues. Germany found it enormously difficult to dispatch even a few dozen soldiers to Afghanistan, France needed months to deploy its aircraft carrier to the operational area; and Italy and Spain were both

132

late and largely irrelevant in sending small forces to Afghanistan. In fact, they contributed fewer troops than Australia or even Canada.

But these facts are, in the short term, less important than the more immediate problem of the extensive linkages between international Islamic terrorism and Western Europe. Of the four elements required for the success of an organization like al-Qaeda—recruitment, funding, logistics and planning, and training—all but one, training, is best obtained in Europe. Basic training was largely performed in countries such as Afghanistan and Sudan, but top-level terrorists—that is, the pilots of September 11—were trained in Europe and the United States.

Recruitment

The most "successful" recruiter for al-Qaeda, responsible for both the terrorist conversion of Moussaoui, Robert Reid, and many others and also supporting the assassins of Afghan anti-Taliban leader Ahmed Shah Massoud, was Abu Qatada, a Palestinian from Jordan, sentenced there for terrorist plots. He and the second most important recruiter, one Al Faisal, apparently of Jamaican origin, were both based in England, and both managed to slip away from the Scotland Yard recently. Indeed, the U.K. is clearly the center of fundamentalist Islam in Europe, followed closely by Germany. The latter still harbors Metin Kaplan, Cologne's self-proclaimed caliph (the spiritual head of all Muslims), whose declared goal is to establish an Islamic state in Turkey. He was accused of trying to reach that goal by, among other means, hijacking a plane and using it to destroy the Ataturk Monument in Ankara. Abu Qatada and Kaplan were both given political asylum—the former also received lavish welfare checks from the British taxpayers—on the grounds that, if returned to Jordan and Turkey respectively, they could be tortured or sentenced to death. Amnesty International's "human rights fundamentalists" clearly defeated both common sense and national security. AI's logic, which has been assimilated into the legal systems of the U.K., Germany, and increasingly the EU as a whole, is that those involved in or suspected of mass murder have a right to asylum if the alternative is capital punishment or whatever fits into AI's ever expanding concept of torture. The inevitable result is that the worst of the worst Islamic terrorist ideologues and practitioners see Western Europe as the safest haven anywhere. Call this the human rights paradox: the more extensive the definition and legal protections of "human rights," the more likely it is that those who disregard any human right would feel comfortable with it—and govern their actions accordingly.

Not surprisingly then, terrorists recruited in England—some Britons, some French or Spaniards—were to be found in Afghanistan, Kashmir, Chechnya, Bosnia, Macedonia, and Kosovo. Even French antiterrorist experts talk about "Londonistan," and there is a connection between one of the worst Islamic terrorists from Britain with the London School of Economics, a center of anti-capitalist, anti-Western miseducation for almost a century.

Soon the United States will be asking various European allies to extradite arrested al-Qaeda operatives. Then, if the current European legal practice, elite reactions, and comments on the treatment of the Guantanamo Bay detainees are any indication, the American public will have a shock. In Europe, Islamic terrorists, recruiters, and trainers are seldom seen or legally treated as criminals, unless they murder French, German, or British citizens. Even then, the punishment is very light. Kaplan is in jail with a four-year sentence for conspiracy to murder a rival imam in Germany—not for conspiracy for mass murder in Turkey, or for trying to destroy the only democratic system in a Muslim Middle Eastern country. AI has already demanded, unsuccessfully, the Bosnian government not to extradite six alleged Islamic terrorists linked to al-Qaeda by U.S. intelligence, because in its wisdom they could not receive a fair trial in the United States. For AI, a fair trial is one where the prosecutors cannot request the death penalty. In AI's judgment, this puts the U.S. legal system in the same category as those of Egypt, Jordan, and Saudi Arabia. And this is the concept shared by most European elites.

Funding and Logistics

A Jan. 27, 2002 London Telegraph headline says it all: "British cash and fighters still flow to bin Laden." Political correctness in Europe, far more advanced and pervasive than in the United States, prevents police from even checking on, let alone acting upon, Islamic preachers, fundraisers, and terrorist recruiters—all in the name of freedom of speech, religion, and expression. Muslim charities, mostly of Saudi origin, are out of bounds in the name of freedom of religion. Because these provide the main instrument for funding al-Qaeda-type cells, there is no legal way to control the flow of funds from European Muslims to terrorist groups and causes in the Islamic world.

Planning

There is little doubt that the planning of the two most important al-Qaeda operations—the assassination of Massoud and the September 11 attacks two days later—were carried out with the decisive support of British-based Muslims, especially Abu Qatada, and a Hamburg-based cell led by Atta.

Training

The general training of al-Qaeda terrorist operatives in the West is of a superior level, concentrated in disciplines of direct application to terrorist operations—electronics/computers, math, biology, and economics. That implies lengthy stays in Western countries and familiarity with the ways and languages of Europe or the United States. Most known al-Qaeda operatives—including those arrested in places as remote as Singapore and Malaysia—were trained in the West, usually in sciences. (No known Islamic terrorist was trained in sociology, psychology, or political science, all disciplines seen as haram (impure) by most Muslim states.

What Europe Must Do

All of these facts would suggest the need for greater transatlantic solidarity, especially on the legal questions where big gaps can be seen. Significant voices in France and the United Kingdom demand that their citizens in Guantanamo be tried under their own laws, laws that have no antiterrorism provisions of any importance and, most important, do not provide for capital punishment. But, whatever one's opinion on capital punishment, as a prudential matter, is it wise to jail for life an Osama bin Laden and thus be a target for terrorist blackmail from his Islamic sympathizers for the duration of his life? For the Europeans to participate fully in a war against terrorism, they will have to recognize their laws, attitudes, and policies must also be changed so that terrorists, Muslim or otherwise, do not find their territories a safe haven.

Reprinted with the permission from http://www.fpri.org, April 12, 2002

THE FRENCH ELECTION: EARTHQUAKE, FASCISM, OR WAKE-UP CALL?

A specter haunts the European Union and the multinational elites behind it: the return of the right among voters in more and more countries. Just three years ago Ireland, Spain, and tiny Luxembourg were the odd men out in a fifteen-member club dominated by the Left; all the other members were socialist. Socialism was tinged with totalitarian Marxism-Leninism in some of these countries (France, Italy, and Portugal, where communist support or membership in government was decisive) or moderate in the U.K. and Germany. Today the balance has been reversed: Italy, Spain, Ireland, Denmark, Luxembourg, Austria, and Portugal all have center-right governments, and conservatives have excellent chances to win this year in the Netherlands, Germany, and even France. Socialist Sweden and Finland, Belgium, and Greece are the last redoubts of socialism—except, of course, for the unelected Eurobureaucrats in Brussels.

Which brings us to the results of the first round of presidential elections in France on April 21, where nationalist candidate Jean-Marie Le Pen overtook socialist Prime Minister Lionel Jospin to win a place in the run-off election on May 5 against President Jacques Chirac. Major European newspaper banners proclaimed this an "earthquake," but then most of those newspapers are on the Left. And as far as the European Left is concerned, it was indeed cataclysmic. But for most of the European and even the French public, the "earthquake" was foreseeable and less than historic.

What occurred is relatively simple: within a complicated electoral system, with a larger-than-usual abstention rate and sixteen (compared to the prior record twelve) candidates, President Chirac, the frontrunner, obtained a mere 19 percent, followed by Le Pen with 17 percent and then Prime Minister Jospin. This was only partly surprising, since pre-election polls had suggested the possibility of Le Pen gaining over Jospin or even Chirac. The May 5 run-off election will be the first second-round elections since the 1960s in which the Left has no candidate. This represents not a significantly larger draw for Le Pen—he polled 5.7 percent in the last elections for the European Parliament—but the deconstruction of the French Left, which produced no fewer than six candidates: some democratic but most antidemocratic. This is what worries the European elites, most of them culturally part of the very Left now being rejected in country after country.

Most commentators have been preoccupied with their "shock" at Le Pen's overtaking Jospin, missing some even more interesting facts to glean from the election results:

- The French Communist Party (PCF), whose boss, Robert Hue received 3.5 percent of the vote, the lowest percent of the vote cast for this party's candidate in eighty-two years. The PCF has most likely receded to history, which is delayed gratification for those who always thought that the fall of the Soviet Union would also lead to the end of its historic puppets, such as the PCF or its Portuguese brother. Better late than never. Ironically, Le Pen received some 30 percent of the "proletarian vote" in France—an order of magnitude higher than the self-appointed representatives of it, the Communists.

- The Trotskyite candidates, who advocated the end of both "bourgeois" democracy and "capitalism" received 10 percent of the vote. Their voters were overwhelmingly young, which suggests that totalitarianism is alive and well in France. The Left-Trotskyites claim the communists are "traitors" to the cause of revolution.

- The main issues of the campaign were crime and Muslim immigration. Both Chirac and Jospin were forced by popular pressure into talking about these issues, which have been Le Pen staples for years. However, after his defeat, Jospin accused Chirac of overstressing the crime problem and making it a key issue. It gives one a sense of his party's disconnection to the voters that he evidently truly saw this as an electoral gimmick rather than an issue about which voters were very concerned. The problem was not the reality of crime or uncontrolled immigration, but talking about them.

There is little question that Chirac will win the presidency in the May 5 runoff: Le Pen has clearly tapped the 20 percent at most of the voters who would support him. There is some, but not much, debate whether Chirac and his conservative allies could win a majority in the June parliamentary elections. What is important is simply how Le Pen was able to do so well.

Bad campaigning by Jospin and the splintering of his "governmental Left" coalition (whose four members presented four presidential candidates) are both factors, but what about the total collapse of the Communist Party vote in working-class Parisian suburbs like Saint-Denis in favor of Le Pen? Why are the proletarians deserting "their party" in droves in favor of Le Pen?

The answer, and ultimately the most significant lesson of the election, is that at least for the workers and lower-income French, immigrants—which is to say Third World immigrants in France as in the rest of the West, usually of a different religion (Islam) and language—are seen as a threat. It also means that the French (and one may say European) establishment—whether the Socialists/ Left (Jospin, the communists, and the Greens), who claim that immigration control is "racist," or the conservatives (Chirac et al.), who prefer not to talk about it at all so as not to invite accusations of racism—all ignored real fears by most voters that their jobs, security, culture, and values are under threat. This is the ultimate, if not the only, explanation of Le Pen's success.

The elites ("Chiraquiens" or socialistes), paralyzed by their culture's basic tenet that Third World people should unquestionably be given victim status, were unable to deal with the issue relevant to French voters who have lost jobs through affirmative action or were victims of criminal acts by aliens. Crime control was seen by French elites as a tool of oppression, implicitly in the service of the U.S.-led war on terrorism. The French-based Muslims engaged in terrorism were explained away by politicians who preferred criticizing the United States to dealing with the activities of Islamists in Paris, Lille, and Marseille, and the problem of an unassimilated mass of Algerian youth hostile to the basics of French beliefs and the rule of law. Why? Because to do so would be "racist" and go against the leftist dominant culture of France.

That is where Le Pen comes in. Often accused of being racist and anti-Semitic—in 1987 he described the Holocaust as a "detail" of European history—he is a former Foreign Legion paratrooper with a big chip on his shoulder. From an American and rational point of view, Le Pen's history is more complicated. A self-proclaimed French nationalist, self-proclaimed leftist on social issues and conservative on economic matters, he is a dedicated enthusiast squaring the circle by some inscrutable (and certainly not Cartesian) logic.

Le Pen believes that immigrants, especially from Muslim North Africa, threaten France's cultural identity and explain the high criminality in France (an exaggerated, but not mistaken notion), but he also sees the Anglo-Saxon and American cultures as equal threats, along with the EU (which he feels threatens French sovereignty). In fact, Le Pen perceives attacks on French culture from the Left, Washington, and everyone else.

Back to the EU and Its Future

Ultimately, what the Brussels elites and their supporters among the ivory-tower inhabitants in Paris, Berlin, and London should be worried about is the "democracy gap" between their nations and an EU interested in ever more regulation, establishing a common currency with no regard to popular opinion (in Denmark, where the voters had the opportunity to vote on this, they rejected it), and generally disregarding popular feelings.

As usual, emotion is the last line of retreat; hence the slogan that opposition to unrestricted immigration is racist. Of course, since all the illegal aliens are from the Third World, this makes attempts at border control "racist" by definition. It is this anti-immigration-control sentiment that explains, at least in part, the appeal of Le Pen and his anti-immigration counterparts elsewhere.

Beyond immigration and sovereignty, however, France (and also Germany, the Netherlands, and Belgium, not to mention Sweden) clings to a truly archaic economic system—"socialism" or the "welfare state—from which the rest of the world is retreating. Globalization, the one object of hatred that Le Pen shares with his leftist enemies, is ultimately anti-capitalism, anti-democracy, and (as usual in France) anti-American. In that sense, France post-April 21 is still the old France: claiming intellectual leadership in support of reactionary and passé ideas. This is no "earthquake." Nor is it a great surprise that Trotskyite totalitarians and "lepeniste" rightwingers have met on the same primitive, emotional, and antidemocratic field.

Le Pen's lasting legacy will be the shock he gave the European Left in general and the EU bureaucracy in particular. His success is a repudiation of the concept of giving non-elected bureaucrats and politicians the right to decide issues of national concern for Frenchmen, Swedes, Greeks, or Spaniards. Paradoxically, a politician who despises democracy may well have brought attention to its importance and the need to safeguard it.

Reprinted with the permission from http://www.fpri.org, May 3, 2002

VICHY THOUGHT POLICE

An interesting, and very French, phenomenon is going on in a Paris court: "l'affaire Houellebecq." A fashionable novelist, Michel Houellebecq, is on trial for calling Islam "stupid" and the "most deceiving of religions"; the formal accusation is "racial injuries" and "incitement to hate against the Muslim community"—all penal infractions under French law. The plaintiffs include the Grand Mosque of Lyon, the National Association of Muslims in France, the World Muslim League and, ironically, the League of Human Rights.

All of this may seem odd to Americans. After all, in a democracy there is supposed to be something called freedom of expression. Furthermore, Houellebecq has made it clear that he has no animus against Muslims as persons, just disdain for Islam, and has never sought to incite anything other than the interest of critics, who were largely unimpressed with his latest novel. He did, however, declare that the Quran is "appalling," referring to its literary style.

Now, Mr. Houellebecq does not read Arabic. Most of those who do, Muslims or not, consider the language of the Quran extraordinarily poetic and expressive. For those who read it in translation it does give the impression of incoherence, but that is perhaps an impression to be laid at the door of the translators.

One, therefore, has to pay far more attention to the opinion of Dalil Boubakeur, Rector of the Paris Mosque, who thinks that Houellebecq has "abused, attacked, and insulted" Islam. "Words can kill. Freedom of expression stops at the point it starts hurting." This, of course, brings to mind the late and unlamented Ayatollah Khomeini's call for the murder of the similarly untalented Salman Rushdie, who, in Khomeini's self-discovered competence in literary analysis, had insulted the Prophet Mohammed.

Boubakeur is a moderate by the general standards of European Muslim theologians, far removed from the ideological recruiters of terrorists ensconced in London: Abu Hamza, Abu Qatada, etc. Still, he is convinced that any opinion unfavorable to Islam, no matter whether informed or not, and whether or not it comes from a Muslim, is a crime. This is also the opinion—and policy—of Saudi Arabia, where it is against the law for non-Muslims to even live in the country. It also flies in the face of everything Western democracies stand for: freedom of expression and, perhaps more importantly, the individual's freedom of thought.

The contrast could not be more apparent: American troops defending Saudi Arabia were prevented from celebrating Christmas, as was former President Bush when he visited them. And of course, there is no church or synagogue in Saudi Arabia, by law. That, however, does not prevent the Saudis from asking for the "right" to build esthetically insulting mosques in Europe, from Spain to Sarajevo. It is a crime, and a serious one, to pray to any God other than Allah even in one's home in Saudi Arabia, but surely Muslims in France (and the rest of the European Union) have arrogated the right to criminalize anti-Islamic thoughts.

With apologies to the American triumphalists of the "democracy is on march throughout the world" school of thought, here is a case of theocracy on the march, on the banks of the Seine. And a smart one, too. The accusation against Houellebecq includes "incitement to racial hatred," a claim guaranteed to attract to the cause all self-proclaimed defenders of "human rights." It was the very same nonsensical accusation that brought the assassinated Dutch politician, Pym Fortuyn, to call an (English) interviewer "stupid:" a correct label. Indeed, there is, and never has been, a "racial" component of Islam. One of the first converts to Mohammed's call in the seventh century was a black slave. Since then Europeans, such as French writer and intellectual Roger Garaudy (formerly a Stalinist, a neoleftist, and a liberal), Hispanics (see alleged al-Qaeda terrorist Jose Padilla), blacks (as much as 50 percent of all American Muslims) are all believers in Islam, but what is their "race?" None, of course, but calling Houellebecq "racist" gives a nice sound, not to mention an effective call to arms to all those who hate the West.

There are perhaps as many as 20 million Muslims in Western Europe today, making an increasingly important political lobby. Some, probably most, are content to practice their faith in peace, but many want more. In the name of Western tolerance for their faith, they want to impose non-Western, especially Islamic, intolerance upon their Western hosts. Call this the Saudi infiltration syndrome, or call it the revenge of multiculturalism.

It is tacitly acknowledged that there is a new wave of anti-Semitism in France (and in the U.K., Netherlands, etc), and an older wave of crime by teenagers. It is not openly acknowledged that both are largely the works of young Muslim men, many born in Europe. The larger number of arrests of Islamic terrorists in Europe than in the United States since 9/11 reflects not better police work there, but that Europe is being used as the perfect petri dish for Islamic radicalism. It allows people expelled from Saudi Arabia for religious extremism—which does actually happen, though one can only wonder how—to live in the U.K. at taxpayers' expense; it allows Islamist totalitarians to recruit, fund, and organize under the umbrella of democratic rights, something they cannot do in Egypt, Tunisia, Morocco, or Jordan—to mention only the most tolerant Arab regimes. Simply put, the worst of the political culture of Islam is moving to Paris, London, and Berlin.

When regimes in truly Muslim states—whether democratic as in Turkey, or less than that in Morocco or Algeria—crack down on Islamic totalitarians, the "human rights" protests get very loud indeed. When the Turkish military, behind the scenes, forced the resignation of the Islamic leader Erbakan, a friend of Iran and Libya, that was condemned as "undemocratic." When in 1992 the Algerian military prevented an electoral victory by the Islamic Salvation Front (FIS), the cries of "democracy above all" were heard all over Europe. No matter that everyone knew that Algeria's election was a case of "one man, one vote, one time." Now Islamic totalitarianism has moved to France, England, and Germany, and its pernicious culture is as accepted there as it was admired by "progressive" intellectuals at home—in Iran or Sudan.

What the Houellebecq case represents, for France and beyond, is a new "l'affaire Dreyfus," a new fight for the very cultural identity of the West. It raises existential questions indeed. Is France's court system to become a tool of Islamist intolerants, aided and abetted by self-hating human rights fundamentalists, or is the secular France going to defeat their attacks against its very nature? Are Muslims in France and elsewhere in Europe going to accept that it was their decision to move there and it is their obligation to accept the rules of the receiving society, rather than use the rules against that society? The case is still open, but the prospects are far from encouraging.

Reprinted with the permission from http://www.frontpagemag.com,
September 20, 2002

BRITISH FIFTH COLUMN

On September 28 a march "against war and for Palestine" was held in London. It was, as The Guardian put it, "a big day out in Leftistan." What the police initially described as "four men with beards and a small dog" became a large-scale demonstration of what is becoming a serious threat to Western values, civilization, and security: the transformation of the remnants of the Left into fellow travelers of Islamic terrorism. The sons of "Uncle Joe," Stalin's admirers, have found a new hero in Yasser Arafat and a new victim to defend against "imperialist" (read democratic Western) aggression in Saddam Hussein. This also explains the simultaneous march in Rome, organized by the unreconstructed Stalinists of the Communist Refoundation Party, with the participation of a PLO representative and Bishop Hilarion Capucci, convicted in Israel's courts in the 1970s for aiding PLO terrorists.

The London demonstrators included the likes of London's independent Lord Mayor, Ken Livingstone (so "Red" that it got him expelled from the Labour Party), the Bishop of Bath and Wells, former Labour candidate for prime minister Tony Benn, the by now ubiquitous nuisance Scott Ritter, and, most interestingly, the Muslim Association of Great Britain.

One may wonder what socialists, who are atheistic by self-definition, have in common with Islamic fanatics. Or what Muslims in Britain (I do not say "British Muslims" since many of their leaders have said they do not see themselves as British at all), mostly from Pakistan or Bangladesh, have to do with Palestine. Indeed, what do "Red Ken" and the imams have in common with each other?

The twin slogans in London were "Don't Attack Iraq" (i.e., "Leave Saddam Alone!") and "Freedom for Palestine" (as in, "Leave Hamas Alone!")—a consistent approach indeed, but one that may be puzzling to those who fail to understand the profound moral and conceptual relationship between the Western Left and the equally anti-Western Muslim terrorism.

We must turn to "slogan analysis" to understand this. Osama bin Laden talks about Western imperialism and considers Muslims its victims, too. When he occasionally remembers the Palestinians, he says that they, too, were victims of

Western and Zionist aggression. This is just how the Marxist and anarchist Left see them. Many spokesmen of Islam describe their religion as one of "peace" (never mind the Islamic empires after empires throughout history, or the actions of Mohammed himself), which is as credible as the claims of the present reincarnation of the Coalition for Nuclear Disarmament to be for "peace" rather than capitulation. In the Islamists' case, the pretext for unilateral Western disarmament against Islamist terrorism is that any use of force is "against Islam." For their leftist allies, the use of force is, by definition, "imperialist aggression" and, hence, evil. The intended result is the same: that when an act of provocation puts a nation into the position of having to choose between giving terrorists immunity or using Western (especially American) force against them, one is morally forced to choose immunity. After all, and here again, Osama and "Red Ken" agree—Islam is the aggrieved side, historically victimized by crusaders and imperialists.

Both the Western Left and the Muslims agree that the Palestinians are victims of Zionist aggression and, thus, indirectly, of the American imperialism behind Israel. Implicitly, they also agree that suicide bombers in Tel Aviv restaurants act in self-defense, just as both agree that September 11 was a response to American aggression. Ultimately, what unites them is a common enemy: the United States. That is what promises to make this de facto alliance a lasting and dangerous one. Viewed in this light, when the Stalinist and the pro-terrorist Bishop march together, they do it for reasons beyond opportunism. They do it because they share the same fundamental values.

Consider the recent statement by the communist parties of Jordan, Sudan, Iraq, Syria, Lebanon, and Egypt opposing a U.S. attack on Iraq, even though they all recognize Saddam's long-standing policy of murdering communists. The implicit argument? That between even the appearance of siding with the Great Imperialist Satan and being killed by Saddam, one has to prefer the latter. When Rev. Garth Hewitt, vicar at All Hallows on the Wall in London, condemns those who "seem to think that violence is the solution," he is not talking about Saddam or Hamas, only about Bush and Blair. This is precisely the implicit sentiment of those, mostly clerics, who say that they oppose war because innocent Iraqis may die, which must mean that they prefer for innocent Iraqis to be killed by Saddam Hussein than by Americans.

Islamists have consistently called for the use of the "oil weapon" against the West. But then, so do their fellow travelers on the Left. "This is all about oil," says "Red Ken" (along with the antiglobalist mobs in Washington). The implication—"this is about keeping capitalism and Western civilization going, so we must oppose it"-mirrors Osama's sentiments.

But there are differences. The Palestinian children marching in London and singing about "Sharon and Hitler" would have it wrong in Osama's eyes: to him and his ilk, Hitler was the good guy. It's only the Stop the War Coalition (SWC) that sees the two as the same. No doubt the Palestinian children's parents will reeducate their children in time.

Morally, all this is repulsive. Logically, it makes as much sense as the London activist hawking T-shirts at the march with the sales pitch "Get your T-shirts here! Say no to war! No to Blair's global imperialism! No to Capitalism! Only ten pounds." An accurate, and capitalist, pricing!

Reprinted with the permission from http://www.frontpagemag.com,
October 3, 2002

EUROPE'S NATIVE TERRORISM

All of Britain, Germany, Italy, Belgium, and France have experienced native, middle-class Marxist/totalitarian terrorism in recent decades: Britain at the hands of the IRA since the late 1960s; in Germany, Italy, and Belgium, by the Baader-Meinhoff Gang, the Red Brigades, and the Combatant Communist Cells, respectively, during the 1970s; and in France by Action Directe during the early 1980s. All have defeated it, often with legislation tougher than the legislation they now condemn when applied to Colombia, a country facing a far more serious totalitarian threat than they ever were.

Today, it is Spain that has the dubious distinction of being the only EU member with a serious terrorist problem—albeit the Italian Red Brigades are increasingly showing signs of revival, and the IRA in Ulster, its protestations to the contrary notwithstanding, is still engaged in violence and helps others—like the Colombian communists of the Revolutionary Armed Forces of Colombia (FARC)—to promote "socialist revolution."

In Spain the Marxist/separatist Basque terrorists of the Euzkadi ta Azkatasuna ("Basque Homeland and Liberty")—infamously known as ETA—have murdered some 800 people since ETA's inception in the late 1960s. Those who cling to the myth that terrorism is the result of "injustice, poverty, and the lack of opportunity" should note that the overwhelming majority of ETA's victims—the latest is a six-year-old girl in an August 4 attack—were murdered after Spain became a model democracy upon Gen. Francisco Franco's death in 1975. As for "poverty" as a determinant of terrorism, the three Basque provinces of Alava, Vizcaya, and Guipuzcoa have Spain's highest per capita GDP and receive massive subsidies from Madrid; with respect to "injustice"—the Basque Country (including the three provinces) government is freely elected (and the Basque Nationalist Party [PNV] is in charge of the local government), has control over education, taxation, police, etc.—everything except foreign policy and defense.

It appears that, none of this withstanding, there is a large Basque constituency (some 10 percent of regional voters), and a total of 200,000 supporters of ETA terrorism, according to Madrid professor and *El Mundo* columnist Felipe Sahagun. The ruling PNV has only a shaky majority, considering that most of the 40-plus percent non-Basques in the region vote for the two major Spanish parties: the ruling conservatives of the Popular Party (PP) and the main opposition, the Socialist Workers Party of Spain (PSOE).

Here is the problem faced by Spain now, and by all democracies at one time or another: The "legal" face of ETA is Batasuna, which is represented in the provincial Basque parliament. Members of this "party" have been arrested for involvement in violence, and its leaders make it their principle to never condemn ETA terrorism, even when the victim is a six-year-old girl. As a party, Batasuna receives massive amounts of money from the regional and national governments—money that goes to help ETA terrorists.

The solution supported by PP and PSOE—i.e., by some 90 percent of Spanish voters—is to make Batasuna illegal, since it is simply a mouthpiece for terrorism. A vote in favor of this took place in the Spanish Parliament on August 26. The Marxist Left of the United Left abstained, though they remain in coalition with the Basque nationalists in the regional Basque government. After all, everything that weakens the Spanish "capitalists and bourgeois classes" is good for revolution; the Catalan autonomists are caught between dismay at ETA's atrocities and fear that they could be next; and the PNV opposed Batasuna's illegalization on various pretexts. The real reason is that the PNV and ETA/Batasuna differ only in tactics—violent or non-violent—rather than the ultimate goal, Basque independence.

That, at least, is what most Spaniards believe, and their tolerance has been sorely tested. The striking similarity in the attitudes of the conservative PP and the socialist PSOE suggests a degree of unanimity that promises violence if Basque nationalists of any stripe ever win independence. The PNV is now pushing a referendum on independence not only in the Basque region but in Navarra, Spain, where the Basques are a minority as well as in the French Basque country.

Indeed, for a very long time, France, which neighbors Spain and also has a significant Basque minority, refused to cooperate with Spain, hoping to contain the ETA's activities in Spain. When ETA started attacking French targets, Paris got tough—so much so that by now ETA "revolutionaries" are extradited to Spain within days of their arrest in France. On September 17, senior ETA leaders Juan Antonio Olarra Guridi and Ainhoa Mugica were arrested in Bordeaux in a joint French-Spanish operation. Not surprisingly, ETA has had to move its logistical rear to friendlier areas—and none is friendlier than "progressive" Belgium.

Considering the Basque nationalists' notion that if independent they will still receive massive Spanish or Brussels subsidies, one might think that some EU statement making it clear that a secessionist Basque state will not automatically acquire EU membership could calm down the large Basque middle-class, which now romantically helps the PNV or ETA. Such a statement would force them to make a clear-cut choice between money and sentimentality. There is a good chance the pocketbook would win among enough Basque hearts to marginalize ETA's thugs. After all, Basques are barely a majority, if they are at all, in one of the three "Basque" provinces (Alava), and their nationalist claims to Navarra are clearly bogus.

So, what does all this mean for the U.S. war on terrorism? First, the Madrid government has, so far, been the most cooperative with the United States on Islamic terrorists, and with good reason: Alicante, in Spain's southeast, is a traditional refuge for Algerian Islamic terrorists of the GIA (Islamic Armed Group), and Spain is highly dependent upon Algerian gas and oil supplies. Cooperation between Madrid and Algiers against GIA is, thus, natural.

Then there is Morocco, with which Spain has a long and tortuous relationship. Most of the 600,000-plus illegal aliens now in Spain are Moroccans, and Rabat still "claims" two Spanish towns in North Africa, Ceuta and Mellilla. Morocco should have no reasonable, plausible legal claim to those cities, the people of which want to be Spanish and a majority of whom are still Christian—both towns were conquered by Spain at least 400 years ago. But then, history is not the same as legal right—after all, depending on what historical point is chosen, all of Spain (and Portugal) could be claimed as Islam (that is the view of Osama bin Laden, who refers to "Al Andalus"), a claim that makes no sense at all, other than to Islamic nostalgics of the eighth century.

It appears that whenever the ruler of Morocco has a problem (usually internal and lately with Islamists) he uses the claim to Ceuta/Melilla as an escape valve—that is, when Western Sahara does not serve. On matters relating to Western Sahara, Spain plays the spoiler. It opposes the obvious and rational solution—a Sahara under Moroccan sovereignty—in the name of "decolonization"—as if a pseudo-state ruled by refugee semi-Marxists from Algerian camps is something to be desired. It would be if the goal was to weaken Morocco, but that is not a goal the U.S. shares. Hence the Washington-Madrid conflict at the UN, with Spain claiming to support some right of nomadic, mostly non-Saharan tribes to "independence." It has to do so, since Madrid has made Gibraltar an emotional issue against fellow EU member Britain. Why Gibraltar should be "Spanish," when most residents prefer to be British, and what difference it makes between two NATO and EU members, is not clear to thinking non-Spaniards; but such is the new "Europe."

What is important here is not Spanish idiosyncrasies, or the rather peculiar problem of the EU community's not providing Spain with significant and effective support. It is the EU's general problem in dealing with, or even understanding, the fact that there is a problem with terrorism—domestic or other. Legalistic approaches, such as Britain's preventive detention of suspected terrorists, or the German ban on groups known to be linked to terrorism—are more often than not rejected by courts. Spain's approach, more radical and realistic, is still limited to domestic (i.e., ETA) terrorists. Indeed, as long as existing legal parameters continue to be applied, the terrorist issue will remain intractable in Europe—just as it may in the U.S., once the legal process weighs in on the Bush administration's post-September 11 decisions. In the American case, however, unlike in Europe, there is some awareness that the rules have to be changed to meet the new times, while in Europe, as a whole, this is far from being the case.

Reprinted with the permission from http://www.fpri.org, October 4, 2002

BELGIUM, ISLAM AND THE BOOMERANG OF "MULTICULTURALISM"

With some 20 million Muslims, Western Europe is increasingly having to face the issue of their unwillingness to play by the historic rules of immigration—assimilation and respect for national laws. Long avoided by the cultural and political elites, the issue is being brought to the fore by radical, vocal, and media savvy, albeit often self-appointed spokesmen of the Muslim populations, as well as by an electorate increasingly fed up with high immigrant numbers, criminality, and refusal to adapt to local customs. Not surprisingly, the more "tolerant, progressive, and open-minded" a country, the more likely that such problems become critical. While few European countries are more "progressive and open-minded" than little Belgium, its recent problems with the Muslims serve as a likely preview for the others.

Belgium was this author's first country of contact with the West, after leaving Ceausescu's Romania some decades ago; it was also the historic source of such artists like Rubens and Van Eyck, and the location of such European artistic jewels as Bruges and Gand - or Brugge and Gent, to be politically, and linguistically, correct. Indeed, Belgium is not a country at all but an unstable arrangement between the majority Flemings and the French—speaking, and culturally dominant Waloons, barely kept together by a King and the money coming from Brussels being the "capital of Europe"—the European Union's center—and the headquarters of NATO.

Since 1999, the Belgian government is an absurd coalition, "arc-en-ciel" (rainbow) government of Socialists, Liberals, Christian Democrats, and Greens—of both the Flemish and Waloon (French speaking) versions. Imagine a U.S. cabinet including Al Sharpton, Ralph Nader, Bush, Daschle, and Kennedy—and one that functions, after a fashion, since 1999, in its Spanish and English versions. But, to quote Mark Twain, "I repeat myself…"

The usual spokesman of this strange formation is Foreign Minister Jean Louis Michel, whose outspokenness is only matched by his country's irrelevance in the eyes of both Europeans and the world. For instance, his government decided that it has jurisdiction over all "crimes against humanity," "genocide," and so on, wherever, whenever, by whomever.

At home, as one may expect, the Belgian government is very "tolerant"—so much so as to be a concrete example of what it means to be so open-minded as to have your brains fall out—and is being awoken, rudely, by its own policies. And, recently, that "tolerance" turned out to be self–inflicted poison—as one may logically expect.

Consider the latest developments in Antwerp, the country's second largest city, with a total population of over half a million, of which some 30,000 are immigrant Muslims (many illegal) and 20,000 Jews, who make one of the oldest (some 400 years before the arrival of the Muslims), richest and largest Jewish communities in Western Europe.

In the last few months, under the pretext of the murder of an Arab by a deranged old Fleming, something called the European Arab League (LAE) started organizing "patrols" in the city, to "watch" over the so- called "racist" police—echoes Al Sharpton's anti–police militancy in the Big Apple.

The LAE founder, Abu Jahjah, is *the* poster boy of everything that is wrong and dangerous in Western European Muslim communities—and with European legal, political, and cultural inadequacies to answering that danger.

Born in Lebanon, thirty-one of age, Abu Jahjah arrived in Belgium at beginning of the 1990s, claiming political asylum, due to alleged problems with the southern Lebanon's dominant terrorist group, Hizbollah. His application rejected, he took a simpler way to stay—married a Flemish woman, got his Belgian citizenship and, promptly, divorced.

Then, at taxpayers' expense, he studied political science at the (formerly prestigious) Catholic (!?) University of Louvain, where he became a Socialist Party activist and union militant.

From that fashionable political base, he founded, first, a pro–Arab group, *El Rabita*, later transformed into the LAE. Asked why he choose Antwerp for his activities, his answer was that he was seeking "new cultures"…But, according to the French newspaper *Liberation*, he sees the city as a "bastion of European Zionism" whom he seeks to transform into a "Mecca of pro-Palestinian action." And, not surprisingly, LAE's finances remain a "mystery."

Abu Jahjah's immediate goal, in addition to preventing the local police from dealing with the enormous criminality among immigrant Muslims, is to "simply demand our rights to housing, employment…while preserving our Arab/ Muslim identity." All that because, as quoted in *Liberation*, December 16, 2002, the State "must accept the reality of multiculturalism." That, presumably, means veils for girls, rejection of "pagan" science studies, taxpayer–paid special meals and vacations for Ramadan, lectures in the Quran, and, specifically, making Arabic an official language, in addition to Dutch, French, and German. All these are the logical conclusion of "tolerance," "multiculturalism," and cultural suicide policies of the Brussels government.

Not surprisingly, the people of Antwerp, including, increasingly, its Jews, find the anti–Muslim, anti–immigration (the same thing in that context) Flemish nationalists of the Vlaams Blok—some 30 percent of local votes the last elections, and growing—more and more attractive—at least in the opinion of Nathan Ramet, leader of the local Jewish community.

And what of the "moderate" Muslims? Noureddin Maloujmaoun, leader of the Executive of Belgium's Muslims, pretends that he criticizes Jahjah's methods, but, as usual, there is always a 'but,' shares his demands.

The situation in Belgium, and specifically in Antwerp, is a case study of what Western Europe is confronted with, and refuses to face, because of its own, self–inflicted, cultural, and political problems. Used for decades to instantly, indeed in a Pavlovian manner, accuse any anti–mass immigration, assimilationist, or national identity–based group, party, or politician of "racism," the European elites are now faced with a popular reaction which, instead of being handled politically and rationally, is channeled by extremists—hence Vlaams Blok, Le Pen in France, etc.

The obvious principles, having to do with common sense and basic legal principles, to be applied to the uncontrollable mass of Muslim immigration from North and Subsaharan Africa—overwhelmingly Muslim—are consistently avoided in the name of political correctness. Thus the question of immigrants' obligations—starting with respect for national laws, which make illegal entry a crime – are never examined—just their real or, more often than not, imaginary "rights."

Is polygamy acceptable? The French legal instances prefer to avoid the issue; same with the veil, and that in a country where "*laicité*" is supposed to be an iron principle—particularly on the Left. Same with arranged marriages, sexual mutilation of girls, etc.—all implicitly, if not formally, tolerated in the name of "tolerance"—open-mindedness to the extreme…

Is this coming soon to an American community near you? You bet—already American Muslims' self-appointed leaders are clamoring for treatment similar to that of blacks and Hispanics—never mind that they are richer than the "oppressor" white group, and nothing good can come of it.

Reprinted with the permission from http://www.frontpagemag.com,
December 19, 2002

OLD EUROPE VS. NEW

It has been said that during the 1930s the *London Times* proclaimed "Dense fog over English Channel. Continent isolated." A similar, and equally amusing claim, is now being made with a strong French accent in Paris, Berlin, and Luxembourg.

Indeed, in January, eight countries, including five EU members (the U.K., Spain, Italy, Portugal, and Denmark) and three new NATO members (Poland, Hungary, and the Czech Republic) signed a statement in Madrid supporting the United States' position on Iraq, and on February 5, in Vilnius, ten East European would-be NATO and EU members (Romania, Latvia, Lithuania, Estonia, Bulgaria, Albania, Croatia, Slovenia, Slovakia, and Macedonia) did the same.

"Parade of vassals," fumed a German member of the European Parliament, clearly convinced that the fog over the German-French axis had isolated Europe. Worse still, coming from a country whose language used to be synonymous with diplomacy, French President Chirac recently asked the Central Europeans to "shut up" and cease being "infantile," while at the same time threatening their accession to EU membership. Such petulant outbursts only prove France's isolation. In fact, it takes a huge amount of Gallic sophistication and arrogance to obscure the simple fact that those isolated are the "old Europe" minority, in the words of Donald Rumsfeld. The reasons for this are not difficult to understand.

For the East European former Soviet satellites (or provinces), there are two existential needs: security and economic development. Security, for them, means protection against the traditional aggressors in the region: Germany and, most of all, Russia. The recent joint position of Russia, France, and Germany against the U.S. policy on Iraq cannot but strengthen Central European suspicions as to what a France-dominated EU may mean for their future security. Luxembourg, Brussels, or, for that matter, Paris, simply cannot provide that security: only Washington can. When it comes to economic development, the EU is the most natural source of support, but the relationship between East and West Europe is different: whereas the military contribution of both East and West European nations (with the possible exceptions of the U.K. and Turkey) is marginal at best, compared to whatever actions Washington may take, the economic equation is more complex. The East Europeans need EU investment and aid, but the EU needs (albeit to a lesser extent) East European markets and labor. Hence, the security relationship is far more asymmetric than the economic relationship, a fact that is well understood in Riga, Warsaw, and Bucharest, but apparently beyond the comprehension of the sophisticates in Paris and Berlin.

And then there is the unquantifiable sentiment, so prevalent in Eastern Europe, that during the dark decades of communist oppression it was Washington, who, at least rhetorically, was on the side of anti-communism. It was certainly not France, which still had communist ministers as late as last year, or Germany, which made concession after concession to Moscow and, even more so, to the late and unlamented regime in East Berlin.

Seen from Paris (and Berlin), the future does not seem bright. With the addition of Poland, Hungary, and the Czech Republic to NATO, and the forthcoming admission next year of seven new East European members, old Europe's isolation is bound to increase. And with Poland, Hungary, and the Czech Republic plus Latvia, Lithuania, Estonia, Slovenia, and Slovakia entering the EU soon, the fog over Europe will increasingly isolate France and, unless it changes course and government, Germany as well.

Germany is a special case, since, until recently, it has been a steadfast U.S. ally in every matter that counted. It was largely the absorption of the former East Germany and its resentful and indoctrinated citizens that have influenced Berlin's attitude regarding Iraq. (Of course, Gerhard Schroeder's desperation during the electoral campaign of last year, and his need to retain the support of the Greens, many of whom remain "like melons—green on the outside, red on the inside.") Add to this the economic stagnation of the past decade, the burden imposed by Berlin's huge contributions to the EU (mostly the price of French amour, and given the enormous cost to the EU, especially to Germany, of subsidizing a noncompetitive Gallic agriculture), and the catastrophic loss of credibility of Schroeder's administration with German voters since its narrow reelection this past November, and the German crisis is structural. Berlin's growing international isolation only makes matters worse.

As to France, its attitudes toward the United States are so regularly peculiar as to be predictable. But this is a power in such a state of decay that it is incapable, at this point, of even controlling events in its former showcase ex-colony, the Ivory Coast. Even its language is losing so much international prestige that the Francophonie—the loose association of countries where French is supposedly spoken—has felt the need to include Bulgaria and Vietnam, and held its last summit in Lebanon—a country whose French-speaking nationals are far more likely to live in Paris or Detroit than in Beirut.

All in all, while only the dreamers of a French-German alliance in control of the EU could still take seriously the notion of a mythical "Europe" as a counterpart to America's "hyper-puissance," the reality checks of Madrid and Vilnius suggest that the political, and indeed ideological, map of Europe is indeed changing for the best: away from isolationist games with an anti-American subtext and toward geopolitical realism.

Reprinted with the permission from http://www.fpri.org, March 12, 2003

HOSTAGES, TERRORISM, AND THE WEST

A number of recent developments in the war on international Islamist terrorism should raise serious questions about the nature of the terrorism threat and the seriousness of the responses to it. These developments, in one week in August, clearly show who the terrorists' targets are, and also what to do and what not to do about the threat.

First, how not to do things. On August 19, fourteen European tourists—nine from Germany, four from Switzerland, and one from the Netherlands—who had been kidnapped earlier in the year—were released by their captors, the Algerian Islamist terrorist Salafist Group for Preaching and Combat (GSPC). These fourteen tourists were part of a larger group of thirty-two who were kidnapped in February 2003, of which seventeen were freed in May by an Algerian military operation. One forty-six-year-old German hostage died in captivity in June.

This saga raises some obvious questions: Why were a group of European men and women ranging in age from fourteen to sixty-two traveling without a guide in one of the most remote parts of the Algerian Sahara—a country that has been convulsed by a civil war since at least 1992 (begun by factions of the Islamic Salvation Front) that has left some 100,000 people dead? And why did the Algerian authorities allow them to enter the country? Why did their own governments not post travel advisories on Algeria?

But there is worse still. Even after the Algerian military successfully liberated more than half of the hostages, it appears—the details remain murky at this time—that there was strong pressure on the military not to liberate the remaining hostages. The pressure appears to have come from Berlin, Bern, and, possibly, the Hague. Instead, the terrorists were allowed into Mali, whose government was forced into the position of main negotiator.

According to past practice and current media reports (German and Algerian), the German, and likely the Swiss government, paid a large ransom: as much as 1 million euros per hostage. This is unsurprising for the German government, which, after all, has a sad history of dealing with terrorists by appeasement and money. In 1974 it paid 2 million marks for the release of a citizen kidnapped in Chad; and according to reliable Turkish sources, it made a deal with the terrorist Kurdish Workers' Party (PKK) to permit the PKK to operate freely in Germany in exchange for not engaging in violence there. To make matters still worse, the Khadafi Foundation, run by Moammar Khadafi's son, Saif al-Islam, claimed to have played a major role in liberating the hostages—just as it had claimed in 2000 that it "mediated" the liberation of French and German tourists kidnapped by another al-Qaeda associate, the Abu Sayyaf group in the Philippines. True or not, this raises questions. The prevailing rumor in Germany is that the Mali government paid the terrorists and that the tourists' home countries will compensate it via "development aid."

Turning now to the beginning of the same week, on August 11, Riduan Isamuddin, a.k.a. Hambali, al-Qaeda's leader for the Southeast Asian region and also leader of the regional al-Qaeda affiliate, Jamaa Islamyyia (JI), was captured in Thailand. Isamuddin was responsible for last year's Bali bombing that left 200 dead and the more recent bombing of a Marriott in Jakarta—operations that resulted from a decision taken in February 2002 at a Bangkok meeting of the JI to shift its attention toward "soft targets" such as hotels and bars, and away from more difficult targets such as U.S. embassies.

Which brings us to the bombing of the UN compound in Baghdad on August 19, in which the UN's chief official in Iraq, Sergio Vieira de Mello, a committed international civil servant, was killed, along with at least nineteen others; with at least another 100 injured.

UN spokesmen expressed "shock" at the attack, since the UN was only doing good works for the Iraqi people. This is a tragic example of blindness. Just as the European tourists acted in disregard of Algerian realities, the UN appears still to be unmindful of the reality of Islamist global terrorism—even in the face of Osama bin Laden's numerous statements that he and his colleagues see the UN as an enemy, a Zionist and American tool, and, thus, a target (and a soft one at that). The problem is not only, or primarily, that Vieira de Melo was murdered: many UN officials have lost their lives throughout the world over the years. The problem is that the UN, by describing the Baghdad attack as "meaningless," is still missing the point, which is that the UN—no matter how consistently it opposes the United States—remains an Islamist target; because the UN is not Islamist, period. Perhaps the tragedy in Baghdad may awaken the UN, but early signs are not encouraging.

All of these recent events are easier to understand if seen in the context of some basic realities of Islamist terrorism and the global responses to it. First, close and persistent cooperation at the intelligence level works, as Hambali's capture in Thailand (a country that, until recently, had taken the very UN-like position that "there is no terrorism here") following his pursuit across Malaysia, Myanmar/Burma, Laos, and Thailand.

Second, paying ransom, no matter how disguised, is worse than counterproductive. The millions of euros the GSPC is rumored to receive will, in no time, translate into thousands of Algerians murdered, and al-Qaeda's being strengthened.

Third, and most important, the attack against the UN should make it abundantly clear that one simply cannot be "half pregnant" when it comes to dealing with international terrorism. This is not some sort of simplistic, neoconservative Manicheism but a fact of global life. There is, indeed, a global conflict between fundamental Islamists and the rest of the world. The Islamists' war is against the UN and hundreds of millions of peaceful Muslims, not just America.

Reprinted with permission from http://www.fpri.org, August 27, 2003

NORWAY'S TERRORIST HAVEN

Norway has long been a reliable NATO member and supporter of U.S. foreign policy. It sent a small number of excellent, mountain-trained troops to Afghanistan and has always been willing to mediate in difficult situations ranging from the Israeli-Palestinian conflict to peace talks between Sri Lanka and its murderous secessionists, the Tamil Tigers. That is why Norway's recent dispute with Washington over a terrorist case is so disturbing. If a normally quiet, reliable ally like Norway could hold the kind of position it did, we should expect even less from the likes of France, Germany, or Belgium.

Faraj Ahmad Najmuddin, a.k.a. Mullah Krekar, is an Iraqi Kurd who fought in Afghanistan against the Soviets and established close links with Osama bin Laden and the al-Qaeda nebula from its beginning. Soon after 9/11, Krekar and some associates established an organization named Ansar al-Islam ("Supporters of Islam") near Halabja, in an area of Iraqi Kurdistan close to the Iranian border. According to Qobad Talabani, the Washington representative of the Patriotic Union of Kurdistan (PU.K.), one of the two major Kurdish organizations, "This is a man who trained in bin Laden camps and has clear ties to al-Qaeda and the Taliban." ("Al-Qaida cohorts still active in Iraq," Insight, Feb. 4, 2003) In fact, Ansar al-Islam was a smaller, Kurdish version of the Taliban. During its control of ten remote villages, it banned music, forced women to wear the burka and men to grow beards, and made collective prayers compulsory. It was Kandahar under Mullah Omar all over again.

Ansar al-Islam, which at the peak of its influence had some 1,000 fighters (including hundreds of Arabs, mostly al-Qaeda types and all fundamentalists), also had close links to, and harbored, Abu Musab Zarkawi, a Palestinian and known al-Qaeda operative who specialized in chemical and biological weapons. More concretely, Ansar al-Islam was involved in a number of assassination attempts on PUK. leaders, some successful. Thus, it murdered a prominent PUK military commander, captured and killed by mutilation dozens of PUK fighters, and tried to kill the PUK's prime minister, Barham Salih (Salih was not killed, but five of his bodyguards were).

Ansar al-Islam is known to be, like its friends in the Taliban and al-Qaeda, ferociously anti-American and anti-democratic. Considering its links with Arab terrorists and dependence on their financial support, it is likely anti-Kurdish as well. Its reign had seemed to come to an end this year, when U.S. airpower, and PUK land forces, dislodged it from its mountainous redoubts and forced the survivors to flee to Iran. However, and with Iran's tolerance, if not support, it has come back again, this time in newly liberated Iraq, and is among the prime suspects behind the chain of bombings in Baghdad, Mosul, and elsewhere. Considering this history, one may think that Krekar is an international terrorist on the run, but one would be wrong.

Indeed, since 1991, Krekar, his wife, children and brother enjoyed comfortable political asylum in Norway, presumably because the nice, humanitarian Norwegians thought that a Kurd in Saddam's Iraq must ipso facto be an innocent victim. The idea that an ethnic Kurd might also be a worse threat in Iraq and elsewhere than Saddam himself never seems to have crossed the mind of Oslo's immigration officials.

But then strange things happened and matters became "curiouser and curiouser." With his Norwegian passport in hand, Krekar repeatedly "visited " Iraq and Iran—the very countries whose alleged persecution of his poor self provided the main argument for his asylum application. In September 2002, while back from Iran, Krekar was arrested upon arrival in Amsterdam (on a KLM flight from Tehran) under suspicion of being just what he was: a terrorist. The Jordanian government asked for his extradition under a drug trafficking charge, and the United States wanted to "visit with him," as Secretary Rumsfeld would call it. Here a disturbing, and indeed a foreboding, pattern emerged.

The Dutch rejected the Jordanian extradition request because they, like all EU governments, believe Amman is too harsh on terrorists—why, they are rough in interrogating them, and if he were found guilty he could even be executed. But they could not just let Krekar go, because Washington was also interested. So Holland threw the hot potato to the Norwegians and expelled Krekar to Oslo.

There, Krekar claimed that he did not want to be "a problem for Norway" but, as the Oslo Aftenposten newspaper noted, he already was. And the strange (for Americans and certainly for Texans) wheels of Viking justice slowly started to move. First, the Ministry of Local Development, finding that Krekar had made false statements upon applying for asylum, withdrew his Norwegian passport and revoked his residence and work permit. But then, Krekar had never had to work in Norway, which had granted him a charitable grant for his religious activities. (Michael Howard, "Kurdish Extremist Leader Arrested at Airport," *Guardian*, Sept. 14, 2002)

Then, after reviewing U.S. information proving the terrorist nature of Krekar and his Ansar al-Islam, Oslo decided to go a bit further and actually expel Krekar, but to where? Jordan, of course, was out of the question, and the United States, too, was cruel and inhumane, with its capital punishment laws. Obviously, a revenge-oriented Iraq was not the place for a terrorist's rights to be protected. So, for now, Krekar remains in detention (complete with marital visits, color TV, etc.) in Norway as a terrorist with no rights of residence. He has started what is sure to be a lengthy appeal process. Since there is now proof that Krekar raised funds for terrorism and had telephone contacts with known al-Qaeda operatives in Italy, he may be convicted, which would be egg on the faces of Norwegian immigration bureaucrats, but then what? At the very worst, a few years in a comfortable prison, liberation in Norway, and then residence there since no country would accept, or be considered by, Norwegian legal lights, safe for a terrorist.

The Krekar case is a clear indication of what Washington can expect from Europe. Hundreds of terrorists, most of them associated with al-Qaeda, Algerian Islamist murderers, or others of the same kind, have been arrested throughout Western Europe, but since most have not committed their most serious crimes there, they are only being charged with the bank robberies or credit card fraud, etc., they engaged in for fundraising purposes.

The most effective recruiters and religious enablers of Islamist terrorism are based in Europe, and they do not, as a matter of course, "kill" anyone. That almost all of them are also under life or death sentences in countries such as Egypt, Jordan, Saudi Arabia, Algeria, Yemen, and Morocco, actually strengthens their case for asylum in Europe. After all, they have a right to freedom of speech, don't they? As long as Norwegians, British, Danes, Belgians, or Dutch do not get killed, they have a right to recruit murderers of Egyptians, Jordanians, Algerians—and Americans.

U.S.-European relations are already frayed, largely over France's position at the UN in the run-up to Iraq. But when Joe Six-Pack finds that terrorists who killed or planned the killing of Americans are let free to do it again in Europe, those animosities will become much deeper than mere disputes among diplomats, turning into real dislike.

Reprinted with permission from http://www.frontpagemag.com,
September 18, 2003

MULTICULTURALISM: SUICIDE OF THE WEST?

Is "Islam," at least the version practiced in the West, compatible with Western values, democracy, traditions, and history? This issue is largely avoided in the United States, under the rug of "diversity" and "multiculturalism." If not, are "Islam" and its never-challenged "representatives" to be seen as a danger? What is to happen when freedom of expression and religion conflict with democratic rule, separation of religion and state, and with the more important, but less legally defined, concept of national identity? Do nations and their voters have a right to a distinct cultural identity and history of their own, or are they forced to give up that identity for the sake of "diversity, " multiculturalism" and "anti-racism?" Americans, or at least American business and cultural elites, in a strange alliance, are still sleep walking around these issues. However, Europeans—especially the French, Germans, and British; that is to say, the largest powers—cannot do so anymore, as a number of cases in France and Germany are proving.

On October 10, Lila, age eighteen, and Alma Lévi, age sixteen, were expelled from their high school at Aubervilliers, in the suburbs of Paris, after repeatedly refusing to remove their Islamic headscarves. At about the same time, Germany's highest court in Karlsruhe decided that an Afghan-born teacher can not be denied employment for wearing the scarf because there is no state law against it. The court also invited German states to pass laws in that respect. Six of those states, including Bavaria and Berlin, already expressed the intention of doing so by banning the headscarf. Some of these states are led by Christian Democrats, some, like Berlin, by Social Democrats and Communists.

But it is in France where the debate is more serious, protracted and, considering France's significant, albeit declining, cultural influence in Europe, most significant. The issue of the Islamic scarf, everybody agrees, goes far beyond the whims of two impressionable teenagers, to the very fundamental issues of *laïcité* (secularism) as a fundamental aspect of the French Republic. It also reflects the ability, or lack thereof, of the country's millions of Muslims to integrate in, or accept the values of, the French society. In a larger context, the issue raises some fascinating dilemmas for the Left, inasmuch as it conflicts between its historic hostility to religion and religious symbols and its beliefs in "multiculturalism," with a promiscuous definition of tolerance.

A case in point is the League of Human Rights (LDH), an organization typical of the "progressive" nature of most such groups everywhere. Founded in 1898, it is older than most. It reacted to Alma and Lila's expulsion by "affirming its attachment to the *laïcité* in schools, and the society as a whole," but, "precisely because it considers *laïcité* one of the fundaments of the Republic," it has taken the position, since 1989, that excluding girls wearing the scarf is a denial of their right to education. This contorted, and ultimately unintelligible, argument is prevalent on the Left—the very Left that, until last year, was in power. Not surprisingly, the same "logic" is used by the two girls, no doubt under the combined coaching of their father, a self-described "atheistic Jew, a man without religion" and lawyer of an "anti-racist" organization. (Their divorced and dissenting mother is an Algerian Berber Catholic convert.) The girls' recruiters to Islam, the Union of Islamic Organization of France (UOIF), is the most fundamentalist Islamic organization in France.

Not all the Left is on the girl's side. SOS-Racisme, an NGO linked to the Socialist Party, approves of the expulsion. Meanwhile, the ruling center-right government is openly split between those, including the Prime Minister, who want to legislate the ban on scarves, and the popular Interior Minister, Nicolás Sarkozy, who does not. What is interesting is that the Left couches its condemnation of Alma and Lila, not in the name of secularism, but of feminism. The scarf is seen by these leftists as an insult to women, women's rights, and feminist ideology, not as its far more important status as a recent symbol of an attack on Western culture and civilization from a *revanchist* trend of Islam.

The problem is that UOIF, an offshoot of the Muslim Brotherhood (which is heavily subsidized by Gulf money), is adept at manipulating existing law and prevailing social mores to promote its own agenda—an agenda that includes Islamic schools, the first of which opened in September. Where the state refused to accept Muslim students wearing Islamic symbols, it would strengthen UOIF's call for more private Islamic schools—soon to become the equivalents of Pakistani *madrassas* and Indonesian *pesantren*: recruitment centers for radicals in the country of the Enlightenment. It is indicative that UOIF's very name, "of France" rather than "French," suggests "exile" in the Islamic sense of the word.

While France, with some 5 million Muslims—or, more precisely persons originating in Muslim states (Morocco, Algeria, Tunisia, etc.), approximately half of whom do not practice Islam—is now forced to face the issue of Muslim integration, so is Germany with its 3 million Muslims. But the United Kingdom (2.5 million Muslims), and other European countries, seem to believe that this is a non-issue, considering it politically incorrect to even discuss the matter.

Thus, a Muslim girl wearing a scarf in a British school has no problems whatsoever. For that matter, an educated Pakistani Muslim businessman who speaks no English after years of living in Britain on an uncertain immigration status, had no trouble being elected to a local city council and demanding the taxpayers pay for a translator in order for him to do his job. That explains why counter-terrorism analysts coined term "Londonistan."

But the U.K. is not alone. In Belgium, Italy, and Netherlands, as well as in Scandinavian countries, the scarves are accepted, although the all-covering, Taliban-style *burka* led to controversy in Göteborg (Sweden). The Danish People's Party also pushed for a ban of the scarf, thus far without success. On the other hand, a group of Gulf-funded Spanish converts recently opened a mosque in Granada—the last place Islam ruled in Western Europe—clearly a provocative and ultimately *revanchist* act, tolerated by a conservative government. To make its intention clearer, the same group is lobbying hard to stop the local annual celebrations of the 1492 conquest of Islamic Granada by the Catholic Christians, much like "Native American" activists trying to throw Columbus out of history in the name of political correctness.

From Aubervilliers to Karlsruhe to Göteborg to Granada—and perhaps soon, Detroit—the issue appears to be more or less the same. It is not nearly as confusing or "complex" as the liberals would make it. Are Western values, like freedom of religion and secularism, to be sacrificed as "outdated" in a "multiculturalist" entity? How ironic that the same people who applaud the prohibition of *any* church or synagogue in Saudi Arabia support a "democratic right" to build Europe's largest mosque very close to the Vatican.

One the positive side, just as half of French "Muslims," like Alma and Lila's mother, are "non-practicing" (or more accurately, practicing their religion at home). Muslims in the West need not lose their faith. But perhaps the nations of the West need to restrain its immigration policies, and beyond that, to discuss the broader question of national identity and *laicité*.

Reprinted with the permission from http://www.frontpagemag.com,
November 5, 2003

THE FALL OF SPAIN?

The outcome of Spain's March 14 elections is the worst news ever since the jihad against civilization began more than a decade ago. More than a tenth of the electorate in a major Western democracy has demonstrated that mass murder pays, and, thus, invited more of it. America is losing a major ally, and the struggle against Islamist terrorism has suffered a major setback. If Spain is a model, the Europeans are clearly not mature enough to understand, let alone deal with, the global threat posed by the Islamist barbarians, and the gulf in the Atlantic is wider than ever.

Prior to the March 11 bombings in Madrid, which left 200 dead and over one thousand wounded, and three days before the general elections, the ruling Partido Popular of Prime Minister José Maria Aznar was ahead in the polls by some 5 percent, and Aznar's designated successor, tough former Interior Minister Mariano Rajoy, seemed a shoe-in to continue the eight-year-old PP government. The latter had a very solid record of accomplishments—it transformed what used to be a large backwater of Europe into the world's eighth largest economy and one of the fastest growing economies in an otherwise stagnant Europe.

Under the PP, Spain became highly respected in Latin America and in European Union's councils; it dealt resounding defeats to the Basque terrorists of the Euzkadi Ta Azkatasuna—ETA. Aznar's foreign policy was that of a true statesman—a rarity in today's Europe. Against the overwhelming sentiments of the majority of his anti–American citizens, he strongly supported the United States in the war against terrorism, sending troops to Afghanistan and Iraq at the cost of Spanish lives, and was both active and effective in hunting down Islamist terror cells in Spanish territory.

By contrast, the internal opposition was playing to a different tune. The Basque politicians of the regional government, insufficiently pleased with enjoying the highest standards of living in Spain, pushed for total independence and took an ambiguous position vis-à-vis ETA's legal fronts. The main opposition, the PSOE (Socialist Workers' Party), trying to ride the anti-American tide, opposed the war in Iraq, and its Catalan branch's allies were dealing with ETA.

And then the bombings took place—and many Spaniards decided that capitulation is the best part of valor, that mindless fear and manipulation are more powerful than common sense, civic values, and pride. Despite public disclaimers by the PSOE leader and next Prime Minister, José Luis Rodríguez Zapatero, and a national period of mourning and a declared suspension of the electoral campaign, PSOE operatives in Estremadura and elsewhere were inciting masses of party militants and clueless students to demonstrate against the government. The slogans used tell it all, in full stupidity and mendacity: "We want the truth before voting," "Our dead, your war," and "The people does not believe the lies of the PP." It all sounded as if Dennis Kucinich was suddenly cloned.

First the mendacity—"We want the truth before voting!" The bombings occurred on Thursday, and the government was rapidly moving the investigation ahead. French, British, American, and Israeli help was requested and received; the Moroccan government, normally not in good relations with Madrid, was cooperating; and arrests were being made. The government, naturally enough, was in the midst of dealing with a humanitarian disaster, while openly informing the public of both main directions of investigation—ETA and Islamic terrorists. No government could have done better or differently, and there were no "lies."

Second, the stupidity—"Our dead, your war!" screamed ignorant youths with "Peace" signs. Translation: Aznar's participation in the war against Islamic terrorism and Saddam's criminal regime was responsible for the deaths on Thursday. To begin with, that assumes that the demonstrators knew better than the government who the perpetrators were, and that they were Islamists—an assumption based on flimsy evidence. While there are some indications that an Islamist group was behind the attacks—and three Moroccan and two Indian Muslims were arrested—that is far from sufficient. The al-Qaeda associated group that initially claimed responsibility for the bombings, has also claimed the same for last August's New York area blackout—a patently false claim. On the other hand, there are also strong indications that ETA could have been behind it, despite its denials.

Further, it assumes that fighting terrorism produces terrorism, an argument repeated here by a number of Democrats and other war opponents who believe that removing Saddam made al-Qaeda mad. Finally, "your war" clearly means Aznar's, and implicitly America's war and, thus, places the blame not on Islamists but on those opposing them, and demonstrates, once again, the intensity of the mindless anti–Americanism haunting Europe. Never mind that Bin Laden has, for years, declared that he sees the Islamic "recovery" of Al Andalus (Muslim Spain and Portugal of the eighth through the fifteenth centuries) as one of his goals. Are those clueless, or ill-intentioned, sloganeers suggesting that Aznar should have returned Spain to Muslim rule in order to prevent the Madrid attacks? This is defeatism of the basest kind.

The result of all this was that from being 5 percent ahead in polls on Wednesday the PP lost 43 percent to 36 percent on Sunday—a shift of 12 percent, the number of clueless and irresponsible Spanish voters. That is a large number and one that raises questions about the maturity of the Spanish electorate, questions that would have appeared preposterous just a week ago.

What are the implications of this for Spain? They may well prove very costly indeed. A successful, market oriented economic policy will be replaced with the very kind of statist, socialist blunders that have brought stagnation to Germany, France, and Belgium. A consistent and tough line on Basque and Catalan separatism will, at best, be replaced by vacillation, inconsistence, and compromise. Economic growth and Spanish competitiveness will slow down. And, from being a staunch ally of the United States, Zapatero's Spain will join France, Belgium, and Germany in opposing Washington on issues ranging from the war on terror to Cuba and Iraq. Indeed, Zapatero already made it clear that he will withdraw the 2,300 Spanish troops from Iraq by August—unless, that is, he obtains the blessing of the United Nations.

In Europe, Aznar was a key member of the group trying to contain the ambitions of the Paris–Berlin axis; Zapatero will likely join or cheer it on. But the most important lesson to be learned from Spain is the most depressing and the one most likely to be assimilated by the terrorist networks the world over—in a Western democracy, terrorism, if massive enough, pays. If the so far unproved suspicion that Islamists were behind the Madrid bombings, on a background of a Pavlovian anti–Americanism, was enough to turn 12 percent of Spanish voters against their own highly successful government, rather than the actual mass murderers, what is there to prevent others like them from thinking that killing a few hundred Britons, Germans or Italians, on a similar background, will be equally successful? If the Madrid bombers were Islamist (and even if not), the murder of 200 innocents advanced one of their strategic goals—intimidating and disarming the West and isolating the United States. If Spaniards are scared enough by terrorism to distance themselves from America, what could we expect from far weaker governments elsewhere? What happened in Spain on March 14 is *jihad*'s greatest victory to date—far greater than September 11, greater than Bali and Madrid or even the temporary takeover of Afghanistan—a dark day indeed.

Reprinted with the permission from http://www.frontpgemag.com,
March 16, 2004

SPAIN'S SOCIALIST SURRENDER

The election of Spanish socialists on March 14 is a major setback for the fight against terrorism, both within Spain and around the world. The Spanish Socialist Workers' Party, whose leaders once colluded with Josef Stalin, are now threatening to become the allies of the worldwide Islamist jihad. If their history is chilling, their plans for the future are even scarier.

On March 14, the Spanish Socialist Workers' Party (Partido Socialista Obrero Español—PSOE) won a relative majority in Parliament, and is likely to form a government coalition with Catalan and Basque left-wing parties. It was an unexpected victory, due to extraordinary events—the Madrid bombings of March 11—and goes against the general trend of European politics where, in country after country, the Left did poorly the last few years. (This is demonstrated most recently by the defeat of the long-ruling Greek Socialists.) But the PSOE had had a rather peculiar history from its beginning in 1879, which makes it the oldest Spanish political party. Its leader, Prime Minister-elect José Luis Rodriguez Zapatero seems to be an odd character himself.

The PSOE began as a Marxist party, and for many decades it lived a precarious existence in the shade of anarchists—Spain was the only European country with a strong and lasting anarchist movement. Its newspaper, *El Socialista*, only began publication in 1886, and a trade union, the UGT (General Workers' Union), was first taken over in Barcelona in 1888. The first Parliament deputy, party founder Pablo Iglesias, was not appointed until 1910. Throughout the convulsed period leading to the Second Republic and the 1936 election, the PSOE was intensively infiltrated by Marxist-Leninist elements, and the massive nationalization of industry was its main political stand. When the PSOE leader,Francisco Largo Caballero became Prime Minister in September 1936, the country was already in the midst of civil war, with the Communists—hence, Stalin's—influence growing. It is indicative of the ideological state of the party at the time that Largo Caballero, leader since 1925, was a relative moderate. Bear in mind, Caballero has called for "the conquest of political power by the working class by whatever means possible" and the "dictatorship of the proletariat organized as a working-class democracy." When this rhetoric made him too moderate for his party, and for Stalin, he was replaced by fellow socialist Antonio Negrín, who, under Communist control, led the Republic to its final defeat in 1939.

Following Francisco Franco's nationalist victory, the PSOE in Spain was virtually destroyed for decades, and the exiled leadership further marginalized itself by retreating into dogmatic Marxism. It was during the 1960s, following a relative liberalization of the regime, that young activists led by Seville lawyer Felipe Gonzalez began the reorganization of the party. Under the moderating influence of the West German Social Democrats, the internal leadership went beyond Marxist dogma and ideological purity and established links with non-leftist opposition to the regime. At the party's 1974 Congress, Felipe Gonzalez was elected Secretary General. Following the first free elections since the Civil War, held in June 1977, the PSOE became the main opposition party, with a little more than 29 percent of the vote.

Nevertheless, the old dogmatism continued, as did the historic attachment to Marxism, even when the Communists themselves became more moderate "Eurocommunists." It was only at the 28th Congress in May 1979 that the issue came to be openly debated, and Gonzales' efforts to renounce Marxism—eighteen years after the German Social Democrats did the same, one may add—were temporarily defeated. He resigned in protest, but an extraordinary Congress (in September 1979) reversed the previous decision, reelected Gonzalez and dropped Marxism from the party's constitution.

In 1982, the PSOE won the elections and formed a government under Felipe Gonzalez, who retained power until 1996. The Gonzalez regime had some clear accomplishments—Spanish membership in NATO and the EU, economic progress, and, most importantly, the transformation of Spain into a "normal" Western democracy. It was also increasingly corrupt, inefficient, and its foreign policy often failed to support pro-Western forces. This is especially true in Latin America, where Gonzalez cozied up to Fidel Castro.

Faced with continuous Basque terrorism, Gonzalez did take a hard line—including the use, or tolerance of secret operations in France, through the Antiterrorist Liberation Group (the Grupo Antiterrorista de Liberacion, or GAL)—admittedly as a result of persistent French refusal to crack down on ETA's activities.[1]

By 1996, the PSOE was clearly compromised in the eyes of the electorate. Corruption scandals and the GAL issue raised questions over its honesty and respect for law, and the party lost the elections to a reconstituted conservative force, the Popular Party of José Maria Aznar—a defeat repeated, in even worse dimensions, in 2000.

The 2000 defeat concentrated minds, and that year the by-then "old guard" around Felipe Gonzalez was replaced by younger leaders of the "Nueva Via" ("New Way"), apparently influenced by the "Third Way" center-left style of Tony Blair and his New Labour Party in Britain. Zapatero became their representative.

José Luis Rodriguez Zapatero was born in Valladolid, on August 4, 1960. His grandfather was a captain in the Republican Army during the Civil War (1936–1939), and was killed in combat. His father was a lawyer; his mother a doctor. Involved in politics since age sizteen, he joined the PSOE in 1978. A lawyer, he taught constitutional law at Leon University from 1982 to 1986, was elected to parliament in 1988, became secretary-general of the Leon Region branch and in 2000 was somewhat surprisingly elected PSOE national leader.

With no government experience whatsoever, Zapatero has no memory of the old internal fights within the PSOE. What he does have is an idealistic and dogmatic attachment to fashionable notions prevailing in the European Left, with a clear dislike of America and, most especially, of George W. Bush. Nor is his political judgmentm in generalm something to encourage hopes for pragmatism and adaptation to reality.

It does not help that he does not even understand the political landscape of Spain. Case in point, this quotation: "WHOEVER wins Madrid, will win the general election in March." So said José Luis Zapatero, leader of Spain's opposition Socialists some months ago. Now that the center-right People's Party has regained control of Madrid, Zapatero has modified his position: "he had expected a far worse result, and his party is in better shape than ever for the spring elections."[2]

Both his dogmatic attachment to the ideas of the European Left, and his lack of political judgment, were demonstrated by his statements following the recent elections. "I said during the campaign I hoped Spain and the Spaniards would be ahead of the Americans for once," he said in an interview on Onda Cero radio. "First we win here, we change this government, and then the Americans will do it, if things continue as they are in Kerry's favor."

"Fighting terrorism with bombs, with Tomahawk missiles, isn't the way to beat terrorism, but the way to generate more radicalism," he said.

First, for a Prime Minister-elect of a NATO ally to openly express support for the U.S. opposition candidate is unheard of, undiplomatic, and imprudent, to say the least. It is also arrogant. Second, whether de facto capitulation to Islamist terror means "being ahead" of the Americans is doubtful; and the notion, shared by others in Europe, that fighting terrorism produces terrorism, is close to inane. Partisans of this view include European Commission President Romano Prodi, who stated, "It is clear that using force is not the answer to resolving the conflict with terrorists." And rolling over for them is?

This is, however, a notion that permeates the PSOE as a whole, as demonstrated by its electoral program, which claims that global terrorism, proliferation of WMDs, organized crime, environmental problems, inequality, illegal immigration, all demand...the eradication of poverty! Problems of such magnitude, said the wise men of the PSOE, "cannot simplistically be reduced...as neoconservative ideologies claim," to transnational terrorist groups, and even less by "recurring unilateralism, preventive attacks, regime changes based on military occupation under the pretext of recuperating democracy." This is an unmistakable assault on U.S. policy and, most clearly, a demonstration of how deeply entrenched political correctness is in the party ranks, from the top to the bottom. It appears that the Marxist nonsense courageously rejected by Felipe Gonzalez in 1979 has returned through the back door in its adulterated form of political correctness. The promise to withdraw the Spanish troops from Iraq, reiterated after the election—unless, of course, there is a UN blessing to keep them—acts upon these innocent premises. Never mind that the UN itself has fled Iraq after last year's attack on its headquarters.

In Europe, Zapatero made it clear that Spain will join and support the Franco-German axis in a "clear European option"; globally, it will support "international legality, represented by the United Nations" (as opposed to the "illegality" of the United States?) and regionally a "just and lasting solution to the Palestinian-Israeli conflict"—whatever that means. A rapprochement with Castro, friendly relations with Hugo Chavez in Venezuela, and withdrawal of Aznar's support for the Alvaro Uribe government in Colombia are all in the cards as well.

In domestic terms, the PSOE record on the most pressing issue, separatism in the Basque Country and Catalonia, is ambiguous. Under Felipe Gonzalez, the PSOE joined the national consensus that separatism is condemnable and violence in its name, criminal. But when its Catalan branch, Partit dels Socialistes de Catalunya, came to power in Barcelona last year, and its Catalan separatist leftists engaged in secret talks with the (Marxist) terrorists of ETA (Euzkadi Ta Askatasuna—Basque Motherland and Freedom), the Socialists' reaction was quite tepid. On the other hand, PSOE's Basque branch, Partido Socialista de Euskadi—Euskadiko Ezquerra (Socialist Party of Basque Country—Basque Left) is in active opposition to the ruling nationalists of the region, and has paid a bloody price for it.

All in all, PSOE's victory is bad news—bad news for Spain, where the successful anti-terrorist, economic, and foreign policies of the Aznar era might well be overturned; bad news for the international struggle against Islamic terror, which has seen its greatest political victory ever on March 14; and bad news for bilateral Spanish-U.S. ties. The fact that even John Kerry, Zapatero's favorite American politician (or is it Howard Dean or maybe even Dennis Kucinich?) felt obliged to ask him to reconsider the troop withdrawal from Iraq suggests that the new Spanish leader is so far off American interests and opinions that normal, let alone friendly, relations are unlikely. Only the terrorists could benefit from this arrangement.

Notes

1. For details, see Antonio Rubio and Manuel Cerdan, *El origen del GAL*, Grandes Temas, Madrid, 1997.
2. "The battle of Madrid. Foreshadowing the next election," *The Economist*, October 30, 2003.

Reprinted with the permission from http://www.frontpagemag.com, March 25, 2004

THE GUANTANAMO FOUR

Their names: Mourad Benchellali, Nizar Sassi, Brahim Yadel, and Imad Achab Kanouni.

Their current status: captured in Afghanistan by U.S. forces, the four—all of whom are French citizens or residents—were held at Camp Guantanamo for over two years. That is, until last month, when they were sent back to France and placed under arrest on charges of "criminal association with the intent of committing acts of terrorism" and, more specifically, of membership in the terrorist "Chechen connection."

The case of these four men is typical of the terrorists held at Guantanamo and, thus, deserves some examination. While we are constantly being told by "human rights" activists that the prisoners at Guantanamo are " illegally" held, and that many, if not all, are "innocent" and have been mistreated by the Americans, the reality is something far different.

Mourad Benchellali, a high school dropout, is a member of a well-known Islamist family that is deeply involved in terrorism. His father, Chellali, was a radical imam in a suburb of Lyons, a would-be combatant in Bosnia (he was captured by the Croatians), a polygamist and, in more general terms, a complete failure. Indeed, he could not hold a job and for a long time lived on welfare (at about $1,200 a month at current exchange rates). That gave him the time necessary to be involved on behalf of the-then main terrorist group in Algeria, the Armed Islamic Group (GIA).

Mourad's brother, Menad, also currently under arrest, is accused of having played a key role in an attempted terrorist attack in France in 2002. He was trained in Afghanistan, and like his father before him, tried, and failed, to join a jihad, this time in Chechnya (he was caught by the Georgians before even getting there). It was Menad who gave Mourad false travel documents that allowed him to travel to London and then to Afghanistan together with Nizar Sassi, another of Menad's recruits. Once there, Mourad joined an al-Qaeda training camp, fought against U.S. forces and was captured.

Menad, joined by yet another Benchellali brother, Hafed, was involved in a number of crimes, including payroll theft, according to *The New York Times*.[1]

Hafed was involved with the Abu Musab al-Zarqawi network, which now leads the terror campaign in Iraq. Also according to the *New York Times*, "the police have found links between both Menad and Hafed and suspected terrorist cells in Spain and London, including one that succeeded in producing an undetermined quantity of ricin."

Nizar Sassi, a night watchman, is described in the French press as Mourad Benchellali's "double." He was recruited by Chellali Benchellali, received false travel documents from Mourad, got al-Qaeda training in Afghanistan (under the cover of "studying in Quran school" in Pakistan), and, like Mourad, was of Algerian extraction.

Imad Achab Kanouni is described in the French press as "the most mysterious and interesting" of the Guantanamo Four. A Moroccan with dual citizenship, he has lived mostly in Germany, where he was involved in firefights with police and was accused of being part of a terrorist plot in Strasbourg. Interestingly, his lawyer claims that he was in Afghanistan just to study the Quran (Taliban-style, of course).

Lastly, Brahim Yadel, who claims to only want to enjoy his first Coca-Cola in two years, is French-born and well known to the police. He was a close friend of a French convert to Islam, Hervé Djamel Loiseau, who died of exposure while fleeing Tora Bora in 2001. Yadel has been accused of involvement in an attempted terror attack during the World Soccer Cop in France in 1998, and sentenced in absentia to a year in prison. According to another Islamist (and convert), Willy Brigitte, Yadel was trained in one of Bin Laden's Afghan camps. He was captured in Tora Bora and delivered to the U.S. forces.

His lawyer claims that, although Yadel did spend three-and-a-half months in a terrorist raining camp, he also spent seven months in an "Arab language Institute" in Kandahar—the Taliban's headquarters. The implication is, obviously, that his primary goal was to improve his education, and terrorist training was just a hobby.

All four men were examined by doctors upon arrival in France and found to be in good physical condition. Their lawyers have tried, so far without success, to get them released on grounds that they have already suffered enough at the hands of the evil Americans, and they consistently mention the Abu Ghraib episode as "proof" of this. Why is all this important? Because the entire episode demonstrates the nature of Islamic terrorism itself and the problems faced by those fighting terrorism.

Let us start with the obvious: all four men were French citizens—born in France, trained in Afghanistan—and captured there as well. All four had extensive police records; and all four were part of an Islamist terrorist movement based in France and Germany, with close ties to London (in addition, the Benchellali clan and, by implication, Nizar Sassi, were directly linked to Algerian terrorism). All were implicated in international terrorism in the Balkans and/or Afghanistan, but also in Western Europe. The four men's backgrounds reaffirm that Islamist terror has no borders, and its best operatives are not the millions of largely illiterate sympathizers in Muslim majority countries but those born and bred in the West—something al-Qaeda itself admits.

Sociologically, the four are personal failures—unable and/or unwilling to hold jobs, poor or insufficiently educated, all with petty crime records, and, in the Benchellali case, a dysfunctional and already radicalized family environment.

Legally, the arguments already presented by the four terrorists' lawyers are telling, and should be seen as a preview of things to come in U.S. courts. First, "study" in Islamist "schools" is a perfectly legitimate way of hiding terrorist indoctrination and, indeed, terrorist training. Second, alleged "abuse" by the evil Americans at Guantanamo plays to an increasingly intense anti–American atmosphere in Europe (expect Abu Ghraib to become standard defense as well).

If all Guantanamo detainees are as "innocent" as the French four, the entire world should thank Washington for taking out of business some 600 professional terrorists, notwithstanding the "human rights" fundamentalists' baseless claim that Guantanamo is a torture center. Medically, the four had nothing to show as far as "torture" is concerned—unless, that is, denial of access to Coca-Cola is indeed "torture" under "international standards" as defined by Amnesty International.

Ultimately, the "Guantanamo Four" are a symbol of the West's ability to deal with Islamist terror, and, unpleasant as the French may be for most Americans, it is clearly better that the standards be set in Paris than elsewhere in "old" Europe. On the other hand, those still claiming that the detainees in Guantanamo are "victims" rather than actual or potential terrorists, should face the reality that defending them is not defending law or Western moral and legal standards, but defending crime.

Note

1.   Craig S. Smith, Web of Jihad Draws In an Immigrant Family in France, *New York Times*, July 31, 2004

HOW CANADIAN TOLERANCE BECAME INTOLERANCE

Sooner or later, the de facto mutual support society of progressives and Islamists had to collapse under the weight of its own contradictions.

The progressives who have supported the claims of Islamists in the West have long chosen to disregard the saying that one cannot be so open-minded as to let your brains fall out. Now reality forces them to wake up and, increasingly in Europe, and now in Canada, realize that the Islamists' goals are incompatible with their own, and that excessive "tolerance" inevitably leads to intolerance.

The days of the joint anti–American demonstrations of the Left and Islamists, of the Communists, Socialists, and Muslim radicals in the streets of Paris or in Trafalgar Square may, indeed, be coming to an end.

The first and most spectacular sign that the progressives and the Islamists seek different, contradictory goals came from the Netherlands—that most progressive of all countries, the land of legal drugs, medical assisted suicide and euthanasia, gay marriages and unionized military. It had a face—Pym Fortuyn, a gay environmentalist who famously declared that Islam is a reactionary and "stupid" religion, and that his country is "full."

Blasphemy? Not really. Shortly after Fortuyn's 2002 assassination by a radical environmentalist, his party came from nowhere to place second in the general elections that year. While the party soon collapsed under the weight of its own incompetence, its radical (by European standards) anti-immigration (read anti–Muslim immigration) program was largely adopted by the present government in the Hague. Meanwhile, the same year, the gay Socialist mayor of Paris, Bertrand Delanoe, was almost killed by a Muslim who did not like gays. No matter how multiculturalists may tie themselves in knots over the issue, Islam and homosexuality are irrevocably incompatible. This is demonstrated by the attitudes of Muslims everywhere. Muslims condemn homosexuality as much, if not more than, fundamentalist Christians. And unlike fundamentalist Christians, they are willing and ready to kill over it.

Then there is Islam's problem with feminism, and women in general. Polygamy, which is illegal everywhere in the West, is quite commonly tolerated, practiced, subsidized in a number of countries, especially France. Then there is the practice of genital mutilation of girls—not an Orthodox Muslim practice, but it happens nonetheless—in many Muslim countries. Finally there is the general—and theologically correct—Islamic denial of the most basic rights to women. Put polygamy, genital mutilation, anti-abortion attitudes, and the *burqa* together, and one is likely to drive feminists wild indeed. It is also a combination that makes all Western women—and most decent men for that matter—question the realism of accepting Islam as just another religion to be respected and tolerated in their midst.

Now, Canada is becoming the Netherlands of North America. Its official ideology is "multiculturalism." Canadians may not like the term, but that is the ruling Liberal Party's entrenched policy since the premiership of the late Pierre Elliott Trudeau in the 1970s. However, multiculturalism is now facing the limits of "tolerance."

Canadian-style multiculturalism, the dream of American academics and the enemy of serious Canadians who care about politics and their own culture, is simple to define: immigrant ethnic minority groups, virtually all from the Third

World, are not only not required to assimilate, but the taxpayers, in the name of "diversity" and "tolerance," are required to pay for maintaining their culture. Hence the plethora of ethnic—Chinese, East and South East Asian, Indian sub-continent, etc. associations, schools, cultural organizations, paid by the tax-payers of Alberta or British Columbia—via Ottawa, of course, since the Canadian West is quite hostile to this.

One may ask the key, common sense question to all pro–immigrant, anti–assimilation groups everywhere: why would anyone choose to emigrate from the balmy climates of the Third World to chilly Canada if their culture—political or otherwise—is so worthy as to be maintained in the new country? Indeed, if Pakistani, Romanian, Bangladeshi, or Jamaican culture are so great, why leave? Or is there no link—logical and practical—between that culture and the push factors for emigration?

In the name of tolerance and multiculturalism, in 1991 the Ontario provincial government passed something called the Arbitration Act, allowing religious (at the time Christian and Jewish) authorities to perform certain legal functions, in family and civil law, rather than having regular courts do it. Of course, as Ontario goes, so goes Canada. Ontario Muslims demanded that Sharia (Islamic law) "courts" be allowed to solve family and other civil matters (divorce, child custody and inheritance, etc.) among Canadian Muslims. And why not? After all, it would be hypocritical to allow a rabbi to deal with kosher matters while denying an imam the right to deal with divorce or child custody, wouldn't it? It is a valid legal point within the moral, cultural, and legal universe of Canadian multiculturalism.

As one may expect, supporters of the sharia as de facto Canadian law for Muslims promise—perhaps sincerely—that no obligatory sharia punishments such as cutting off the hands of the thieves, stoning adulterers, etc., associated with strict application of sharia in Saudi Arabia, would happen in the snowy towns of Ontario. However sharia is divinely ordained, in its totality, in Muslim eyes. It is a matter of faith, and choosing and picking among its rules is not for Canadian (or any other) imams to decide. But that essential issue is not what has provoked a strong feminist reaction in Ontario and among those Canadians not in Barbados or Florida at this time; it is the relationship between sharia and women rights—and feminism.

"It's shocking to see the seeds of an Islamic republic being sown here in Canada," one young woman shouted to vociferous applause at a recent Toronto rally, organized to denounce the practice of sharia in Ontario. "Sharia doesn't work anywhere else in the world. Why does the government believe it will work here?"[1]

This is a clear case of "tolerance" gone wild and becoming intolerance—and it is a double one. On the one hand, Muslims in Canada (at least some of them) claim that, in the name of Canadian "tolerance" and "multiculturalism," they have a right to live by their own legal rules (sharia), which is, by definition, intolerant (to non-Muslims), "morally conservative," and gives Muslims a legal domination over all others. On the other hand, the Left—of which feminism, here, in Europe and in Canada, is one of the strongest contingents—believes in erasing religious moral standards, indiscriminate "equality" between sexes and to gays, bisexuals, etc. The problem for Western leftist politicians and their media sidekicks is that, sooner or later, their gay, feminist, and "tolerant" constituencies would rebel and prove that they are still more numerous at the ballot box than those immigrant Muslims who cannot adapt.

Note

1.   Susan Bourette, "Can tolerant Canada tolerate sharia?" *Christian Science Monitor*, August 10, 2004.

Reprinted with the permission from http://www.frontpagemag.com,
August 18, 2004

PART 3
THE PLAGUE OF OUR TIME—TERRORISM

THE PLAGUE OF OUR TIME—TERRORISM

Despite apologists' efforts to deny the obvious, terrorism, and Islamic terrorism in particular, remains the main security and, indeed, civilizational threat today. Its nature, after more than two decades, is still uselessly debated, despite overwhelming data suggesting that its roots are cultural, rather than economic or political. The methods of combating it are similarly "debated"—or, more accurately, impeded, in the name of promiscuous, fanciful, and dangerously irrelevant definitions of "human rights."

The pseudo issue of whether combating Islamist terror is the same as combating Islam is a red herring, an excuse for those who choose to avoid the answer. Islam—especially its majority Sunni version—has no recognized theological authority, no Vatican that could define what is inside, or outside, the bounds of orthodoxy. No Muslim scholar, theologian, or politician could declare al-Qaeda and its nebula of associates as "unorthodox" and be accepted as authoritative. Even less so can non-Muslim, Western politicians persuade that Bin Laden & Co. have "hijacked" Islam, a "peace" religion. A Muslim is a Muslim, says the Quran, as long as he does not openly declares otherwise. Any other distinctions are for God to make.

The problem with Islamist terrorism is that it is gaining sympathizers all the time, not because of American attacks on Afghanistan, Iraq, or any other place after 9/11, but because Islam, as a self-defined cultural, moral, economic, and political system, has lost traction and credibility, as well as military victories, for some three centuries. To claim, as some do, in the Muslim and Western world, that democracy is the solution, is to disregard reality. In Algeria in 1991–1992, voters did express their will, and it was in favor of a party (the Islamic Salvation Front—FIS) that made it clear that democracy is an instrument and, ultimately, one to be discarded—a "one-man, one-vote, one-time" pattern. And in Bahrain and Qatar's relatively free elections, who won? Well, mostly the Islamists.

What "democracy" means in a place like Saudi Arabia is not clear: a free-for-all ballot that would make Bin Laden the president of a (Sunni) Islamic state of Arabia? Did nobody in Washington even think about this? If they did, then multiculturalism and political correctness most likely obscured it all.

I do not pretend to be expert on Middle Eastern politics, political culture, or demographics. I speak no Arabic or Farsi, let alone Kurdish dialects. But common sense would say that a people such as the Palestinians, who have been well described as "never missing an opportunity to miss an opportunity," are never going to solve their conflict with Israel through violence, and, yet, since the second intifada began in September 2000, they have killed as many Jews as they could, losing some five of their own for each one.

But when bin Laden describes his cause as one directed against "Christians and crusaders," Jews, Hindus, communists, and Muslim regimes that are insufficiently religious, such as Saudi Arabia's, and claims "al-Andalus" for Islam (al-Andalus is not the Spanish region of Andalusia but the Arab-controlled Iberian Peninsula, which includes Portugal and Cataluña), he is serious—and should be taken seriously.

Al-Qaeda has became a shortcut to Islamist terror, from Chechnya to Pakistan, Bali, and New York. Its core leaders are still around, deciding the strategy and ideology of Islamist terrorism everywhere, but they do not control, finance, or direct attacks in faraway places by sympathetic locals in Morocco, Spain, Turkey, or Indonesia, even if they do provide helpful "visitors."

SEPTEMBER 11, 2001: TEN WAYS TO LOOK AT WHAT HAPPENED AND WHAT TO EXPECT

As the nation—or nations, since some forty countries lost citizens in the New York City attacks—recovers from the immediate shock and outrage over the events of September 11, it is necessary to understand the phenomenon that led to the atrocities, lest our response be incomplete or misguided.

1.   This is not a war between the West and Islam but between the West and a large segment of the Islamic world, the fundamentalist minority. For the fundamentalists, the problem is not U.S. policy toward Israel, the Gulf, or anywhere else, the problem is the United States itself—not what we do, but who we are.

2.   While Arab leaders and our own leaders are right to admonish us to avoid confusing Muslims with terrorists, the fact is there are no known cases of contemporary mass terrorism in the name of Judaism, Christianity, Confucianism, Buddhism, or Hinduism. There, thus, appears to be something in Islam that allows the likes of the Taliban or bin Laden to thrive. Only the Muslims themselves can root it out. What America needs from the Islamic world, far more than military or political support, is for Muslims themselves—from the smallest mosques in New York City, Peshawar, or Hamburg to the largest in Mecca—to read the fundamentalists out of Islam. In the long run, the most effective counter-terrorist force—potentially—is Muslims who proclaim that terrorism is anti-Islamic.

3.   It is said that Pakistani President Musharaf sees Mustafa Kemal "Ataturk," the builder of modern Turkey, as his model. Let us hope that is true, and that more Muslim leaders see Ataturk as a model. For Turkey, alone, in the Middle East has succeeded in demonstrating that Islam and Western political values are not incompatible. It is ironic, in this respect, that our European friends often think that Ankara's crackdown on Islamic fundamentalism is an infringement on human rights.

4.   Speaking of our European friends, their expressions of solidarity cannot help but move us all. Let us hope, however, that we don't find ourselves debilitated by unrelenting objections over strategy and tactics, or, even worse, the attempt to solve the "root causes" of terrorism—the surest path to retreat. It was not a European, however, but a prominent American professor at MIT, Noam Chomsky, who interpreted the events of September 11 as "an atrocity answering American atrocities."

5.   There are innumerable Islamic terrorist cells throughout Western Europe taking advantage, as they do in the United States, of democracy's openness. When we hear that some Islamic leaders in England or Germany still preach support for the perpetrators of the crimes in New York, Washington, and Pennsylvania—and do so publicly—one has to wonder. When dozens, or hundreds, of Islamic terrorists indicted, or even sentenced, for crimes in Egypt, Algeria, Morocco, Turkey, and so on are still being given asylum in Western Europe, one has to question how serious our allies are. What we need to know from the Europeans is whether they are in this for the long haul and whether they are prepared to take stiff measures to stem the terrorist threat. Judging from the European press, not all the signs are encouraging, for the Atlantic may be wider than we thought.

6.   President Bush has described the terrorist attack and its aftermath as "a different kind" of war. How "different" is it? To begin with, it is a protracted conflict in which the distinction between domestic and foreign, police and military, can no longer be made. It is a seamless conflict in which the link between the internal and international operations has a clear name—intelligence. Indeed, in the long run, the most important and decisive role is going to be played not by the military but by institutions that Western democracies do not normally see as associated with war: police and intelligence. The U.S. and allied militaries obviously have an important role in the short term, but, ultimately, this is a war to be won or lost on the streets of New York, London, Hamburg, and Paris, by innumerable policemen and plainclothes FBI and other security personnel, as well as by plainclothes men of the Jordanian, Egyptian, and Algerian secret services.

7.   Legislation has to be dramatically changed in Washington as well as Ottawa, Brussels, Strasbourg, and all the EU member states. If this war

is to be won, the European obsession with American death penalty legislation has to give way to higher priorities, such as extraditing or putting down terrorists for good. The politically correct campaign in Europe and the United States against "racial profiling" has to stop: after all, looking for tall, blond and blue-eyed persons in order to stop Middle Eastern terrorism makes no sense.

8.   The terrorists of New York have many potential allies in the anti-globalization movement who share anti-capitalist, anti-democratic, and anti-Western ideas. It is not that the "anti-globalists" are terrorists, or even support them, but they will likely oppose the tough anti-terrorist measures that are required to meet the threat.

9.   In the short run, the military questions most often mentioned are targeting, logistics, and numbers. The targets could be limited, at least initially, to the Taliban and Osama bin Laden leadership. One has to remember that many, probably most Afghans, are at least tired of, if not hostile to, the Taliban rule. The notion that myriads of Afghans, plus some refugees in camps in Iran or Pakistan, would join the "jihad" requested by the Taliban is probably nonsense; it may well be a call to war few would rally around. Logistically, Pakistan, Russia, and Russia's protectorates in Central Asia (all of whom are Turkic speakers) are the keys for a ground operation. That operation has to be short, sharp, and effective. At the same time, we must get out the word to the Afghan people that the Taliban rulers and their criminal guests are the enemy, not the Afghans themselves. Many Afghans would cooperate with the U.S. if that understanding is clear in their own minds, and if the idea of an American occupation of Afghanistan is dispelled beforehand.

10.   Ultimately, this is a protracted conflict, to be won by Western police, intelligence, and military forces, with the vital support of Muslim intelligence resources. It is not, as I said earlier, a war between Islam and the West, though irrationality and fear could make it so. And, whether we like it or not, the map of the Islamic world is going to be different from what it is today—politically and culturally.

This said, we should not forget that international terrorism is not limited to Islamist fanatics, even if they are the most numerous, best organized, and wide-spread. There are still the Basque Euskadi ta Askatsuna (ETA), the Irish Republican Army, and the Tamil Tigers lurking in the shadows, planning murder and mayhem in many countries, and receiving support from many more. They are part of the enemy in this war.

Reprinted with the permission from http://www.frontpagemag.com,
September 18, 2001

WHY WE FEAR AFGHANISTAN AND WHY WE SHOULDN'T

Much of the current analysis of the U.S.-British military actions against the Taliban and al-Qaeda in Afghanistan seem to accept unquestioningly conventional wisdom on the prospects for military success in that country. But the major premises of this conventional wisdom are simply myths that have developed over the years, either from ignorance or malevolence. The facts, it will be seen, simply do not support them.

Myth #1: The U.S. is bound to be Defeated in Afghanistan, just as the British and the Soviets were

The myth that the U.S. is destined to follow in the footsteps of the two prior great powers who suffered disastrous defeats there, Great Britain (in the First Afghan War, 1838-1842) and the Soviet Union (1979-1989), has gained wide currency.

In the First Afghan War, the British tried, and failed, to impose an unpopular puppet king, Shah Shuja, in Kabul, thus uniting all the fractious Afghans who, then as now, united only when threatened by the possibility of an effective central government. The British garrison in Kabul was completely wiped out, with enormous losses of life and blows to British prestige.

Britain would again fight in Afghanistan in 1878-1880 and 1919, but these were mostly limited operations, since London had realized its error and turned to a policy of manipulating (often financially) the various Afghan groups. The success of this policy is demonstrated by the transformation of Afghanistan into an effective buffer state between the competing ambitions of the British and Russian empires. (Perhaps a better term would be "buffer territory" since "Afghanistan" always was, and still is, a geographic expression more than a real state, let alone a "nation.")

The Soviet experience in Afghanistan was equally ill-fated, and caused enough bitterness at home to help contribute to the fall of the Soviet Union. But the reasons for this have as much to do with factors on the Soviet side— including the large number of soldiers lost to preventable disease, inappropriate military tactics, and poor national morale—as Afghanistan-specific factors. Furthermore, the very ideology of Marxism-Leninism coming on the back of Soviet tanks was rejected by virtually all population groups.

Importantly, unlike nineteenth-century Britain or the twentieth-century Soviet Union, the United States has neither interest in, nor geopolitical reasons for, wanting to control, let alone occupy, Afghanistan. And unless there has been a miserable failure to communicate, all Afghans know this. Moreover, developments in recent decades, exacerbated by the incompetence of the mujahideen regime (now represented by the United Front, also known in the West as the Northern Alliance) of 1992-1996 in Kabul, have achieved what all of prior history had not: sharpening ethnic divisions within the country. While all the ethnic groups united against outsiders in the earlier conflicts, now the Tajiks, Uzbeks, Aimaks, Hazaras, Nuristanis, and Turkmen—ethnic minorities that collectively make up over half the country—are only loosely and sporadically "united" against the Pashtun-dominated Taliban regime. (The Pashtuns are the largest ethnic group but only 40 percent of the population.) It is no coincidence that the Taliban's political and ideological center is not multiethnic Kabul, but all-Pashtun Kandahar.

Myth #2: The terrain in Afghanistan renders modern military technology largely irrelevant.

The implications of this myth are: (a) that an almost Stone Age military would defeat a twenty-first century power; and (b) that the country's terrain is the same and equally important everywhere.

While a great deal of Afghanistan is indeed mountainous and exceedingly difficult for infantry operations, key areas—the Uzbek border, the Shamali Plain north of Kabul and the entire southeast around and including Kandahar—are perfect operational areas for heliborne forces. These are also, in fact, the areas of major Taliban force concentrations.

As for the truly difficult mountainous regions, the worst of those, the Badakshan Wakhan Corridor, is under Northern Alliance "control," but certainly not under the Taliban's. The strategic Panjhir Valley remains, as ever, under Tajik control, as does the entire area around Herat, although not the city itself—yet. It is only in the mountainous east, around Jalalabad and the Pakistani border, that Pashtun ethnics may—if the price is right—continue to support the Taliban-cum-al-Qaeda. But would the latter have the money to continue its control, or the aura of success following the U.S.-British air attacks? That is doubtful.

Actually, the very fact that the Taliban was able to conquer so much of Afghanistan from 1994 on points to other factors more relevant to the potential for success here. First, there was the desire of many—in fact, most—people for some order and discipline to be imposed in their regions, so long as it was not imposed by a foreign (i.e., Soviet) force. Many wanted an end put to the banditry and warlordism, in order to stanch the emigration flow to Pakistan that this caused. But consider the recent history of the city of Herat: under Ishmael Khan, a former Royal Afghan Army officer, it successfully fought the Soviets and in 1989 established an enlightened system in which girls and boys had equal access to education. Escaping after being captured by the Taliban in 1998, Khan is now close to retaking the city—Afghanistan's most multicultural and historic. Helping Ishmael Khan means helping everyone in Afghanistan.

The second reason for the Taliban's success was its ability to buy local military-cum-religious leaders—particularly in Pashtun and Nuristani areas. With al-Qaeda and Pakistani help, that was doable. With the money flow from Islamabad cut off and al-Qaeda now centered on its own physical survival, the ability to buy local warlords is limited at best—and the U.S.-led allies could buy them instead, at least temporarily.

Myth #3: This is an irregular campaign for which the U.S. is ill-prepared.

Many of the large number of former military officers, civilian analysts, and journalists now offering "expert opinion" have made the claim that U.S. forces will face an endless guerrilla campaign in the mountains (see above) and plains of Afghanistan. They generally base this claim on the Soviet experience. But the claim is wrong.

Unlike the Soviets, whose support was limited to a very thin group of urban intelligentsia and (Soviet educated and indoctrinated) military officers vulnerable to communist atheistic and secular propaganda, the U.S. does not proclaim, or harbor, any cultural or religious (including anti-religious) goals. Hence the Northern Alliance—all Sunni Muslims but moderately so—and the Shi'a Hazaras see nothing wrong with the U.S. Air Force being their air force against the Taliban. The implication should be obvious. While U.S.-British Special Operations forces may, and should, play a key role, most of the hunting for bin Laden and his crowd—most of whom are Arab or other foreigners—will be done by Afghans themselves once the Taliban loses control over the major cities and regions.

And where would a Taliban guerrilla fight, if they are seen as losers and no longer benefit from Pakistani intelligence and military support? With the major air bases of Shindand in the West, Bagram in the Kabul area, and Mazar e Sharif in the north already out of commission, and some minor ones already under anti-Taliban control, U.S. forces will have free access to operations throughout the country.

Myth #4: It is impossible to find Osama bin Laden in Afghanistan.

This theory is based on all the above fallacies. It assumes that al-Qaeda's Arab (or foreign) militants could find refuge inside Afghanistan, without the locals knowing their whereabouts or acting upon the usual Afghan dislike and suspicion of all foreigners, especially the more recent dislike of "Islamic" foreigners.

In truth, any Afghan worth his history and tribal traditions would readily join the winners (i.e., the anti-Taliban forces) and capture or kill bin Laden, especially if doing so made the Afghan or his group wealthy. So it might be asked where, and for how long, a foreigner and his large group of "Arabs" could hide in a country where the population wants, and needs, international aid, money, and food, and is historically xenophobic?

Myth #5: Since the United Front is made up largely of ethnic minorities, it cannot form a stable government in Kabul and hence there is no realistic long-term alternative to the Taliban.

This is the Islamabad thesis—but then, Islamabad is not exactly an objective observer. The theory's flaws are many. To begin with, as noted above, the non-Pashtun ethnic minorities, who make up the United Front, which is recognized by the UN as the government of Afghanistan, collectively make up a large majority of the Afghanistan population. The Islamabad thesis may hold for Pakistan itself, which, incidentally, has more Pashtuns than does Afghanistan, but for Afghanistan? That does not mean leaving the Pashtuns entirely out of a future new power distribution.

Second, the Pashtuns are not, as Secretary Rumsfeld has begun calling them, "southern tribes." They are, to use George Bernard Shaw's phrase, "a people separated by a common language." The Durrani confederation in the east and south is the Taliban's power base. But—and this is a very large but—the Ghilzai confederation in the east (with Jalalabad its center) is unhappy with the Durrani/Taliban power-sharing arrangements. They are equally represented in Pakistan, hence Musharaff's admittedly daring challenge to the Taliban. The former King Zahir Shah is a Pashtun, he is recognized (probably temporarily, as all things are and always will be in Afghanistan), and he could probably rally enough of his people to get rid of the bin Laden gang of foreigners, with some financial backing.

We must all consider these facts in thinking about Afghanistan and the success probabilities for the U.S.- British led military action—especially when we are barraged with ill-informed arguments to the contrary.

Reprinted with the permission from http://www.fpri.org, October 12, 2001

GUIDE TO THE PERPLEXED ON AFGHANISTAN

As a student of Afghanistan throughout the 1980s—albeit from outside, since I never traveled there—and based upon all I have learned from real experts who did, like David Isby and others, here is my take on the commonly vented myths regarding Afghanistan and future U.S. policy toward it.

There are a number of myths, some based on ignorance, some on malevolent intention, regarding what we could, or could not, should, or should not, do in Afghanistan.

Myth # 1—The British (in 1840-1842) and the Soviets (1979-1989), both world empires at the time, broke their teeth in Afghanistan. Hence, the U.S., today's dominant world power, will suffer the same fate.

This is a myth equally supported by the Taliban, some of their not-so-well-disguised Muslim fellow travelers and useful idiots, and, naturally enough, by the purposefully ignorant Western Left fringes.

Reality check

The British in 1840 tried, and failed, to impose an unpopular puppet king in Kabul, thus uniting all the fractious Afghans who, then as now, could only be united against any effective central government. Later on, the British realized their error and engaged in a policy of manipulating (mostly with money) the various Afghan groups, and did so successfully, as demonstrated by the transformation of Afghanistan into an effective buffer state (or, perhaps, better put, a buffer territory, since "Afghanistan" was always, and still is, a geographic expression more than a real state, let alone a "nation") between the competing interests and ambitions of the British and Russian Empires.

The United States in 2001 has no interest, capability, or geopolitical reasons to control, let alone occupy, Afghanistan—and unless we fail absolutely in our propaganda efforts, all "Afghans" know it. Moreover, the recent (as in "before the Soviet invasion of 1979") developments, made worse by the incompetence of the Mujahedeen regime of 1992-1996 in Kabul, now represented by the "Northern Alliance," have done what history has not done—sharpen ethnic divisions within the country, with Tadjiks, Uzbeks, Aimaks, Hazaras, Turkmen—together a majority, loosely and temporarily "united" against the Pashtun-dominated Taliban regime. It is no coincidence that the Taliban 's political and ideological center is not multi-ethnic Kabul, but all-Pashtun Kandahar.

Myth # 2—The terrain in Afghanistan is such that modern military technology is largely irrelevant. The implications are: 1) that an almost Stone Age military would defeat a twenty-first century power; and b) that the terrain is the same and equally important everywhere.

Reality check

The two main reasons the Taliban did conquer so much of Afghanistan since 1994 are the following:

1. The desire of many people, in fact most people, to have some order and discipline imposed in their areas, as long as that was not done by some foreign (e.g., Soviet) force. Simply put, an end of banditry and warlordism, and the reason for mass emigration to Pakistan. But consider Herat's recent history: under Ishmael Khan, a former Royal Afghan Army officer, it successfully fought the Soviets, and since 1989

established an enlightened system in which girls and boys had equal access to education; captured by the Taliban in 1998, and then escaping, Khan is now close to retaking the city—Afghanistan's most multicultural and historic. Helping Ishmael Khan is helping everyone in Afghanistan.

2.   The Taliban's ability to buy local military *cum* religious leaders—particularly in Pashtun and Nuristani areas. With Al-Quaeda and Pakistani help, that was doable; with no more money flows from Islamabad, and Al-Quaeda now centered on its own physical survival, the ability to buy local warlords is limited at best – and we could buy them instead—at least temporarily.

While a lot of Afghanistan is mountainous and exceedingly difficult for infantry operations, a look at the map would make it clear that key areas—the Uzbek border, the Shamali Plain north of Kabul, and the entire southeast around and including Kandahar, are perfect operational areas for heliborn forces. These are also the areas of major Taliban force concentrations. As for the truly difficult mountainous regions, the worst of those, the Badakshan Wakhan Corridor is under Northern Alliance "control"—whatever that means—but certainly not under the Taliban's; the strategic Panjhir Valley remains, as ever, under Tadjik control, as is the entire area around Herat. It is only in the mountainous East, around Jalalabad and the Pakistani border that Pashtun ethnics may—if the price is right—continue to support the Taliban *cum* Al-Quaeda group. But would the latter have the money? Or the aura of success following the U.S./British air attacks? Considering the past, that is at best doubtful.

Myth # 3—This is an irregular campaign the U.S. is not prepared for or competent to win.

We are bombarded with analyses from former military officers, with no experience in Afghanistan whatsoever, civilian analysts having a hard time reading the maps of that country, and all-knowing journalists. The general theory of those claiming that U.S. forces will be faced with an endless guerrilla campaign in the mountains (see above) and plains of Afghanistan is based upon the experience of the Soviets—precisely the Taliban's main ideological point—and is all wrong.

Reality Check

Unlike the Soviets, whose support was limited to a very thin group of urban intelligentsia and (Soviet educated and indoctrinated) military officers vulnerable to communist atheistic and secular propaganda, the present U.S. campaign does not try, or claim, any cultural and religious (or anti-religious) goals. Hence the moderate Northern Alliance and the Shi'I Hazaras see nothing wrong with the U.S. Air Force being their Air Force against the Taliban.

The implications are obvious—or should be to some of those "experts." While U.S./British Special Operations forces—the British Gurkhas look very much like the central Bamyan province's Hazaras—may, and should, play a key role, most of the hunting for bin Laden and his crowd—most of whom are Arab or other foreign fanatics—will be done by Afghans themselves—once the Taliban loses control over the major cities and regions. "Let a thief catch a thief" will clearly apply.

A Taliban guerrilla war? Where, if they are seen as losers and do not enjoy Pakistani intelligence and military support, as they did until recently?

With the major air bases of Shindand in the West, Bagram in the Kabul area, and Mazar e Sharif in the north out of commission already, and some minor ones under anti-Taliban control already, U.S. forces will have free access to operations throughout the country.

Myth # 4—It is impossible to find Osama bin Laden in Afghanistan.

This theory is based on all the above fallacies. It assumes that Al-Quaeda's Arab (or foreign) militants could find a refuge inside Afghanistan, without the locals knowing their locations or acting upon the usual Afghan dislike and suspicion of all foreigners, or the more recent dislike of "Islamic" foreigners.

Reality Check

Any Afghan worth his history and tribal traditions would join the winners (i.e. the anti-Taliban forces); capture and/or kill bin Laden if that makes him, or his group, very wealthy.

Finally, where, and for how long, could a foreigner and his large group of "Arabs" hide in a country where the population wants international aid, money, and food, and is historically xenophobic?

Myth # 5—Since the Northern Alliance, though recognized by the United Nations as the government of Afghanistan, is made up largely of ethnic minorities, it cannot form a stable government in Kabul. Hence there is no realistic, long-term alternative to the Taliban. This is the Islamabad thesis—but then Islamabad is not exactly an objective observer.

Reality Check

To begin with, ethnic "minorities" (Tadjiks, Uzbeks, Turkmen, Aimaks, Hazara, and Nuristanis) make up a large majority of the Afghanistan population – the Pashtuns are under 40 percent—the largest ethnic group but clearly a minority themselves. It is true that, for Pakistan—which has more Pashtuns than Afghanistan does—that is the key element. But for Afghanistan?

Second, the Pashtuns are not as Secretary Rumsfeld called them, "southern tribes." They are, to paraphrase Oscar Wilde, "a people separated by a common language." The Durrani confederation in the east and south is the Taliban's power base, BUT—and this is a very large but—the Ghilzai confederation in the east (with Jalalabad its center) is unhappy with the Durrani/Taliban power sharing arrangements. And they are equally represented in Pakistan—hence Musharaff's admittedly daring challenge to the Taliban.

The former King Zahir Shah is a Pashtun—and he is recognized (probably temporarily, as all things are, and always will be, in Afghanistan) and he could bring enough of his people around to get rid of the bin Laden gang of foreigners. As usual, money will talk also.

We should consider all these facts in talking about Afghanistan—the chances and probability of success of our military action—and in dealing with nonsensical, ahistorical and ignorant arguments to the contrary.

Reprinted with the permission from http://www.frontpagemag.com,
October 16, 2001

AFGHANISTAN: THE ENDGAME

As of this writing, the military situation in Afghanistan is increasingly clear. The Taliban remnants are cornered in their traditional bastion of Kandahar in the southeast, the center of power since 1994 for Mullah Mohammed Omar, the self-appointed Amir al-Mumemeen ("Commander of the Faith"), and also survive in an isolated pocket in the northeastern town of Kunduz. Otherwise, all other cities and towns of the country are under the control of anti-Taliban (or at least non-Taliban) forces.

In Kunduz a large Taliban force—variously estimated at between 5,000 and 20,000—is completely isolated and surrounded by Northern Alliance troops. Some top Taliban leaders are also there: its defense ministry has relocated to Kunduz. A very large number of the Taliban forces are foreigners, mostly al-Qaeda elements: Arabs, Uzbeks, Chechens, and Pakistanis. This explains their ferocious resistance against all military sense. They know full well that they have no place to go, and, in fact, the Northern Alliance commander on that front, Mohammed Daud, has made it clear that he will only accept the surrender of Afghans, not foreigners, in Kunduz. The likely scenario, guaranteed to send shudders among human rights activists, is that any foreigners captured will be dealt with summarily. Irene Kahn, Secretary General of Amnesty International, has already "expressed concern about the summary execution of soldiers," saying "Human rights abuses committed by the Taliban cannot be used to justify new abuses by the Northern Alliance; these killings must be stopped" (AI News Flash, 11/13/01).

But would one really expect the Northern Alliance to keep in camps, feed and respect the thousands of the aliens who brought disaster upon the country for seven years? That is not the Afghan way of warfare, nor would it make much practical sense. One would hope that some trials will take place, but that is just a hope. The fact remains that, from an American (and world) viewpoint, the more al-Qaeda members who are eliminated, the smaller the future pool of trained and indoctrinated terrorists.

Taliban resistance continues in Kandahar, not least because all indications are that Mullah Omar remains in the city. As in Kunduz, the fact that the hardcore Taliban and al-Qaeda are concentrated makes them vulnerable and facilitates our own goal of eliminating them.

Present Dangers from the Past

It is important that the Pashtun tribes of the south and southeast have finally found the resolve to act against the Taliban in their midst rather than continue with their complaints that the Northern Alliance's victories threaten their traditional claims to control in Kabul. But this also poses the main threat to the future of Afghanistan: a return to the bad habits of the past.

Even during the rule of the strongest of Afghanistan's kings, the reach of Kabul over the provinces was relative at best. The basic principle of Afghan politics was that the less control the government had, the better. That fit with the fact that Afghan loyalties were never with a country called "Afghanistan" but with their own ethnic group, their own version of Islam (Sunni, Shi'I, or Ismaili), and the traditional leaders of their own local clans and tribes, in that order.

The Soviet occupation of 1979-1989 did little to change this. The communist puppets of Moscow were virtually all Pashtuns, and they were divided between two factions of the Communist Party: one based on the Ghilzai and the other on the Durrani Pashtun tribal confederations.

Today, following the collapse of the Taliban, one sees the potential for the rapid return of that pattern and the revival of warlordism. In Mazar-e Sharif the wily Uzbek warlord Abdul Rashid Dostum, head of the National Islamic Movement (Jombesh-e Melli Islami), is back in control, as he was between the last years of the Soviet occupation and the fall of that city to the Taliban in 1996. He is also repeating his old patterns of behavior: ruthless persecution of enemies combined with a relatively enlightened social policy (religious tolerance, rights for women, and competent administration).

Further southwest, in Herat, another warlord, Ismail Khan—less ruthless than Dostum but equally "progressive"—is back in control as well, and more popular than ever. In the hardcore Tajik areas, the relatives and proteges of the late Ahmed Shah Massoud are in control—albeit still without a clear leader. And in the Pashtun regions in the south and northeast, the number of local warlords is proliferating again. In the provinces of Pakhtia, Paktika, and Khost, former Taliban minister of borders Jalaludin Haqqani has "retired his turban," as Le Monde put it. In Ghazni, the Taliban themselves left control to their previously submissive local leaders—to the good luck of the eight Western humanitarian workers left there and immediately released. In Kandahar and north of it, King

Zaher Shah loyalist Hamid Karzai is trying to wrest control. In Jalalabad, to the northeast, a multitude of warlords jockey for control, including Haji Kadeer, the former governor and brother of the murdered Abdul Haq. The Hazara Shi'i leaders in Bamyan have emerged in the center of the country and in Mazar-e Sharif, and so on.

Some of these warlords are relatively modern-minded: Ismail Khan, Dostum, and the Massoud successors being the cases in point; others, such as Younis Khalis, are only slightly more enlightened than the Taliban, which originated as a splinter from Khalis' Hezb-e Islami Party; and there are dangerously fundamentalist and anti-American warlords in search of a base of support—the worst being Gulbuddin Hekmatyar, now a protege of Iran, a pathologically anti-Western and fundamentalist character and the individual most responsible for the destruction of Kabul in 1992-1994.

Any international force deployed to Afghanistan will have to follow three basic principles:

- Disregard the noise from Amnesty International and related human rights utopians demanding trials of warlords guilty of human rights abuses in the past or since October. That would only be a recipe for the beginning of an anti-Western, anti-international resistance—and we all know what united Afghans can do in those circumstances.

- Make distinctions between malleable, adaptable, and rational warlords á la Dostum, Ismail Khan and the Tajik leadership, and fundamentalist fanatics a la Khalis, Hekmatyar and others.

- Accept for the short- and medium-term the reality of warlord control in Afghanistan, and use development and humanitarian funds to slowly and carefully erode their control and strengthen Kabul's, while remaining aware of the strength of regionalism in Afghanistan.

For these and many other practical reasons, if an international Islamic force is to be sent to Afghanistan, its core and commanding structure should be Turkish—respected, tough, no-nonsense forces, rather than the UN's usual forces of Fijians, Swedes, etc.

And the Taliban?

We are being bombarded with rumors and dire predictions of a likely Taliban retreat into a guerrilla mode of warfare—and, at least by implication, into a Soviet- or Vietnam-like nightmare. These predictions come either from military experts with minimal understanding of Afghan sociology and history or from ill-informed academics and journalists.

As Olivier Roy, perhaps the West's best scholar of Afghan affairs, has stated, "If the Taliban lose Kandahar, they are done in." (See interview in Le Monde, "Les talibans ne sont pas des gu‚rrilleros, c'est un mouvement urbain," November 16.) Why? Because, as he correctly explained, the Taliban are a basically urban movement, and Afghans are not a mobile people. In other words, they could only operate within their own tribal-controlled area. And where are the Taliban controlled areas now? Most of the remaining Taliban forces are Arab foreigners—hated by the locals, unfamiliar with the terrain, and lacking outside logistical, military, or indeed any other form of support, resupply, and reinforcements. Add to that the attractiveness of the $25 million price on Osama bin Laden's head and the future of al-Qaeda in the mountains of southern Afghanistan is dim indeed.

The bottom line is that the military aspect of the first phase of the war on terrorism—what could be described as "the Afghan lesson"—is close to completion with practically no American casualties. Meanwhile, arrests and the subsequent dismantlement of al-Qaeda cells in Western Europe are proceeding apace—much more quickly, one might add, than in the United States. Which only proves, if proof is needed, that this is a strange war: one in which computer software engineers, accountants, and law enforcement officials—including your friendly neighborhood cop—are as important as the special operations commandos and the Marines.

Reprinted with the permission from http://www.fpri.org, November 15, 2001

THIS AFGHAN WAR IS DIFFERENT

Early analysis of the U.S.-British military actions against the Taliban and al-Qaeda in Afghanistan seemed to accept that the prospects for military success in that country were poor. The major premises of this conventional wisdom, however, were simply myths that have developed, either from ignorance or malevolence. The facts do not support them.

Myth #1: U.S. military leaders are planning their strategies for the present conflict according to the patterns established by the Soviet Army during its failed 1979-1989 invasion and occupation of Afghanistan.

Nothing whatsoever in the known U.S. and British military operations of the present campaign supports this assumption. There are no massive concentrations of conventional armor or heavy army divisions in the countries neighboring Afghanistan, nor is there any indication of a massive conventional ground effort being prepared.

Myth #2: The United States is bound to be defeated in Afghanistan, just as the British and Soviets were.

In the First Afghan War (1838-1842), the British tried and failed to impose an unpopular puppet king, Shah Shuja, to unite all the fractious Afghans who, then as now, united only when threatened by the possibility of an effective and foreign—supported central government. The British garrison in Kabul was wiped out, with enormous losses of life and British prestige. Britain would fight again in Afghanistan in 1878-1880 and 1919, but these were mostly limited operations, because by then London had realized its error and turned to a policy of manipulating (often financially) the various Afghan groups. The success of this policy was demonstrated by the transformation of Afghanistan into an effective buffer zone ("state" would be too much to describe Afghanistan) between the competing ambitions of the British and Russian empires.

The Soviet experience in Afghanistan was equally ill fated, and caused enough bitterness at home to help contribute to the fall of the Soviet Union. The reasons for this, however, had as much to do with factors on the Soviet side—including the large number of soldiers lost to preventable diseases, inappropriate military tactics, and poor national morale—as Afghanistan-specific factors.

Unlike nineteenth-century Britain or the twentieth-century Soviet Union, the United States has no interest in controlling Afghanistan. The U.S. military does not intend to impose a Jeffersonian democracy on Afghanistan, and it does not intend to occupy the country. Instead, it supports all anti-Taliban forces—and not just the United Front (popularly and misleadingly known as the Northern Alliance). Moreover, most of Afghanistan's people know all this. Like ghosts, U.S. or British special forces units will appear and disappear, presenting no fixed targets for the Taliban and their supporters-and certainly they will not be laying the groundwork for occupation.

Myth #3: The terrain in Afghanistan renders modern military technology largely irrelevant.

While a great deal of Afghanistan is mountainous and exceedingly difficult for infantry operations, key areas-the Uzbek border, the Shamali Plain north of Kabul, and the entire southeast area around and including Kandahar, are perfect for heliborne operations. These also happen to be the areas of major Taliban force concentrations.

As for the truly difficult mountainous regions, the worst of those, the Badakshan-Wakhan corridor bordering China, is under United Front "control." The strategic Panjhir Valley remains under Tajik control, as does the entire area around Herat (although not the city itself). It is only in the mountainous east, around Jalalabad and the Pakistani border, that Pashtun ethnics may-if the price is right-continue to support the Taliban and al-Qaeda.

Afghanistan

The fact that the Taliban were able to conquer so much of Afghanistan from 1994 onward points to other factors more relevant to the potential for success here. First, many if not most people desired some order, so long as it was not imposed by a foreign (i.e., Soviet) force. Many wanted an end to banditry and warlordism, and the emigration flow to Pakistan that these caused. Another reason for the Taliban's success was their ability to buy local military/religious leaders—particularly in Pashtun and Nuristani areas—with al-Qaeda and Pakistani help. With the money flow from Islamabad cut off and al-Qaeda now focused on its own survival, the Taliban's ability to buy local warlords is limited at best.

Myth #4: This is an irregular campaign for which the United States is unprepared.

Based on the Soviet experience, many of the former military officers, civilian analysts, and journalists now offering "expert" opinions claim that U.S. forces will face an endless guerrilla campaign in the mountains and plains of Afghanistan. This claim is wrong.

Unlike the Soviets, whose support was limited to a very thin group of urban intelligentsia and military officers vulnerable to communist propaganda, the United States does not harbor any cultural or religious goals. Hence, the United Front (all Sunni Muslims, but moderately so) and the Shi'a Hazaras see nothing wrong with the U.S. Air Force being their air force against the Taliban. The implication should be obvious: while U.S.-British special operations forces will play a key role, most of the hunting for Osama bin Laden and his crowd will be done by Afghans themselves once the Taliban lose control over the major cities and regions.

Moreover, the Taliban are not a "guerrilla" army anymore. They have become a quasi-regular force, and like most former guerrillas (e.g., the Khmer Rouge in Cambodia, Frelimo in Mozambique, and the Sandanistas in Nicaragua), they are performing badly in their regular posture.

Myth #5: It is impossible to find Osama bin Laden in Afghanistan.

This assumes that al-Qaeda's Arab (or foreign) militants can find refuge inside Afghanistan without the locals knowing their whereabouts or acting on the historical Afghan suspicion of foreigners, Muslim or otherwise.

In truth, most Afghans would join the winners (i.e., the anti-Taliban forces) and capture or kill bin Laden, especially if doing so made them wealthy. So it may be asked where, and for how long, a foreigner and his large group of Arabs could hide in a country where the population longs for international aid, money, and food, and is historically xenophobic?

Myth #6: Because the United Front is composed largely of ethnic minorities, it cannot form a stable government in Kabul. Therefore, there is no realistic long-term alternative to the Taliban.

This theory's flaws are many. First, the non-Pashtun ethnic minorities that make up the United Front (which is recognized by the United Nations as the government of Afghanistan) represent the majority of the Afghan population.

Second, the Pashtuns are not, as Secretary of Defense Donald Rumsfeld has begun calling them, "southern tribes." They are, to paraphrase George Bernard

Shaw, "a people separated by a common language." The Durrani confederation in the east and south is the Taliban's power base, but-and this is a very large "but"-the Ghilzai confederation in the east (with Jalalabad at its center) is unhappy with the Durrani/Taliban powersharing arrangements. They are equally represented in Pakistan, hence Pakistani President General Pervez Musharaff's admittedly daring challenge to the Taliban. The former Afghan King Zahir Shah is a Pashtun and probably could rally enough of his people to get rid of the bin Laden gang of foreigners, with some financial backing. The Taliban's army, which held out defiantly for five weeks of U.S. air bombardment, crumbled once the ground war began in earnest.

By mid-November, all these myths have been exploded by the reality in the field. In four days the Taliban lost all but one of the country's major cities (Kandahar), and the fate of that city was sealed as well. Moreover, none of this was accomplished by U.S. ground forces, but by native Afghan elements on their own—albeit with the decisive support of U.S. air power. Thus, none of the mistakes made by the Soviets was repeated and the results were both rapid and spectacular.

The issue that still worries the proponents of the above myths is the possibility that the Taliban will revert to irregular warfare and, thus, enmesh the United States in a messy counter-insurgency campaign similar to the Soviet experience. That scenario is based on a misunderstanding of history. The anti-Soviet mujahedeen enjoyed widespread international support-military, financial, and logistical—and had a reliable haven in Pakistan. These are advantages the Taliban and their foreign mercenaries of al-Qaeda do not have. Furthermore, as the Taliban ranks have shrank dramatically through casualties and defections, their remaining core of support is precisely those foreign elements—resented by the population and, thus, unable to survive for long in a hostile environment.

There remains the issue of Osama bin Laden's fate. This, however, is closely linked to that of the Taliban leadership, which looks bleak. After the United Front took control of Kabul, the Pashtuns have to prove, through action, that they deserve the important role they claim they should have in a future government. The most likely way they will try to do that is the destruction of the Taliban/al-Qaeda leadership, now cornered in their territory. While this probably will require a more extensive role for U.S. or British special forces than before, it is not just a plausible scenario-it is the most likely.

We must consider all these facts when thinking about Afghanistan and the probabilities for success for the U.S./British—led military action-especially when barraged with ill-informed arguments to the contrary.

THE FUTILE SEARCH FOR "ROOT CAUSES" OF TERRORISM

Socioeconomic grievances, or so some assert, explain (though they do not justify) terrorism in general and Islamic terrorism in particular—the factors Al Gore called this past February "another axis of evil in the world: poverty and ignorance; disease and environmental disorder; corruption and political oppression," all of which lead to terrorism. But do they?

It is hubris to attempt to explain terrorism in general, let alone in its many different forms across time and place. The following observations are therefore intended only to refocus the debate, not to "explain" terrorism.

The desire to identify "root causes" and so be able to correct them is natural. Root causes "have" to be there—at least in the American mind. There must be an explanation for the inexplicable: Why a teenaged Palestinian girl would blow herself up in an attempt to kill as many Jews as possible, or privileged young men of the Arab world plot to kill themselves while murdering thousands of American civilians. But much as the frequently asked question this fall, "Why do they hate us?" had flawed premises and yielded flawed answers, framing the question as "What are the root causes of terrorism?" leads too easily to looking at the usual suspects: "poverty," "injustice," "exploitation," and "frustration." Like the man in the parable who looks for his lost keys under the streetlight instead of where he lost them because "the light's better," it's easier to look in these familiar areas than to face and address the real problems.

Those who hold to "poverty as the root cause" do so even though the data does not fit their model. Even leaving aside multimillionaire Osama bin Laden, the backgrounds of the September 11 killers indicates that they were, without exception, scions of privilege: All were either affluent Saudis and Egyptians, citizens of the wealthy Gulf statelets, or rich sons of Lebanon, trained in and familiar with the ways of the West—not exactly the victims of poverty in Muslim dictatorships. Many poor Egyptians, Moroccans, and Palestinians may support terrorists, but they do not—and cannot—provide them with recruits. In fact, al-Qaeda has no use for illiterate peasants. They cannot participate in World Trade Center-like attacks, unable as they are to make themselves inconspicuous in the West and lacking the education and training terrorist operatives need.

Indeed, ever since the Russian intellectuals "invented" modern terrorism in the nineteenth century, revolutionary violence—terrorism is just one form of it—has been a virtual monopoly of the relatively privileged. Terrorists have been middle-class, often upper-class, and always educated, but never poor. The South American Tupamaros and Montoneros of the 1970s were all middle-class, starting as café Jacobins and graduating into urban terrorism, as were their followers among the German Baader-Meinhof Gang, the Italian Red Brigades, France's Action Directe, the Sandinista leadership in Nicaragua and, before it, Fidel Castro's Cuban revolutionaries. Considering the composition of many of the antiglobalist groups today, it is a safe bet that middle-class, prosperous, and self-righteous as they are, they will soon provide the recruits of a new wave of terrorism in the West—as we may already be seeing in the revival of Italy's Red Brigades.

To say that economic conditions are not the root cause of terrorism is not to say that the there are no conditions that correlate strongly to political violence and terrorism. There are phenomena we should be concerned about in this regard, it is just that they are far less obvious than poverty and much more complex to address.

Environmentalist extremists, their animal-rights friends, anti-international corporation militants, anti-genetically modified plants fanatics á la Jose Bove—the world's best known vandal—none of them poor or underprivileged, have already demonstrated a propensity for violence and should be expected to do so in more deadly and organized manners in the future.

That is where the Osamas of the world meet the Western rejectionists of what the West is all about: rationality, individual as opposed to collective rights and interests, secularism, and capitalism. True enough, there is little common ideological ground among French Trotskyite Arlette Laguiller (who, with colleagues, has reached 10 percent in the polls in the first round of France's presidential elections) and Marxist-cum-separatist groups like the Turkish PKK, the Basque ETA, the Sri Lankan LTTE, and the Irish Republican Army. But they share a common enemy. That enemy is the Western culture of democracy (which is correctly declared un-Islamic by all ideologues of Islamic terrorism), capitalism (hated in a very ecumenical way by Marxists of all stripes and Islamists), and individualism (opposed by Marxist totalitarians dreaming of Marx's stateless communist Utopia, as well as by Islamic believers in a new Caliphate to lead the community of Muslims worldwide).

But, we are told, the Islamic states are poor and undemocratic, which justifies rebellion against their tyrannical rulers. Why is that so, and what can be done about it by Muslims and others? Perhaps most Muslim countries are undemocratic because they are Muslim. When given an electoral choice in 1992 in the first and last democratic elections in the Arab world, most Algerians preferred the Islamic Salvation Front (FIS) over the secular (and corrupt) ruling socialist party—although perfectly aware that FIS's ideology meant not just "one man, one vote" but "one man, one vote, one time." Which raises a very uncomfortable question for both conservatives in the U.S., who routinely blast the lack of democracy in the Arab world, and the human rights fundamentalists such as Amnesty International on the left, who support absolute democracy and at the same time condemn the Islamist disregard of all freedoms, as in Iran.

The apologists of Marxism and Islamism also need to answer another basic question. Did such regimes as, say, Iran, Afghanistan under the Taliban, or the late regimes in Eastern Europe and the Soviet Union, actually make the life of ordinary citizens better, or worse? And why would "democracy" be better in Saudi Arabia morally, ideologically, and practically, where the chances of an Islamist getting elected are at least as great as in Algeria? Does it make sense for the European Union to condemn Turkey for proscribing (constitutionally, one might add) Islamist parties? Does Brussels really believe that an Islamic-governed Turkey is better than the current, secular Turkey, a NATO ally?

The poor in Muslim states may be the popular base of terrorist support, but they have neither the money nor the votes ("who votes doesn't count, who counts them does," in Stalin's immortal words) the privileged do. Ultimately, Islamic terrorism, just as its Marxist or secessionist version in the West and Latin America was, is a matter of power—who has it and how to get it—not of poverty. Accepting this as a fundamental aspect of terrorism does not suggest any immediate solutions, but can direct further study toward better explanations of terrorism and theories with some potential predictive value.

Reprinted with the permission from http://www.nationalreview.com/ comment/comment-radu042902.asp, April 29, 2002

OBSERVATIONS ON THE IRAQ WAR DEBATE

Brent Scowcroft, Presidents Ford and George Bush senior's national security adviser ("Don't attack Saddam," *Wall Street Journal*, August 15), and then Zbigniew Brzezinski, Scowcroft's counterpart in President Carter's administration ("If we must fight . . . .," *Washington Post*, August 18), have both questioned the very idea of attacking Saddam Hussein's Iraq. No one questions that the Baghdad regime is indeed threatening, and both authors agree that the world would be better off without Saddam. But are they advocating caution more than inaction, or are they making the dividing line between them so thin as to be invisible? Both either state or imply that the Bush administration has not yet made the case for war; and that a war on Iraq will not be an easy war. So the questions are narrowed to three: when to start the war, how to conduct it, and "What next?"

Scowcroft argues that any war against Saddam must come after the war on terrorism has been concluded and the Israeli-Palestinian conflict resolved. Only then "it may at some point be wise to remove [Saddam] from power." There are major problems with Scowcroft's argument, however. First, by its very nature, the war on terrorism is a very long, perhaps generations long, protracted conflict. For how long should we allow Saddam, and perhaps also his son and/or successor, to continue in power in Iraq, threatening regional stability and amassing weapons of mass destruction? Second, Scowcroft's distinction between Saddam and terrorism is artificial. He seems to disregard the fact that, whether or not Iraq supports terrorist groups elsewhere (and he does openly do so, at least in the cases of Israel and Lebanon), the Saddam regime itself is a terrorist organization.

As for resolving the Israeli-Palestinian conflict, Scowcroft makes two dubious assumptions: (1) that the Arab states now opposed to the removal of Saddam are serious (or correct) in believing that they cannot survive the continuation of the Al Aksa intifada simultaneous with a U.S. attack on Iraq; and (2) that there is a solution to the Israeli-Palestinian conflict in the foreseeable future. But Arab regimes may well be less vulnerable than is assumed by both Scowcroft and his opponents among the supporters of war with Iraq in the Bush administration. But what better encouragement for the growing number of Palestinian terrorists and their supporters, prominent among them Saddam himself, to do everything in their power to sabotage any and all attempts to find a solution to their conflict with Israel? And what if, as many observers have noticed and many Israelis and Palestinians believe, the Israeli-Palestinian conflict is, indeed, an existential one, a zero-sum struggle to death between two peoples, rather than a conventional struggle over land, water, borders, and the like ? If that is so, no solution can be possible in the foreseeable future.

The "how" of the war is a serious issue indeed, and caution is needed, as Brzezinski and Scowcroft both argue. The Gulf War is an imperfect model in every respect. To begin with, in 1991 Saddam knew that his removal from power was unlikely. In 2002 he knows the opposite. This should have a very concentrating effect on minds in Baghdad. The predictable result is some very strong resistance from those-mostly the Sunni Arab minority in power now-who have benefited from the regime.

It may well be, as Scowcroft points out, that Saddam will decide to drag Israel down with him-a very real possibility. However, it is equally plausible that, left unchecked, Saddam will try to destroy Israel anyway. Indeed, if Saddam thirsts for weapons of mass destruction as a deterrent, they can only be meant to deter both those who threaten his regime and those opposing his regional goals-one of which is the destruction of Israel.

Then there is the issue of allies. Militarily speaking, the U.S. only needs the significant support of a handful of countries: the U.K. for its forces, Turkey, and some smaller Gulf states for basing rights. It has no particular need for Syria, Argentina, or some of the other dozens of members of the 1991 alliance-nor even for its NATO allies, whose capabilities are minimal against their extensive claims to a right to participate in decision making.

On the other side of the argument, the war advocates' claims will soon have to be lucidly examined, both with respect to the questions "How?" and (especially) "What next?" It is unlikely that some serious, organized, and capable internal Iraqi force will assist, let alone be assisted by, the U.S. forces. The Kurds are, as always, divided and unreliable; the Shias are divided and unarmed; and the rest is largely in London. We can expect only tacit or post facto support from most Iraqis. At least in the important early stages, it would be our war alone. This brings us directly to the matter of "What next?"

In Iraq, the only lid on internal strife and protection from division is Saddam. Once he and his Baath party apparatus are removed, some external force will have to keep the country together. It would have to be an international force, perhaps along the lines of Bosnia—with the UN's blessings, a de facto (Muslim) administrator with extensive powers and, yes, some U.S. forces in the (deep) background. The difference, pace Brzezinski, is that Iraq's extensive oil resources would pay for most of this. The notion that the "Iraqi people" want "democracy" is unrealistic-and against the traditions of Iraq and every other Arab country. The advocates of war need to offer us much better arguments in support of this notion than they have offered so far. The experience of Afghanistan since October should remind us to have extremely modest expectations from a post-Saddam Iraq.

Nor is the issue of Iraq's neighbors an easy one to deal with. For instance, Turkey, the irreplaceable ally for military action, is at one with Iran and Syria in opposing the creation of a Kurdish state, de facto or otherwise, in northern Iraq. If Saddam is to be removed, the Kurds' desire for independence would have to go unfulfilled. The Kurds best chances are with the present de facto Turkish zone of influence in northern Iraq.

All of this said, the removal of Saddam is a necessity, and time is short. The war opponents have no case. The postponement advocates risk making Saddam more, not less, of a threat. But the war advocates must soon make a clear-visioned, well-argued case.

Reprinted with the permission from http://www.frontpagemag.com,
August 21, 2002

ISLAM ON THE DEFENSIVE

The recent spate of arguments and judicial actions in France against intellectuals accused of insulting Islam—first Michel Houellebecq, then Oriana Fallaci, continues a line which started with Salman Rushdie—any criticism of any form of Islam is blasphemy and, thus, a crime. While the Rushdie scandal could be laid to the doorstep of Khomeini, the others are the result of Western confusion over its own values and the culturally suicidal impact of mindless "multiculturalism." The latest spate was provoked by the British author's Martin Amis criticism of Islamic militants as humorless and sexually insecure. While such frivolous criticism could, and should, be, itself, criticized on its merits, the problem is that rational criticism was not what Islamic spokesmen in Europe choose to do.

Less than surprising, according to the *London Times*, Sheikh Omar Bakri Muhammad, of the extremist al-Muhajiroun group [and a major recruiter of

Islamists in the United Kingdom], said: "When people speak about radical Islam it conflicts with so-called human values. I believe this is a war against Islam. Any comment on radical Islam is a hidden attack on Islam. Islam is for the whole of mankind. Muslim sisters are as active as Muslim brothers. What he has said is a way of subverting Islam." Interestingly, Omar Bakri probably meant "human rights" when he referred to "so-called human values"—"so-called" because his brand of Islam does not accept such thing—for it humanity is restricted to (radical) Islam.

However, according to the same source, Dr. Zaki Badawi, Principal of the Muslim College, said: "Can he say the same about radical Christianity or radical Judaism? Radical Islam is very difficult to defend, but radical Judaism is offensive to women, and there is no sense of humour at all. I cannot criticise him. I agree with him. But I think that *non-Muslims are very unwise to comment on Islam*, [emphasis added—MR] particularly a man like Martin Amis, a novelist, because he has not studied it. They should be a little more cautious. They should leave it to the specialists." From there to the claim of the main ideologue of South East Asian Islamic terrorism, Abu Bakar Bashir, who claims, like his friend Ossama, that his being accused of the Bali mass murder is a "grand ploy against Islam" is only a small step.

Translation—even if September 11 proved, as the very moderate (but still a plaintiff in the Houellebecq case!) Rector of the Paris Grand Mosque, Dalil Boubakeur put it, that " a certain [type of] Islam" could be dangerous for the West," Muslims should be the only ones entitled to criticize that "certain type of Islam." Indeed, non-Muslims trying to do so are immediately accused of "orientalism," one of the most poisonous and, indeed, dangerous concepts ever invented—creation of a Christian Palestinian professor at Columbia, Edward Said. Hence, Western specialists on Islam are, ipso facto, expressions of Western imperialism (Said), or ignorant (Badawi), or criminally blasphemous (Omar Bakri). Islam is a world by itself, to be understood and examined by its inhabitants only, whether they live in the West or in the Muslim world. And here lies the problem, as well as, optimistically, the opportunity.

During the early 1980s a political joke circulating in Cuba claimed that Cuba was the largest country in the world—with its government in Moscow, army in Africa, and economy in Miami. To paraphrase, and this is definitely not a joke, al-Qaeda is the largest Non-Governmental Organization (NGO) in the world: its recruiters are largely in London, its recruits in Western Europe and Saudi Arabia, its leaders in Pakistan, its dead ideologues were in Egypt, its actions everywhere, from Bali to Lackawana and from Morocco to Yemen. So then, where do we start in dealing with it?

The recruits and operatives are being dealt with most effectively in Muslim countries, where terrorist organizations like Hizb-ut-Tahrir are treated as terrorist organizations—which they are, in Egypt and Central Asia, while they are legal in "Londonistan." Human rights fundamentalists á la ACLU or Amnesty

International may not like it, but in a war friends are more important than nice friends—after all the United States was the ally of "Uncle Joe," was it not? Would they have objected to the anti-Nazi alliance on the ground that Stalin was a mass murderer?—one could never know, but one suspects not. The al-Qaeda International's operations in country after country are a matter of intelligence, police, and, occasionally, military action.

Which brings us to the crux of the matter—the recruiters and ideologues, the ideological struggle within Islam between "modernizers," to use an admittedly loose term, and terrorist fundamentalists. In the long term, it is just this aspect of the "war on terrorism" which will decide the outcome, and the statements and actions of non-fundamentalists are not very encouraging at this point.

There is a defensive reaction of Muslims of all kinds when al-Qaeda and its nebula of associated groups is criticized as an Islamic phenomenon—and that is the main obstacle in the ideological war—which is what has to happen and has to be won within Islam—and it could only be described as the circling of the wagons, as demonstrated above. To state that attacks against the al-Qaeda nebula, let alone the musings of Houellebecq, Fallaci, and Amis, are "anti-Islamic" or dangerously close to an attack on "Islam" is to play into the hands of the Omar Bakris, Bashirs, and Bin Ladens. Islamic solidarity, the notion of *umma*, (Islamic community) is far easier to manipulate by terrorist fundamentalists than by the ambiguous attitudes of a Boubakeur or Badawi. Indeed, for centuries now, self-analysis, logical and rational, has not been the Islamic culture's strong point—and that is what has to be revived, if the intra-Islamic ideological conflict between modernists (or "moderates") and Islamists is to be won in the long run.

All of this brings us to the center of the current debate about the nature of Islam, its ability to live with, or adapt to, Western laws, values, and rules—the real key on the cultural war within Islam and the only way to avoid al-Qaeda's march through the Islamic world.

Reprinted with the permission from http://www.frontpagemag.com,
November 1, 2002

THE PECULIAR CASE OF AL-QAEDA

al-Qaeda is giving lawyers, politicians, and analysts a lot of headaches because it is, indeed, the first "post modern" terror organization. Its modus operandi is perfectly adapted to a post-Cold War environment, far more so than the international and domestic legal systems and governments everywhere are—no matter the nature of those governments, democratic and Western, third world, transitional. or whatever.

While it is never prudent to underestimate one's enemy, it is even less so in the case of al-Qaeda, whose entire leadership—not just Osama bin Laden or

Ayman al Zawahiri—is adept at understanding and taking advantage of today's uniquely fluid geopolitical map.

With the fall of the Soviet bloc, a large number of states—particularly in Africa, but also in the Muslim world as a whole—collapsed into black holes of anarchy (Somalia or Sierra Leone come to mind). Many of the post-colonial states were not viable to begin with, but prior to 1989 were kept afloat after a fashion, and with only a small investment, by Soviet, Warsaw Pact, or, indeed, Western (primarily U.S. and French) military and economic aid. That aid gone, such nominal states finally faced their inherently artificial nature—and promptly collapsed.

And so we have places like Somalia and Sudan, Sierra Leone, Nigeria, Yemen, and, indeed, Pakistan, where the writ of the government—if any—hardly runs beyond the suburbs of the capital city, the rest of the "country" being a wildly anarchic area where a few thousand dollars and a few simple (they have to be simple in a mass of illiteracy) ideas take over.

It is precisely these holes in the Swiss cheese of the "international system" that make groups like al-Qaeda possible: the savage frontier provinces of Pakistan and Yemen, northern Nigeria, parts of Sudan and the whole of Somalia, most of West Africa, the infinite islands of Indonesia, the ethnic mish-mash of Northern Caucasus, the "triple border" area of Brazil, Paraguay, and Argentina—and the list goes on and on. al-Qaeda discovered this reality long before Washington did and moved into those interstices where the rule of law is a joke, where children use guns larger than themselves, where power comes from bullets rather than electoral mandates, and where mad dictators run amok.

And then there is the West. European countries as well as the United States have lost control of their borders and their cultural destinies. Airline tickets to move terrorists across countries are easily enough obtained that a critical mass of potential recruits to Islamists' dream of universal power exists in virtually all of Western Europe. Legal systems increasingly prove inadequate in dealing with terrorism, as demonstrated most recently by the acquittal of four al-Qaeda operatives in a Rotterdam court, but also by the United States' confused legal approach vis-á-vis Islamist terrorist suspects. Some are kept in a legal limbo in Guantanamo, some in military brigs in the United States; some are tried in federal courts, some are killed in the sands of Yemen, etc.

And then there is the inherent confusion of the Western cultural elites. Some are still trying (uselessly, but, hey, it's all at the taxpayers' expense) to find "root causes" of Islamist terrorism in American policies or the West's past colonial guilt, as if they could not read Bin Laden's own statements: he wants Spain back, he wants Alabamians to convert to "his" Islam—or else! As for the Muslim world, when many Indonesians, Pakistanis, or Malays, even Turks, not to mention Arabs, think that al-Qaeda's massacres in New York was justified by the "victimization" of Palestinians, we have an international dysfunctional culture better understood by psychologists than politicians.

Then there is the biggest problem counterterrorist operatives face: that al-Qaeda is a new animal. Sendero Luminoso in Peru (actually the communist party of Peru, according to its own description), even the Khmer Rouge or the Marxist drug dealers of Colombia's guerrillas, all had immediate political goals, as did the plane hijackers of the Palestinian "cause" during the 1970s: things that could presumably be approached in a political manner. So do ETA in Spain and France, the IRA in Britain, the Corsican separatists, etc. Even the East German-manipulated terrorists of Germany, Italy, France, and Belgium during the 1970s had immediate political goals, but not al-Qaeda.

Indeed, when terrorists are prepared to kill themselves, deterrence—a major tool in dealing with traditional terror groups—becomes futile. Before 1989 the threat of retaliation from Moscow's puppeteers of terror could work—it was all a rational, albeit deadly, game. But for those whose game is the "recovery" of the Iberian Peninsula, life is of no significance.

al-Qaeda has also been extraordinarily successful in eliminating national and cultural distinctions among its members: Algerians and Moroccans, Egyptians, Indonesians, Pakistanis, Yemenis, and French converts, Puerto Ricans, and Californians, Lackawana, New York Yemeni-Americans, British mullahs on phony welfare, all make this terror organization a global, indeed a globalist, one.

Culturally, Bin Laden has clearly won one argument—despite President Bush's disclaimers, he did make the current war one between cultures: between his version of Islam and the rest of the world. Not just the West, but the rest of the world. Since 9/11, this war has claimed Hindus murdered in Bali, Buddhists everywhere, Confucians and Marxists in China and Uzbekistan, a Bulgarian Eastern Orthodox killed off the coast of Yemen, Catholics and Protestants in the United States and Europe. It is indeed a war between religions, if not cultures. And, most importantly, Bin Laden has largely won this argument among the world's fifth largest religious group: the Muslims. Faced with the choice of eliminating Bin Laden or defending him, most Muslims tend toward the latter. There are too many "but" defenses among mainstream Muslims to think otherwise.

True enough, as we all know, there is no Muslim Vatican, no single authority deciding what or who is universally accepted as beyond the bounds of "orthodox" Islam—at least not among the majority Sunni Islam. Islam is not the Catholic Church. But even so, one may wonder. The King of Morocco, self-proclaimed "Commander of the Faithful" insists (quite effectively, one might add) that the (largely illegal) mass of Moroccan residents in Europe remain his subjects—no assimilation, please! The secular regime in Algiers claims control over former Algerians in France, and the Saudis...well, the Saudis do and fund everything possible to ensure that Muslims in the West answer only to the rules of Wahabbism, not the law of their new countries, not reason, not anything other than their own eighteenth-century ideology.

Unless there is an extraordinary birth of a Western Islam—one that breaks some basic rules and historic traditions, accepts the reality of Muslims as a minority with no more or fewer "rights" than the existing populations in countries to which they choose to relocate, the Islamic diaspora is going to continue to be a deadly threat everywhere, and has to be contained.

Reprinted with the permission from http://www.frontpagemag.com,
December 20, 2002

WHAT WE DO NOT KNOW ABOUT TERRORISM

The media, members of Congress, and Democratic presidential candidates—all of whom should, and do, know better—have made it a favorite sport to criticize our intelligence on terrorism, both domestic and international. The problem is that intelligence, by its very nature, is vulnerable to malicious or uninformed criticism—when successful, it has to be quiet; when unsuccessful it becomes a target for free-for-all criticism. However, occasionally enough, information filters out to the public to suggest that the critics of the CIA, FBI, and the Bush Administration's alleged "unilateralism" are badly off base.

Three recent cases may serve as a reminder to the uninformed and overcritical that there is much more they do not know than there is what they know, or think they know.

Item # 1—On August 12, a British citizen and arms dealer of Indian origin, was arrested at Newark International Airport while trying to sell an undercover FBI agent a Russian-made a shoulder-fired anti–aircraft missile. The sting operation started in Moscow, where the dealer approached a Russian officer with a request to buy such a missile. The Russian informed his government, which contacted the FBI, which contacted British domestic (MI5) and foreign (MI6) intelligence. As a result, the FBI Arab speaking operator approached the dealer with an offer to buy the missile for an Islamic terrorist group, for an attack against an U.S. airliner. Meanwhile, closely monitored, the missile made its way as a "medical supply" shipment to Baltimore. Once the dealer was in the United States to finish the transaction, he was arrested. The entire operation took more than a year.

Item # 2—According to reputable French media, at the end of 2001 the Canadian intelligence—which, by the way, is far more effective and cooperative with the U.S. on counter terrorism than the Ottawa government—discovered that one of its Canada-based Algerian terrorist suspects was in Cuba, and informed the U.S. Apparently surprised by his existence, the NSA started intercepting his communications. That led to the location of the Algerian's ultimate boss—the "amir" of the Islamic Armed Group (GIA), Antar Zouabri, inside Algeria, and so informed the Algerians. The result was that in February 2002, Zouabri shared the fate of six of the GIA's previous leader—he was killed by government forces. It should be pointed out that Zouabri was correctly described as "the worst criminal in Algerian history;" indeed, under his leadership (1996–2002) the GIA was probably responsible for tens of thousand of murders. The reason was that he declared the entire Algerian people—or at least the 99.9 percent who did not support the GIA, as "infidels" and, thus, as legitimate targets for murder.

What is particularly significant in these two cases is that effective international counter terrorism cooperation was with two governments with a very long history of political hostility or, more recently, political differences with the United States. Indeed, the Russians (and their present intelligence is the direct successor of the KGB, one of whose members was President Vladimir Putin himself) have for decades been our main intelligence enemies. Algeria, at least until it was shocked by economic bankruptcy and the Islamists' electoral victories in 1989–1991, was a "socialist" Arab regime, closely aligned with Moscow and a strong supporter of Palestinian terrorism.

One could go further, and note that intelligence cooperation between American and French organizations is far better, indeed one may appear as surprisingly better that the obviously difficult political relations between Washington and Paris.

Surprises of this kind do not stop here—Libya has cooperated, at least marginally, with the U.S. in pursuing Islamist groups in Europe and elsewhere – not least because Qaddafi himself is threatened by an Al–Qaeda associated group, Al–Jama'a al-Islamiyyah al-Muqatilah bi-Libya (Libyan Islamic Fighting Group—FIG). Syria did the same, and for similar reasons—as its former counterpart in Iraq, the Damascus regime is a sectarian minority regime disguised as Baath "socialist"—Sunni in Baghdad, Alawi in Syria, and is threatened by Sunni majority Islamists under the control of the Muslim Brethren. And the Saudis, occasionally, but more and more consistently lately, have also increased their cooperation with the U.S., despite public denials.

There are some, mostly human rights fundamentalists á la Amnesty International, as well as a variety of neoconservatives, who believe, for distinctly different reasons, that U.S. cooperation, including in intelligence matters, with such regimes is shortsighted, politically wrong, and morally unpalatable. That, of course would also imply that World War II alliance with Stalin was shortsighted, politically wrong, and morally unpalatable—an arguable notion, considering Hitler's threat to civilization as we know it, and a threat similar to that posed by the likes of Osama bin Laden or Antar Zouabri today. It should be clear to any serious observers that intelligence cooperation with such as the Libyans, Syrians, Saudis, even Russians is not, and should not be, based on common values but on common, immediate interests and enemies—which simply defines what intelligence is all about.

The Russians have suddenly become our partners on counterterrorism because they face Islamist terrorism in Chechnya, not because they share our

interests—witness their counterproductive policy of selling Iran nuclear technology. Moscow has long, and wrongly, claimed that all Chechen opposition
to Russian rule is terrorist—but the Chechens have also demonstrated, and for
many years, that they would rather have solidarity with openly declared and al-
Qaeda associated Islamist terrorists, such as Shamil Basayev, ex-prime minister
of the short–lived independent Chechnya of the mid-1990s. It is not hypocrisy,
as human rights and pro–Chechen groups in the West still claim that Chechen
Islamists have taken over the legitimate cause of Chechen self–determination.

Furthermore, it is only common sense to accept cooperation from Damascus
if the alternative may well be another Sunni terrorist regime; the same applies
to Libya; and, most importantly, to Saudi Arabia.

Once again, we are faced with a regime which, on the one hand, pays and
exports the ideology, Wahhabism, that creates Islamist terrorism world wide; on
the other hand, the very same regime is the only game in town—any free elections in the kingdom are likely to result in a victory for al-Qaeda, with Osama
bin Laden as the leader. Do we really want that?

And so we go back to the intelligence cooperation aspect—it is going on
under the horizon of most media, media pundits and running politicians; it is
cheap, easy, and commonly manipulated for equally cheap political reasons.
And it is wrong. Humility and modesty are needed, but not found.

Reprinted with the permission from http://www.frontpagemag.com,
September 4, 2003

THE SEAMLESS WAR ON TERRORISTS

Now that the Democratic primary season is upon us, we being inundated
with non-sequitors on the issue of terrorism—and not just from the candidates.
Senator Ted Kennedy contends that the war on Saddam Hussein was cooked up
in Crawford, Texas. Many of his party colleagues claim that they were taken for
a ride when they voted to authorize the war, because some malevolent Texas
Svengali had duped them into believing that Saddam and Bin Laden were
connected. (And a handful of these now hope to bring their perceptive insight
into the Oval Office.) Others who should have known better and who are *not*
presidential candidates, mostly retired generals, also claim Bush convinced the
American public there was a connection between Saddam and 9/11, despite the
fact that nobody in the administration has ever claimed such a link and everyone has repeatedly stated that there is no evidence of a connection.

Opinion polls show the American public also overwhelmingly believes there
was a direct link. Whatever the merits of this particular belief, the public *has*
intuited correctly that terrorism—whether the al-Qaeda suicide version or
Saddam's more calculated variant—is not a scattered set of unrelated episodes
but a seamless continuum.

The facts, such as they are in the murky world of intelligence, are simple: the Bush Administration made no serious attempt to tie Saddam's regime to the planning or carrying out of 9/11. However, there are indications of some contacts between Iraqi intelligence and disparate parts of the al-Qaeda nebula. But then, it would have been absurd for Saddam's people, or, for that matter, *our* intelligence, *not* to try to establish links with, infiltrate, or manipulate as many segments of that nebula as possible. If nothing else, Iraq would have appreciated that "the enemy of my enemy (the U.S.) is my friend."

In more specific terms, by the end of the Saddam regime Iraq was combining a number of elements common to terrorist hotbeds elsewhere. In the northeast, outside Baghdad's control, a Taliban-like group, Ansar al Islam, was spreading its influence, and attracting professionals of terror from Afghanistan to Lebanon—precisely the type of black hole familiar from Somalia, Liberia, and Afghanistan. Meanwhile, volunteers for *jihad* were pouring into Iraq from Algeria and Egypt, Saudi Arabia and Pakistan.

Then there is the support Saddam gave to Islamic Jihad and Hamas, including as much as $25,000 per case "life insurance" (i.e. support for "martyrs") to the families and enablers of suicide bombers in Israel. Like al-Qaeda, Hamas and Islamic Jihad are Islamic fundamentalists, and, therefore, ideologically incompatible with the Ba'ath Party ideology, which is minority secular (in Iraq) or heretical (in the case of the Alawis, the secretive sect now ruling Syria). But Islamic sectarianism (Islamic, that is, if the Alawis are Muslims, which is not what most orthodox Sunnis would accept) mixes well with radical, even Marxist, "surface" politics in the Middle East. For instance, the Revolutionary People's Liberation Army/Front (DHKP/C) of Turkey, an ostensibly Marxist-Leninist urban terrorist group with Maoist nuances is 80 percent or more Alawi. Incidentally, the DHKP/C is now larger and more active inside Turkey than even the equally Marxist-Stalinist Kurdistan Workers' Party (PKK), now called Kurdistan Freedom and Democracy, or (KADEK).

One can thus reasonably dismiss the claims that Saddam's secularism makes cooperation with Islamists impossible, or even unlikely. Would anyone claim that the World War II alliance of Churchill's Britain, FDR's America, and Stalin's Soviet Union never existed? Nor does it make sense to distinguish between "Palestinian Islamic terrorists," who, so far, have not specifically trained their murderous eyes upon Americans, and the al-Qaeda nebula, whose stated goal is precisely the wholesale murder of American and Jewish "pigs and monkeys." Worse still, some human rights groups, self-appointed spokesmen of the American Islamic anti-anti-terrorist elements, and European governments, are trying to make another absurd distinction between "social" and "political" branches of known and active terrorist groups such as Hamas

It seems, and indeed is, absurd to believe, as the Europeans pretended until very recently (when the EU finally banned the "political" branch of Hamas) that Hamas' "social work" organizations—schools, kindergartens, clinics—are somehow the "good" side of that group, or that the newly minted KADEK is somehow the "peaceful" reincarnation of the same PKK that has murdered some 30,000 Turkish citizens since 1984. What those are, in a non-coincidental echo of the old communist "peace," "labor," or "legal" fronts, is clear: tools for recruitment, mobilization, and indoctrination.

Where the administration is misleading, or simply incorrect, is in repeatedly claiming that al-Qaeda is just a radical fringe of Islam, which is supposedly inherently pacific. In fact, many wealthy and middle-class Muslims, half educated in half-baked notions of historic victimhood, make up a minority (but *the* politically relevant and articulate one) that is actively or otherwise on the enemy side. And even a minority of the world's some 1.2 billion Muslims equals a group much too large to define as "fringe."

Islamist preachers in London take advantage of Britain's rights of free speech to recruit members of al-Qaeda, to raise funds, and to stir up opposition to the very Western values they have taken advantage of to pursue their agenda. The Muslim Brotherhood, the font of contemporary Islamist radicalism, and its legitimizer and organizer, controls France's largest, most aggressive, and best-organized Islamic organization. Thanks to that, and the oil resources of its Saudi/Wahhabi allies, the Brotherhood controls Muslim missionarism in the United States' military and prisons, has a growing and increasingly sophisticated lobby structure in most European capitals, and has been able to forge an alliance with irresponsible multiculturalism and anti-capitalist *altermondism* throughout the West.

But to return to Saddam: does his removal make Islamist terrorism weaker? Yes, inasmuch as at the very least it denies resources to Hamas & Co. And a defeat of Islamism (whose Sunni supporters are now flocking into Iraq) along the Tigris and Euphrates, would be one step toward victory over Islamist terror in general. Ultimately, the practitioners of *jihad* pursue their actions on behalf of the world-wide Islamic community—*umma*, and that explains the presence of Chechens and Moroccans, Pakistanis and Indonesians in Afghanistan and now in Iraq. For the al-Qaeda nebula is engaged in a global struggle against civilization, and not in a series of spasmodic acts of violence. Bin Laden has a global strategy, well planned and steadily pursued, and Iraq fits perfectly into that strategy. Just as "Che" Guevara was seeking more and more "Vietnams" in South America as part of a global pursuit for socialism and the defeat of the United States, so Bin Laden is pursuing a strategy of more and more Afghanistans (or Somalias or Lebanons) with the goal of purifying the world from the baleful influence of the United States—and forcing Americans to turn and run out of Iraq is, in his view, one more step toward that goal.

Conversely, a defeat for fundamentalists anywhere, especially in a place as historically and culturally important as Baghdad, is a victory against terrorism everywhere.

Obviously, it is hard for political candidates seeking office now to acknowledge that this conflict is open-ended, cultural, and ideological *as well as military*. Few voters want to hear that patience, restraint, and perseverence are the best steps to take. Yet it is not impossible for politicians to be serious, and so far the public seems to comprehend the reality of Iraq better than the Democrats do. With the toppling of Saddam, an avowed enemy of this nation, the enemy of the United States is now less than clear but the terrorist foe remains deadly. This enemy is a cultural nebula that includes Saddam, Osama, and every America-hating Islamic extremist dedicated to toppling the Great Satan via deadly force—a seamless unity of seething anti-Western hatred. The components will likely have to be taken apart piece-by-piece rather than with one fell swoop, as in previous wars. This war, which will likely grind on in one skirmish after another over the course of several presidencies, requires vigilance and sacrifice, as well as the clear understanding that eliminating one part of the terrorist apparatus sets back the entire movement of murder. None of this could serve as an election-winning slogan, but they could, and should, serve as education to the "public" . . . if only both parties were willing to take up the call.

Repritned with the permission from http://www.frontpagemag.com,
October 1, 2003

THE U.S. VS. THE UN: THE STAKES

UN Secretary General Kofi Annan recently stated that his organization should have a decisive political role in Iraq because, as one of his aides was quoted by the *Financial Times*, it's "not possible to have two jockeys on the same horse." Annan, along with the Security Council's anti-U.S. trio of France, Russia, and Germany, was wrong on the first matter and correct on the second. But the issue of UN's role goes well beyond Iraq, to the very core of international order and the role of states in general and the United States in particular. Is the mythical "international community," as represented by the UN, going to be the ultimate guarantor of global security and the maker of rules of international conduct, or are individual states, or groups of states, entitled to decide on security matters and act accordingly?

In Iraq, so far, the UN has acted as it usually does. Toothless on its own, when its chief envoy to Baghdad was killed in the August truck bombing of the UN's headquarters there, it pulled out most of its personnel "until security circumstances" improve—that is, until somebody else dramatically improves those circumstances. Imagine that the Paris/Annan idea of the UN role in Iraq becomes reality and the UN, put in charge, quickly transfers authority to whatever Iraqi institutions it finds in place. It would be protected, most likely, by Fijian, Bangladeshi, and perhaps a few better battalions of UN blue helmets. This author's own experience with the UN's biggest-ever operation, in Cambodia in

1993, suggests that rules of engagement, that could only be described as irresponsible (e.g., no shooting back unless headquarter bureaucrats give a green light) will be the rule. And Cambodia was not the only, just the biggest, example of the UN at work in dangerous environments, including Bosnia prior to NATO's intervention, Kosovo, Sierra Leone, Liberia, and Rwanda.

Security aside, what would be the most likely UN political approach to Iraq? First, no controversial decisions, since France, or whoever replaces Syria as the Arab/Asian member of the Security Council (Syria was elected on October 8, 2001, for a two-year term that began in January 2004), may object. Second, decisions by committee (or the Security Council) ensure that a consistent UN approach on Iraq will be easier than herding cats. Finally, it will live up to its reputation as a well-intentioned but weak and bumbling entity. Less than major powers ranging from Liberia to Rwanda, from Israel to Lebanon, have challenged, manipulated, disregarded, and gotten away with humiliating the UN. Even sub-state entities such as Hezbollah in southern Lebanon or the Khmer Rouge in Cambodia have managed to do this.

None of this even takes into account the specific realities in Iraq. The Kurds, the best organized and, for now, most militarily efficient element there, are strongly pro-U.S. and autonomy-minded. Would they allow UN bureaucrats from Belgium or New Zealand to tell them how to organize their society? For the Shia majority, the issue is ultimately power, and Iran, among others, will make sure that this remains their objective, UN or not. For the historic losers, the Sunni, terrorism would seem to work as political leverage. In their eyes, the UN retreat from the country after the August bombing of the UN compound seems a vindication of what can be achieved through terrorism. And while some Iraqis may hate the U.S. and others like or manipulate it, at least it is respected by all. The UN is disrespected by all, hated by a few Islamist bombers, and feared by nobody.

Looking closer at what happened in Bosnia, the same UN representative who ran the operation in Cambodia was put in charge in Sarajevo, with similar results: failure. The runners-up in the election the UN arranged there were allowed to wrest power from the victors with guns. Indeed, the men with guns were allowed to run wild in the Balkans until somebody else—the United States, under NATO's flag—could impose temporary order, working outside of the UN's "legitimacy" umbrella. The difference between Bosnia and Iraq is that Bosnia was a regional (and a marginally regional at that) problem, whereas Iraq is a major Arab and, indeed, Muslim country.

All of this bring us to a more fundamental problem with the UN: its General Assembly. The Assembly is the perfect example of bogus democracy; Nauru, Lebanon, and the Maldives have votes, just as the United States, Japan, and Germany do. But the U.S., Japan, the EU nations, Canada, China, and Russia (a total of nineteen states, or 10 percent of the 191 member states) are asked to contribute over 85 percent of the UN's budget, from which the remaining 90 percent of members benefit.

It is not much better in the Security Council, whose five permanent members in fact control whatever decisions are needed. Russia, with a smaller GNP than Brazil, is one of the five, because Stalin was a founder of the UN; France is another nostalgic relic, as, in truth, is the U.K. Mr. Annan's reform efforts offer no real solution. Will the UN have any better decision-making ability or legitimacy if it makes Brazil (whose current regime subsidizes Cuba), India (which is obsessed with offering hypocritical lessons on morality to anyone who might be paying attention), or Nigeria (which is eternally on the brink of fracture) permanent, veto-wielding members?

Viewed in realistic, if unflattering, light, what is the UN, and what is the basis of its claims to a dominant role in Iraq? Kofi Annan's job is to promote the UN, but this is as dangerous as it is understandable. Americans, who have traditionally been skeptical of what ultimately was their own creation in 1945, tend to remember past irresponsible and outrageous votes in the General Assembly ("Zionism is racism," "The media has to be controlled") and the Security Council's vote on Iraq this year, where France managed to block resolutions supported by the U.S. and common sense.

The problem, that neither the Bush administration nor its opponents running for office have proven good at explaining, is that the UN is not an either/ or matter. Most UN agencies do a decent job at helping people everywhere, albeit at a high bureaucratic cost. It can, and often does, help solve humanitarian, health, postal, and communications issues. But on security or nation-building matters, the UN is, at best, ineffective, and more often than not, counterproductive. Americans should make this distinction—or be educated into making it.

On the other hand, the Bush administration should also be educated into renouncing its present notions of somehow having the UN as an equal or "vital" partner in Iraq, and remember what Kofi Annan's people said: there can't be two jockeys on the same horse.

Reprinted with the permission from http://www.frontpagemag.com,
October 6, 2003

RADICAL ISLAM AND SUICIDE BOMBERS

To most Westerners, especially Americans, the almost regular and predictable murder of Israeli civilians of all ages seems both incomprehensible and, precisely because of its regularity and frequency, unsurprising. The phenomenon has, however, stirred some interest in a media previously immune to serious analysis of terrorism in general and within American academia, which was traditionally uninterested in terrorism.

Since the early 1980s, when the Lebanese Shia Hezbollah (with Iranian Khomeinist funds and training) and the Sri Lankan Liberation Tigers of Tamil

Eelam—LTTE (Marxists/Hindus/Tamil secessionists) initiated the routine use of suicide terrorists as an instrument of war, suicide bombers have been active in Sri Lanka, Turkey, Kashmir, India, Lebanon, Israel, Russia, the U.S., and Indonesia. Failed suicide bombing attempts (including the use of aircraft) are known from France, Spain, and Turkey, and successful attempts have been made elsewhere by citizens or residents of Germany and the U.K. A *New York Times* op-ed by Robert A. Pape, "Dying to kill us" (Sept. 22, 2003), therefore concludes that suicide terrorism transcends religious, ethnic, and political boundaries.

But with the exception of the LTTE's acts, all other terrorist acts were committed by Muslims, and of those, all except those by the PKK/Kadek in Turkey and Arafat's Al-Aksa Martyrs Brigades were committed by members of openly Islamist groups. The LTTE/PKK cases led some to dismiss the role of religion in the motivation of suicide terrorists, but on further analysis, the exception indeed proves the rule.

The LTTE are Marxists, Hindus, and Tamil separatists; the PKK/KADEK are self-proclaimed Marxists and Kurdish separatists; and Arafat's Fatah is "secular." But the religious element, properly and unconventionally understood, applies equally to these apparent exceptions. Indeed, the LTTE under Velupillai Prabhakaran (who has been involved in this year's Norway-arranged peace talks between LTTE and Sri Lanka but remains wanted around the world) and the PKK under Abdullah Ocalan (who has been imprisoned in Turkey since his 1999 arrest) are groups that operate more like religious sects under the absolute control of a charismatic leader.

An excellent case could thus be made that the LTTE and PKK are, in a sense, "religious" despite their Marxist/separatist claims, inasmuch as they operate like sects (Jim Jones of Guyana fame was also mixing Marxism and religion) and the leaders are God-like figures of absolute political and spiritual authority. Ocalan was known as "Apo" (uncle), a mysteriously grand and omnipresent figure.

By contrast, "orthodox" Marxist-Leninist groups, including Sendero Luminoso and Colombia's Revolutionary Armed Forces (FARC), do not use suicide bombings, presumably because they claim a "scientific" ideological base, hence one critical of religious fanaticism. Al-Aksa's bombers, some of whom had been rejected by Hamas (!), operate in a political and cultural, not to mention educational, environment increasingly dominated by Islamism, and, thus, are more the result of peer pressure than of secularist convictions. Chechens began to use suicide bombers only once they were infiltrated by Wahhabis.

And then there is suicide bombers' targeting, again a religiously related variable. The LTTE targeted politicians—they murdered a former Indian prime minister and a Sri Lankan president—but not civilians, unless as "collateral damage"; the PKK suicide bombers also targeted Turkish military or jandarma, not civilians. By contrast, the Islamist terrorists have targeted civilians since the start: Jews if possible, Americans, Australians, Indians, or other Western "crusaders" and assorted "non-believers."

The suicide bomber terrorist phenomenon is a growing element in international terrorists' arsenal, but it remains a weapon with religious background. It was, and is everywhere, a weapon of the relatively educated: Tamil Hindu women who were able to mix well at Buddhist electoral meetings in Sri Lanka, Palestinian high school and university students posing as Israelis; and it was Western-educated Islamists who trained to murder thousands in America on 9/11, hundreds in Bali, many in Casablanca and Riyadh.

Ultimately, the suicide bomber is just another tool in the arsenal of the international terrorist groups. For the bomber, religion is the basic motivation or excuse. Their mission is legitimized by a supreme charismatic leader or Islamic cleric; special recruiters bring the suicide candidate together with the group. Eliminating the enablers—the recruiters and ideologists—wherever they are (mostly in London, Pakistan, and Saudi Arabia) must therefore be the first step in eliminating the problem.

Who, exactly are these suicide bombers, widely described as "martyrs" in Muslim, not just Islamist opinion? They are not certainly "martyrs: in the Christian sense—people who were killed for their faith, but murderers—people who killed themselves in order to murder others. Most choose innocent and defenseless victims simply for the psychological value of their actions—the "theater" aspect of terrorism. Most are relatively privileged, educated young people, and a growing number are women. A few (such as Chechnya's "black widows") have deeply personal reasons, primarily revenge for the loss of family members; others are simply lost souls who have lost all moral standards; but most are fanatics, products of well planned recruitment and indoctrination schemes. But what they all share is Roman philosopher Seneca's opinion that "he who does not prize his own life threatens that of others." And suicide terrorism works—according to Israeli souces, during the past three years suicide bombers were responsible for 50 percent of Israeli fatalities, while making only 0.5 percent of the total number of terrorist attacks.

Is there a "solution" to the suicide bomber phenomenon? If "solution" means putting a stop to it in absolute terms the answer has to be negative—precisely because Seneca was right. Could the incidence of such actions be limited and drastically reduced? Yes, and it has been done, in Algeria, Turkey, and Israel. At the same time, we must provide support and understanding for, rather than persistent criticism of those Muslim regimes, whether in Cairo, Islamabad, Rabat, or Algiers, undemocratic as they may be for the human rights fundamentalists of the UN and nongovernmental organizations, not just because perfection is often the enemy of good, but also because, being the first on the line of fire from terrorists, they have the motivation and the record of success against them. It remains a mystery why the World War II alliance between Western democracies and Stalin's criminal and aggressive regime was, and still is, seen as acceptable, and the one between Washington, Riyadh, Cairo, and Islamabad should be rejected for human rights reasons. The war is similar in scope, the danger is similar in nature, and the future hard to predict, but the essential point for now is that the enemy is the same.

Reprinted with the permission from http://www.frontpagemag.com,
October 9, 2003

TERRORIST WEDDING

Are American (especially American-born) citizens who are members of terrorist organizations abroad entitled to special (i.e. American-style) treatment, at a time when the United States demands all countries to choose between being with us or against us in the war on terrorism?

Lori Berenson thinks so. The thirty-four-year-old New Yorker, who is serving twenty years in a Peruvian prison on terrorism charges, criticizes the authorities for keeping her groom from the wedding they just recently arranged. The groom, Aníbal Apari, a forty-year-old "law student" recently released from prison after serving twelve and a half years of a fifteen-year sentence as a member of the Castroite Tupac Amaru Revolutionary Movement (MRTA), was represented by his father, since the authorities did not permit him to leave Lima.

Very moving, indeed, at least in the Manhattan circles in which her progressive and vocal parents, both academics, move. They joined their "persecuted" daughter in protesting that the groom was unable to participate in the happy event.

The newly wedded Mrs. Apari, a former MIT student, has a romantic penchant for terrorists. Apari is her second husband. Her first was another "idealistic" Marxist gunfighter she met in El Salvador, who later left her. She arrived in Peru and rented a home with Panamanian MRTA member Pacifico Castrellon, who later testified against her.

The Berenson case is a study of everything wrong with American mentalities, including wrongheaded Congressional behavior, at least prior to 9/11. Arrested in 1995 on charges of collaborating on a planned MRTA seizure of Congress—she had used questionable U.S. press credentials to gain access to Peru's Congress—she was tried for treason and given a life sentence by Peru's military courts under then President Alberto Fujimori. Average Peruvians, weary of terrorism, were unanimously unsympathetic to her cause, but American and international human rights groups succeeded in obtaining a new civilian trial, which was held in June 2001. For this trial, she had the charges reduced to terrorism, which carried a lesser minimum sentence, even though she has consistently maintained that MRTA is revolutionary, not terrorist. On these charges she received a twenty-year sentence.

Following the first verdict, Berenson shared the same uncomfortable prison in the Andes as others MRTA and Shining Path members, except that she had weekly visits and comfortable help from the U.S. embassy. Later, she was moved to a lowland prison, where she is free to communicate with family and write nonsensical screeds, which are immediately posted at her parents' website. (Peruvian prisoners, especially terrorists, barely have access to outside food or family contacts, let alone the ability to communicate with the world at large.)

Berenson complains about the prison conditions, but she was, and is, able to finish her sentence in U.S. jails. She has refused to do this out of solidarity with her MRTA. She remains a terrorist, a totalitarian, and ideological dinosaur: a Stalinist/Castroist long after even committed communists departed from solidarity with Fidel & Co.

The MRTA was founded during the 1980s by the kind of people with whom Berenson was comfortable. The leader, Victor Polay Campos, was son of a senator, brother of a congressional candidate, and roommate of future President Alan García at the Sorbonne. Originally, MRTA was a faction of García's Popular American Revolutionary Alliance, which is still Peru's best-organized political party, with García well placed to win the next presidential election. At no time more than a few hundred strong, it engaged in spectacular kidnappings of businessmen, keeping its victims in narrow holes in the ground, where they sometimes died of starvation. It assassinated military personnel—usually retired ones, who made easier targets. In desperation, in 1996 it undertook its largest operation ever, taking hundreds of hostages at a ball at the Japanese ambassador's residence (this after the Congress operation Berenson was involved in, up to drawing the building's floor plans and giving her rented house to the MRTA for planning, was thwarted).

The December 1996 operation ended up badly for Berenson's MRTA friends. All the hostages were released following a commando operation, and all the kidnappers were killed. But, she was still "different," born in Manhattan, a fashionable "professional revolutionary" with many friends—including some at the *New York Times*. Few congressmen were informed, or cared, about what she did in South America. Before 9/11, more than 100 members of Congress, Republicans included, signed letters to the Clinton and then the Bush White House, demanding special treatment for Berenson. But this died down after John Lindh and other U.S. citizens demonstrated that there is a problem with Americans training abroad for terrorism. September 11 was, for Berenson, a worse defeat than her arrest. Americans started learning, and stopped sympathizing, with fellow Americans who were involved in murdering strangers in exotic places.

So now Berenson is again "married" to a fellow terrorist and expects to be treated preferentially—not, she says, because she is American, but because of some "universal human right" to the pursuit of happiness. Peruvians, even under the present confused and weak government of Alejandro Toledo, object to this and remain unmoved the persistent demands of a *gringa* who sought to kill their countrymen.

Ultimately, the "wedding" of a convicted terrorist and a paroled one—neither of whom has expressed any regret for their actions—seems yet another attempt to "humanize" them and make us forget their shared past. Apari's comment that "People understand that Lori and I are human beings and like everybody else we have every right to make a life, to find happiness, and love" seems not much different than the Free Lori website's assertions that Lori "could be anyone's daughter, raised by caring, intelligent parents." It is not going to work in Peru and it should not work in post-9/11 America, either.

Westerners have obtained a habit in joining murderous terrorist groups in the Third World, without renouncing their citizenship. Germans in Turkish Kurdistan, Americans in Latin America, and Britons in Israel or Afghanistan who kill or help others kill seem confident that they can expect assistance from their embassies or bleeding-heart NGOs if their actions land them in hot water. But Western governments cannot give these terrorists special rights just because the victims are non-Westerners, nor can they expect other nations to assist in the war on terrorism if their own citizens are exempted from prosecution. There is no legal, moral, or political reason to take seriously Berenson's incessant demands for yet another trial, or for American terrorists abroad to be given any more rights than those we would be prepared to give the foreign terrorists whom we want in our custody.

Reprinted with the permission from http://www.frontpagemag.com,
October 24, 2003

THE ENEMY IN IRAQ

On October 27, four suicide bombers in Iraq killed over forty people, mostly Iraqis. The targets were the Red Cross headquarters and Iraqi police stations. The suicide bombings continue to target Iraqis or international organizations such as the UN or the Red Cross and to occur in the "Sunni triangle"—the Sunni areas of Baghdad and north/northeast of the city. What does this pattern tell us about the nature of the enemies that the U.S. troops in Iraq face? A lot. But judging from the administration's and the military's statements, the nature of the enemies remains obscure in Washington—and among Democratic would-be presidents, complete confusion reigns.

We are being told, repeatedly, by sources ranging from the president to military spokesmen in Baghdad and the Pentagon, that there are three basic types of enemies engaged in violence in Iraq: Saddam's Baath Party stalwarts, criminals, and foreign terrorists. This is correct enough, but it misses significant differences and similarities among the three groups, as well as their relationships to each other.

The first enemy identified by Washington, Baath stalwarts, are largely Sunni. They seek a return to power and the perks associated with it, are secular to the extent they have a clear ideology, and enjoy support among the 20 percent of the Iraqi population that is Arab Sunni, a minority used to dominating the other 80 percent ever since Iraq was invented by the British in 1921. While not all Sunnis are Baathists and vice versa, both have a lot to lose in a new Iraq, even a remotely democratic one (which actually is the best of the possible outcomes of the U.S. intervention).

The Saddam stalwarts have a number of tactical advantages. They are native; they possess a strong collective motivation to hate any post-Saddam regime; and (for now) they still have a leader to motivate and finance them. But they also have a number of serious disadvantages, beyond just being a minority. Their region is flat semi-desert or urban, unlike Kurdistan, which is the only region in Iraq that offers a friendly terrain to guerrillas (and is also the most friendly to the U.S. and hostile to Saddam). The Sunnis/Baathists are dependent upon a leader whose future survival is doubtful at best, and they are disliked by everyone else.

Suicide bombing would not help the Baathists, especially since their goal is to recover political and economic power. Unlike fundamentalists, they do not seek Paradise but ministries and oil deals. If Saddam ever did a good thing, it was to cut down and prevent the growth of Islamism in the country, which he did far more effectively than the leaders of most other Arab states. It helped that Iraq's political culture was also resistant to fundamentalism, whether the Muslim Brotherhood or the Salafi/Wahhabi version.

The second identified enemy, the criminal element, includes the some 100,000 inmates—few, if any, were political prisoners—Saddam released prior to the latest war. This group has contributed to the current instability, especially since the end of the war. They played the largest part in the massive looting that took place after the end of the conventional stage of the war, and have been known to place bombs and mines and serve as snipers against coalition forces (for a price). But criminals seek fortunes, not Paradise. They do not normally blow themselves up in order to get rich. And Iraq's criminals have their own problems. Saddam's people are running out of money to pay them, as the new diners replace the old and as other funds inevitably dry up.

So, which of the three identified enemies has the motivation required for suicide bombings? The Islamists, some belonging to the few and small Iraqi groups such as Ansar al-Islam, but most connected to organizations belonging to the al-Qaeda nebula: the Algerian GIA and GSPC, the Sudanese and Yemeni organizations that are still semi-legal at home. They include the usual Saudi fanatics, assorted Syrians, Pakistanis, European Muslims, and others in search of jihad, excitement, Paradise, and a utopian purity of the *umma* (the Muslim community worldwide). In short, people whose motivation is religious. The goal of their recruiters and manipulators is global, anti-Western, anti-U.S., and anti-Judeo-Christian.

The suicide attacks in Iraq are quite similar in technique and pattern to al-Qaeda attacks in, among other countries, the U.S., Indonesia, and Saudi Arabia. Whether one likes it or not, the al-Qaeda nebula has now decided that Iraq is now the best place—politically, strategically, and tactically—to continue their battle against "Crusaders and Jews." What the U.S.-led forces, which include more and more Iraqis, face in Iraq is less (and less every day) the remnants of Saddam's system than the present phase of al-Qaeda's war against the world. The world? Yes, when one considers the growing list of bin Laden's enemies— from the *jahiliyya* (pagan supporters) in power in just about every Muslim country to the U.S., EU, India, China, and Russia.

Foreigners (who are not hard for even ordinary citizens to detect) murdering Iraqis are bound, sooner or later, to make even Sunni Iraqis, who did the same to Shiias and Kurds, resentful. al-Qaeda's grasp will once again exceed its reach, and it will accumulate more enemies than it can reasonably handle. But are Americans in Peoria prepared to accept the present rate of U.S. casualties and costs, for and in a country few could locate on a map? That—not the military balance or the success of Iraqi recruitment for the police and military—is the real bet. Here, and only here, might the Vietnam analogy apply.

Which leads to the key element of al-Qaeda's strategy in Iraq and elsewhere in the *umma*—Americans, because they are democratic and have no standing power: kill enough of them, regularly and sufficiently far away, and, "just like in Vietnam," political dissension within the U.S. will result in retreat and, thus, strategic defeat. When al-Qaeda hears some Democratic presidential candidates—even marginal ones like Dennis Kucinich, Carol Moseley Brown, and Al Sharpton—promising retreat, they hear capitulation and have all the more reason to murder American GIs and cooperating Iraqis and to scare away they very international organizations that American politicians are offering as the alternative to the Marines. What is happening in Iraq is more and more directly linked to what happened on September 11, and it is time for the Administration to make it clear to the public. Iraq is now a battle in the general war against terrorists, regardless of the specific reasons that led to the Operation Iraqi Freedom.

Reprinted with the permission from http://www.frontpagemag.com,
October 31, 2003

TERROR OVERREACH

With the murder of Muslim Arab children in Riyadh, Turks and Jews in Istanbul and Italian carabinieri in Nassiriya, al-Qaeda has once again demonstrated its major strategic error, one any successful military strategist from the time of Hannibal to the present has avoided: Do not make new enemies faster than you are prepared to cope with them. It was Hitler's error in attacking Stalin before finishing off Churchill, with well-known results.

Arab analyst Abdulwahab Badrakhan writes that with the new terrorist strike in Riyadh, "sabotage becomes just sabotage; killing becomes just killing," with no overarching purpose. No one is interested anymore in the "excuses," which became irrelevant. Terror has become "a plan for permanent and general chaos," not only destabilizing society but also dashing any hope for reform and development ("Terror for Terror," *Al-Hayat*, Nov. 10, 2003). Amen.

Until Riyadh, al-Qaeda's declared enemies already included the U.S., Russia, China, India, Western Europe, and most Muslim governments. Now added to the list are Muslims as such, as people, not only in Saudi Arabia but also in Egypt, Lebanon, and beyond. In expanding its scope, al-Qaeda demonstrates the truth of what the Bush administration has claimed ever since 9/11: that al-Qaeda is at war with civilization writ at-large, including the mainstream Islamic one. It was a truth that should have been obvious to all, but was rejected by the famously undefined "Arab street," as well as by anti-American elites in the West—all the stubborn seekers of some remote but plausible (and possible to pin on the U.S.) "root cause" of Islamist terrorism. Now, at least the Arab world has finally realized that killing has become "just killing," as Badrakhan put it, and that terrorists are just terrorists.

After Riyadh, the young Saudi cellphone chatterers, who felt subliminal or even open satisfaction when al-Qaeda murdered thousands of Americans, have to now look over their own shoulders for bombs, snipers, or knife wielders targeting them and their families. One could also hope, but not too much, that Westerners who have remonstrated about America's "insensitivity" in fighting terror during Ramadan will consider that the terrorists do not seem to be observing the holy month.

It has all happened before. In the 1980s and 1990s, the Egyptian Jamaa Islamiyya and Islamic Jihad—main sources of bin Laden's ideology and support—drew its own support from the slums of Fayum, Cairo, and Alexandria. But then it murdered Western tourists in Luxor, ruining the Egyptian tourism industry and the hundreds of thousands of jobs it provided until the regime finished it off. al-Qaeda's inability to learn from its predecessor's mistakes is great news for its enemies. Saudi Arabia's monarchy, which has long been ambivalent in its dealings with Bin Laden & Co., balancing bribes, threats, and crackdowns within its country with tolerating financial support for it from abroad, has finally had enough. Until the May attacks in their country and these most recent attacks, the Saudis largely made only sympathetic noises and symbolic moves in support of the U.S. war on Islamists. Now their support is serious. Nothing better concentrates the mind, particularly an Arab ruling family's mind, than an open threat to its physical survival.

al-Qaeda's attacks on the UN and the Red Cross in Baghdad arguably should have taught the West the same lessons. But, as usual, it is the "progressive" Western establishment that has the hardest time getting the point. Even after the UN headquarters there were blown up and its representative killed, a large majority of West Europeans still believed that the UN was better prepared to deal with Iraq than the U.S. And after sixteen Italian carabinieri and soldiers were killed in Nassiriya this week, the usual suspects in Rome—unreconstructed as well as "democratic" ex-communists—called for withdrawal, evidently taking a page from the book of a majority of U.S. Democratic Party presidential candidates.

For Italians as for Americans, withdrawal from Iraq will do nothing but invite additional terrorist attacks. This is a lesson the Turks may have learned last week as well—after its reluctance to support the U.S. at the beginning of the war in Iraq, and the withdrawal of an offer to deploy troops in that country, Ankara may have believed that it could stay away from the unpleasantness in Baghdad. Instead, the bombing of two Istanbul synagogues last week demonstrated that Turkey is a natural target for al-Qaeda and associates, regardless of any specific position on Iraq, because it is secular, friendly to Israel and tolerant.

In the U.S. the issue has become a clash of wills between those led by George Bush, who see this as a war to be won, and those who see it as a marginal but politically useful instrument for gaining elections at home. It may seem paradoxical that ordinary Saudis could get the point of al-Qaeda's unadulterated terrorism sooner than comfortable and opportunistic Western politicians, academics, and intellectuals, but it is true.

This is even more important because the entire conflict between Islamists and the world is now at a crucial, psychologically decisive point. If Rome, Washington, or any other Western power give up now, when Muslims everywhere, especially in Saudi Arabia, are finally beginning to unite against the terrorists in their midst, the two trends will cancel each other, and the al-Qaeda nebula will retain its lease on life. The two immediate centers of confrontation are Iraq and Saudi Arabia, and it is in those countries that the war on Islamic terrorism will be won or lost—as much as in the Western media, Iraqi Sunni attitudes, and Saudi mentalities.

As long as Western media, from the *New York Times* and CNN to *Le Monde*, continue to describe the conflict as one between American "occupation" and some hypothetical "Iraqi resistance," the conflict will continue, innocents will die, the costs will rise, and the terrorists' theater of operations will expand. Nothing produces more incentives for al-Qaeda to murder more Americans and other Westerners than Western calls for concessions, "understanding" or pullouts from Iraq. French sniping at U.S. operations, Italian communists' calls for withdrawals, and the Kucinich/Sharpton brand of defeatism, kill.

As long as the American forces in central Iraq continue to treat the Sunni minority's reluctance to accept the reality of their minority status in the new

Iraq as something to be dealt with by "conquering minds," rather than representing common sense and historical inevitability, the problems and attacks there will continue. In the cities of Faluja and Tikrit we do not need to convince their inhabitants that democracy, or at least an equitable redistribution of power, is good for them, but that they can either accept the new reality or face their cities' destruction at the hands of either the other Iraqis or the coalition. Period.

No doubt we will soon hear the complaints of Amnesty International, Human Rights Watch, and assorted European human rights groups regarding a Coalition crackdown on Iraqi Sunnis or the Saudis' treatment of captured al-Qaeda terrorists. But we must not give the terrorists legal defense at taxpayer expense, or move to prevent some undefinable "psychological" torture of those under interrogation. There can be no suicidal interpretation of the "rights of terrorists." Permitting the Saudis to do what they must may sound regrettable, but recall that Stalin's treatment of his own people, and of occupied Poland and the Baltics, didn't prevent—nor should it have prevented—the West's alliance with the Bolshevik mass murderer against the Nazi one.

Reprinted with the permission from http://www.frontpagemag.com,
November 20, 2003

MOROCCO'S FEMINISM—FROM ABOVE

"I cannot authorize what God forbids and forbid what God has authorized." So King Mohammed VI of Morocco recently stated when instructing his (elected) parliament to pass a new family and revolutionary family code (*moudawanna*), thus reforming the status of women. This demonstrates how progress in the Arab world could realistically be made—from above. This legislation has shown the way for a transformation of the Arab world and demonstrated that Islam and human rights are not necessarily on a collision course. It also provides a valuable lesson for Iraq, one that will hopefully be learned by all concerned.

The proposed family code declares that marriage is the "joint responsibility" of the two spouses. It abolishes "matrimonial guardianship," which required even adult women to obtain a male guardian's approval for marriage. There will be no more "proper women's duties, but reciprocal obligations," including a duty of consultation on matters regarding family planning and children. Polygamy, while not formally banned, becomes so difficult, and subject to a judge's decision, as to be virtually impractical. Divorce becomes a "right exercised by both spouses" under a judge's control. Islamic repudiation remains on paper, but is now conditioned by a court's decision and only after reconciliation fails, thus de facto making it a *legal* act; furthermore, it only becomes legal when the husband guarantees the woman's rights and the children's income, allows the woman to retain the house or its equivalent, and agrees to the equal division of common property. An abused wife can now initiate a divorce proceeding.

The context of this revolutionary reform is revealing. A somewhat more limited reform proposal was put forward in 1999 by Socialist then-Prime Minister Yousouffi Abderahmane, only to be massively opposed in the streets by Islamists and conservatives, leading to the Islamists' spectacular electoral victory in the 2002 parliamentary elections. In a manner familiar to Western politicians, the reform was sent to a commission for further study and what appeared to be certain political death. Then came the May 16, 2003, terrorist suicide bombings by al-Qaeda's local affiliate, Salafiya Jihadiya, in Casablanca, and everything changed—in precisely the opposite direction the perpetrators intended.

First, the secular intellectuals and middle-class became scared, with many of them demonstrating against terrorism. Second, and more important, the bombings gave the king a reason to arrest hundreds of Islamists and force the others to take a low profile. Radical Islamism, as such, was cowed and abruptly discredited in the eyes of a majority, at least in the cities, while the king's authority and legitimacy increased. As a result, the presumably dead commission (which, by the way, did include a woman, Zoulikha Naciri, the only woman member of the Royal cabinet) was resurrected.

To this, one has to add the fact that, as (claimed) descendants of Prophet Mohammed, Morocco's monarchs (like the Hashemites of Jordan) are also "Commanders of the Faithful," the supreme religious authority in the realm. Hence King Mohammed's ability and credibility to impose his interpretation of Islam on the matter of women's rights. By invoking the *jihad*, the ability to interpret the Quran given to legitimate individuals, the king could institute precisely what the radical Islamists totally reject. This trapped the Islamists. To deny the right of the Commander of the Faithful to interpret the Quran and the Sunna is tantamount to lèse majesté—a very dangerous, indeed un-Islamic, position. Saadedin el-Othmani, the leader of the Islamist Justice and Development Party, could only lamely claim that the king had "from the beginning to the end insisted on an Islamic reference framework."

That the king cleverly did, indeed. Hence repudiation and polygamy were not "abolished," just made practically impossible, and all in the name of Islam. But, as Naciri stated, "it was necessary to reconcile modernity and Islamic references." Polygamy is a good example. According to the commission's president, former minister and Nationalist Party leader M'hamed Boucetta, it was not abolished, since the Quran allows it, but it was regulated into virtual extinction because, while the Holy Book allows a man to marry up to four women, if the man is not righteous, he can only take one. And what man is perfectly righteous? Let a judge decide…

What do the Moroccans think about all this? According to the *Economist*, some 65 percent are in favor of the new family code, leaving a minority of hardliners to mutter that it was all done in order for Morocco to obtain Western support to host the World Soccer Cup in 2010…hmmm!

What does all this mean in the larger scheme of the Arab world? To provide a context, in North Africa, only Tunisia has passed similarly enlightened legislation on women's rights, which it did when it gained independence in 1957; Algeria and Libya at least pretend that women can vote. In non-Arab Turkey, women gained the right to vote in 1934, ahead of women in some Western countries. The Arab countries of the Middle East, by contrast, seldom even pretend to offer women any rights.

Women's rights aren't the only issue on which Morocco is ahead of most other Arab countries. Morocco also has the only significant Jewish community left anywhere in the Arab world (followed closely by Tunisia), has ties to Israel, and is generally friendly to the United States and, of course, France. Which raises the question why other absolute monarchies in the Arab world, all of which, aside from Jordan, are more absolute than Morocco's, refuse to do what Mohammed VI did. Is it lack of will, fear, disinterest, or indeed, dislike of modernity?

Similarly, why isn't the United States doing more to applaud Morocco as an example of what the other Gulf states could do? All the Gulf states are dependent on Washington for their security, and controlled by absolute monarchs. Liberating women need not be presented as a human rights issue. It could be presented as a matter of economic common sense and national security. Indeed, when a majority of the labor force in the Gulf state is foreign and potentially threatening national security, what is the logic of denying education, skills, and jobs to half of the native population?

Most important, however, the Moroccan case demonstrates that progress in the Arab (and indeed Muslim) world is far more likely to come from above, through "undemocratic" means—such as decisions by the hereditary ruler—than through the "will of the people." Most people are not aware that the reason Turkey is now the model of the potential for democracy in an Islamic context is because the founder of the Turkish Republic, Kemal Atatürk, did not consult the people when he eliminated the Caliphate, proclaimed the Republic, separated Islam from the state, liberated women, and established secular public education. He and his close advisers just decided to do so and imposed their decisions on the people, often by brutal and undemocratic means. It took decades, not to mention a few military coups, for the Turkish public to internalize and accept the reforms and to proceed to a democratic system—an imperfect one, but no more so than that of some of Ankara's European critics.

Which raises the issue of Iraq. What kind of democracy, if any, is realistically obtainable in Baghdad, by what means, and when? Is a multi-party system, inevitably arranged along ethnic and confessional lines, viable or desirable? Is a Shiite-dominated, mildly authoritarian but tolerant regime acceptable—not just to us, but more important, to the Sunnis and Kurds? Should a nice constitution patterned after some Western lawyers' notions be preferred to a messy text resulting from political bargains reflecting the balance of demographic, economic and military forces among Iraq's fractious society?

None of these questions are easily answered. But the case of Morocco should suggest a new angle of seeing these issues—that there are some real virtues to imposing reform from above in the Arab world, the greatest among them being realism.

Reprinted with the permission from http://www.frontpagemag.com,
December 15, 2003

TERRORISM IS FREE SPEECH

Freedom of speech permits supporting terrorism, as long as you are only providing "expert advice and assistance" to groups the federal government has designated as "foreign terrorist organizations." So says a California district judge, in a decision that can only be disheartening for those on the frontlines of the struggle against terrorism. We can hope the decision will be set aside on appeal, but it nevertheless shows how vulnerable our legal instruments are against international terrorism—and how powerful the influence is of those who would dismantle existing Homeland Security legislation.

The Decision

In a decision released January 26, Federal Judge Audrey B. Collins (Central District of California), ruled in *Humanitarian Law Project,* et al. *v. Reno* et al. that the U.S. Departments of State and Justice cannot stop groups from providing "expert advice and assistance" to either the Kurdistan Workers' Party (PKK) in Turkey or the Liberation Tigers of Tamil Eelam (LTTE) in Sri Lanka.

The plaintiffs had brought their suit in 1998, after passage of the Anti-Terrorism Law, most of which was initially upheld by Judge Collins. However, she agreed with the plaintiffs that the prohibition against providing "expert advice and assistance" was "impermissibly vague." The newest decision comes in a new phase of the case based on the post-9/11 Patriot Act's similar prohibitions. "The USA Patriot Act places no limitation on the type of expert advice and assistance, which is prohibited, and, instead, bans the provision of all expert advice and assistance regardless of its nature," said Collins. She specifically cited the provision that makes it a crime to provide personnel and training to designated terrorist groups as unenforceable, saying that it was sufficiently vague to raise First and Fifth Amendment issues. (Surprisingly, she rejected arguments by the plaintiffs that the law was too general and that it gave the Secretary of State "virtually unreviewable authority" to designate a group as a foreign terrorist organization.)

As the *New York Times* noted,[1] Judge Collins is the first federal judge actually to strike down part of the Patriot Act. But this is not the first legal challenge to aspects of the war on terror. California courts have made earlier attempts to weaken anti-terrorism legislation introduced in 1997. In 1998, the infamous Ninth Circuit Court of Appeals ruled that fundraising for the lawful activities of a foreign terrorist organization is protected by the First Amendment, if there is no specific intent to further the group's illegal ends.[2] That decision, resulting from a complaint by pro-terrorist Arab groups, would have allowed Hamas, Palestinian Jihad, and others to openly raise money in the United States. Had it not become moot after 2001, the decision also would have allowed most of those tried or indicted since 9/11 to remain free, and the terrorist-funding Islamic "charities" the Bush administration has closed down, to remain open and active.

Judge Audrey Collins, who was appointed to the court in 1994 by Bill Clinton, is a product of Affirmative Action. Her decision follows a familiar pattern of California jurisprudence that the Supreme Court routinely overrules in some 80 percent of the cases, far more than for any other court. Indeed, California judges are the ones who declared that God has no place in the Pledge of Allegiance and who have twice attempted to cripple the nation's already limited legal defenses against terrorism.

The Plaintiffs

The plaintiffs in the case were suing for the right to provide support "to the political and humanitarian activities" of the PKK and LTTE. One of them, the International Educational Development-Humanitarian Law Project (IED-HLP), has long provided aid to the PKK, and was joined in the suit by five Tamil organizations who aided the LTTE.

The IED-HLP said that, since 1992, it had conducted fact-finding investigations of human rights violations by the Turkish government against the Kurds, published reports on their findings that were supportive of the PKK, and provided training to the PKK on how to advocate for their "rights" under international law. The five Tamil organizations support the LTTE with donations of food, clothing, books, and educational materials for its orphanages, refugee relief centers, and schools. These groups also wanted to make cash contributions to the LTTE to finance both its 1997 lawsuit challenging its terrorist designation and the distribution of LTTE literature in the United States.

So who are the terrorist beneficiaries of this court case, the PKK and LTTE? Both the PKK (now going under the name of the Kurdistan Freedom and Democracy–KADEK) and the LTTE are separatist, terrorist, Marxist organizations, whose actions have so far led to more than 100,000 deaths over the past two decades.

The PKK

The PKK has always been defined not by Kurdish nationalism but by Marxism. Founder Abdullah Öcalan was half-Turkish, as he himself reminded his Turkish commando captors in Kenya in 1999; its other early leaders included ethnic Turks as well as Kurds, but no "workers." In the "Party Program of the PKK," adopted at the Fifth "Victory" Congress of January 1995, the organization portrays itself as the vanguard of the new global socialism movement. On the subject of the decline of the USSR, it claimed that Soviet socialism was a rough, wild, even "primitive" deviation. By contrast, its own approach to socialism was "scientific and creative."

The Party's internal structure also demonstrates its Leninist character. Öcalan's continuous control was only obtained by ruthlessly eliminating challengers, "the most deviated" of whom, he says, "could only be neutralized." Even journalist Chris Kutschera, a sympathetic but knowledgeable analyst of the PKK, has acknowledged that five or six of the Party's original leaders were killed. Three others committed suicide, and others have been driven underground.

After training in PLO-run international terrorist camps in Lebanon, the PKK opened its military campaign against the Turkish state in 1984, largely from its secure bases in Syria. By 1990-1993 it was able to take advantage of the post-Gulf War environment (specifically, the power vacuum created by the de facto creation of an autonomous Iraqi Kurdistan), and it became a real threat to Turkey's territorial integrity. The PKK engaged in a massive rural insurgency in southeastern Turkey, which, by 1999, resulted in some 30,000 fatalities. These deaths were mostly insurgents, civilians and anti-PKK village guards—and almost all were Kurds. Indeed, far more Kurdish civilians have been killed by the PKK than Turks, some as reprisals for suspected collaboration with Ankara, others during clashes with rival clans. Kurds in Europe and Lebanon who disagreed with Öcalan were murdered. Throughout the 1990s the PKK in Iraq enjoyed Saddam's support and regularly engaged in clashes with local Kurdish forces.

At its Fifth Congress the PKK decided to engage in suicide bombings and, by 1997, the group had formed "Suicide Guerrilla Teams." The early "volunteers" came from the most vulnerable segments of society: young, impoverished, poorly educated women. The group's ambitions went even further: in November 1996, thirteen PKK members arrested on the Syrian border with the Hatay Province were found to possess antimony, which they thought was uranium.

PKK operations in Western Europe are led by relatively well-educated people. They enjoy support from governments and groups in Western countries (Germany, Benelux, Scandinavian states), local governments such as the Basques in Spain, prominent individuals and member parties of government coalitions in Italy, France, Russia, and Greece, and most of the remnants of Germany's and

Italy's Marxist terrorists. These latter occasionally participated (and were killed or captured) in PKK combat operations.

In addition to its key role in PKK propaganda and political support, Europe was, and still is, the major source of PKK funding. European assessments of the PKK's income generally placed it at between $200 and $500 million a year for the mid-1990s. The German government has asserted that the PKK collects millions of deutsche marks at its annual fundraising events, and some sources have estimated PKK's annual income from these along with drug trafficking, robberies, extortion, and emigrant and arms smuggling at $86 million (U.S.). Considering the range of PKK drug trafficking in Europe (Germany, France, Denmark, Romania, Switzerland, Belgium, Netherlands), the group is wealthy indeed. None of this dissuaded such self-proclaimed "human rights" militants as Danielle Mitterand, the radical widow of former French president, from addressing Öcalan as "Dear President Öcalan" in a 1998 letter which ended with: "Looking forward to an initial result, rest assured, Abdullah, that I am committed to be beside you in the bid for peace, Sincerely yours, Danielle Mitterand."

This, then, is the organization the HLP managed to get Judge Collins to allow open support for in the United States in the name of the First and Fifth Amendments. Karen Parker of IED-HLP, an NGO accredited by UNESCO, has called it "an affront to humanitarian law" that Turkey and the United States designate the PKK a terrorist organization. IED-HLP president Ralph Fertig, a retired administrative law judge with the EEO Commission in Los Angeles, claims that the Kurdish civilian population is being "terrorized" by the Turkish armed forces and that the PKK elements are being denied protections they should have under humanitarian law.

The Liberation Tigers of Tamil Eelam (LTTE)

Ever since the group's founding in 1976, the LTTE have been led by a high-school dropout and perhaps the world's most successful terrorist, Velupillai Prabhakaran. His main spokesman is Anton Balasingham, a Marxist and former journalist. The group's goal is to establish a totalitarian, ethnically pure Tamil state in northern and eastern Sri Lanka.

Whereas the PKK engaged in suicide bombings only sporadically, the LTTE were the world's main practitioners of suicide terrorism until very recently, when Palestinian groups overtook them. Their more prominent victims include former Indian Prime Minister Rajiv Gandhi in 1991 and Sri Lankan president Ranasinghe Premadasa in 1993. Since 1987, at least 243 Tigers, all members of a special "Black Tigers" unit, have blown themselves up, including fifty-three women ("the Birds of Freedom," in LTTE parlance). In addition, just about every LTTE member captured has followed Prabhakaran's strict orders and swallowed the cyanide pill that is an obligatory part of terrorist equipment.

In the book *Inside an Elusive Mind: Prabhakaran. The First Profile of the World's Most Ruthless Guerrilla Leader* (Delhi, 2003), M. R. Narayan Swamy writes that LTTE managers in the Western world use coercion to force Tamils to support them, "keeping tabs on Tamils, their incomes, and names and addresses of their relatives back in Sri Lanka." Considering the enormous size of the Tamil diaspora in Britain, Canada, Australia, and the fact that many of its members are professionals with high incomes, these are huge sums of money—to which one can add the "taxes" imposed on inhabitants of LTTE-controlled areas in Sri Lanka and international drug and precious stones trafficking. Judge Collins' decision would open the gates for a flood of legal contributions from the likes of Parker and Fertig, as well.

Where are these contributions going? To LTTE's de facto statelet in Sri Lanka, where "illicit" sex, smoking, liquor, and homosexuality are forbidden and rules are enforced by a secret police at Prabhakan's arbitrary will. That is the future of the "free Tamil state" which the LTTE fights for, and in the name of which the group has left 60,000 dead. This is also the militant aim of the Humanitarian Law Project (HLP). Nonetheless, the HLP describes itself as "a Los Angeles-based not-for-profit organization that advocates for the peaceful resolution of armed conflicts and for worldwide compliance with humanitarian law and human rights law before the United Nations, where it has consultative status as an NGO, and in other arenas." Or, alternatively, in a purely Orwellian manner, HLP states it is "a nonprofit organization founded in 1985, dedicated to protecting human rights and promoting the peaceful resolution of conflict by using established international human rights laws and humanitarian law" (See http://hlp.home.igc.org/) it works for the PKK's right to kill).

The HLP's Goals

The HLP is open about its goals within the United States. As Parker puts it, "Citizens, wherever they are, pay taxes. Our taxes have gone to perpetrate atrocities and gross violations of human rights and the humanitarian law around the world. Now, as we succeed in unraveling and curtailing that involvement, less tax money is required in those areas." In fact, by making PKK and LTTE "taxes" [read: extortion and crime proceeds] legal, Judge Collins' ruling would permit further atrocities by those groups, precisely because "less tax money is required in those areas."

A Canadian Security Intelligence Service report asserts that a "quasi-diplomatic" LTTE organization had cells and offices in some fifty-four countries in 1998. The most important are in Western nations with large Tamil expatriate communities, most notably the U.K., France, Germany, Switzerland, Canada, and Australia. Most LTTE international propaganda tends to be conducted through politically sympathetic pressure groups and media units, the activities of which are coordinated through umbrella front organizations such as the

Illankai Tamil Sangam in the United States. The LTTE uses its "peace" slogan to attract NGOs such as the IED, whose support has helped the LTTE internationalize their cause.

The Implications

Nancy Chang, senior staff attorney at the leftist Center for Constitutional Rights (CCR), asserts that the Anti-Terrorism Law effectively intimidates the plaintiffs from exercising their First Amendment rights. She contends that convictions under this law can result in up to ten years imprisonment and substantial fines. The plaintiffs' counsel, David Cole, a professor at Georgetown University Law Center, was an attorney for one of the al-Arian defendants who was subsequently deported. He explains the legal theory behind the case: "The Anti-Terrorism Law violates a cardinal principle of the First Amendment: it imposes guilt by association, rather than on the basis of one's acts. The Anti-Terrorism Law makes it a crime to send blankets to a refugee relief center, not because doing so is wrong, but because the government has designated the group that runs the center as 'terrorist.' This is guilt by association, which is prohibited by the First Amendment."

This is the faulty logic accepted by Judge Collins.

In a globalized world of mass communications, travel, and instant financial transactions, the PKK and LTTE cannot survive without international help. The same can be said of al-Qaeda, Hamas, the Philippines' New People's Army, the Basque ETA, and many other violent groups. And, as Clausewitz put it, war is the continuation of politics by other means. Giving "political and humanitarian" aid to terrorists is paying for murder.

Prof. Cole's claim that the Anti-Terrorism Law "imposes guilt by association, rather on the basis of one's acts" is made in apparent blissful ignorance of such legal concepts as "accessory to crime" or "conspiracy to commit murder." It makes one wonder about the legal training that is being inflicted on his Georgetown students. According to this kind of thinking, Hitler or Osama bin Laden would be untouchable. After all, neither committed a physical crime. So would Sheik Omar Abdel Rahman, convicted in connection with the February 1993 bombing of the World Trade Center. He was merely a poor, blind old man, obviously incapable of personally inflicting violence.

How much should we excuse supporters' purported ignorance of the nature of these groups? Ignorance should be no defense here: a search for PKK on Google brings 355,000 results; one for LTTE returns 278,000. These are not exactly obscure sects. In fact, the plaintiffs in Judge Collins' court made no secret of their being well aware of the nature of these groups.

The IED-HLP or CCR say that the First Amendment is being violated by the application of the Anti-Terrorism Law's restrictions to legitimate activities of supporters of international human rights. This means that the providers of funds, recruiters, and ideologues of terrorism are immune from punishment, while their homicidal rank-and-file recruits are unpunishable under "human rights" protections ("human rights" that 100,000 victims of terrorism by the PKK no longer enjoy). No one is to blame.

One can only hope that Judge Collins will be overruled, if not by her colleagues on the Ninth Circuit (yes, miracles do happen), then by the Supreme Court. But regardless of what happens, we can draw valuable observations from these developments. The War on Terror has numerous fronts, many of them, unfortunately, within America itself, where sympathetic lawyers, "human rights" militants and inane judges can be the most dedicated enemies to national security.

Notes

1. "Citing Free Speech, Judge Voids Part of Antiterror Act," Eric Lichtblau. *New York Times*. January 26, 2004.
2. American-Arab Anti-Discrimination Committee v. Reno, 9th Circuit Court of Appeals, 1997.

Reprinted with the permission from http://www.frontpagemag.com,
February 3, 2004

THEY'RE HERE! THE BAD GUYS CAN ALWAYS COUNT ON USEFUL IDIOTS

For a decade at the very least, Osama bin Laden and his lieutenants and associates, from Indonesia to Morocco, have made it clear that they are at war with everyone—Muslims included—who does not completely agree with their goals and methods. Contrary to popular opinion, their list of enemies includes not just the Western world, let alone the United States, or the "Crusaders and Jews" often railed against. Japan and India, Russia and China—not exactly "Western" in the usual sense—as well as Hindus, Buddhists, and Communists, East African blacks, and Turks, not to mention "the U.N., which is opposed to Islam." All figure quite prominently on the Islamists' "people to murder" list. And, as Casablanca and Istanbul, Djerba and Riyadh, Baghdad and Karachi have demonstrated, the "wrong" kind of Muslim is on that list too. Not surprising, since, for Osama bin Laden, "the general aim of the jihad and the mujahadeen is to strike at the foundations and infrastructure of the Western colonialist program or at the so-called world order....Their defeat means, simply, the elimination of all forms of nation-states, such that all that remains is the natural existence familiar to Islam—the regional entity under the great Islamic state."

Simply put, Islamic terrorists are not involved in a war of civilizations as much as a war against civilization of any kind—pure barbarism against culture.

But this is barbarism with a very dangerous twist—in its skilled use of technology, communications, and the media, the al-Qaeda nebula is the first "postmodern" terror movement—certainly compared to the still-active Marxist insurgent and terrorist groups in Latin America, or the largely defunct ones in Western Europe. Its strategy is global, its tactical modus operandi is perfectly adapted to the post-Cold War environment, and its leadership—not just, or even primarily, Osama bin Laden or Ayman al Zawahiri—is adept at taking advantage of today's uniquely fluid geopolitical map. But, to take just the West, "[its] occupation of our countries is old, but takes new forms. The struggle between us and them began centuries ago, and will continue. There can be no dialogue with occupiers except through arms. Why? Because "believers are in one tent and the infidels are in another," and "you should know that seeking to kill Americans and Jews everywhere in the world is one of the greatest duties [for Muslims], and the good deed most preferred by Allah, the Exalted." So said Osama bin Laden, on many occasions.

One would think that all of this widely available information, and the actions of the jihadists themselves, at least since 1993, would be enough for any rational and thinking person anywhere to understand the global and deadly threat Osama bin Laden and his cohorts represent for humanity—but one would be wrong. The incredulity and blindness of so many people, in the West and elsewhere, multiply the effectiveness of the Islamist barbarians—and until disbelief and ignorance are dealt with, no amount of military force, technology, intelligence, or money could keep the new barbarians from the gates of civilization. Here is a preliminary roster of the blindness-and-idiocy types:

The Umma Solidarity Crowd. Since the jihadists began their activities in the early 1990s, a large majority of their victims has been Muslim—beginning with those killed in Afghanistan by bin Laden's Brigade 52 unit, but also including those killed in Saudi Arabia, Turkey, Morocco, and Indonesia. In Algeria alone some 120,000 people—virtually all Muslims—were killed since 1991 by two Islamist terror groups, one of which is closely associated with al-Qaeda. Nor did Osama bin Laden make a secret of his priorities: "The most qualified regions for liberation are Jordan, Morocco, Nigeria, Pakistan, the land of the two holy mosques [Saudi Arabia], and Yemen."

One would think that enough to trigger the hostility of most Muslims—but it wasn't. It almost appears that the Muslim masses are waiting to see who will win, prepared to quietly accept the outcome. In the case of the Palestinians, it is even worse—the masses won't even stay neutral, instead actively sympathizing with the likes of Islamic Jihad and Hamas—especially among the young. The Muslims in the West are too busy complaining about alleged discrimination to bother with the bomb throwers in their ranks. If the iron rule of guerrilla and terrorist success is that the passivity of the majority is more important than its active support, the jihadists are winning in Pakistan as much as in Detroit and Saint-Denis. For the majority of the world's Muslims, bin Laden may be misguided, but ultimately he is *their* misguided devil. For bin Laden & Co., this is a religious war—and most of the world's Muslims seem to agree, at least implicitly. Ultimately, the Muslim masses and bin Laden share one key psychological trait—a persecution mania of historic and mass proportions in which all that is wrong in Islam is everybody else's fault.

Nor is it surprising for the largely illiterate "street Arab" to think that way—if "think" is the term—when prominent intellectuals, in prestigious newspapers, deliver pearls like "the Afghani experience and then the Iraqi one—despite their differences—have confirmed that the concept of independence related to free will and self-determination has no place in the new world order as long as the Americans are the ones to choose the regimes, the men in power, the laws, and even the constitutions."

We are being told ad nauseam that "most Muslims do not support terrorism"—a very dubious claim in places like Gaza and the West Bank, Pakistan, and Yemen—and, at best, irrelevant elsewhere, since we know that all that is necessary for the triumph of evil is for good men to do nothing.

The "It Cannot Happen Here" Believers. For a multitude of reasons, governments like those of Indonesia, Nigeria, Pakistan, and Thailand have persistently denied the obvious jihadist threat—out of narrow-mindedness, fear, incompetence, or expediency. It took some bloody and rude awakenings for these governments to finally admit the existence of an "Osama bin Laden," and some have yet to draw the necessary conclusion: that they are also targets.

The Delusional Neutrals. Some African governments labor under the illusion that the present conflict is somehow going to avoid their shores. Similarly, some Western governments (especially Scandinavians) prefer to see the present conflict as one between a disliked United States and a misguided minority of violent Muslims. Or they prefer to see what is a declared war against civilization itself as only a regrettable result of the unfortunate conflict between Israel and the Palestinians.

The "Altermondist" Fellow Travelers. It may be little known, but Osama bin Laden supports the Kyoto Treaty, considers capitalism as one of the main pernicious influences of the infidel West on the Islamic world, and is a great supporter of the rights of the Guantanamo detainees. Hate for America is a strong unifying factor, and the altermondists, formerly known as the anti-globalists, also share his desire to get off the train of global cultural and economic integration. While only the anarchist fringes of the altermondists openly express solidarity with the jihadists' anti-Western goals, the entire movement protects or legitimizes that fringe. Groups like the remnants of the Italian Red Brigades are in open solidarity with al-Qaeda—and hyperactive altermondists as well.

The "Blame-the-Yanks" Crowd. Anti-Americanism is so widespread throughout the world, and is so intense, that the "enemy of my enemy is my friend" dictum has global effects benefiting the Islamist terror networks. America exploits the world, and makes it poorer, more unjust, and more polluted: "Right on!" says the bearded prophet out of the Middle Ages into his cell phone. "The U.S. is the main terrorist force in the world," says an MIT professor, "absolutely!" say those proud perpetrators of September 11 and Bali; if only the Americans would let that Israeli tumor be neutralized or removed from the Middle East, the "democratic" lamb and the Islamic lion could peacefully lie together.

The altermondists meet this crowd in their explanation of the "real causes" of cowboy Bush's assault on Afghanistan and Iraq; "On one hand he (Bush) is carrying out the demands of the Zionist lobby that helped him to enter the White House. These demands are to destroy the military strength of Iraq because it is too close to the Jews in occupied Palestine, regardless of the harm that will happen to your people and your economy." On the other hand, Bush is concealing his own ambitions and the ambitions of the Zionist lobby and their own desire for oil. He is still following the mentality of his ancestors who killed the Native Americans to take their land and wealth. Sounds familiar? We heard this from members of Congress, Democratic presidential candidates and huge European crowds—but the quote is from a statement of Osama bin Laden, in October 2003.

The Idiots Savants of Academia and Media—"Poverty and Injustice" as Bomb Makers. There was a time, not so long ago, when Galbraith was detecting a convergence between Marxist totalitarianism and American capitalism; when political pilgrims "discovered" Ho Chi Minh's peasant nationalism, Castro's egalitarianism, and Mao's intellectual prowess, or saw the "future that works" in Lenin's Soviet nightmare. Today our academic "experts" on Islam claim that poverty and lack of democracy are the root causes of Islamist terror: Have free elections, and bin Laden will go into the honey-export business.

Never mind that bin Laden disagrees: "Democracy is deviation. Voices have risen in Iraq as before in Palestine, Egypt, Jordan, Yemen, and elsewhere, calling for a peaceful democratic solution in dealing with apostate governments or with Jewish and crusader invaders instead of fighting in the name of God. Hence, it is necessary to warn against the danger of this deviant and misleading practice that contradicts Allah's teachings to fight in the name of God. They have chosen democracy, the faith of the ignorant." Indeed, "It is not the American war machine that should be of the utmost concern to Muslims. What threatens the future of Islam, in fact its very survival, is American democracy." This according to Issue al-Ayyeri, a.k.a. Abu Muhammad, a now-deceased (killed in action by the Saudis in 2003) associate of bin Laden in the *Future of Iraq and the Arabian Peninsula After the Fall of Baghdad*, published by al-Qaeda.

Do the experts—the same types who have long told us that the Vietcong, Shining Path in Peru, or FARC in Colombia, are "peasant reformers," despite the "reformers'" insistence that they are Marxist revolutionaries — know better what Osama bin Laden seeks?

The Clueless and the Absurd. Those "peace activists" with no hidden agendas, and the clueless youths at good colleges, think that if only Bush and his misguided (or militaristic) allies would stop persecuting the jihadists, terrorism would stop. Hence the strange argument that the removal of the Taliban and Saddam is the *cause* of Bali, Madrid, and Istanbul, and the pathetic spectacle of Spaniards reacting to the Madrid massacre by holding signs of "Paz!"

Perhaps the most spectacular combination of the clueless and the absurd is to be found in the person of the Archbishop of Canterbury, Dr. Rowan Williams, who "urged America to recognize that terrorists can 'have serious moral goals.'" He said that, while terrorism must always be condemned, it was wrong to assume its perpetrators were devoid of political rationality. "It is possible to use unspeakably wicked means to pursue an aim that is shared by those who would not dream of acting in the same way, an aim that is intelligible or desirable."

He said that in ignoring this, in its criticism of al-Qaeda, America "loses the power of self-criticism and becomes trapped in a self-referential morality." After this, what can one expect from politically illiterate college students?

The Blind Mice of Human Rights. "You have claimed to be the vanguards of Human Rights, and your Ministry of Foreign Affairs issues annual reports containing statistics of those countries that violate any Human Rights. However, all these things vanished when the mujahadeen hit you, and you then implemented the methods of the same documented governments that you used to curse. In America, you captured thousands of Muslims and Arabs, took them into custody with neither reason, court trial, nor even disclosing their names. You issued newer, harsher laws....What happens in Guatanamo is a historical embarrassment to America and its values."

If one believed this to be part of a press release by Amnesty International or Human Rights Watch—as it may very well be—the error would be understandable. It is, in fact, a quote from bin Laden's November *2002 Letter to America.*

Much as when, during the Cold War, anti-Communists were the most effective de facto fellow travelers and useful idiots, human-rights fundamentalists and libertarians are serving in those roles now. They see terrorism as no different from ordinary crime, and think terrorists have the same rights as soldiers—while implicitly accepting the fact that they play by different, or, more accurately, no rules. Thus, interrogation becomes "psychological torture," underage bombers are "children" to be protected, focus on statistically and culturally likely suspects is "racial profiling" (Muslims are now a "race"), as if the same resources should be devoted to old Lutheran ladies as to young bearded Muslim men; and, in the memorable words of the late foreign minister of Sweden, Anna Lindh, killing a prominent al-Qaeda operative in the deserts of Yemen is "extra-judiciary execution"—a crime itself. Moreover, at least in the opinion of a California judge, supporting officially defined terrorist groups is a constitutional right.

One does not have to support or share the jihadists' goals or methods in order to promote their cause and help their activities, just as before it was not necessary—in fact it was often counterproductive—to be a card-carrying Communist-party member or even a Marxist, if one wanted to promote the victory of the "socialist camp." All that is needed is to weaken the immune system of society in its struggle against barbarism, to unilaterally disarm civilization, and to dilute its moral and legal standards and values. For that, the useful idiots and fellow travelers are well trained—and they're back.

Reprinted with the permission of http://www.nationalreview.com/comment/radu200404130904.asp, April 13, 2004

VISITORS OF DEATH

The recent arrest of al-Qaeda operative Eisa al-Hindi in Britain gives one an idea about how Islamist terrorists prepare for their attacks. Al-Hindi is a convert from Hinduism who had done surveillance of New York targets in 2001 and is suspected of planning additional operations in the U.K. or US.

Prior to attacks in Casablanca in May and Istanbul in November of 2003, Madrid in March, 2004, and probably in Bali in October, 2002, it appears that a high-ranking associate of Osama bin Laden traveled to the target cities beforehand to provide advice to the local activists who would actually perpetrate the attacks. The visitor was usually based in Pakistan or elsewhere in the Indian subcontinent, or in Saudi Arabia, the two major centers of Islamist terrorism in the world. Al-Hindi is of Indian extraction, a natural choice, since most Muslims in Britain are from the Indian subcontinent.

The general consensus now is that al-Qaeda is no longer a tightly structured organization with a well-defined hierarchy. However, al-Qaeda, which means "the base" in Arabic, remains active. The usual analogy is with a franchised global company, but this "McDonald's model" is an imperfect comparison.

When the Taliban lost control over most of Afghanistan by the end of 2001, al-Qaeda lost access to its own extensive network of specialized training camps. Since al-Qaeda was no longer an alien terrorist organization that largely controlled a government, it reverted to an older pattern—being a terrorist organization with transnational reach but no fixed base.

In the thirteenth century, St. Bonaventura defined God as a circle whose center is everywhere and circumference nowhere. That is a good way to describe the al-Qaeda of today. On the one hand, bin Laden has lost many of his tactical capabilities. It is one thing to control specialized training camps (some for Western operatives, some for ordinary combatants, etc) but another to be pushed into hidden jungle camps in places such as Indonesia and the Philippines. On the other hand, strategically, Osama bin Laden and Ayman al Zawahiri have made great progress towards their first and most important goal: transforming the virtually dormant concept of jihad from an Islamic religious and political recovery into a serious cultural reality.

In that sense, al-Qaeda's dominance is clear, no matter how often President Bush and others assert that al-Qaeda does not "represent" Islam. At least in majority Sunni Islam, there is no legitimate, universally recognized authority to define what "orthodox Islam" is. Certainly not Saudi imams, whose Wahhabi interpretation of Islam would have been seen as heresy before oil made them rich and influential; nor al-Azhar in Cairo, let alone Kairouan in Tunisia. All would have been seen, correctly, as co-opted, if not bought, by their respective governments.

As the Quran and Hadith make clear, Osama remains a Muslim unless he publicly renounces his faith. If Osama operates within the accepted or implicit bounds of Islam, what should stop any Muslim from accepting or following his (or al Zawahiri's) ideas and tactics? This explains why al-Qaeda has, indeed, won the first round. It has convinced millions of Muslims everywhere that this is a conflict between Islam and the rest of the world rather than what it really is—a civil war within the Islamic world.

While the list of states Osama considers enemies is large—the US, Israel, France, the U.K., Russia, India, and China are all on it—we also have the normally moderate Council of British Muslims complaining about harassment by the authorities, thus implicitly accepting the Islamic quality of the terrorists arrested. The claim is taken to further, laughable lengths by the British Parliament's Joint Committee on Human Rights, which, in an Orwellian outburst of absurdity, claimed, "There is mounting evidence that the powers under the Terrorism Act are being used disproportionately against members of the Muslim community in the U.K." Did they expect some proportional action against Methodists and Anglicans?

To accept that Islamism is a lasting cultural phenomenon, as well as arguably an immediate terror threat, is to also admit that al-Qaeda is everywhere going back to Bonaventura's definition of God. By becoming fundamentally synonymous with Islamism, al-Qaeda has established a "presence" in all countries with significant Muslim communities. There are national Islamist terror groups everywhere, from Indonesia and the Philippines to Morocco and the U.K.. These groups were not invented by someone hiding in the mountains of the Afghanistan/Pakistan border. They are the products of a global Islamist revival—one defined by al-Qaeda and its way of thinking.

Thus, national Islamist terror organizations and al-Qaeda have two things in common: ideological similarity and persistent strategic (not tactical) cooperation. The Algerian Salafist Group for Preaching and Combat or the Moroccan Islamist Fighting Group, or the even more dangerous and larger Islamic Group in Southeast Asia, were not founded by al-Qaeda, but it ideologically energizes them and gives them technical advice. McDonald's—to push the analogy a bit further—does not allow the use of its name to just any entrepreneur. It imposes standards—and so does al-Qaeda. They maintain a degree of quality control to protect the company's logo.

The al-Qaeda visitor, therefore, has a role. The targeting has to be accepted, if not approved, by the "owners of the logo" in Pakistan, and it has to be done right: hence the use of al-Qaeda's technical expertise. Virtually all known al-Qaeda-linked operatives are experts in computers and engineering. This means that while al-Qaeda is just a base, its role and degree of control over operations everywhere cannot be discounted as far too many countries are wont to do.

For counter-terrorist organizations everywhere, catching the visitor is tantamount to preventing an attack. The visitor is an essential ingredient in any successful terror attack, and is also the proof that al-Qaeda is not only a form of Islamic ideology, but also the engine behind the entire problem of Islamist terror. Hence, we are back to basics. We must continue to improve intelligence and border controls, for detecting the "visitor." And we must admit that the problem is not some fringe, pseudo-Islamic minority but a significant proportion of the global Muslim community.

Reprinted with the permission from http://www.frontpagemag.com,
August 23, 2004

RUSSIA'S PROBLEM: THE CHECHENS OR ISLAMIC TERRORISTS?

Russia is under assault by Islamic terrorists. On August 24, two Russian airliners were blown up, leaving ninety people dead. A week later, a car bomb near a Moscow subway station killed another ten people, and the next day, September 1, Islamist terrorists took hundreds of hostages in a North Ossetia school, including many children. At this writing, scores of people are reported to have died. Far from remaining a localized affair, the Chechen conflict is becoming an open wound in Russia's flank, a cultural, ethnic, and religious clash with no end in sight and with growing international ramifications.

Two common aspects to these attacks deserve highlighting: their Middle Eastern roots and their being carried out by women. Based on the limited intelligence available, none of these attacks was a strictly Chechen operation. The Islambouli Brigades, an al-Qaeda-associated group previously known for attacks in Pakistan, has taken credit for the plane and subway bombings. The Brigades is named for Egyptian army lieutenant Khaled al-Islambouli, the main author of the assassination of President Anwar Sadat (for which he was executed). Islambouli, whose brother Mohammed is an al-Qaeda operative, was a member of the Egyptian Islamic Group, led by Ayman al Zawahiri, now Bin Laden's second in command.

The link between Chechen rebels and international terrorism, including al-Qaeda, is not new. Indeed, ever since the first Chechen war (1992-96), Islamists from all over the Middle East and beyond have gone to Chechnya to fight the Russian infidel. While it is true that Chechen Islam was traditionally rather syncretic and mostly under the influence of Sufi brotherhoods, some warlords, most prominently Shamil Basayev, have been attracted to Wahhabism—and by Saudi and other Gulf money, weapons, and volunteers. It was one of those volunteers, Bin Saleh al-Suwailem, Samir, a.k.a. Khatab—a Saudi whose life and career strongly resembled Bin Laden's—who, together with Basayev, invaded the Russian province of Daghestan in 1999, thus provoking the present Chechen war. A number of European Muslims, from France and the U.K., have also joined the Chechens, while the self-proclaimed Chechen Islamic Republic was only recognized by the Taliban. Chechens were trained in al-Qaeda camps in Afghanistan and fought against the United States in that country in 2001.

The extent to which Russian brutality and clumsiness have radicalized many Chechens could be debated, as could Moscow's often exaggerated claim that all Chechen resistance is Wahhabi and attributable to non-Chechen mercenaries. What is not arguable is the fact that the most effective, violent, and well-trained elements in Chechnya are indeed Islamists, part and parcel of the al-Qaeda nebula, whose methods are imports from the Middle East.

The perpetrators of those attacks were Chechen women, the so-called Black Widows, who are specially trained for suicide operations and have committed such acts in the past. The involvement of women in suicide terrorist attacks is becoming more and more common both in and beyond Russia, where they began in 2002. Indeed, the two suicide bombers who killed three policemen and a child in Tashkent on March 29, 2004, were women. One of them, Dilnoza Khalmuradova, was nineteen-years-old.

One may wonder how the use of women suicide bombers is consistent with Islamic views of the role of women. In May 2003, Yusuf al-Qaradawi, who is dean of Islamic Studies at the University of Qatar, a regular al-Jazeera contributor, and perhaps the most influential Sunni cleric today, managed to find a way: "The act [of suicide terrorism] is a form of martyrdom for the cause of Allah. . .A woman should go out for jihad even without the permission of her husband." Qaradawi notes that terror groups could benefit because women "may do what is impossible for men to do." Hence, these women are allowed to violate Islamic teachings, "avoid wearing the veil, and be without a male escort." (Cited in Clara Beyler, "Female Suicide Bombers: An Update," www.ict.org.il)

The Russian response to these developments has been, so far, a mixture of denial, incompetence, contradictory policies, and naivete. Moscow has repeatedly denied either that there is a war in Chechnya or that the conflict involves a significant portion of the Chechen population, instead claiming that it is all about Wahhabi terrorism incited by outsiders. It has organized several meaningless "elections" in Chechnya, the latest on August 29, notwithstanding that as long as it does not control the territory, no elections in Chechnya could conceivably be legitimate. In military terms, four years into the recent round of violence, the Russian military still cannot even seal the borders of Chechnya—a small state, even if its terrain is difficult. The fact that Chechnya-based terrorists could repeatedly strike into Russia proper, including Moscow, and that the recent mass kidnapping took place in North Ossetia, historically the most pro-Russian (and the only Orthodox) of all the northern Caucasian regions, only underscores this fact.

Nor has Russia's policy of blackmailing the southern Caucasus states of Georgia and Azerbaijan in an effort to elicit their help in dealing with Chechnya been successful. Indeed, what is the incentive for Georgia, which borders Chechnya, to help the Russians seal the border, with Moscow openly arming and encouraging separatists in Georgia's Abkhazia and South Ossetia? Or why should nearby Azerbaijan stop arms shipments to Chechnya, if Moscow is encouraging Armenia to annex a third of the Azeri territory?

So far, Moscow's response to the school kidnapping has been to convene a meeting of the UN Security Council. What exactly Moscow intends by this—to have blue helmets replace the Russian troops in the Caucasus mountains? To ask the UN declare the Chechen resistance a terrorist organization?—is not clear.

That said, the Chechen conflict has clearly become an open-ended problem in international politics. Unless some drastic—and improbable—reforms make the Russian military become efficient and the government pulls itself together, Moscow will have no "victory" any time soon. At the same time, the increasingly Islamist Chechen leadership, with its persistent use of terrorism and its close ties to international terrorist networks, makes the possibility of a Chechen state a frightening, if remote, prospect. Indeed, even before Chechnya was infiltrated by Islamists, during the country's brief independence (1996-99), the Chechens had demonstrated a complete inability to operate as an independent state. Chechnya (or "Ishkeria") became a black hole of criminal gangs, smuggling, and crossborder violence—and matters have only gotten worse since.

The Chechnya conflict has itself begun to spawn international terrorists. According to France's antiterrorist judge Jean-Louis Bruguiere, the authors of a planned 2003 chemical attack in Paris that was prevented at the last moment were a network of Islamists trained in Georgia's Pankissi Gorge area. Their leader was one Menad ben Chellali, the oldest son of a radical imam from near Lyons who had trained in Afghanistan in 2001. Menad's brother and imitator, Murad, was captured in Afghanistan, detained in Guantanamo, and is now in a French jail.

Western sympathy for the Chechens should be reassessed in light of these developments. Perhaps, unlikely as it may seem, even the *New York Times* will bring itself to label as terrorists (rather than "guerrillas" or "armed insurgents") those who take school children hostages and murder their fathers. (See "Hostage Crisis Unfolds in Russia as Guerrillas Seize School," *New York Times*, September 1, 2004.) The understandable initial sympathy for the Chechens—a people treated atrociously by Russia and the Soviet Union—should not excuse what is done in their name today.

Reprinted with the permission form http://www.fpri.org, September 3, 2004

PART 4
THE AMERICAS

More than two decades of travel, research, and contacts in Central and South America have only made it clear to me that, if there is any clarity in the region's culture, either political or elite, it is either nonexistent or beyond my grasp. Where is "Central America" when the differences between El Salvador and Honduras—neighboring countries with a combined area smaller than Pennsylvania's—are greater than between Germany and Algeria, their common language notwithstanding? Or a "South America" including (again neighboring) fast-developing Chile and perennially confused Peru, entrepreneurial Colombians and eternally resentful Argentines?

Cuba's Transition: Institutional Lessons from Eastern Europe

An emerging consensus holds that Cuba's communist regime is moving away from Fidel Castro's brand of orthodox Marxism-Leninism and toward—something else. Cuban officials now publicly profess their indifference to labels such as "socialism" and "communism," referring, instead, to some vague "Cuban way" of social and economic organization. Even Castro himself claims that his hostility to multiparty politics stems less from an adherence to Marxism and owes more to the calls of José Martí, Cuba's national hero, for national unity of purpose and organization.

All of this may point to a growing belief in Havana that communism cannot long endure as a legitimizing factor for the regime and a corresponding attempt to locate a new source of legitimacy in the alleged uniqueness of Cuba's socialist system. The implication of such an attempt would be: (1) that the Cuban regime differs fundamentally from the collapsed Eurasian communist regimes; and (2) that its future is therefore likely to differ also—and fundamentally. In other words, it has a future.

The purpose of this article is to examine the validity of such a claim by comparing the institutional changes that have taken place in Cuba since 1990 with those that have already occurred in the Eurasian communist regimes, principally the satellite members of the now defunct Warsaw Treaty Organization (WTO), during their final decade.[1]

The Cuban System in Perspective

The communist system of Cuba differs from the communist systems of most of the Eurasian communist states in six significant ways.

First, the Cuban regime is younger. If its commencement is dated from Fidel Castro's format proclamation of his Marxist faith, circa 1961 (two years after his victory over Batista), then the communist regime in Cuba is now thirty-three years old. By contrast, Soviet communism started in 1917 and its East European offshoots just after World War II. Thus, only one generation of Cubans has been socialized under Marxist rule *versus* two or more generations in the case of the Eurasian states.

Second, Cubans are less isolated. The process of socialization in Cuba has never been as tightly controlled as it was in the Eurasian communist states. Apart from the East Germans, no subjects of communist rule in Eurasia enjoyed as much access to outside, non-Communist media as do the Cubans, for the latter are exposed daily to broadcasts from their co-nationals across the Florida straits and, in growing numbers, to tourists from the West and Latin America.

Third, the Cuban revolution, in its initial stages, was a genuinely popular, non-ideological movement that succeeded on its own.

Whereas the regimes in Eastern Europe (Yugoslavia and Albania aside) were imposed by the armies of Joseph Stalin.

Fourth, the Cuban regime has followed an institutional trajectory quite different from that of its East European counterparts.

The latter originated in the assumption of power by communist parties, however small and unrepresentative. In Cuba, the personal rule of Fidel Castro long preceded attempts to institutionalize Marxism-Leninism. As a result, it was only by the mid-1960s that Castro saw fit to establish a new Communist Party of Cuba (Partido Communista de Cuba, or PCC), and, even then, it was more of a facade for "Castroism." Only in the 1970s did the PCC begin to take on a life of its own, and even today it is not in real control of the traditional pillars of communist rule, such as the Fuerzas Armadas Revolucionarias (FAR)[2] and the forces of the secret police and/or internal security known as the MLNINT (that is, the Ministry of the Interior). On the contrary, Fidel Castro is Commander-in-Chief; Raúl Castro, his brother, is Minister of Defense; their close associate, Gen. Abelardo Colomé Ibarra, is in charge of the MININT; and Raùl's wife, Wilma Espin, controls the women's organization, one of those ancillary institutions that, in Eastern Europe, were typically run by the party. All this suggests that the ECC still does not hold a position comparable to that enjoyed by the Communist parties in Eastern Europe.

Fifth, the role of the leader in Cuba makes the Cuban system more like pure Stalinism, with its "personality cult."

And less like the communist East European regimes (except for those of Ceausescu in Romania, Hoxha in Albania, and Tito in Yugoslavia). Castro's role in Cuba also puts the Cuban system rather close to the Latin American (and Iberian) tradition of *caudillismo.*

Sixth, the Cuban regime's role within the "socialist community" prior to 1989 was quite peculiar.

With the only analogies, again, being with such "marginal" or "special case" communist regimes as Mao's China after the late 1950s (and, by extension, Hoxha's Albania); Tito's "nonaligned" Yugoslavia; and Ceausescu's "Romanian way." Castro saw his revolution as a model for Latin America and for the Third World in general. Hence, despite Soviet reluctance (and even outright opposition), Havana tried to serve as an alternate center of revolution in Latin America. Castro's creation, the Organización Latinoamericana de Solidaridad

(OLAS), for example, was intended as a Havana-based mini-Comintern. Similarly, Cuba's expeditions in Africa during the 1970s and 1980s were examples of Third World solidarity as well as communist solidarity.

On the other hand, and despite Castro's current claims, his is indeed a communist regime, based on the same ideological principles as those of pre-1989 Eastern Europe: hostility to private property; state control of the "principal means of production" (that is, virtually all enterprises); and control over economy, culture, social life and politics by an unelected minority.

Institutional Analysis

One must grasp a few basic points to understand the predicament of the Havana regime today and that of the 1989 East European communist governments. Virtually all institutions in these communist political systems are (or were):

A. Recent. Even in the former Soviet Union (longest lasting of the communist systems), institutional experiments from Lenin to Gorbachev insured that most social institutions were fairly recent, either in their essence or in their form. Even the Communist Party, the military, and the internal security apparatus—the three institutional pillars of all communist regimes—repeatedly shifted their positions relative to one another. This fluidity, however, should not be confused with imaginative change. Sometimes all that changed was the name (from Cheka to NKVD to KGB, as the Soviet security apparatus was variously named, for example), while most of the time change involved only formal functions, or perhaps the size of an institution's area of control.

B. Created from the top and highly centralized. Because institutions in a communist country are creations of the party leadership, itself a self-appointed elite ("the vanguard of the proletariat"), such institutions are intrinsically authoritarian, as proved by their formal and de facto definition as instruments of the Communist Party ("transmission belts," in Marxist parlance). Labor unions, youth groups, women's organizations, and so forth, have the same leadership as the Communist Party, not only ultimately, through the domination of the party over society as a whole, but also in quite direct ways. Thus in the Eurasian communist states, it was a routine fact of life for a national trade union leader to become the secretary for ideology (or organization, or personnel, or security) of the Communist Party's Central Committee, then the secretary responsible for media operations, and then (even if male) leader of the national Women's organization. This interchangeable leadership simply reflected the all pervasiveness of party control, but it underscores the almost total lack of autonomy of virtually all institutions.

Indeed, not only are communist institutions under the formal control of the party (the "leading force" in society), their leaders are invariably part of the party leadership as well, and thus subject, first and foremost, to party discipline.

Furthermore, in the East European regimes, individual leaders of various institutions—labor unions, military, internal security—were quite often shifted from their positions in order to avoid the creation of personal, autonomous power bases.

C. Political in their goals and claims to legitimacy. In communist systems, the state strives for omnipresence and omnipotence. Inevitably, therefore, the daily life of the individual is political (or at least superficially politicized) because everyone must deal with the state: as employer, educator, pension administrator, media manager, and so forth. Old ladies and teenagers alike are forced to face regime politics, for the state controls both pensions and dance halls. By the same token, since the legitimacy of the regime lies in its political claim to represent "the masses," objections to any of its myriad activities becomes a political act. Naturally enough, this forced politicization of the population led, after decades, to cynicisms, disgust for politics in general, and distrust of politicians.

D. Lacking inflexibility. Because all institutions are directly controlled by the party leadership, all important decisions, from management to personnel to planning and production targets, are dependent upon the central policymaking apparatus, the Politburo. Hence, the ability to respond promptly to any challenge or unexpected development is severely hindered, and individual responsibility by institutional leaders is inhibited. Attempts at institutional reform—whether "workers' self-management" in Yugoslavia, or decentralization of planning in Hungary—failed because they did not (and, by the logic of communist system, could not) escape from the party's ultimate control.

Institutional Change and Decay

Little argument exists over the basic similarities of the institutional framework employed by the regimes of both Cuba and Eastern Europe. By the same token, there should be small room for dispute regarding some of the important differences. How else could one explain why the government of Fidel Castro is still in control (even if shaky), while those of the Eastern European regimes have all collapsed?

The obvious starting point is with a brief comparison of the social and political bases of the East European and Cuban models.

Social Base

Between 1944 and 1947, the Eastern European Communist Parties came to power riding the tanks of the Red Army and with little or no popular support on the part of the people they were to govern. For instance, the Romanian Communist Party, put in power by the Soviets in March 1945, had only 800 to 1,000 members at the time, and a majority of these came from the ranks of ethnic minorities who were widely resented: Hungarians/Szeklers, Jews, Gypsies, Ukrainians, Bulgarians (Tismaneanu, 1986:325). Two decades later, in most cases, those parties had vastly expanded their base of popular support, as expressed by the number of members, to anywhere from 10 to 15 percent of the adult population. By 1980, according to official (if dubious) figures, communist party membership totaled 16 percent of Romania's entire population, the largest proportion anywhere in the communist world. During the 1980s, however, support for the ruling Communist Party declined dramatically in Eastern Europe, as demonstrated by official statements, defections, declining membership, increased dissidence, and public protests involving both active and former party members.

The PCC in Cuba, on the other hand, had virtually no role be; in carrying out Cuba's 1959 revolution, although individual members (notably, Raúl Castro) took an active part. Indeed, the PCC was tainted by its long history of submission to Moscow and collaboration with the Batista regime. Far from being the means for installing Marxist rule in Havana, the PCC was seen as an enemy by Fidel and his group, a dangerously subversive element, and anti-national to boot. Simply put, although Fidel declared his loyalty to Marxism-Leninism, he did not accept the PCC as a legitimate vehicle for communist rule in Cuba—until it was his communist party, rather than Moscow's. Only after the party was reconstituted in 1965, and its members subjected to a dramatic purge (including the elimination in 1968 of its historic leadership under Aníbal Escalante), did the PCC begin to play the formal role traditionally assigned to Communist Parties in other communist regimes. But the operative word here is "formal" because, even today, the PCC is Fidel's creation, albeit an increasing independent one, and remains relatively small by the standards of Eastern Europe: just 600,000 members in 1990 (Volsik, 1991:77). By contrast, Kadar, Zhivkov, and even Ceausescu were creations of their respective parties.

In this respect, then, Castro had a major advantage over his East European colleagues. He came to power on his own, was known for his anti-U.S, sentiments all his life, and created at least the impression autonomy from Moscow. Of course, informed observers realized that whatever independence Havana once enjoyed had ended by the time Fidel was forced to support the 1968 invasion of Czechoslovakia. However, most Cuban citizens are not informed observers, for obvious reasons.

The Leader

Because Castro's nationalist credentials are infinitely stronger than those of any East European regime and, in fact, comparable only to those of Ho Chi Minh, Kim Il Sung, and Mao, and because he is undoubtedly charismatic, Fidel enjoys a highly unusual position as communist leader. Just how unusual is best demonstrated not by his complete domination of party and state institutions—

after all most East European communist bosses ultimately reached positions of unchallenged domination—but by the widespread popular conviction that communism, the Cuban revolution, and Fidel cannot be separated. Moreover, this is a conviction shared by the regime's supporters and enemies alike.

No serious observer of Cuba would deny the dominant role of Fidel Castro in that country's present or future.[3] The question is: to what extent does Fidel's role differ from that played by the other supreme leaders in either the Soviet Union or Eastern Europe? Clearly, Fidel has a unique position in the history of communist states. Unlike all other communist leaders, he did not come to power as a Communist Party first secretary (that is, through intra-party bureaucratic maneuvering), who then took over as chief of state. Castro took power as the institutionally undefined leader of the revolution. Only later did he become the PCC's first secretary and, later still (de facto), chief of state and head of government. While even Fidel's worst enemies admit that there are significant numbers of *fidelistas*, few people, either inside or outside the former East! European regimes, ever spoke of "Ceauscuists," "Zhivkovites," or "Husakists!" ("Titoists" may constitute a limited exception). Moreover, Castro is also highly unusual in having an ideology to himself, however undefined that ideology may be (something between a historic Latin American *caudillismo* and the peculiar revisions of Marxism-Leninism that go by the names of Stalinism, Titoism, Maoism, and—in Kirn Il Sung's North Korea—*Juche*).

Over the past two years, however, Castro seems to have kept himself in the background, at least on specific issues, for the first time in his adult life. Gone are the days when he engaged in Ceausescu's favorite sport, e.g., visiting all types of institutions and providing advice in all fields. Economic policy or at least its implementation, seems to be largely in the hands of Carlos Lage; foreign policy in those of Robaina and Alarcón and the actual supervision of the regime's survival strategy in those of Raùl Castro and his military associates.

All of this suggests that Castro's popularity peaked in January 1959; had experienced a sharp drop by 1962, as the Cuban middle-classes emigrated or opposed the radicalization of the regime; reached a new high point with the period of Latin American revolutionary expansion led by Havana in the mid1960s; reached a plateau with: (a) the apparent economic boom of the late 1970s and early 1980s; and, (b) the apparent successes in Angola and Nicaragua; and has gone downhill ever since, dramatically so since 1989.

The PCC

The position of the PCC in society and in Cuba's institutional structure differs considerably from that of its counterparts in Eastern Europe and USSR. To begin with, in the latter cases, the Communist Party was the instrument and beneficiary of the country's communization; in Cuba, it was Castro's first victim. Later (in its post-1965 incarnation), the party was part of Castro's attempt to provide ideological legitimacy to his already existing Marxist-Leninist regime. Except for Fidel, no communist leader has reached supreme power other than by rising through the party. Even those (like Stalin, Hoxha, Mao, Ceausescu, and Tito) who later reached a position that enabled them to emasculate and eclipse, or even destroy (Gorbachev and Yeltsin, Brazauskas in Lithuania, Posgay in Hungary), the party were initially the direct creations of that party.

In Cuba, by contrast, the pre-1959 communists of the *Partido Socialista Popular* (PSP)- pro-Soviet from beginning to end, anti-Castro, and occasionally pro-Batista—played no role in Castro's revolution (excepting individuals like Carlos Rafael Rodríguez and Raùl Castro himself). Moreover, because the PSP was a pro-Soviet organization, Cubans looked upon it as anti-nationalist and controlled from outside. Since it consistently described Castro as an adventurer, it was viewed as anti-Fidel, not least of all by Fidel himself. Hence the hostility exhibited by Castro in the 1968 purge of PSP leadership under Aníbal Escalante.

Even after the party's recreation in Fidel's image (in 1965), and despite a brief rejuvenation of sorts after 1968, the PCC continued to play a far lesser role in Cuba than did its counterparts in the Soviet bloc, with the exception of the last years of Ceausescu's Romania. One example of this institutionally limited relevance was the irregularity with which it convened its party congresses, of which it has held only four to date: in 1975, 1980, 1986, and 1991. The closest analogy is Stalin's suspension of the party congresses of the Communist Party of the Soviet Union (CPSU) from the late 1930s to the 1950s, which could be explained, at least in part, by the intervention of World War II.

That the armed forces (FAR) are not only independent of the PCC but superior to it in terms of actual influence has as much to do with history as with Fidel's idiosyncrasies. Those include his stormy past relations with the communists and his position as the ultimate arbiter of all institutional, sectoral, and social conflicts in Cuba. Given his military credentials, his resentment of the PSP and its history, and any caudillo's distrust and dislike of institutions (since they only magnify his sense of mortality), Fidel Castro was never a vocal champion of the PCC, at least in practice, except when the party was useful as an instrument of his policies or for purposes of legitimacy.

Unlike its East European counterparts, the PCC is too recent to have experienced that ultimate test of institutional resiliency, a change of leadership at the very top, especially as Fidel, Raúl, and Carlos Rafael Rodríguez have all maintained their positions since 1965. Nevertheless, the PCC has exhibited some of the symptoms of fatal decay witnessed in communist parties of Romania and the USSR during the 1970s and 1980s. The first of these is the rather abrupt ouster of relatively strong leaders who are perceived either as potential challengers to the leader or as having established autonomous bases of power. In the Eurasian communist states, such demotions were usually accomplished by removing the person from the Politburo. Thus did Gorbachev discard Romanov and Grishin, the local bosses of Leningrad and Moscow respectively; thus Ceausescu did the same to his ideological chief Iliescu, and to his youth leader and, later, union boss Trofin. Ever since the mid-1980s, Castro has been following the same pattern, discarding his chief ideologue Antonio Pérez Herrero, Minister of the Interior Ramiro Valdes, union boss Roberto Veiga, and Deputy Prime Ministers Pedro Miret and Carlos Aldana—a process that has been somewhat euphemistically described as the "destruction of the bureaucratic oligarchy," (Domínguez, 1994: 2-3).

In every case, the replacement of the old-timers was attributed to personal failings (e.g., corruption), as in the cases of Romanov, Grishin, Aldana, and Trofin, or to the party's need to rejuvenate itself. Whether the latter claim was plausible or not, the process did result in the appointment to the Politburo, and to lesser positions, of younger people who were distinguished from their older predecessors by two characteristics: a better education (if only a "socialist" one) and, by virtue of their age alone, the lack of an independent political base. Thus provincial boss Yeltsin became a Politburo member in Gorbachev's scheme, Dumitru Popescu attained prominent positions in Ceausescu's Romania, and Carlos Lage and Roberto Robaina became Politburo members of the PCC.

Robaina and Lage offer good examples of the threat that the PCC establishment could pose to Fidel and his clique. Both are, by age if nothing else, separated from the *Granma* mythology (the *Granma* being the name of the boat which bore Fidel and comrades back from exile). Both are now supposed to enjoy extensive privileges and the right to express opinions different from Fidel's—and to do so in English. Robaina's "promotion" to Foreign Minister from leader of the Union de Jóvenes Comunistas (UJC) or Young Communists League (and a popular one at that) was probably intended to limit his influence, but it may well create new expectations both at home and abroad. Lage's rational economic analyses might do the same. And both men might then take on lives of their own (Gonzalez, 1994: 24-25). After all, this process has all happened before: for example, with Bulgarian Foreign Minister Petar Mladenov, who led the party-army coup against Zhivkov in 1989.

The Military

While the military is one of the three pillars of any communist regime (the others being the internal security apparatus and the party), the role played by the military has differed from one communist country to another.

Throughout Eastern Europe, the military was created *after* the communist takeovers that followed World War II (once again, Tito's Yugoslavia was the exception). Because, during the early postwar period, few of the officers and soldiers had belonged to the pre-communist military, the institution itself was not only the creation of the party but, from the very start, the party's instrument. Secondly, the military forces of East European communist states functioned largely as extensions of the Soviet military, under the fig leaf of the Warsaw Treaty Organization. Although attempts were made, at times, to project a more nationalist image of those military institutions, most East Europeans remembered that Soviet Marshal Konstantin Rokossovsky was the first Defense Minister of communist Poland and that Soviet citizen Emil Bodnaras was Romania's. So, while it is true that a subliminal faith in the national character of some East European armies persisted (particularly in Romania, and in Poland until 1981), the fact remains that, at best, the popular legitimacy of those armed forces remained quite limited.

Nevertheless, the leadership of the various communist parties in Eastern Europe displayed a certain degree of ambivalence towards the loyalty and political role of their respective military establishments. On the one hand, the military leaders at the very top—including the Defense Minister, the Chief of the General Staff, and a few more high-ranking officers—were routinely coopted as members of the Central Committee of the Communist Party. The Minister of Defense, in particular, who was almost always a military man (at least formally), was generally a member of the Politburo. Moreover, the party also controlled the personnel policy of the military, either directly or through the security apparatus (understood as the combination of secret police, members of the Internal Ministry and its informer apparatus, border guards, and the military's political commissars). However, that was the catch. For the national security apparatuses were, in their turn, controlled by the Soviet KGB. Thus, no matter how pro-Moscow the East Europe's communist leaders might be, they could only be discomfited by the sense that their militaries were likely to be more loyal to Moscow than to their own national leaders. Indeed, in every instance elements of the military of an East European communist state acted against (or separate from) the state party, they acted in support of Soviet goals rather than in support of national anticommunist goals. The one exception to this pattern was in Romania. In that state, the leader's personal (rather than party) control over the military was ensured, or supposedly ensured, by the simple practice of nepotism: Ceausescu's brother, Ilie, was in charge of the military's personnel policies right up to the very end of the regime.

The ambiguous position of the military was reflected in the social status of the military as an institution, and of its officer corps as a group. To start with the latter, officers in Eastern Europe had certain advantages, such as access to special stores, relatively high salaries, privileged access for their children to university education, and so forth. At the same time, however, the military were reminded daily that they were not completely trusted. In all East European countries, the political reliability of the military was ensured by outsiders, that is, by political commissars who operated under various names, but who were not subject to the military hierarchy. Also, and without exception, military intelligence was directly subordinated to the internal security apparatus (Watts, 1992: 995-97).

Most important, however, no communist regime ever succeeded in resolving the key dilemma of defining the essence of its military institution: is it to be purely professional, that is, apolitical and unflinchingly loyal to the civilian (party) authority? Or is it to be politicized and socialized into Marxist-Leninist ideology? And, thus, into an arm of the ruling party? The first option is incompatible with the totalitarian, ideological nature of the communist regime; but the second is incompatible with the goal of keeping generals out of politics.

Thus, "Bonapartism," the Marxist term for the threat of a military inclined to take political action, has been a specter haunting communist governments, and not only in imagination. In China, Lin Piao's control over the military threatened the rule of Mao until that threat was finally terminated by Lin's death in 1971 (Rice, 1974: 505-9). Incidents that are much less well known include the attempts at a putsch that took place in both Bulgaria (in 1965) and Romania (twice during the 1970s). A more confusing, complicated case occurred in Poland in 1981 where the military takeover and imposition of martial law under General Wojciech Jaruzelski could be interpreted as either an attempt to save communism, despite the Communist Party, or as recognition of the party's terminal illegitimacy. With the possible exception of the Chinese case, however, all those military Interventions in politics were on behalf of the Soviets or at least of important Soviet factions, rather than against the system as such. In other words, the Bulgarian, Polish, and Romanian military involvement in communist politics was in support of Soviet, rather than institutional or national, interests.

Turning to Cuba, the case of General Arnaldo Ochoa might seem very different on the face of it, but there are similarities. Like his Bulgarian and Romanian colleagues in 1965 and the 1970s, and like General Nicolae Militaru of Romania in particular,[4] it would appear that Ochoa was eliminated in 1989 because the Castro brothers viewed him as pro-Moscow (i.e., pro-*perestroika*) and, thus, a potential leader of reformist communism (Oppenheimer, 1992:101-104).

However, it is important to note that none of communism's "Bonapartists" have had any known political ambition, let alone an alternative public program. In most cases, certainly in those of Militaru, Ochoa, and (paradoxical as it may seem) Jaruzelski, the threat that those military men posed to the communist establishment originated in their apparent indifference to politics and ideology. They represented a commonsensical approach, potentially appealing to a depoleiticized population, but highly threatening to a leadership whose raison d'etre was ideology.

The only exceptions to this pattern in Eastern Europe were the nationalist, arid implicitly anticommunist, behavior of the Hungarian military in 1956, under Defense Minister General Pal Maleter, and that of the Romanian Army under Defense Minister General Vasile Milea in 1989. Though both men were responding to, rather than leading, popular anticommunist revolts, they did command the loyalty of most of their troops at the time of their anti-regime, or anti-Soviet, acts. Those two examples and the fact that the Polish military's rank-and-file obeyed Jaruzelski's orders in 1981, suggests that some professionalism (at least some acceptance of orders by superiors) persisted in Eastern Europe.

What then is the position of the Cuban FAR and its institutional expression, Raúl Castro's MINFAR, vis-à-vis the regime as a whole, the regime's other institutions, and the military's experience in Eastern rope prior to 1989?

First and foremost is the question of relative institutional legitimacy. The FAR first assumed power as a nationalist force. Only later (as much as a decade later) was there a Cuban Communist Party sufficiently loyal to Fidel to pretend to control of the military. Among the members of the Warsaw Pact, Ceausescu alone—plus Tito in Yugoslavia and Enver Hoxha in Albania—also managed to project the state military as an instrument of nationalism. However, in the first case,

> By stressing Romanian nationalism, Ceausescu has gained national support but he has also undercut the ideological supremacy of the party by introducing a competing set of values. (Price, 1986: 292)

Mutatis mutandi, is the problem facing the Cuban regime, and it is apt to become more serious after Castro since, like Tito and Hoxha, he alone can serve as an effective mediator between the two institutions and their competing values.

Next are questions of perception and self-perception. The more a military institution was socialized as professional (something Ceausescu tried to do in the late 1960s and Cuba in the 1970s, though both tried to undo it later) or had combat experience, as did the FAR in Africa, the more painful was the shock of being forced into doing extensive civilian work. Indeed, the key word here is "extensive," since militaries in all modern societies have engaged in some civilian work, whether in emergencies or natural disasters, often on a frequent, but still irregular, basis. Thus, some Cuban or Soviet military personnel engaged in construction or agricultural work, often on a large scale. Nevertheless, they did so, at least in the public's understanding and in the official propaganda, as a secondary, and largely marginal, endeavor. From the very beginning, the Red Army built concentration camps and canals, harvested turnips, and constructed dams—just as the FAR cut sugar cane. That was, and was largely seen as, yet another proof that these militaries were true "people's armies." In all those cases, however, the military's civilian engagement was balanced, in both the public eye and official propaganda, by its heroic role abroad. For the Soviet military, their traditional status as national guardians remained the supreme image; for the FAR, their civil activities were balanced by their "internationalist" successes.

But just as Ceausescu went beyond such uses of the military and ultimately saw them only as a virtually free, but disciplined, labor force (Gitz, 1992: 108-109), Rail Castro, in a distinction without a difference, now thinks that

> defense includes everything. Right now it involves providing food for our people, which along with sugar production, has been designated by our commander in chief as the main strategic task [emphasis added]. (FBISLAM, 1994)

Naturally enough, a military regularly engaged in infrastructure and agricultural work—two types of work avoided and despised by the population at large—tends to provoke questions about its professionalism, in its own mind as well as in the minds of others. The Cuban military suffers all the problems, and faces all the dilemmas, as the militaries of communist Eastern Europe, only more acutely. To begin with, the FAR not only preceded the PCC (in its Castroite version) but was also Fidel's favorite institution, as demonstrated by his fondness for the uniform, his official title of *Comandante* rather than "Comrade Secretary" or "President." Similarly, Fidel's obvious successor, Raúl, while "just" second PCC secretary and MINFAR boss, has six of his generals in the Politburo (the ministers of defense and interior, the FAR chief of staff, and three assorted friends of Raúl, including the Minister of Transportation). In this respect, Cuba's position in the history of communism is unique. By contrast, when Ceausescu tried to use nepotism as a vaccine against military political autonomy, the attempt failed, as demonstrated by the events of December 1989. The reason for the difference is clear: the top leaders of the FAR, Raúl included, are all veterans of the revolution, from which they derive their legitimacy. Ceausescu's obscure brother had no such legitimacy.

Furthermore, the FAR is increasingly in direct control of key, albeit new, activities of all sorts of traditional Communist Party auxiliary institutions, such as the UJC (FBIS-LAM, 1993). Thus, the military leadership's area of influence and control is steadily expanding at the expense of all other political and social institutions. A good example is that of General Senen Casas Rigueiro, one of Raùl's intimates and a co-founder of MINFAR (in which he is still active) while serving, at the same time, as Minister of Transportation. Last year, he stated that "civilian life will certainly have to move step by step toward what is done in the Armed Forces" Juventud Rebelde, 1994). Such a statement could hardly have come from any Soviet or Central European general prior to 1989, and Casas went even further by proclaiming (in both his capacities) that the goal was to "*follow faithfully Raùl's guidance and Fidel thinking,*"[emphasis added] (Juventud Rebelde, 1994). Simply put, now that Fidel is providing only general direction, Raúl, due to his military background, is in charge of implementing all policies.

These facts suggest that, de facto although not de jure, the FAR is seen as the regime's main pillar of support. Furthermore, in a unique reversal for a communist state, and certainly in sharp contrast with all East European cases, in Cuba it is the military (or more precisely that segment of the military loyal to the Castro family) who control the MININT, at least since the downfall of Abrantes in 1989. In Eastern Europe, it was the party, the departments of interior and defense, in that order, who played the key roles in deciding the fate of their regimes (in the case of the latter two, this was accomplished primarily by staying out of the political struggle which led to the system's demise). In Cuba, on the other hand, it is primarily the military who will decide the fate of Castroism.

All of which raises the question of the FAR's loyalty to the regime. Even if one dismisses the testimony of Cuban military detectors, including those of such prominence as General Rafael Del Pino, one must recognize that the very size of the Cuban military establishment means that the regime, in its present state of economic collapse, cannot maintain the military at its historic levels. According to reports, the disappearance of free (or almost free) supplies from the USSR and Eastern Europe has led to acute shortages of spare parts, the cannibalization of tanks and fighter aircraft, and to reduced food rations for low-ranking personnel; in short, it has led to advanced decay and very poor morale at the lower and intermediate levels.

Even the regime's attempts at economic reform, feeble as they are, have had a perverse effect upon the morale of the FAR. Hence the 1993 decision to allow citizens to own U.S. dollars led to the ironic situation where politically unreliable relatives of the despised Miami *gusanos* (literally, worms) could afford better food than captains in the FAR. Legalization of small private shops has resulted in independent shoemakers or car repairmen earning more money than non-commissioned officers (NCOs) in the FAR, and so forth. Not only does this have an unsettling effect upon the military ideologically, but it also undermines the FAR's previously exalted moral and social status, which now appears under attack, not from an enemy, but from Fidel himself. Retired officers now find themselves pressed into working as taxi drivers and tourist guides (*Wall Street Journal*, 1994), a situation comparable to that of former personnel of the Soviet army, who engaged in operations on the black market towards the close of the old USSR.

Thus, even as members of the FAR are required to assume more and more non-military tasks, as admitted by Raùl Castro (see *supra*), they are also losing ground socially and economically—a dangerous combination. It is a combination made even more dangerous by the events of 1989, when General Arnaldo Ochoa and Colonel Antonio de la Guardia were both shot after what was widely perceived as staged trials. Leaving aside the dubiousness of the entire affair, a person of Ochoa's ideologically pure background, rank, social prominence, and record of service cannot be so violently and dishonorably removed without creating a potentially large, disgruntled element made up of his sympathizers and admirers in the ranks. While Ceausescu's murder of General Milea was an important element in the decision of the Romanian army not to fight for the regime less than a week later, Ochoa's death may be more of a time bomb for Fidel, but a bomb nevertheless.

Lastly, the issues of the FAR's training and doctrine, and its impact on loyalty, need to be examined as well. Despite its beginnings as a genuine Cuban and revolutionary institution, the FAR has, ever since the early 1960s, increasingly come to resemble its East European and Soviet counterparts. All officers have been trained in former Warsaw Pact countries, most in the USSR; they use the same equipment and most have shared combat experience with their WTO colleagues in places like Ethiopia and Angola.

The record of 1989-1991 shows that in no Eastern European country did the military support the communist regimes under attack, that in Bulgaria they played a key role in pushing Zhivkov aside, and that, in Romania, they joined the anti-Ceausescu forces. From this perspective, therefore, the widespread speculation that Ochoa's death was directly tied to Castro's suspicions regarding his ties to the Soviet military, makes sense.

On the other hand, the fact that Ochoa (and Abrantes, for that matter) went down so meekly, and that the clique of generals around Raùl Castro-Ulises Rosales del Toro, Leopoldo Cintra Frías, Abelardo Colomé, and Julio Casas (all Politburo members)—seem in clear control of both the FAR and the MININT, may suggest that the FAR's loyalty to Fidel is, at least for the moment, stronger than institutional dissatisfaction.[5]

Nevertheless, the question must be asked: for how long? Post-1989 developments in former WTO militaries all point toward the previous existence of a very deep ideological, political, and economic cleavage between generals and admirals on the one hand, and the rest of the officer corps, colonels included, on the other. In post-Ceausescu Romania, for instance, officers below flag rank have (briefly and with limited success) created their own organization, pushing for purges at the top and a deepening of democracy within the military. Similarly, deep differences, albeit with a different ideological twist, occurred in Russia itself, where most generals were supporters of the civilian, reformist leadership, while most subordinate officers (such as Colonel Viktor Alksnis and then-Colonel Aleksandr Rutskoy) were distinctly more nationalist and chauvinistic. Given Cuba's circumstances, as well as evidence from defectors and other sources that is still unclear, it appears that such cleavages exist in Cuba as well, and that their direction tends to parallel the Romanian, rather than Russian, case.

The Internal Security Forces

Throughout the history of communism, the internal security apparatus—generally associated with the Ministry of Internal Affairs and the generic term "secret police"—has played a decisive role in maintaining the regime in power. That said, some clarifications are in order. First, in both the USSR and Eastern Europe, the term "secret police" was a misnomer: it was never really "secret," nor was it really a "police" in the sense of maintaining law and order. Second, the reach of the internal security apparatus has always gone way beyond the Ministry of the Interior. It included large, well-armed border troops and internal security units armed with heavy weapons; it controlled the regular police as well as military intelligence and all counterintelligence services (military and national); it had the ultimate word in all personnel decisions, even down to marginal military, economic, professional, and cultural positions; and it controlled, paid, and recruited literally millions of citizens as informers. Not only did this apparatus serve as the armed branch of the communist party, it also acted as its eyes and ears, as its public opinion pollster, and its chief psychologist. Furthermore, in its military capacity, the internal security apparatus was routinely used as a counter to the regular armed forces. In places like Ceausescu's Romania, internal security forces were actually more heavily armed, almost as large as, and better trained, than the military, and were never used for harvests or road construction.

Compared to the Soviet KGB, East German Stasi, Albanian Sigurimi, or Romanian Securitate, the Cuban MININT was always an exception, and became even more so after 1989. Indeed, while the FAR has always played a more important political and social role than the MININT, it was in 1989, with the destruction of the latter's entire leadership, that Cuba's internal security apparatus was practically put out of business as an institution. In July 1989, MININT Minister General José Abrantes and three associates were arrested; Abrantes later died in jail under suspicious circumstances. Soon after, five MININT division generals and dozens of mid-level officers were fired, as were ministry informers and representatives throughout the entire government bureaucracy (Oppenheimer, 1992: 121). That action was unprecedented in communist annals. When Khrushchev shot KGB boss Lavrentyi Beria in 1953 with the help of the military, he limited the purge to a few individuals. Ceausescu's 1966 dismissal of party rival and Minister of Interior Minister Alexandru Draghici was also limited and less violent (Fischer, 1989: 132-135). In neither case was the autonomy of the institution threatened.

While it is true that Abrantes's demise was due, in part, to having provoked the resentment and envy of Rail Castro, it is also true that the issue went beyond a fight over personal turf. The arrest of Abrantes led to the entire M1NINT leadership being replaced by MINFAR cadres, from the new Minister—General Abelardo Colomé Ibarra—on down. With the MININT thus becoming a branch of the MINFAR (Baloyra, 1994: 5+61), the general pattern of Eastern Europe and USSR was turned upside down, and with potentially deadly consequences for the regime. Indeed, as mentioned before, the MININT has played a double role, just as had its counterparts in Europe: as enforcer of loyalty to Fidel, and as a listening post on the population as a whole. While the Castro brothers may think that the first role is better served by having their loyal army generals run the MLNINT, the second role requires a kind of training and access to the nation's sociological and psychological nooks and crannies that is completely alien to military people, who rest on the glories of Ogaden, Angola, and Mozambique. That was something that both Khruschev and Ceausescu, different as they were, understood well, but to which the Castro brothers seem oblivious. In addition, former members of the internal security apparatus—highly trained, well-informed, and now disgruntled at having lost posh jobs and finding themselves in the position of being ordered around by their traditional rivals—are not a safe group for the regime. They may well decide to take a leaf from the book of their counterparts in Eastern Europe and do as they did after 1989: that is, prepare to play the role of former secret dissidents and discreet opponents.

Auxiliary Organizations

With regard to traditional communist party auxiliary organizations, Cuba seems to repeat, in a condensed way, the history of post-1945 Eastern Europe. Initially created to expend and legitimize the party's role and to socialize the population into the values of the new regime, such organizations (primarily the unions, cultural, women's, and youth organizations) had, by the late 1960s, become largely irrelevant. Indeed, by that time, the ruling parties had come to realize that such efforts were essentially futile, and their leaders began to fear that such groups might provide a political base for challenges to their own position. Once again, it was Romania where developments most closely parallel those in Cuba.

After coming to power in 1965, Ceausescu found it helpful to forge alliances with young cadres against the old guard inherited from the Gheorghe Gheorghiu-Dej regime. Hence he used the Communist Youth Organization (UTC) in particular, and its branch, the Students' Union (USR), as instruments for strengthening his own legitimacy, appointing young, relatively charismatic leaders to the top positions. Subsequently, he turned against his erstwhile allies. Thus, Virgil Trofin became UTC leader, only to be fired later on; he was ultimately driven to "suicide" when his popularity with the nomenklatura appeared threatening to the Ceausescus. Ion Iliescu, Romania's president today, used to be a leader of both the USR and UTC and then Minister for Youth, finally rising to become the party's Secretary of Ideology before being removed and appointed director of an obscure publishing house once *he* was seen as a threat to the ruling family. By the late 1970s, the UTC had became so irrelevant that even Iliescu's successor to the UTC post, Ceausescu's own son, relinquished it. By then, both the student and the communist youth organizations had practically ceased to serve a political purpose, even for the regime, and they degenerated into failed attempts to divert the youth away from attention to politics and into various forms of entertainment that were more or less controlled.

By 1989, the auxiliary organizations of East European Communist Parties were moribund; none played a role in the events of that year, either in support of, or opposition to, the anti-communist movements. The same year a local poll in Santa Cruz del Norte (Havana Province) showed that only 10 percent of the respondents said membership in the PCC or the UJC (Young Communist League) was a factor in persuading them to vote for a candidate in local elections (Domínguez, 1994: 10). The following year, a nationwide survey was taken which suggested "the Communist Party and the Communist Youth Union as institutions lacked the appeal to elicit vote support at the local level" (Domínguez, 1994: 11). Even the leader of the UJC, Juan Contino, complained (October 1993) his organization was being marginalized by the Committees for the Defense of the Revolution (CDRs). He admitted that "at this time lack of social discipline has increased" and recognized that there is a "marked tendency" toward pessimism, opposition to training, criminality, and prostitution (Juventud Rebelde, 1993). Not surprisingly, the treatment of the auxiliary organizations of the PCC at the last party congress was described in the following terms:

> Mass organizations mattered the least. The heads of the committees for the Defense of the Revolution, the Women's Federation, and the Peasants' Association were absent from the Political Bureau; nor was there anyone from the top leadership of such organizations in the Political Bureau. (Domínguez, 1994: 3)

Collapse of the Communist Party auxiliary organizations is no minor issue. Western media consistently, but wrongly, assume that the Cuban Committees for the Defense of the Revolution (CDRs) are somehow unique to Cuba. They are not, All over Eastern Europe, during the early 1950s, the newly established ruling Communist Parties tried to expand their political base and ability to control the society as a whole by establishing neighborhood watch committees under various names. The intention was to expand the regime's political base by mobilizing popular sentiment against crime and delinquency in general; but throughout Eastern Europe the attempt had failed by the late 1950s and was never again attempted.

What we now witness in Cuba in regard to the communist auxiliary organizations is the same institutional decay that was experienced in Eastern Europe forty years ago. Their active membership has decreased sharply, actual participation of remaining members is in steep decline, programs like nightly vigilance patrols or block meetings are practically defunct, and the regime itself seems to have accepted their ineffectiveness insofar as it felt it necessary to create the Rapid Response Brigades, made up of the few remaining core supporters of the "Revolution." (*New York Times*, 1993).

Conclusion

Is Cuba today in a situation of advanced institutional decay similar to that of Eastern Europe in 1989? or is its situation completely different? One cannot dismiss Cuba's peculiarities, among the most important of which are the role of Fidel and the relationship between the FAR and the MININT. On the other hand, the cancerous growth of MINFAR's power (or that of its historic leadership group) seems to be as much a cause, as a result, of the atrophy of the regime's other institutions.

Since the late 1980s, the Cuban regime has undergone significant shifts in policy, particularly in the economic area, while its institutional base has failed to keep up with the new circumstances, has lost prestige, authority, and the ability to mobilize—a phenomenon seen in pre-1989 Eastern Europe and the USSR and highly suggestive of institutional sclerosis. The militarization of the regime, expressed by the overwhelming role of the FAR in all aspects of policy and economics, seems to be the answer to this situation. The risks involved are quite clear, ranging inflexibility to the decline of the ruling party and its ancillary organizations. The lack of flexibility associated with the military institution threatens to make the regime as brittle as it may seem strong. Not surprisingly, perhaps, the most militarized regime in Eastern Europe, General Jaruzelski's Poland, was also the first to fall. The "Bonapartist" danger that frightened Marx, Lenin, Stalin, and Khruschev, because they all realized that a politically, economically, and socially dominant military, will, inevitably, become politically divided, may yet come to fruition in Havana as party and national politics—from economic strategy to the succession of Fidel—are translated into military politics. Political divisions, when supported by guns, can be deadly, a fact of life that applies equally to communist and noncommunist regimes alike. The events of 1989, which led to the execution, death in jail, or public disgrace of prominent leaders of the FAR and MININT, suggest that Fidel has not been immune to such fears though he may have taken action too late. The date may not have been completely accidental, and it was certainly symbolic—an independent-minded military may well become neutral when the regime's fate is at stake—for that was precisely the pattern that prevailed throughout Eastern Europe during that year.

While it is true that the Cuban regime has a history of heavy military involvement in politics, the present situation is still unusual inasmuch as today Castro has to rely on the FAR because all other institutions, the PCC above all, are failing to perform—a situation not dissimilar from that of Poland in 1981, when the political power vacuum, created by the party's weakness, forced the military to step into the breach. The general evolutionary progression of Eastern European communism—first the attempt to mobilize the "masses" under the control of the Communist Party and its auxiliary organizations, then the acceptance of the decay of those very organizations, and ultimately a retreat into reliance upon the institutions of law and order—secret police in Eastern Europe, the military in Cuba—appears to be operating in Cuba, albeit with different accents. Cuba's strongest accent in this respect is the fact that not only is the MINFAR politically dominant (it controls the MENINT and plays the key role in PCC decisions), but it has also become an essential economic factor in the country, a situation with some analogies to China, though nowhere else in the communist world.

Indeed, all of Cuba's civilian institutions are in a state of decay—clear in the cases of Women, Youth, Labor, and CDRs, less obvious, but nevertheless detectable, in that of the PCC. The process as a whole is quite similar to that of the 1989 European communist systems, all of which were, by then, mere empty shells in institutional terms. Even the last of them to fall, Ceausescu's Romania, was an empty shell, superficially filled by the personality cult of the leader himself (and his family), not exactly the kind of analogy that would encourage Fidel as he looks into the future of his revolution.

While such analogies are clear and attractive, they should not be exaggerated—Cuban communist institutions are not exact replicas of Eastern Europe and, in fact, exhibit significant differences: the question is whether or not these are differences without a distinction.

Just as in pre-1989 Eastern Europe, the institutional edifice of Cuban communism is collapsing; the difference is that Castro apparently realizes it and is prepared to resist. The main form of resistance to such decay is militarization; as General Casas Rigueiro put it, the civilians better learn to behave like soldiers.

Comparisons between the present Cuban regime and those of pre-1989 Eastern Europe are inevitably limited in scope and may even, to some extent, be artificial. However, they are clearly relevant inasmuch as they suggest long-range trends, possible regime answers to noncommunist challenges, and ability to adapt to pro-market and pro-democracy pressures from the outside world. In all these respects, Cuba is both different in detail and similar in principle. The outcome of such an analysis is that, while no assessment of Castro's future is likely to become more or less plausible by comparison to Eastern Europe, the examination of the latter's terminal days is bound to be relevant to Castro's future—if any.

Notes

1.   Those states were: Poland, the German Democratic Republic (GDR), Czechoslovakia, Hungary, Romania, and Bulgaria. To a lesser extent, this article will also consider the former Union of Soviet Socialist Republics (USSR).
2.   Originally, the acronym FAR stood for Fuerzas Armadas Rebeldes, later transmuted into Fuerzas Armadas Revolucionarias as an indication of their institutionalization.
3.   The partial exception is Jorge Domínguez, who claims that the regime "became depersonalized" between 1965 and 1980, "after which it once again reverted to the pattern of domination by Fidel" (Domínguez, 1994: 2).
4.   Suspected of plotting a pro-Moscow coup against Ceausescu in the late 1970s, Militaru's life was apparently saved by the Soviet ambassador. After redefining his past as one of anticommunism, Militaru staged a brief comeback in 1990 as the first post-Ceausescu Defense Minister (Watts, 1992:100 and 102-4).

References

Baloyra, E. (1994) *Where Does Cuba Stand?* Carlisle, PA: US Army War College, Strategic Studies Institute.

Dominguez, J. (1994) "Leadership Strategies and Mass Support: Cuban Politics before and after the 1991 Communist Party Congress," pp. 1-19 in Jorge F. Pérez-López (ed.) *Cuba at a Crossroads." Politics and Economics after the Fourth Party Congress.* Gainesville, FL: University Press of Florida.

Fischer, M.E. (1989) *Nicolae Ceausescu: A Study in Political Leadership.* Boulder, CO: Lynne Rienner Publisher.

Foreign Broadcast Information Service-Latin America (FBIS-LAT) (1994) "Raùl Castro on Internal Situation," Havana PRENSA LATINA, 17 September; in FBIS-LAT-94-181 (19 September): 9-15.

__ (1993) "Rosales del Toro Presides over UJC," Havana Radio Reloj Network, 3 December; in FBIS-LAT-93-232 (6 December): 8.

Gitz, B. (1992) *Armed Forces and Political Power in Eastern Europe*: The Soviet/Communist Control System. New York, NY: Greenwood Press.

Gonzalez, E. and D. Ronfeldt (1994) *Storm Warnings for Cuba.* Santa Monica, CA: RAND Corporation, National Defense Research Institute.

Juventud Rebelde (Havana) (1994) "Interview with General Senen Casas Rigueiro." (16 October): 5.

__ (1993) (10 October): 6. *(The) New York Times* (1993) (7 November).

Oppenheimer, A. (1992) *Castro's Final Hour.* New York, NY: Touchstune Press.

Price, G. (1986) "Nationalism in the Romanian Military: Ceausescu's Double-Edged Sword," pp.277-294 in Jeffrey Simon and Trond Gilberg (eds.), *Security Implications of Nationalism in Eastern Europe.* Boulder, CO: Westview Press.

Rice, E. (1974) *Mao's Way*, (2rid ed.). Berkeley, CA: University of California Press.

Tismaneanu, V. (1986) "Romania" pp. 344-355 in Richard Staar (ed.) *Yearbook of International Communist Affairs.* Stanford, CA: Hoover Institution Press.

Volsky, G. (1991) "Cuba," pp. 71-77 in Richard F. Staar (ed.) *Yearbook of International Communist Affairs.* Stanford, CA: Hoover Institution Press. *(The) Wall Street Journal* (1994) (12 August).

Watts, L. (1992) "The Romanian Army in the December Revolution and Beyond," pp. 95-126 in Daniel Nelson (ed.) *Romania after Tyranny.* Boulder, CO: Westview Press.

Michael Radu, "Cuba's Transition: Institutional Lessons from Eastern Europe," in Irving Louis Horowitz and Jaime Suchlicki (eds.), *Cuban Communism*, Ninth Edition, Transaction Publishers, New Brunswick (USA) and London, 2001, pp. 697-718.

AN APOLOGY INSTEAD OF POLICY: U.S. BLUNDERS IN LATIN AMERICA

On March 10, while on a visit to Guatemala, President Clinton apologized for the U.S. role in the 1962-1996 civil war in that country: "For the United States, it is important that I state clearly that the support for military forces or intelligence units which engaged in violent and widespread repression. . .was wrong. . . . The United States must not repeat that mistake." The Guatemalans were neither impressed nor particularly interested. Amidst cries of "Viva Monica" they protested against the apparent refusal of the United States to grant residence to tens of thousands of Guatemalan illegal aliens who have abused immigration laws. The president has, once again, decided that rewriting history and blaming his predecessors is the easy way to avoid hard decisions and cover up the almost total failure of his Latin America policies.

The facts show that a presidential apology in Guatemala was hardly warranted. Between 1962, when the Marxist insurgency began, and 1977, when Guatemala rejected the Carter administration's conditions for a $2.1 million military aid package, that country received $2 million per year, or about $30 million in military aid—a pittance by any reasonable standard. Aid was never restored, and after 1977 Guatemala was even denied the right to buy parts for American military equipment previously provided or sold.

One might also point out that the most intense phase of the insurgency in Guatemala, claiming the greatest number of casualties, took place after the discontinuation of all U.S. military aid, during the military governments of Romeo Lucas García (1978-1982) and Efraín Rios Montt (1982-1983). Those two regimes finally broke the communist insurgency's back—and they did it without any American "support."

Of course, throughout the insurgency period the CIA was present in Guatemala and no doubt aware of the brutally effective counterinsurgency methods used by government forces—in other words, doing precisely what an intelligence service is supposed to do. Since aid was nonexistent, the United States had no leverage left with the Guatemalan military—unless the president suggests that we should have used force in support of the insurgents.

It is easy to rewrite history now to feel good and make revisionists feel even better, but at the time the possibility of a Marxist Guatemala—the largest Central American country and Mexico's neighbor—joining totalitarian Nicaragua was deemed unacceptable by responsible policy makers in Washington.

Whatever the state of the president's knowledge of history, the Guatemala apology is indicative of a more profound problem: the administration's unwillingness to accept disturbing political realities in Latin America today. The Cold War may have ended elsewhere, but someone forgot to tell that to the increasingly victorious Marxist guerrillas in Colombia or their less successful comrades in Mexico and Peru.

And the Clinton administration doesn't know what it should do about that. Despite the State Department's characterization of the communist Revolutionary Armed Forces of Colombia (FARC) as terrorists and drug traffickers, Peter Romero, acting assistant secretary of state for Western Hemispheric Affairs, held a meeting last December in Costa Rica with "Raúl Reyes," one of FARC's leaders. The dilemma posed by that meeting was plainly evident in February after FARC murdered three American leftists (not their first U.S. victims), when the State Department was reduced to lame protests and demands for the extradition of those responsible (perhaps Comrade Reyes?). Nevertheless, the administration is still supporting the "peace process"—the fashionable code word for Colombian President Pastrana's capitulation to the Marxists.

After Hugo Chávez, a leftist demagogue, tried to overthrow the democratically elected government of Venezuela, he was denied a United States visa. When he was elected president, however, all was forgiven—as if that victory suddenly made him a democrat. Now Venezuela's government is full of military officers, its congress is under threat, and Chávez has recognized the belligerent status of Colombia's terrorists.

In 1994 American forces were sent to "restore democracy" to Haiti, a country which has never known it. The only restorations were those of Jean Bertrand Aristide—a defrocked Marxist priest—and of chaos and violence. On February 25, Gen. Charles Wilhelm, the commander of the U.S. Southern Command, called for a complete U.S. pullout from Haiti because "we see little progress toward creation of a permanently stable internal security environment. . . .In fact, with the recent expiration of parliament and the imposition of presidential rule. . .we have seen something of a backsliding." Naturally enough, the main cause of this situation, Aristide, is also the overwhelming favorite to win the next presidential election. As the president of Haiti's Chamber of Commerce and Industry accurately put it, "The country is dying." Meanwhile Haitian illegals are again invading Florida's shores.

As for Cuba, the Clinton administration is trying to weaken the embargo and "improve" relations with Castro. In January the administration decided to increase the amount of remittances from family members in the United States, and to allow direct flights. In response, the Havana regime has heated up its anti-American rhetoric and put its kangaroo courts to work full-time against political dissidents.

Closer to home, the drug certification policy is in shreds because of the administration's lack of will. The recertification of Mexico, which is now the main source of drugs to the United States, and (according to the Drug Enforcement Administration itself) increasingly uncooperative and corrupt, makes a mockery of the law. Colombia has gotten off just as easily: although drug production there has skyrocketed, the country has been recertified after a two-year pause. The administration cannot make up its mind whether to continue its head-in-the-sand certification policy or discard the entire process and start over.

Against this background of wrong directions and dashed hopes, the two successes—NAFTA (negotiated by the Bush administration and passed with Republican support in Congress), and its role in the resolution of the Peru-Ecuador border dispute (in which most of the credit should go to Ambassador Luigi Einaudi, a hard-nosed survivor from the Reagan and Bush administrations)—appear nearly accidental.

Washington may not realize it but Latin America is undergoing a general swing leftward, against the democratic and free market developments of the past decade. The signs cannot be clearer: the election of Chávez in Venezuela; probable victories by the Left in Argentina and Mexico; the lethal Marxist threat in Colombia; Ecuador's descent into chaos; Brazil's economic crisis; Castro's new political and diplomatic relevance; and the dangerous vacuum left in Panama by the departure of U.S. forces that may be filled by FARC and its narcotrafficking friends. All of these require a coherent and steady strategy from Washington.

Instead, we get the president's apology in Guatemala; Justice Department cooperation with a Spanish judge's dangerously broad proceedings against former Chilean President Augusto Pinochet; the high-level meeting in Costa Rica with the hemisphere's most dangerous totalitarian group; the misguided embrace of Aristide and the refusal to admit that error; the search for some accommodation with an unrepentant Castro; and they all seem to suggest that a feel-good posture on the "right side of history" (the Left, openly Marxist or not!) has replaced a coherent Latin America policy based on the national interests of the United States.

Reprinted with the permission from http://www.fpri.org, March 19, 1999

FESTINA LENTE: UNITED STATES AND CUBA AFTER CASTRO

It may appear that dealing with a post-Castro, probably post-communist and per hags (in the short term) "neo-communist" Cuba, is a simple matter. After all, we have a 20/20 hindsight, based upon the experience of 1989-1991 in Eastern Europe and Russia. Russia aside, given her size, mythical proportion in the American political mind, and nuclear arsenal, what, if anything, are we to "learn" from the experience of the United States—specifically the Executive and Congress—relations with, activities in, and ultimate impact on the former Soviet satellites in Eastern Europe—the late East Germany excepted for obvious reasons?

The first, and most fundamental lesson is that chaos theory, rather than market logic and democratic rules of the game, is the most applicable road map to a post-Castro environment. Cuba's underlining Latin American political culture, albeit heavily distorted by four decades of communism, will play an essential role; but so would the decades of Marxist rule.

The second factor to be assumed, and is assumed by this author, is that we now know more, and better, what Castroite Cuba is all about than we ever did in 1989 about Poland, Hungary, and Russia, not to mention such exotic places as Romania, Bulgaria, Albania, or Mongolia. On the other hand—and these words are inevitably present throughout this article—since this author does not claim prophetic powers and not every problem faced or error made in Eastern Europe should be expected to reappear in a post-Castro Cuba, there are limits to what this comparative analysis could provide.

The most important caveats in this respect are related to Cuba's historic relations with the United States and the uniquely close overlap between American domestic politics and policy toward Havana, which make the third factor in assessing American policy toward a post-communist Cuba.

Without entering into details—most of which well known to this audience—two immediate political realities have to be faced by American policy makers in respect to post-Castro Cuba. First, that whereas Eastern Europe in 1989 was, and remains to this day, the most unambiguously "pro-American" region of the world, ambiguity defines the Cubans' attitude vis a vis the United States. Second, the importance of domestic factors in the making of the United States' policy toward Havana virtually guarantees a greater and more complicated role of Congress in the formulation and implementation of that policy than was the case with Eastern Europe a decade ago.

For these reasons, this article will concentrate on the role of the Executive Branch (henceforth USEB), while aware of the role of Congress.

All these being said, however, the likelihood of the USEB (United States Government) repeating, or engaging in, the same mistakes it made in Eastern Europe and Russia since 1989 and, until recently—when domestic developments in the United States and common sense in the former Soviet bloc began a reassessment of those policies—is high.

The general assumptions upon which this presentation is based are that:

a)   in practical political terms the transition from communism in Cuba will only start after Fidel's death;

b)   the social and economic transition has already started;

c)   Castro's immediately successor regime, whoever happens to lead it, will formally discard Marxism Leninism and Communism in favor of "social democracy "or some form of "socialism with democracy and a human face";

d)   such regime will formally and publicly discard anti-Americanism as its basic ideology, while at the same time use it internally, albeit discreetly for electoral and political gain;

e)   in a dramatic reversal of decades of "revolutionary" rhetoric, such a regime will actually ask for U.S. aid, while proclaiming a continuous commitment to Cuban "nationalism and values."

In light of these assumptions, the question raises as to the extent to which the experience of the USEB, European Union, and various Western private foundations and organizations in post-communist Eastern Europe and former USSR may be relevant in a post-Castro Cuba.

In this respect one may well start by stating a few obvious facts. First, Cuba in the late 1990s or whenever the required and inevitable political change will take place, provides a clear opportunity to learn, or unlearn from the experience of Eastern Europe and the former USSR a decade earlier. Second, that one may well assume that some of those lessons will be disregarded, particularly in light of Cuba's peculiar position within the U.S. domestic political discourse.

The Political Culture of Transition

Without going into a lengthy discussion over whether Cuba is "different" or "similar" to other former communist regimes, there are a number of aspects related to the political culture of all post-communist transitions, which are likely to be present in Cuba as well. Those are clear in the common experience of Mongolia and Cambodia-obviously "different" in so many other ways—as well as in Poland, the Czech Republic, Russia, Romania, and Bulgaria.

The first is the fragmentation of the political scene, demonstrated by the mushrooming of "political parties." Most of those parties were simply vehicles for personal ambitions; some were grandiose titles for what, in other political systems, would simply be interest groups of various sizes or just NGOs; some were disguises for criminal groups; and some, very few, proved to have the potential for becoming effective political parties.

Russia had hundreds of "political parties" competing in the 1993 elections; so did Romania in 1990, and virtually every other former communist state in Eurasia. A simple look into the composition of the Concilio Cubano's member organizations strongly suggests that this process has already begun in Cuba as well. Indeed, we find there socialists, social-democrats, Christian democrats, agramontistas, liberals, and everything in between, at least as tendencies and claims, if not yet as ideologically coalesced "parties."

The second, and related, reality is that the initially dominant and by far the largest (and most "real") party in a Havana transition period will, most likely, be the Cuban Communist party (PCC), under whatever name it will chose—very probably something including the words "social" and "democracy." That party will also engage in extensive efforts, again in the name of "democracy," to encourage further proliferation of "parties." That is the very pattern exhibited in 1990 Romania (where this author was an electoral observer) and Bulgaria, where the dominant ex-or neocommunists promulgated electoral laws allowing for the registration of groups as small as 250 as "political parties." The reasons are quite obvious—the more fragmented the opposition, the more confused the electorate and, hence, more likely to prefer the discipline of the PCC successor to the cacophony of the available alternatives.

Recommendation

Unlike the behavior exhibited in Eastern Europe, the U.S. Administration should not encourage the proliferation of "parties," regardless of how vocal demands to the contrary—at home or in Havana—may, and likely, will be. While a good case may be made that Washington's ability to influence the process of political fragmentation will be quite limited, it should not be dismissed. The point is not that Washington—or at least the Executive—should decree how many parties Cuba should have, but that resources should be concentrated and high standards of proven organizational ability and programs, compatible with democratic and capitalist values, enforced.

That attitude should particularly be encouraged by organizations funded, related, or perceived to be related to the United States Government—such as the National Endowment for Democracy (NED) and its various party-controlled segments (National Democratic Institute [NDI] and National Republican Institute [NRI]). As an aside, the experience of Eastern Europe suggests that, regardless of their actual legal status in the United States, such organizations are very likely to be perceived as representative of the United States. Hence, their support is likely to be interpreted locally as an "American" accolade.

To the contrary, funds, technical support, and advice, indeed the weight of the American private and public attitudes, should discourage party proliferation and, at least for the first two electoral cycles, make it clear that coalitions, rather than individual parties, are to be preferred.

It would also be important for the Cuban American members of Congress, and their friends in both parties, to realize that such a discerning attitude is also likely to be more productive, in the medium- and long-run, than support for some misguided notion of an open ended "democracy" risking to result in anarchy and a PCC victory.

Finally on this point, the West Europeans will likely play a significant role—and if Eastern Europe is a model, they will be quite selective in their support for Cuban political parties. Indeed, the Socialist, Liberal, and Christian Democratic Internationals have all tended to select one party per country for technical, financial, and political support.

Social Realities

The third aspect of political culture in a transitional Cuba is largely sociological and, hence, difficult to "prove." However, there are both some common occurrences in all Eurasian former communist states, and indications of their existence in today's Cuba.

The most significant of these is the fact that for most of the population, and particularly its younger segments, hostility to the communist regime does not inevitably, or even necessarily, translate into support for a political alternative to it, whatever its nature. At least among the youth, nihilism and political cynicism are far more important than positive beliefs in political, as different from social, cultural, or economic-freedom. Indeed, in virtually all former communist regimes the electoral participation of the youth has been small to begin with, and has declined with every free election since 1989.

There is no reason to believe that Cuba will be different—indeed, the opposite seems to be true. As far as we know—or at least this author knows from his admittedly limited knowledge of Cuba—general interest in politics there is quite low. This also seems to be proven by the reverse relationship between the time of emigration to the United States and the intensity of political interest and participation among Cuban emigres: the later their arrival and more protracted their experience with the Castro regime, the lower their interest and participation in local ethnic Cuban-American or American electoral politics. This is a pattern also to be found among East European immigrants—the more recent their arrival to the U.S., the less involved in politics, American or of country of origin, they appear to be.

What this suggests is that communism, and life under communism, has generally resulted in general political cynicism and apathy, rather than what we may all prefer to believe and certainly hope—an insatiable thirst for political democracy and political freedom. It also suggests that a revolutionary political wave against Castroism is less than likely.

Recommendation

The U.S. Executive Branch, its agencies, and congressionally funded organizations, as well as private organizations, should understand that attempts to overly politicize their activities in a transitional Cuba will likely backfire, to the advantage of the successor to the PCC. Hence, efforts should be concentrated less on the ideological and political aspects of their activities than on the organizational, economic, and social ones. Of particular importance are the groups most likely to be attracted by the PCC's siren song—the retired persons, the employees of large state enterprises, and a large number of Cuba's black population. For these groups the economic interests—dependence on state-provided pensions and jobs—is more important than any political and/or ideological consideration.

With that in mind, if any official U.S. aid to Cuba is to be provided, it should be directly, openly and strictly centered on: (a) support for the pension, health, and social security funds for the retired, and (b) retraining of public employees below managerial level. That would weaken, if not eliminate, those two groups' natural drift toward the appeal of a "welfare state," likely to be offered by the PCC and/or its successor, and one Cuba itself—now or later—cannot realistically afford. As for the black population, its possible support for the successor of the PCC will also be grounded on economic motivations, related to that group's already disadvantaged position in society and fear of further deterioration in a free market environment.

General Considerations

Starting from the experience of Eurasia, and the nature of communism itself, one may assume that transition should concentrate upon dismantling key elements of communist power.

One of those elements, in the case of Cuba (but also of Latin American states in general) and other communist systems, is centralization of power, decision-making, and bureaucracy. That means the capital—whether Moscow, Bucharest, Warsaw, or Sofia, but also Lima, Ciudad de Mexico, and Havana—absorbs and consumes a disproportionate share of national resources, enjoys absolute national political power, and concentrates the country's cultural, political, and economic decision-making. However, unlike most of those other cases, Cuba does not have a separatist, ethnic, or otherwise, or even a regionalist, problem, and, thus, political, economic, and administrative decentralization is both feasible and necessary. Indeed, this is a clear case of Cuban exceptionalism in the context of post-communist transitions, and allows for support of local initiatives and leaders—some of whom may be younger PCC officials—in a way that does not threaten national integrity the way support for Hungarians in Romania or Slovakia, Turks in Bulgaria, or Albanians in Serbia, did.

Recommendation

The USEB will have to avoid, publicly and concretely, any concentration of support, aid (financial or otherwise), or encouragement of the Havana bureaucracy, and encourage, mostly by distribution of funds, regional and local decision-making, in both economic and political terms.

Local interests, long-time neglect, and control from Havana, combine to allow development of regional (Oriente, Matanzas, etc.) projects, require, both economic and social, creation of healthy competition and, ultimately, healthy political debates within the island.

The NGOs

A general phenomenon in post-communist Eurasia is the proliferation of NGOs, largely, in fact, almost exclusively funded, advised, and trained by large American and European foundations, some with their own political and ideological agendas.

While such groups are legitimate, and perhaps natural, results of democratization, their activities, importance, and influence in a transitional period, when political parties and government decision-making are at their weakest, often tend to increase confusion. NGOs, particularly those involved in human rights, also tend to create unrealistic demands and heighten expectations that are often unrealistically high. When those expectations are not fulfilled by weak governments lacking experience, a supporting national consensus, and the necessary judicial and legal instruments, the result is a reinforcement of existing political apathy and cynicism toward institutions. The latest aspect is particularly relevant since NGOs are often seen as alternatives to parties, and found convenient by many—particularly the young—and those uninterested in electoral politics. The fact is that the proliferation of NGOs weakens still shaky political institutions in ex-communist states. Furthermore, while NGOs may increase participation, they do not promote representative institutions.

Recommendation

None of the earlier statements should be interpreted as hostility to NGOs in general. Some play an important role in encouraging participation and mobilization of the population in causes directly relevant to their lives: associations of producers, small businessmen, and professionals are good examples.

However, the USEB and Congress alike would be wise to avoid interference, whether through statements or funding, with post-Castro NGOs, because of their potentially ambiguous impact on the political and market transition. Furthermore, notwithstanding their likely claims to the taxpayers' support, Cuban NGOs will probably have abundant private outside sources of support.

The Political Economy of Transition and USEB Aid

While economics are well above this author's pay rank, some basic facts of political realities in transition states are inevitably economic in their nature. Furthermore, rightly or wrongly, the Cuban population as a whole will inevitably—whether consciously or not—judge everything happening during a transitional regime as valid on the basis of economic realities.

To Aid or Not to Aid

Is there a need to provide U.S. aid, financial or otherwise, to a post-Castro Cuba? While many today, and more in the future, will claim that USEB aid is essential, and a few will oppose it, the fact is that reason, Cuba's peculiar position in U.S. strategic considerations and domestic politics, and common sense, all suggest that American aid of some sort will be needed, provided, and should be strictly limited.

That being said, there should be some strict rules as to the nature, focus, and distribution of such aid. Billions of dollars in U.S. aid to Eastern Europe, and even more in Russia, have produced little, if any, change in political and economic developments in those areas that would not have occurred in the absence of most of that aid. Here are some specifics:

Education and Personnel Exchange Support

Tens of thousands of Eurasian ex-communist states' citizens have benefited from research, education, and training fellowships, scholarships, and travel support grants to the West. The overwhelming majority of those beneficiaries have been former nomenklatura products, able to speak foreign languages and to establish useful contacts with relevant Western European and American groups, organizations, and individuals.

Most of those stays in the West have only reinforced existing opinions, ways of thinking, and personal "self-esteem," and a disturbing number of beneficiaries have put those interests above their self-assumed role as vanguards of their peoples' road to free markets and democracy. That being said, there is no reason a new generation of Cuban technocrats, intellectuals, and general elites cannot be trained in Cuba, by Cuban exiles or Latin Americans.

Nor is there any reason why scholarships should be provided to Ivy League schools, especially at taxpayers' expense (or even at the schools'), for existing Cuban elites. On the other hand, some small USEB support for Latin American universities to enable them to accept students or open branches in Cuba could be far more effective. Such institutions could include Universidad Francisco Marroquin in Guatemala, the Monterey Technological Institute of Mexico, or the Catholic Universities of Lima and Santiago—all private institutions.

Finally in this regard, one of the most egregious mistakes made in Eastern Europe and Russia, and one with serious political implications, has been the invasion of those countries by Western experts, real or pretended, often paid by the taxpayers, and always very expensive. Their presence—whatever the merits of their activities—has often created resentment, inferiority complexes, and nationalist reactions. All of these negative effects, and more, should be expected in Cuba. For all these reasons, U.S. funding for academic, technical, and cultural personnel exchanges should give first priority to the training of Cubans in Cuba; second, training of Cubans in the United States; third, training in Latin America; and only as a last resort should funds be spent on American personnel in Cuba.

Distribution of Funds

In Eurasia the USEB, mostly through AID, has tended to distribute funds through non-competitive awards. The case of the Harvard Institute for International Development (HIID) in Russia was typical: it did not work, and it had to be changed, in light of the close, indeed unseemly, connections between HIID and prominent members of both Russian and U.S. Administrations.

Furthermore, USAID should only provide limited funds, on the basis of competitive bids from Cuba, rather than the United States, and those funds should be limited in both time and amount. Such a process would eliminate the trouble of irresponsible behavior by local, subcontracting organizations, supported by their main contractor in the United States, an all too common pattern in Eastern Europe between 1989-1994.

Economics

Any analysis of Cuban economics, present or likely in the transition phase, implies a level of expertise this author is not best qualified to comment on.

However, there are certain political, as well as economic, considerations to be examined and considered. The first and foremost is that capitalism, rather than central planning, is more likely to serve the economic interests of the Cuban people in the long term.

The very nature of communism requires concentration of economic activity (and thus political control) in large units—hence "industrialization" from Stalin to Mao to Ceausescu to Castro. In the case of Cuba, "industrialization" meant, as in Eurasia, the creation of massive state enterprises producing large financial losses and little else, but employing large numbers of people.

It may be, and it will certainly be so-described by political demagogues, that a policy of "de-industrialization" of Cuba will be seen as hostile to the national interest. However, the elimination of communist era large industrial companies is necessary in economic, political, and social terms.

This may sound like old wisdom, but it is true nevertheless. In Cuba's case, unlike most of Eastern Europe, this is also made more politically acceptable as the regime itself has, in fact, admitted its mistake in creating huge industrial enterprises, by the recent dismissal of many of their employees.

The more people are involved in free market economics, the less support is likely to be given to the PCC successor. That also means that services, including tourism, are more likely to provide such involvement than the state enterprises, most of which are already unprofitable by the Cuban regime's own admission.

Similarly, for a brief period—no more than one year or two—the USEB may provide training support for Cuban state employees likely to be laid off by the restructuring of the state sector. Most of those are already underemployed, and few should, or are, seeking alternative employment by the government. In fact, most are already involved in the informal sector, the one the USEB should support. Ultimately, the key problems facing the USEB in transitional Cuba will be related to the economic, social, and political fallout from the restructuring of the economy and the shrinking of the State.

Obstacles

One of the main problems to be dealt with in terms of economic and social policies, is that the post-communist transition government in Havana is likely to be faced with a wave of anti-free market rejection policies throughout Latin America—from Argentina to Mexico—demonstrated by left wing populist electoral victories. When possible, or already existing, left-of-center governments in Buenos Aires, Mexico City, or Caracas trying to find a "third way" between capitalism and socialism, it will be so much more difficult to counter a post-Castro, new-fangled "ex"-PCC demagoguery. Whether there is any short-term "solution" to this problem is doubtful, and whether the USEB could do anything about it even more so.

Recommendation

Absolute priority should be given to the privatization of the Cuban agricultural sector, particularly to its division into individually-owned properties and, with absolutely necessary, albeit temporary, USEB financial aid, associated technical and financial support.

In this respect, a USEB-supported Agrarian Bank in Cuba, with small loan insurance provided for small loans, would probably produce more anti-communist electors than any NED effort with similar money expenditure. It would also serve to wean Cuba from its fateful, harmful, and ecologically destructive, sugar cane industry.

USEB should concentrate on small, rather than big, enterprises—a seemingly obvious statement, but not one followed in Eastern Europe or Russia.

Against conventional wisdom, one should leave aside the inevitable issue of the sugar quotas. Any reduction of quotas to old and loyal U.S. allies and friends in favor of a transitional Cuba will be counterproductive to both Cuban and American long-term interests. Therefore, Cuba should not be allowed anything but, at the most, a one- or two-year additional quota, and no more—the only true "shock therapy" the USEB can, and should, impose unilaterally.

The clear, stated, and practical goal should be the elimination of sugar as Cuba's main export. Land, even marginal ones, now dedicated to sugar, should be used for other crops. Sugar growers should be encouraged to shift to either food or alternative export products (such as palm hearts), as they individually see fit. Ultimately, no successful transition from communism, economic or political, is possible unless sugar is displaced from its dominant position in the island's economy—the very same slogan Castro proclaimed in 1959, and never fulfilled since. Simply put, dependence upon sugar and its producers, all large agricultural enterprises, state-owned or not, is incompatible with the existence of free markets or political democracy in Cuba.

Furthermore, regardless of the advice of experts, land now dedicated to sugar, even marginal ones, will, anyway, shift to food crops once the alien and oppressive hand of Havana is removed. While such a shift may be theoretically disruptive, it would allow peasant economic freedom—including the freedom to fail—and destroy Havana's main lever of control over the rest of the island.

Ultimately, the USEB should reject the demands—likely to come from PCC as well as opposition parties—for an increased sugar quota for Cuba. To the contrary, it should make it clear that sugar is not, and should not be, seen as an essential part of Cuba's economy, and that it should be eliminated as a major national export asset. If that will be seen as "tough love" by many Cubans, so be it. That, by itself, would prevent the survival of the politically poisonous communist, managerial type, political influence and interests in rural Cuba, and encourage small farm production of food crops.

Once again, regional and international support, rather than aid through Havana, would be most effective, and recommended for the USEB and particularly the U.S. Congress.

An important, perhaps decisive role in helping the future transitional government in Cuba, should be played by multilateral institutions in which the United States plays a key role—the International Monetary Fund (IMF), World Bank, and Inter American Development Bank (IDB). The first two institutions have played a key role in Eastern Europe's economic restructuring; their ability to condition funding on reform has proved to be largely effective, and that very capacity has channeled local resentment from Western capitals to international bureaucrats.

The same pattern should be encouraged in Cuba—limited United States official aid should be provided and targeted on institutions and areas outside the reach of international financial institutions, while the bulk of financial support for Cuba should come through multilateral organizations.

Dealing with the Institutions

At the time of transition, whether we like it or not, Cuba will still be dominated by the institutions established during the Revolution—particularly the military, Communist Party and its associate organizations, and state bureaucracy. Unlike the situation in most of Eastern Europe, one of the key such institutions, and the most difficult to reform, the internal security apparatus (Interior Ministry—MININT in Cuba's case, Securitate in Romania, Stasi in East Germany, Sigurimi in Albania) will be less of a problem in transitional Cuba, since it lost its institutional autonomy and strength as a result of the 1989-1990 purges following the Ochoa and Abrantes affairs.

As a result, MININT is controlled by the military, a fact that, in addition to weakening the loyalty of its professionals, will also simplify efforts to dismantle or reform it—through the military.

The Military

Throughout Eastern Europe, at the time of transition and since, the military has consistently remained (generally with the Church—Catholic or Orthodox) the most respected institution in popular eyes. There is no reason to believe that the Revolutionary Armed Forces (FAR) will be in any way different. Hence, attempts to dismantle or reform the FAR in a wholesale manner—beyond the removal of the older and most loyal Castroite generals—will be not just unrealistic but counterproductive.

For this reason, pressure from exile or dissident groups to drastically change, or even dismantle, the FAR should be resisted. As for bringing it under direct civilian control—a desirable but not required element of democracy, as demonstrated by the numerous uniformed defense ministers throughout Latin America today—it should be seen as a medium- or even long-term proposition. While the experience of post-Sandinista Nicaragua should not be repeated, it should certainly be kept in mind. Unlike the FSLN, however, the PCC control over FAR is more theoretical than practical, and, thus, the nature of the problem is different.

A number of steps could and should be taken, however, in order to change the FAR's role in society. These include:

a)   Retirement of all senior generals, and certainly of those closely associated with the Castro brothers, occupying party or government positions; as a general proposition, the top-heavy institution should be streamlined, its size reduced, and younger officers promoted;

b)   Every form of formal link between the FAR and the PCC or government should be immediately severed—including links with the Interior Ministry. All forms of political activity within or by FAR should also be curtailed;

c)   FAR economic activities (ex. Gaviota, etc.) should be curtailed, and military expenditures provided exclusively from the state budget;

d)   Draft should be eliminated and replaced by a voluntary force, with members carefully screened and retrained—preferably by Latin Americans (from Brazil and Argentina, for instance) rather than the United States, although funds for this will have to be provided by the USEB.

The Cuban Communist Party

It is quite likely that in a post-Castro transition period the PCC itself will try to change its image and name, probably seeking to acquire a social-democratic facade. This "social-democratic" (i.e., neocommunist) successor of the PCC will try, and probably succeed, in associating itself with the Socialist International.

Whether such ideological esthetic surgery is ultimately "sincere" or not may be less significant in the short-term than the changes it will necessarily imply.

At least two of those changes will be very real—a purge of those senior cadres most publicly associated with the Castro regime and a dramatic reduction in total membership. Furthermore, it is likely that at least some hardline Castroites will split and form an "orthodox," still Marxist party—the pattern that occurred in Russia, Romania, the Czech Republic, or Moldova.

The first, and foremost, measures to be taken by a new Cuban government—with the support of the USEB—should be the dismantlement of the PCC auxiliary organizations: the Committees for the Defense of the revolution (CDR'S), party-controlled unions, youth, and women organizations. Unions aside, this should not be as difficult as it may appear—most of those organizations are already in an advanced state of decay and will most likely disband with, at best, a whimper. This, indeed, is what happened in the Eurasian ex-communist states once the Communist parties began losing power and the massive patronage associated with it.

Second, all PCC property should be transferred to the government—a key step if meaningful multi-party competition is to develop. Wherever in Eastern Europe that was not done—Romania being the best example—the neocommunists had an insurmountable financial advantage over non-communist parties.

Third, the PCC's control over the media should be immediately eliminated—but not replaced by that of the new government. As an aside, Radio Marti should certainly continue its operations—despite likely Congressional objections similar to those against post-1989 Radio Free Europe—as an alternative to what will likely be an enthusiastic, but not overly professional, objective, or responsible, post-communist media in Cuba. TV Marti, however, is another matter, and its continuing operation will be hard to justify.

Even if all these measures are rapidly and effectively implemented, however, the future "new style" PCC will remain the largest Cuban political party, with an electoral base among older people, bureaucrats, professionals, and industrial workers. This has been the pattern in each and every Eurasian former communist country, and, Cuba's sociological realities being what they are, should be expected to occur there as well.

In the short-term at least, there is little that could be done to avoid this pattern. To the inevitable extent that the already moribund Cuban industrial state sector will have to be dramatically pared down, the resulting unemployment will strengthen the appeal of neocommunist, populist appeals among former state employees. While private investments from abroad—which should be encouraged, perhaps with tax incentives—may create a force of well-paid and efficient workers—they will inevitably be a small minority for a long time.

However, one key factor that could be influenced from outside—that is, by the USEB—is the attitude of the rural population. In most ex-communist countries it has tended to support the neo-communists (Poland, Russia, Moldova), but that attitude was not universal—in Hungary, Bulgaria, and the more developed parts of Romania, it did not. To the extent agricultural prices remain stable and relatively high (i.e., if food imports are kept under control) and the baleful impact of the sugar industry, with its large labor force, on Cuba's agricultural sector is reduced or eliminated—small producers of food staples could support economic and political change.

The USEB could help in this process by strongly encouraging the development of a small and medium farm sector. This could be done by:

a)   Massive land reform, directly targeted to the elimination of all collective farms, rapid and complete privatization of land, including rapid provision of property titles to individuals. In Eastern Europe (Poland and Hungary, not collectivized during the Communist period, being the exceptions) postponement of land privatization has led to decline in production, higher food prices, and imports—themselves resulting in huge trade deficits—rural unemployment, and dissatisfaction with reform.

b)   Limiting the sugar quota given Cuba and denying support to that industry. To the extent foreign companies will become involved, their impact will not necessarily be negative: mechanization, higher efficiency, and a drastic reduction in labor requirements will likely force many Cubans to leave the industry and shift to other crops.

c)   Encouraging the formation of and providing short term financial support to private or cooperative agrarian banks; temporary (three to five years) technical support, subsidized prices for fertilizers, seeds and equipment should also be considered by the Department of Agriculture.

Justice and Public Order

Ordinary crime—from prostitution to theft of state property to corruption—is on sharp rise today—as the Cuban regime itself now admits, and as demonstrated by the recent changes in the penal code. During the post-Castro transition that trend should be expected to gather even more speed.

The first reason for this is the universal trend in all recent post-authoritarian and post-totalitarian regimes, from post-Franco Spain to post-communist Eastern Europe and Russia, and is directly related to the general relaxation of repression and internal control and the de-legitimization of the old law and order institutions (courts and police).

The second is related to the fact that while the old legal system has rapidly ceased to be applied or accepted, an alternative one requires a long time to be formulated, understood, and applied.

Dramatic increase in crime will be the most immediate challenge facing any transitional democratic government. It will provide neocommunists with anti-democratic arguments, creating the impression that criminality and democracy come hand in hand.

The USEB influence in this area is probably limited to the following:

a) to dissuade transitional authorities from giving up to the expected pressure from European governments and international human rights groups to abolish the death penalty, even if it would be applied in only a few cases. The issue is one of political perceptions rather than practical impact—whereas for some elite elements, particularly intellectuals, abolition is a proof of democracy and Westernization, for most Cubans is likely to be seen as capitulation to the criminal elements—elements whose influence, size, and role will be likely overestimated in popular eyes. That type of reaction was demonstrated in Russia and Romania, Ukraine and the Caucasian successor states of the USSR, but also in such "liberal and westernized" states as Lithuania, Estonia and Slovakia.

b) to cooperate with the few Latin American democracies with a functioning judiciary and a relatively low level of criminality: Costa Rica and Uruguay.

c) help train and fund the development of a small police detective force-like in Costa Rica—strictly centered on crime control, and recruited from MININT members fired in 1989, new personnel and/or Latin American expatriates.

Finally there are tow basic political and indeed moral issues to be considered: dissidents and the Church.

The Dissidents

The present Cuban dissidents exhibit the very same characteristics as those in Russia and most of Eastern Europe (Poland and Hungary aside) and the same delicate dilemmas as those did. To begin with, they are largely unknown by the overwhelming majority of Cubans, particularly those outside Havana.

Second, they are seen as suspicious supporters of the Left—a democratic one to be sure—and thus irrelevant in a post—and likely anti-communist, Cuba. Indeed, for the ordinary Cuban with political interests, it is not clear why dissident intellectuals, mostly descendants of the ruling nomenklatura, and still committed to some form of "socialism" should be preferred to neocommunists.

Third, the dissidents are mostly intellectuals, a protected and relatively privileged urban group, even if they were successfully marginalized socially by the Castro regime. A persecuted intellectual is seen by most Cubans—when they ever heard of him—as it was seen by most Romanians, Russians, or Bulgarians before 1989: as a spoiled rebel.

Finally, dissidents in Eastern Europe have a poor record of post-communist political savvy, performance and popular—including electoral—acceptance in each and every former communist state. From Russia to Poland (Maszowiecki), Romania (Doina Cornea), The Czech Republic (Havel's party), to Slovakia, to former East Germany, parties run by intellectuals, or those so perceived, lost elections badly—most of the time to neocommunists. Considering the social origin, even the names (Roca) of Cuban dissidents, they will likely fare no better. Regardless of their individual courage and suffering in resisting Castro, present dissidents in Cuba are best seen as the moral heroes many of them are—but certainly not as automatically plausible future political leaders.

Recommendation

The USEB should in no way—including statements by high officials—confuse respect for dissidents, their courage and commitment to democracy, with a willingness to support their specific political projects—no more, and no less, than doing so in regard to emigre organizations. While members of Congress are likely to press for preferential treatment of specific groups, such pressures should be strongly resisted.

The Church

The Catholic Church in Cuba today is, as this author has repeatedly and publicly made it clear, the only autonomous institution. As such, it should be, and it is, supported by the USEB through the channeling of aid via Caritas.

On the other hand, given reality, and based upon the experience of such Catholic countries in Eastern Europe as Poland, Lithuania, and parts of Ukraine, there is no reason to believe that the likely post-Castro revival of Christianity and its public expressions, mostly Catholic, will either last or translate into acceptance of Catholic political influence.

Indeed, any transitional government in Havana will likely face the same problem post-communist governments in Warsaw and Vilnius faced—how to combine popular respect for the Church with Catholic social and economic agendas largely opposed by the population. To the dismay of the Vatican, in Poland and Hungary the Church consistently lost public and political support for its pro-natalist, anti-divorce, and education policies—and perceived hostility to free market economics.

Therefore, the USEB should make, now and certainly during the transition, a clear distinction between the interests of the Catholic Church in Cuba and its own. That is a distinction the Catholic Church and Cardinal Ortega himself are already making by their vocal disagreement with both the embargo and, more importantly, capitalism in general.

Since Catholic influence in a post-communist Cuba is bound to decline—as it did in post-communist Poland, Lithuania, Croatia, and Slovenia—certainly at the political and legal levels, there is no reason for the United States, Executive and Congress alike, to operate on the assumption that the present de facto coincidence of interests with the Cuban Church—and the Vatican's policy in Cuba—will have to continue. While mutual respect is a permanent fact, Catholic insistence on population growth, family integrity (i.e., rejection of divorce), and opposition to free markets are not likely to be accepted by most Cubans— nor are they issues Washington should be associated with.

As a specific suggestion, once the Catholic Church loses its present status as the only autonomous institution in Cuba, official United States aid should cease to be channeled through Caritas and instead be distributed through Executive Branch agencies.

Preparing for the Transition

Some of the possible USEB reactions, policies and attitudes vis-á-vis the post-Castro, post-communist Cuba were already mentioned. In light of the East European/Russian experience, with its failures and successes, a few additional measures could and should be taken now to avoid some of the problems likely to be faced in Cuba.

From a policymaking viewpoint, inter-departmental and inter-agency competition and differences, inevitable as they are, should be minimized before the specific chain of political events leading to the post-Castro transition begins. Unlike 1989, when surprise at the extent and speed of communism's collapse was perhaps understandable, that should not be the case in Cuba.

To that effect, within the Executive, a coordinating group should be established, bringing together State, Justice, Commerce, Defense, and Trade representatives, as well as the FBI, CIA, and USAID (also Radio Mart, in a coordinating and permanent decision-making group.

Second, a parallel, bi-partisan group of experts and opinion makers, including representatives of the Cuban American organizations (i.e., excluding extreme groups, such as pro-Castro elements or violent anti-Castro factions) should be established, with the task of providing a clear and specific program for USEB policies in Havana after Fidel and Raul Castro disappear from the scene. Most importantly, such a group should include members of the Congressional staff. This group should be jointly appointed by the Administration and the Congressional leadership of both parties.

References

*Since this is not intended to be an academic paper, I neither expect the audience to have much time to spend on what academics have to say, nor blame it for not doing so. There are, however, a few relevant studies from which lessons relevant to Cuba could perhaps be drawn. The best analysis of the pitfalls and mistakes made by Western governments and aid agencies in Eastern Europe and Russia, and one strongly recommended to all those likely to be involved in Cuba is Janine R. Wedell's *Collision and Collusion: The Strange Case of Western Aid to Eastern Europe 1989-1998*, St. Martin's Press, New York, 1998. A more general description of the problems related to the pain associated with the transition to free markets in Russia is to be found in Rose Brady, *Kapitalizm: Russia's Struggle to Free its Economy*, Yale University Press, New Haven and London, 1999. For the role of the military in the transition, a useful volume is *The Military and Society in the Former Eastern Bloc*, edited by Constantine P. Danopoulos and Daniel Zirker, Westview Press, Boulder, 1999. For a more general comparative overview of the issue of transition, specifically centered on Cuba and the former Soviet Bloc, Michael Radu's *Collapse or Decay? Cuba and the East European Transitions from Communism*, The Endowment for Cuban American Studies, Miami, 1998, may be of some use.

Michael Radu, "Festina lente; United States and Cuba after Castro," in Irving Louis Horowitz and Jaime Suchlicki (eds.), *Cuban Communism*, Tenth edition, Transaction Publishers, New Brunswick (USA) and London, 2001, pp.768-86.

VENEZUELA'S CASTRO

Hugo Chávez Frías's presidency in Venezuela has caused an opposition coalition to form that, uniquely in Venezuela's history, breaks all class distinctions: middle-class professionals and mid-level military and police officers; unionized workers and business associations; the Catholic Church and virtually all the normally competitive media, have come together.

This poses a major problem for the United States. Chávez is elected freely, and democracy—or at least free elections—has been a sacred cow of U.S. foreign policy in Latin America for decades. But most of Chávez' policies are distinctly anti-democratic, often unconstitutional, and usually anti-American and pro-Castro. Furthermore, Venezuela is a major supplier of oil and oil byproducts to the United States, and the civil conflict there has reduced those supplies from 3 million barrels per day (bpd) to less than 200,000.

Chavez was first elected in 1998 and again in 2000. Since then, a number of populist/leftist South American presidents have been elected, including most recently Luiz Inácio Lula da Silva in Brazil (inaugurated 1/01/03) and Lucio Gutiérrez (inaugurated 1/15/03) in Ecuador. All have contempt for free markets, are distinctly anti-American and pro-Castro, albeit they operate under different constraints and in distinct national political and economic environments.

To begin with, Chávez's own democratic credentials are dubious. He first gained notoriety in 1992 when, as a paratroop lieutenant colonel, he staged a failed coup against the democratically-elected president Carlos Andrés Perez. Arrested and jailed, he was released by Perez' successor. Taking advantage of the profound popular discontent with the Venezuela's decaying two-party system, Chávez ran in 1998 on an anti-corruption, nationalist, and populist program, strongly supported at the time by all the numerous and disparate leftist groups and mini-parties. He blamed the country's structural problems on one cause—elite corruption, avoiding the more profound national corruption, decades of which had accustomed the entire population to little work and unsustainable social services, all excused by the myth of infinite oil revenues.

Ideologically, Chávez is a wooly rethread of the quasi-Marxist, demagogic populists who have ruined Latin America during the 1970s and 1980s. His declared hero is Simón Bolívar, the father of South American independence two centuries ago, and, indeed, Chávez has changed the country's name to the Bolivarian Republic of Venezuela. His "Bolivarian" ideology includes nationalism, "solidarity" and, last but not least, anti-Americanism.

His first visits abroad were to Baghdad, Tripoli, and Teheran. His friendship with Castro is both personal and concrete: in accordance with a 2000 agreement, Venezuela provides 50 percent of Cuba's oil imports, some 53,000 bpd, with 25 percent of the cost payable over fifteen years and a two-year grace period—all of which amounts to a vital lifeline to Cuba's dismal economy. Castro has paid a long visit to Venezuela (reminiscent of his three-week visit to Allende's Chile) and provides doctors (which Venezuela does not need) and experts on internal security (which the Chávez regime does need), including some involved in the formation of the "Bolivarian circles," a local copy of Cuba's infamous Committees for the Defense of the Revolution. Like the CDRs, the Bolivarian circles are basically mobs of the unemployed, unemployable, and social misfits paid and armed by the government.

To make his ideological allegiances and the threat he poses to regional stability clearer, Chávez' security services are actively cooperating with the Colombian Marxist-Leninist terrorists/narcotrafficantes of the Fuerzas Armadas Revolucionarias de Colombia–Ejército Popular (FARC-EP), including providing arms, safe havens, and transit facilities—at least according to the Colombian government and high-ranking defectors from the Venezuelan military.

All of this raises a crucial issue regarding the Chávez regime's chances of surviving: the loyalty of the armed forces. Indeed, with his popularity in the 20-percent range among all social and economic sectors of the population, including the poor and disadvantaged he is supposedly championing, it is becoming clearer by the day that Chávez' ability to stay in office, just as Allende's before him, is almost completely dependent on the military.

The problem is that the Venezuelan military has a dislike of Castro and Castroism that goes back to the early 1960s, when Fidel and his sidekick, Che Guevara, prepared and led a failed insurgency against the recently established democratic government in Caracas. And although in April 2002 segments of the military briefly removed Chávez from power, only to have others bring him back, the country's almost total militarization in recent months—the armed forces have taken over the oil fields, ports, and police armories in Caracas, the transportation and distribution sectors, etc.—increases the stress on an institution that has had no decisive political role since the 1950s. Chávez' habit of appearing in public ceremonies with the generals in his lieutenant colonel uniform, rather than as the civilian supreme commander he is supposed to be by the Constitution, does not help with the military's institutional pride—or speak well for his political judgment.

Since December 2, 2002, the usually disorganized and divided opposition has engaged in a general strike that, so far, resulted in the collapse of the oil industry, currency, and financial system, causing some $3 billion in economic loses so far. Chávez' answer has been to fire the entire management and thousands of workers of the national oil company (PDVSA, which provides half the government's budget), and to try to split the company in two. He knows he has a problem (no alternative workers, managers, or administrators), so he is now asking Lula to provide them. This is a very unrealistic idea is based on fluffy sentiments of solidarity rather than serious considerations, since Brazilian union workers are refusing to do this and, in any event, Lula has no surplus of workers. And this is one area where Castro cannot help

In the short term, Chávez just may survive the "fascist" and "terrorist" challenge of the general strike (never mind that the "fascists" are a majority of the people, from taxi drivers to bankers and bishops, to union leaders and the "terrorists" are all those who do not like him), albeit at an enormous cost to his country. His Bolivarian and Popular Organizations have written him demanding the nationalization of all media (or at least the anti-Chávez outlets) and the financial sector, and that oppositionists be tried for "sabotage." Does all this sound like Stalin or Castro? Yes, because the ideology behind such claims is the same.

Meanwhile, Washington is at a loss how to deal with the situation. Not surprisingly, a group of eighteen leftist Democrats in the U.S. House—John Conyers (D-MI), Jesse Jackson Jr. (D-IL), etc.—joined by that body's sole Socialist (Bernie Sanders, I-VT) took sides (for Chávez, naturally) and decided that "it is against the best interests of Venezuela and its people" to accept the opposition's (66 percent) demands for new elections.

A "friends of Venezuela" group of governments is suggested as a mediator, but since Chávez has managed to transform Venezuela's consensus-based politics into a zero-sum game, that idea seems to be a loser, as demonstrated by the failed attempts by the Organization of American States' president to mediate between Chávez and his opponents. Ultimately—back to Allende—the civil strife in Caracas will be resolved by the least democratic but still most effective institution: the military. The tragedy is that the longer Chávez stays, the more devastating the economic impact on the country and, equally important, the bloodier the outcome.

Reprinted with the permission from http://www.frontpagemag.com,
January 23, 2003

CASTRO, HUMAN RIGHTS AND LATIN ANTI-AMERICANISM

Recently, following a pattern understood by all but American liberals, Fidel Castro again did something he always does in response to U.S. efforts to improve relations with Cuba. He answered renewed congressional efforts to weaken the embargo by cracking down on the opposition. In the past, when then-President Jimmy Carter tried to improve ties, we wound up with the Mariel exodus and the emptying of Cuba's jails through migration to the U.S.; when Bill Clinton tried to improve relations, it ended up with American citizens being blown out of the skies by Castro's fighter planes and yet another mass send-off to Florida. This time, when a combination of greedy Republicans from farm states and leftist Democrats tried to weaken the embargo in the name of free trade, Castro answered by jailing seventy-nine dissidents for sentences totaling over 2,000 years.

Even the communist, Portuguese José Saramago, a Nobel laureate in Literature and supporter of any leftist cause this side of the Milky Way, declared in an interview with Spain's *El Pais* that "This is my limit." ("Saramago critica ejecuciones en Cuba," AP, April 14). This reminds one of the late 1960s, when Castro's Stalin-like purges of intellectuals forced Jean-Paul Sartre, another life-long fellow traveler, to reach his limit with Fidel. And Miguel Vivanco, of Human Rights Watch, whose goal seems to be indirectly helping the Marxist-Leninist terrorists/drug traffickers of Colombia's Revolutionary Armed Forces (FARC) by blasting every effort of that country's democratic government to fight FARC, also seems to have seen the light. He criticized the UN Human Rights Commission's proposed resolution condemning Castro's persecution of dissidents and demanding that they be released as "weak. . .a slap on the wrist."

Those conversions, along with the fact that the UN resolution was submitted by Costa Rica, Nicaragua, Uruguay,and Peru, are the good news from a UN organization now improbably chaired by Libya. Costa Rica aside, the Latin sponsors have paid heavy prices in fighting and defeating Marxist-Leninist insurgencies over the past few decades. They know what communism is, does, and may lead to.

There is another, less symbolic, but darker side, to the issue. Argentine president Eduardo Duhalde, a lame duck but nonetheless representative of his people's feelings, declared that Argentina will abstain from voting on the Resolution, calling the timing of the vote "inopportune" given the "unilateral war [in Iraq] that has violated human rights." Brazil will also abstain and in Mexico some fifty leftist intellectuals and the majority in the Mexican Congress have asked President Vicente Fox to abstain as well. They could not bring themselves to support Havana, but, again using Iraq as a pretext, claimed that abstention is the best way to deal with Castro. As Mexico's human rights ombudsman stated, regretfully, "only poor countries are condemned" and, thus, in his logic, condemning Cuba is unfair—in effect asking for some kind of proportional condemnation, regardless of realities.

Ultimately it comes down to fundamental differences among the Latin countries. The politics of most of the larger of them, vis-à-vis the United States, are adolescent, based on the desire to demonstrate independence from Washington. Nowhere is this more evident than in Mexico. To support the U.S. position on any matter, from the treatment of rocks on Mars to dissidents in Cuba, is politically dangerous, opening a leader to accusations from the intellectual elites of being a "gringo puppet." These elites have a disproportionate, and usually nocive impact, on politics. In Brazil those sentiments are enhanced by most Brazilians' emotional belief that their country, by virtue of its size and relative economic power, is entitled to a leading role that Washington unfairly challenges.

It was the very same adolescent politics that led the left-of-center governments of Brazil, Ecuador, and Venezuela to recently refuse to do the obvious, common-sense thing: to declare as terrorists the three irregular forces—FARC, the smaller, also communist National Liberation Army (ELN), and the anti-communists of the United Self-Defense of Colombia (AUC)—that are trying to destroy or avoid the democratic government of neighboring Colombia. They refused to do so despite the fact that FARC at least, and certainly soon enough the AUC, which is hunting them, operates across the borders in Panama, Ecuador, Brazil, and especially Venezuela, whose government is openly supportive of the insurgents.

In the case of Mexico, which has a seat in the UN Security Council (likely to the chagrin of President Fox), not supporting the U.S. approach to the Iraq issue was not a foreign policy or national interest issue, but one of national identity. Supporting the United States is a "sell out to the gringos." Teenagers of the world, unite!

In Chile, the most rational and pragmatic country in Latin America, and certainly the most successful in economic, free-market terms, the story is the same, and equally depressing. President Lagos, a Socialist leading a coalition with the Christian Democrats, had never behaved as a socialist in either economic or political terms until Iraq, when he had Chile withhold support for the United States in the Security Council. Why? Because of anti-Americanism. It does not cost much and is popular—especially in a country where hating capitalism and the United States is still popular among elites and the small (3 percent in the last elections) but organizationally effective Communist Party. Likewise with enthusiastically supporting whatever Havana does. Furthermore,

Santiago, like Ciudad de Mexico, Brasilia, and Buenos Aires, still has difficulty understanding that Washington is less tolerant of adolescent games now than prior to 9/11. When President Bush stated that "those who are not with us are against us" in the war on terror, most Latins did not take it seriously. They may well have to now.

Ultimately, abstaining on, or voting against, a largely meaningless UN criticism of Cuba, is, itself, irrelevant. However, a combined accumulation of Latin American positions suggests that when it comes to choosing between the obvious violations of freedom by one of their own (Havana) and supporting anything proposed by the United States, most Latin American governments will choose opposing Washington.

Understanding this, now let's consider both Castro's recent summary execution of thee ferryboat hijackers and the broader issue of how these Latin American attitudes toward U.S. global positions will affect their U.S. relations.

On the first issue, there is only one thing to say: a hijacker is a hijacker, period. As for capital punishment, it remains what it always was—a matter of political culture. Latins are fast to condemn U.S. executions, especially when they involve their own citizens, but have little or nothing to say when Castro sentences people to death.

As to the price Latin America will pay, some sort of price for their recent behavior? Mexico is clearly doing its best to diminish, if not destroy, whatever support there was in Congress for the legalization of millions of its nationals living illegally in the United States. Chile was a legitimate applicant for NAFTA membership and possessed all the right social, economic, and political credentials, but it has how raised questions about its belonging there. Instead of facing Congressional opposition only from U.S. Democrats opposed to free trade, it will also now face opposition from Republicans, whether they are for or against free markets.

Washington must make clear that being "anti-gringo" just on principle cannot continue in the age of international terrorism. Behavior should cost in terms of how many benefits one can expect to continue from Washington. Opposing the United States on matters of American security should have a cost in that regard, and Washington should impose it. Mexico, Chile, Brazil, and Argentina should be convinced that the cost is real and immediate.

Reprinted with the permission from http://www.frontpagemag.com,
April 21, 2003

BOILING BOLIVIA

Bolivia is on the brink of a constitutional, indeed societal, collapse. It seems headed for a military coup d'état and general chaos. In the overall scheme of things in Latin America, Bolivia is of only marginal economic or political significance. But as the most acute case of a more general and disturbing set of problems affecting far more important countries in the region—an increased radicalization (and anti-democratic manipulation) of indigenous peoples, the return of long-discredited populist and Marxist ideologies, general government incompetence, and pathological anti-Americanism—it is a country we should be paying attention to.

The immediate cause of Bolivia's current anti-government protests, which have included riots and highway blockades erected by the protesters (leading to several deaths and serious food shortages in the capital), is the issue of natural gas exports. Once a major tin producer, Bolivia today depends almost completely on hydrocarbons (oil and natural gas) for its legal export revenues; coca makes a significant and growing illegal contribution to revenues. Coca growers have increasingly sought to see coca be treated the same as hydrocarbons. Congressman Evo Morales Ayma, the coca growers' leader, chief of the Movement Towards Socialism (MAS) party, and runner-up in last year's presidential election, said in an interview last year, "Now is the moment to see the defense of coca as the defense of all natural resources, just like hydrocarbon, oil, gas; and this consciousness is growing....Five or six years ago I realized that one day, coca would be the banner of national unity in defense of our dignity, and now my prediction is coming true."

To start with oil and gas, Bolivia has plenty of both—especially the latter, of which it has the second largest reserves in Latin America. Until recently most was exported to neighboring Brazil, but that country has reduced imports as it exploits domestic deposits. One would think that the alternative would be export elsewhere, and the United States and Mexico are, indeed, highly interested. But any pipeline linking Bolivia to world markets must cross another country's territory, since Bolivia is landlocked. To get gas to the Pacific, Bolivia would have to transport it through Peru or Chile, the latter of which would provide a much shorter path. However, Bolivia is landlocked precisely because it lost its Pacific coast to Chile in 1883, following an ill-advised war that Bolivia initiated. No Bolivian has forgotten, forgiven, or gotten used to this— indeed, the country still pretends to have a Navy (on Lake Titicaca) and makes claims to the lost territory, usually to the Chileans' amusement. The Bolivian military strongly opposes any pipeline through Chile.

The MAS, a collection of cocaleros, old-fashioned communists, Trotskyites, Castroites, and racialist indigenous peoples nostalgic for pre-Colombian times, is opposed to the export of gas per se, claiming that it would only enrich the United States and multinational corporations. This even though a pipeline through Chile would bring Bolivia close to $500 million a year in revenues. Such revenue, however, would be dirty money in the eyes of Evo Morales and his followers, unlike the proceeds from coca, which is worshipped as part of "ancestral tradition."

The problem with this rationale is that coca, in Bolivia as in Peru, where similarly false claims are being made, is being grown in areas and quantities that have nothing to do with indigenous traditions and everything to do with greed, criminal enterprise, and leftist propaganda. Most Bolivian coca is now grown in the lowland tropical jungles of Chaparé rather than in the highlands of Yungas, as was traditional. And none was grown there before the Europeans arrived, when it began to be grown during the 1980s not by Indian communities but by former tin miners who moved to the area in search of more money and less work, who brought with them a socialist ideology and trade union organization. This may, in fact. be the only case in the world where a criminal enterprise is heavily unionized and has its own political party—the MAS.

Like Morales himself, MAS is not just an open advocate of drug production, which is a crime under Bolivian and international law, but also advocates (re-)nationalization of all large enterprises, natural resources, and large farms, non-payment of external debt, and anti-globalization, all mixed with a "return" to the pre-Colombian paradise of the Aymara and Quechua of half a millennium ago.

Perhaps such notions seem ridiculous, but Morales and the MAS believe in their rhetoric and seek to "liberate" their fellow Amerindians and coca growers throughout Latin America. In the same October 2002 interview, Morales acknowledged that "of course, sometimes it is the coca growers that set off the spark" if there is still violence and military repression. The advent of MAS will make it harder than ever for Bolivia, with its nationalist military, a tradition of about one coup d'état every ten months since it gained independence in 1825, an unstable government coalition of ex-leftists, opportunists, and the simply corrupt, to function as a democracy or achieve economic development.

La Razón columnist José Gramunt de Moragas put it well when he recently described Bolivian politics as a pendulum eternally moving between unsolved problems, to violence, and back to the status quo.

Bolivia is not alone in this predicament. Ecuador's recently elected president, Lucio Gutierrez, a former coup-making colonel, lost the support of the powerful Indian socialist organizations when he tried to impose some economic common sense. He is in danger of becoming the fifth elected president in so many years to lose his job before the end of his mandate. In Peru, another former officer and (failed) coup-maker is also increasing his popularity on an indigenous/socialist platform. All in all, and considering also the pseudo-indigenous Zapatista socialists of Mexico (led by a Marxist, blue-eyed former academic), it appears that the indigenous Latin American peoples' growing political power represents not progress, but simply anti-democratic, socialist nostalgia and a profoundly reactionary, and illiterate, approach to economics. The tragedy, of course, is that these people are the most likely victims of the type of politics they advocate. Their future seems destined to look much like their past of poverty and backwardness, all in the name of a "progressive" agenda.

Reprinted with the permission from http://www.frontpagemag.com,
October 8, 2003

CHAVEZ THE CHEAT

The results are in, and they are not pretty. Venezuelan President Hugo Chavez Frias, amigo and financier of Fidel Castro and of all radical, anti-American, anti-capitalist organizations in Latin America, won his country's August 15 referendum to remove him by a hefty 1.5 million votes. After receiving 58 per cent of the popular vote, the Organization of American States and observer Jimmy Carter accepted Chavez's victory claim.

But all did not come up roses in this seemingly sweet victory for the South American leftist, who calls himself the leader of the "Bolivarian Revolution." A medley of incoherent and leaderless opposition groups is claiming fraud, putting forward some good (but not good enough) explanations for their defeat. Many of their recall petitions, for example, were rejected in May by a Chavez-appointed electoral commission and had to be re-signed in an atmosphere of intimidation; the Supreme Court had been "enlarged," that is, stuffed with Chavez loyalists in a move that would have made FDR proud; and on election day voting hours were moved at the whim of the authorities, to list only a few.

But the size of Chavez's victory cannot be explained entirely by fraud in a country of relatively well-educated people with access to information and to a mostly anti-Chavez media. The main explanations for the referendum's failure to remove him lie elsewhere, and are far more serious and extensive. Besides the incompetent opposition, the other major one responsible for Chavez's survival is oil.

Venezuela is a major producer and exporter of this very valuable commodity, ranking fifth overall in the world in production, first in the Americas, and third as a source of U.S. imports, a position it has occupied since the 1960s. Oil has done to Venezuela what it has done to every large, oil-exporting, Third World country where the consequences of total dependence on its export have become predictable and poisonous. Even developed Norway suffers some of the symptoms.

Like in these other countries, oil revenues in Venezuela have encouraged a widespread aversion to work, so most of it is now done by immigrants from the rest of Latin America. That, combined with the creation of high-paying, money-losing, state-owned "industries," has created an entire nation of rent-seekers, widespread corruption, and an almost total dependence on government hand-outs.

When oil prices started to fall during the 1990s, all these pathologies came to the fore. Venezuela's comfortable two-party system, established in 1958, whereby the social-democratic Democratic Action (AD) and the equally redistributionist Social-Christian Party controlled national politics, ended when high national debt and low oil prices forced AD President Carlos Andres Perez Rodriguez to impose belt-tightening measures. This, in turn, caused army officers, led by then Lt. Col. Chavez, to try and overthrow Rodriguez twice in 1992, failing both times.

But Perez was subsequently found guilty of corruption in 1996, completely discrediting the two-party system. This, along with popular frustration and the widespread, popular belief that Venezuela was a "rich country," combined to produce the Chavez's election in 1998 and his reelection in 2000.

The disarray and incompetence of the Venezuelan opposition played a contributing role in each of Chavez's victories. In the August one, opposition leaders assumed that Venezuelans, anxious for democracy, would rise up and get rid of Chavez democratically. The Sumate ("Join In") opposition umbrella included the Catholic Church, most trade unions, the middle-class, those few remaining members of the upper-class who have not yet relocated to Miami, and politicians from the far left to the center right. The problem is that many Venezuelans belong to none of those groups.

High oil prices also helped Chavez. Indeed, once he took over the state-owned oil company last year, he used the cash bonanza to basically buy a majority of the voters. The government's recent campaigns to establish schools and clinics in remote areas and destitute neighborhoods in Caraca and to organize, arm, and control "Bolivarian" militias—that is, organized and government-controlled thugs that intimidate, beat, and sometimes murder opponents—were similarly successful.

To be fair, credit for Chavez's August 15 victory has to be shared with Fidel Castro. Not only did the Cuban leader add hundreds of security and secret police cadres to Chavez's own, he also provided essential advice derived from his earlier, but less successful, attempts to create mirror-image communist regimes in Salvador Allende's Chile in 1973 and in Sandinista Nicaragua in 1979.

However, while both those ventures failed, Castro did learn some valuable lessons, unlike the anti-Chavez opposition. One of the first was the importance of controlling the military, something that Allende failed to do and paid for with his life. This lesson was applied after Venezuela's 2003 pseudo-coup that removed Chavez for a few hours. His opponents made every possible error and then some, the outcome being the reinstatement of the Bolivarian hero. Helped by his regular meetings with Castro, Chavez then launched a purge of the Venezuelan military, which is now a reliable instrument in the president's hands.

Another lesson was learned from the Nicaraguan experience of 1990, when the Sandinistas expected an electoral victory but were defeated. Castro expressed to his admirer from Caracas that he should be sure to actually buy, rather than just rent, the mobs, and to give them something more than rhetoric to ensure their support. Here circumstances came to Chavez's aid in the form of oil prices. The Sandinistas, on the other hand, had no oil-based bonanza to offer their voters.

As a result of Chavez's referendum victory, the United States and the Western Hemisphere are still faced with a "legitimate," subversive regime in Caracas, propelled by oil and intent on promoting its (or Havana's) policies. A Chavez-led Venezuela is also capable of acting as a potential, new life preserver for the otherwise sinking Cuban regime.

As a result, Washington should question its concern with the democratization process, at least in Venezuela's case. America should not meekly accept either Chavez's claims to democratic legitimacy or his subversive activities in this hemisphere. Venezuela needs the U.S. market at least as much as the United States needs its oil, and Washington should make other Latin Americans leaders aware of the fact that playing Chavez's game has costs, which could indeed be high.

Reprinted with the permission from http://www.frontpagemag.com,
August 27, 2004

GUATEMALA VOTES DOWN THE CONVENTIONAL WISDOM

The conventional wisdom took a beating at the polls on November 7, when Guatemala held its presidential and congressional elections. In the presidential race, lawyer Alfonso Portillo, representing the Guatemalan Republican Front (FRG), received 48 percent of the vote, well ahead of the ruling party's candidate, who obtained only 30 percent, and of the candidate of the former Marxist guerrillas, who received 12 percent. While a runoff is necessary, it is clear that Portillo, who lost the 1996 presidential election by a whisker, will be the next president of Guatemala.

The FRG also seems to have obtained at least a large plurality, if not an outright majority, in the newly elected Congress. Both Portillo and the FRG came out on top in each of Guatemala's twenty-two departments, from the purely Maya Indian Huehuetenango and Quiché, to the mostly *ladino* (mixed blood or assimilated Indian) Zacapa and Escuintla. The party's founder, Efraín Rios Montt, was reelected in Guatemala City and is poised to reclaim leadership of the Congress, a position he held from 1994 to 1996. Rios Montt, Guatemala's most popular politician, is the real engine driving the party's— and Portillo's—success, but as a former junta leader he is constitutionally forbidden from running for president. Portillo (intriguingly, a former leftist himself) has twice been his hand-picked candidate for the top office.

Although polls consistently predicted the outcome of the election, Western media reacted with amazement to the victory of Portillo and the FRG. Such news agencies as Reuters, the *Washington Post*, the *New York Times* and *Le Monde* all felt compelled to remind readers that Guatemala went through a long civil war (1960-1996) which left some 200,000 people dead (a figure both implausible and unverifiable), mostly due to atrocities allegedly committed by the military against innocent Indians.

These reports display two incriminating weaknesses. The first is their suspiciously uniform and uncritical acceptance of the version of Guatemalan history purveyed by the Guatemalan Left, Western academics, and the human rights community. The second is their inability to make sense of the Guatemalan voters' unambiguous rejection of precisely that historical slant. The journalists are befuddled at the FRG and Rios Montt's consistent electoral success because, in their view of Guatemalan history, Rios Montt committed atrocities against the very people who now embrace him and his party. But instead of disbelieving the voters, the media representatives should look elsewhere for an explanation.

These are the indisputable facts: As Guatemalan Army chief of staff at the end of the 1960s, Efraín Rios Montt led a highly effective counterinsurgency campaign that virtually ended Castroite rural guerrilla activities and urban terrorism. He then ran for president on the Christian Democratic ticket in 1974 and, by all objective accounts, won a large majority of the votes, only to be defrauded by his erstwhile military colleagues and sent into exile. Following that episode, he converted to Evangelical Protestantism (ironically, his brother is now Guatemala's highest-ranking Catholic bishop) and largely retired from politics. In 1982, following a coup by junior officers that brought down the corrupt military junta that was losing the war against revived insurgents, Rios Montt was brought in to lead the new regime—the first Protestant president ever in a Latin American country. During his seenteen months in power, Rios Montt once again crushed the insurgency—this time permanently—reestablished law and order in the cities, and tried, unsuccessfully, to put the government's finances in order by introducing taxes (unheard of in Guatemala). This last issue triggered his downfall at the hands of a pro-business and pro-Catholic military faction.

But it was the methods Rios Montt used to combat totalitarianism and crime that brought the ire of the Left upon his head. His regime's arming of civilians, mostly Indians, led to the insurgents' collapse by denying them the capability to recruit freely and intimidate the population. And as an unabashed proponent of strict justice, he introduced capital punishment (Guatemala is still the only Latin American country that applies it) against not only terrorists, but common rapists and murderers as well—including members of the police forces. For all this, he is consistently described as "genocidal" by his enemies at home and abroad.

But if that is true, why on earth did the very victims of his alleged atrocities—the Indian Guatemalans—vote for him, his party, and its presidential candidate in such overwhelming numbers? Indeed, in an election whose freedom and legitimacy is undoubted, the current ruling party's candidate got most of his votes from the capital's largely non-Indian, *ladino* and business classes. The FRG's overall victory throughout the country, therefore, indicates that most of the FRG/Portillo support came from the 50 percent or more Guatemalans of Mayan origin. That is, if the "common wisdom" is to be believed, the FRG's largest constituency comprises people that the party's standard-bearer once sought to eradicate.

It is time to abandon such common wisdom in favor of true common sense. Obviously, most Guatemalans simply do not buy the standard "history" of their country's civil war, no matter how many outsiders try to explain it to them. In light of the electoral evidence (including the minuscule popular support given the former Marxist insurgents), the historical record is in need of serious revision.

To begin with, the decades-long civil war pitted the army *and most of the society* against the guerrillas; it was not a government campaign against the

Indians, let alone a race war. Indeed, Indians constituted the overwhelming majority of the army and the "civil patrols" it armed and controlled. Indians served on both sides in the conflict, suffered abuse by both, and doubtless inflicted it as well.

Equally clear is that the ex-guerrillas and their associated "popular" groups cannot claim to represent the Indians. The Indians, given a voice at the polls, soundly rejected them—a shocking display of "ingratitude" toward the very people who supposedly protected the Indian population from "genocide."

What Guatemalans in general, and Indians in particular, do seek protection from is the country's rampant criminality, and for help they turned to the FRG. They are also wary of those who attempt to win their support either for a leftist agenda or for an irresponsible elite that refuses to pay its taxes, cannot control crime, and in the name of democracy has sought only its own continued dominance.

Unless one accepts the implicit paternalism of the reports in "reputable" media outlets, one is forced to reconsider the standard interpretation of recent Guatemalan history. If not, one is left to explain the Indians' embrace of an alleged anti-Indian, and their rejection of their supposed defenders. To put it slightly differently, one would have to ignore the voice of the voters for the sake of political correctness.

Reprinted with the permission from http://www.fpri.org, November 17, 1999

GUATEMALA ELECTION REFUTES THE RIGOBERTA LEFT

The conventional wisdom took a beating at the polls on November 7, when Guatemala held its presidential and congressional elections. In the presidential race, lawyer Alfonso Portillo, representing the Guatemalan Republican Front (FRG), received 48 percent of the vote, well ahead of the ruling party's candidate, who obtained only 30 percent, and of the candidate of the former Marxist guerrillas, who received 12 percent. While a runoff is necessary, it is clear that Portillo, who lost the 1996 presidential election by a whisker, will be the next president of Guatemala.

The FRG also seems to have obtained at least a large plurality, if not an outright majority, in the newly elected Congress. Both Portillo and the FRG came out on top in each of Guatemala's twenty-two departments, from the purely Maya Indian Huehuetenango and Quich, to the mostly ladino (mixed blood or assimilated Indian) Zacapa and Escuintla. The party's founder, Efraín Rios Montt, was reelected in Guatemala City and is poised to reclaim leadership of the Congress, a position he held from 1994 to 1996. Rios Montt, Guatemala's most popular politician, is the real engine driving the party's—

and Portillo's—success, but as a former junta leader he is constitutionally forbidden from running for president. Portillo (intriguingly, a former leftist himself) has twice been his hand-picked candidate for the top office.

Although polls consistently predicted the outcome of the election, Western media reacted with amazement to the victory of Portillo and the FRG. Such news agencies as Reuters, the *Washington Post*, the *New York Times* and *Le Monde* all felt compelled to remind readers that Guatemala went through a long civil war (1960-1996) which left some 200,000 people dead (a figure both implausible and unverifiable), mostly due to atrocities allegedly committed by the military against innocent Indians.

These reports display two incriminating weaknesses. The first is their suspiciously uniform and uncritical acceptance of the version of Guatemalan history purveyed by the Guatemalan Left, Western academics, and the human-rights community. The second is their inability to make sense of the Guatemalan voters' unambiguous rejection of precisely that historical slant. The journalists are befuddled at the FRG and Rios Montt's consistent electoral success because, in their view of Guatemalan history, Rios Montt committed atrocities against the very people who now embrace him and his party. But instead of disbelieving the voters, the media representatives should look elsewhere for an explanation.

These are the indisputable facts: As Guatemalan Army chief of staff at the end of the 1960s, Efraín Rios Montt led a highly effective counterinsurgency campaign that virtually ended Castroite rural guerrilla activities and urban terrorism. He then ran for president on the Christian Democratic ticket in 1974 and, by all objective accounts, won a large majority of the votes, only to be defrauded by his erstwhile military colleagues and sent into exile. Following that episode, he converted to Evangelical Protestantism (ironically, his brother is now Guatemala's highest-ranking Catholic bishop) and largely retired from politics. In 1982, following a coup by junior officers that brought down the corrupt military junta that was losing the war against revived insurgents, Rios Montt was brought in to lead the new regime—the first Protestant president ever in a Latin American country. During his seventeen months in power, Rios Montt once again crushed the insurgency—this time permanently—reestablished law and order in the cities, and tried, unsuccessfully, to put the government's finances in order by introducing taxes (unheard of in Guatemala). This last issue triggered his downfall at the hands of a pro-business and pro-Catholic military faction.

But it was the methods Rios Montt used to combat totalitarianism and crime that brought the ire of the Left upon his head. His regime's arming of civilians, mostly Indians, led to the insurgents' collapse by denying them the capability to recruit freely and intimidate the population. And as an unabashed proponent of strict justice, he introduced capital punishment (Guatemala is still the only Latin American country that applies it) against not only terrorists, but common rapists and murderers as well—including members of the police forces. For all this, he is consistently described as "genocidal" by his enemies at home and abroad.

But if that is true, why on earth did the very victims of his alleged atrocities—the Indian Guatemalans—vote for him, his party, and its presidential candidate in such overwhelming numbers? Indeed, in an election whose freedom and legitimacy is undoubted, the current ruling party's candidate got most of his votes from the capital's largely non-Indian, ladino and business classes. The FRG's overall victory throughout the country therefore indicates that most of the FRG/Portillo support came from the 50 percent or more Guatemalans of Mayan origin. That is, if the "common wisdom" is to be believed, the FRG's largest constituency comprises people that the party's standard-bearer once sought to eradicate. It is time to abandon such common wisdom in favor of true common sense. Obviously, most Guatemalans simply do not buy the standard "history" of their country's civil war, no matter how many outsiders try to explain it to them. In light of the electoral evidence (including the minuscule popular support given the former Marxist insurgents), the historical record is in need of serious revision.

To begin with, the decades-long civil war pitted the army and most of the society against the guerrillas; it was not a government campaign against the Indians, let alone a race war. Indeed, Indians constituted the overwhelming majority of the army and the "civil patrols" it armed and controlled. Indians served on both sides in the conflict, suffered abuse by both, and doubtless inflicted it as well.

Equally clear is that the ex-guerrillas and their associated "popular" groups cannot claim to represent the Indians. The Indians, given a voice at the polls, soundly rejected them—a shocking display of "ingratitude" toward the very people who supposedly protected the Indian population from "genocide."

What Guatemalans in general, and Indians in particular, do seek protection from is the country's rampant criminality, and for help they turned to the FRG. They are also wary of those who attempt to win their support either for a leftist agenda or for an irresponsible elite that refuses to pay its taxes, cannot control crime, and in the name of democracy has sought only its own continued dominance.

Unless one accepts the implicit paternalism of the reports in "reputable" media outlets, one is forced to reconsider the standard interpretation of recent Guatemalan history. If not, one is left to explain the Indians' embrace of an alleged anti-Indian, and their rejection of their supposed defenders. To put it slightly differently, one would have to ignore the voice of the voters for the sake of political correctness.

Reprited with the permission from http://www.frontpagemag.com, November 30, 1999

CLINTON'S HAITIAN NIGHTMARE

Ten years ago, in September 1994, U.S. troops invaded Haiti under the auspices of restoring democracy, human rights, and the rule of law. At the time, the Clinton-conceived operation was hailed by leftists as a model of liberal interventionism, as former Catholic priest Jean-Bertrand Aristide was restored to power and an oppressive military regime was ousted. There was only one problem with this scenario: not only was Aristide vehemently anti-capitalist and (ironically) anti-American, he was every bit as brutal a despot as his predecessors. To make matters worse, the Clinton administration knew beforehand of Aristide's radical pedigree but chose to prop him into the dictator's chair anyway, in one of foreign policy's all-time worst liberal bungles. Today, the disastrous results of Clinton's experiment in Caribbean colonialism are painfully evident.

Despite the fact that Haiti, the second oldest independent state in the Americas, just recently marked its 200th anniversary in November 2003, freedom and prosperity remain sadly elusive for the country's citizens.

While the country, or more precisely the Jean-Bertrand Aristide regime, celebrated this bicentennial, most Haitians were too busy demonstrating against Aristide or simply scrounging for food—or a raft to Florida—to take part in any festivities.

In 2004, Aristide himself will celebrate the tenth anniversary of Operation Restore Freedom, which returned him to power. Friends of his, like Jesse Jackson and Randall Robinson, had helped pester the Clinton administration into undertaking this intervention. At the time, I pointed out that such an operation was an oxymoron, for how could one "restore" Haitian freedom, when the Haitian people have always been denied such freedom?

Ten years later, despite claims that Operation Restore Freedom was a great foreign policy triumph for the Clinton administration, the failure of Aristide's regime to transform Haiti's profoundly dysfunctional society into a functional one is all too evident. Indeed, if ever there was a case of a country hopelessly dysfunctional, from its civil society to its elected leadership, it is Haiti, which has become an almost perfect example of a society beyond salvation. Its problems are stubbornly rooted in violence and terror, which continue to enjoy mass support.

Aristide's election in 1990 (when he promised to "necklace" his opponents, or burn them alive) is often declared to have been Haiti's first free election, despite the notorious François "Papa Doc" Duvalier's election in 1957. Besides this ongoing democratic charade, since 1994 the Catholic Left in Haiti has destroyed what little remained after two centuries of savagery in the name of social justice and heretical liberation theology.

But Haitian corruption and misery are threats that reach well beyond the borders of Haiti. Washington has proven unable to do anything about Haiti, or even to protect the U.S. against wave after wave of Haitian émigrés coming to Florida. Haiti has also repeatedly invaded—raping, destroying, and stealing as much as possible—today's Dominican Republic, while always managing to remain eras behind it in terms of development.

The U.S. and European Union have suspended aid after the fraudulent 2000 elections that returned Aristide to power. Even Paris and Ottawa now agree with Washington that no more of the $500 million promised to Port-au-Prince in the ebullient days of 1994 should be delivered to Aristide.

Such a decision is absolutely necessary, since Haiti has always pursued the same solution to its problem of ungovernability: deflect blame and ask for money from outsiders. Hence, "You owe us $21,685,135,571.48, screams the bankrupt regime in Port-au-Prince" (*London Telegraph*, Oct. 10, 2003). This refers to the 90 million francs Haiti alleges it wrongfully had to pay France in 1825 in connection with Haitian crimes under founding father Dessalines as the country fought for independence, including murder, rape, confiscation of property, and similar actions against white French civilians, mostly women and children. That was the amount demanded by Paris in return for granting independence. With good reason, since Jean-Jacques Dessalines' 1805 Constitution clearly stated that "No white man of whatever nation he may be, shall put his foot on this territory with the title of master or proprietor, neither shall he in future acquire any property therein."

Such racist constitutions in Haiti have since changed, but the behavior of its government has not. The French are right to dismiss this monetary claim, not just because it is extortion, but also because—due largely to Paris' influence— the EU has already wasted almost $2 billion on Aristide's thuggish regime. And no matter how much Aristide and his lackeys spend on lobbying in Washington, it appears that even his racialist supporters in the United States are embarrassed by him now.

The *Washington Post* reported (on November 18, 2003) that, at the 200th anniversary celebration, Aristide told Haitians, "After 200 years of economic violence, the traces of slavery are still here. Poverty today is the result of a 200-year plot. Whether it be slavery or embargo, it's the same plot. You are victims." Referring to the aid suspensions—which he calls "economic sanctions," he said, "We got out of the blockade then, now there's another one. It's the same conspiracy. We won that victory. We can walk toward another victory."

The undeniable truth is that Aristide is merely the latest incarnation of an uninterrupted chain of murderous tyrants who have ruled Haiti over the centuries. In fact, the country still glorifies the racist Jean-Jacques Dessalines (Emperor Jacques I) as its "founding father." That a genocidal murderer is the national hero makes perfect sense in Haiti, where Dessalines' assassin, Henri Christophe (King Henry I, 1806-1820), is also glorified as a founding father. Although many Haitians excuse Christophe's act as a part of Haiti's independence struggle, it is obvious that Haiti's history of bloodshed, from the lines of succession to the lush fields of the countryside, underpins its current political and social culture.

And the tragic spin of Haiti's history wheel continues. Whereas under Francois Duvalier the sinister "tonton macoute" gangs controlled the population, now it is Aristide's "chiméres" gangs doing the killing and beating. Members are recruited from the worst ghettos. Formed for the purpose of beating up, or even murdering, opposition, some of these gangs themselves are now considered "opposition." One famous thug, Amiot Metayer, the alienated leader of a formerly pro-Aristide "community organization" called the "Cannibal Army," was found dead on a roadside in Gonaives with his eyes shot out. His gang's members blame Aristide.

Even a cursory understanding of Haitian history should have taught the Clinton administration that to speak of "Restoring Freedom" in a country that never had it—or wanted it—is ridiculous. The real reason for Clinton's intervention was the invasion of Florida by Haitians, an invasion that has not abated and never will, because of the very fact that, by per capita income, Haitians today have only 60 percent of what they did in 1800. "Restore Freedom?" Freedom has not yet dawned upon Haiti's bloodstained shores. To insist Bill Clinton restored freedom insults the meaning of the word itself.

Reprinted with the permission from http://www.frontpagemag.com,
January 22, 2004

A THUG'S LEFTIST GROUPIES

According to Senator Christopher Dodd (D-Conn) in an interview on CNN, the administration is responsible for the overthrow of Haiti's former president, Jean-Bertrand Aristide; Aristide was "a democratically elected," albeit "not perfect" figure. The opposition is comprised of "thugs," although Dodd does not know anything about their leader, Guy Philippe. According to Dodd, the administration weakened democratic legitimacy in Latin America by not supporting Aristide, because it did not like him. Of course, the fact that two presidents of Ecuador, one of Argentina and, more recently, the very pro-U.S. president of Bolivia, Sanchez de Lozada, all democratically elected, were overthrown during the past few years, with no U.S. intervention, conveniently escapes Senator Dodd's memory. That, considering Mr. Dodd's well-established romance with the unsavory Left in Latin America, is no surprise; the fact that such statements make him a moderate among Democrats, is one.

Indeed, Rep. Maxine Waters of California claimed that Aristide's wife told her that she and her husband, "'"felt like [Aristide] was in jail…Yes, he felt like he was under arrest and in jail." Whether that is true or not, and Waters is known to have peculiar feelings of her own—she described the racist Los Angeles riots as "rebellion" and was a promoter of the notion that crack was introduced by the

CIA as a plot against blacks. Randall Robinson, self-exiled black racialist, apologist for Aristide, and noisy promoter of the notion that "America owes" its wealth to blacks and, thus, "owes" them "reparations," repeated the claims. Clearly, Haiti's voodoo-laced conspiracy culture is not limited to that country.

Referring to Aristide as having been democratically elected is a misnomer. For example, when Saddam Hussein declared himself elected with 100 percent of the Iraqi vote in 2002, just about everybody laughed (I cannot vouch for Rep. Waters or Mr. Robinson); when Aristide was "elected" in 2000 with 97 percent of the vote, which the opposition boycotted (only 15 percent bothered to participate), that, according to Sen. Dodd, Mr. Robinson and Rep. Waters (and mindlessly joined by the media) makes him "democratically elected." And, implicitly, the fact that one year later he blatantly rigged parliamentary elections presumably strengthens his Jeffersonian credentials.

But none of that matters for the Congressional Black Caucus—Aristide was a "democrat" overthrown by the implicitly racist Bush gang, yet another demonstration of the Caucus' increasingly pernicious irrelevance. Aristide was black, anti-American, a "progressive" who made it rich in the Hemisphere's poorest country—all endearing characteristics, apparently. Never mind that 99 percent of Aristide's opponents, and all his victims—the Haitian people—were also black, or that a few hundred (black and poorly armed) opponents drove him out amidst mass sympathy or indifference from the population—evidently those were neither black enough, nor "progressive" enough, nor, presumably, aware of what is good for them. As for the "racists" in the Administration, such as Powell and Rice, we all know, because Harry Belafonte told us, that they are just "house slaves." Aristide's racialist "progressivism" evidently has an echo among some in Congress.

As Garry Pierre-Pierre, publisher and editor-in-chief of New York's *Haitian Times*, put it in the *Wall Street Journal*, "[Aristide's] detractors included the intellectual left, instrumental in forming the Lavalas popular movement which swept him into power fourteen years ago; and they also included women's groups, church groups, and the labor unions, which, all taken together, made clear that there was no part of his original radical base that was not against him. (Only the U.S. Congressional Black Caucus, far removed from Haiti and from reality, stood by its man.).".

Aristide, always the Orwellian, told state radio in Bangui, "By toppling me, they have cut down the tree of peace, but it will grow again." Indeed, peace is not exactly the word one would immediately associate with Aristide—after his first, and only legitimate election in 1990, this former man of the cloth was openly encouraging the mobs of Port-au-Prince to enjoy themselves with "Pére Lebrun"—the creole term for "necklacing" (burning people with gasoline filled tires around their neck) made famous by the other famous racialist "progressive"—convicted thief and kidnapper Winnie Mandela. That was then—after regaining power on the backs of the Marines, the now defrocked ex-priest took more than a page from the Duvalier regime he helped overthrow—the new pro-regime mobs were renamed—from Tontons Macoutes into chimères. When the CIA accurately predicted all this, its analyst was criticized, implicitly—or not so implicitly—accused of racism.

Is "America" guilty of anything in Haiti? The answer should be obvious: "America" is not; the race-obsessed Left is. But do not expect Waters, Robinson or Jesse Jackson to ever admit it—no, it is always somebody else's fault. That is just like Aristide's claim (perhaps inspired by Robinson) that France "owes" Haiti (or him?) some $21 billion—precisely the sort of claim that would make a Dominique de Villepin furious and revengeful—and that Franco-American "colonialism" is the cause of Haiti's misery.

What next? "We have seen quite a few revolutions, but this is the weirdest one," said Walter Bussenius, a retired hotelier in Cap-Haïtien," quoted by the *Economist*. Indeed, Haiti had thirty-two prior violent changes of government in 200 years of existence—an average of one every six years, and this one is the weirdest because it was probably the least violent (so far), started by Aristide's thugs turning against him, and implemented by only a handful of men. That said, it is unlikely to be the last—or the weirdest, for long. The middle-class is virtually non-existent or in New York and Miami; the political parties are fictional; the decent opposition to Aristide has no guns, and the successful one has guns but is far from decent.

Next question: does the United States owe anything to Haiti? The answer is, again, no, but Washington has an obligation to prevent yet another uncontrollable wave of illegal Haitian immigrants. That means that the Coast Guard will be in view of the Haitian coast for a long time. Other than that, here is the perfect opportunity for the United Nations to demonstrate that it could do what France and the Democratic candidates for president claim it could, and should have done, in Iraq—fix a broken society, dysfunctional political culture, and tradition of violence. Perhaps France, which, for once, has demonstrated more clarity and steadier will than Washington, would take the leadership of a UN force of Fijians and Bangladeshis and do what U.S. interventions in Haiti (one lasting between 1915-1931) have failed to do. We should cheer them on.

Reprinted with the permission from http://www.frontpagemag.com,
March 10, 2004

THE LOOMING MEXICAN CRISIS

Mexico has a tradition of regional conflicts and political instability dating back to the days of independence from Spain. Although the country has been ruled by the same authoritarian and corporatist party since 1929—the Institutional Revolutionary Party (PRI)—that older tradition largely explains why such a vast and rich country, and its talented and fast-growing population of 94 million, are still struggling with dismal poverty and instability. Many Mexicans among the political and business classes are increasingly willing to admit these obvious facts in private, but virtually no politician, in Mexico City or Washington, will face them publicly. Out of fear of the politically correct accusation of "insensitivity," an accusation equally encouraged by the Mexican government and multiculturalists in the United States, Washington today has adopted an "ostrich" policy vis-á-vis Mexico.

Nevertheless, Mexico today is in deep, if not terminal, trouble, and once more its roots are political. After examining three of the major aspects of Mexico's present crisis—the 1994 peso crisis, the two Marxist insurgencies now active in the South, and the twin issues of migration and drugs—I will then look at the causes of the crisis.

Currency in Crisis

The 1994 peso crisis was the direct result of fundamentally political decisions made by then-Mexican president Carlos Salinas de Gortari (1988-1994). In the middle of difficult negotiations with the United States and Canada over the North American Free Trade Agreement (NAFTA)—negotiations that came about largely at Mexico's insistence—and in the midst of a presidential campaign, the Salinas government decided to take the attitude of the proverbial monkey: hear no evil, see no evil. As a result, the wildly overvalued peso was not brought back to its real value through a slow and steady process; instead, to avoid scaring away foreign investors and the U.S. Congress, it was allowed to remain at unsustainable levels until Washington approved NAFTA and, not coincidentally, until President Salinas left office. That left his successor, Ernesto Zedillo Ponce de Leon, to pick up the pieces. Ignorance of economics was clearly not an excuse; Salinas, like Zedillo, is a competent economist.

Nor was this type of behavior unique to Salinas. In 1982, again at the end of a presidential term, then-President Jose Lopez Portillo nationalized the banks and virtually declared Mexico bankrupt, thus leaving a messy economic inheritance to his successor, Miguel de la Madrid, a situation that took almost a decade to correct.

State of Instability

Another major aspect of the current crisis involves the political unrest and insurgencies in various Mexican states. In January 1994, just as NAFTA went into effect, the Zapatista National Liberation Army (EZLN) began an insurrection in Chiapas, Mexico's southern-most state. To most Mexicans, and to virtually all foreign media, it was a great surprise. It should not have been. Not only do EZLN communiques mention that theirs is a fourteen-year-old organization—thus dating its founding to 1983—but the U.S. Central Intelligence Agency and, presumably, the Mexican government knew of the organization's existence for more than ten years, as demonstrated by now-available internal Mexican intelligence reports dating back to 1990.[1]

Furthermore—and here is the crux of Mexico City's current guerrilla problem—the Salinas government not only knew far in advance of the budding EZLN insurgency, but it tried for years prior to 1994 to deal with it the only way it knew how: by throwing money at the situation. Hence, before 1994, Chiapas, Mexico's poorest state, received more funds per capita than any other—and the trend accelerated after 1994, with thousands of new schools being built and thousands of isolated communities provided with electric power and medical clinics.[2]

When the far more violent People's Revolutionary Army (EPR) began its insurgency in 1996 by attacking some of Mexico's most economically sensitive areas in the state of Guerrero (which includes the Acapulco resort area), once again the Zedillo administration behaved as if caught by surprise—even though the EPR had been active in that region for at least a decade.

The PRI had additional political and ideological reasons to try to keep the very existence of the EZLN and the EPR under wraps: its own "revolutionary" status was under attack. Although PRI's left-wing revolutionary credentials are by now largely rusty and dubious, its core claim to legitimacy is not that different from those of either the leftist opposition Party of the Democratic Revolution (PRD) or even the two guerrilla groups. They are all socialist, anti-American, and anti-capitalist—except that PRI, having had the responsibility of governance since 1929, and also having had to face the reality of living with the United States and Mexico's inescapable dependence on foreign investments.

One result was that PRI governments, for the sake of immediate political advantage, allowed the EZLN and EPR to transit their initial stage of recruitment, indoctrination, and mobilization unmolested. Now, Mexico as a whole is paying the cost.

During the last days of May 1997 alone, two EPR clashes with the army in Guerrero led to the loss of a military plane, the deepening of cleavages within the Mexican political debate, and the deaths of at least thirteen people—a majority from the military. As in the previous EZLN case, the Mexican military and police demonstrated poor tactical intelligence prior to the ambushes, and their ineffective reaction—massive air and infantry search-and-destroy operations—suggested a structural inability to learn from decades of prior counterinsurgency experiences elsewhere, from Vietnam to El Salvador to Anastasio Somoza's Nicaragua.

Twin Issues of Anti-Americanism

The third key aspect of the Mexican crisis, in part, concerns migration, which in the Mexican context means migration to the United States. This is a particularly difficult combination of issues related to political survival, nationalist rhetoric, and economic necessity. It is especially challenging for the United States because an overwhelming majority of Mexican individuals, political parties, and pressure groups have all developed a strong belief that Mexicans have a *right* to emigrate to the United States. Even the Catholic Church considers the distinction between legal and illegal migrants morally misguided.[3] Mexican leaders thus feel entitled to complain about U.S. immigration policies, general legislation vis-á-vis immigrants, and even the application of the death penalty to Mexican murderers convicted in the United States.

Ironically, the same government in Mexico City that considers the activities of foreign human rights groups on its territory a threat to its sovereignty, manipulates vaguely defined "human rights" to protect its migrant citizens' "rights" to speak Spanish rather than English, receive foreign welfare, and avoid summary deportation from the United States. In autumn 1996, in a sharp departure from historic policies, the Mexican Congress voted to allow migrants to vote in national elections and own land in Mexico. Central American migrants to Mexico are routinely deported, abused, and jailed, but nothing less than preferential treatment for Mexican illegals north of the Rio Grande is considered acceptable.

The very nature of Mexican migration to the United States—mostly from the backward central and southern states of Zacatecas, Oaxaca, Michoacan, and Chiapas; disproportionately Indian; and often illiterate and ignorant of Spanish—helps explain Mexico City's historic refusal even to pretend to guard its northern border. Indeed, such migration not only helps siphon off ethnic elements hard to assimilate into Mexico's mythical "cosmic race," but it also limits, to some extent ,what, in any other developing country, would be the first migratory step—to the capital city and, in Mexico's case, the relatively developed North.[4]

A report from Mexico's National Council on Population (CONAPO) recently confirmed the importance of (mostly illegal) migration to the United States. According to CONAPO, Mexico annually receives between $3 billion and $4 billion in remittances from its 7 million emigrants to the United States, more than the value of the country's agricultural exports.[5] Indeed, there is very limited permanent (as opposed to transitory) internal migration to the northern

Mexican states, although Mexico City is rapidly caving under the burden of waves of poor and unskilled provincial immigrants, for whom it is clearly unprepared.

Some readers may be surprised that I have left drugs—the second most important U.S. preoccupation regarding Mexico and the other example of ailing U.S.-Mexican relations—to this point in my essay. The reason is that drug trafficking, probably Mexico's largest employer and certainly the largest hard currency source, is not a cause of the general weakening of the country's main institutions and the growing popular cynicism—it is a symptom. For that reason, although the drug issue is important to U.S. citizens, it is not an issue that merits further attention in this essay. Rather, I will turn now to the causes of Mexico's problems.

An Accumulation of Threats

Although many analysts in the last century and a half have predicted Mexico's collapse and were proven wrong, it is also true that, while Mexico has long lived perilously on the verge of chaos and violence, the current crisis may well be the most dangerous. The reason is that virtually all of Mexico's historical cleavages—social, geographic, political, ethnic—seem to be converging at a moment when the central government is weaker than at any time since the revolution.

Zedillo's administration is widely, and correctly, perceived as the weakest in the PRI's history. Not only is Zedillo himself an "accidental" president—he was the second and unexpected PRI choice to be the 1994 nominee, after the assassination of the popular Luis Donaldo Colosio—but he, unlike most of his predecessors, is hardly able to control his own party. A Yale-trained technocrat without a strong personal political base, Zedillo was a lame duck from the day of his election, having received only 48.8 percent of the vote.[6] He was humiliated by PRI old-timers when the party's congress resoundingly defeated his 1996 plan to privatize parts of Mexico's cash cow (and heavy burden on the country's budget), the oil industry. To add to this problem, Zedillo has a rather uneasy relationship with the armed forces, which although admittedly not as strong politically as elsewhere in Latin America, are, nevertheless, a pillar of PRI's rule.

Zedillo is the third of a line of Ivy League-trained, technocratic presidents, following de la Madrid and Salinas, and he has had to face the impossible task of combining PRI's historic socialist rhetoric and corporatist practices with Mexico's contemporary free-market needs; not surprisingly, he has run into obstacles in many areas. Privatization of the bloated public sector upset PRI's more socialist-minded voters, limited the corruption opportunities of its power-minded, and alienated most nationalists. Worse still, for himself and the future of the PRI, Zedillo seems to be a democrat at heart—hence his efforts to make the electoral process more transparent and free, with the not-unexpected result that the PRI's electoral losses, accumulating since the 1980s, have become an avalanche.

This July, Mexico had elections for Congress as well as for mayor of Mexico City, a previously appointed position. Given the capital's enormous population and political importance, the newly elected mayor, Cuauhtemoc Cardenas, will inevitably become the second-most-important political figure in the country and a natural presidential candidate. The victory of Cardenas, the PRD presidential candidate in 1994 and 1988, represents the Mexican Left's biggest electoral triumph ever. Moreover, in the congressional elections, the PRI's mere plurality means that the PRD, together with the more right-wing National Action Party (PAN), have put PRI in a minority position for the first time in its history.

To advocates of democratic politics, competition, and the division of power, such an outcome may look like decisive victory. But in terms of Mexico's long-term future, such an outcome is far more disturbing than encouraging, because of the nature of each party's electoral base.

The "National Party"

The PRI is the party of power, the status quo, and clientelism, but it is also the only truly national party, with a presence throughout the country. On the other hand, it is plagued by corruption and internal divisions between minority technocratic modernizers like Zedillo and a semisocialistic, semifascist corporatist majority of cadres and union bosses who are aware that free markets and democracy are incompatible with their continued careers, power, and ideology.

Accusations made by Carlos Castillo Peraza, the PAN's candidate for mayor of Mexico City, that the PRI and the PRD colluded against him, make sense, considering that most of the capital's population is fundamentally dependent upon transfers from the federal budget—and that both the PRI and the PRD candidates promise to increase them.

The "Traditionalists"

The PRD is, today, Mexico's most traditionalist post-1910 party. Rejecting economic reality and common sense, the populist, antidemocratic, and semi-Marxist organization plays a political double-game: vocally supporting human rights and democracy when they fit its interests; engaging in extraparliamentary, often violently illegal actions when they do not. This party has consistently helped legitimize the violence of the EZLN and has broken the law through violent demonstrations and the open persecution of its opposition in areas it dominates. When the EPR killed a number of Mexican soldiers in Guerrero in May 1997, the PRD local congresswoman demanded that the military be withdrawn from her state; the PRD minority leader in the Mexican Congress, Hector Sanchez Lopez, went even further and claimed that, because the EPR is not a military threat, the national army should not attack or "provoke" them. Such responses should not be surprising because, as respected commentator Enrique Krauze accurately assessed, "The PRD was born from two profoundly anti-democratic currents: Communists and ex-*priistas.* . . .The PRD is an authoritarian wolf in a democratic sheep's clothes."[7] This raises the serious question of the extent to which the PRD is a "loyal" opposition— inasmuch as it publicly condones violence from the Left, occasionally engages in it itself, and tries to disarm the Mexican state despite a violent challenge from the totalitarian Left.[8] Cardenas himself, and his colleague and co-leader of PRD, Porfirio Munoz Ledo, are both former PRI leaders—Cardenas as governor of Michoacan, Munoz as PRI secretary general—and their party includes all the remnants of Mexico's Communist Left that did not join the guerrillas.

The PRD's main electoral strongholds are in the most backward, most Indian southern states—Guerrero, Oaxaca, Michoacan, and Chiapa—and among a combination of leftist students, intellectuals, and unurbanized recent migrants in Mexico City.

The "Free-Marketers"

The PAN is a (mostly) free-market conservative party, the oldest in Mexico since the PRI imposed its rule almost sixty years ago. Its support is concentrated mostly in the North and among conservative, mostly middle-class elements in the center of the country. It is only spottily represented in the southern areas. Unlike the PRD, before the July elections the PAN already controlled a number of important political offices: governorships in Baja California Norte and Nuevo Leon and the city hall of Monterrey—the city that is, for all practical purposes, Mexico's capitalist center.

The fact that the PAN-dominated North perceives itself to be subsidizing the rest of Mexico only sharpens the regional conflict. It also considers itself different from—and implicitly superior to—the South. When the faculty of the modern Colegio de la Frontera Norte in Tijuana was asked for its opinion on the economic gap between northern and southern Mexico, the answer was unanimously pessimistic: comparing the levels of income, health, and education of the two halves of the country, it commented that the southern states were about twenty years behind. Yet, the major demands of the southern EZLN dealt not with health, education, and welfare, but with political, cultural, and territorial autonomy for Indians—virtually the creation of a state within a state in Chiapas and a few other regions—and their "right" to massive economic subsidies from the rest of the country.

The distinct differences between economically efficient Northern Mexico's ideological inclinations toward the PAN, and the dependent South's support for PRD and elements further to the Left, call into question Mexico's long-term prospects for territorial integrity and political stability. But even the North is not without its problems: The very economic success it has witnessed can be attributed, at least in part, to the region's heavy involvement in, benefits from, and control over cocaine, marijuana, and heroin trafficking to the United States. There is little good news from Mexico indeed.

A General Collapse of the System

The most immediate issue most Americans associate with Mexico—other than immigration—is drug trafficking. Extensive areas—ranging from entire states, like Sinaloa, to major cities like Juarez, Tijuana, Guadalajara and Hermosillo—are virtually outside government control and dominated socially, politically, and economically by drug traffickers—just as Medellin and Cali were a decade ago in Colombia.

But again, drug trafficking is a symptom rather than a cause of Mexico's political problems. The corruption of PRI politicians and political clients explains why Mexico has no functioning drug enforcement agency, for example, or more generally, *any* police force. At best, the many Mexican police organizations—some not controlled by the federal government, some escaping control by state governments, some immune to local authority—are a threat to law and order. At worst, they have openly joined the criminal organizations—all the way to the formal leadership of Mexico's supposed drug enforcement agency.

When Zedillo placed the military in charge of policing the capital in May 1997, the police violently opposed the move and fought with the military police.[9] Media reports of police cooperation with the major drug cartels are routine, and they are routinely confirmed by the highest political authorities. Nor are the police forces of much use in controlling the insurgencies, as demonstrated by the militarization of Chiapas and Guerrero.

Likewise, the Mexican military is a good example of what happens when the armed forces are so removed from politics as to have no input whatsoever. Allegedly apolitical, but, in fact, an obedient instrument of the PRI, the Mexican military has a long history of being underpaid, undertrained, and isolated from the rest of Latin America, with the result that it is reluctant even to begin to learn—let alone apply—any counterinsurgency lessons from Mexico's neighbors to the south.

Military intelligence in the insurgency areas is dismal—a fact most recently demonstrated by the EPR ambush of an army patrol in Tepozonalco, Guerrero, on May 24, 1997, in which six soldiers died for lack of basic tactical intelligence. The Mexican military rejects help from the United States, dismisses as irrelevant and inferior the successful counterinsurgency of Guatemala, and remains unconvinced that it needs to learn anything from the recent Colombian and Peruvian experiences.

A Call for Realism

The U.S. government, admittedly following a long, bipartisan tradition of being "sensitive" to Mexico's real or alleged perceptions of grievances, is making things worse. The reality is that no Mexican institution is functioning properly and most are dysfunctional. The PRI, accurately, if self-servingly, described Cuauhtemoc Cardenas as "the smiling face of violence," and President Zedillo himself has recently called for a new political culture in his country. Former PAN attorney general Antonio Lozano, equally accurately, stated that any law-and-order strategy in his country is hindered by corruption and lack of continuity. If Mexico today looks like, feels like, and kills like Colombia during the late 1980s it is because it most definitely is like Colombia at that time.

Nor is the Catholic Church—repressed since 1929 and only able to resolve its problems with PRI in 1992—any different. Like other elements of Mexico's political culture, large segments of it too seem to be bent upon catching up with the failed Marxist utopias the rest of Latin America experimented with, and discarded at high human cost, since the 1960s.

What, then, remains? Certainly not the overproliferating "human rights" and "Indian rights" groups, most of which are simply subsidiaries of Western pacifist, leftist, or ecologist organizations; with few exceptions, these Western groups' interest in protecting Mexico's Marxist insurgents, or their recruits, overrides both common sense and the interests of most Mexicans in maintaining the integrity of their country and improving the safety of their lives.

Ultimately, Mexico is a long-term problem for. . .Mexico, yes, but also for the United States. Polite avoidance of that reality in Washington, or phony indignant rejection of it in Mexico City, is no solution. Unless a real, responsible answer is found—one that treats Mexico as a responsible but clearly sick society and its people as responsible for their own problems—the disturbing developments south of the Rio Grande will become a cancer that destroys both Mexico and the United States.

There is no simple solution to Mexico's crisis, and there is certainly no U.S.-made solution. But Washington may start by at least admitting the existence of a serious problem instead of avoiding reality behind a fog of banalities. Serious congressional hearings should be convened without consideration of Mexican "sensitivities" or political correctness. In more specific terms, and particularly in regard to the three major problems facing Mexico—drug trafficking, emigration, and political violence—certain unilateral measures could make a difference.

First, the border should finally be brought under control, perhaps even militarized, and Mexican policymakers told in no uncertain terms that they cannot expect the United States to absorb their labor surplus anymore. Second, Mexico should not be recertified for compliance with anti-drug-trafficking efforts; at best, it should be put on "probation" like its neighbor Belize. Washington should insist that U.S. Drug Enforcement Agency personnel be allowed to increase their numbers in Mexico and to carry weapons, and that Mexico allow extradition of important traffickers. At the same time, financial support for drug enforcement efforts in Mexico should be substantially increased.

As far as the insurgencies are concerned, the U.S. role has to be limited, but Washington could help in at least two areas: Congressional restrictions on Mexico's use of U.S. weapons, particularly helicopters (now specifically limited to narcotics control), should be lifted—there is no reasonable way to separate drug trafficking from insurgencies in Peru or Colombia or to expect the situation in Mexico, particularly as it concerns the EPR, to be any different. Nor would it do much good to provide helicopters for anti-drug operations in a country weakened by revolutionary violence. Although the Mexican military is unlikely soon to discard its anti-American mentality and resistance to U.S. advice, it may—just may—be more open to such advice from countries like Peru and Colombia; the United States should, therefore, encourage and support such cooperation.

In the long term, the present trend of state-to-state cooperation (such as between Texas and Nuevo Leon or Arizona and Sonora) should, at least, solidify northern Mexico's economy and help to stabilize it; Washington should, therefore, encourage such interaction. Furthermore, the United States has to be very careful in its assessment of Mexico's political future. Although the PRI has committed many sins and will continue to do so in the future, its loss of control in the event of a PRD or PAN electoral victory should not necessarily be seen as a demonstration of democracy, but as the beginning of a period of chronic and probably violent instability. That would be particularly true if the PRD makes significant gains: Its visceral anti-Americanism, anticapitalism, and dubious democratic credentials could only threaten both bilateral ties and NAFTA. None of this suggests that the United States should interfere in Mexico's domestic affairs—a dangerous proposition to begin with—but that it end its many years of bipartisan failure on relations with Mexico. For now, Mexico is not moving toward democracy and prosperity, but toward instability and internal conflict, and that realization should be the basis of a new approach in U.S. policy toward its southern neighbor.

Notes

1.   Andres Oppenheimer, *Bordering on Chaos* (Boston: Little, Brown, 1996), pp. 45, 47.
2.   Ibid., p. 68
3.   See "Celebrar un *tratado de libre trabajo,* plantea el Episcopado a los dos mandatarios" ("Celebrate a *Free labor treaty,* proposes the Episcopate to the two presidents"), *La Jornada,* May 6, 1997.
4.   The Mexican North is defined as the states of Sinaloa, Baja California Sur and Norte, Sonora, Chihuahua, Coahuila, Nuevo Leon, and Tamaulipas, with all but the

first two bordering the United States. Baja California Sur is totally dependent on tourism, and many facilities are owned or controlled by U.S. interests.

5.   CONAPO figures quoted in Mexico City's *El Universal,* May 27, 1997.

6.   Zedillo's poll results demonstrated the steady erosion of PRI's control over elections: During the 1920s, General Alvaro Obregon won his election with 1,670,456 votes in favor and 0 (zero!) against; by 1988, Salinas won—and then only fraudulently—with 50 percent. See Oppenheimer, *Bordering on Chaos,* p. 180.

7.   Enrique Krauze, *Tiempo contado* (Mexico City: Editorial Oceano, 1996), p. 53.

8.   Not surprisingly, because their local militants in Guerrero are often interchangeable with those of the PRD, the EPR also has a high esteem for that party; a "Commander Antonio" of the EPR made it clear that his group's "main difference" with the PRD, which he described as "contributing to the democratization of the country" is that the latter limits its activities to electoral politics—thus implying that they have no substantive political differences. See *La Jornada,* June 1, 1997.

9.   See, for example, "Formal prision a otros 9 policias" ("Formal prison term to nine other policemen"), *Novedades Editores,* May 20, 1997

Michael Radu, 'The Looming Mexican Crisis,' *Washington Quarterly,* 20:4 (Autumn, 1997), pp. 117-127. ©1997 by the Center for Strategic and International Studies (CSIS and the Massachusetts Institute of Technology).

MEXICO'S ELECTIONS: A TRIUMPH FOR DEMOCRACY?

On Sunday, July 6, Mexico held its most important elections ever. At stake were all 500 seats in the Lower House of Congress, thirty-two of 128 seats in the Senate, six state governorships, the mayoralty of Mexico City (marking the first election for this position after years of presidential appointments), and thousands of state and local offices. The results were largely predicted by the Mexican pollsters, and their increasing accuracy indicates the nation's growing pluralism and freedom of expression. For the first time since its establishment in 1929, the longest-ruling party in the world, the Revolutionary Institutional Party (PRI), lost its majority in the Lower House. It needed 42 percent of the popular vote to gain an absolute majority, but it received only 39 percent, followed by the socialist Party of the Mexican Revolution (PRD) with 26 percent, and the conservative National Action Party (PAN) with 25 percent. Of the six state houses at stake, PRI lost two very important ones, both to PAN: Nuevo León, located on the Texas border, and considered the second most important industrial center in the country, and Querétaro, in central Mexico. On the other hand, PRI held on to the important border state of Sonora, as well as to Campeche, Colima, and San Luis Potosí. Nonetheless, PRI finished a poor second, and PAN an even poorer third, in the Mexico City race. Here PRD founder and leader Cuauhtémoc Cárdenas, a former PRI boss and governor of Michoacán, won with a landslide 50 percent of the vote.

According to most Mexican and international observers, the election was the fairest Mexico has ever had, and the game of interpreting the elections' impact has already reached gargantuan proportions, both in Mexico and around the world. Cárdenas, a two-time presidential loser (in 1988 and 1994) has been presented, by some, as a virtual shoe-in for the presidency in 2000. This may look as absurd as declaring the mayor of New York City an automatic front-runner in a U.S. presidential election, except for Cárdenas' national prominence and the city's disproportionate size (about 10 percent of the total population) and political role. Indeed, if there is any beneficiary of Mexico's wrong-headed economic policies during the past seven decades, it is the population of the capital. Add to that the huge number of students who are both attached to romantic notions of socialism and dependent upon the state for their largely parasitic existence as wards of the state, and Cardenas's victory seems preordained.

But how representative of the nation is Mexico City? Not very—as northerners of the PAN-controlled states of Baja California Norte, Chihuahua, Jalisco, Guanajuato, and now Nuevo León and Querétaro—would tell anyone ready to listen. These states make up 40 percent of Mexico's population and 60 percent of its economic base. What the elections illustrated is that Mexico is increasingly divided along economic, political, and party lines that coincide with regional fault lines. PRI remains the dominant party in most rural, depressed, and backward areas; the PRD is now legitimized as the party of the resentful poor and of the self-segregated Indians, the lower-class former beneficiaries of PRI's clientelism, mostly concentrated in the south and the capital; and PAN has strengthened its influence over the most modern, entrepreneurial, and usually northern regions, those that provide the tax base for PRI's clientelism and PRD's redistributionism. As for the two Marxist insurgent movements in Mexico, the Zapatistas in Chiapas and the Popular Revolutionary Army (EPR) in Guerrero, the latter was seen as the more radical, but it suspended activities prior to the elections, while the former succeeded in preventing the electoral process in the areas of Chiapas that it influenced. The Zapatistas prefer blackmail and the threat of violence to democratic balloting.

What next? In countries with a democratic tradition—and Mexico is not among them—there would normally arise a compromise between the congressional majority and the executive (what the French call "cohabitation"). That scenario will not work in Mexico, despite President Ernesto Zedillo's ostensible willingness to work toward compromise. The reason is that PRI, still the largest party, is by now little more than a collection of pressure groups. Some will align themselves with the PRD to push left. Some, including the technocrats around Zedillo, will establish an alliance with the PAN to push toward further economic opening. All in all, the only reason PRI was able to maintain a facade of unity during the past decade was its members' desire to be part of the controlling party—but that control was eliminated with Sunday's elections. The result is that the Mexican political system, as it has been known for half a century, is defunct. Party leaders, their clients, and various contesting groups, are, thus, operating in completely new and unfamiliar territory. If various coalitions cannot be stitched together, then Mexican politics will become incoherent, the government may be paralyzed, and chaos will result. Should that happen, this election will be remembered not for the triumph of democracy but for the victory of instability.

Reprinted with the permission of http://www.fpri.org, July 16, 1997

MEXICO: SLOUCHING TOWARD NORMALITY

For the foreseeable future, Mexico will perplex the United States, because what is going on there remains as opaque as ever to most Americans. This doesn't have to do with the North American Free Trade Agreement (NAFTA) alone, even though the complexities underlying that agreement are formidable. Unlike Canada, our other NAFTA partner, the differences go beyond arcane disputes over fishing rights and lumber. Over the next decade Mexico will present U.S. policymakers with a baffling array of rapidly changing political, cultural, economic, and social issues. These changes bear uncertain results for Mexico, which—because of a growing economy; a population of 93 million, plus millions of legal and illegal Mexicans living in the United States; 3,000 miles of common border; and the position as America's third largest trading partner—will have enormous implications, positive and negative, for its northern neighbor.

North of the Rio Grande, Mexico often appears to be America's inescapable poor relative, the unruly bad boy of the neighborhood. In Mexico on the other hand, the United States has historically been seen as the neighborhood bully and imperialist—to be wary of, albeit not feared anymore. Thus, when U.S. ambassador Jeffrey Davidow recently stated the obvious, that Mexico is, today, the Western Hemisphere's epicenter of drug mafias, the reaction, as filtered through a heated electoral campaign and its associated nationalist rhetoric promoted by the Left, was instant condemnation. The ambassador's statements provoked a self-righteous nationalist outcry from all Mexican political parties. There is nothing new in that, but this time the hullabaloo was far from convincing, and much attenuated from the response such a remark from such a source would have elicited in years past. As if to underscore Davidow's point, within days the Tijuana chief of police was murdered by drug traffickers. What is new and interesting in the past three years or so is that the response of Mexico's powerful cultural, social, and political elites to criticism of their country by outsiders, particularly in the giant El Norte, has become a matter of selective, rather than reflexive, indignation. This is a dramatic change.

Despite its admission to the elite club of the Organization for Economic Cooperation and Development (OECD) and membership in NAFTA, Mexico is a country starkly in transition: between quasi-socialist statism and free markets, between a de facto one-party systems and a multi-party democracy, between nationalism and globalism (in all its aspects, human rights included), and attempts to press all of the above to the advantage of party, ideological, and particular group interests. In economic and social terms, the transition is toward what is usually described by the catchall term used and abused in the political discourse of all candidates for presidency and Congress—*"neoliberalismo."* More than a coherent economic and political philosophy, this describes an attitude of acceptance of free markets and participation in the global economic system.

Just as important, the slow grind of demographics is inexorably obliterating memories of the bitter past. Nearly 50 percent of the population was born after Ronald Reagan became president of the United States. The epic struggles that went into the making of modern Mexico's identity—such as the nationalization of the oil industry in 1938—are little more than ancient history to the Nintendo generation. What makes today's Mexico different from the country Americans pretended to know just a decade ago is the simple, albeit understandable, fact that past *gringo* confusion over politics and economics south of the Rio Grande is now being shared by many Mexicans as well.

Mexico's Democracy: Progress and Paradox

Nothing encapsulates this new level of confusion more than the present political campaign, which culminates in the July 2, 2000, presidential and congressional elections. Mexico ceased to be a de facto one-party state after the 1988 presidential campaign, in the sense that the long-ruling (since 1929) Institutional Revolutionary Party (PRI) has actually had to go out and compete for votes, by hook or by crook, to stay in power. In 1988, the PRI had to cheat in order to prevent its defector, Cuauhtemoc Cardenas, from winning the presidency with his Marxist allies of the newly formed Revolutionary Democratic Party (PRD). In 1994 the PRI's accidental candidate, incumbent President Ernesto Zedillo (chosen after the assassination of the party's initial standard bearer), barely won a relative majority, and this primarily because the opposition divided between the PRD and the traditional conservative choice, the Party of National Action (PAN). In the 1997 congressional elections, the PRI, for the first time, lost its absolute majority in the lower house of Congress to the PAN, the PRD, and two minor parties. The PRI also lost the first-ever free election for mayor of Mexico City's 8 million inhabitants, to the PRD's Cardenas. Almost half of Mexicans since then have, at least temporarily, lived under opposition governments in major states such as Jalisco, Guanajuato, Sonora (since lost to the PRI), Chihuahua, Nuevo Leon, Baja California Norte, as well as Baja California Sur, Zacatecas, and Oaxaca. No serious observer can claim that Mexico is still fundamentally "undemocratic" or authoritarian in any meaningful sense—not that the facts have kept some malcontents from making such manipulative claims, as will be discussed shortly.

Many Mexicans are discovering that the problem with democracy is that the opposition, once in power at all levels other than the presidency, turned out to be no better than the PRI in fulfilling popular expectations, exorbitant as many of those may be. The PRD government in Mexico City, under Cardenas, produced a nonstop show of politically correct gimmicks (such as replacing corrupt male traffic policemen with women, only to discover that Mexican feminists' gender equality claims were right all along—policewomen turned out to be just as corrupt as their male counterparts). The government failed to reduce crime, improve housing, or do anything about pollution. And the long-serving PAN administrations in Baja California Norte, and Tijuana in particular, proved no better at controlling local drug trafficking (one of the region's economic mainstays) than the PRI at the federal level. There were a few exceptions, the most important being the Guanajuato PAN administration of Governor Vicente Fox Quesada. As governor, Fox was relatively successful and highly visible in addressing poverty, increasing foreign investment, and producing new employment opportunities.

Among the opposition groups, the PRD has been especially disappointing. The party's whole raison d'etre was its ostensible claim to offer an alternative to the PRI's corruption and clientelism. Yet the PRD's election for party chairman in 1999 was so tainted that it had to be held again; the fight over the selection of congressional candidates in 2000 has demonstrated the depth of factionalism within the party and the pervasiveness of clientelism; and the PRD has repeatedly (since 1994 publicly) supported groups or activities which are, and openly claim to be, antidemocratic (i.e., against "bourgeois democracy"), most notoriously the Marxist "Strike General Council" (CGH) of the National Autonomous University of Mexico (UNAM) and the continuing armed threat to Mexican democracy in Chiapas, in the shape of the Zapatista National Liberation Army (EZLN).

The UNAM was a hotbed of left-wing activism in the 1960s but had hitherto been relatively quiescent. Although committed Marxists make up less than 10 percent of the students (but more among faculty), their ideology has long dominated the curriculum, causing a steady decline in the university's prestige and credibility—a trend accelerated by the nine-month strike. This notwithstanding, the PRD, and Cardenas personally, went out of their way to show steadfast support and solidarity for the Marxist strikers. The PRD administration in Mexico City refused to act on the strikers' violence, looting, and vandalization of the university. This raised, for many Mexicans, legitimate doubts about the party's and candidate's commitment to real democracy, as distinguished from demagogic protests against all government attempts to maintain order. Not surprisingly, local and national PRD politicians also supported, and still seek to curry, the electoral favor of the EZLN, in Chiapas and nationally, despite that group's oft-declared goal of seeking a new national government that would reject, out of hand, the principles of capitalism, competition, and individual, as opposed to "collective, Indian" rights (as defined by the Zapatistas' non-Indian leadership). Historian Enrique Krauze's description of the PRD as a combination of PRI authoritarians and Communist totalitarians has been proven accurate indeed.[1]

The good news is that the PRD, its ideology, and its presidential candidate, Cardenas, are all losing steam. As Cardenas's credibility evaporates, his base of support is increasingly reduced to the numerically small (though socially influential) Mexican intelligentsia, some inefficient state employees, and peasant farmers afraid of free-market competition. He is currently stuck at 10 to 15 percent of the popular vote in all opinion polls.

As for PAN, its choice as a presidential candidate is Vicente Fox Quesada, the successful governor of Guanajuato. Fox is largely an opportunistic politician; his past participation in a conclave of the Hemispheric Left does not seem to bother those who see him as the new great hope of what passes as Mexican conservatism. His career includes a Harvard business degree and a stint as a former manager at Coca-Cola, but his campaign persona is that of a common-sense, straight-talking rancher. A man for all seasons, Fox has been able to obtain financial support from moneyed interests throughout Mexico and has a credible chance of winning the presidential elections. His recent standing in public opinion polls has held, or grown slowly, at close to 32 percent, compared to the PRI candidate, Francisco Labastida, steady at 42 percent, and Cardenas's rapid decline from a high of 16 percent.[2] Fox's problem is that, unlike previous PAN presidential candidates, he has no strong emotional support from his already weakly institutionalized party. This is partly explained by the fact that he made much of his career by running as a maverick within his own party; many old-time PAN loyalists would go further and say he made his career running against his own party. His repeated appeals to PRD sympathizers, while apparently successful, suggest a lack of serious ideological or programmatic goals beyond simply dislodging the PRI. Conversely, Cardenas' low standing in polls reflects the fact that a large part of the electorate—especially among PRD's traditional supporters—is also less interested in ideology or committed to a party than in kicking the PRI out of the Los Pinos Presidential Palace and see Fox as the best opposition choice.

Fox's trip to the United States in March 2000 suggests a dramatic change in Washington's attitudes toward Mexico. The trip was noteworthy in itself, but it was also the first instance in which Washington has treated a Mexican opposition leader as a possible future leader of its southern neighbor. But, as demonstrated in Fox's interview with PBS's *News Hour* on March 21, Fox is basing his campaign on many demagogic and unrealistic promises. Just as Labastida promises computers and English as a second language for all kids in a society with intolerably high illiteracy rates and poorly trained teachers, Fox promises better education while evading a position on the UNAM strikers' attempt to destroy the pinnacle of Mexico's public higher-education system. He also advocates revising the terms of NAFTA to include free population movements across the U.S.-Mexican border in a few years, along European Union lines, a utopian proposal guaranteed to raise hackles in the United States when the news travels across the border and into the U.S. Congress.

The interesting truth is that far from being the "dinosaur" among Mexico's three major political parties, the PRI alone has been able to systematically revamp its structures, its method of selecting its candidates, and its public image to reflect modern reality. Envious opponents lash out at this "Americanization" of Mexican politics, though not without attempting to emulate it with varying degrees of enthusiasm. Only the PRI organized, and held, transparent primary elections to select its presidential candidate. Those primaries had massive popular participation; were fair enough to have all contenders accept the results and declare their support for the winner, Francisco Labastida; and were later held, at least occasionally, to select candidates for a number of governorships.

By contrast, the PRD split over its election. Co-founder (and former PRI chairman) Porfirio Munoz Ledo is running on a separate ticket, while the party's usual ally, the Green Party, joined the PAN. The PAN seeks victory behind a traditional *caudillo* (leader) with indefinable opinions and a demagogic program, with a less than enthusiastic party behind him. None of these alternatives seriously offer "change" to the PRI. Even when opposition alliances won governorships in states like Zacatecas and Baja California Sur, they had to do so behind locally popular, independent, former PRI candidates.

As Mexico's political campaigns go into high gear for the July 2 elections, there are only two viable presidential candidates: Labastida and Fox. It would be premature to hail this as the consolidation of an incipient bipartisan system. More likely, it suggests that Mexico's political system, though far more open and fair than ever before in its history, is not yet completely modern or, indeed, rational. More than anything else, the fact that so many "natural" supporters of Cardenas are clearly prepared to vote for Fox—ostensibly his ideological opposite—indicates a vaguely defined itch for "change" rather than any clear understanding of what change really entails. All in all, the general trend is toward the weakening of all of Mexico's political parties, a disturbing long-term development,[3] but one common throughout Latin America, in Peru and Venezuela, Guatemala, Brazil, and Colombia. For better or for worse, in this sense, as in many others, Mexico's exceptionalism is being diluted.

As if Mexico's political situation were not muddy enough, it is further complicated by the large and expanding role of nongovernmental organizations (NGOs), particularly the dozens, if not hundreds, of the ubiquitous, self-proclaimed "human rights" groups. These are moving into the political vacuum opened by the decline of the parties, with the distinct difference that human rights NGOs are not subject to any form of legal, popular, or financial control, are responsible to no one (other than, perhaps, their U.S. and Western European financial backers), and are uniformly opposed to any federal, state, or local legal action against political minority groups or individuals. While this may be seen, from a politically correct perspective, as a positive development, the fact remains that some of Mexico's major problems—like ordinary crime, insurgency, and self-described violent "political protest" such as that at UNAM—are made all the more intractable by an absurdly expansive definition of "human rights" promoted by well-funded (mostly from abroad) private groups.

So politically potent is the collective voice of the "human rights" NGOs that the Mexican government is increasingly unable to enforce the rule of law over extensive areas of the country. Thus, it has long become a key demand of such NGOs, their associates among the PRD, and fringe elements of the Catholic Church, that the Mexican Army withdraw from EZLN-dominated areas of eastern Chiapas. Many claim that counterinsurgency operations against the Maoists of the ERP (*Ejercito Revolucionario del Pueblo*) or its splinter group, ERPI (*Ejercito Revolucionario del Pueblo Insurgente*), in Guerrero and Oaxaca are nothing short of "repression," thus, by definition, "violations of human rights." This cry is particularly shrill when the operations are successful. Likewise, the NGOs (and the PRD) raised a furor charging that the federal police's intervention at UNAM on February 6, 2000, and arrest of CGH leaders accused of looting, vandalism, and violence, was "repression," regardless of obvious facts, and a valid court warrant, allowing it. Largely due to the activities of domestic (and particularly international) NGOs, the Zapatistas have been able to reign over their dwindling Marxist ministate within a state in the eastern fringes of Chiapas—to the incalculable detriment of the respect for law and order nationally.[4]

The Clinton administration, just as its Republican predecessors, has long demonstrated that it is not particularly interested in judging, let alone condemning, Mexico. Yet even it has felt obliged to reinterpret a relatively simple and rare, successful Mexican military counterinsurgency operation (in Guererro, against the ERPI) as a questionable "human rights" matter—based on the fact that "human rights NGOs found it suspicious that. . .the military suffered no casualties."[5] As in so many other cases, the State Department's human rights professionals seem unaware of the fact that most of the "human rights" NGOs in Mexico are foreign-subsidized groups that reflexively condemn whatever the government does to limit or stop the breaking of the law by politically correct (or self-proclaimed "progressive") groups, individuals, or causes.

The most obvious, and obnoxious, indication of the weakening of Mexico's rule of law (never strong to begin with) and of PRI's grip over the country, crime and drug trafficking aside, is the very survival of the Zapatistas. The EZLN first engaged in military attacks against the government in Chiapas on January 1, 1994, in what Mexico's *intellectuel a la mode,* Carlos Fuentes, blessed as the "first post-modern insurgency."[6] Thousands of foreign "revolutionary tourists" flocked to "share the experience." When they were expelled for the simple reason that they were flouting the Mexican Constitution, which prohibits foreigners from being involved in domestic politics, the Mexican Left, including the PRD and its galaxy of fronts and fellow travelers among the "human rights" groups, vociferously protested the government action as a violation of freedom and repression. This pattern was repeated when the police took over the UNAM, sought to control crime in Mexico City, led a successful counterinsurgency in Guerrero, or in any way attempted to impose the rule of law. These, one may keep in mind, are the very same groups which protested Ambassador Davidow's factual observations as an insult to the pride, laws, and Constitution of Mexico.

The UNAM Strike and Its Impact

On April 20, 1999, a small and violent group of Marxist-Leninists, Maoists, Castroites, and similar groups decided to close down the world's largest university. This group was comprised largely of students, outside ideologues, professional agitators, and professors, united by their common sympathy for Ho Chi Minh and Che Guevara. The group defined itself as the General Strike Council (*Consejo General de la Huelga,* or CGH). The initial pretext involved a threatened increase of tuition from virtually nothing to as much as $120 per year! The rector immediately capitulated and made the tuition increase voluntary, sacrificing the very rational policy he had started with. This failed to work. The CGH was, by this time, going after a far larger game than UNAM's tuition (which, incidentally, swallows about $1 billion a year in government subsidies, much of it paid for by uneducated or privately educated Mexican taxpayers).

The university held a referendum, in which 80 percent of the students and faculty participated, to discuss the strike. Ninety percent voted against the strike. This outcome, however, did not faze the CCH revolutionaries. The imbroglio ended on February 6, 2000, with the Federal Preventive Police occupying the campus and expelling the Marxists. Not only did the PRD—at the local level as Mexico City authorities—refuse to enforce the law against UNAM's radicals, but it became an advocate of a blanket pardon of those involved—including vandals, hooligans, convicted drug dealers, and looters—all in the name of "human rights" and freedom of speech.

The outcome of the UNAM melee was the virtual destruction of an institution built by the government of Mexico in the 1920s; the loss of one year of study by 260,000 mostly lower-income students; and the additional unmasking of the highly dubious commitment to democracy of the PRD. Yet more disturbingly, the UNAM episode, like the Chiapas insurgency, demonstrated the profoundly reactionary, and antidemocratic, nature of the Mexican Left,

PRD included. On the other hand, it also demonstrated the weakness of Mexican institutions in general. After one year of a radical minority having hijacked the country's largest and proudest institution, the Mexico City government remains all but an accomplice, and the federal government is still struggling to bring the issue under control. Under such circumstances it is clearly unrealistic to expect Mexico—at state or national levels—to deal effectively with the far larger, richer, and, indeed, popular drug trafficking networks in Baja California Norte, Sinaloa, and Chihuahua.

Expanding a Divided Economy

Incredible as it may seem to most Americans, Mexican migration to the United States is driven less by an absolute lack of jobs in Mexico than by Mexico's shortage of educated and competent technical personnel—at least in most of the country. What is happening is the redundant export of uneducated labor from specific areas and social classes. This probably has as much to do with Mexico's dependency on U.S. economic cycles as with Mexico's regional differences regarding general development. Indeed, between 1994 and 1999 over 90 percent of all foreign investments in Mexico went to the capital and five states (Jalisco, Mexico, Nuevo Leon, Chihuahua, and Baja California Norte) while only 0.7 percent went to the southern states of Chiapas, Guerrero, Oaxaca, Campeche, Yucatan, and Quintana Roo.[7]

Not surprisingly, in Guadalajara, capital of the state of Jalisco, some local entrepreneurs are now asking for a suspension of outside (mostly foreign) investment, because their demand for local and national skilled labor competes with that of local companies and drives all wages higher.[8] In the border state of Nuevo Leon alone, 30,000 technical, skilled jobs are going unfilled, in a market where wages of technical personnel are 40 percent higher than the national average.[9] Simply put, the areas of the country most adapted, and adaptable, to private enterprise in general, and benefiting from NAFTA and market globalization especially, are experiencing labor shortages for the first time in Mexican history.

More generally, after receiving a $1.218 billion standby IMF loan, benefiting from dramatic increases in oil prices, and expressing worries about the general problem of foreign investments, Mexico's modern sector is clearly faced with an overheated economy. Rising oil prices have lifted the peso to 9.20 to the dollar, the highest level since 1998. The February 2000 trade deficit, at $320 million, was well below the expected $540 million, and the inflation trend is encouragingly downward, from 12.3 percent in 1999 to an expected 10 percent this year.[10]

This economic context is quite remarkable, considering Mexico's tradition of "the curse of the *Sexenio*," an economic downturn at the end of every six-year presidential term since 1982. This is the result of prudent economic management by the outgoing Zedillo administration. It also reflects the PRI's confidence in winning the coming elections, which makes massive public spending during the electoral campaign less necessary than in the recent past.

Not all of the economic news is positive, however. Sometimes it seems as if, NAFTA or not, everyone is still seeking government subsidies or tariffs on imports. A vast gulf persists between the increasingly competitive modern sector in the northern and central states, and the inefficient small and medium agricultural producers, particularly in the south. These differences have rock-hard political implications. Most Mexican small producers are unable to compete with their U.S. and Canadian counterparts, even, or especially, on staples such as beans or corn. They correctly blame NAFTA for their woes; likewise, the coffee sector, significant in places like Chiapas, suffers from low world prices and demands subsidies.

The oil industry, long seen as a symbol of Mexico's sovereignty, is doing well with the current high prices, but remains undercapitalized after years of austerity and skimping on new technology. Furthermore, considering Mexico's economic links with the United States, high oil prices may well backfire by slowing down economic growth north of the border and hurting Mexico's exports. Thus, although not a member of OPEC, Mexico did shadow the oil cartel's moves by reducing production last year by 325,000 barrels per day. This measure has been partially reversed recently, at some political cost for the government. [11]

Generally speaking, the Zedillo administration has followed a highly pragmatic and depoliticized approach to economic policy, which has put the country back on the steady growth track, and there is no reason to believe that a Fox administration would return to past habits of nationalism as a rationale for economic decisions. Campaign rhetoric aside, there are few substantive differences between Fox and Labastida on the fundamentals of Mexico's economic policy. Cardenas, to the contrary, tends to retain reactionary and primitive nationalist positions, the hallmark of these being his insistence on posturing as the sole defender of sovereignty as symbolized by the oil industry. After all it was his father, Lazaro Cardenas, who, as president, expropriated the oil companies in the 1930s in what was regarded as a landmark assertion of Mexican nationalism.[12] Yet even Cardenas has been forced to tone down some of his anti-NAFTA sentiment. After initially opposing the trade agreement, Cardenas now says that he only intends to renegotiate certain bits of it—a highly unlikely possibility.

Ultimately, neither Labastida nor Fox could forget that more than ever before, Mexico's economic destiny is linked to the United States. In 1998, 88 percent of Mexico's exports were directed to U.S. markets. Mexico's recent (March 23, 2000) free trade agreement with the European Union (EU), even if ultimately successful, will have only a marginal impact; both the United States and the EU will simply use Mexico as a conduit for bilateral trade without tariffs rather than as a bona fide trade partner. Small Mexican businesses and independent agricultural producers are left open to overwhelming competition from major European companies. Indeed, it is difficult to see how such Mexicans can compete, since they "do not have access to credit, to technology, and their management practices are not modernized" according to Pedro Xavier Gonzalez, chief economist of the independent Institute of Political Studies (IMEP).[13]

Misunderstanding Chiapas

Mexico's economy today—at the macroeconomic level and in the formal, large-scale sectors at least—is closer to the developed world than to the developing. The problem is that "macroeconomics" means little, if anything, to many Mexicans—a minority, to be sure, but one numerous enough for the intellectual class and political demagogues to manipulate effectively. When this minority, which is unable or unwilling to adapt, or take advantage of, Mexico's economic transformation, includes elements of racial grievance, the result is a heady brew that makes it all the more difficult to provide realistic structural solutions to the genuine problems of Mexico's poor.

The EZLN masquerade in Mexico's southern state of Chiapas is a case in point. It was made worse, and more politically relevant, than it should have been, by fashionable intellectuals whose sympathy for a utopian "revolution" runs far deeper than any real concern for the realistic future of Mexico's Indian population.[14] In this sense, the EZLN propaganda[15] is accurate. The insurgents, a minority within a minority in Mexico's poorest state, have long been able to manipulate the political parties, especially the PRD, to complicate Mexico's relations with Western Europe, and serve as little more than convenient tools for U.S. politicians and special interest groups which seek to denigrate Mexico and attack NAFTA.

The EZLN supporters are still manipulated by outsiders, such as the former bishop of San Cristobal de las Casas, Samuel Ruiz, a practitioner of liberation theology or, worse still, Marxist militants such as Rafael Sebastian Guillen Vicente (a.k.a., "subcomandante Marcos"), the white, middle-class, and highly educated leader of the EZLN. Nevertheless, the organization is increasingly marginalized and ignored by most Mexicans—although one would never know this, if one were merely to judge from the noise made by European and U.S. professional activists and assorted members of the fashionable Left. After negotiating fruitlessly with the insurgents for three years, the Zedillo administration finally devised a working strategy for dealing with them—a combination of military containment, reliance on local anti-Zapatista forces (a growing, though unruly, and occasionally criminal, element), increased subsidies to the region, and official public silence. Labastida has made it clear that he will pursue the same strategy. Fox pays lip service to negotiations, but is unlikely to concede the kind of semi-autonomous, socialist utopia that Marcos demands. Only Cardenas promises to give in to the insurgents' demands.

Crime, Drugs, and Human Rights: Beyond Wrongdoings

The chorus of Zapatistas, UNAM strikers, Mexican intellectuals, radical clergy, journalists and professional "human rights" activists, as well as United Nations (UN) European human rights militants, harps consistently on a single theme: Mexico's human rights record is abysmal, and repression, lawlessness, corruption, and official abuse of citizens' rights, are rife. Reality is far more complex. Mexico is in the irritating situation of a country whose government is too weak, or vacillating, to guarantee law and order throughout the national territory—but which, nonetheless, is accused of brutality and routine disregard for law. Hence the strange fact that the latest State Department Country Report on Human Rights Practices, although claiming that "the government generally respects many of the human rights of the citizens," devotes thirty of the thirty-one pages of its Internet version to human rights violations.[16] Mexico is, in fact, far more sensitive to outside human rights accusations than ever in its history. At the same time, it is subject to more domestic and international scrutiny than ever—a case of the Heisenberg principle as applied to social sciences—the more and the freer the scrutiny, the easier it becomes to find, or invent, practices to condemn. It makes little sense, however, to accuse the government of failing to prevent abuses in remote corners of Chiapas when it could not prevent the assassinations of the PRI's own presidential candidate and party chairman, both in 1994.

This is not to deny that Mexico has a grave and growing problem with law enforcement, particularly in the area of drug trafficking and production, and that the United States is acutely sensitive to this problem. The Mexican police, judiciary, and increasingly the military, are plagued by corruption—driven largely, though not exclusively, by drug traffickers. While the police force, despite regular efforts to reform it, is hopelessly inefficient, corrupt and brutal, the military's track record is mixed. Better intelligence and improved operations have allowed it to virtually destroy one of the three Marxist insurgencies in the country, the Guererro- and Oaxaca-based ERPI, but their involvement in drug control is having a growing negative impact on their institutional integrity and respect from the populace.

Mexicans hate being thought of as a drug haven—which often leads to denial of reality. In fact, the mayors of Ciudad Juarez and Tijuana have indignantly protested that naming narco-trafficking mafias after their cities is "insulting" and should cease—a hard case of denial if there ever was one. Indeed, as the State Department's 1999 report described it, "Mexico continues to be the principal transit route to the [United States] for up to 60 percent of South American cocaine sold in the [United States]."[17] Add to this the similar, perhaps higher, percentage of Colombian heroin transiting through Mexico, and the domination of the production and distribution of amphetamines by the cartel led by brothers Luis and Jesus Amezcua, and it becomes undeniable that Mexico is the source of the most pressing problem for drug control in the United States. NAFTA's liberalization of truck traffic from Mexico (limited as it is to date) has only facilitated this role.

Former prosecutors (some of them drug-tainted) are murdered in broad daylight in downtown Mexico City; the Tijuana police chief is assassinated; and Mexican Army patrols stationed across the U.S. border are suspected of trying to shoot U.S. border patrol officers for the $200,000 bounty Mexican narcos have set on their heads. Few criminals get caught, none of them the big shots from the drug mafias of Ciudad Juarez or Tijuana. The lone exception was the arrest in February 2000 of Jesus Labra Aviles, a major leader of the Arellano Felix cartel of Tijuana.

It is painfully apparent that Mexico's campaign against drug trafficking and production is not going well, despite a projected $450 million counter-narcotics budget for the year 2000.[18] This lack of success has a negative impact on attempts to deal with crime in general, as well as on respect for law and institutions. Nor are the politicians immune from the corruption associated with drug trafficking. Mario Villanueva, the ex-governor of Quintana Roo, is in hiding, accused of involvement with the drug cartels, and Fox routinely accuses Labastida, a former governor of Sinaloa, a state long dominated by drug production and trafficking, of similar involvement, though, so far, without proof.[19] Worse still, a growing number of Mexicans blame the United States for the problem.[20]

Neither the Clinton administration, nor most Mexicans—from Zedillo to Fox and down—see the yearly "certification" process as anything but an insulting charade. This despite the fact that for years Mexico has had scant success in controlling drug trafficking to the United States, and for just as many years successive administrations in Washington have "certified" Mexico in defiance of overwhelming evidence to the contrary. All this says more about the trouble with the certification process than about Mexico's below par performance on drug control. If Fox is elected that performance is likely to be poorer still: he opposes any physical presence by U.S. Drug Enforcement Agency (DEA) personnel within Mexico, but rather seeks some undefined association of drug producing and consuming states.

While the Clinton administration has repeatedly ignored Mexico's underperformance on drug control by certifying the country on the basis of official effort, rather than actual results, Republicans in the U.S. Congress have criticized the White House but proved unable, or unwilling, to offer an alternative. Indeed, decertification could mean a sudden revival of Mexican nationalism and the death of NAFTA, something that is not in the interest of Mexico or the United States. Additionally, neither party in Washington has been able to successfully address the other major bilateral issue—immigration.

With many skilled jobs in northern and central Mexico remaining unfilled, or filled by expatriates, and the continuous economic crisis in particular regions, one might have expected a decline in Mexican emigration to the United States, but this did not happen. What did happen, paradoxically, is that both "modern" Mexico and the United States are equally reluctant, or unable, to use redundant Mexican labor—mostly rural, often Indian, uneducated, and unskilled. On the other hand, the millions of legal and illegal Mexican immigrants to the United States are becoming a juicy target for Mexican politicians, hence the 1999 decision of Mexico's Congress to grant them property rights back home, growing support for the idea of granting them voting rights, and the increased activities of Mexican consulates in the United States on behalf of the real, and alleged, rights of Mexican citizens. It is not clear, however, whether the PRI regime's selective encouragement of this trend is a concession to nationalist opponents today or a serious policy for the future.

In the long-term, millions of Mexican immigrants, many of them illegal, encouraged and organized by the Mexican consulates, and allowed to vote in both U.S. and Mexican elections, would raise serious constitutional problems in both countries. The educational level of migrants is becoming steadily lower, a trend which applies both to those who leave Mexico to go north and to those who come to Mexico from elsewhere, chiefly Central America. Mexico reacts by further limiting and discouraging (none too delicately) the immigration or passage of thousands of Central American emigrants. It is hardly a secret that Mexico's treatment of these migrants is far more restrictive than the U.S. immigration policies it so often, and so bitterly, condemns. Ultimately, Mexico should understand that the United States has no moral, or other, obligation to accept redundant Mexican labor and that, at the very least, Mexico should help by cutting the transit flow of illegal migrants from third countries.

Understanding the New Reality

For the first time in its history, Mexico in 2000 has a real choice for president and the United States faces the real issue of dealing with an alternative party in power in Mexico City. The ruling PRI candidate, Labastida, and the opposition's Fox, are close enough in the polls to make the July elections' outcome hard to call. To its credit, the Clinton administration has recognized this reality and has treated Fox the same way it has traditionally treated opposition leaders in Western Europe—by officially welcoming him. Nevertheless, that did not prevent Fox from accusing Washington of "interference in Mexican affairs," while speaking from a pulpit at an official Washington event.

The Mexican government, and many in the opposition, have played down nationalism and claims of Mexican exceptionalism, further deepening a positive trend in bilateral relations. Gone are the days when Mexico felt that it has to define its identity by reflexively opposing Washington's policies in Latin

America. Indeed, recently the Mexican government opposed Venezuela's pro-Castro government attempt to give Cuba preferential oil prices, criticized Havana's human rights record, and has even had officials meet with Castro's opponents in Cuba and with anti-Castro exiles. Under the cautious, realistic, and genuinely courageous Zedillo administration, Mexico has taken huge, albeit discreet, steps toward a mature relationship with the United States, based on real economic and political interests rather than the traditional manipulation of nationalist emotions and demagoguery. If, as seems increasingly likely, Cardenas's attempt to go back to the past will fizzle at the polls on July 2, that trend will continue, to the mutual benefit of both countries, regardless of which of the leading candidates wins. That does not mean that a Fox victory would not introduce some new elements and uneasiness into bilateral relations. It does mean, however, that such a scenario will not result in a traumatic reassessment of those relations. As Mexico's political scene becomes more "normal," so do its relations with the United States—a development scarcely perceived, let alone understood, by most Americans and their representatives, but which should be appreciated and encouraged.

Notes

1.   Enrique Krauze, *Tiempo Contado* (Mexico: Editorial Oceano de Mexico, 1996), 56.
2.   Sam Dillon, "In Mexico's Election, the Race Is Real," *New York Times,* March 12, 2000.
3.   For a good analysis, see Jesus Silva-Herzog Marquez, *El antiguo regimen y la transicion en* Mexico (Mexico: Editorial Planeta, 1999), 93-110.
4.   For a devastating, well-documented analysis of "zapatismo" and its leader, Rafael Vicente Guillen (a.k.a. "Subcomandante Marcos"), as well as of the methods, ideology, foreign and domestic supporters, and ultimate impact on the further impoverishment of the very Maya Indians it claims to represent, see Bertrand de la Grange and Maite Rico, *Marcos. La genial impostura* (Mexico: Nuevo Siglo, 1997). The authors were both correspondents of socialist newspapers — France's *Le Monde* and Spain's *El Pais.*
5.   U.S. Department of State, *Country Reports on Human Rights Practices: Mexico,* February 25, 2000, <http//www.state.gov/www/global/human_rights? 1999_hrp_report/mexico.html>.
6.   Carlos Fuentes, "Chiapas: Latin America's First Post-Communist Rebellion," *New Perspectives Quarterly* 11, no. 2 (spring 1994).
7.   Victor Osorio, "Accentua TLC brecha entre ricos y pobres," *Reforma,* April 3, 2000
8.   Carlos Elizondo Mayer-Serra, "La demanda de empleo," *Reforma,* March 17, 2000.
9.   Ibid.
10.   Rodrigo Martinez, "Mexican Peso Reaches 19-Month-High Against Dollar," Reuters, Mexico City, March 24, 2000.
11.   Julia Preston, "Mexico to Raise Oil Output, but Tells U.S. Not to Be Pushy," *New York Times,* March 23, 2000. Ultimately, however, following OPEC's March decision to increase oil outputs, Mexico only increased its by 125,000 barrels per day — nowhere near the 1999 decrease.
12.   "Petroleo, Ejercito y education, pilares de la soberania: Cardenas," *La Jornada,* March 19, 2000.

13.   Adriana Barrera, "Free Trade with EU Won't Loosen Mexico-U.S. Ties," Reuters, Mexico City, March 23, 2000.
14.   Martinez, "Mexican Peso Reaches 19-Month-High Against Dollar."
15.   Ejercito Zapatista de Liberacion Nacional (EZLN) — the best of its many sites is <http://www.ezln.org/>.
16.   U.S. Department of State, *Country Reports on Human Rights Practices: Mexico.*
17.   Ibid.
18.   "Las accusaciones 'colombianizan' la batalla por la presidencia de Mexico," *El Nuevo Herald,* March 17, 2000
19.   Ibid.
20.   For a lucid analysis of the impact of drug trafficking on Mexico see Jorge Chabat, "La Guerra imposible," *Letras Libres* 2, no. 15 (March 2000): 56-58; see also the map of Mexican drug mafias and their U.S. connections at 48-51.

Michael Radu, "Mexico: Slouching toward Normality," *Washington Quartery*, 23:3 (Summer, 2000), pp. 41-56. ©2000 by the Center for Strategic and International Studies (CSIS and the Massachusetts Institute of Techology).

MEXICO'S ZAPATISTAS: ANOTHER FAILED REVOLUTION

For how long can the international Left sustain its ideological dinosaurs? On January 1, the Zapatista National Liberation Army (EZLN) in Mexico's southern state of Chiapas celebrated two dubious anniversaries: twenty years since its formation as an underground Marxist-Leninist guerrilla organization and ten years since it propelled itself onto the international scene—on the very day NAFTA became a reality—with an armed uprising in San Cristóbal de las Casas that left some 150 dead.

Flash back to 1994, when the EZLN was the darling of the Mexican and Western Left. Its blue-eyed, white-skinned, pipe-smoking leader, Sebastian Guillén Vicente (a.k.a. "Subcomandante Marcos") was the heartthrob of Mexican and "progressive" women from across the Atlantic realm. Leftist intellectuals like Carlos Fuentes, Pablo Gonzalez Casanova, John Berger, and Roger Burbach anointed the Zapatistas the first "postmodern insurgency"—whatever that means—and the likes of Oliver Stone and Danielle Mitterand made obligatory pilgrimages to the poor villages of Zapatista-controlled areas. In addition, European (and some American) human rights NGOs showered the Zapatistas with publicity and, equally important, money.

Today, even in Mexico's Leftist media, there are fewer and fewer mentions of the EZLN, whereas, just a few years ago, there was serious hope that the group was key to the survival and success of a socialist/indigenous territory within Mexico. Even Zapatista sympathizers admit that they now have the support of only 10 percent, or one-third (and rapidly decreasing) of Chiapas' Indian population—less than half of what it used to be. Moreover, Marcos' long-running logorrhea (he used to publish his quasi-political poetry rants on websites and even had a "children's book" published in Texas) seems to have slowed down markedly. After organizing an "intergalactic" assembly and a march to Ciudad de Mexico in 2001, Marcos has fallen into obsolescence in the West, in Mexico, and, most importantly, in Chiapas. Such are the difficulties of a virtual guerrilla trapped in the midst of rapid globalization.

Founded as the product of another reactionary Mexican (and Latin American) force—the radical Marxisant sector of the Catholic Church—the EZLN originally operated under the misleading label of "liberation theology." This was the very same movement (one which was repeatedly disavowed by John Paul II) that gave the Sandinistas their priestly ministers and made Brazil a haven of Catholic radicalism. In Chiapas, its promoter was Bishop Samuel Ruiz (since forcibly retired), whose search for revolutionary help led him to invite first Maoists and then Castroite intellectual organizers from the North to help create a Marxist Utopia in his bishopric. One of those outsiders was Guillén, a former Mexico City University professor of design, committed Marxist, and scion of a radical and well-connected Tampico family.

Guillén came to Chiapas and decided to start a Sandinista-type Marxist revolution among the local Tzotzil, Tzeltal, and Tolojobal Maya groups. He took over Ruiz' radicalized catechists and prepared for war, which he started in 1994, using the neglected Maya as cannon fodder. Prior to that, he tried, and failed, to obtain armed support from Cubans and Sandinistas, who knew that the ideological winds at the time were blowing away from radical Marxism. Nevertheless, the EZLN began its violent insurrection in 1994 as a typically Marxist one, and Marcos settled back into more fashionable discourse on "indigenous" collectivism. His education and public relations talents led to success on the Internet and in the media, and many of the orphans of the global Left—still reeling from the collapse of the Soviet bloc—were happy to support him.

Increasingly devoid of political support in Chiapas and credibility in Mexico, Marcos & Co. tried to organize their Utopia in isolated mountain villages. The result was predictable: rejecting, by force, any aid from Mexico City, the caracoles—groups of villages led by so-called "good government" councils—are now even worse off than they were before the progressives took over decades ago. In Oventic, a large Zapatista-controlled area, there are no doctors or teachers, which has led former supporters to migrate into government-controlled (and abundantly subsidized) areas. That leaves the "good government" councils with only the "brotherly" 10-percent tax they levy on all foreign-funded projects in the region, which pays for a Che Guevara cafeteria/cooperative, a Women for Dignity folk art store, and, of course, guns.

Meanwhile, as elsewhere in Latin America (Guatemala comes to mind), former Bishop Ruiz' efforts to introduce Marx into the Gospel led to the collapse of Catholicism and made Chiapas the first Mexican state with a neo-Protestant majority. Zapatista threats and pressures on non-radical Catholics only hastened that process. On December 8 for example, in the main Zapatista center of Altamirano, there was a demonstration of hundreds demanding a return to government control and the cessation of Zapatista "arrests, humiliations, and abuses."

Considering its previous record of relentless repression and successful eradication of guerrilla groups, the Mexican government, under the Revolutionary Institutional Party (PRI) that ruled until 2000, and the independent Fox government since, has acted subtly in Chiapas. In a word, it has decided to let the Zapatistas die a natural death. No open crackdown, but support for mass defections and paramilitary groups reacting to Zapatista repression, social and economic investments in Chiapas, and public silence. PRI is now regularly winning elections in Chiapas, Marcos is regularly ignored and, since his offer of support for the murderous ETA terrorist group in Spain (which was ridiculed by Spanish judge Garzón and rejected even by ETA), spiraling toward obscurity. Meanwhile, the victims of Marcos' attempts at Utopia are becoming poorer and poorer in Mexico's poorest state. Thus, the world's first "virtual insurgency" has ended where all things virtual do when confronted with real life: in an increasingly remote corner of our memory. And that is where it should remain.

Reprinted with the permission from http://www.frontpagemag.com,
Janurary 16, 2004

WHY DEMOCRACY IS DOOMED IN COLOMBIA

Colombia is a country on the verge of political collapse, a putative democracy where communist terrorists control a third of the municipalities and national territory; where high-ranking ministers regularly resign, or are fired, for blatant corruption; where congressional members of both chambers are routinely accused, and often convicted, of corruption; where the president is elected with the help of drug traffickers' money while his party's congressmen, who do the same, excuse him on the pretext that "he didn't know."

One of South America's largest and richest countries, a major producer of precious stones, gold, coffee, and oil, and possessed of one of the continent's most talented and entrepreneurial-minded people, Colombia is also the victim of a badly distorted political culture that is encouraged by Western European and American forces seeking to impress their own notions of perfect democracy upon the struggling state.

On the face of things Colombia's politics have been democratic for almost four decades, bolstered by regular and relatively free elections, occasional changes in government, civilian control over the military, and the existence of a free press. Yet for most of those years the two major parties, Liberals and Conservatives, have, in fact, perpetuated a formal arrangement whereby they rotate the presidency between them. While such an arrangement proved useful, and necessary, for ending the civil war between the parties in the 1950s, it became a recipe for corruption, and the marginalization, of other parties. In Colombia, as in most Latin American countries, the president holds extensive powers, often abused, and left unchecked, by a Congress usually controlled by the president's own party.

Indeed, the very existence of the Colombian state is in danger today as a discredited, thoroughly corrupt, and incompetent lame duck president (he has stated he will leave the country when his term expires next August), Ernesto Samper Pizano, oversees the collapse of the state. Samper has already agreed to "demilitarize," that is, withdraw the national military from a territory larger than the size of Luxembourg, in exchange for the freedom of seventy military personnel captured by the Revolutionary Armed Forces of Colombia (FARC), the country's largest guerrilla group. The president promises to do the same for a much larger region if FARC and the smaller, but nastier, Marxist terrorist group, the National Liberation Army (ELN), agree to talk "peace," and proposes to meet with FARC's old, dyed-in-the-wool leader Manuel Marulanda Velez, and the ELN's Manuel Perez, a turncoat Spaniard and ex-priest, in the Presidential Palacio de Narino to discuss the terms. To show his commitment to "peace," Samper fired Colombia's most competent, lucid, and efficient military leader, armed forces commander General Harold Bedoya Pizzaro, whom guerrilla forces accused of not respecting "human rights."

So while the Colombian military grows weaker under attacks by guerrilla forces, and withering criticism from Western "human rights" organizations, the president retreats, the FARC continues to advance territorially, the ELN destroys the country's oil infrastructure, and the Colombian Congress votes to equip its members with bullet proof vests. Indeed, such bullet proof wear, including vests, party gowns, tuxedos, and blue jeans, have become the new national fashion among the country's elites, small business owners, and middle-class professionals.

In a struggle to survive, Colombia must face the world's highest crime rate (eight times that of the United States), the planet's main drug trafficking network (in cocaine, heroin, and lately, marijuana), and the only Marxist-Leninist guerrilla groups to maintain an offensive stand since the collapse of world communism. To complicate matters, the three elements are intertwined, with the "noble idealists" of FARC/ELN self-interestedly involved in protecting the narcotraficantes and their laboratories. While FARC actively conspires in drug trafficking, ELN blackmails the oil companies to the tune of some $300 million a year, and both organizations do a big business in kidnapping, a major industry in Colombia, and in extorting "war taxes" from businesses in guerrilla-controlled regions. Such lucrative criminal activities enable the terrorists to pay, train, recruit, and equip their members better than the national police and military.

As law and order comes under siege from guerrillas, narcos, and out-of-control criminals, Colombians react peculiarly to the situation by clinging to the myth of "democracy at any price," and suffering Samper to remain in the Palacio de Narino instead of sending him to jail with his closest advisors and friends. With the national military underfunded, overextended, and largely forbidden to intervene, collective and regional self-preservation has forced Colombians to form paramilitary groups, including the Rural Vigilance Cooperatives (Convivir) and peasant self-defense organizations, sometimes with the covert support of the military.

In this respect, General Bedoya's firing, largely under pressure from FARC's political arm, the legal, and highly vocal, Communist Party of Colombia, may have backfired. The now retired Bedoya has become one of the most popular candidates for president and an outspoken supporter of law and order.

All current talk of "peace" in Colombia, whether from the discredited president, the leftist fellow-travelers of the guerrillas who are disguised as "human rights activists," or the "international community" of well-meaning but innocent, or socialist, West Europeans and Americans, is tantamount to capitulation by the state to the Marxist cum drug-trafficking FARC and ELN. The situation also evokes an eerie reminder of the situation in Nicaragua in 1979 wherein "human rights" and "democratic" activists supported the Marxist Sandinistas only to get an unpopular, violent, and anti-national regime that the people rejected at first opportunity.

The U.S. Senate, made none the wiser by past experience, has, unfortunately, passed the "Leahy Provision" accepted by the Clinton administration, which conditions the transfer of military equipment to Colombia on its being used exclusively for drug control operations and specifically prohibits the use of the equipment for counterinsurgency operations. This provision can only be described as the "guerrilla support" amendment since it is impossible to distinguish between the Marxist FARC/ELN and the drug industry on which the guerrillas thrive.

Colombia stands at a threshold in its history: it can continue on its rapid descent towards collapse in the name of a phony "democracy" that produces more Sampers, more chaos, more terrorism, more criminal infiltration of its institutions, and more advances by narco-Marxists, or—perhaps prompted by the election of Bedoya as president—endure a period of all-out anti-terrorist, anti-Marxist, anti-corruption war to save the state.

Argentina in 1976, Mexico today, and, perhaps most relevant, Peru in 1992, serve as examples of partial, and corrupt, pseudo-democracies in Latin America that opened the way for chaos and totalitarianism. They were all sacrificed, or only temporarily revived, at the cost of loud howls from distant, and misguided, "human rights" purists who persisted in their formal, and suicidal, notions of "democracy."

The end of the Cold War may be a reality in Eastern Europe, but its democratizing trend clearly missed Colombia where Marxists terrorists, made wealthy by cocaine and heroin trade, are closer than ever to gaining power. Colombia is too far-gone to afford the niceties of German, Swiss, or American democratic formalities. What it needs is not another "election" providing "democratic continuity" and further decline toward chaos, but a revolution. Revolution could come through a military coup—a distinct possibility—or a national decision to adopt emergency measures, á la the "Peruvian" solution. Either way, Colombian "democracy" as we know it is doomed, and deservedly.

Reprinted with the permission form http://www.fpri.org, November 1997

THE SUICIDE OF COLOMBIA

In most of the world, Marxism-Leninism has been discredited. But in Colombia, it seems that the two major communist organizations—the Revolutionary Armed Forces (FARC) and the National Liberation Army (ELN)—have won their three-decades-old war against Colombia's decaying democracy. Now, with the August 7 inauguration of President Andrés Pastrana, the insurgents are about to receive what amounts to the government's capitulation disguised as "peace negotiations:" an effective end to democracy in Colombia that the United States should by no means support.

To understand why Pastrana's offer of peace—supported by his predecessor, his opponent in the presidential election, and most elites and voters—amounts to potential national political suicide, consider the strong position currently enjoyed by the FARC and ELN:

  *   The insurgents control and administer almost half the national territory, including areas where there is no government presence to speak of; half the country's mayors support or obey the insurgents.

  *   The estimated 15,000 Marxists are better armed, equipped, and trained than the Colombian armed forces, and certainly better led. The result is that for more than two years, they have won major battles with the military in what now amounts to a conventional war. Guerrillas obtain tactical superiority at will in most areas outside major cities, and have heavily infiltrated the latter. Whereas the ideal ratio of counterinsurgency forces to guerrillas is 10:1, in Colombia it is close to parity.

  *   Insurgent fighters are better paid than the military or the police, a result of the communists' huge revenues (estimated at more than $700 million a year) from drug trafficking, kidnapping ransoms, and protection rackets imposed on oil companies, ranchers, and industrialists.

Pastrana's "peace" follows a trend of irresponsible decisions established by successive Colombian governments since 1982. For example, this would not be the first time that concessions to the insurgents have been made in the name of peace: a blatant example is the legal ban on police and armed forces draftees' participation in counterinsurgency operations. In addition, Bogotá has brought on the present situation by:

  a)   diverting increasingly scarce resources from counterinsurgency to anti-drug trafficking—as if the two could be separated;

  b)   allowing the "legal" face of armed totalitarians, particularly the Communist Party (whose military branch has been FARC) and its front, the Patriotic Union, effectively to subvert institutions, particularly the mushrooming "human rights" organizations;

  c)   not only limiting the use of the most effective instrument of counterinsurgency in a country as large as Colombia—an armed population organized for self-defense—but lately actually making the paramilitary and self-defense peasant anti-communist forces a target of government prosecution—exactly what the guerrillas and their "human rights" de facto allies have dreamed for years. In so doing, Colombia has disregarded the lessons of neighboring countries, particularly Peru, whose experience in the early 1990s paralleled Colombia's. Indeed, faced with national collapse in 1990, Peru mobilized and armed the people, with the result that Marxist terrorism was largely stamped out and drug production and trafficking were dramatically reduced.

Instead, Pastrana is now leading his nation to self-destruction, and, although he has a fresh electoral mandate, it is not clear that the Colombians would have voted for him had they known his definition of "peace." Consider that as he met the leadership of FARC—in their territory—he promised the following before the start of "peace negotiations":

* the withdrawal of all military and police from an area more than half the size of New England, thus recognizing the existence of Marxist "liberated areas" and condemning thousands of his citizens to life under unreconstructed Stalinism;

* a crackdown on the "paramilitary" enemies of the insurgents, the same forces that kept them out of crucial areas like the Middle Magdalena. This opens a third front (in addition to the drug traffickers and insurgents) for the demoralized, and undermanned, military and police, indirectly strengthening the hand of the Marxists;

* a likely change in current law to allow for exchanges of army and police personnel captured by the Marxists for imprisoned (and legally tried) terrorist leaders.

Most amazingly, these concessions were offered not amidst a peaceable atmosphere among the parties but during the guerrillas' largest offensive in years, described by the insurgents as a "send-off message" to the outgoing Samper government: one that resulted in some 200 military and police killed, a similar number wounded, and yet another 260 captured.

While the Colombians' right to capitulate to anti-democratic forces is theirs alone, there is no reason for their neighbors, or the United States, to support it. But these outside parties *will* feel the consequences. Both FARC and ELN operate in Ecuador, Panama, and Venezuela, mostly to support their kidnapping and drug operations. And FARC is, by now, probably the largest single collective drug lord in Colombia.

Not only should the United States refuse to support Pastrana's "peace" program, but it should make it clear that it is politically and morally wrong. Instead, Washington insists that (noncommunist) drug traffickers should remain the main target of Colombia's demoralized armed forces and police. Both the Clinton administration and the congressional Left still believe and act as if elimination of "human rights abuses" by, and only by, the military or the anti-communist self-defense groups are *the* essential precondition for any American aid to the Colombian armed forces. That, of course, plays right into the hands of the insurgents and their "legal" fronts and allies in Bogotá and Washington, and, in turn, encourages defeatism in Colombia.

That Colombia has ceased to be a real state, inasmuch as it has lost its legitimate monopoly over organized force and ability to protect its citizens, is now a fact; so is the reality that the majority of the Colombian citizenry and elites are unwilling to defend their freedom against a totalitarian assault. Neither of these facts, however, should be a reason for the United States to support capitulation in Bogotá, let alone to pay for its implementation. Though we may have to live with a narco-Marxist regime in Colombia, at least we should not, directly or otherwise, help it come to power.

The options facing the United States in Colombia today are few and bleak:

*   Recognize that the main, and most immediate, threat to Colombia's existence as a non-Marxist state is the insurgents rather than the remnants of the drug cartels, some of whom have been replaced by the narco-Marxists anyway.

*   Stop pretending that Colombia is a "democracy"; it is a collapsing state lacking any legitimate and effective institution, despite the rearguard efforts of isolated, but heroic, Colombians. While normal trade could continue for the time being, support for narcotics control should be linked to, conditioned on, and combined with counterinsurgency efforts, or alternatively stopped as a waste of money.

*   Recognize that the Colombians' decision to capitulate, as demonstrated by the election and early decisions of the incoming Pastrana administration, is a threat to the stability of neighboring countries and to the security of the United States. Hence, efforts should be made to help those countries contain the spread of instability from Colombia, through military and political support.

Reprinted with permission from http://www.fpri.org, September 3, 1998

AID TO COLOMBIA: A STUDY IN MUDDLED ARGUMENTS

A Clinton administration proposal for $1.57 billion in aid to Colombia now seems likely to win approval from the Congress. That the Republican leadership should agree with the White House on such an enormous foreign aid package is indeed remarkable. But this consensus masks a disturbing lack of clarity as to the goals of the aid program and the means to achieve them.

Arguments on both sides of the aid issue largely ignore the real danger facing Colombia: the Marxist-Leninist rebels who now control 40 percent of the country's territory. But under current conditions, even if Washington were to provide aid with the clear intention to deal with that danger, the money would be wasted on a weak and irresolute Colombian government unprepared to defend its own citizens.

The Argument in Washington

Administration and Republican congressional leaders claim that the major problem in Colombia is drug production and trafficking. The head of the White House's drug control office, Barry McCaffrey, stated that without U.S. aid, Colombia "is unlikely to experience the dramatic progress in the drug fight experienced by its Andean neighbors." That Colombia has failed to control drug production is obvious. According to the CIA, Colombian coca cultivation areas have increased from 126,000 acres in 1995 to over 300,000 acres in 1999. By contrast, in Peru coca cultivation decreased from 285,000 acres to 96,000, and in Bolivia from 120,000 to 54,000 during the same period.

Has no one in Washington thought to ask why the Colombian statistics are so discouraging? Obviously not, as McCaffrey himself repeatedly stated that the US aid is intended to support the Colombian Government's "Plan Colombia"—a vague "plan" that Bogotá itself has yet to define or approve.

Apparently content to remain oblivious to the larger currents of Colombia's problems, aid supporters strive to tackle the drug issue as though in a vacuum—and the result will be both predictable and tragic. For example, Rep. Benjamin Gilman, Chairman of the House International Relations Committee, thinks that most of the aid should go to the Colombian police. To be sure, the police force is an unusually corruption-free institution by Latin American standards, but one completely inadequate to deal with anything beyond the marginal effects of drug production. The police alone cannot even address the source of the drug problem: the not-so-innocent coca-producing peasants looking for a fast buck, and the Marxist-Leninist "protectors" who exploit them. Giving military aid—modern Black Hawk helicopters, in this case—to the Colombian police is akin to sending untrained neighborhood crime watchers to fend off Uzi-toting drug dealers. And it is guaranteed to produce more deaths than results.

To their credit, the minority in Washington opposing the Colombian aid package (a predictable coalition from the Left) have, at least, acknowledged that more is at stake in Colombia than drugs. Unfortunately, this insight does not make their arguments any more convincing.

Some, such as Rep. Janice Schalkowsky (D-IL), fall into the trap of believing that drugs are the real problem and object to the aid program because "treatment" is preferable to a "militaristic approach."

Most, however, have taken a broader view of Colombia's problems while rejecting the proposed remedy. Prominent in this camp are Democratic Senators Kennedy, Dodd, and Leahy, who consistently voted against U.S. support for Central American governments threatened by Marxist insurgencies during the 1980s. Advising them are experts such as Robert White, President Carter's envoy to Cuba and El Salvador, another long-standing opponent of any U.S. attempt to stem the tide of Marxist insurgency anywhere in the Americas.

Allied with these politicians, and in some cases advising them, are real, and alleged, "human rights" groups so obsessed with "respect" for human rights that any aid to the Colombian armed forces is unthinkable, despite Amnesty International's own estimate that the military is guilty of only 3 percent of all violations. And no matter that the leftist alternative is predictably worse. One suspects that among these human rights groups the most objectionable position would be to support Colombia's elected government. For they are notably quieter about the mass kidnappings, murders, and economic destruction perpetrated by the leftist rebels of the FARC (Revolutionary Armed Forces of Colombia) and ELN (National Liberation Army). This is, at best, a clear case of perfectionism encouraging totalitarianism, and it was made obvious by Human Rights Watch's recent publication of allegations (presented as "facts") of military and paramilitary collusion.

Human rights groups, and their congressional allies, also complain that the aid package does not provide for more government intervention against the Colombian paramilitaries. But clearly, it is the very weakness of the government of Colombia that led to the creation of the paramilitaries in the first place. Moreover, escalating the fight against those groups would, necessarily, increase the level of military activity in Colombia—and with it, the need for U.S. military aid.

Finally, the claim by aid opponents that "development," rather than force, is the way out of Colombia's predicament conveniently forgets that no development is possible under present circumstances. Bogota lacks control of over 40 percent of the national territory, and the insurgents are destroying roads, power lines, oil pipelines, and villages faster than any government could hope to replace them.

In short, the proponents of the aid package in Washington have failed altogether to confront the fundamental truth of the communist threat to Colombia's government. Opponents of aid, on the other hand, have acknowledged a struggle broader than the war on drugs, but discount the obvious, but unfashionable, significance of the war against totalitarian insurgents. Meanwhile, Colombia stumbles closer to chaos.

What is to be Done?

Colombia's predicament need not end so tragically, however. It is worth noting that Peru also confronted the dual problems of drugs and insurgents, and the government successfully dealt with both. The Shining Path established close ties with Peru's drug mafias, much as FARC and ELN are now doing in Colombia. Lima recognized that the Shining Path was the greater problem and—with almost no aid from the United States—defeated it. Once the insurgency was destroyed, the cocaine producers—deprived of the Shining Path's arms (and the funds used to purchase them)—were far more easily defeated.

Tackling the drug problem first—or at the same time—would have been impossible, just as it is in Colombia.

The example is instructive. Aid to Colombia, if it is to have any effect at all, must be directed against the FARC and ELN. This is not merely a drug control issue, it is a military and ideological one, and it is high time Washington be candid about that. The greatest problem Colombia faces is not the criminal trafficking of drugs, but the spread of the criminal ideology of Marxism-Leninism, from which, today, the drug problem arises.

That said, it is equally true (and clear from the Peruvian example) that no amount of U.S. aid to Colombia will matter unless Bogotá's ruling elites cure themselves of defeatism. At the moment, President Andres Pastrana and his advisers (particularly the "peace negotiator" Victor G. Ricardo) have either underestimated, or miss the point, regarding the real threat to their country's existence. Until their "peace at any cost" policies change, Washington can expect no success from its own efforts—and should provide no aid.

But Colombia is too important for Washington simply to walk away from. The ills of the "sick man" of Latin America are spilling over borders, threatening Panama, Ecuador, Peru, Venezuela, and Brazil. And Colombia is the main source of drugs on America's streets.

Therefore, rather than fighting Bogotá's losing wars with American funds—and lives—Washington must seek to change Colombian attitudes. It can do this, first, by declaring the absolute primacy of the war against the communists, rather than the war on drugs. Beyond that, Congress should make the passage of any aid package contingent upon the following changes in Colombia:

*   Reversal of the policy of surrendering territory to Marxists. Specifically, that implies a refusal to give away areas of the Bolivar state to the ELN (a capitulation opposed by the vast majority of residents there); and recovery of land already ceded to FARC, unless that group becomes serious about negotiating peace.

*   A public, strategic decision by the military to launch nationwide offensive operations against the communists. At the moment, the military is being undermined by politicians trying to "convince" hardline Stalinists to model themselves after Sweden. If Colombia has the money to sponsor a bizarre visit by the New York Stock Exchange Chairman to FARC-controlled land, and to take FARC terrorists to Western Europe to "learn" the nature of capitalism and democratic socialism, as it is doing now, it does not need, or deserve, US aid.

*   Cessation of the government policy of "understanding" the Stalinists' claims to legitimacy, or of talking to them on matters political and economic. To ensure the credibility of the new stance, the government's negotiator Victor Ricardo, who is currently escorting FARC personnel on their visit to Sweden, must be dismissed immediately.

    *   An increase in the Colombian military budget, reversing recent reductions. If Bogota refuses to fund its own defense, Washington should not pick up the slack.

All of these conditions should be included in any bill considered by Congress, or else it will be subsidizing a lost cause. To be sure, the resources of the United States could play a significant, positive role in Colombia's efforts to defend itself—but only when that country's leaders and elites commit themselves to the cause.

Washington should be clear about what its aid should accomplish. It needs to be equally clear about what it can never hope to accomplish on its own.

Reprinted with the permission from http://www.fpri.org, February 25, 2000

THE PERILOUS APPEASEMENT OF GUERRILLAS

The collapse of East European communism in 1989 and the dissolution of the Soviet Union two years later had an immediate impact on the fortunes of Marxist-Leninist revolutionary groups in Latin America. They lost not only their rear bases in Nicaragua (because of a regime change) and Cuba (because Castro abruptly lost the resources to promote revolution elsewhere), but their discredited ideological underpinnings as well. All this seemed to spell the end of Marxism-Leninism as a military threat in Latin America. Conservatives and liberals agreed that communism was dead. Hence the decisions of El Salvador's Farabundo Martí National Liberation Front (Frente Farabundo Martí de Liberación Nacional—FMLN) and Guatemala's National Revolutionary Unity (Unidad Revolucionaria Nacional Guatemalteca—URNG) in 1992 and 1996, respectively, to make their peace with the government and become "normal" political parties. Even earlier, the remnants of the Argentine Montoneros and the Uruguayan Tupamaros had made similar transitions, but only after they were already militarily defeated and saw legal acceptance as their only chance for survival. All of these groups participated in elections and, with one exception, fared poorly at the ballot box in 1999. The URNG was a poor third in the Guatemalan elections, the Tupamaros and assorted allies narrowly lost the Uruguayan presidential race, and Gladys Marín, the unreconstructed Stalinist candidate of the Chilean Communist Party, received 3 percent of the vote in that country's presidential contest. Only the main splinter faction of the FMLN has had some success: after losing two consecutive presidential elections, the party won the race for mayor of the capital and, in March 2000, a plurality in the Salvadoran legislature.

The Exceptions

Against this background of renounced violence and disavowed ideologies across Latin America, three countries appear anomalous. In Peru, Colombia, and Mexico, Marxist-Leninist organizations continued to thrive and wage deadly insurgent campaigns long after most others had disappeared or been defeated. Peru was, for years, plagued by the Communist Party of Peru (better known as Shining Path—Sendero Luminoso, henceforth Sendero) and the Tupac Amaru Revolutionary Movement (MRTA). Next door, Colombia continues to struggle with the Colombian Revolutionary Armed Forces (Fuerzas Armadas Revolucionarias de Colombia—Ejército del Pueblo, known as FARC), the National Liberation Army (Ejército de Liberación Nacional—ELN), and the Popular Liberation Army (Ejército Popular de Liberación—EPL). Mexico faces the Zapatista National Liberation Army (EZLN), the People's Revolutionary Army (EPR), and the Insurgent People's Revolutionary Army (ERPI).

Several preliminary observations can be made about these groups. First, Marxism-Leninism is far from dead in Latin America, regardless of its fate elsewhere, because the politics of the Latin American Left do not always mirror its West European and American counterparts. Secondly, the persistence, or public appearance, of insurgent groups cannot be explained by a country's lack of democratic political systems. Although opinions differ as to the real level of democracy, the three countries in question were at least as democratic as most of the other states in the region, which do not now face armed insurgencies. Indeed, some facts suggest that democratic practices coincided with, even if they did not facilitate, violence by groups seeking a totalitarian solution to social, economic, or political problems. Sendero's first violent action took place on May 17, 1980, in the Andean village of Chuschi, on the same day that electoral politics returned to Peru after a seventeen-year interruption. The EZLN made its first public appearance the day Mexico formally renounced economic nationalism by joining the North American Free Trade Agreement, and during the campaign for what was the most open, fair, and closely contested election in Mexican history.

The present analysis is limited to Colombia and Peru, two neighboring Andean countries that, at different times during the past two decades, faced similarly grave revolutionary challenges. Mexico is beyond the scope of this paper because the EZLN, EPR, and ERPI are not, and never were, serious military threats or nationwide movements.

The insurgents in Peru and Colombia share a similar ideology, the main enemy of which is democracy. Sendero consistently described leftists who participate in elections as "parliamentary cretins," and proudly admitted that the date of the Chuschi attack was selected because the organization wanted to "expose the whole 'return of democracy' as a patent fraud, a sham manipulated by the US."

That Peru won its war against Latin America's most vicious communist insurgency is indisputable. In addition to the Sendero threat, Lima also had to deal with the Castroites of the MRTA and a large drug production and trafficking network. Colombia, faced with a similar constellation of threats, has failed to defend itself and is now desperately seeking outside military and diplomatic help. The question immediately arises as to why Peru, with a shorter history of uninterrupted electoral politics than Colombia and a considerably smaller population, was successful in prosecuting its war, while Colombia is close to defeat. Perhaps the different outcomes can be traced, at least in part, to practical and cultural differences between the two countries. Specifically, two matters seem essential: different perceptions, among both the elite and the general population, of the nature and seriousness of the threat, and differing assumptions as to whether the population is hostile to, and, thus, could be mobilized to resist, Marxist rebels.

Resolve in Peru

In 1990, Peru was under siege. Enormous areas in the hinterland were devoid of any state presence, the police were consistently being routed in small-town skirmishes, and Sendero insurgents openly controlled neighborhoods in Lima. Many of the country's roads were cut, severely curtailing movement in provincial cities (particularly at night), and the economy was collapsing because of governmental incompetence and the damage inflicted by insurgents. Entire universities, such as San Cristóbal de Huamanga in Ayacucho and La Cantuta in Lima functioned as indoctrination and training camps for the rebels. Reputable analysts in the United States predicted imminent victory for Sendero. In light of the civil war's death toll of at least 25,000 since 1980, direct economic damages of $25 billion, and the regime's clear inability to cope with the challenge, such estimates seemed entirely realistic.

Prior to 1990, Peruvian political leaders failed to perceive the nature of the threat posed by the Communists. Between 1980 and the end of 1982, President Belaunde Terry and his government derided Sendero as "cattle rustlers" and "bandits"—a criminal problem, not a serious political danger.[1] The American Popular Revolutionary Alliance (APRA), a left-of-center party with ties to the MRTA, advocated dialogue with Sendero. Alan García of the APRA, Peru's president from 1985 to 1990, publicly expressed admiration for the Senderistas' commitment and willingness to sacrifice themselves, and his prime minister, Armando Villanueva, professed his belief in "convincing" the rebels to see the light of peace. The García administration appointed a peace commission in September 1985 that included Bishop Augusto Beuzeville, whose nephew, Edmundo Beuzeville Cox, was a known Sendero military leader in Puno.

By the end of the García regime, however, things started to change—not because the government reassessed the threat, but because the insurgent groups rejected APRA's peace offerings. The MRTA, after declaring a cease-fire upon García's election in 1985, reopened its war against the state a year later and assassinated a retired admiral and Peru's first defense minister. In 1986, Sendero embarrassed President García by staging a violent prison riot when APRA was hosting a Socialist International meeting. Sendero also murdered APRA leader Rodrigo Franco and made it clear that it had no interest in negotiations with "imperialist puppets" such as APRA (which was, in fact, one of the most anti-American governments in Peru this century). But despite this unquestionable hostility toward the government, when MRTA supreme leader Victor Polay was captured for the first time in 1989, he was visited by the prime minister (an old friend of his father) in prison. A year later, most MRTA leaders, Polay included, escaped from prison. Clearly, the APRA never understood the nature of the Marxist threat and never fought adequately against it.

With the arrival of President Alberto Fujimori in 1990, the fight against the Communists took a decisive turn. Civilian administration in most departments of the country was replaced with politico-military rule under army generals. The government in Lima abruptly stopped all talk of negotiations with Sendero and the MRTA. Both groups were treated as treasonous, tried in military courts before anonymous judges, afforded limited appeal opportunities, and given lengthy sentences in isolated and well-guarded prisons. Innumerable Sendero and MRTA members are now serving life terms. Members of front groups and other associates of the rebels, including a former member of the national legislature, were also tried and sentenced, and the military was given a free hand to deal with insurgency. Only a few, isolated negotiations took place: with the imprisoned Sendero leader Abimael Guzmán in 1993 (which improved his jail conditions in exchange for a call to remaining followers to lay down arms), with MRTA during the Japanese hostage crisis (which was cut short by military attack), and with one of the remaining Sendero factions in 1999 (in a failed attempt to obtain its surrender). What is important to note is that these instances did not constitute a policy to negotiate with armed rebels.

By 1992, the top leaders of both Sendero and the MRTA had been captured, and incidents of terrorism declined dramatically. In 1997, the last MRTA leader, Nestor Cerpa Cartolini, was killed by security forces after holding hostages for four months at the Japanese ambassador's residence in Lima. In June 1999, the last active Sendero founder, Oscar Alberto Ramirez Durand ("Comrade Feliciano") was captured, summarily tried, and jailed for life. By the beginning of 2000, the MRTA was defunct, and Sendero was confined to a few territorial pockets in the drug-producing areas in Alto Huallaga and jungle regions in Junín and Ayacucho. The Peruvian population, now freed of the fear of terrorism, has turned to other concerns—crime, inflation, and freedom of the press. Peru's Marxist-Leninist terrorism outlasted most of its regional counterparts, but is for all practical purposes finished.

Colombia on the Verge

The picture in Colombia could not make a sharper contrast. During 1999, according to the military, 2,465 persons were kidnapped—more than six per day—mostly attributable to the insurgents, for whom ransom is a major and growing source of income. A special thousand-member unit of FARC, based near Bogotá, specializes exclusively in the taking and keeping of hostages. The total number of Colombian military and police personnel held captive by Marxists reached a staggering 1,632. By comparison, the Colombian military claimed to have killed 1,019 guerrillas and captured 786, and to have confiscated nineteen tons of coca and fourteen tons of heroin. These accomplishments, however, ultimately amount to very little, given that the number of Marxist combatants in Colombia is estimated to be between 17,000 and 20,000, of which perhaps 15,000 belong to FARC, 5,000 to the ELN, and 500 to the EPL. The two larger groups control between them 40 to 60 percent of Colombia's territory and have sufficient strength to launch offensives against major military installations in even the largest cities.

The insurgents are far from united, however. While sharing a general ideology, the three major guerrilla groups are competitors, generally operate in different areas, and seldom cooperate militarily. ELN and FARC, despite their formal membership in the so-called Bolivarian National Coordination Board, are, at times, deadly enemies. In December 1999, five ELN commanders were shot by FARC in Antioquia, and the latter regularly tries to attract ELN's members and trespass upon the lands it controls.

By 1998, FARC and the Colombian security forces were waging quasi-conventional warfare, with some engagements involving thousands of combatants. The government forces, facing an enemy whose weaponry and communications are often superior, are losing ground and unable to turn the tide. The ratio of regular combat forces to insurgents is close to three to one, whereas the generally accepted minimum needed for a successful counterinsurgency campaign is ten to one. As a result, the guerrillas have achieved tactical superiority across a vast area. They are also rich. FARC was estimated to have taken in $350 million in 1998 alone—a sum comparable to any of Colombia's largest enterprises—from extortion, drug trafficking, cattle rustling, kidnapping, and bank robberies.

Tracing the Origins of Success and Defeat

In 2000, the difference between the fortunes of Peru and Colombia is striking. Peru is now enjoying the benefits of relative stability and increasing economic vigor, while Colombia is on the brink of collapse under the joint assault of Marxist guerrillas and drug traffickers. To be sure, the divergent outcomes cannot be reduced to any simple algorithm, but it is clear that the political and military decisions of the governments, the attitude of the population at large, and the tactical and strategic choices made by the insurgents are all significant factors.

There is no question that the Marxist insurgents in both countries enjoyed little popular support. Although opinion polls prior to the capture of Abimael

Guzmán in 1992 suggested some sympathy for Sendero's goals, and he has been rated among the most powerful Peruvian political figures, these data indicate Sendero's undeniable impact on the country rather than support for its goals and methods. In Colombia, FARC promised in 1985 to participate in elections under the banner of the Patriotic Union (UP), but the party's best electoral result was a paltry 4.5 percent for its presidential candidate in 1986. If impressions of popular support often indicate otherwise, that is because many academics and journalists have mistaken the guerrillas' military prowess for the backing of the population. It is precisely the matter of political skill, however, that is an important key to FARC's success and Sendero's failure. FARC generally succeeded in infiltrating the legitimate political scene by using legal allies, or fronts such as the Colombian Communist Party and the UP, adopting the language of human rights causes, and manipulating some domestic human rights groups (a tactic first used during the mid-1970s by Nicaragua's Marxists). FARC was, thus, assured of support among a segment of the (mostly rural) population. Similarly, the ELN has long influenced the leadership of some trade unions, particularly in the oil industry. To be sure, such tactics tend to give an exaggerated impression of the groups' actual political strength because the union leaders' politics are not representative of their members, and the links with insurgents are not openly admitted.

Rather than cultivating pockets of support, Sendero did the opposite, and this decision contributed substantially to its defeat. Abimael Guzmán miscalculated badly when he declared Peru's "legal" Marxist Left an enemy before he had won the military conflict against the government, instead of following Lenin's pattern of forming alliances with others on the Left first, and eliminating them later. The murders of prominent local leaders (e.g., Elena Moyano in Lima in 1992) deprived Sendero of important support it would have otherwise enjoyed. At the international level, instead of appealing to the sympathies of human rights groups, Sendero condemned notions dear to them. For example, Alfredo Crespo Bragayrac, leader of the Democratic Lawyers Association, a Sendero front, explicitly disavowed the concept of human rights as a goal: "[W]hat we assume is the defense of the rights of the people. We consider human rights as a bourgeois concept, and people's rights as those won by our people with its struggles, blood and dead. . . ." Through such expressions of contempt for widely accepted legal and moral categories, Sendero isolated itself abroad and at home. Its small support groups in Spain, Sweden, and California never ceased to attack every leftist group not openly dedicated to the form of Maoism known as "Pensamiento Gonzalo" (literally "Gonzalo Thought," after Guzmán's *nom de guerre*).

Sendero's error was especially damaging because the leftist parties held far more political power in Peru than did their counterparts in Colombia. Indeed, in the mid-1980s, the Marxist Alfonso Barrantes was elected mayor of Lima and in 1985 came close to victory in the presidential election against Alan García.

After long denying the existence of a Sendero problem (or, as during Barrantes's campaign, advocating negotiations), the Left only joined the state campaign against the guerrillas when it became the main target of their aggression. As a result, Sendero had no broad support in Peruvian civil society. Ultimately, this proved decisive because the resolve to fight terrorism was not forthcoming from the political establishment, which consistently underestimated the challenge confronting the state. But the Peruvian establishment and its mistakes were not so firmly entrenched that they could not be dislodged—which Fujimori, a newcomer to national politics, did in 1990. Sendero itself also pushed the middle classes from relative indifference to active hostility toward the rebels by means of a bombing campaign in the fashionable part of Lima in 1992.

Colombian politicians seem to have learned nothing from their neighbors to the south. Their insurgents benefited not only from alliances with legitimate political actors, but also from the defeatism of a conservative oligarchy that has failed to wage war decisively against them, and even lent them credibility on the national stage. Perhaps nothing encapsulates better one of the main reasons Colombia is losing its war than the following headline in the Bogotá daily *El Tiempo*: "FARC again uses cylinders against civilians: In Santander and Metá, civilians, among them two minors, were once again victims of FARC. Meanwhile, in San Vicente del Caguán, 'Tirofijo' met with the president of America Online." The American visitors—AOL's Jim Kimsey, and Joe Robert, the founder of a major real estate firm—"invited the guerrillas to their country and offered them support so that they could travel in safety." Such contacts are hardly unique: in 1999, the chairman of the New York Stock Exchange, Richard Grasso, and Congressman William Delahunt (D-Mass.) also visited FARC's headquarters. All of these meetings took place, with the *encouragement* of the government, in Bogotá. Indeed, Kimsey explicitly stated that, prior to his trip, he had contacted Victor G. Ricardo, President Andres Pastrana's confidant and high commissioner for peace. And in February 2000, the Pastrana administration underwrote and organized a trip to Western Europe by FARC leaders, ostensibly to have them learn what Grasso, Kimsey, and Robert failed to teach them: the virtues of "democratic capitalism." Instead, the FARC leaders were quite clear that they went abroad in order to reinforce their position.

If the Colombian government and numerous outsiders have failed to appreciate the danger posed by FARC, it is hardly surprising that the mainstream opposition (mostly the Liberal Party) has done no better. Daniel Samper Pizano, a prominent Colombian journalist, brother of former president Ernesto Samper, and a Liberal stalwart, had only criticism for President Pastrana's "Plan Colombia," the request for U.S. aid: "We all know it—Plan Colombia is a war proposal, intended to settle a problem that could only be truly corrected with economic, social, and peaceful solutions." He went on to suggest that the proposed $1.6 billion in U.S. assistance be distributed among the FARC and ELN guerrillas "in exchange for their laying down arms and dedicating themselves to peace, which would deactivate the paramilitaries." That, as it happens, is precisely FARC's propaganda theme: the insurgency is legitimated by economic and social problems and will not cease until those grievances are corrected. As Raúl Reyes, FARC's top negotiator, told an interviewer in Spain, "[P]eace will come when people cease to suffer of hunger, when they have jobs, when they are not killed, when they have guarantees to think differently, so that those who dissent are not assassinated or have to exile themselves." He did not mention that for forty years his organization has murdered its political opponents, intimidated and kidnapped journalists, and destroyed economic targets.

But the respectability conferred upon FARC by its international contacts, and de facto recognition by Bogotá, was hardly proof that the terrorists had turned over a new leaf. To the contrary, they admitted killing three Indian-rights activists in February 1999, and even "declared war on the United States." And if the visiting Americans sought to persuade FARC of the virtues of democracy, Reyes, for one, was unconvinced. In his interview in Spain, he made it clear that "we are revolutionaries, not electoralists," and that the guerrillas intend to dispute the power of the traditional parties "in the streets and plazas," not at the ballot box.

As for FARC's remedies to the ills plaguing Colombia, a hint was evident in FARC's demand, made in discussions with the government on economic policy, that half of the national budget be spent on social welfare—employment, housing, health, wages, education, and recreation. But details aside, the very fact that the elected president held talks with terrorists about such matters as the employment policies of his own administration is indicative of the degree to which Bogotá has given up any pretense of controlling the agenda.

At heart, a major part of the problem is that Pastrana, the rest of the establishment, and most of the media, underestimate the threat to their country. Pastrana managed to give an hour-long interview on American television without once mentioning the words "communism" or "Marxism," and made the same omission in an opinion piece in *El País*, probably the most widely read Spanish language newspaper in the world. Victor Ricardo, the government's peace negotiator, thinks "FARC are a peasant guerrilla movement."

His government and many elites also appear ambivalent about communism, as demonstrated by the reactions to the death in March 2000 of Gilberto Vieira White, the secretary general of the Colombian Communist Party between 1947 and 1990. In the early 1990s, Vieira stated, "I am a communist, will die a communist, and socialism is the future of the world," and reacted to the collapse of the European communism by saying, "I am re-reading my Marxist library to see where the error was." He admired Stalin, lived in Mao's China, and was instrumental in the formation of FARC, which he also controlled until the late 1970s. Pastrana's own government called him "the symbol for many who saw in him a talented statesman who fought to his last days for his political ideals, using democratic channels." Colombian media from across the political spectrum eulogized him as a "good citizen" and "gentleman," apparently over-looking his ties to a group threatening to overthrow the state.

Certainly, a strong current of defeatism—or, at the very least, an unwilling-ness to confront the real problem directly—runs through the Colombian elites as well. The case of Francisco Santos, a member of one of Colombia's wealthiest families and editor of *El Tiempo*, is instructive. He recently decided to leave the country, and in a moving address to his readers avoided any mention of the reason for his self-imposed exile. His newspaper, however, made it clear that a notorious FARC expert on kidnapping planned to murder him for organizing a peace march in 1999. Santos's own notion of peace included criticism of FARC atrocities, and his newspaper has been more critical of the government's capitulationist approach than most other Colombian media outlets.

The lack of resolve pervading the Colombian establishment became crystal clear in 1998, when FARC actually *supported* Pastrana's presidential campaign because he offered more concessions than his opponent. But his electoral vic-tory also suggests that the Colombian populace bears a heavy responsibility for thinking that peace could be reached by surrender, rather than struggle. In October 1999, millions of Colombians demonstrated in favor of peace, proving that they are ready to countenance defeat in order to see the war ended, no matter the cost. The Colombian elites and electorate have failed to realize that in this war, their country's democracy is under a deadly threat, and that the solution must be unambiguous victory, rather than surrender.

If the rebels' shrewd politics, support from within society for their move-ment, and defeatism among broad segments of the population, all played roles in the insurgents' success, Colombia's *coup de grâce* may have been delivered by Pastrana himself, for his first decision upon being elected in 1998 was a strategic blunder of gross proportions. He ordered the withdrawal of all police, troops, and even civilian administrators, from five counties in central Colom-bia—an area the size of El Salvador—in effect conceding it to FARC. This "demilitarized zone" was supposed to be a haven for insurgents during nego-tiations with the government. Instead, predictably, it became a state within a state, with its own police, courts, and administration. From this large and secure base, the guerrillas launched attacks in other regions and established new coca plantations.

Unsurprisingly, once the ELN perceived the advantages FARC enjoyed as a result of the demilitarized zone, it sought similar treatment—specifically, four counties in the south of the Bolivar department. That area, particularly the San Lucas mountains, had long been the ELN's logistical center and emotional stronghold. But there were important differences from the region abandoned to FARC. Whereas in the largest of its five counties, FARC already had some contro,l and considerable influence, even before the government relinquished it, the ELN had been expelled from San Lucas by the anticommunist paramilitaries of the United Self-Defense of Colombia (Autodefensas Unidas de Colombia—AUC) during fighting in 1998-1999. The AUC leader Carlos Castaño made it clear that, regardless of the government's decision, his organization would not allow the ELN to take over the area. Furthermore, local mayors, and the governor of the Bolivar, state all opposed demilitarization, and let Bogotá know it. The president's response was to accuse the governor of being an "enemy of peace."

Military effectiveness has been curtailed in other ways as well. In 1998, when General Harold Bedoya, commander of the armed forces, challenged the government's anemic approach to the rebels, he was dismissed. Additionally, the government has decided to destroy its landmines. In some contexts that may be a laudable decision, but when the ELN has been staging regular attacks against oil pipelines that security forces are patently incapable of protecting, it will lead to severe economic losses. Finally, by constitutional amendment (enacted after a deal with Marxist groups in the early 1990s), some 16,000 high school graduates are exempt from military service in counterinsurgency operations, thereby depriving the armed forces of much-needed strength. Instead, it is the FARC, ELN, and EPL—and the AUC fighting against them—that still show signs of strength and resolve.

The People Armed

It is certainly ironic, but the Marxists may have had a point after all. Ultimately, it will be "the people" who decide the outcome of wars such as those in Peru and Colombia, although that term may not encompass the revolutionaries who claim to fight in their name. Since the 1950s, the experiences of the Philippines, Malaya, Thailand, Guatemala, Oman, and Peru have demonstrated that governments invariably win when they have the courage and skill to mobilize their populations against guerrillas. Peru and Colombia provide vivid demonstrations of what happens when a government is prepared to do what it takes to win—or when it is not. After Fujimori's election in 1990, he armed the Peruvian population, and Peru won the war against Sendero. Bogotá went in the opposite direction. The government disarmed the population and made criminals of those who defended themselves, even as it welcomed terrorists to the negotiating table.

In the Peru of the early 1990s, huge swaths of the national territory were denied any government presence, let alone control. Terrorism was so pervasive in Lima itself that nobody felt safe—not leftists assassinated in their houses, not prominent military officials murdered by the MRTA, not the previously aloof middle classes who found that their apparently submissive maids were actually Senderistas with machine guns under their beds. The military was incapable of stopping Sendero's descent into the cities. In January 1990, General Howard Rodriguez, just returned from a quasi-dictatorial position as political and military leader in Ayacucho, rejected the very notion of arming civilians.

Yet only a few months later, following Fujimori's election, Rodriguez and his fellow generals began supporting village self-defense units—the *rondas campesinas*—which blended peasant self-defense, military training, and the limited provision of arms to civilians willing to resist Sendero pressures, atrocities, and forced recruitment. This strategy was based on long-extant groups. In the northern department of Cajamarca, peasant vigilantes (long known as *rondas*) had targeted cattle rustlers for decades. In the central jungle areas of Junín, and particularly in the Satipo province, native Ashaninka Indians, victimized first by the MRTA and then by Sendero, had also organized resistance movements on their own. Nor was Peru a unique case: peasants in Colombia, Mexico, and Guatemala organized themselves—in the absence of effective administration by the state—according to community rules and enforced their own "laws." To its credit, the Peruvian government recognized the advantage of arming, training, and maintaining military control over these peasants' natural self-interests. In 1991, the government decreed that each *ronda* had to be authorized by the Joint Command of the armed forces, and "operate under the control of the respective Military Commands." That policy did spark opposition, of course, from leftists whose interest was not in a government victory, Catholic prelates worried about even more bloodshed, conservative officers, and international human rights groups. But the government had only two choices—coopt the peasants, or lose the war against the rebels. By 1991, the self-defense groups served as a major obstacle to Sendero advances in the countryside. The Ashaninkas permanently eliminated MRTA's presence, and Cajamarca never became a favorable area for Sendero. But it was in Ayacucho, Guzmán's original staging point, that the *rondas* made the greatest difference. Traveling through that department at the beginning of 1999, I witnessed firsthand the high level of security, despite the almost total absence of the military. To be sure, some of the armed groups also took the opportunity to abuse their power. *Rondas* in the Apurimac Valley used their weapons, and legal status, not only to eliminate the terrorists' local presence, but also to engage in drug trafficking once Sendero was unable to impose its own "tax." On balance, however, their transgressions must be weighed against the progress made in defeating Sendero.

In contrast to Peru's relative success, Colombia, again, was a failure. The administration of César Gaviria Trujillo (1990-1994) legalized self-defense groups known as CONVIVIR, but the military never controlled, armed, or trained them at a level sufficient for them to become effective counterinsurgent forces. More importantly, they lacked the support of the political leadership. In 1999, the Pastrana administration allowed the legislature to dismantle the groups, which, in any case, had already grown weak and ineffective. As a result, the ranks of the AUC swelled as CONVIVIR members joined them.

While communist activity throughout most of the hinterland increased dramatically, the Colombian government's hostility to the population's right to self-defense, and its obvious inability to provide protection itself, led to a loss of state control over resistance to the insurgents. Innumerable rural Colombian communities, with no hope of even minimal government support, formed independent paramilitary organizations. The AUC emerged with a nationwide structure, strategy, and, yes, a web site. Carlos Castaño proved to be a talented political organizer and military strategist, and the AUC's membership—conservatively estimated to be between 5,000 and 7,000—became a potent counterinsurgent force. Instead of making use of the organization, however, the government in Bogotá, because of concerns about human rights violations, outlawed it, forcing the beleaguered military to open up another front to curtail it.

The AUC membership, to be sure, includes criminals, and some of the disparate groups filling its ranks pursue legitimate interests, while others have more unseemly agendas. Among them are local groups of peasants who reject FARC/ELN social and economic policies, cattlemen and rural business owners victimized by the costs of the war, and drug traffickers resentful of the guerrillas' "taxes" on their profits. Equally indisputable are crimes committed by the AUC, including drug trafficking that it has even admitted.[2] More serious are AUC massacres of innocent civilians suspected of being insurgent sympathizers or militants. The pattern is always the same: paramilitary members enter villages with lists of Marxist sympathizers, or recruiters, and they murder them. This tactic, however, is also used by FARC and ELN.

Contrary to the widely held position of human rights advocates, the AUC is not part of the problem, but a *result* of the state's failure to maintain law, order, and its own credibility. It should come as no surprise that some military commanders view the paramilitaries as allies—although they do so at peril of criminal prosecution—for the AUC does not seek to overthrow the government, eliminate democracy, or free markets, or make kidnapping an acceptable form of fundraising (as the ELN openly claims to have a right to do). The paramilitaries have also been effective in the field, having done more than the army to weaken the ELN and FARC in crucial regions of Bolivar and Cordoba states, the Middle Magdalena River valley, and the Panamanian border.

It is a paradoxical and even difficult truth, but Peru's experience shows that the legalization, and military control, of the *rondas* actually helped *reduce* human rights violations. Bogotá's policy of criminalizing the AUC, and dismantling the CONVIVIR, increased criminality while lowering the morale of the overextended state forces. Combating the paramilitaries when the guerrillas have yet to be defeated will, ultimately, benefit the enemies of the Colombian state.

Conclusions

On February 6, 1999, speaking at the Inter-American Defense College in Washington, Peruvian president Fujimori stated that Colombia's guerrillas, and their links to the narcotics trade, were a regional threat. He then undiplomatically offered his opinion on the peace negotiations in that country: "We can't imagine what kind of concessions a state could offer to obtain peace with those who want to destroy it." He was right, although his comments were bitterly criticized in Colombia. Fujimori's government, whatever its other sins, decided from the start to concentrate on defeating Marxist terrorism, and it was ruthless—but successful. Peru's victory, moreover, was achieved with minimal U.S. economic or military aid, but with the overwhelming support of the Peruvian population, as demonstrated by Fujimori's consistently high levels of approval in opinion polls and his landslide reelection in 1995. Only after the Marxist threat was eliminated could Peru address the problem of drug trafficking, whereupon it was able to reduce the area under coca cultivation by half. The political cost of Peru's success was the virtual destruction of its traditional party system, which proved unable to cope with the threat to the state.

In Colombia, by contrast, the political establishment has made concession after concession for almost two decades. It tried—and failed—to negotiate its way out of the civil war, and is now obliged to ask for massive outside military and financial aid. At the same time, it has also become the world's largest coca producer. Instead of learning from Peru's experience, the Colombian establishment seems bent on the destruction of the state. Rather than focusing on defeating the Marxist insurgencies that pose the greatest threat, it offers them further concessions, opens a new military front against the organizations that might, in the short-term, be useful allies, and pretends that the drug problem can somehow be separated from the rebellion. Worse still, these futile pirouettes receive the active support of the United States.

All this raises the question of what the United States could, or should, do regarding Colombia. A few issues are clear. For one, considering Colombia's dominant role in world production of cocaine and the export of heroin to the United States, domestic reasons alone would prevent a policy of neglect. Moreover, Colombia's dysfunctional institutions, and inability to protect its borders or its citizens, also suggest that neglect is out of the question. Its failure has already directly affected the security of Ecuador, Panama, and Venezuela. (Brazil and Peru are somewhat insulated from the turmoil by the largely impenetrable nature of their border areas.)

On the other hand, massive U.S. military aid to Colombia is unlikely to be effective so long as Bogotá's political elites lack the will and courage to pursue a policy leading to victory. Nor is aid to the police likely to produce results in the fight against drug production and trafficking when the government has lost control over so much territory. Economic aid to a country whose economy is severely harmed by insurgents is costly to taxpayers and holds no hope of success.

In the short-term, the United States could probably be most effective by providing military support to Colombia's neighbors in order to contain the war, and by sending helicopters, communications equipment, and intelligence to the Colombian military. More important—and less expensive—forms of aid are political. Above all, Washington must finally understand that the primary problems in Colombia are FARC and the ELN, and that no solution to the drug problem is possible while the insurgents operate at will. The lessons of Peru should be heeded.

First, Washington must cease to pressure Bogotá to give priority to narcotics control rather than counterinsurgency. Secondly, the United States (and especially Congress) should understand that unrealistic, and occasionally absurd, human rights demands are paralyzing the Colombian military. In the midst of a war for national survival, and absent a functioning justice system, that approach can only lead to defeat—and far worse abuses by victorious insurgents. A third, and related, point is that forcing the Colombian state to engage the paramilitaries in yet another war only helps the rebels. Washington should, instead, encourage Bogotá to reorganize, discipline, and strengthen those natural allies of the state in its ongoing civil war.

Ultimately, the best that Washington can do is to state unequivocally that U.S. aid cannot truly help Colombia until Colombians themselves abandon their futile "peace at all costs" approach.

Reprinted with the permission from http://www.fpri.org, Summer 2000

COLOMBIA: A TRIP REPORT

After a recent three-week trip to Colombia, Ecuador, and Peru, I returned as pessimistic, and confused, about the region's immediate future as ever. The most serious problem, at least in the short-term, remains Colombia, a dysfunctional country of dubious prospects. After numerous interviews with active and retired military leaders, businessmen, journalists, and politicians, I drew the following conclusions about Colombia's leadership, its dealings with Marxist rebels, and its relation to U.S. interests.

The good news is that the military, or at least the army, remains loyal to the constitution and obedient to their commander in chief, President Andres Pastrana. The bad news is that the words most often heard in private about Pastrana are "weak," "deluded," "stubborn," and "contemptible"— with the latter most often used.

Consider the case of when Pastrana requested a military report on the links between the major Marxist-Leninist insurgent group, the Revolutionary Armed Forces of Colombia (FARC), and drug trafficking. Upon receiving the report, Pastrana implicitly castigated the armed forces chief, Gen. Fernando Tapias, for writing it and for concluding the obvious: that the FARC are, as everyone knows, Colombia's major drug traffickers.

The April 22 capture of the top Brazilian (and, probably, South American) cocaine trafficker, Luiz Fernando da Costa, a.k.a. Fernandinho, dispelled all reasonable doubt about FARC's narco connections. Indeed, Fernandinho admitted that he paid FARC some $10 million a month for the cocaine they supplied. This news rightly upset Pastrana, since he has long claimed that FARC are not drug traffickers and that he would never talk to them if they were—which sets his increasingly controversial pursuit of negotiations with the group on its ear.

At the beginning of his presidential mandate in early 1999, Pastrana granted FARC a zona de despeje, or ZD (roughly translated as an area of withdrawal of government presence) the size of Switzerland, in exchange for peace negotiations. These negotiations never went beyond "talks about future talks," and the FARC's ZD became a cocaine-producing, totalitarian, fortified state-within-a-state, whose status has been renewed periodically by Pastrana ever since. Even in light of the ZD's failure, Pastrana wants to grant a similar area in the south of the Bolivar Department to the National Liberation Army (ELN), the smaller of the two Marxist-Leninist insurgencies operating in Colombia. The area, in this case, is smaller and is being granted with some additional, though dubious, guarantees, such as an "international observers' team" to include Cuba-ELN's creator and supporter.

Still, there are a number of problems here. First, the civilians in the area, who have experienced ELN's totalitarian atrocities for years, want nothing to do with it and are quite organized and vocal on the matter. Secondly, the ELN is a spent force. Its membership declined by half during the last four years, and it is militarily defeated in the south of Bolivar—not by the government, but by a nationwide paramilitary group, the United Self-Defense Forces of Colombia (AUC). Giving the ELN an area of control now is tantamount to reviving a communist force on the brink of terminal defeat— but something two previous Colombian presidents also did in the 1970s and 1980s.

Apparently, that is precisely what Pastrana seeks: the rescue of ELN in order to "negotiate" with it. If the idea seems absurd, that's because it is. And, it should be pointed out, it is an absurdity paid for — at least in terms of promises, if not in cash deliveries—by ELN's European Union supporters. Basic common sense would suggest that the army should be unleashed to finish off the ELN, and then concentrate on the main enemy, FARC. It is this observation that, more than anything else, explains the military officer corps' disdain for their civilian commander in chief.

The solution to Colombian political violence is as obvious as it is untenable— arm the civilian population, which is sick and tired of the systematic atrocities, theft, and totalitarian rule of FARC and ELN. But the Colombian political class simply hates civilian participation in the war more than they hate the communists of FARC and ELN. Ordinary Colombians, however, not to mention landowners, businessmen, and ranchers in the conflict area, feel differently. They openly support the AUC. In fact, opinion polls suggest that AUC leader Carlos Castano has at least twice the approval of FARC supreme Manuel Marulanda.

Let us be clear: Carlos Castano is no angel— but then there are no angels in civil wars. He admits to taking drug money to compete with the FARC and ELN; he admits to killing "civilians"—that is, un-uniformed recruiters, suppliers, and supporters of the guerrillas; and he underestimates the number of innocent civilian victims of his forces, of which there are many. On the other hand, Castano is no enemy of the state. He does not seek a totalitarian Colombia, nor does he fight against state army or police—a great difference from FARC/ELN. Nor is AUC an enemy of the United States. Indeed, while the organization has this year been included in the State Department's list of terrorist organizations, it was included among "other terrorist groups"—that is, groups which do not attack U.S. citizens or interests— again, in sharp contrast to FARC/ELN.

AUC forces clearly have better tactical intelligence than the military, as many of their members are former guerrillas themselves, and operate without the shackles imposed by Colombia's human rights groups. Add to this the fact that many of AUC's members are former soldiers, and the difficulty of any officer's ordering an assault on AUC in his area becomes clear. What is also clear is that the AUC, and not the Colombian armed forces, is the main reason that ELN is on the ropes militarily. Therefore, for Pastrana to declare war on AUC in the name of human rights is tactically wrong, morally irresponsible, and strategically misguided. He does so to the dismay of his own military, and at a cost of exacerbating the splits within Colombia's political elite.

It is time for the United States to see Andres Pastrana as most Colombians do: a disastrous failure and, more relevant, a lame duck. To express support repeatedly for such a failure does nothing for American credibility in Colombia, and less for U.S. interests in the long run. If anything, Pastrana is a perfect example of what is wrong with the Colombian political culture at both the elite and popular levels: stubbornness, a lack of realism, belief in corruption as a solution to all problems, and a lack of common sense, all combined with an extraordinary tolerance of violence. The issue should be less what the United States could do for Bogotá than what Bogotá is prepared to do for itself and for Colombia. Pastrana and his increasingly small circle of defeatists send all the wrong signals—and Washington should put more distance between U.S. interests and them.

Reprinted with the permission from http://www.fpri.org, June 1, 2001

Colombia: Lucidity at Last

On February 20, President Andres Pastrana of Colombia, whose term ends in August, finally realized he had no chance of achieving peace with the Colom-

bian Armed Revolutionary Forces (FARC) and garnering the Nobel Peace Prize
he seems to have coveted. Giving in to reality and common sense after thirty-
seven months of assiduous work on the "peace process" with the communist
insurgents, he formally declared an end to the peace discussions that have been
the centerpiece of his presidency.

The immediate result was the abolition of the 42,000-square-kilometer demilitarized zone (the size of Switzerland) he granted FARC in 1998. Pastrana
purportedly decided to abolish the zone in response to FARC's hijacking of an
airliner, and the kidnapping of a senior Colombian senator aboard it, earlier
that week. Few in Colombia, or elsewhere, accept this explanation, since throughout Pastrana's presidency FARC has engaged in kidnappings, hijackings, recruiting, coca cultivation and cocaine trafficking, and imposed "Stalinist-style
people's law" in the demilitarized zone, without serious reaction from the "peace
president."

However, it would be unfair to blame Pastrana alone, or even primarily, for
the failure of the peace process. Considering Colombia's dependence on foreign support—military, political and economic—outsiders must share some of
the blame.

Sponsors of Failure

To begin with, the European Union has consistently conditioned any mea-
ger economic aid it might give Colombia on the continuation of the "peace
process," a behavior consistent with its insistence on a failed peace process in
the Middle East and its present opposition to any military action against Iraq.

Others also contributed to keeping Pastrana on the "peace course." These
included Lutheran churches in Germany, which sponsored and financed similar
and equally fruitless "talks" with FARC's little Marxist brother, the National
Liberation Army (ELN). The European Union also implicitly recognized FARC
as a legitimate political actor by granting its representatives quasi-diplomatic
status while restricting legitimate Colombian military responses to the insurgency by invoking human rights.

Human rights NGOs are also responsible for the bloody course of events,
most notably Amnesty International and Human Rights Watch, not to mention
openly leftist groups such as the Washington Office on Latin America (WOLA)
and their supporters or elected spokesmen in the U.S. Congress, such as Sen.
Patrick J. Leahy (D-Vt.), all of whom weakened the Colombian government's
ability to establish its authority throughout the national territory.

The pretext used by the rich international NGOs, their Colombian branches
and local satellites—Colombia has almost half of Latin America's "human
rights" NGOs, most funded externally and by some FARC fronts—was the activities of Colombian anti-Marxist vigilante groups, now organized, centralized, rapidly growing, and led by the Colombian United Self-Defense Forces

(AUC). AUC does, indeed, depend on drug trafficking (as well as voluntary support from FARC's victims), but less so than FARC; they engage in the killing of "civilians"—usually (but clearly not always) the "civilian" FARC/ELN militants (the classic "peasant by day, guerrilla by night" types). What is different is that the AUC, though using unorthodox guerrilla-type tactics and unsavory funding sources, have never engaged in any form of attack, or even rhetoric, against the United States (or other foreign) interests, citizens or companies.

On the other hand, the almost total destruction of the pro-Castro ELN is due far more to the AUC than to the Colombian armed forces. The AUC see themselves as (and act like) allies of the state. Hence they are not involved in attacks against the military or police. While certainly often criminal in their behavior, they do not seek to overthrow the democracy or capitalism in Colombia. The AUC problem grows out of state weakness, and the resulting citizen demands to take law into their own hands in self-defense.

By contrast, the main target of the NGO-EU-Leahy axis, however good their intentions may be, was always the AUC and the Colombian armed forces and police, rather than the far more deadly Stalinist project of the FARC/ELN. As a result, for years the U.S. Congress, the EU, and associated NGOs, have worked together effectively to force the Colombian government to open a third, tactically unnecessary, and, indeed, self-defeating, front—against the AUC—at a time when the Colombian military was obviously unable to cope with the main enemy: the Stalinist totalitarian FARC/ELN threat.

Which brings us to the role and responsibility of the United States—both its executive and the legislative branches. For almost a decade, and certainly since the 1990s, the lingering legacy of Vietnam and Central America, as well as sympathy for the Left on the part of influential members of Congress, made Congress leery of supporting effective military aid to Colombia, out of fear of another counterinsurgency, another hopeless imbroglio. On the other hand, no one in U.S. government could deny Colombia's role as the main provider of cocaine and heroin to the United States.

The solution was to formally separate the "war on drugs" approach from the anticommunist (after all, is communism not supposed to be dead?), counterinsurgency reality. Hence, the Clinton and Bush administrations, with Congressional support, both represented their aid to Colombia as counternarcotics efforts rather than as attempts to address the more threatening, and closely related, insurgency problem. Hence the tragicomic decision by the Bush administration (and the Clinton administration before it) to make a deal with the Congressional (and Democratic) Left, whereby the U.S. will help Colombians fight drug production and trafficking, but it must remain only an open secret that such aid is actually intended to fight the communist protectors, sellers, and beneficiaries of that production and trafficking. Hence, the U.S. could sell, or give, helicopters to Colombia under Clinton's $1.2 billion Plan Colombia (which Bush recast as the Andean Initiative), but only if Colombia somehow distinguished between "real" narcos and FARC's Stalinists in using it. No counterterrorism, please! On September 10, Secretary of State Colin Powell designated the AUC a "foreign terrorist organization," putting it officially in the same category as the FARC and ELN whose continued existence—under a government hamstrung from taking strong action against them—had led to the formation of the AUC, to defend against the FARC and ELN.

Presidents Clinton and Bush both made the mistake of confusing matters, such as the already vague definition of "international terrorism" the U.S. is at war with, in order to obtain help from the Congressional Left, only further confusing the situation for Pastrana.

The Impact of September 11

September 11 helped Pastrana see the light, as indeed it similarly helped President Bush, but Washington deserves only secondary credit: the Colombian people also finally realized that "peace" at any price—the slogan of most of their elites, NGOs and outside helpers—is suicidal. The proof of this is the polling trajectory of the presidential candidates for the May 26 elections.

The year-long frontrunner, Horacio Serpa, boss of the Liberal Party machine and a strong advocate of Pastrana's "peace at any price" approach toward FARC, went from leading in the polls in January, to running nineteen points behind at the beginning of February, to less than 30 percent support at the end of that month. He is now unlikely to even make it to the second round, if one is required, of the presidential election.

Noemi Sanin, a nice successor to Pastrana's conservative candidacy, is sliding into oblivion. Ingrid Betancourt, a rebel scion of one of Colombia's aristocratic families, founder of the Oxygen-Green Party, and favorite of the American and European Left, had only 0.6 percent support before she was kidnapped by FARC this past weekend at a roadblock on the way to the demilitarized zone (a trip that was either motivated by solidarity with townspeople, as her supporters claim, or irresponsible, as government and military officials who had warned Betancourt against the trip assert; see "Colombian Candidate Noted for Flair," *New York Times*, Feb. 25, 2002).

So far, the winner would be Alvaro Uribe Velez, a dissident former Liberal governor of Antioquia, Colombia's most populous province, who, virtually alone and for months, declared Pastrana's policy morally and politically bankrupt, and advocated firmness, law and order, international military and security help, and the arming of civilians against the Stalinist Left. From being irrelevant in 2001, Uribe went to 39 percent support in the polls in January and is now at 53 percent. If this support holds, it will eliminate the need for a second round. Uribe's popularity seems to indicate that the Colombian people have finally recognized the nature and the goals of the FARC.

Changing the Campaign

The Bush administration, to its credit, took advantage of Pastrana's "decision" to discard the pretension of separation between counternarcotics and counterinsurgency U.S. aid and is now supporting aid to Colombia against terrorism. One could only hope that democrats in Congress, especially in the Senate, will agree. That the FARC/ELN terrorists happen to be Marxist-Leninist, involved in drug trafficking, and internationally connected (with the Irish Republican Army, Chilean Marxist terrorists, and the Spanish ETA Marxist separatists) is no accident: it is natural, and it is why they should naturally be a target in America's war on terror.

Hence, all the previous artificial requirements that U.S. aid to Colombian military units be restricted to counternarcotics operations should be removed. Indeed, all notions that U.S. help to Colombia's law-and-order organizations should be conditioned according to standards set by Sen. Leahy, and assorted human rights NGOs, should be rejected in the name of the higher goal of defeating international terrorism wherever it is. Sen. Leahy expressed concern in his February 4 reaction statement on the president's proposed FY2003 budget, which increases aid to Colombia, that "For the first time, the administration is proposing to cross the line from counternarcotics to counterinsurgency. Now, as a matter of our national policy, this is no longer about stopping drugs but about fighting the guerrillas." One might add "And it's about time."

Fortunately, Pastrana's term in office is virtually over, and hence Washington would gain little from commenting on his actions. Nor does sending U.S. troops to Colombia even need to be considered. Colombians themselves, if properly supported, armed, and politically protected from the European Left and the associated NGOs, can, and should, be able to defeat the FARC/ELN themselves. That, ultimately, is the best contribution Colombia could offer to the war on terrorism.

Reprinted with the permission from http://www.fpri.org, March 1, 2002

COLOMBIA'S STRUGGLE AND ITS ENEMIES

This past May, Alvaro Uribe Velez was elected president of Colombia in the first round, with an overwhelming mandate to deal with the country's main problem: the Leninist insurgencies of the Revolutionary Armed Forces of Colombia (FARC) and the Castroite Army of National Liberation (ELN). Uribe (a lapsed Liberal) received 51 percent of the vote in a crowded field, despite being an independent, rather than a Liberal or Conservative, the traditional parties that have controlled Colombian politics since the nineteenth century. His support, as this author witnessed at the time of the elections, crossed all lines—economic, class, and political. There was good reason for this: Colombians were tired of the violence that made their country the world champion of kidnapping and murder, and realized that appeasement of the communists—the failed policy of President Andres Pastrana (1998-2002)—only increased the violence and led to the country's descent into chaos.

By contrast, Uribe was clear and decisive in his electoral program, advocating a hard-line approach to FARC, which, with some 17,000 combatants, is the deadliest threat to Colombia's existence as anything resembling a democratic country. Uribe's position was made credible by his being the only major politician who had criticized Pastrana's naiveté and appeasement policy from the start.

After taking office on August 7, Uribe did exactly what he promised to do as a candidate: he announced the formation of a million-strong system of citizen collaborators with the government against the guerrillas, a dramatic increase in defense spending, to be paid for by levying a special tax on the rich, and, in the medium-term, the formation of armed citizen groups controlled by the military to combat leftist terrorism.

Surprisingly to many, including this author, who has consistently criticized the Colombians' general reluctance to join in the struggle against Marxist terrorism and their toleration of Pastrana's suicidal "peace" policy, the large and competent business community not only supported Uribe politically, but accepted, without complaint, the one-time, 2 percent defense tax on the "rich" (defined as all those with income or assets of over $60,000).

One result was that the cooperation of the military and police with the government, plagued by their distrust of Pastrana, has improved dramatically, as has the effectiveness of the government forces' counterinsurgency operations. Another is that the Colombian Congress, where Uribe has no organized majority, has, so far, supported legislation introduced by the president intended to give the forces of order more leverage in pursuing, arresting, and interrogating terrorists and the criminals they associate with. Even more spectacular is the Congress's willingness to discuss Uribe's proposal to cut down on its own numbers and expenses—again, in order to husband the nation's resources against the main enemy, FARC.

To its credit, the U.S. Congress (which has long been more important in deciding Colombia's capacity to deal with its internal threat than its counterpart in Bogotá), under strong prodding from the Bush administration, finally gave up its pretense that the problem in Colombia is drug production and trafficking, rather than a Leninist insurgency. It has finally recognized that the two are one and the same. Indeed, FARC is, without any question, the largest single producer of coca and cocaine in the world and will soon match the unlamented Taliban in heroin exports—at least to the United States.

Not surprisingly, Colombia's old enemies here were upset, and unrelenting, in attacking Uribe's policies. Some U.S. liberal and left-wing congressmen, the usual spokesmen of self-proclaimed "human rights" pressure groups, were positively scared at the notion that Uribe could, in fact, mobilize the nation for victory against the FARC (the ELN is militarily close to extinction already—mostly due to the self-defense forces). Their favorite approach, as ever, is to state that the Colombian military is at least as (morally, if not technically) guilty of "human rights violations" as the insurgents, and that the former are still in cahoots with the United Self-Defense Force of Colombia (AUC).

The AUC is a mixed bunch, to be sure. But that is why the very idea of treating them as a unit is misguided (with apologies to the State Department, which has declared them a "terrorist organization" on par with al-Qaeda and FARC). Indeed, the 15,000 strong (and growing) AUC is the result of the successive Colombian governments' patent inability to fulfill the most basic function: protecting the citizenry against communist predation. Many AUC members are former military men; as many, if not more, are former FARC and ELN militants. Most are just peasants and laborers tired of being terrorized. A significant portion, however, are former, and present, criminals and narcotraffickers taking advantage of the lawlessness of Colombia's outback. These latter are the natural target of Uribe, the military, and, indeed, the healthier majority of AUC leaders and members themselves. It is clear, however, that no AUC element, criminal or just vigilante, has ever attacked Colombian police or army units, nor (something the State Department should understand) have they ever attacked U.S. citizens or interests. This in contradistinction to FARC, which has kidnapped and murdered Americans (including leftists) and makes no secret of its anti-American strategic goals. It seems that the only reason AUC, as a whole, was put in the same basket as FARC, was to make sure that enough Congressional Democrats would agree to help Colombia.

Unfortunately, there are still Colombians whose actions help, if their sympathies do not belong to FARC. Some trade union leaders, especially in the influential Ecopetrol (the state oil company) union, are ELN- or FARC-infiltrators. But on September 16 most Colombian trade unions declared a general strike, justified by Julio Roberto Gómez of the General Confederation of Democratic Workers (CGTD), as a rejection of Uribe's freeze on public-sector hirings (he has not cut existing employees)and decrease in public spending—or "social investment," as Gómez calls it. Simply put, while the business class (and indeed the middle-class) was prepared to contribute toward defending Colombia, the leaders of the "progressive" public sector unions were not. The "rich" would pay; the privileged "progressive" employees of the state would not. And who would benefit from further damage to the economy and to the health, oil, and telecommunications sectors, of whose paralysis union leaders are particularly proud? FARC, of course.

And then there are the professional "human rights" NGOs of Colombia, who make up half the total number of human rights groups in all of Latin America. As REDEPAZ, an umbrella organization for such groups, stated on September 15, for Uribe to ask citizens to arm themselves to defend themselves and democracy is to "convert [the citizens] in part of the conflict"—as if they were not already the unarmed victims of it. Keeping the population—the citizens—of Colombia unarmed against well-armed terrorists is to give FARC a free hand to continue its massacres. FARC's main propaganda target is precisely the idea of an armed citizenry, and REDEPAZ is on FARC 's side.

The remnants of the Pastrana defeatist approach are not entirely gone. In fact, sixteen of Colombia's thrity-two state governors are (unsuccessfully) pressuring Uribe to allow them to engage FARC in "regional dialogues"—that is, to make deals allowing terrorists to act in a neighboring state in exchange for immunity in their own . As the courageous Elsa Gladys Cifuentes, governor of Risaralda, has put it, that would transform Colombia into thirty-two "Caguans"— the name of the ill-fated, Switzerland-size area given by Pastrana to FARC in exchange for what amounted to failed negotiations about negotiating. Cifuentes is still one of the few governors to speak out like this.

Alvaro Uribe has his work cut out for him. Spectacular as the Colombians' change of mind, and return to common sense, which expressed itself in his own election, is, many—too many—politicians, union leaders, and "human rights" fundamentalists, both in Colombia and in the United States, are still prepared to capitulate to FARC's openly manifested totalitarianism—whether in the name of "human rights," "economic justice," or "peace," well-intended, just misguided, or treasonous—as if there is a practical difference.

Uribe tries, and does a better than job than many, to deal with all these problems, and he has enormous popular support. It is time for the United States to help him more, in turn, especially by making it clear that Uribe's enemies are also enemies in our war on terrorism.

Reprinted with the permission from http://www.frontpagemag.com,
September 19, 2002

COLOMBIA'S "REVOLUTIONARIES" AND THEIR HELPERS

During the January 19 Stalinist-organized, and allegedly "peace"-motivated, demonstration in Washington, one of the speakers was described as "representing" a previously unknown, and probably nonexistent, organization, "Colombian Trade Unionists in Exile." His language, and indeed his very presence— together with such old hat pro-Latin American terrorist groups—Nicaragua Network, CISPES (Committee in Support of the People of El Salvador) and other Leninist nostalgic of the Cold War—clearly demonstrated the hard Left's desperate search for some communist cause, any cause, in the Americas. Indeed the Revolutionary Armed Forces of Colombia–Popular Army (FARC-EP) the speaker implicitly endorsed, is such a dubiously "progressive" cause that even

Amnesty International and Human Rights Watch, not known for their hostility to the Left, have occasionally felt compelled to complain about its barbarity—which included the murder of three "pro-native" ecologists from the United States—"an error" said FARC—mass murders of Colombian Indians, and indiscriminate kidnappings for ransom—including those of "progressive politicians. All this without mentioning the direct link—admitted by FARC—with massive cocaine and heroin trafficking.

With some 17,000 armed combatants, and about 4,000 underground urban "militias," FARC is the world's largest insurgent group. Established in 1964 as the military arm of the pro-Soviet Communist Party of Colombia, it is also the world's oldest. And with an annual income of over $600 million (from cocaine and heroin trafficking, kidnappings, and protection rackets), it is by far the wealthiest terrorist group.

Paradoxically, FARC's real growth in size, and strength, occurred even as it was losing whatever popular support it may have had at the beginning. Recent polls have shown its public support to be declining, generally dropping closer to 2 percent of late than the 4 percent of a few years ago. The main reason for this is the idiocy and incompetence, often bordering on treason, of large sectors of Colombia's elites since the early 1980s. But there is also the unwillingness, and/or inability, of the U.S. Congress, and successive administrations, to understand the nature, and magnitude, of the threat FARC poses and FARC's own successful evolution from Moscow-supported to self-sufficient military organization.

To begin with, ever since the presidency of Belisario Betancour (1982–1986), and until last year's election of Alvaro Uribe, government after government in Bogotá treated the Marxist insurgencies—FARC was never the only one—less as a matter of national security and more as a political issue to be "solved" by negotiations. Negotiations were often accompanied by orders to the military to withdraw at the very moment they were close to eliminating the insurgent leadership. After a middle/upper-class Castroite group decided to lay down arms in 1991, a new Constitution was adopted, in the name of "democracy," which effectively paralyzed the government. Among other things, the new constitution dismantled self-defense forces in the countryside and banned the use of draftees with a high-school diploma for combat—in effect making the war one between the poor and the Marxists.

This pattern of national suicide reached an apogee during the presidency of Andrés Pastrana (1998–2002), who simply "gave" FARC a "demilitarized area" larger than El Salvador in the center of the country in exchange for...discussions about future negotiations. The military, judges, and police were withdrawn from the safe-haven area, and FARC established there what its declared goal is for the country as a whole—a Stalinist mini-state, complete with "revolutionary justice," luxurious houses complete with pools for the "people's leaders," a place where international figures such as the Chairman of the New York Stock

Exchange could meet the Irish and Basque ETA terrorists training FARC in the finer points of urban terrorism: a safe haven for FARC to recruit and train and to keep its hundreds of kidnap victims.

However—and one has to be open and blunt about this—far too many ordinary Colombians were demanding "peace" at any cost—exactly what Pastrana was trying to deliver. These Colombians had been encouraged by the burgeoning human rights NGOs—Colombia harbors half of such groups in Latin America, virtually all leftist and subsidized from abroad, largely by groups in Europe but also by U.S. organizations, and most are infiltrated by or sympathetic to FARC and its smaller Castroite rival, the National Liberation Army (ELN).

The predictable result is that FARC doubled in size, by 1999–2000 reaching a level of military effectiveness that allowed it to defeat large units of the Colombian military in what amounted to conventional battles; to briefly occupy a remote provincial capital; and to threaten the existence of not only Colombia's imperfect democracy, but the very existence of the Colombian state. The police were always outgunned and outnumbered, and, thus, deserted huge swaths of territory. The military was too small, and demoralized, to replace the police, and most of the country became a no-man's land, where insurgents threatened to replace whatever pretense of national sovereignty Bogotá had.

Meanwhile, Washington under the Bush Sr. and Clinton administrations, was alternately asleep, or had its head in the sand. The FARC problem was seen as one of drug producing and trafficking, rather than one of a serious communist threat to a major country in the Americas. Hence the opinion expressed even in Congress that since the USSR was dead, *there couldn't be a communist threat* anywhere, except in the feverish imagination of reactionaries. The Democratic Left's customary manipulation of the lingering "Vietnam syndrome," together with the enormous influence of NGOs such as Human Rights Watch and Amnesty International, blocked any understanding of FARC, let alone any support for U.S. aid to Colombia in its war against totalitarianism.

Prominent Democrats like Senators Patrick Leahy (D-VT) and Christopher Dodd (D-CT), who have never seen a threat from any self-declared Marxist-Leninist terror group in the Americas, successfully blocked help to the Colombian military by charging human rights violations—as defined by HRW and Amnesty—and forced the separation between anti-drug and anti-insurgency support to Colombia. The fact that by the end of the 1990s FARC had become the world's largest single cocaine supplier (and the United States' largest heroin supplier) was pushed under the carpet.

The Clinton administration, therefore, implicitly supported Pastrana's irresponsible schemes, refusing to provide military training or equipment to the Colombian military unless strictly used for drug control, and—here the Republicans proved to be no more serious or helpful—showing an irrational preference for the Colombian police, the least effective counterinsurgency force, over the military. In short, Washington has, for a decade, gone along with Bogotá's irresponsibility.

By the beginning of 2002 things started to change, in Bogotá as well as in Washington. To begin with, Colombians, in their huge majority, realized FARC's game—to use "negotiations about negotiations" as a tool to advance their totalitarian project. Hence the overwhelming votes for Alvaro Uribe as president, although he ran as an independent and, for the first time, won in the first round. Uribe was, and is exactly, what previous Colombian presidents were not: clear in his program, realistic in his approach to FARC and ELN, and, most important, wildly popular. This makes the U.S.-FARC sympathizers unhappy (see e.g., the article at www.iacenter.org, the website of the International Action Center, founded by Ramsey Clark, "The Election of Alvaro Uribe Velez in Colombia: Why it bodes ill for the people of Colombia"). Evidently what Colombia's voters think is both wrong and irrelevant—so what else is new?

The events of 9/11 changed some minds in Washington, and the Democrats' loss of Senate control diminished the power of the "there is no enemy on the left" senators, á la Dodd and Leahy. The false distinction between anti-drug and anti-insurgency in Colombia became less viable, and the Bush administration, with Congressional support, did finally get rid of it. That decision was made easier by newly elected president Uribe, making it clear after his election that any negotiations by his government with FARC would depend entirely upon FARC's seriousness and, ultimately, its renunciation of arms and terror. Otherwise, it will be war. The Colombian military are better prepared, and more effective, than at any time since the late 1970s, when Bogotá began its ill-fated appeasement approach. And FARC is back to where it feels most comfortable—killing and kidnapping innocents, occasionally murdering policemen, and destroying the country's infrastructure.

Finally, the Colombian people and establishment are on the same wavelength—defeat the terrorists, put an end to their country being the place where 70 percent of the world's kidnappings occur, and support the military. Uribe, who has been the target of at least three FARC assassination attempts, is their vehicle.

And "Human Rights?"

For decades now, the international human rights establishment, and the Colombian franchises it subsidizes, have used Colombia as an instrument of international activism. It is time to see this for what it is—outsiders with money helping to destroy an important country. It's not that AI and HRW never condemned the FARC atrocities—they did so repeatedly, but strategically. Their goal in Colombia remains paralyzing the government's anti-insurgency operations. They, therefore, condemn the government "equally" with the insurgents. The UN and governments, under the human rights establishment's influence, are vulnerable to such lobbying, while irregulars are not—a double standard there for the exploitation.

The human rights' groups targets are always (and this is quite helpful for the insurgents) the most effective military officers. They are seldom proven to be legally guilty of cooperating with independent self-defense groups, but are always suspended from office before being found innocent, as most are found to be.

And the Self-Defense Groups?

Created by the Colombian state's inability, and unwillingness, to protect its own citizens against Marxist terror, the AUC (Colombia's United Self-Defense Groups) were created by an organizational genius, former FARC victim, and narcotrafficker, Carlos Castaño. For FARC and ELN supporters, mostly among human rights NGOs, countering Castaño is the perfect cover for helping FARC without being seen to do so. He and his associates, it is claimed, committed atrocities against "civilians" (usually known FARC/ELN underground and informers) and, it is less credibly claimed, were in cahoots with the Colombian military.

That the absence of the Colombian state in large areas was the ultimate cause of the formation of self-defense forces, or that facing the highly organized FARC and ELN those forces had to imitate the Marxists methods—which Castaño proudly admits—does not seem to matter to Bogotá 's "human rights" critics. Nor does it seem to count that the AUC does not seek to overthrow the state in favor of Stalinism; that they never fight the legitimate Colombian forces; or that they have been more successful than the army in eliminating communist terrorism (especially ELN) in large areas. The obsession with eliminating the AUC is the ever-present pretext of NGOs sympathetic to FARC for preventing any U.S. support for the war against FARC.

President Uribe has engaged in what amounts to a political and economic, revolution and, yet, still enjoys enormous popular support. He has strengthened the military and, despite the corrupt and inept judiciary, stuck with it; he is limiting the numbers and perquisites of congressional members; and he is serious about actually winning the war against Marxist totalitarians—none of which makes his natural enemies comfortable.

FARC, on the other hand, behaves as if nothing can damage its international image—and is usually correct. Thus they kidnapped Ingrid Betancourt, a marginal candidate to the presidency in February 2002—and made her a martyr in France, where her fashionable citizenship and wooly ideology were popular (her latest book was a best-seller in Paris, ignored in Bogotá). They have murdered Native Americans/environmentalists—and had their friends blame...the United States. The EU did, finally, declare FARC a terrorist group, but the temptation to negotiate with them, or press Colombia to do so, remains strong in Paris, Berlin, and the Hague. FARC did manage to get a representative, masquerading as a "trade unionist" to Washington to appear on C-Span on

January 18—in which appearance he linked their "revolution" to the efforts of the PLO and Hamas—an accurate association.

There is nothing easy in the war against terror, but it cannot be used by prominent American politicians as a pretext to protect the largest terrorist group in the world. In opposing Colombian popular opinion, these American politicians become responsible for thousands of Colombian deaths in the name of appeasing—or sympathy for—totalitarians.

Reprinted with the permission from http://www.frontpagemag.com,
January 28, 2003

FROM HARVARD TO MASS MURDER

Facts and reason are still rare commodities among academics studying political violence and terrorism. Nowhere is this more obvious than in their persistent, and futile, search for a root cause of such phenomena in some deep flaw of society, whether it be injustice, poverty, or inequality. This is, at best, subliminally Marxist "class analysis," and like Marx's other theories, has no real basis.

For example, a recent intercept of al-Qaeda recruiters quoted by the *Observer* made it clear who the most effective terrorists are: "We need foreigners. We have Albanians, Swiss, and English. All that is important is that they are of a high cultural level ...businessmen, professors, engineers, doctors, and teachers." Not exactly the natural victims of injustice, poverty, and inequality, but similar to the perpetrators of 9/11 and indeed the entire al-Qaeda leadership.

However, Islamist terrorism is not the only example of mass murder committed by, or under the orders of, the privileged. A recent event in South America demonstrates, once again, that the engine of terrorism everywhere is largely a dysfunctional middle- or upper-class seeking power. This time the "hero" was Ricardo Ovidio Palmera Pineda, a.k.a. Simón Trinidad, ideologue and a member of the supreme leadership of Colombia's Revolutionary Armed Forces (FARC), who was captured January 2, 2004 in Quito, Ecuador. This was the first time a top FARC leader was ever captured.

A FARC member since 1987, Trinidad (born in 1950) belongs to a wealthy family of ranchers from Valledupar. He graduated from a prestigious private Catholic high school and studied economics at the Jorge Tadeo Lozano University, where he later became a faculty member. He also did post-graduate work in business administration at Harvard, and, upon returning to Colombia, worked as a manager of Banco del Comercio. His wife was also a bank manager, his father a prominent lawyer, and his two sons live safely abroad. Nevertheless, in 1987, Trinidad fled to the mountains and joined FARC—but not before stealing 30 million pesos from Banco del Comercio's coffers, as well as a list of the main depositors' accounts. The list was later used by FARC to select targets for kidnapping and assess the amount of their ransom.

According to the Bogotá newspaper *El Tiempo*, Trinidad stated upon his arrest that, although it was hard to leave behind his children, "dignity comes first." What dignity? As commander of one of FARC's main units, he kidnapped and murdered Consuelo Araújo Noguera, a former minister and Trinidad's own relative! By 2001, after propagating FARC's cause in Denmark, Sweden, Spain, and Italy as its chief "peace negotiator," Trinidad was a prominent hardliner within FARC. In talks with the government, he repeatedly emphasized on FARC's behalf that, "We want power."

Apparently ill with leishmaniasis (a parasitic disease transmitted by sand flies), and diagnosed with prostate cancer, Trinidad may have sought treatment in Ecuador, where he was finally arrested before being extradited to Colombia, to face sixty-nine charges of terrorism, rebellion, kidnapping, extortion, forced displacement of civilians, multiple homicide, recruitment of minors, conspiracy to commit crimes, property damage, etc. He is also accused of ordering the destruction of the oil, hydroelectric, gas, and water infrastructure, and the kidnapping and assassination of former governor and minister Gilberto Echeverri, for which he could face a sixty-year prison sentence. In addition, he is presently being sought by the United States for being responsible, with his colleagues in the FARC leadership, for the kidnapping and subsequent murder of American pilots in February of last year.

Not surprisingly, considering the longstanding and intimate ties between FARC and the "legal" Communist Party, the Party's boss, Jaime Caycedo, "did not find any pleasure" in Trinidad's capture. This for an individual accused by the Colombian justice of being the intellectual author of the Bojayá massacre of May 2, 2002, when FARC blew up a chapel full of civilians, killing 119. Comrade Caycedo also stated that Trinidad is a "political prisoner in a foreign country," and that Colombia, as a result, had to think about a "political solution and humanitarian accord." Considering that the "political prisoner" himself, while "negotiating" with the government in October 2001, made it clear that FARC will use military or political means, or both, to obtain power, Caycedo's statements are laughable at best.

What made Trinidad, a Harvard graduate from among Colombia's elite, join, and ultimately become a leader of, a murderous Marxist organization? Did he feel that he did not have enough power for someone with his education, social standing, and income? That is precisely the motivation of Islamist terrorists, from Osama bin Laden on down to Mohammed Atta. These characters are no more representative of the real victims of existing poverty or injustice than the unanimously elected former dictators of the Soviet bloc or Saddam Hussein. They are equally criminal, especially as they exploit and manipulate their poor followers. Those in the frontlines of combating terrorism know this, and the public should be helped to understand it-but don't count on the academic experts or the media to help.

Reprinted with the permission from http://www.frontpagemag.com,
January 9, 2004

LETTER FROM LIMA

Last December 17, as the Japanese ambassador to Peru held a reception in honor of his country's national day, a group of about twenty gunmen entered the ambassador's residence and made hostages of the host and all his guests—a total of almost 600 persons. It was one of the most spectacular acts of terrorist kidnapping ever, and it continues to this day February 7, 1997.

The Terrorists

The group that seized the compound is the last significant organized unit of the Tupac Amaru Revolutionary Movement (Movimiento Revolucionario Tupac Amaru—MRTA), a Marxist-Leninist organization established in 1984. The MRTA emerged from the division, and fusion, of many minuscule, and frustrated, groups of the Peruvian Marxist Left, including leftovers of the failed Castroite insurgencies of the mid-1960s and the socialist military regime of General Juan Velasco Alvarado (1968-1975).

From the start, the MRTA was a mostly urban, middle-class-led group with an ambiguous commitment to revolutionary violence. Like its mentors and initial sponsors from among other Latin American guerrilla groups, such as the Sandinistas in Nicaragua and the M-19 in Colombia, MRTA established legal fronts and kept open channels to legal leftist parties.

In its brief history, the MRTA has been known for some spectacular assassinations, including those of a former defense minister, as well as dissident members of the group's leadership. It has also been linked to sixteen kidnappings for ransom, two of which ended in the death of the tortured prisoners; fifteen car bombings; and close ties with the drug traffickers of Peru's Upper Huallaga valley. A particularly gory event was the 1989 murder of an ex-member—a recent mother and young lawyer—who had complained about the murder of her son's father. She was first shot in the street, and then, as she was recovering after months in hospital, was finished off in her recovery bed.

The supreme leader of the MRTA is Victor Polay Campos, last arrested in 1992 and now serving a life sentence in a solitary cell in a navy prison. Like all but one of the MRTA's founders and leaders, Polay comes from a middle-class family—his father was a senator, his mother a member of Congress, his sister a congressional candidate. He was a friend, and university roommate (at Sorbonne), of former president Alan Garcia (1985-1990). When initially captured in 1989, his first visitor in jail was then prime minister Armando Villanueva, his father's long-time friend. The next day he gave press conferences from his comfortable cell. Both Polay's lieutenants, and his former rivals for the leadership of the MRTA, also hail from the privileged, but traditionally leftist, Peruvian middle-class. Perhaps it is not surprising, then, that during the last days of the Garcia government, Polay and all other MRTA leaders, imprisoned at the time, somehow managed to escape through a tunnel from a maximum-security prison. Two university graduates who escaped are now among the lesser leaders of the hostage seizure.

There is one major exception to the middle-class MRTA leaders: Nestor Fortunato Cerpa Cartolini, a.k.a. "Evaristo," the man leading the hostage seizure and the last MRTA leader of stature who remains outside prison. Cerpa is a poorly educated former worker and trade unionist who became the MRTA's supreme leader after the December 1995 capture of Polay's one remaining middle-class lieutenant, Miguel Rincón. (Americans may be interested to know that one of the main links between Cerpa and Rincón was a middle-class radical from Manhattan named Lori Berenson, currently serving a life sentence in Peru, after being arrested together with Cerpa's common-law wife.)

Cerpa, now forty-three-years old, first came to public attention during a violent strike in Lima in February 1979—a strike that resulted in five deaths and Cerpa's imprisonment for four months. The next year, he apparently briefly joined Peru's most deadly guerrilla organization, the Shining Path, but went on to join the MRTA in 1985. In 1990, he organized the prison escape that freed so many of his comrades.

The Hostages

Among the hostages taken by the MRTA are politicians (including five members of Congress, Supreme Court justices and two ministers, one of whom is the popular foreign minister, Francisco Tudela), a brother of the Peruvian president, and a who's who of the Peruvian security forces: the chief of state security, two former directors of the special anti-terrorist unit of the national police, and some seven police generals, as well as army, navy, and air force officers. Also being held captive are Japanese and Peruvian-Japanese businessmen.

The Media

After the attack took place, the international media invaded Lima's middle-class San Isidro neighborhood, where the ambassador's residence is located. For the most part, the journalists who came behaved responsibly, if somewhat foolishly. When there was no immediate news, for instance, they made news of each other. And a few stupid stories were published, notably the attempt by the *New York Times* to find some "deep social roots" of the terrorist attack.

But for true irresponsibility, one must turn to the Japanese media. On December 31, a Japanese journalist broke through the police cordon and created a free-for-all media invasion of the ambassador's residence, as well as a free international press conference for Cerpa. At just that time, the government thought it had reached a deal with the terrorists whereby controlled media access would be exchanged for fifty hostages. As a result of the journalist's irresponsibility, Cerpa freed only seven captives.

When another Japanese reporter entered the residence illegally, on January 4, he was arrested, his material—which included a ransom message from the kidnappers—was confiscated, and he was summarily expelled to New York. Encouragingly, most of the media disapproved of these journalists' behavior, apart from the left-wing Peruvian newspaper *La Republica* and a few marginal outlets.

The Government

The government of Peru may be faulted for police incompetence around the residence during the media interferences (the colonel in charge was replaced) and for the failure to counter MRTA propaganda, which includes a very active page on the World Wide Web. Those deficiencies aside, the government, and especially President Alberto Fujimori, played its cards correctly. Unlike Jimmy Carter during the 1979 hostage seizure in Tehran, Fujimori speaks rarely and with purpose. He made clear that the terrorists' main demand— freedom for imprisoned MRTA leaders—is not negotiable. And he soon put the government back to its ordinary work, not allowing officials or himself to become obsessed with the hostage drama. That Fujimori's brother, Pedro, is a hostage helped the president fend off emotional pressure from the families of other hostages.

The International Response

The governments of the G-7 countries have backed the tough line of the Peruvian government, especially President Fujimori's rejection of the terrorists' main demand. Russia even offered military support—which is unlikely to be accepted by Lima. However, British and U.S. intelligence and technical support are being quietly accepted, though this is publicly denied.

Save for the government of Uruguay, which capitulated abjectly to the terrorists in a way that raises doubts about Uruguayan democracy itself, other governments, whose diplomats were taken hostages, behaved wisely. The supreme court of Uruguay (after a talk with President Mario Sanguinetti) released two MRTA terrorists; mere hours later the Uruguayan ambassador in Lima was released by the MRTA. That surrender contrasted with the attitude of Bolivia, which has staunchly refused to release the four convicted MRTA terrorist kidnappers in Bolivian jails and which has bravely borne the price: its ambassador is now the only remaining foreign diplomatic hostage, apart from the ambassador of Japan.

Prospects

It would take prophetic gifts to predict the outcome of the hostage crisis in Lima. However, the impression I gleaned from lengthy talks with Peruvian, particularly police, officials, is that a military solution, despite the risks involved, is increasingly under consideration. Cerpa Cartolini has renewed his insistence on the release of his comrades, as, indeed, he must. The group in the ambassador's residence is, for practical purposes, the MRTA's last organized unit of any importance. The MRTA's future now depends on Cerpa's success; he is, thus, as much a captive as his victims. By the same token, the government can close the sorry MRTA chapter of Peruvian history with one swift, but competent, stroke.

Weighing against a commando attack is the danger an attack would pose to the life of hostages and especially that of popular Foreign Minister Francisco Tudela (an old friend of this author). The government may find cause for optimism in Cerpa's acceptance of Ayacucho Bishop Luis Alberto Cipriani as a negotiator, for Cipriani is Peru's most conservative bishop, a member of Opus Dei, a vocal enemy of communist terrorism, and a friend of President Fujimori.

After changing his demands daily—initially, Cerpa demanded a drastic change in the government's free market policies—Cerpa now seems to stick to his primary goal, the release of his comrades from jail. On the other hand, President Fujimori has dismissed that demand out of hand too many times to be able to give in without losing face, and perhaps any chance of running for re-election in 2000. Yet another solution, the integration of the MRTA into Peru's political life, is dismissed by Fujimori as unrealistic given the lack of popular support for the MRTA. With the remaining seventy-two hostages increasingly showing increasing signs of desperation, a show of force appears almost inevitable, despite both sides' promises to avoid it.

Reprinted with the permission of http://www.fpri.org, February 7, 1997

THE ELECTION IN PERU: A FIRST-HAND ACCOUNT

On April 9, under the gaze of observers from around the world, Peru's presidential and congressional elections probably created more uncertainty than they resolved. Amidst the flood of allegations and counterallegations of corruption and conspiracy, the country is left with both a runoff election in the presidential race, and a divided, and ideologically confused, legislature. But for all the foibles that have come to light, the most important question has already been answered: Peru's democratic institutions, immature though they may be, are strong enough to weather the storm.

Because of the extensive constitutional power placed in the hands of the chief executive, the presidential contest was far more important than the congressional races. Alberto Fujimori, president since 1990, faced eight challengers, ranging from a discredited populist, to a cult leader, to representatives of long-moribund parties, to a forgotten former vice president, to the mayor of Lima. The most significant challenge came from Alejandro Toledo, who won 40 percent of the vote and will face Fujimori in the runoff.

Toledo, who was a lackluster presidential candidate in 1995, holds degrees from Stanford (MA in economics and education, Ph.D. in education) and is also a "cholo"—a Peruvian term for (mostly) Indian citizens (hence his common nickname today, "Choledo"). During the campaign, Toledo made much of his ethnicity, concentrating his efforts in cholo areas, even though he speaks much better English than Quechua. He even vowed to accept the presidential oath of office in Machu Picchu, the lost Inca city. Fujimori has never been popular in some cholo areas anyway, and has tended to draw his support from Lima's poor and those provinces with bad memories of terrorism. Thus, Toledo's racially polarizing strategy actually had only limited impact on his rise.

The real key to Toledo's support may lie in the Peruvian electoral system itself. Constitutional rules require a second round of elections unless one candidate receives an absolute majority (50 percent of valid votes, plus one) in the first. During the final two weeks before the election, when it became clear that Fujimori had a good chance of winning in the first round, his hitherto divided opposition saw the benefit in uniting behind a single candidate. Toledo was sufficiently vague in his economic and other positions to have relatively broad appeal, and so he became the empty vessel into which the diffuse anti-Fujimori votes were poured. He also became the unabashed favorite of the international media, and even some European governments, who insisted on a second round even before the results of the first round were known.

For his own campaign, the president took full advantage of the perks of incumbency. The man universally known as "El Chino" ("the Chinese")—a term he himself approves of, despite his Japanese ancestry—trumpeted his accomplishments around the country at countless openings of new schools, bridges, roads, and clinics. He also made use of the omnipresent intelligence services to obtain information on opponents, disseminating scandalous tidbits via pro-government television outlets (most cable channels were hostile to the government) and government-subsidized tabloids. And, shrewdly, he selected as a running mate Francisco Tudela, one of Peru's foremost intellectuals and diplomats, a former foreign minister and ambassador to the UN who has occasionally been critical of the regime and was held hostage by Marxist terrorists in 1996-1997.

Observing the election were numerous international and Peruvian groups, including the Organization of American States, the Carter Center, and the National Democratic Institute (NDI), as well as an "independent" Peruvian group named Transparencia, which receives support from the United States. As it happens, the leader of Transparencia was a prominent collaborator of the pro-Soviet military dictatorship of 1968-1975 and its official press organ.

At the end of the voting, at 4 P.M. on April 9, some Peruvian opinion poll-sters proclaimed that Toledo had won the first round 46 to 43 percent—but also said that there was a 5 percent margin of error. "Toledistas" were euphoric, having clung to the first part of the announcement and ignored the second. As it turned out, those numbers had nothing to do with either actual votes or reality. When the real returns started to show Fujimori on top, his opponents claimed fraud.

Toledo clumsily proclaimed himself president, then discounted the same polls he had initially believed once they no longer favored him. He compounded the foolishness by claiming that only Transparencia's figures were to be be-lieved, only to have that group give Fujimori 48 percent to his 42 percent, this time based on actual vote counting—at which point Toledo cried foul. In a potentially dangerous move, he then invited thousands of his excited followers to "march to the palace" to protest the "fraud"—before any official results were even known. Fortunately for Peru, the president's supporters in the Presidential Plaza were evacuated, avoiding a confrontation, and the Toledistas were met by tear gas from the police—all things considered a responsible reaction by the government. Toledo's dramatic gesture, however, was later rejected as irrespon-sible by over 60 percent of Peruvians polled.

Ultimately, Fujimori was declared to have won 49.86 percent of the votes, compared to 40.16 percent for Toledo. The numbers, to be sure, are, at best, questionable, no doubt reflecting both government shenanigans and the sheer incompetence of the chief of the official vote-counting office. Whatever their veracity, the numbers put the incumbent ahead by one million votes, but some 14,000 short of outright majority. There will be a second round of voting on May 28.

Meanwhile, the government lost its majority in congress, and now holds only fifty-two seats of 120, with the rest distributed among nine other groups. Adding to the confusion is the disarray of the Peruvian party system. Of the 120 legislators just elected, only 30 percent are incumbents—and of those, none was a member of the same "movement" or "alliance" ten years ago. The vast majority of the winners are what might be described as political nomads, shift-ing allegiances as the electoral winds dictate. Whoever wins the presidency, in other words, may have a hard time dealing with the divided and undisciplined congress.

That opportunism and "fluidity," however, might also help the presidential winner to a certain extent. A Fujimori victory, for instance, would likely give his "Peru 2000" coalition a congressional majority by attracting the support of members who are nominally part of the "opposition." If Toledo wins the runoff, he might enjoy the same sort of swing in his direction from the divided "fujimoristas."

Perhaps most important, the congressional elections finalized the disinte-gration of Peru's traditional parties. Popular Action, which once dominated

Peruvian politics and whose founder, Fernando Belaunde Tery, was president from 1980 to 1985, lost its legal status as a party, as did the Popular Christian Party (PPC). Former UN Secretary General Perez de Cuellar's Union for Peru has disbanded. The Popular American Revolutionary Alliance (APRA), which was in power from 1985 to 1990, barely survived, capturing only five seats.

Both the presidential and congressional campaigns were dominated by rumor posing as strategy. The government accused the European Union, and various nongovernmental organizations, of favoring Toledo, and its charges were correct. Moreover, according to high officials interviewed by this author, the U.S. ambassador demanded a second-round election—*regardless* of the official results. Normally serious middle-class Peruvians are now fervent believers in all sorts of conspiracy theories, from blackouts planned by Fujimori to the increasingly bizarre claims by Toledo that he was kidnapped and drugged by the intelligence service. Toledo also stated that he had official support from the French government, only to be publicly rebuffed. He said he had held talks with military representatives and made agreements with the prime minister, and was later forced to retract those claims.

The best that can be said of the Peruvian media is that any accusation of being "yellow" has to apply to all sides. The pro-government tabloids dwell on Toledo's somewhat mysterious personal life and his penchant for half-truths and vague statements. On the other side, the media tend to overstate the strength of Toledo's support. This author actually counted heads at a pro-Toledo demonstration in Arequipa, Peru's third largest city, and arrived at a figure of 500. The following day, a major newspaper, *La Republica*, reported that no fewer than 11,000 people were there.

What should not be overlooked, despite the flaws in the process, is the real issue: Peruvians themselves must decide who their next president is, and they have some critical questions to answer. On the one hand, most Peruvians realize, and enjoy, the accomplishments of the Fujimori regime: domestic peace, quiet borders, better roads, more schools, more clinics, more foreign investments, virtually no inflation. On the other, many think that the price of those achievements—authoritarian government, an omnipotent and omnipresent intelligence service, a prominent and influential military—is too high, and that any alternative (Toledo, in this case) is better.

In the runoff, the margin of victory is likely to be very narrow, despite Fujimori's clearly superior strength in the first round. Indeed, pressure from the international media, foreign governments, and NGOs may sway enough middle- and upper-class voters (the only ones with access to outside information) to decide the outcome in favor of Toledo. Just at the moment when Peruvians are demonstrating the vigor of their own civil society that would be a pity indeed.

Reprinted with the permission from http://www.fpri.org, April 26, 2000

Peru's "Democratic Opposition" Plays with Fire

On July 28, the date of Alberto Fujimori's inauguration as president of Peru, mobs set fire to the Education Ministry, the National Bank, and the Palace of Justice—the culmination of Alejandro Toledo's "national march for democracy."

Toledo first ran for president against incumbent Alberto Fujimori in 1995 and drew a scant 3 percent of the vote. In 2000 he became the surprise front-runner among opposition candidates, obtaining 41 percent of the vote in the first round—a million votes behind Fujimori but enough to force a runoff election. Toledo then withdrew from the runoff, claiming the election was fraudulent.

Throughout the campaign Toledo made a number of allegations that had no basis in reality: he declared himself president before *any* first-round results were known; he claimed to have had discussions with military leaders and the prime minister, which never took place; he boasted of having officially received support from the French government when none was given; and he and his wife charged that the Fujimori government had hatched conspiracies involving secret tapes and plans to kidnap them, though none appears to have come to fruition. His supporters made wild accusations of torture and stolen tapes supposedly "proving" government collusion with election officials—and then fled the country never to be heard from again. The allegations and unsubstantiated rumors created an atmosphere of national paranoia, no doubt encouraged by President Fujimori's secretive and authoritarian style, and the almost universally poor quality and partisanship of the media, whether for, or against, the government.

Toledo's claim to represent democracy in Peru lies solely in the real, but not decisive, irregularities that occurred during the first round of elections. That they were real was demonstrated by the objections raised by the Organization of American States mission of observers, and by their refusal to observe the second round. That they were not decisive was demonstrated by independent polls, which largely confirmed the election results, and by the OAS's own refusal either to declare the elections invalid or demand new ones. In fact, the most recent polls suggest that if a new election were to take place today, Fujimori would win with an even greater majority. Ultimately, what Fujimori did was what incumbents everywhere routinely do—use the advantages of incumbency to the limit of the law, and occasionally beyond.

Most revealingly, in the same first round election that Toledo rejected as fraudulent, Fujimori's supporters (the movement known as Peru 2000) lost their majority in congress—hardly an outcome that suggests a rigged vote. To be sure, Peru 2000 soon regained its majority after defectors from the divided opposition joined Fujimori's camp. But when Toledo predictably accused defectors of corruption, he was able to offer no proof. He then announced that some Fujimori supporters would defect to him; none did. It is indeed telling that, despite their cries of vote fraud, not a single one of Toledo's followers who won a seat in the new congress refused to accept it.

Toledo seems bent on destroying the nation's hard-won gains for the sake of his own personal ambitions. First, he has tried to capitalize on his ethnicity, repeatedly describing himself as "Indian, stubborn, and rebellious," thus threatening to reopen old cleavages that Fujimori had begun to heal. Fujimori, Peru's first non-white president, continues to enjoy the loyalty of many Indians. Toledo, who holds two degrees from Stanford, draws his support mostly from urban middle classes, disgruntled intellectuals, and especially radicals.

Because he lacks a real party of his own, Toledo has only been able to mobilize large numbers of people by appealing to a core constituency of radical leftists, and the results have been disheartening. One may wonder, for example, why "democrats" would burn the Education Ministry. As it happens, the teachers' union, which has long been a bastion of Maoism, Trotskyism, and related ideologies, has become one of Toledo's key supporters. In addition, the traditionally communist-dominated General Confederation of Labor, badly hurt and marginalized by privatization programs under Fujimori's government, has been involved in Toledo's marches, as was a minority of Marxist students (interestingly, the national organization of students refused to participate). Thus, the specter of a revived anti-democratic left, which nearly destroyed Peru only a decade ago, again looms large. It also explains the growing doubts about Toledo's political judgment among many Peruvians, including members of his own movement.

Peru is all too familiar with the ravages of violence linked to politics, but has been largely free of that misery since the 1992 capture of the chieftains of the two Marxist terrorist groups—the Communist Party of Peru, better known as Shining Path, and Tupac Amaru Revolutionary Movement. What Toledo is now doing is reintroducing violence as a justifiable means of political expression in Peru. Unbelievably, he has repeatedly declared his commitment to "peaceful" action and has even compared himself to Mahatma Gandhi and Martin Luther King, Jr. But his inflammatory rhetoric and encouragement of volatile demonstrations prove that such a flattering comparison is either delusion or doubletalk. After the first-round results were made public, he incited a midnight "march to the palace," knowing full well that rioting, vandalism, and a forceful police response were likely to ensue. In June, he did the same on the occasion of the OAS mission's visit. He then spent most of the next two months urging people throughout the country to join demonstrations explicitly designed to prevent Fujimori from taking office. Now, Toledo feigns surprise that Lima is burning. (The six people who died in the bank building fire were neither demonstrators nor police; they were private guards. Toledo never designated a representative to attend the funeral.)

A political pyromaniac, Toledo is now the greatest threat to Peruvian democracy. Human rights groups should reconsider their support of him and reflect on the fact that the alternative in Peru to a flawed democracy is not democracy but mob rule.

Reprinted with the permission from http://www.fpri.org, August 9, 2000

CHAOS IN THE ANDES

President George W. Bush's first international trip was to Mexico—a historic novelty, but not an unexpected event, considering Mexico's size, importance as our second-ranking foreign trade partner, and geographic position. U.S.-Mexico relations are on an even keel, with many matters of bilateral interest on the agenda but none that are threatening or of immediate concern.

The same cannot be said about the Andean region (Colombia, Venezuela, Ecuador, and Peru), where recent explosive developments make it likely to pose the new administration's first crisis. The region, with some 100 million people, is an essential supplier of both U.S. oil and most of the drugs infesting America. While the states as a group are an important trading partner, the region is now a threat to the economic, political, and military stability of South America, and, as such, threatens large U.S. interests at home and in the Caribbean.

Ecuador

The most immediate, if not the most important, problem is in Ecuador, now overtaking Colombia as Latin America's "sick man." Simply put, the country is ungovernable. It has had five presidents in as many years, and has a divided military of dubious loyalty to democracy and the elected government. Moreover, there are huge segments of the population that are simply unwilling to understand, or to accept, simple economic facts: that the government is bankrupt, that it cannot afford subsidies, and that the country can no longer live beyond its means. Added to these problems are ethnic cleavages: Marxist-led Indians have already used force to overthrow an elected president in February 2000, and are prepared to do so again now. There also is a growing regionalist movement centered in the country's largest city, the port of Guayaquil, based upon resentment of paying taxes on production to the profit of a largely parasitic Quito and the highlands in general. It is, thus, easy to see why Ecuador's political class is in immediate danger of losing control and being replaced by chaos—and a Marxist-type chaos at that, just as the equally suicidal Venezuelan elites did two years ago.

How does this affect the United States? The air base at Manta, Ecuador, is slated to replace the lost facilities in Panama in the United States' fight against Colombian drug trafficking. The implications of Ecuadoran unrest for the entire strategy of coping with the cocaine/heroin problem are ominous.

Colombia

Given its size, Ecuador's problems pale in comparison with Colombia's. There, the government of Andres Pastrana has tried for more than two years to "make peace" with the two communist insurgent groups destroying his country—the Revolutionary Armed Forces of Colombia (FARC) and the National Liberation Army (ELN). The Pastrana government is, again, proving its inability to learn or to adapt. This time, however, it is having to deal with an increasingly restive, but still professional, military and a better organized anti-communist populace.

Indeed, if there is a case study of how not to deal with a Marxist revolutionary challenge, Pastrana's policies could be the perfect model. After the 1998 surrendering of national sovereignty—no police, no army, no administrative government presence—over an area the size of Switzerland to the 17,000-strong FARC in exchange for vague promises of "talks about peace talks," the government has nothing to show for it. Nonetheless, Pastrana decided, against overwhelming local opposition, to give the ELN its own chunk of national territory as well, in the San Lucar Mountains in the South Bolivar department.

What makes the ELN deal so incredibly inane is that, unlike the still growing FARC, the ELN (whose original stronghold was the San Lucar) is on the ropes, militarily and politically. Long specialized in destroying Colombia's largest source of income, oil, by blowing up pipelines on a weekly basis, the ELN has largely been dislodged from most of its areas by the activities of the paramilitary Autonomous Self-Defense Forces of Colombia (AUC). Thus, at the very time that ELN could be finally defeated, Pastrana decided—against the loudly voiced interests of the tens of thousands of men, women, and children soon to be ELN subjects—to give that group a lifeline. No wonder the military was at last ready to manifest its unhappiness.

As for FARC, their lack of interest in serious negotiations is matched only by their arrogance. Indeed, FARC's main precondition for resuming "talks about talks amidst war" is that the government destroy their most effective enemy—the AUC! Simply put, and obvious to all but Pastrana and his closest advisers, FARC's precondition for continued talks, other than retaining its control over what amounts to a state within a state, is government disarmament.

One of the reasons Pastrana has brought Colombia to the brink of collapse in the name of "peace" is the extraordinary influence wielded by nongovernmental organizations (NGOs), mostly those specialized in human rights. These groups—some well-intentioned but obsessive; some dominated, controlled, or penetrated by Marxist sympathizers of the insurgents—have made not the FARC and ELN but the AUC their main enemy. They are convinced that the paramilitaries are somehow the cause of violence in Colombia, rather than the natural result of Bogota's inability to protect its citizens against guerrilla kidnappings, racketeering, and murder. The report on the conflict just published by the Colombian Defense Ministry (February 3, 2001—see http://eltiempo.terra.com.co/04-02- 2001/judi_0.html), suggests that the AUC was responsible for fewer civilian deaths than the insurgents during the past three years. It also suggests that they were far more likely to surrender to the police or military than to fight them—which is borne out by the fact that the number of soldiers or policemen killed by the AUC is quite small. The number of those murdered or captured by FARC and ELN, however, reaches into the thousands.

The AUC enjoyed success against the insurgents because they hit them where it hurts—in their recruiting, intelligence, and financing activities. It is made up of about equal numbers of deserters from the insurgents, disillusioned army and police personnel, and civilians who suffered from the Marxists' abuses. While there is nothing glorious about the AUC—they are also involved in drug trafficking and other forms of criminality—they do not seek to overthrow the Colombian democracy, imperfect as it is, and replace it with a Stalinist system, as the FARC and ELN do.

President Pastrana seems bent on making everything more complicated than it need be. There is no other explanation for his insistence on bringing the European Union—whose sympathy for the insurgents and a "peace at any cost" strategy does not match their scarce promises of funds—into the negotiating process. Worse still, as far as symbolism is concerned, Pastrana has chosen Havana (!) as the location of his talks with the ELN.

Peru

After the collapse of the Fujimori regime last year, it appears that Peru is going back to its bad reputation as a country of wild political gyrations. The fall of Fujimori and his corrupt security adviser, Vladimiro Montesinos, has, so far, led to political revenge, economic chaos, and further institutional decay. A weak, unelected, transitional regime is busy dismantling everything Fujimori did in ten years. That has meant a witch hunt of all associates of Fujimori, legal or otherwise—including some surprises, such as opposition parliamentarians bought by Montesinos. Also targeted was Fujimori's sound economic policy of the past decade. Worse still, the anti-Fujimori hysteria in Lima includes a de facto pardon for former President Alan Garcia, who is now back after fleeing from corruption charges for almost a decade. Indeed Garcia is running for president, in a field of seventeen! Antiterrorist legislation, which played an essential role in eliminating Latin America's worst terrorist threat in the 1990s, is being dismantled in the name of "human rights." One can only hope that such "democratization" will not lead to a revival of the terrorist groups—the Shining Path and Tupac Amaru Revolutionary Movement—that almost destroyed Peru a decade ago and were so adept at taking advantage of misguided definitions of "democracy."

The silver lining in Lima is Lourdes Flores, a centrist politician who is in a good position to win the April presidential election. She is a free marketeer realist and seems to be the first woman ever with a chance to win the presidency of a Latin American country on her own merits (in contrast to those who won elections for their name—as in Nicaragua, Panama, and Argentina).

Venezuela

It is hard to see the administration of President Hugo Chavez—with its anti-Americanism, economic illiteracy, admiration for Fidel Castro (including oil subsidies to a bankrupt Havana regime), and its militarization of politics—as anything but reminiscent of Salvador Allende's Chile of the early 1970s. Not surprisingly, exactly two years after the beginning of his "Bolivarian revolution," Chavez's popularity declined by 20 percent, to some 40 percent—and his main institutional prop, the military, nearly overthrew him in January. He destroyed the country's political institutions—with the "help" of decaying and corrupt parties, judiciary, and economic elites—but built nothing but rhetoric in their place. He did succeed in scaring national capital and the educated out of the country. Chavez also managed to antagonize Washington and his own neighbors by, for instance, openly helping FARC and ELN, as well as leftist groups in Bolivia and Ecuador, while allowing his own borders to become lawless areas.

Prospects

The failed Ecuadorian state cannot cope with any spillover of Colombia's conflict over its unprotected borders. A weak Peruvian regime will more likely need to deal with its own revived insurgencies rather than with an expanding Colombian one. The radical regime in Caracas is more likely to run into border conflicts with Colombia and Guyana than to help stabilize the region. And a collapsing Colombia will immediately threaten defenseless Panama as well as its other neighbors. Rather than concentrating on Mexico, the Bush Administration must turn its attention to our serious interests south of the Panama isthmus.

Reprinted with the permission from http://www.fpri.org, March 20, 2001

PART 5
AFRICA

In the forty-five years since 1960, the "Year of Africa" in which seventeen African nations gained independence, the Subsaharan region has been the world's problem child. The same issues and false solutions seem to appear again and again—Africa as "victim" of colonialism, racism, poverty, injustice, and a variety of crimes, almost always somebody else's. What they have in common is a paternalistic approach, characteristic of Western (especially American) scholarship. An obsession with race is rooted in its domestic politics, influenced by the heavy lobbying of Black American elites and their manipulation of white guilt—over slavery, over colonialism (not ours, but generically Western), over a complex history. For years the alleged need to "aid" Africa was seen as obvious, and taken seriously in some quarters, with the Scandinavian countries, for instance, subsidizing most of the failed, and almost criminal, socialism of Tanzania or Seychelles, which are both now recognized as historic failures by Dar es Salaam and Mahè. It seems that four decades of independence—almost half as long as European colonialism lasted, other than by the Portuguese and Arab (yes, Arab—ask the Zanzibar and East African coast towns)—have changed little in Western academic and African political minds.

It used to be that "development aid" was deemed politically, economically, and, indeed, morally necessary—now it's subsidized medicine for AIDS—never mind, in both cases, that African self-sufficiency, rational policies, and changes in personal and collective behavior all got shortchanged in the process, and never mind that Africa's capacity of absorbing foreign aid continues to be quite limited.

Then there is the issue of racism, not as a cause of African underdevelopment, but as contemporary African practice. It is suicidal and immoral, and goes largely unnoticed or excused. The expulsion of Asians from Uganda, and the official mass theft of white agricultural property in Zimbabwe and Namibia, are both examples of racism that have caused economic collapse.

Nor is the politically incorrect issue of the viability of some post-colonial states mentioned, let alone dealt with. But the Sierra Leones, Liberias, and Zaires are no accidents, nor can they be fixed by UN blue helmets or ridiculously expensive and inefficient UN-sponsored international tribunals.

Ivory Coast and Zimbabwe:
Two Tales of Self-Destruction

It is no secret that signs of social, political, and economic progress in Africa have been rare indeed. What is less often discussed is the responsibility borne by African leaders for the misery of their own people. But powerful Western nations hardly deserve to escape some criticism. Nowhere is the truth of these observations more clear than in Ivory Coast and Zimbabwe, two countries that, until not too long ago, appeared to offer a glimmer of hope for a better future. Now, both have slipped to the brink of disaster.

Since independence from France in 1960, the Ivory Coast has been, by far, the most stable and economically successful country in Francophone Africa. Under the leadership of the authoritarian, but benevolent, Felix Houphouet-Boigny from 1960 to 1993, the country prospered. Lacking in natural resources, the Ivory Coast's economy was driven by small-scale agriculture, and was so successful that the country had a chronic shortage of labor for decades. Stability was guaranteed, in part, by ensuring that the small, and politically irrelevant, military stayed that way. That was by no means accidental: France maintained a strong military presence, which served both as a protector of extensive French investments and as an effective deterrent against an institution that in so many other African states has been a source of instability and ruin.

All this ended in December 1999, when the military overthrew the corrupt and ineffective, but elected, government of Henri Conan Bedie as France stood by. Not long ago, this would have been inconceivable, but France's Socialist-Communist government now ostensibly eschews "interference" in other countries' internal affairs and, therefore, contented itself with impassivity in the face of the emerging crisis.

In the short time since the coup, the disastrous results have been almost mind-numbingly predictable. The economy collapsed, and as resources grew increasingly scarce, ethnic and religious cleavages surfaced and conflicts between natives and immigrants became acute. The initial coup was followed by other attempted coups. Mutinous soldiers exacted tribute from their nominal boss, General Robert Guei, and looted what had been one of Africa's most attractive capitals. Foreign investors fled.

The Ivory Coast's crisis has also left West Africa without a political and economic counterbalance to Nigeria, which has long dreamt of regional hegemony. Charles Taylor, the bloody tyrant of Liberia, is now the unlikely successor in that role, but he (along with like-minded rulers and warlords in Burkina Faso and Sierra Leone) thirsts for diamonds, blood, and brute power, far more than regional stability. Paris's political correctness in December will prove horrendously expensive, in financial and in human terms.

At the other end of the continent, Robert Mugabe appears to be leading Zimbabwe inexorably toward economic and social destruction through a combination of socialism and racism. Mugabe, whose claim to power rests largely on the results of phony elections, has begun to destroy his country's economy by dismantling the only sector that is productive and employs large numbers of people—agriculture. What is more, he has blatantly made race the sole determinant for land redistribution. Land owned by whites is simply being confiscated and occupied by blacks. As Mugabe put it, "As a collectivity, they (white farmers) are a natural fissure and beachhead for the retention or re-launch of British and European influence and control over our body politic."

Even aside from the illegality and incendiary effect of the land seizures, the redistribution of farmland will lead to enormous economic hardship. The agricultural industry has, until now, been Zimbabwe's major source of jobs and hard currency. Competent management is a key factor, along with economies of scale that, in a capital-intensive commercial sector, will be lost if land is given over to small-scale subsistence farming. Zimbabwe will lose not just jobs and foreign exchange reserves, but food production as well.

Family farmers will probably require subsidies from the government eventually, but the state coffers, deprived of the income formerly generated by agricultural exports, will soon empty. Food shortages—in a country that, along with South Africa, has been one of sub-Saharan Africa's few self-sufficient food producers—are a real possibility, along with the inevitable requests for foreign aid.

It is worth noting that, despite Mugabe's obvious reliance on race to drum up support, many Zimbabweans see beyond color lines to the dangers of his policies: in marginally fair elections in June, the majority of educated blacks in every city voted against him. He nonetheless maintained a majority nationwide thanks to the support of the rural and largely illiterate population swayed by his promises of land ownership.

If Zimbabwe's slide has been truly disheartening, South Africa's reaction to it has been, at the least, disappointing. Rather than issuing stern criticism, President Thabo Mbeki has supported his neighbor in Harare. His message seemed to be that stealing property in order to redress racial grievances was acceptable—even at the cost of economic and social self-destruction. That hardly helps South Africa's standing with foreign investors; nor does it inspire optimism in regard to Africa's financial, racial, or economic future in general.

The West, largely responsible for putting Mugabe in power, has been, as so often in Africa, unwilling to do much about his racism, economic primitivism, and irresponsibility. The United Kingdom complained vocally, but stopped there; the United States did even less. No economic or trade sanctions were ever mentioned.

Nevertheless, the West's fault, in both instances, is one of omission: ultimately, France did not overthrow the civilian government in Abidjan, nor did the British destroy Zimbabwe's economy. On the other hand, had France intervened to stop the coup in the Ivory Coast, or Britain to block Mugabe's racism, the cries of "colonialism" would have been universal.

In the Ivory Coast and Zimbabwe—both considered bright spots in a troubled continent up until recently—the future appears bleak. But as depressing as that observation is, the fault lies overwhelmingly with Africans themselves. The complaints of nongovernmental organizations about "donor fatigue" are correct—and justified. How long is a huge swath of the world going to avoid responsibility for its own mistakes, fail to correct them, and expect taxpayers abroad to subsidize them? It is time for a change.

Reprinted with the permission form http://www.fpri.org, August 4, 2000

Does Africa Exist?

The Organization of African Unity (OAU), founded in 1963 in Addis Ababa, is attempting a transformation of sorts. Last week in Lusaka, Zambia, it changed its name to the African Union (AU) in imitation of the European Union, mostly as a result of Libyan Col. Moammar Khaddafi's latest brainstorm and spending spree. The "new" body also decided to establish a continental Central Bank, Court of Justice, parliament, and, in the future, a single currency. Considering the realities of the African continent, and its real needs, this seems like the reshuffling of the chairs on the deck of the Titanic.

To the superficial observer, all of this may be seen as a step forward. After all, who could be against African unity? But there is no such thing as "Africa" in any meaningful political and cultural sense, and there is no reason to think that the newly minted AU will be any more effective than the OAU was. What the continent needs is not another fictional show of unity or layer of bureaucracy.

Africa, like Asia and unlike Europe or Latin America, is not a cultural, political, or economic entity. It is a geographic collection of fifty-three states, virtually all postcolonial and recent inventions.Some countries have French as the official language, some Portuguese, Arabic, or English. Some have a mostly Black population, some Arab or mixed. Some are mostly Christian, some Islamic, some a mix. A handful has functional democratic systems, most are autocracies, many are kleptocracies, and all but a few (South Africa, Libya) are among the poorest in the world. Simply put, beyond accidents of geography, there is no such thing as "Africa"—except vis-á-vis the rest of the world.

For more than four decades, African elites and their intellectual mentors in the West have comfortably lived with a fiction: that whatever is wrong in the

continent—tribalism, corruption, genocide, failing states, poverty, and HIV/
AIDS—is somebody else's fault, that is, the rich West's. Genocide in Rwanda?
Blame the Belgians. Rampant anti-Asian racism in East Africa? Blame the British. Even more blatant anti-white racism in Zimbabwe? The British again. A
string of spectacularly bloody tyrants, including Idi Amin in Uganda, Bokassa
in Central Africa, Macias Nguema in Equatorial Guinea? The really guilty ones
are in London, Paris, and Madrid; "Africa" is innocent.

But the problems go beyond denial. Take the case of Zimbabwe. Formally
independent under black rule since 1980, the former Southern Rhodesia was
one of the most economically developed states in Sub-Saharan Africa. It formed
one-half (along with South Africa) of an exclusive club of continental food
exporters, mostly due to a large, white-owned agrobusiness sector. Corn, wheat,
and tobacco made famine unheard-of and produced large surpluses of hard
currency.

But then in 1980 Robert Mugabe, a committed Marxist, came to power, a
strong believer in socialism and "racial justice." He imposed a one-party system, aggravated ethnic cleavages—for example, unknown thousands of Ndebele
were murdered by Mugabe's Shona-based regime—and, during the past few
years, fomented anti-white racism mixed with anti-free-enterprise ideology,
leading to the virtual destruction of the agricultural sector. He is also giving
asylum to his friend and ideological comrade-in-arms, one of Africa's worst
criminals, former Ethiopian Stalinist dictator Mengistu Haile Mariam.

First, members of Mugabe's party took over large farms and, in no time,
managed to ruin them. Then, beginning in 1999, pro-Mugabe thugs, disguised
as "war veterans," invaded white-owned farms, killed their owners (Zimbabwe's
managerial class), evicted thousands of Black workers, and transformed one of
Africa's bread baskets into a famine area.

The international response was entirely off the mark. It is best characterized
by a *New York Times* headline that read: "Zimbabwe seeks international aid to
prevent famine" (July 6, 2001). Said Mugabe's Finance Minister, Simba Makoni:
"Where human life is concerned, we can find common cause to mitigate [fam-
ine]." It is the old story of the perpetrator of patricides asking for pity because
he is now an orphan: the clear creator of famine is asking for the taxpayers of the
West to pay for his crime, all in the name of a level of "humanity" to which he
does not subscribe. Unfortunately, it is only a matter of time until misguided
relief organizations will flood our TV screen with malnourished Zimbabwean
children and ask for our help without mentioning either the cause or main
beneficiary of the famine—Robert Mugabe himself.

At the same time, the old British—and, indeed, Southern Rhodesian—political culture still survives. A multiracial opposition movement with majority
support in the country has been able to defeat Mugabe's attempt to make himself president for life, organize massive strikes, and, despite assassinations and
the president's open disregard of Supreme Court decisions, put serious pressure

on the regime. None of this, however, is due to any pressure or influence of pan-African opinion. To the contrary, one of the AU's first decisions was to rally behind Mugabe—the continent's poster boy for racism, kleptocracy, and totalitarianism.

Indeed, as the *New York Times* (July 10, 2001) put it in another headline, "African leaders accuse Britain of attempting to isolate Mugabe." A group made up of Nigeria (Africa's most populous country), South Africa (the continent's prime industrial, economic, and military power and Zimbabwe's enabler), Kenya, Zambia, Algeria (itself under ethnic and religious attack), and Cameroon declared that the real problem is "British moves to mobilize European and North American countries to isolate and vilify Zimbabwe, leading to imposition of formal and informal sanctions against it."

The problem, then, according to the AU, is not Mugabe's destruction of his own country, but Britain's campaign to make the facts known. While the final draft did not explicitly support Mugabe—an encouraging sign—neither did it condemn him, let alone draw useful lessons from Zimbabwe's collapse. The African continent is depending upon international (read "Western") welfare, with no appreciation of the real problem: postcolonial African political culture and its often-disastrous results. One of those is the irresponsible "solidarity" among its corrupt elites, with Mugabe the present beneficiary.

Another is the persistence in recognizing the fictitious Sahrawi Arab Democratic Republic—which is neither "Arab," nor "democratic" nor a "Republic"—in fact, it is a non-entity whose "people" (most of whom never lived in Western Sahara) and radical leadership live in Algeria. The price of this example of "solidarity"? Morocco stayed out of the AU.

All this comes while Africa begs for billions of Western aid to deal with its problems. Where is Africa's responsibility? It does not seem that its leaders even accept the notion of responsibility, let alone the idea of using what resources it has to address its own problems. The result is that thuggery unchallenged leads to thuggery legitimized—or emulated. For example, South African president Thabo Mbeki's reluctance to condemn, and, thus, remove, Mugabe has only encouraged illegal land grabbing in his own country, a racist as well as anti-capitalist issue. To its credit, the government in Pretoria has put a stop to that—for now.

If the new AU paymaster is Khaddafi and the result is solidarity with Mugabe's totalitarian racism, why should Africa deserve Western tax money? Is this the best way to attract investments (the answer is already clear and negative) or international aid? The answer, coming from Lusaka, is a definite "no." If Libya wishes to buy its way back into international respectability, let it pay not just for the AU's new stationery, but for substantive solutions to its continent's problems as well. However, even were Libya to do so, it is unlikely that a change of label and higher still unrealistic ambitions would change Africa's abysmal situation. Only serious self-criticism and steps toward more honesty, free markets, and elite accountability could do that—and only the Africans, not the outsiders' money, could accomplish that.

Reprinted with the permission from http://www.frontpagemag.com,
July 26, 2001

COMRADE MUGABE'S "STATE OF DISASTER"

With famine now threatening the country, Robert Mugabe's regime in Zimbabwe has declared a state of disaster. Considering that Mugabe is the main reason for the disaster, there is a tragic irony in his implicit admission of the calamity he has brought to his country.

True enough, there is a drought in Southern Africa today, affecting all the region's countries—Lesotho and Mozambique, Swaziland, Zambia, Botswana, and Namibia—the only exception being, not surprisingly, the most important country: South Africa. Western humanitarian agencies and NGOs are now rushing food aid to the region, and, as usual, avoiding "judgments" as to the causes of the calamity.

Those causes range from simple bad luck and a backward infrastructure in cases like Lesotho and Mozambique, to incompetence and corruption in many instances. Only in Zimbabwe is the famine a manmade (by Mugabe) crisis. In a sub-Saharan version of Stalin's policies of the 1930s, the state created famine to physically get rid of its opponents, a faster and cheaper way than murdering them on a wholesale basis (although, like Stalin, it is not that Mugabe has any compunction about doing this, too). In Stalin's case, the enemy was hard-working kulaks—peasants, mostly in Ukraine, who, by becoming prosperous, became a "class enemy."

Marxist Mugabe went even further than the Soviet model. He added race to the poisonous mix that is now killing the people of Zimbabwe when he began a new "freedom fight" against the white minority in 1999. There is no lack of implicitly racist or ethnically exclusivist regimes in the world today, from Malaysia to Kosovo, but only Mugabe's is explicit and gets away with it. (As Mr. Mugabe said of whites at a September 2000 Harlem event during his visit to the U.S. for the UN millennium summit, "What we hate is not the color of their skins but the evil that emanates from them.") This is all the more horrifying because his destruction of Zimbabwe has an immediate impact on the entire region. Until a few years ago, Zimbabwe was, with South Africa, part of the "happy duo" of sub-Saharan countries that possessed a quasi-permanent food surplus, the result of a modern, efficient, large-scale—that is, capitalist—agricultural sector. That meant that South African and Zimbabwean surpluses of maize and wheat, by and large, filled the gap in less efficient countries in the region. The agribusinesses of Zimbawbe and South Africa also provided thousands of jobs both for locals and for illegal migrants from other countries, primarily Mozambique. They kept food prices relatively low and absorbed huge numbers of peasants who would otherwise have headed to the already crowded cities.

The problems begin with the fact that in both countries, but particularly in Zimbabwe, the owners and managers of the agribusiness sector are white Africans, an ethnic minority. These businesses are also capitalist, giving Mugabe, a professed Marxist, the needed excuse to expropriate the farms under the auspices of "land reform."

Another and immediate issue is political unrest. After wielding absolute power for twenty-two years, the aging Stalinist knows that "his people" have discovered that *Das Kapital* does not feed them and Leninism has deprived them of freedom and jobs (one half of Zimbabweans are unemployed). Threatened by a newly coalesced and ably led opposition, Mugabe did what any Stalinist has to do: impose terror, first on the spirit, by destroying any remnants of press and university freedom, and then physically, by creating poverty and famine.

The small white minority, owners of some 30 percent of the agricultural land and the employers of tens of thousands of relatively well-off black laborers, were demonized as "colonialists" despite having been born in the country. Some, like former prime minister Ian Smith of then-Southern Rhodesia, were even stripped of their citizenship, although native born. (Mugabe, however, points to the fact that Smith is still alive as proof that he is a kind, non-vengeful person.) Others, even less fortunate, were murdered by thugs from Mugabe's ZANU-PF party, often in front of their families, sometimes in the most barbaric manner. White-owned farms were either confiscated by Mugabe's clique of government thieves or ruined by his corps of "war veterans"—that is, self-proclaimed combatants of the pre-1980 civil war. The black employees of those farms lost everything: their jobs, security, and more often than not their lives. Having decimated the white population, Comrade Mugabe is now focusing his attention on the even smaller Asian community, mostly small traders and professionals. They are the newest "intruders" and "exploiters" the regime needs to inspire and legitimize its crimes.

After destroying his country's economy in the name of Marxism and overt racism, Mugabe's gang still had to deal with a stubborn opposition. It took another page from Uncle Joe's book. In the March elections it made sure that it counted the votes. Unsurprisingly, Comrade Mugabe's gang "won"—but even by their own count they got only 54 percent of the vote against the opposition Movement for Democratic Change's Morgan Tsvangirai. In a meeting with UN representatives, Mugabe dismissed U.S.-U.K. concerns about the validity of the March elections (the U.S. barred him from traveling to the U.S. following the elections) by saying "To this day we still do not know who actually won the presidential election between Bush and Gore." (*Herald*, Harare, May 1) He also told the mission "We view the voice of the U.S. and Europe as the voice of the whites against blacks." In all events, Mugabe's government is proceeding with its prosecution of Tsvangirai for treason with highly questionable evidence.

Meanwhile, most of Zimbabwe's military has been busy looting what passes as the Democratic Republic of Congo (formerly Zaire) since war began in that country in 1998.

How does Mugabe manage to survive, even when many of his fellow Zimbabweans cannot? Exploitation of the Congo's diamonds, cobalt, and titanium is part of the answer; Qaddafi's supplies of cheap oil are another. But the ultimate answers lie in Pretoria, Brussels, and London, in that order.

Without South African trade, migrants, and access to oil supplies, Mugabe would have lasted an even shorter time than Smith. But South African president Thabo Mbeki has refused to apply any but the mildest political pressure on Mugabe, who helped Mbeki's own African National Congress to power in Pretoria. This has been a misguided policy, regardless of its motivations. Sooner or later, the seventy-eight-year-old Mugabe is going to go away, one way or another. Mass illegal Zimbabwean immigration across the Limpopo River is already creating unrest among Northern Transvaal black South Africans, who correctly perceive it as a threat to their own jobs and security. The inevitable chaos of a post-Mugabe Zimbabwe cannot be good for South Africa or the greater region, of which Pretoria is the natural leader. As for the Zimbabwean market for South African products, it is gone—and will remain so for a long time.

However, when Britain tried in January to have Zimbabwe expelled, or at least suspended, from the fifty-four-member Commonwealth, South Africa, together with Nigeria and Botswana, and with the support of leaders of the Southern African Development Community states, blocked this. Why? Because of a dubious notion of "solidarity" with a fellow Third Worlder. Mugabe's blatant racism met the more discrete racism of his colleagues in the Commonwealth. (In March, following the elections, Zimbabwe was finally suspended from the Commonwealth for a year.)

And where is the African American community on this? There has been little to no comment from the Revs. Jesse Jackson, Al Sharpton, and Louis Farrakhan. Rev. Jackson has distanced himself from the violence of his erstwhile friend's party, but hopes that funding to Zimbabwe will not be reduced. In a February 21 press release, he argued against sanctions, saying "the international community should not punish innocent Zimbabweans because of policy differences with their government."

Tragically, there may be no other way to help Zimbabwe but to do just that. The G8 meeting on African development to be held in Canada this June will provide an opportunity to send a strong message. Western nations and NGOs can make an exception of Zimbabwe and suspend aid as long as Mugabe and his gang are in power, as countries such as Denmark and Norway have done. The funds could, instead, be spent helping the MDC and the majority eliminate his criminal regime, or reallocated to help countries like Mozambique, whose government has had the sense to offer land to Zimbabwean farmers fortunate enough to survive Mugabe's thugs.

Reprinted with the permission from http://www.fpri.org, May 17, 2002

AFRICAN NIGHTMARE

"Fears of famine in Ethiopia," says the *New York Times*; "Mugabe's "surreal" policies ravage Zimbabwe's economy," adds the *Washington Post*—and those headlines are just from the past two weeks. Meanwhile, a civil war rages in the Ivory Coast, and generalized famine threatens most of Southern Africa—Zimbabwe, Zambia, Mozambique, and Malawi. And in the continent's most populous country, Nigeria, fundamentalist Islam, complete with the stoning to death of adulterers and the chopping off of thieves' hands, is on the march.

All that in countries that still have governments, because places—one cannot call them states in any meaningful sense—like Somalia, Sierra Leone, or "The Democratic Republic of Congo" (formerly known as Zaire) do not enjoy even that dubious advantage. And then there are the civil wars: in the Sudan, between Arab Muslims and black Christians; and in Zaire, between Ugandans and Rwandans on the one side (or are there two?) and Zimbabwe, Angola, Namibia on the other. al-Qaeda has a presence in Somalia, Kenya, Sierra Leone, Burkina Fasso, and Liberia, and Libyan troops operate in Central Africa and run interference in West Africa. And, last but far from least, up to 40 percent percent of the adult population in countries like Lesotho and Zambia, to name but a few, are suffering from HIV/AIDS.

The more recent AIDS pandemic aside, and with a few names changed, similarly depressing headlines could have been read twenty years ago: let us remember Idi Amin, the cannibal ruler of Uganda; Jean-Bedel Bokassa, the convicted cannibal and emperor of Central Africa; Francisco Macias Nguema, the self-described "sole miracle" of Equatorial Guinea, who publicly shot most of his ministers as the band played "Happy Days are Here Again"—all prior to 1979.

It would seem that Sub-Saharan Africa today, just as yesterday, remains behind all other areas of the world—in economic, political, and social terms. There are many reasons for this, and, one must say, there are a few flickerings of light at the end of the tunnel.

To begin with, most of the continent's problems today are inherited from the time of independence. With the exceptions of Liberia, Ethiopia, and South Africa, not one of the contemporary subsaharan countries has any history of independent statehood. They are all creations of European rivalries and European bureaucrats in London, Paris, or Lisbon. Nor, again, with a few exceptions (Botswana, Somalia, and the island states), do they have any pre-independence

sentiment of nationhood, divided as they were, and are, along ethnic and linguistic lines. Declaring the former colonial language the official one is recognition of this reality: only a foreign language could provide a minimum of
internal unity.

Once independent, in many cases without any popular demand for independence, country after country fell under the control of European-educated (at the
Sorbonne or the London School of Economics) and influenced (naturally
enough, by the leftist ideas prevailing there) elites. Socialism, occasionally
Marxism-Leninism, was the favorite among the various ideologies that failed
in richer countries but devastated Africa. All this was encouraged by Western
intellectuals and often paid for by Western taxpayers.

Thus, for decades, Tanzania's ruinous experiment with socialism was subsidized—at the highest per capita rate in Africa—by the Scandinavian countries.
Julius Nyerere, the country's first president and "father" of African socialism,
admitted upon retirement "We failed."

And then there was the Cold War. The countries under Soviet rule aside,
no other region has lost more during it than Africa. Non-viable country after
non-viable country had muddled through for four decades because outside
support kept them together: Western economic and military aid; East German, Cuban, or Soviet arms, secret police advisers, and political support.
Fear of some marginal state going to the other side attracted attention and
support, out of proportion in many cases, to the state's importance in the
larger scheme of things. By 1989 it all came crashing down, and Africa was
faced with the unpleasant reality of its actual status in the world. It turned
out that the emperor had no clothes. Their vision no longer clouded by
perceived geopolitical or strategic interests, outsiders began to see Africa in
its real dimensions.

In fact, with some 650 million people, Subsaharan Africa's combined GNP is
somewhat smaller than that of Belgium (population: 10 million). As for per
capita income ($474 in 2000), it had a negative growth rate of 0.6 percent over
the years 1988-2000—or 0.3 percent excluding the region's economic superpower, South Africa. All this despite the fact that a few, usually small, countries
(Saõ Tomé and Principe, Equatorial Guinea) are experiencing a major oil boom,
and a handful (Botswana, Uganda and Mauritius, e.g.) have competent and
successful economic policies and healthy growth rates. Simply put, in the new
world of globalization, a few commodities aside, Africa isn't a significant market, competitor, or exporter.

Nor has Africa's longstanding ability to exploit Western guilt over colonialism retained its potency. Increasingly, taxpayers in the West, if not many intellectuals and the Left, find it harder and harder to attribute forty years of postindependence decay to eighty years of colonialism—especially since in many
countries the statistics suggest that the majority were worse off in 1990 than at
the end of the colonial era.

The fiasco of the 2001 UN Conference on Racism in Durban was both significant and, in some ways, encouraging. It was significant because it demonstrated that attempts to mine Western guilt, at the cost of insulting both history and common sense, are still popular in some quarters; encouraging because the most vocal advocates of the most preposterous ideas advanced—"reparations for slavery" and open anti-Semitism—were American racial demagogues and Arabs, rather than Africans.

This is not to say that Africans did not engage in racism, often with economically suicidal consequences. In the 1970s Idi Amin expelled the prosperous Indian community of Uganda and stole their property; Lebanese in West Africa have occasionally been expelled and their property confiscated; and today Comrade Mugabe in Zimbabwe is engaged in a massive ethnic cleansing of whites and Asians and stealing their property, with dire consequences for most black Zimbabweans. A case could be made that Mugabe is a Stalinist dinosaur and Idi Amin was certifiably unhinged, but the fact remains that there was no pan-African condemnation of their actions.

All of which should bring to light the obvious fact, avoided for decades by both African elites and well-intentioned Westerners, that outside the conceptual framework of racism there is no such thing as "Africa." Yes, there is the creation in 2002, through Muammar Qaddaffi's brainstorm and oil dollars, of the African Union, successor to the famously irrelevant Organization of African Unity, likely to make the latter an example of effectiveness. But to understand how shallow the concept of African unity is in the real world one only has to look at the post-1994 events in the Great Lakes region of Central Africa.

In 1994 the ruling Hutu regime in Rwanda engaged in the world's most obvious case of genocide since the Holocaust, with as many as 750,000 minority Tutsis murdered in a matter of weeks. An invading force of Uganda-based Tutsis then took power and the defeated perpetrators fled to Zaire. The Rwandans pursued them, and the result was an all-African free-for-all war that, for once, involved only African armies (at least six of them) and their local proxies. It would be hard, indeed, to blame that war, fought over diamonds, titanium, manganese, and copper, as much as over territory, on Belgian colonialism. Nor is it easier to blame the recent Ethiopia-Eritrea war over a few patches of bush, with up to a million casualties, on Mussolini's Italy.

All of these are tragedies, but they are strictly African-made tragedies, and the good news is that Africans and outsiders alike are coming to see them as such. After decades of lies, blaming others, and irresponsible elites and outsider interveners, today Africa is forced to live in a global environment in which responsibility is what matters.

In economic terms, some African states are fighting to erase their well-deserved reputation of corruption and bureaucratic red tape and attract foreign investment. Many are oil producing countries, but Uganda and Mauritius are succeeding, even without oil. And West African oil is not to be sneezed at: it is clean, offshore (thus minimizing frictions with the locals) and abundant. Though hopelessly corrupt, divided, and increasingly threatened by Islamic fundamentalism, Nigeria is, for now, the major producer. That will change in favor of small states with a need for protection against the likes of Nigeria—which is where U.S. technology, power projection capabilities, and capital could come in.

If there is any positive political sign coming from Africa, it is that democracy is making some progress after decades of dictatorships and kleptocracies. A number of the continent's "big men" have lost elections (Kaunda in Zambia, Diouf in Senegal, Ratsiraka in Madagascar) or have retired voluntarily: Moi in Kenya, Rawlings in Ghana, soon Chissano in Mozambique. That does not a democratic march from Dakar to Khartoum, or from Bamako to Harare, make, but at least the signs are not all negative.

Because Subsaharan Africa is, and is likely to remain, marginal in economic, political, and strategic terms, regional self-sufficiency is the key to progress. To a decisive extent, that means South African supremacy. South Africa is the only country in the region with the capital, technological and professional resources, and the obvious interest (dictated by its location and experience) to help the entire region, or at least the southern and central areas of Africa. It controls the transportation hubs (ports and railroads all the way to Zaire); it produces the bulk of manufactured goods and energy; and it has a still large (albeit diminishing due to massive emigration) professional and technical mass of qualified experts. If South Africa fails politically or economically, Subsaharan Africa has no future outside a few isolated oil enclaves.

The problem is that South Africa does not play the role one would expect or hope. The case of Zimbabwe is a good example. While Mandela or Tutu pontificate about U.S. imperialism and cruelty in using the death penalty, their country's labor minister, Membathisi Mdladlana, just claimed that South Africa "has a lot to learn" from Mugabe's Stalinist "land reform," which has destroyed the economy one of Africa's few formerly prosperous countries. The minister's opinions may have been disavowed by his government, but the fact remains that it is Pretoria's tolerance and, indeed, active political and economic support, that keeps Mugabe's criminal regime afloat.

Nor is Pretoria the only one at fault. The African Union itself had nothing to say about Zimbabwe's self-immolation—naturally enough, since Mugabe's financial sponsor, Muammar Qaddafi, is also the Union's promoter. And African members of the Commonwealth blocked efforts to suspend Zimbabwe's membership. Racial solidarity, once again, as in the cases of Bokassa, Idi Amin, etc., trumped decency and indeed rational self-interest.

If there is any problem that attracts the same old tired and demonstrably ineffective calls for more aid, more sympathy, and more misguided, and indiscriminat,e outside interference in Africa, is the issue of AIDS. Since the pandemic originated in Africa, the continent has suffered longer than any other part of the world from its impact. Today, although Subsaharan Africa represents only 10 percent of the world's population, it has 67 percent of known AIDS/HIV cases.

There are many reasons for this, and objective causes why it is so difficult to cope with the problem, some independent of whatever African governments could do. A very young population (in some cases 50 percent under the age of twenty) means that the most irresponsible age group is unusually large; mass illiteracy and poor infrastructure make education and prevention difficult; and poor health services make treatment almost impossible. More important, however, is the attitude of African governments. With the laudable exception of Uganda, for years they have denied the very existence of an AIDS problem. Even today, the president of South Africa, Thabo Mbeki, denies that AIDS is the result of a virus, and, thus, provides the worst possible example to other, far less developed, countries in the region.

Western pharmaceutical companies have given up their patents for AIDS medication, and relatively cheap generics exist—enriching Indian and Brazilian manufacturers. Massive Western infusions of medicines, medical personnel, and funds are now available, but, as is the case with aid in general, these only lead to waste, corruption, and demands for more.

Massive amounts of free U.S. food aid to southern African countries afflicted by famine are being rejected by Zambia and Malawi because they are genetically modified types of corn or wheat. Suddenly, starving people are denied food because, under the influence of paranoiac European Greens, their governments have decided to be politically correct.

All of this raises the question, is Africa going anywhere? The answer is unclear, and it all depends on how African states and Western partners treat each other. If African states finally decide that they have distinct interests, rather than pretending to belong to a non-existent "Africa," they could enjoy the fruits of their sound decisions—where those decisions are sound. If not, they should pay the price of failure, just like any other country, whether Bolivia, Nepal, or Romania. As for the West, it should finally stop its irresponsibly paternalistic treatment of "Africa" as a perennial victim of everyone except its own rulers, reward the successful and leave the failed to pay the price.

Reprinted with the permission from http://www.frontpagemag.com, January 15, 2003

South Africa: The Downside of Liberation

Nelson Mandela, South Africa's first black president, who is widely admired across the political spectrum more for his performance in office than for his beliefs, is now retired and, thus, free to express his long standing Marxist, and often bizarre, beliefs freely. He continually attacks U.S. "imperialism" and "arrogance" while voicing support for the likes of Libya, Iraq, and Cuba. This is not surprising. Despite the well-deserved Nobel Peace Prize (shared with F.W. de Klerk) and his relatively moderate behavior while in office, Mr. Mandela did support violence in the past—a fact that is largely forgotten or trivialized. Indeed, in 1961 he was the founder of Umkhonto we Siswe ("Spear of the People"), ANC's terrorist arm, and never during his long years in prison did he condemn that organization's acts of indiscriminate terrorism. Moreover, throughout his career, Mandela has remained close to regimes actively supporting terrorism—the former Soviet Union, Libya, Cuba.

There were good reasons for such fears, not the least being the decades old cohabitation of Mandela's African National Congress (ANC) with, and its penetration by, the Communist Party of South Africa (SACP), one of the world's most committed Stalinist parties. There were also the ANC's close links with the militantly leftist (and SACP-dominated) trade union federation, COSATU. However, most of those fears turned out to be exaggerated. Once in power, the ANC (the leadership of which has since passed from Mandela to Thabo Mbeki) understood, or was made to understand, by the collapse of the Soviet bloc, that capitalism is not a "white" thing, but, rather, is the reason South Africa is the continent's superpower, with half of Subsaharan Africa's GNP. Capitalism was the only way it could remain in that position.

And importantly, despite the rhetoric about black economic oppression under apartheid, the fact remains that a black middle- and, indeed, upper-class had developed in South Africa, the interests of which had little to do with the traditional socialism advocated by the ANC throughout its history.

Yes, Mandela implemented an aggressive affirmative action policy once he took office—which slowed down the economy. His government established a criminal law code on the European model—abolition of the death penalty, excessive rights for accused criminals, etc., with destructive results. South Africa today competes with civil war-torn Colombia for the dubious distinction of being the world's most crime-ridden country. Interpol's International Crime Statistics say it all: in 1999 South Africa had 121 murders and 119 rapes per 100,000 inhabitants, compared with Colombia's sixty-nine and six respectively (and the United States' five and thirty-two). The trends are no more encouraging considering that in 1994 the world's average murder rate was 5.5 per 100,000, compared to South Africa's forty-five. In such circumstances, and with a slow justice system, which only produces a 10 percent conviction rate, South Africa has seen the rise of vigilante groups filling the void left by an incompetent (affirmative action, again—one third of policemen are functionally illiterate) and violent police—who between 1997 and 2000 killed 1,550 people, compared with 2,700 killed by the apartheid regime in thirty years.

The high crime rates, and a decline in educational standards, led to a massive emigration of white professionals to the United States, U.K., Canada, and Australia. A 1998 poll of 11,000 skilled professionals suggested that 74 percent wanted to emigrate—with then-president Mandela responding with "Good riddance" to them. The problem is that not just professionals leave South Africa— major corporations also moved out, including mining giant Anglo American Co. and South African Breweries, both of which are now headquartered in London.

Most South African companies, including the largest, which are in the mining and energy fields, have black shareholders, whose interests are the same as those of shareholders everywhere: maximizing profits. And the economy is doing relatively well, at least by African standards. Indeed, the nation experienced a 2.6 percent growth rate in 2001 and, according to the CIA, had a GNP of $412 billion that year ($9,400 per capita). However, the unemployment rate remains very high among the black majority—with a lack of education and an inflexible labor market being the primary causes.

It used to be fashionable to accuse the apartheid regime of racism when it tried to control immigration from the rest of Africa. The issue remains even now that South Africa's president is black. The people most hostile to African immigrants, most of them illegal aliens, are South Africa's blacks themselves, who see their jobs lost to cheap immigrant labor and their opportunities lost in competing with foreigners. (Sound familiar?) The result is that today South Africa is implementing increasingly draconian immigration restrictions for foreign Africans and considering even more.

South African companies are involved as investors or consultants in most Subsaharan countries, continuing a process started during the apartheid regime. Since then Pretoria has refrained from exerting its natural influence, and its restraint has only made things worse in most of Africa. A clear instance is the situation in Congo (formerly Zaire and now officially the Democratic Republic of the Congo), where an all-African war pitting six different countries killed hundreds of thousands while Pretoria remained largely ineffective. Even closer to home, while the criminal regime in Harare goes its way in transforming the once-prosperous nation of Zimbabwe into a basket case, Pretoria has had little to say, despite the Zimbabwe regime's open disdain for South Africa. Although Pretoria has a decisive say on what Zimbabwe does, or does not, do, it elects to protect Robert Mugabe's Stalinist clique.

When it comes to African opinions at the UN, Pretoria also prefers to side with the worst. Libya for chairmanship of the UN Human Rights Commission? Yes, said Pretoria, and so did the rest of the African bloc. Support Mugabe's "right" to be invited to Lisbon for the EU-African Summit? Yes again, at the cost of billions of dollars in aid to Africa. Mandela's ideological legacy seems to be alive in Pretoria's international behavior.

None of this should come as a surprise. The once dominant South African National Defense Force (SANDF) is now only a shadow of its past self, largely as a result of budget cuts and affirmative action, which put former ANC terrorist thugs and gang members in charge and led to a massive exodus of white and colored (mixed race) officers.

Since elections in South Africa are largely decided by race, the ANC is, for all practical purposes, the only political party that matters, and the distribution of power is decided by intra-party debates, rather than by negotiations with the largely ineffective opposition.

President Mbeki has a problem with his own ANC party, specifically with Nelson Mandela's former wife, Winnie. Mrs. Mandela is the loose cannon of the ANC. A convicted torturer and felon and thoroughly corrupt, she remains a very popular figure with black South African youths and was repeatedly elected to the ANC leadership. The disturbing thing here is not so much Winnie's criminality, awful as it is, as the general decline of South Africa's judiciary, which is becoming increasingly more "African" and less and less Western.

Finally, there are Mr. Mbeki's autocratic style and personal beliefs—such as those regarding AIDS. South Africa has the world's largest number of persons living with HIV/AIDS: 5 million of its 44 million citizens are HIV-positive. Only 42 million are infected worldwide (Anne-Marie O'Connor, "S. Africa Has Doubts on U.S. AIDS Proposal," *Los Angeles Times,* 1/30/03). But Mbeki has repeatedly stated that he did not believe the "thesis" that AIDS is caused by HIV, or that it is a virus at all. Until last week, he even resisted making available, at foreign subsidized prices, the anti-retroviral drugs that have proven effective in preventing mother-to-child transmission of HIV. (South Africa already has 660,000 AIDS orphans.) Considering that South Africa has the only real health care system in sub-Saharan Africa, such an attitude is nothing short of suicidal for the region.

Ultimately, it is South Africa that will decide the future of sub-Saharan Africa as a whole. But South Africa's policy vis-à-vis the rest of the continent is still in flux, with many discouraging signs crushing hopes of a better future under its democratized rule. One must hope Pretoria will take the direction of common sense and free markets. South Africa has the responsibility for, and would deservedly benefit from, making the right choice. If it does not, Africa is doomed.

Reprinted with the permission from http://www.frontpagemag.com,
February 6, 2003

PAN-AFRICAN RACISM

For Westerners today, "Africa" still sounds exotic and somehow "victimized"—it conjures past images of blacks being enslaved to the Americas (conveniently forgotten are those shipped to Oman, Arabia or the Gulf); and the present day visions of starving children, genocide, and AIDS. For better or for worse, the combined impact of these perceptions has somehow given "Africa," at least in naïve Western eyes, a moral credibility of victimhood it never deserved and, most importantly, it is now doing its collective best to destroy. After decades of manipulating, and extorting, aid over Western guilt over colonialism, "Africa," or at least its loudest voices, is now increasingly turning toward what could only be called a politically incorrect name: racialism in the name of a phony continental solidarity. Just as Western universities, academics, media, and experts used to help African states along the self-destructive road to "socialism" during the 1960s and 1970s, they are now playing along the game of blaming non–black outsiders for the continent's woes. A few recent examples are very enlightening.

An EU-African summit meeting scheduled for March 2003 in Lisbon was postponed indefinitely because of Africa's insistence that Zimbabwe's President Robert Mugabe be invited and Britain's refusal to attend if he is. South Africa and Nigeria also insist that Zimbabwe's suspension from the Commonwealth be lifted, which Australia strongly opposes. The EU has renewed sanctions against Zimbabweans' travel to the EU, but only after accepting as a fait accompli France's decision to invite Mugabe and his high spending wife to Paris.

Meanwhile, on January 20, at the insistence of the African bloc at the UN, the UN Human Rights Commission—the same commission that in May 2001 voted to replace the U.S. on that commission (the U.S. only regained its seat beginning January 2003)—elected Libya to assume its chairmanship. Finally, among his more notable recent comments, Nelson Mandela has claimed that the United States is only pushing for war on Iraq because...UN Secretary General Kofi Annan is a black man. That, to put it politely, is racialist obsession.

The newly minted (at Libyan insistence) African Union includes some fifty-two countries. Some are "African" strictly by virtue of geography (Arab North Africa, Somalia, Mauritania, Mauritius) and a handful are democracies of sorts, but most are kleptocracies, and many—with Mugabe's Zimbabwe as the poster boy—are murderous tribal dictatorships. "Democracies of sorts?" Indeed, since, ultimately, most AU decisions are taken by a handful of countries, most prominently (aside from Libya) Nigeria and South Africa, both of which have elected governments, albeit Nigeria's cannot control the march of Islamic fundamentalism in its north and South Africa's is increasingly collapsing into a crime ridden, race-defined one-party system.

Alas, most of Africa, at least Subsaharan Africa, clearly is, and for at least three decades has been, the world's sick continent. It is the only part of the world that is consistently behind, and falling further behind, on all economic, social, and political rankings. It is the most dependent on debt forgiveness for its very survival as a plausible collection of states, and often dependent on food and health care handouts for the survival of its people.

One would hope that "Africa" could understand and, at the very least begin to seriously examine, the causes of its condition. There was a fleeting moment at the beginning of the 1990s when such a self-examination seemed possible, mostly because the end of "existing socialism" discredited an ideology which had a major role in Africa's pitiful state. Unfortunately, the moment passed, and now we see a return to the patterns of the past—racism elevated to the level of continental "solidarity," blaming selectively chosen "others" (i.e., the "whites"), singing the song of anti-Western sirens from Tripoli, etc. Meanwhile, Nigeria is descending into confessional conflict, with Islamists persisting in cutting off the hands of thieves and in stoning women; South Africa continues on its suicidal course of "Affirmative Action," resulting in an illiterate police and an increasingly politically correct media; while in Zimbabwe, Mugabe brings all these political and cultural diseases onto the front page—with "Africa" supporting him.

Why "Africa" when there are some countries on the continent that, in practice at home, does not share the AU's values, as expressed by the "big men" in Lagos or Pretoria? Because too many people outside Africa—and not just in Tripoli or the UN's New York headquarters, but also in the press rooms of major European and American newspapers and elite universities—long ago decided that "Africa" has to have one voice—implicitly a "black" one, a vicarious way of fighting against the despised capitalism and democracy of their own societies.

Do the relatively effective governments of Uganda, Mauritius, Senegal, and Botswana really represent the same "Africa" as the murderously corrupt Stalinist Mugabe does in Zimbabwe? Obviously not, and the question is why they implicitly accept the "leadership" of an impotent Obasanjo of Nigeria, incoherent Mbeki of South Africa, not to mention Qaddafi. The answer is because they believe to have no alternative to such specious, and dangerous, "solidarity." Not all—fortunately, and this makes the point—Mozambique, itself ruined by decades of "socialism," has invited (yes, invited !), the very "white colonialist" farmers Mugabe has expelled and persecuted to set up farms on government provided land. But that example of common sense is more than obscured by the anti–white rantings of Sam Nujoma, the aging Marxist dictator of Namibia, and even by some voices in South Africa, all of whom think that today's stealing of "white" property by their clique's aces the inevitable starvation of blacks that will follow tomorrow.

When President Bush talks about spending billions of dollars in "Africa" to eradicate AIDS, he only promotes the illusion of a unified Africa that doesn't exist now and never did, and which should not be treated as a fact. President Bush never speaks of "Asia" or "Latin America" in this way, and it does not make sense here either.

As long as Washington, Brussels, or especially the UN continue to speak of "the continent of Africa," as Bush did in his recent State of the Union Address, they only encourage racist demagogues à la Mugabe and his enablers in Pretoria and Abuja, rather than treating the various countries of that continent as the separate and different countries they are. As for the French, who invited Mugabe to Paris last week, well…they are enablers, French and, thus, desperate to maintain what used to be an effective influence and is now badly slipping away throughout the continent—the latest humiliation coming in what used to be France's model ex-colony, Côte D'Ivoire. Uganda is not South Africa, certainly not when it comes to dealing with AIDS; Kenya is not, especially now that an elected government is in power, the racially obsessed, anti-Semitic place Sudan is; well-governed Botswana is certainly not anarchic Somalia, etc.

If African racism is to be contained, the idea of African "solidarity," whether coming from within, or encouraged from without, must be discarded as a bad and dangerous habit. Outsiders, on whose investments, aid, and general help the future of all countries in Africa depend, have to treat each country as an individual case—and, expect the government, if any, to behave according to its citizens' interests, not according to some vague and irresponsible notions of African solidarity. And well-intentioned Western NGOs have to accept that the declining support for aid to Africa is not just a matter of "donor fatigue"—although that is an understandable reality—it is also a reaction to the unending assaults of self-appointed "African" voices against those very donors.

Ultimately, the future of many countries in Africa depends on the deconstruction of this false and dangerously self-defeating concept of African unity among the region's different peoples and governments. The future of "Africa" is dependent on the end of the very notion of "Africa" as some kind of ethnic, racial, and historic unity that never did, and does not, deserve to exist.

Reprinted with the permission from http://www.frontpagemag.com,
February 28, 2003

WINNIE MANDELA: SOUTH AFRICA'S MOTHER OF THIEVES

Once upon a time, Winnie Madikizela-Mandela's admirers thought of her as the "mother of the nation" of South Africa. Today, Madikizela-Mandela, the ex-wife of Nelson Mandela, stands convicted of massive theft and faces sentencing to up to fifteen years in jail by a court appointed by her own party, the ruling African National Congress (ANC). This on top of a previous conviction for kidnapping (that, but for the politics involved, should have been a conviction for murder and kidnapping). Simply put, the "mother of the nation" is a career criminal.

Winnie's nature is nothing new. From the early 1980s she was using anti-apartheid supporters' financial help to maintain a life of luxury, encouraging the infamous "necklacing" of that decade (the practice of placing a rubber tire filled with gasoline around the neck of suspected apartheid collaborators and setting it on fire), and running a gang of adolescent thugs grotesquely called Mandela's United Football Club, etc. (Her husband eventually divorced her for adultery after he was released from prison.)

Nor is Winnie the only prominent South African "freedom fighter" involved in criminal affairs. Alan Boesak, another hero of the anti-apartheid struggle, was also convicted of stealing money from the cause (for his and his white mistress's use). A general sense of corruption within the ANC is common in South Africa—making that party just another among the depressingly familiar list of permanently elected organizations destroying Africa. As encouraging as it is that Winnie was convicted, it is equally troubling that she remains popular even though she has now been convicted twice of serious crimes.

Even more troubling, Winnie has been elected to parliament twice (in 1994 and 1999) and to the leading forums of the ANC largely on the basis of her popularity with the youth wing of the ANC. Indeed, she is the poster girl of South Africa's "lost generation:" the generation now in its thirties who, at her incitement, eschewed schooling in response to the irresponsible slogan of "No education before liberation." These uneducated masses are now the main reason South Africa is at the very top among the world's most violent nations, as confirmed by a November 2002 UN report (Pretoria has not released statistics recently). With a huge number of guns available, the country leads in rape, carjacking, murder, armed robbery, and assault. These are Winnie's constituency: the unemployed and unemployable—unless they are hired by the National Defense Force or police under their affirmative action policies, and, thus, free to pursue a criminal career legally armed and in uniform.

Madikizela-Mandela was convicted this week of forty-three counts of fraud and twenty-five of theft involving $120,000 from the African National Congress Women's League, which she heads. But outside the court, "Madikizela-Mandela was met by a group of about thirty students, chanting 'Viva Winnie viva,' with raised fists. Madikizela Mandela smiled at the group and raised her fist" (AP, April 24, 2003).

Winnie's prominence and political significance raises the general issue of South Africa's future. During the unregretted apartheid era, South Africa's elites saw the country's future as being part of the West, which they felt irrationally kept them aside. Both the Afrikaans speakers who supported the system, and their English-speaking opposition, tried, or pretended to try, to follow Western patterns. The idea was that South Africa, a Commonwealth member (if suspended) that enjoyed cooperative relations with the United States, etc., was part of the vaguely defined "West."

The non-elite view of the country's future, radically represented by groups such as the quasi-Maoist Pan-African Congress, saw the country as part and parcel of the Third World in Africa (whatever that continental demarcation might mean), and were, thus, opposed to all that is Western and "exploitative."

This brings us to the ANC, which is not really a "party" in the usual sense but more an umbrella "movement" of ideologically disparate groups united by the desire of power. Within the ANC, Winnie was a typical opportunist. She liked money, enjoyed Western luxuries, wore couture fashion, and thrived on media adulation, while also encouraging some practices commonly associated with African politics: terror, violence, and one-party rule. Not surprisingly, given the influence the unreconstructed South African Communist Party (SACP) has always exerted within the ANC, Winnie represents the ANC's totalitarian wing.

It is too early to say whether the ANC's leadership has yet made a choice between South Africa's being a Western or an African country. The corruption, tolerance of criminality, and irresponsibility of the leaders—President Thabo Mbeki Mbeki, it will be recalled, still claims that he does not believe the "thesis" that AIDS is caused by HIV, or even that it is a virus—suggest an "African" choice. But its still relatively independent judiciary, free press, and refusal to emulate neighboring Zimbabwe's racist, anti-white, and economically suicidal policy of confiscation of white owned farms, and its encouragement of foreign investment, suggests otherwise. Hence the confusion when Nelson Mandela bizarrely accuses the United States of being guilty of "racism," or when President Mbeki tries to negotiate between Washington and Baghdad. Pretoria supports some of the worst human rights violators in the name of African solidarity, and, yet, has, by far, the most liberal constitution in Africa: homosexual rights, no capital punishment, etc.

It is precisely this confusion that ultimately explains South Africa's absence from the space it occupied for decades, up to 1991, on the front pages of Western newspapers. And then there is the Western media's reluctance to admit that past heroes like Winnie and Boesak were just crooks taking advantage of an ideological, liberal fashion.

Winnie's conviction is also a challenge to President Mbeki. His options are to do nothing, as a Western leader would, or to do the "African" thing: pardon her because of her political influence. That would be an insult to Africa, a demonstration of South Africa's descent into the third world, and a disappointment for all those who placed their hopes for African renewal on an apartheid-free South Africa.

Reprinted with the permission from http://www.frontpagemag.com,
April 28, 200

WHAT DO WE OWE LIBERIA?

Liberia is a mess. As usual we are being blamed for the mess. The reason Liberia is a failed state? It's the United States' neglect. That is the expressed opinion of Liberian president Charles Taylor, and there are many in the United States, and elsewhere, who share Taylor's premise that Washington is somehow responsible, at least morally, for Liberia's predicament, and, hence, somehow obliged to fix it, by sending troops there.

We are being told that, since Liberia was established by freed American slaves more than a century and a half ago (in 1847), America remains responsible for its fate, a paternalistic, but convenient, position. Not surprisingly, such claims come from the very same U.S. liberals (along with the Moravian mobs) who opposed the Iraq intervention but strongly pushed for the use of the Marines in Kosovo, Bosnia, Somalia, and Haiti—in short, everywhere some mushy "humanitarian" cause popped up, but not where the security and national interests of this country were clearly involved. Marines as social workers are fine, but Marines as Marines are proof of American imperialism.

It is useful to review the actual history of Liberia's founding. Quakers, who were skeptical of America's ability to fully integrate liberated slaves, and Southern slave holders, who were disturbed by the "bad example" of free slaves in their midst, combined to find a solution by relocating them to Africa, as if that were some homogeneous and unified place all blacks came from and any part of it would do. They followed the precedent of the British, who dumped slaves found on trading ships captured by their Navy on the west coast of Africa, in what has recently became both Liberia's victim and fellow failure, Sierra Leone.

At the time, nobody in official Washington considered Liberia a "moral obligation," and, indeed, the United States did not even recognize the country until after the American Civil War, and with good reason. The behavior of the transplanted former American slaves was already nothing to be proud of, and it got worse with the time. As Liberian columnist Tarty Teh put it, "These returned slaves kept us, African Liberians, as field slaves for well over 130 years in the land of our ancestors. For nearly a century and a half they gradually promoted us into the rough equivalent of house slaves when they domesticated a few of us by helping us sport such names as George Washington, Robert Kennedy, George Wallace, etc., as our new identities and as testimony of our acquired elegance. But the bulk of us remained Africans because we could not help it. For daring to remain Africans we, in the eyes of the ruling Americos, forfeited our rights to any aspiration beyond being tolerated by the snobbish descendants of ex-slaves." (Tarty Teh, *Liberia Is Being P.U.S.H.ed by Rev. Jesse Jackson*, May 24, 2000, http://members.aol.com/csiedit/liberia_is_being_push.htm).

Indeed, the small American-Liberian elite established what amounted to official apartheid for the duration of its rule, which lasted up to 1980. Native tribal blacks, always a huge majority, were treated as obviously inferior, remained uneducated and poor, were often sold as de facto slaves ("contract laborers") to plantations in Spanish Guinea (now Equatorial Guinea) and only received the right to vote in 1946, ninety-nine years after independence. From the late 1860s until 1980 Liberia was a one-party state, under the True Whig Party. Seen in this context, Liberia's mimicking the American flag, using the American dollar, and naming its capital, Monrovia, after James Monroe, appear more as insults to Americans than a cause for emotional and historic fellowship.

And then, in 1980, the oppressed tribals had their revenge: a coup led by the illiterate Sergeant Major Samuel Doe captured and shot President William

Tolbert and his cabinet members. Following a by-then rich African tradition represented by the likes of Idi Amin, Jean Bedel Bokassa, and Macias Nguema, Doe gave himself phony titles, including "doctor," and misruled the country until other tribes rebelled. In 1990 Doe was captured, mutilated, and murdered—all on videotape.

Meanwhile, Charles Taylor, educated in part (and jailed) in Boston, escaped prison and obtained the support of Muammar Ghadafi and his regional proxy, the leader of one of the world's smallest and poorest nations, Burkina Faso, and made his own bid for power. By 1997 he has killed or intimidated enough people to be "elected" president. In no time at all he had invented "opposition groups" in neighboring Sierra Leone, Guinea, and Ivory Coast—and cashed in diamonds and other booty. None of this, naturally enough, prevented the likes of Rev. Jesse Jackson from visiting Taylor and treating him as a long-lost brother.

But Taylor overextended himself, and his neighbors realized that his was a game that others could play as well. Guinea, with American support, and Ivory Coast, with French support, encouraged, armed, and paid some of the masses of unemployed young Liberian refugees in their territories to go back, and soon a number of anti-Taylor "national" and "democratic" organizations had appeared, who are now cornering Taylor in the capital. Meanwhile, a UN-sponsored tribunal in Sierra Leone has indicted Taylor for crimes against humanity—an indictment that does not seem to impress the government of "Africa's giant," Nigeria, the self-proclaimed regional power, which offered him a comfortable and safe asylum. Nor did it prevent the Rev. Pat Robertson from making deals with Taylor and from realizing that the latter's Baptist faith (?) gives all Baptists a bad name.

This is the "country" we are supposed to have a moral obligation to and to which we are asked to send troops to restore a "democracy" that never existed, the power of a corrupt, and by now largely dead or emigrated, American-Liberian elite? A country with no institutions, no sense of nationhood, no infrastructure, no limit to its needs or, worse still, to the exaggerated expectations of a destitute and chaotic population? If the Haiti intervention was a failure, an intervention in Liberia would be a tragedy, and for similar reasons. Where there is no country and there are no citizens or institutions, no amount of Marines or dollars can invent them.

If the newly established African Union wants to be taken seriously, it should prove that it is capable of doing something for and in Liberia, rather than spend its energies debating whether the AU parliament should be located in Capetown or Tripoli. The British have temporarily stabilized Sierra Leone, which should remain "stable" as long as the paratroopers stay there, and not one minute longer. The French are doing the same in Ivory Coast, with similar short-term success. Whatever Paris and London's reasons for deciding to get into the swamps of their former colonies, their actions do not mean that Washington has to do the same in a place that, far from being a former American colony, was a caricature of America.

President Bush should make it clear that Liberia is not a place of national interest for the United States, that we have no moral or other obligation toward it, and that no commitment of American lives should be expected, only possibly some (very) temporary logistical and financial support for an African or UN force. As a good Texan would put it, the U.S. does not have a dog in the Liberian fight.

Reprinted with the permission from http://www.frontpagemag.com,
July 14, 2003

DEAD CANNIBAL

According to the news agencies, Idi Amin, a.k.a. "Big Daddy" or, more formally "His Excellency President for Life Field Marshal Al Hadj Doctor Idi Amin Dada, VC, DSO, MC, Lord of All the Beasts of the Earth and Fishes of the Sea and Conqueror of the British Empire in Africa in General and Uganda in Particular" has died on August 15.

Amin's name was synonymous with tyranny during his presidency of Uganda, from 1971-1979. Amin's career took him from illiterate national boxing champion to chief of staff, "doctor" to military dictator, mass murderer to chairman of the Organization of African Unity (OAU). In the nearly twenty-five years since his rule ended, has the behavior of African regimes or outside observers and aid donors changed?

"Tell me who your friends are and I will tell you who you are," the saying goes. Amin's friends included the communist Red Brigades and Palestinian terrorists he aided in their 1976 hijacking of an Air France airliner to Entebbe. The Jewish passengers being held on the plane (who were rescued in the spectacular Israeli raid that ended the hijacking) had been carefully selected: Amin, who publicly praised Hitler for murdering Jews, had become an admirer of the Fuhrer after Israel, which he visited, refused to provide him with modern weapons.

Idi Amin was a declared racist. He confiscated the wealth and expelled from Uganda all Asians, whose crime was being hard working, and Asian. (Neither India nor Pakistan would receive them: it was the United Kingdom that gave them asylum, and another chance to use their talents and get rich again.)

But the West's blind eye toward Amin was such that, as the U.S. ambassador to Uganda at the time, Thomas Melady, recently noted, the human rights-oriented administration of future Nobel Peace laureate Jimmy Carter refused to impose even the most minimal sanctions (such as on Ugandan coffee) on Amin's regime. And this was an administration that unhesitatingly penalized Argentina for human rights abuses against educated, middle-class Marxist terrorists.

That Amin was a member of Uganda's small Muslim community allowed him ultimately, after sometime in Libya, to reach safe and comfortable asylum in Saudi Arabia. He was granted asylum, thereby avoiding a trial in his own country for the 100,000 to 300,000 murders committed by his regime, in the name of *umma* (worldwide Muslim community) solidarity. Reporters describe the Saudi-funded exile's life in Jeddah as one of a comfortable suburban home, driving Cadillacs, BMWs and Mercedes-Benzes, lunching at the Meridien, having tea at the Sofitel, and swimming and taking massages at the Intercontinental.

The UN (which, interestingly, has been less vocal about Amin than it has been about Milosevic or Mladic), and the human rights NGOs were all disturbingly mute about Amin's comfortable asylum. Because Amin has enjoyed exile as a Muslim, the world must tolerate it, fearful as the West is of holding Muslims to the same human rights standard as others are held to.

Indeed, while 1979 was a bad year for African dictators-cannibalistic Jean Bedel Bokassa, the "Emperor" of Central Africa was overthrown by his erstwhile French protectors; sadistic Macias Nguema of Equatorial Guinea was shot by a Moroccan squad (locals did not believe he could be killed, considering his voodoo talents)—Amin at least survived, no matter how many of his countrymen he fed to the crocodiles. Interesting for those who still believe, or claim to believe, in "international law," Bokassa, a recent convert to Islam, was removed by a perfectly illegal French Foreign Legion intervention; Moroccans tied up Equatorial Guinea after Nguema, and it was an illegal Tanzanian invasion that liberated Uganda from Amin.

After becoming chairman of the OAU in 1975, Amin was able to use that platform to rant about Israeli "racism" and other causes. At the time Amin became chairman, chairmanship of the OAU—which has since been renamed the African Union (AU)—was a matter of rotation. The chairman's values were assumed to be "African" because he was president of a member state. The Libyan-backed AU does not seem troubled by its history of glorifying mass murderers such as Amin, Bokassa, or Nguema. Old habits are hard to break, and the AU continues to preclude discussion of this by labeling it "racism" to question Africa or an African leader.

"African solidarity," a racialist term if ever there was one, remains the AU's approach to the rest of the world. Amin may have been a criminal, but non-Africans have no right to say so. The same AU nations that judge other nations' pasts harshly (Europeans, for instance, were "slave-owning criminals") is mute about Amin (and Bokassa, Nguema. etc.). But that was in the past, some would say—wrongly. Today Amin's successors, Mugabe in Zimbabwe, Taylor in Liberia, are still protected by their African colleagues. Mugabe is still in power (and harboring fellow murderer and former Ethiopian version of Stalin, Mengistu Haile Mariam) and still ruining what was once one of Africa's prosperous countries, simply because South Africa does not want him out. Nigeria, which vies with South Africa for African leadership, has long allowed Taylor to stay in power and create havoc throughout the region, and now has given him asylum—despite his indictment by a UN court in Sierra Leone.

And then there is Central Africa, a bloody mess the size of Western Europe. In 1994 the majority Hutus in Rwanda murdered at least half a million Tutsis, in a mass frenzy of genocidal proportions. What did "Africa" and its Western supporters, or enablers, do? Blame the West for not stopping Africans from butchering Africans, and have the UN establish a court to try the perpetrators. That court, in Tanzania, has managed to convict fifteen persons in seven years at the cost of sixty million dollars...Meanwhile in neighboring Burundi the Hutus are trying hard to come to power—with the potential of a Rwanda repeat.

As for the Democratic Republic of Congo (!!!), the continent's second largest "country," it is a huge sore on the map, robbed blind by "friends" like Angola and Zimbabwe, with large areas under Ugandan or Rwandan control, a political fiction but a much too real tragedy. After Mugabe and the Angolans stole enough and left (just as the Nigerians did in Liberia a few years back), it was left to...the French to establish temporary order in a small region.

Collapse in Sierra Leone ? Call the British. Collapse in Côte d'Ivoire? Call the French. Collapse in Liberia? Call the Marines. Where is the African Union, so aggressive in condemning colonialism and slavery (but only the European part in it) and demanding universal respect and "a voice" in world affairs? Well, the AU did take a position on Zimbabwe—it elected Mugabe as one of its vice presidents.

There are, of course, notable and decent exceptions—Senegal, Botswana and...Senegal and Botswana. Uganda itself has recovered from Amin's reign of destruction and is now doing better than most. But all in all it does not seem that "Africa," or at least its self-proclaimed spokesmen have internalized the lessons of Idi Amin's rule. He may be dying but the evil he represented still haunts the continent.

Reprinted with the permission from http://www.frontpagemag.com,
August 19, 2003

The Nigerian Threat

It is by now a common, if mysterious habit of American media, to treat Nigeria as an important country—"Africa's largest," etc. Not so long ago there was even talk about an "African bomb" to be built by that country, the pride of the continent. The problem is not that Nigeria is unimportant—as millions of Americans receiving email offers of fraudulent riches from Nigerian crooks know. The problem is that Nigeria is a major criminal center, specialized in financial fraud and drug trafficking.

It may have a population over 100 million—the CIA assumes some 133 million—but we will never really know, since no national census has been taken since just after independence in 1960. This is because any result (more Muslims or more Christians?) is too politically dangerous for the region. Nigeria is also a major exporter of oil to the U.S.—when, that is, oil pipelines are not blown up, workers are not killed for being on the wrong side of local tribal conflicts, and tankers are not attacked in daylight by pirates in the main ports.

For those who know Sub-Saharan Africa and have no illusions about it, none of this is new or particularly shocking—nor are Nigeria's claims to "leadership" in a morally and politically leaderless subcontinent. What makes this huge country suddenly relevant is its growing role in producing, recruiting, and, indeed, acting, on the principles of Islamist radicalism.

Not that this is particularly new either—in the early 1980s a fundamentalist Islamic sect, the Maitatsine, was active in northeastern Nigeria, influencing neighboring Chad, Niger, and Cameroon. Today, Islamist customs are applied in Northern Nigeria, with twelve of its thirty-six states officially adopting Sharia Law as their legal practice.

What is different about the rise of Islam in Nigeria than in other countries in Africa or the Middle East is that it all happened in a rather unusual period of "democracy"—perhaps better described as chaotic, free-for-all politics. Since the collapse of the latest military junta in 1999, Nigeria has a weak, but elected, government, led (if that is the word), by a former military dictator, retired general, and friend of Jimmy Carter's, Olusegun Obasanjo; a Christian in a country divided, equally it seems, between Christianity and Islam—a division largely parallel to its major ethnic and tribal cleavages. Muslims, who until recently dominated the Nigerian military, make up a far more significant percentage of the population in the northern parts of the country, as opposed to a mostly Christian population in the south.

To make things worse, Nigeria's only source of revenue (other than widespread fraud and drug trafficking) is oil and gas—which provide 20 percent of its GDP, 95 percent of its foreign exchange earnings, and about 65 percent of its budgetary revenues, and is all concentrated in the south-east, the mostly Ibo and Ijaw, non-Muslim areas of the country.

Add to this the fact that the Ibos, who tried unsuccessfully to leave Nigeria in the late 1960s, at the cost of hundreds of thousands of citizens (remember Biafra?), are Christian and have a strong entrepreneurial spirit; unlike the Hausa and Fulani. The latent problems between the rich non-Muslims and the numerous, militant, but largely unproductive Muslims becomes a time bomb—one that is now close to exploding, due to a weak and vacillating central government.

Furthermore, due to the way the newest Nigerian Constitution (1999) is written, local governors have had a free hand to manipulate religion, especially Islam, and one ends with the cutting off of hands and stoning of "adulterous" women in Kaduna, Kano, Katsina, Sokoto and Zamfara —all centers of Islam and Islamism.

Recently, when a unit of GSPC (Jamiyy'a Salafiyya li'l-Daw'a wa-'l Jihad— a Salafist Group for preaching and combat), the main Algerian Islamist terrorist group, led by Amari Saïfi, a.k.a Abderezzak el Para, was decimated or captured in Chad, it turned out that a large part of its members were Nigerians.

This is no surprise, for in addition to the irresponsible political ambitions of northern state governors, Islamic fundamentalism is encouraged there by Saudi funding and Wahabbi-trained imams. As a result, the old and respected Islamic-tradition cities of Kano and Sokoto increasingly serve as secondary recruiting, and indoctrination, centers for unemployed and unemployable youths from throughout the Sahel.

And this is no small problem, for the Sahel is a huge breeding ground for terrorism, since this area on the margins of the Sahara extends from Mauritania on the Atlantic to the Darfur in Western Sudan, and includes Mali, Niger, and Chad. Compounding this Islamist expansion is the further problem that in Darfur these Nigerian influences meet those of Khartoum, Subsaharan Africa's main Islamist center.

The most immediate threat posed by the rise of Islam in Northern Nigeria is to the unity and very existence of Nigeria itself. Clashes between the dominant Muslims and the minority Christians in the North have occurred for a long time, and the introduction of sharia has not helped matters.

Recently, Christians have begun to answer in kind, especially in the central state of Plateau. There, some 1,000 people, mostly Muslims, were killed in September 2001, and hundreds more in April and May of this year. In response, Christians were slaughtered in Kano, while the central government declared a state of emergency in Plateau and appointed a retired general as governor.

While these clashes are routinely described by the Western media as "sectarian," they are far more than that: they are religiously tinged clashes of ethnicity and tribal identities over increasingly scarce resources—land and oil money. The Hausa and Fulani think they have the numbers, but little else, not even food; the mostly Christian Yorubas and Christian Ibos have the skills and the oil.

The central government has enough power to provoke some envy and resentment, but it is too weak to control regional bosses. All this makes for a potentially explosive situation, which could be ignited by a major decline in oil revenues or another major religious clash.

What such a scenario may mean for an already unstable West Africa, sprinkled with failed states like Sierra Leone and Liberia, and weak ones throughout the Sahel, is anyone's guess—but it can only be catastrophic. Nor is it clear what, if anything, outsiders can do about it—unless, that is, they are participants in the radicalization of Islam in Northern Nigeria. Numbers alone suggest that Nigerian radical Islamists would have a dramatic impact in the Sahel, an area already threatened by fundamentalists from the north in Algeria, and east in the Sudan. In short, we would have another major terrorist front on our hands.

Reprinted with the permission from http://www.frontpagemag.com, June 11, 2004

Index